THE
NYSTROM

DESK ATLAS

Fifth Edition

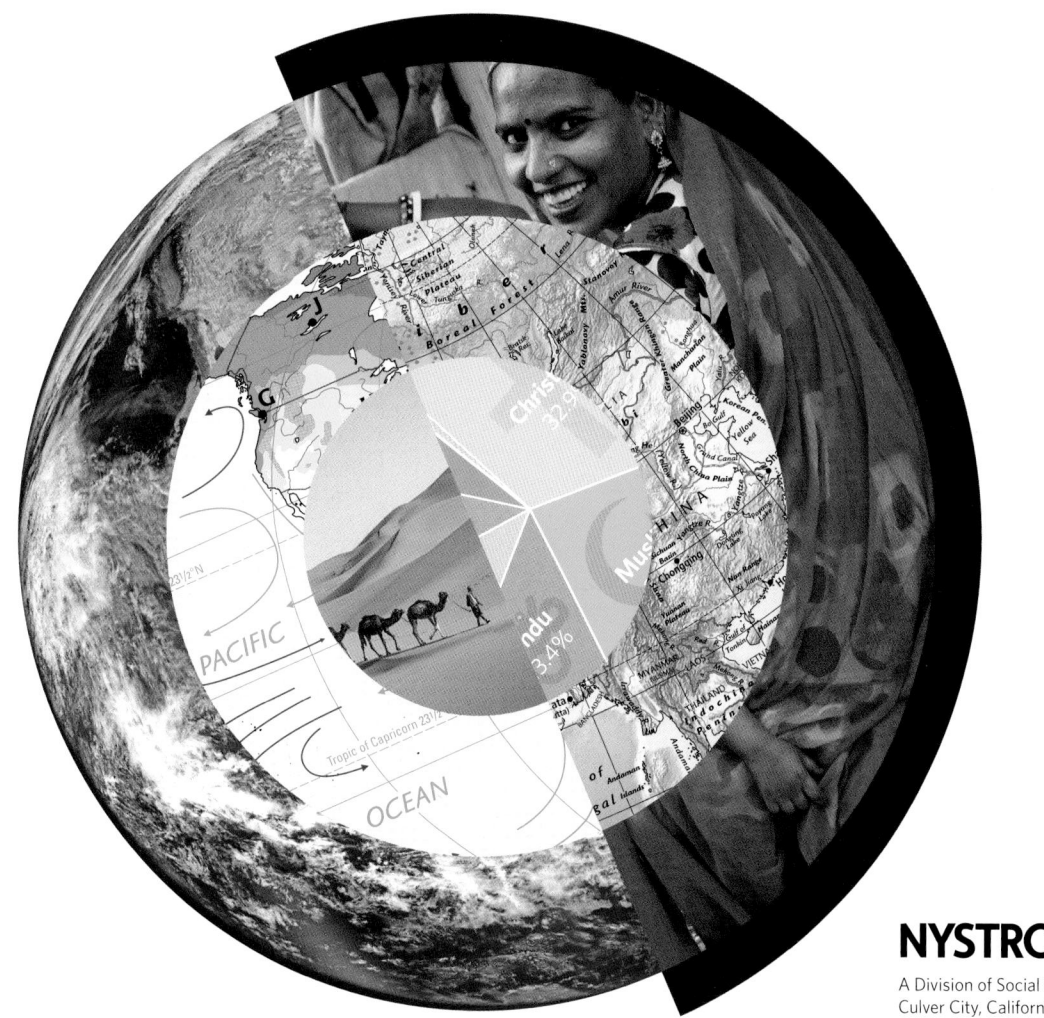

NYSTROM

A Division of Social Studies School Service
Culver City, California

Contents

Introduction

How to Use This Atlas	4–5
Understanding Map Projections	6
Issues Today ▪▪▪ Map Projections	7
Detailed Legends	8
Thematic Maps	9

World 10–49

World Reference Maps

Political Relief Map	12–13
Land Cover Map	14–15
Elevation Map	16–17

World Matters

Elevation and Landforms	18–19
The Moving Earth	20–21
Oceans	22–23
Weather Patterns	24–25
Climate	26–27
Energy Resources	28–29
Metals	30–31
Using the Land	32–33
Environmental Issues	34–35
Growing Population	36–37
Health Concerns	38–39
Feeding the World	40–41
Rich and Poor	42–43
Global Economy	44–45
Cultural Diversity	46–47
Human Migration	48–49

North America 50–117

Political Relief Map	52
Land Cover Map	53
Elevation Map and Cross Section	54
Thematic Maps	55–58
Issues Today ▪▪▪ Immigration	59

Canada

Political Relief Map	60–61
Land Cover Map	62
Elevation Map and Cross Section	63
Thematic Maps	64–67
Regional Maps	
Western Canada	68–69
Central Canada: Ontario	70
Central Canada: Québec	71
Eastern Canada	72
Issues Today ▪▪▪ Mining	73

United States

Political Relief Map	74–75
Land Cover Map	76–77
Elevation Map and Cross Section	78–79
Thematic Maps	80–87
Regional Maps	
Northeastern U.S.	88–89
East Central U.S.	90–91
Southeastern U.S.	92–93
South Central U.S.	94–95
Central U.S.	96–97
North Central U.S.	98–99
Northwestern U.S.	100–101
Southwestern U.S.	102–103
Alaska	104
Hawaii	104
Issues Today ▪▪▪ Military Power	105

Middle America

Political Relief Map	106–107
Land Cover Map	108
Elevation Map and Cross Section	109
Thematic Maps	109–113
Regional Maps	
Mexico	114
Central America	115
Cuba and Its Neighbors	116
Puerto Rico and the Lesser Antilles	116
Issues Today ▪▪▪ Indigenous People	117

2019 update of names and boundaries
© 1994, 2003, 2008, 2018 Social Studies School Service
Nystrom Education, a division of Social Studies School Service
PO Box 802, Culver City, CA 90232

Printed in Hong Kong

Statistics and estimates are from government and United Nations sources: populations for the most recent available date, other data averaged over the three most recent available years.

ISBN: 978-0-7825-2658-5   Product Code: NYS1351   v5.13

To order: socialstudies.com or 800-421-4246

Photo Credits

front cover, back cover, title page Courtesy of NASA/NOAA/GSFC/Suomi NPP/VIIRS/Norman Kuring; iStock.com/yavuzsariyildiz; iStock.com/hadynyah

10 Courtesy of NASA/NOAA/GSFC/Suomi NPP/VIIRS/Norman Kuring; **11** Physical World: Courtesy of Dr. Steve Ross, UNC-W. NOAA Office of Ocean Exploration; iStock.com/tiero; iStock.com/hanhanpeggy; iStock.com/Jorisvo; Human World: © Ggia/CC BY-SA 4.0; iStock.com/yavuzsariyildiz **18** left: iStock.com/erikjohansson78; right: iStock.com/hanhanpeggy; **19** left: iStock.com/shunjian123; right: iStock.com/Tarzan9280; **20** Courtesy of Philip A. McDaniel/U.S. Navy; **21** Courtesy of Jeff Schmaltz, MODIS Rapid Response Team/NASA; **22** Courtesy of Dr. Steve Ross, UNC-W. NOAA Office of Ocean Exploration; **24** iStock.com/BlueJayPhoto; **25** iStock.com/FlavioVallenari; **28** iStock.com/GaryKavanagh; **29** iStock.com/LUKASZ-NOWAK1; **30** iStock.com/THEGIFT777; **32** left: iStock.com/spooh; right: iStock.com/chrishowey; **33** left: iStock.com/tiero; top right: iStock.com/Jorisvo; bottom right: iStock.com/MarcPo;

South America 118-129

Political Relief Map	120
Land Cover Map	121
Elevation Map and Cross Section	122
Thematic Maps	123-125
Regional Maps	
Northwestern South America	126
Southern South America	126
Brazil and Its Neighbors	127
Issues Today ▰▰▰ National Development	128
Issues Today ▰▰▰ Rain Forest Deforestation	129

Africa 130-143

Political Relief Map	132
Land Cover Map	133
Elevation Map and Cross Section	134
Thematic Maps	135-137
Regional Maps	
Northern Africa	136-137
Western Africa	138
Central Africa	139
Eastern Africa	140
Southern Africa	141
Issues Today ▰▰▰ HIV/AIDS	142
Issues Today ▰▰▰ Refugees	143

Europe 144-163

Political Relief Map	146-147
Land Cover Map	148-149
Elevation Map and Cross Section	150-151
Thematic Maps	152-156
Regional Maps	
British Isles	156
Northern Europe	157
Western Europe	158
Central Europe	159
Eastern Europe	160
The Caucasus	161
Issues Today ▰▰▰ Industrial Pollution	162
Issues Today ▰▰▰ International Organizations	163

Asia 164-185

Political Relief Map	166-167
Land Cover Map	168-169
Elevation Map and Cross Section	170-171
Thematic Maps	172-177
Regional Maps	
Southwestern Asia	178
Central Asia	179
Southern Asia	180
Southeastern Asia	181
Eastern Asia: China, Mongolia, and Taiwan	182
Eastern Asia: Japan and the Koreas	183
Issues Today ▰▰▰ Population Growth	184
Issues Today ▰▰▰ Urbanization	185

Australia and Oceania 186-197

Political Relief Map	188-189
Land Cover Map	190
Elevation Map and Cross Section	191
Thematic Maps	192-194
Regional Maps	
Australia	195
New Zealand	195
Issues Today ▰▰▰ Invasive Species	196
Issues Today ▰▰▰ Sea Level Rise	197

Antarctica and the Arctic 198-201

Land Cover Maps and Cross Section	200-201

Geographic Facts and Index

World Facts	inside front cover
Country Tables	202-207
Glossary	208-209
Time Zones Map	209
Index	210-240
Abbreviations	240
Thematic Index	inside back cover

34 top: iStock.com/Vasca; bottom: © Frank Vassen/CC BY 2.0; **35** left: Courtesy of NASA/Goddard Space Flight Center Scientific Visualization Studio; right: Courtesy of NASA/Goddard Space Flight Center Scientific Visualization Studio; **37** iStock.com/yavuzsariyildiz; **38** iStock.com/ Bartosz Hadyniak; **40** © Robert Oxley/ DFID/CC BY 2.0; **42** © Aleposta/CC BY-SA 2.0; **46** iStock.com/ SmileKorn; **48** © Pedro Szekely/CC BY-SA 2.0; **49** iStock.com/Tigeryan; **50** iStock.com/Arpad Benedek; **56** top: iStock.com/Maksymowicz; bottom: iStock.com/ChrisBoswell; **57** Courtesy of Guldhammer; **58** iStock.com/Vadim_Nefedov; **59** Courtesy of U.S. Customs and Border Protection; **63** iStock.com/ KathrynHatashitaLee; **65** iStock.com/shaunl; **66** iStock.com/Pgiam; **73** iStock.com/dan_prat; **80** iStock.com/ Wendy Olsen Photography; **81** iStock.com/GomezDavid;

82 iStock.com/IMNATURE; **83** iStock.com/ DarcyMaulsby; **84** left: iStock.com/ SumikoPhoto; right: iStock.com/Mlenny; **108** left: iStock.com/tonda; right: iStock.com/Focus_on_Nature; **111** iStock.com/ aureliavalema; **114** © Valerie Hinojosa/ CC BY-SA 2.0; **115** iStock.com/onlymehdi; **117** iStock.com/ SimonDannhauer; **118** iStock.com/PatricioHidalgoP; **124** iStock.com/Alfredo Allais; **125** iStock.com/ hadynyah; **128** iStock.com/dabldy; **130** iStock.com/ hadynyah; **135** © rolandh/CC BY-SA 2.0; **138** © Vgrigas/CC BY SA-3.0; **139** iStock.com/Robert_Ford; **141** iStock.com/nicolamargaret; **142** Courtesy of Victor Balaban/CDC; **143** © Ggia/CC BY-SA 4.0; **144** iStock. com/Madzia71; **151** iStock.com/AlpamayoPhoto; **154** iStock.com/danielsnaer; **156** iStock.com/Westbury; **161** iStock.com/art33art; **162** iStock.com/Mlenny;

163 iStock.com/Koutsaftikis; **164** iStock.com/WitR; **171** iStock.com/perreten; **173** iStock.com/Danielrao; **176** iStock.com/maomaotou; **179** left: Courtesy of NASA Earth Observatory; right: Courtesy of NASA Earth Observatory; **180** iStock.com/SoumenNath; **183** iStock.com/Nikada; **184** iStock.com/Bartosz Hadyniak; **185** iStock.com/Spondylolithesis; **186** iStock. com/MelanieMaya; **190** iStock.com/AndrewHalsall; **192** iStock.com/BentheBeeMan; **193** iStock.com/ AL-Travelpicture; **194** © jeanfrancoisbeausejour/CC BY 2.0; **195** iStock.com/eyecrave; **196** iStock.com/ JohnCarnemolla; **197** © Government of Kiribati/CC BY-SA 3.0; **198** iStock.com/Mlenny; **200** iStock.com/ Bernhard_Staehli; **201** iStock.com/Wildnerdpix

How to Use This Atlas

The Nystrom Desk Atlas is a collection of maps—and much more. Its reference and thematic maps, graphs, photos, and explanatory text explore key concepts and processes. These tools will help you understand important environmental, humanitarian, economic, and cultural issues affecting the world today. To get the most out of *The Nystrom Desk Atlas*, follow these steps.

A

Get acquainted with the three styles of **Reference Maps** in this atlas. See the **Political Relief**, **Land Cover**, and **Elevation Maps** of the world on pages 12–17. Their detailed legends are on page 8.

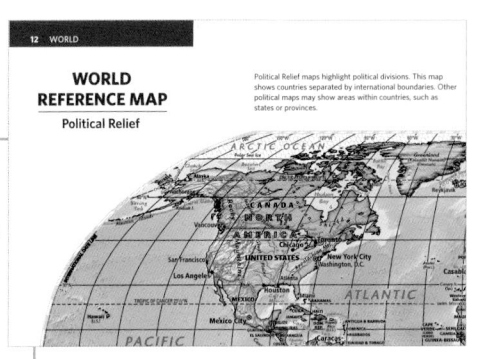

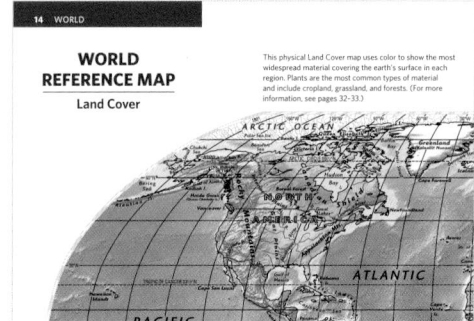

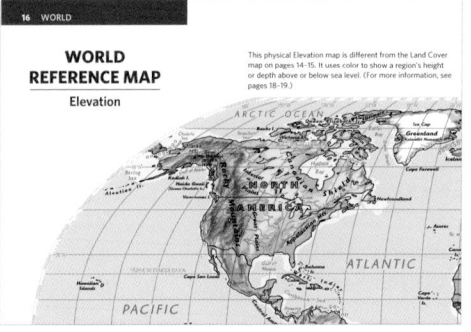

B

Check out World Matters on pages 18–49. They provide a foundation for understanding themes that are repeated throughout the atlas.

1. Look at the title, which tells you what the two-page spread is about.

2. Then read the introduction. It provides an overview of the theme addressed on the spread.

3. Look at the maps. Their legends explain what the main colors and symbols on the map mean. Always read the legend before examining a map.

4. Also look at the graphs, photos, and diagrams. Read their captions too. They help you understand the significance of each image.

5. Watch for Sparks, which share interesting facts. Some define important terms; others provide helpful examples.

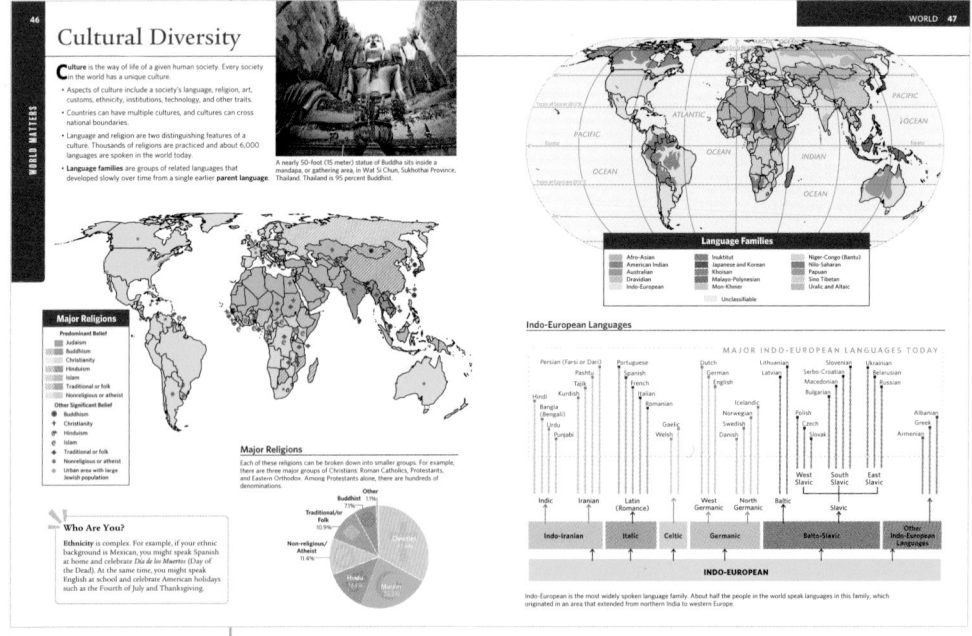

C

For each continent, start with the first two pages, the Continent Overview. It provides key facts and shows the areas covered by regional maps.

Locator maps show the location of the continent in relation to the world or a region in relation to the continent or a larger region.

Area comparisons compare the size of a continent, country, or state with the familiar size and shape of the contiguous United States.

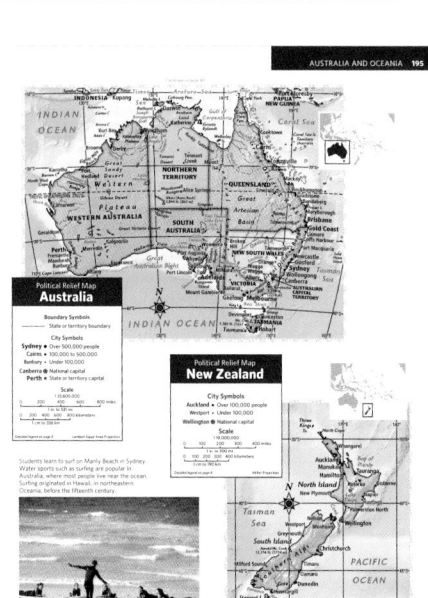

D

Then page through the section. First you'll find reference maps, followed by thematic maps for the full continent, and then maps for regions on the continent.

Diagrams illustrate concepts that are difficult to show in a map, graph, or photo.

Thematic maps focus on single topics or themes. Often the patterns on one thematic map become more meaningful when compared to the patterns on another. The five types of recurring thematic maps are shown on page 9.

Graphs summarize facts in a visual way, making it easier to see trends and make comparisons. Four recurring graphs appear throughout the atlas: Climographs, Balance of Trade, Natural Population Growth, and Ethnic Composition.

Regional maps are provided for nearly every populous part of the world. Because they appear at larger scales than maps of continents, they can name more cities and show more features.

Photos show people and places in a geographic context. Some provide examples of map categories. Others bring abstract ideas to life.

Cross sections show slices of the earth, to make landscapes easier to comprehend. Their exaggerated height and depth make features easy to see.

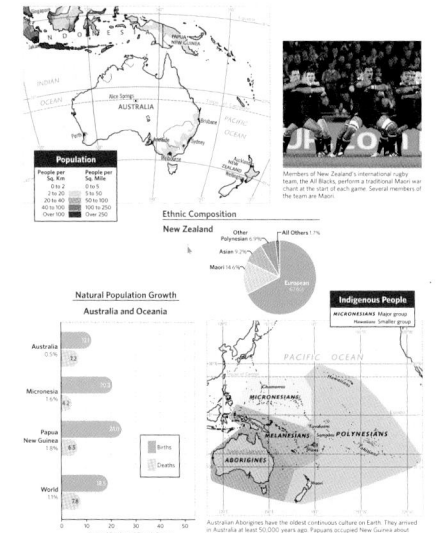

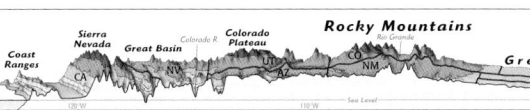

E

Finally, read **Issues Today**. Each article looks at a global issue that has particular relevance for the continent or region—from two perspectives.

Other Reference Tools

Country Tables, organized by continent, list key facts about every country in the world.

Unfamiliar terms in **bold** type are defined in context. Other terms are defined in the **Glossary**.

The complete **Index** gives the page, latitude and longitude, and description of every place named on the maps.

The **Thematic Index** lists thematic maps and graphs by theme.

This symbol lets you know that there are related maps or graphs available in the digital atlas.

Understanding Map Projections

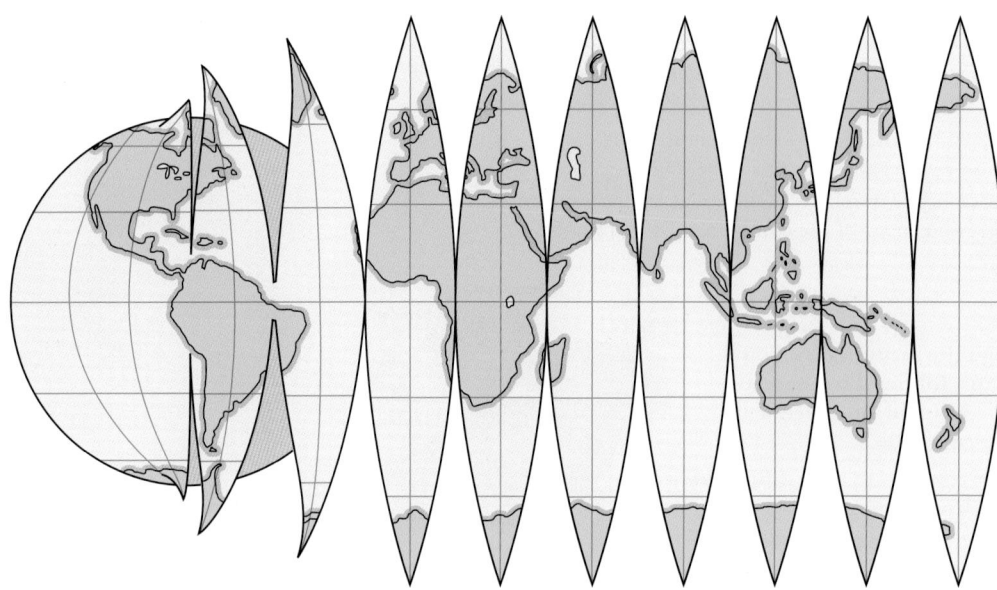

A map of a round object would be like a peeled and flattened orange peel if cartographers could not transform the information from the segments to make them fit together. No flat map can be a true model of the earth. There will always be distortion in shape, direction, or relative size. The distortion is the inevitable result of trying to show a curved surface on a flat surface. Only globes can accurately depict shape, direction, and relative size, but a globe cannot show the entire world at once.

Properties of Map Projections

Map projections are the means by which the curved surface of a globe is transformed onto the flat surface of a map. There are hundreds of map projections. Different map projections accurately depict different aspects of the earth, so the projection used depends on the information that the map is presenting. Map projections are often classified by their properties.

Conformal projections, like this Mercator projection, show true shapes but distort sizes. World maps of this type are mainly used for navigation, because the direction from any point is accurate to the real world.

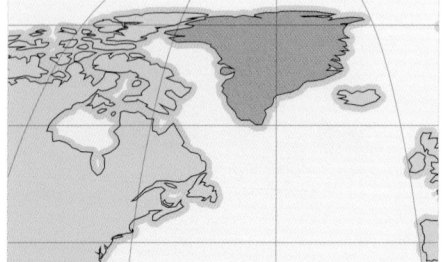

Compromise projections, like this Robinson projection, allow some size distortion in order to portray shapes more accurately. World maps of this type are mainly used for reference maps because the overall shape and size are less distorted than in other types.

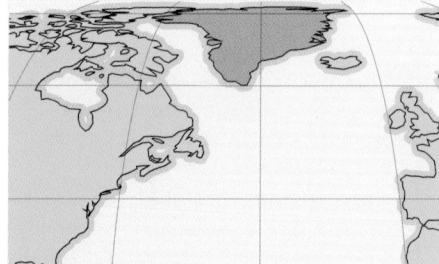

Equal-area projections, like this Eckert IV projection, show all areas in their true relative sizes, but distort shapes. World maps of this type are mainly used for thematic maps because they show the relative area affected by the subject of the map.

Centering and Orientation

Two other considerations are a map's centering and orientation.

Centering refers to the central horizontal and vertical lines of the map. Nearly all world maps use the Equator as the central horizontal line. The vertical central line is usually the Prime Meridian. The vertical central line affects what geographic feature will be divided by the left and right edges of the map.

Orientation refers to what direction is found on the top of the map. Most world maps have north at the top of the map, but this is strictly a convention and doesn't reflect physical reality.

The Nystrom Desk Atlas uses a compromise projection called the Robinson projection for world reference maps. The Eckert IV projection, an equal-area map, is used for most thematic maps.

To allow for easy comparison, the atlas uses the conventional centering and orientation for most world maps. However the ocean maps on pages 22 and 23 are centered on 90°W, a centering that allows both the Atlantic and Pacific Oceans to be shown uninterrupted.

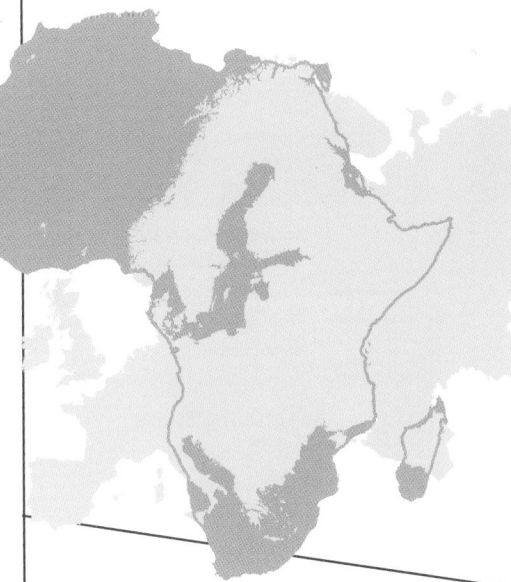

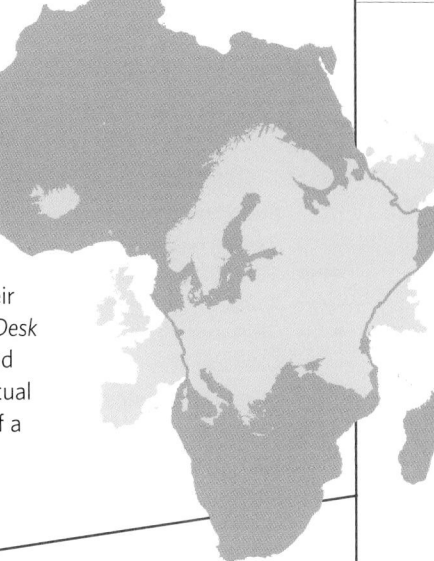

Some educators and cartographers believe that the most common centering, orientation, and map projections can lead to a distorted view of the world that emphasizes the wealthier areas of the Northern Hemisphere. Compare the Mercator projections of Europe and Africa to their actual sizes. Throughout *The Nystrom Desk Atlas*, Area Comparisons use the United States for scale to demonstrate the actual size of a place without the distortion of a map projection.

Mercator Projection

Actual Size

Conventional designs are easiest to use.

- The most conventional arrangement for a world map is centered at the Equator and Prime Meridian and oriented with north on the top edge.

- These designs have been used for decades, in some cases centuries. This allows people to easily use maps from different eras without confusion.

- Because no map can perfectly reflect the world, students should learn the advantages of different types of maps and the appropriate uses of different projections.

Mercator Projection

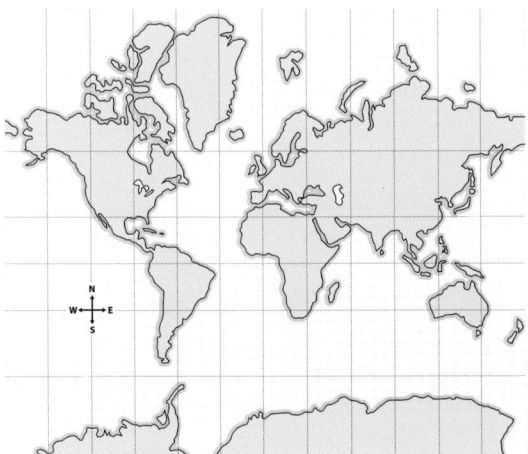

Developed in 1569 by Gerardus Mercator, the Mercator projection is a conformal projection. Features nearer to the poles like Europe and Greenland appear much larger than they actually are. This has led to significant controversy.

Conventional designs do not properly reflect the world today.

- For many generations students were given a distorted view of the world, emphasizing Europe and the United States over all other areas. Conventional map designs emphasize these areas by exaggerating their size and placing them in the visual top and center of the map.

- Asia and the Pacific region are major economic and population centers, but conventional map design puts these areas on the edges of the map.

- The explanation that no map can perfectly reflect the world should not excuse design decisions that continue to emphasize the old colonial powers and de-emphasize poorer, but more populous, regions of the world.

Inverted Eckert IV Projection Centered at 160° E

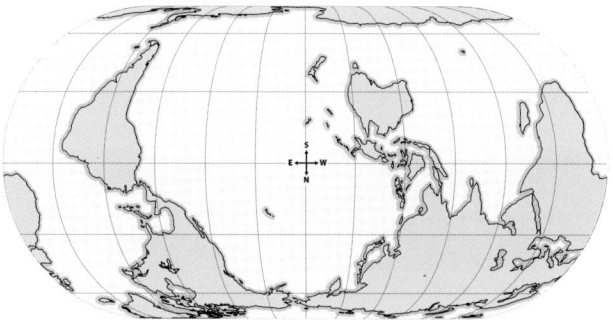

This map places the Pacific Ocean in at the center and puts the south at the top. The Eckert IV projection is an equal-area map that shows the relative sizes of landmasses. This design emphasizes the Pacific Rim and the Southern Hemisphere.

Detailed Legends

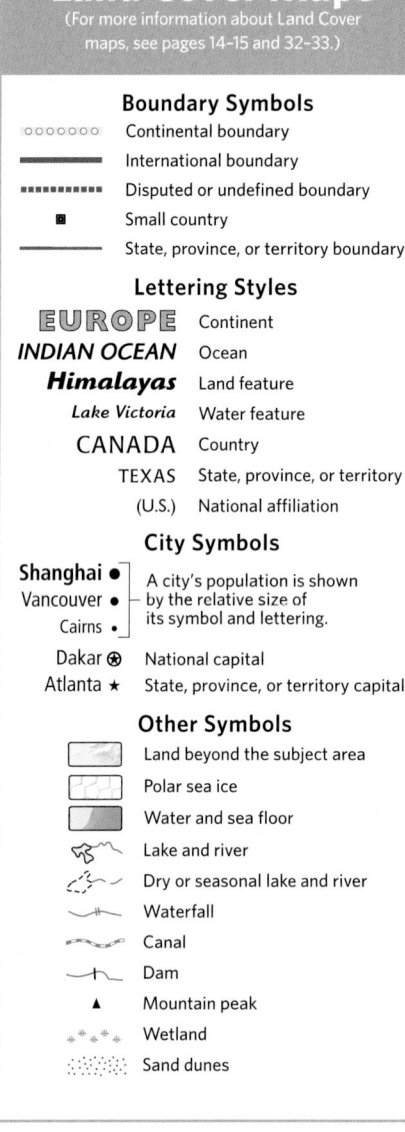

Political Relief Maps

(For more information about Political Relief maps, see pages 12–13.)

Boundary Symbols

- Continental boundary
- International boundary
- Disputed or undefined boundary
- ■ Small country
- State, province, or territory boundary

Lettering Styles

- EUROPE — Continent
- *INDIAN OCEAN* — Ocean
- *Himalayas* — Land feature
- *Lake Victoria* — Water feature
- **CANADA** — Country
- **TEXAS** — State, province, or territory
- (U.S.) — National affiliation

City Symbols

- **Shanghai** ● — A city's population is shown by numbers in the legend and by the relative size of its symbol and lettering.
- **Vancouver** ●
- **Cairns** ·
- **Dakar** ⊗ — National capital
- **Atlanta** ★ — State, province, or territory capital

Other Symbols

- Land beyond the subject area
- Polar sea ice
- Water and sea floor
- Lake and river
- Dry or seasonal lake and river
- Waterfall
- Canal
- Dam
- △ Mountain peak
- ⬡80 U.S. Interstate highway
- ⬡ Trans-Canada Highway
- ⬡101 Other highway

Land Cover Maps

(For more information about Land Cover maps, see pages 14–15 and 32–33.)

Boundary Symbols

- Continental boundary
- International boundary
- Disputed or undefined boundary
- ■ Small country
- State, province, or territory boundary

Lettering Styles

- **EUROPE** — Continent
- *INDIAN OCEAN* — Ocean
- *Himalayas* — Land feature
- *Lake Victoria* — Water feature
- CANADA — Country
- TEXAS — State, province, or territory
- (U.S.) — National affiliation

City Symbols

- **Shanghai** ● — A city's population is shown by the relative size of its symbol and lettering.
- **Vancouver** ●
- **Cairns** ·
- **Dakar** ⊗ — National capital
- **Atlanta** ★ — State, province, or territory capital

Other Symbols

- Land beyond the subject area
- Polar sea ice
- Water and sea floor
- Lake and river
- Dry or seasonal lake and river
- Waterfall
- Canal
- Dam
- ▲ Mountain peak
- Wetland
- Sand dunes

Elevation Maps

(For more information about Elevation maps, see pages 16–17 and 18–19.)

Boundary Symbols

- Continental boundary
- International boundary
- Disputed or undefined boundary
- ■ Small country
- State, province, or territory boundary

Lettering Styles

- EUROPE — Continent
- *INDIAN OCEAN* — Ocean
- *Himalayas* — Land feature
- *Lake Victoria* — Water feature
- CANADA — Country
- TEXAS — State, province, or territory
- (U.S.) — National affiliation

City Symbols

- **Shanghai** ● — A city's population is shown by the relative size of its symbol and lettering.
- **Vancouver** ●
- **Cairns** ·
- **Dakar** ⊗ — National capital
- **Atlanta** ★ — State, province, or territory capital

Other Symbols

- Land beyond the subject area
- Ice covered land
- Water
- Lake and river
- Dry or seasonal lake
- Waterfall
- Canal
- Dam
- ▲ Mountain peak

Each region has a color theme

A legend's header and frame color match the region's color theme.

World	North America	South America	Africa
Pages 10–49	Pages 50–117	Pages 118–129	Pages 130–143

Europe	Asia	Oceania	The Poles
Pages 144–163	Pages 164–185	Pages 186–197	Pages 198–201

Thematic Maps

Thematic maps focus on single topics or themes, and the subject can be anything that is mappable. The following thematic maps appear throughout the atlas.

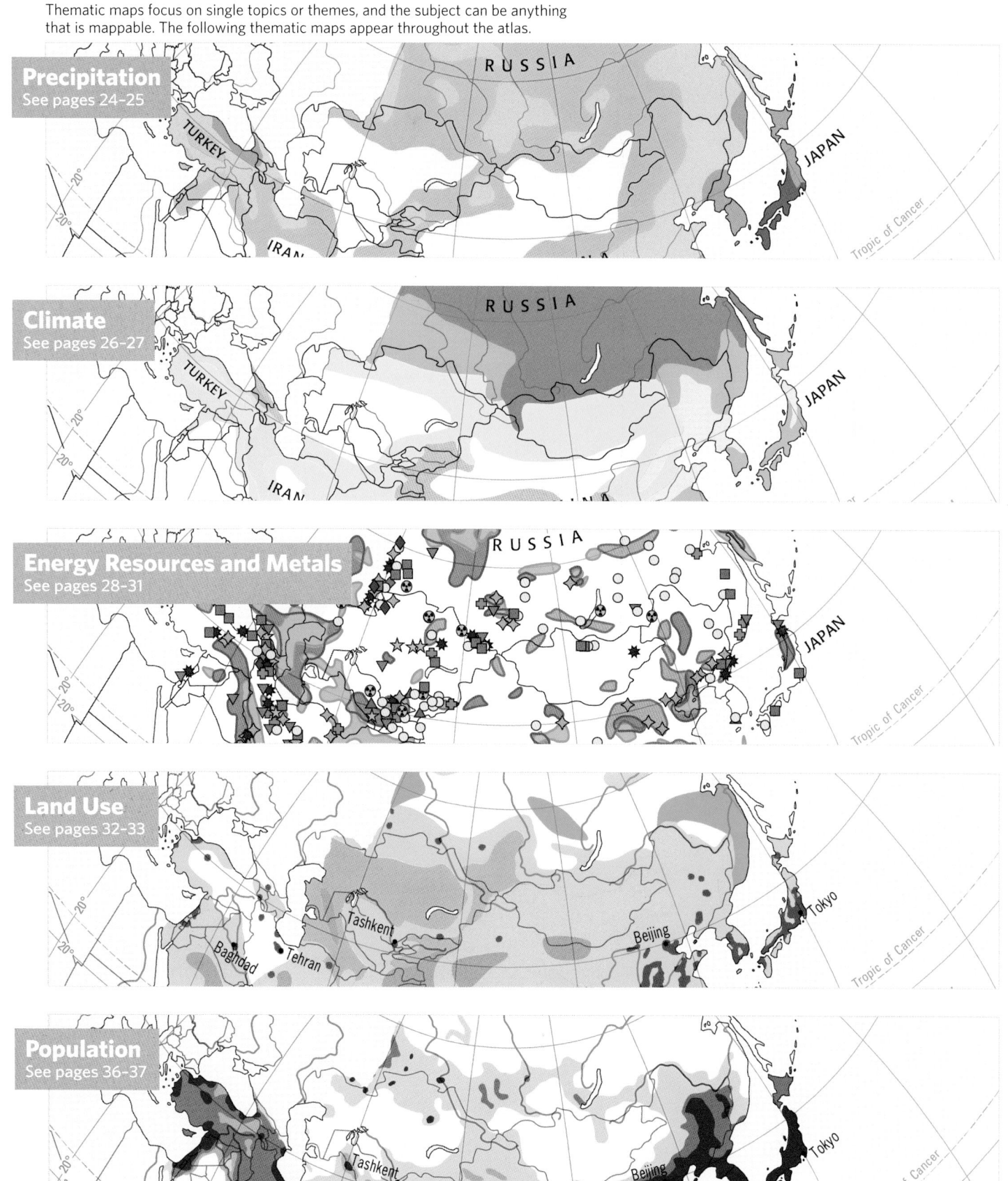

Precipitation
See pages 24–25

Climate
See pages 26–27

Energy Resources and Metals
See pages 28–31

Land Use
See pages 32–33

Population
See pages 36–37

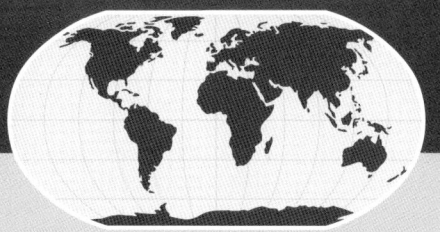

World

Earth is known as the "blue planet" because 71 percent of its surface is covered with water. The planet has five oceans and seven continents.

Physical Features

Longest mountain range
Andes Mountains 4,500 mi. (7,200 km)

Largest plain
West Siberian Plain 1,200,000 sq. mi.
(3,000,000 sq. km)

Deadliest earthquake
830,000 people
Shansi, China
January 23, 1556

Strongest earthquake
9.5 on Richter scale
Valdivia, Chile
May 22, 1960

Average ocean depth
12,100 ft. (3,688 m)

Average temperature
59°F (15°C)

Most abundant metal
Aluminum (8.1% of Earth's crust)

Cultural Features

Population
7,400,000,000

Most densely populated
Monaco 39,288.5 people per sq. mi.
(15,170.7 per sq. km)

Least densely populated
Greenland 0.1 people per sq. mi.
(0.03 per sq. km)

Longest life expectancy
Monaco 89.5 years

Shortest life expectancy
Chad 50.2 years

*Highest GDP (Gross Domestic Product)
per capita*
Liechtenstein US$179,478

*Lowest GDP (Gross Domestic Product)
per capita*
Burundi US$312

Physical World

Landforms, Plates, and Oceans • pages 18–23
Weather and Climate • pages 24–27
Resources, Land Cover, and Environment • pages 28–35

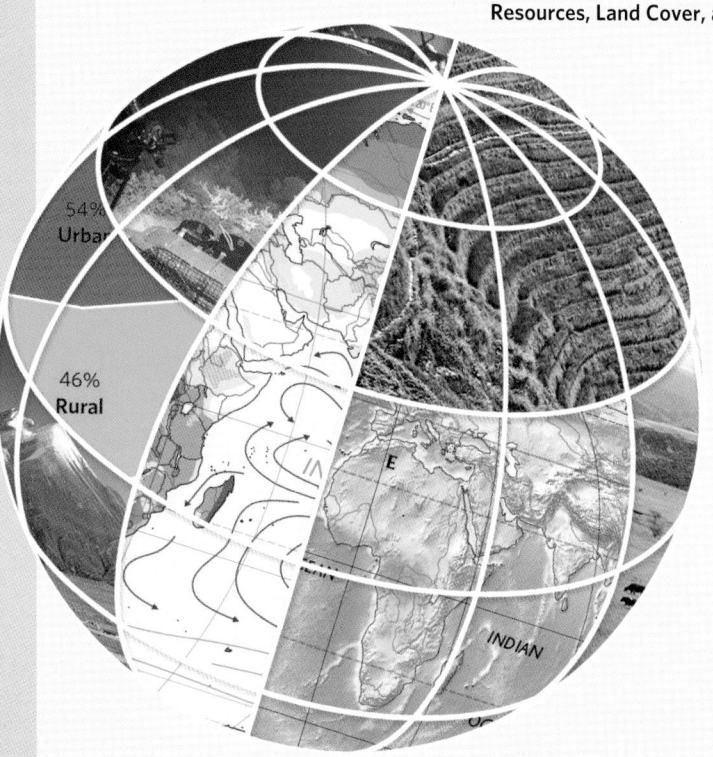

Human World

Population, Health, and Food • pages 36–41
Economics • pages 42–45
Cultures and Migration • pages 46–49

WORLD REFERENCE MAP

Political Relief

Political Relief maps highlight political divisions. This map shows countries separated by international boundaries. Other political maps may show areas within countries, such as states or provinces.

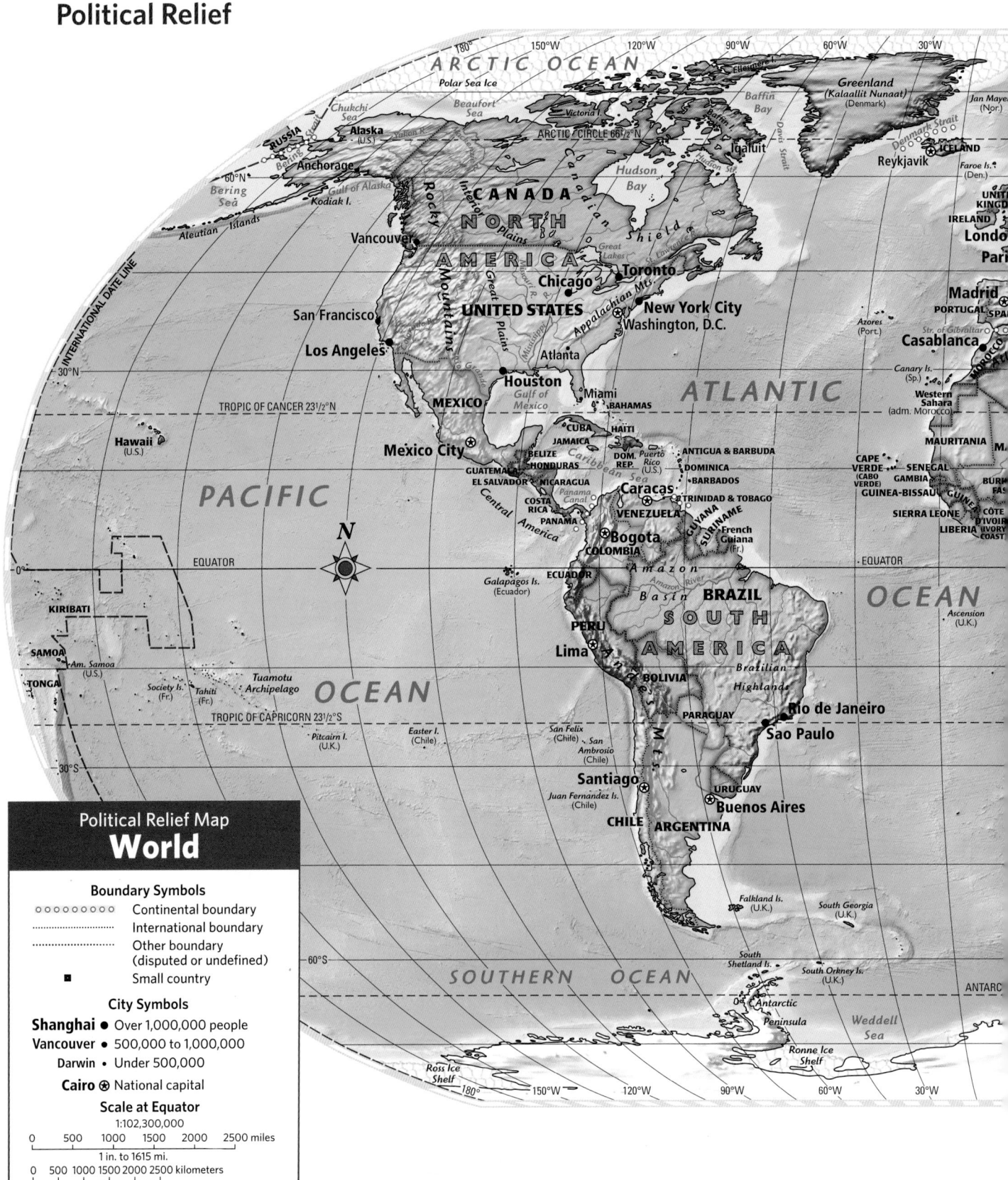

Political Relief Map
World

Boundary Symbols
∘∘∘∘∘∘∘∘∘ Continental boundary
·················· International boundary
·················· Other boundary (disputed or undefined)
▪ Small country

City Symbols
Shanghai ● Over 1,000,000 people
Vancouver • 500,000 to 1,000,000
Darwin · Under 500,000
Cairo ⊛ National capital

Scale at Equator
1:102,300,000

0 500 1000 1500 2000 2500 miles
1 in. to 1615 mi.

0 500 1000 1500 2000 2500 kilometers
1 cm to 1023 km

Detailed legend on page 8   Robinson Projection

North Polar View

South Polar View

WORLD REFERENCE MAP
Land Cover

This physical Land Cover map uses color to show the most widespread material covering the earth's surface in each region. Plants are the most common types of material and include cropland, grassland, and forests. (For more information, see pages 32–33.)

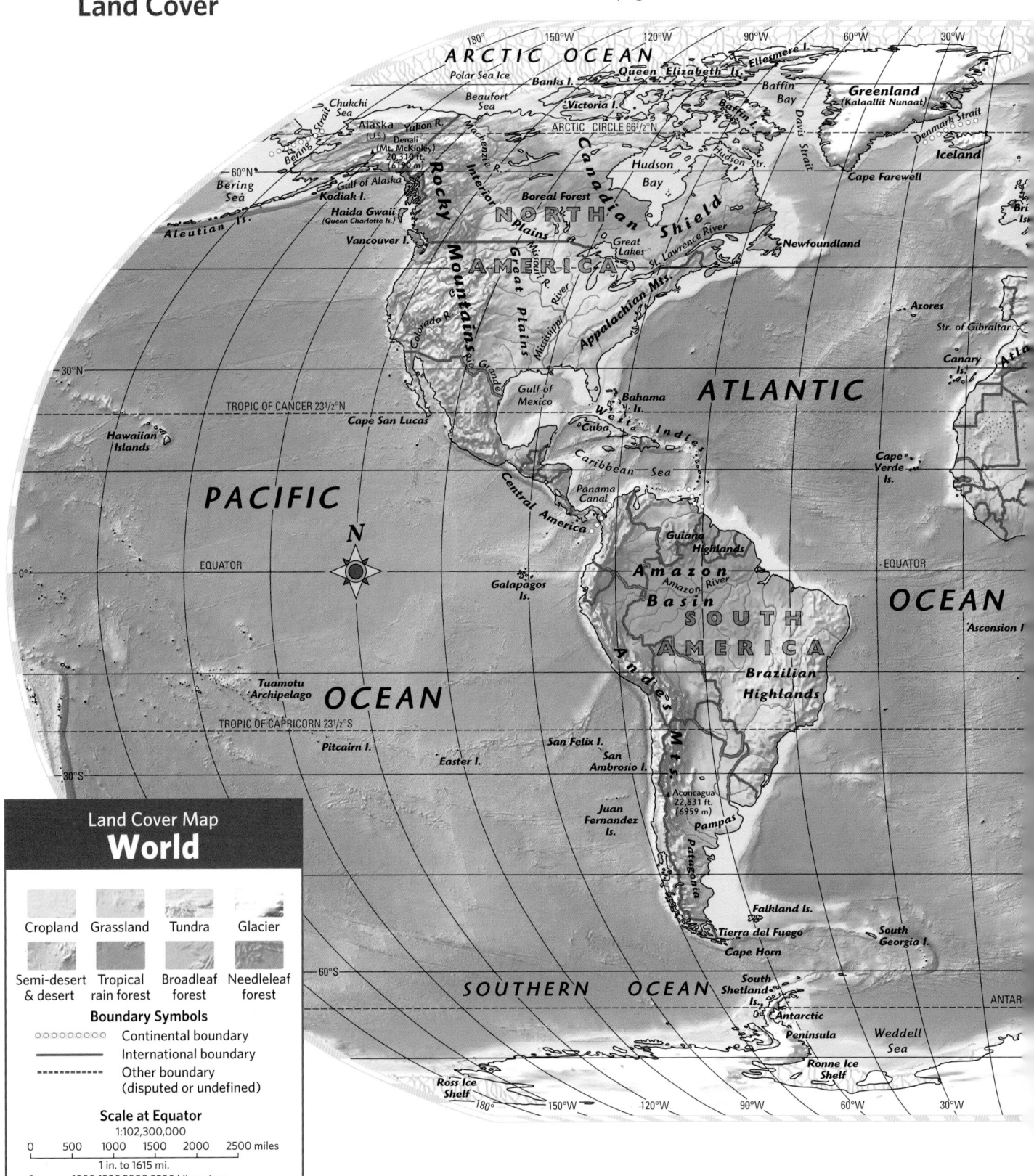

Land Cover Map
World

Cropland	Grassland	Tundra	Glacier
Semi-desert & desert	Tropical rain forest	Broadleaf forest	Needleleaf forest

Boundary Symbols

ooooooooo Continental boundary

——————— International boundary

- - - - - - - Other boundary (disputed or undefined)

Scale at Equator
1:102,300,000

0 500 1000 1500 2000 2500 miles

1 in. to 1615 mi.

0 1000 1500 2000 2500 kilometers

1 cm to 1023 km

Detailed legend on page 8   Robinson Projection

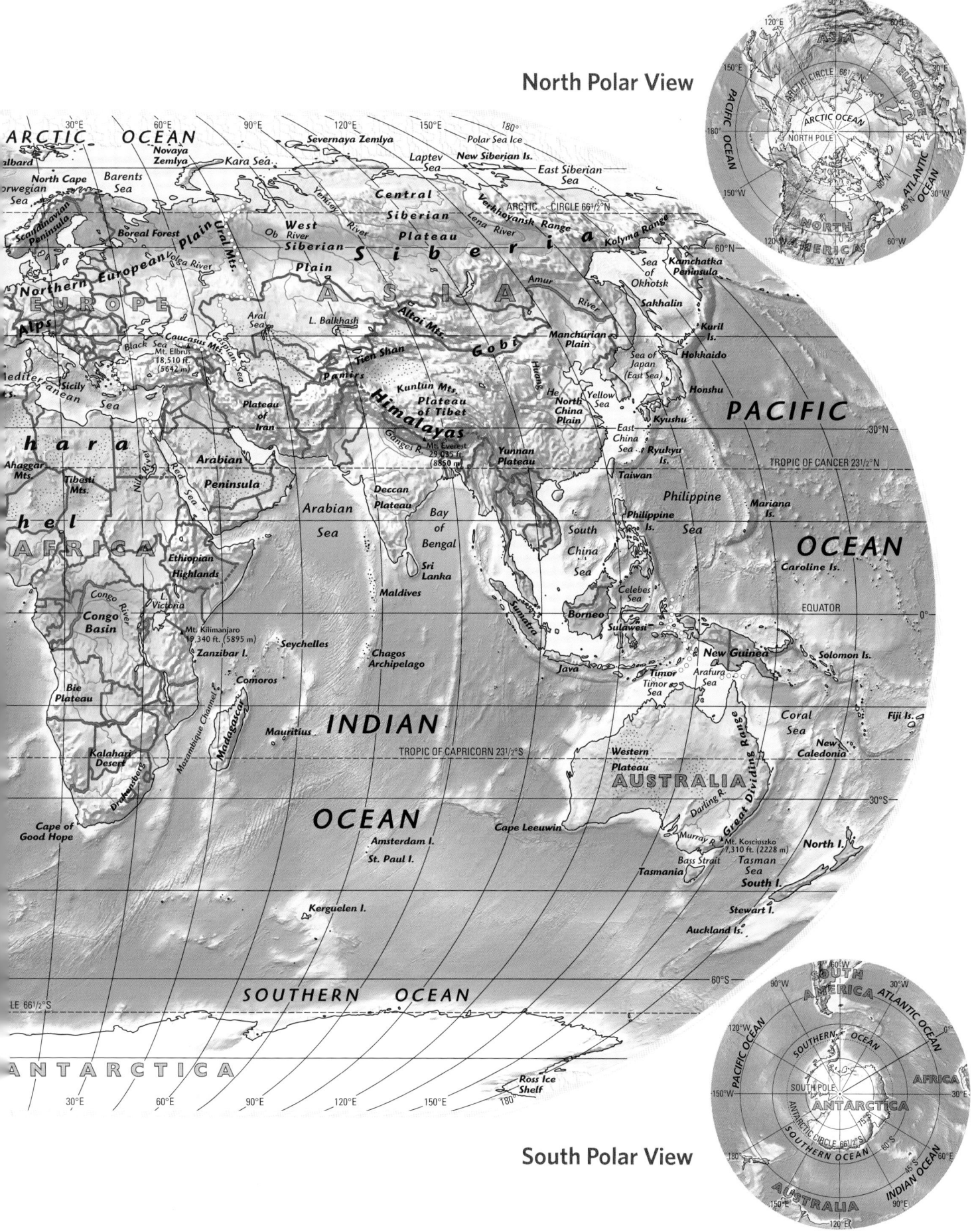

North Polar View

ARCTIC OCEAN

ASIA
ARCTIC CIRCLE 66½°N
EUROPE
PACIFIC OCEAN
180°
ARCTIC OCEAN
NORTH POLE
ATLANTIC OCEAN
150°W
45°N
NORTH AMERICA
120°W
60°W
90°W

ARCTIC OCEAN
Svalbard
30°E
60°E
90°E
120°E
150°E
180°
Novaya Zemlya
Severnaya Zemlya
Polar Sea Ice
Kara Sea
Laptev Sea
New Siberian Is.
North Cape
Barents Sea
East Siberian Sea
Norwegian Sea
Scandinavian Peninsula
Central Siberian Plateau
ARCTIC CIRCLE 66½°N
Boreal Forest
Yenisey River
Verkhoyansk Range
Kolyma Range
Northern European Plain
West Siberian Plain
S i b e r i a
60°N
Ob River
Ural Mts.
Volga River
A S I A
Amur River
Sea of Okhotsk
Kamchatka Peninsula
EUROPE
Aral Sea
L. Balkhash
Altai Mts.
Sakhalin
Alps
Black Sea
Caucasus Mts.
Caspian Sea
Gobi
Manchurian Plain
Kuril Is.
Mt. Elbrus 18,510 ft. (5642 m)
Tien Shan
Pamirs
Hokkaido
Mediterranean Sea
Sicily
Plateau of Iran
Kunlun Mts.
Plateau of Tibet
Huang He
North China Plain
Yellow Sea
Sea of Japan (East Sea)
Honshu
PACIFIC
Sahara
Himalayas
Mt. Everest 29,035 ft. (8850 m)
Ganges R.
Yunnan Plateau
East China Sea
Ryukyu Is.
Kyushu
30°N
Ahaggar Mts.
Arabian Peninsula
Taiwan
TROPIC OF CANCER 23½°N
OCEAN
Tibesti Mts.
Nile River
Red Sea
Deccan Plateau
Philippine Sea
Mariana Is.
Sahel
Arabian Sea
Bay of Bengal
South China Sea
Philippine Is.
AFRICA
Ethiopian Highlands
Sri Lanka
Caroline Is.
Congo River
L. Victoria
Maldives
Celebes Sea
EQUATOR
0°
Congo Basin
Mt. Kilimanjaro 19,340 ft. (5895 m)
Zanzibar I.
Seychelles
Chagos Archipelago
Sumatra
Borneo
Sulawesi
New Guinea
Solomon Is.
Bie Plateau
Comoros
Java
Timor
Arafura Sea
Madagascar
Timor Sea
Mozambique Channel
Mauritius
INDIAN
Coral Sea
Fiji Is.
Kalahari Desert
Drakensberg
TROPIC OF CAPRICORN 23½°S
Western Plateau
New Caledonia
Great Dividing Range
AUSTRALIA
30°S
OCEAN
Cape of Good Hope
Amsterdam I.
Cape Leeuwin
Darling R.
Murray R.
Mt. Kosciuszko 7,310 ft. (2228 m)
North I.
St. Paul I.
Bass Strait
Tasman Sea
Tasmania
South I.
Kerguelen I.
Stewart I.
Auckland Is.
60°S
SOUTHERN OCEAN
LE 66½°S
ANTARCTICA
Ross Ice Shelf
30°E
60°E
90°E
120°E
150°E
180°

South Polar View

SOUTH AMERICA
60°W
30°W
90°W
ATLANTIC OCEAN
PACIFIC OCEAN
120°W
SOUTHERN OCEAN
AFRICA
150°W
SOUTH POLE
30°E
ANTARCTICA
ANTARCTIC CIRCLE 66½°S
SOUTHERN OCEAN
75°S
180°
60°S
INDIAN OCEAN
AUSTRALIA
150°E
90°E
120°E

WORLD REFERENCE MAP

Elevation

This physical Elevation map is different from the Land Cover map on pages 14–15. It uses color to show a region's height or depth above or below sea level. (For more information, see pages 18–19.)

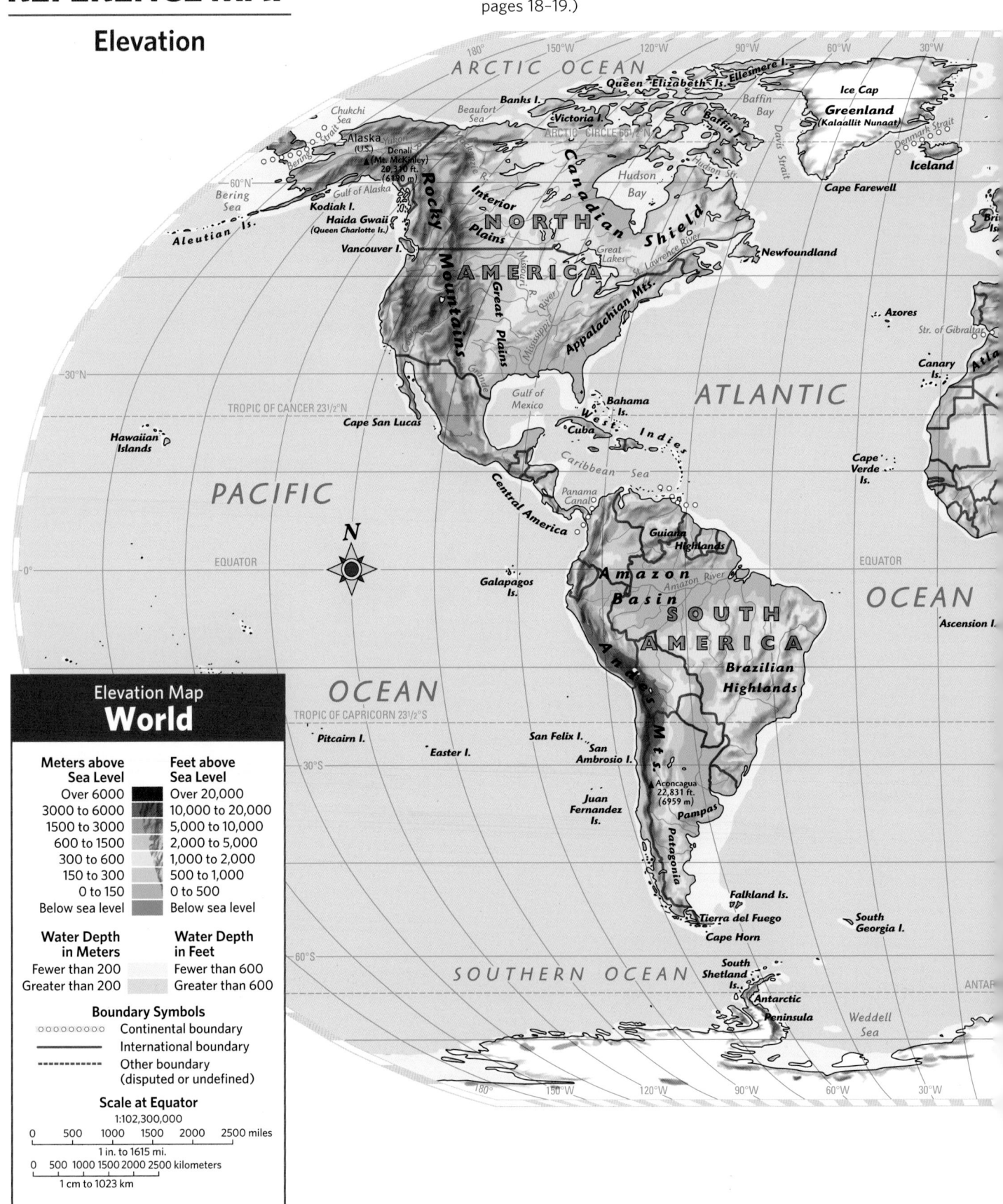

Elevation Map
World

Meters above Sea Level		Feet above Sea Level
Over 6000		Over 20,000
3000 to 6000		10,000 to 20,000
1500 to 3000		5,000 to 10,000
600 to 1500		2,000 to 5,000
300 to 600		1,000 to 2,000
150 to 300		500 to 1,000
0 to 150		0 to 500
Below sea level		Below sea level

Water Depth in Meters	Water Depth in Feet
Fewer than 200	Fewer than 600
Greater than 200	Greater than 600

Boundary Symbols

ooooooooo Continental boundary

———— International boundary

– – – – – Other boundary (disputed or undefined)

Scale at Equator

1:102,300,000

0 500 1000 1500 2000 2500 miles

1 in. to 1615 mi.

0 500 1000 1500 2000 2500 kilometers

1 cm to 1023 km

Detailed legend on page 8   Robinson Projection

North Polar View

South Polar View

ARCTIC OCEAN

Svalbard
North Cape
Barents Sea
Novaya Zemlya
Kara Sea
Severnaya Zemlya
Laptev Sea
New Siberian Is.
East Siberian Sea
Norwegian Sea
Scandinavian Peninsula
Northern European Plain
Ural Mountains
West Siberian Plain
Central Siberian Plateau
Verkhoyansk Range
Kolyma Range
ARCTIC CIRCLE 66½°N
60°N
Sea of Okhotsk
Kamchatka Peninsula
Sakhalin
Amur
EUROPE
Volga River
Ob
Yenisey River
Lena River
Siberia
ASIA
Aral Sea
L. Balkhash
Altai Mts.
Gobi
Manchurian Plain
Kuril Is.
Alps
Black Sea
Caucasus Mts.
Mt. Elbrus 18,510 ft. (5642 m)
Caspian Sea
Tien Shan
Pamirs
Kunlun Mts.
Plateau of Tibet
Huang He
Sea of Japan (East Sea)
Hokkaido
Honshu
Mediterranean Sea
Sicily
Plateau of Iran
Himalayas
Mt. Everest 29,035 ft. (8850 m)
North China Plain
Yellow Sea
Kyushu
Sahara
Ahaggar Mts.
Tibesti Mts.
Arabian Peninsula
Ganges River
Yunnan Plateau
East China Sea
Ryukyu Is.
Taiwan
PACIFIC
30°N
TROPIC OF CANCER 23½°N
Nile River
Red Sea
Deccan Plateau
Bay of Bengal
Philippine Sea
Mariana Is.
OCEAN
Sahel
AFRICA
Arabian Sea
Philippine Is.
Ethiopian Highlands
Sri Lanka
South China Sea
Caroline Is.
Congo River
Victoria
Maldives
Celebes Sea
EQUATOR
0°
Congo Basin
Mt. Kilimanjaro 19,340 ft. (5895 m)
Zanzibar I.
Seychelles
Sumatra
Borneo
Sulawesi
New Guinea
Solomon Is.
Chagos Archipelago
Java
Timor
Arafura Sea
Bie Plateau
Comoros
Timor Sea
Coral Sea
Fiji Is.
Mauritius
INDIAN
Madagascar
Mozambique Channel
Kalahari Desert
Western Plateau
Great Dividing Range
New Caledonia
Drakensberg
TROPIC OF CAPRICORN 23½°S
AUSTRALIA
30°S
OCEAN
Cape of Good Hope
Amsterdam I.
St. Paul I.
Cape Leeuwin
Darling R.
Murray R.
Mt. Kosciuszko 7,310 ft. (2228 m)
North I.
Tasmania
Bass Strait
Tasman Sea
South I.
Kerguelen I.
Stewart I.
Auckland Is.
60°S
SOUTHERN OCEAN
ANTARCTICA
Ice Cap
30°E
60°E
90°E
120°E
150°E
180°

Elevation and Landforms

Elevation is the measure of land's height or depth above or below sea level. **Landforms** are the physical features of the landscape. Most extensive landforms have patterns of high, low, or changing elevation.

- Most vast, level landforms are sections of the relatively flat tectonic plates that make up the continents.

- High landforms are produced when plates collide and push up the earth's crust or the magma below.

- Other landforms are carved or deposited by wind, water, and living beings.

- **Relief** is the difference between the highest and lowest elevation of a feature or region. Shading on a map shows landforms with rugged relief, such as mountains and hills.

Every Breath You Take

The higher you travel above sea level, the thinner the air is and the less oxygen you get with each breath. That is why climbers aiming for the world's highest peaks must first acclimatize or get accustomed to the oxygen level at one elevation range before attempting the next.

A **Mountains** can be single peaks or part of a range. The summit of Lhotse Mountain in Nepal lies at 27,940 feet (8,516 meters). Lhotse is part of the Himalayas, the highest mountain range in the world. (For more information, see page 171.)

B **Plateaus** are vast areas of relatively flat land at high elevation. The Plateau of Tibet, located in China, is the world's highest plateau. It has an average elevation of more than 14,800 feet (4,500 meters).

Elevation

Meters above Sea Level	Feet above Sea Level
Over 6000	Over 20,000
3000 to 6000	10,000 to 20,000
1500 to 3000	5,000 to 10,000
600 to 1500	2,000 to 5,000
300 to 600	1,000 to 2,000
150 to 300	500 to 1,000
0 to 150	0 to 500
Below sea level	Below sea level

Scale at Equator
1 in. to 2,860 mi., 1 cm to 1800 km

Area shown on cross section

Cross sections use **vertical exaggeration** to make shapes and elevation patterns of landscapes easier to see. Vertical exaggeration sets the vertical scale several times larger than horizontal scale.

Cross Section
Vertical exaggeration 67 to 1
Scale at 28°N: 1 in. to 425 mi., 1 cm to 270 km

Plateau of Tibet
Himalayas
Sichuan Basin
North China Plain
Yangtze R.
Sea Level

A   B   C   D

C **Basins** are low areas surrounded by higher ground. The Sichuan Basin, along the Yangtze River in southern China, is surrounded by rugged mountains. It has an elevation range between 700 and 2,500 feet (200 and 750 meters).

D **Plains** are broad stretches of nearly level land, usually found at low elevations. The fertile lowlands of the North China Plain have the best farmland in China. The elevation of the North China Plain ranges from 0 to 500 feet (0 to 150 meters) above sea level.

The Moving Earth

The land and water features of the earth appear stable, but actually they move between 1 to 5 inches (2.5 to 15 centimeters) each year.

- The earth's crust is made up of about 30 **plates** that float above the molten interior of the planet. Lighter, thicker areas of the plates form the continents. Denser, thinner areas form the ocean floors.

- Plates slide along, bump into, and move away from each other.

- **Earthquakes** and **volcanoes** are common near the boundaries between plates. When an earthquake takes place beneath the ocean, a massive, destructive wave called a **tsunami** may result.

In December 2004, a massive earthquake hit off the coast of Sumatra, Indonesia. The coastal village Aceh was destroyed by the tsunami that followed the 9.1–9.3 quake.

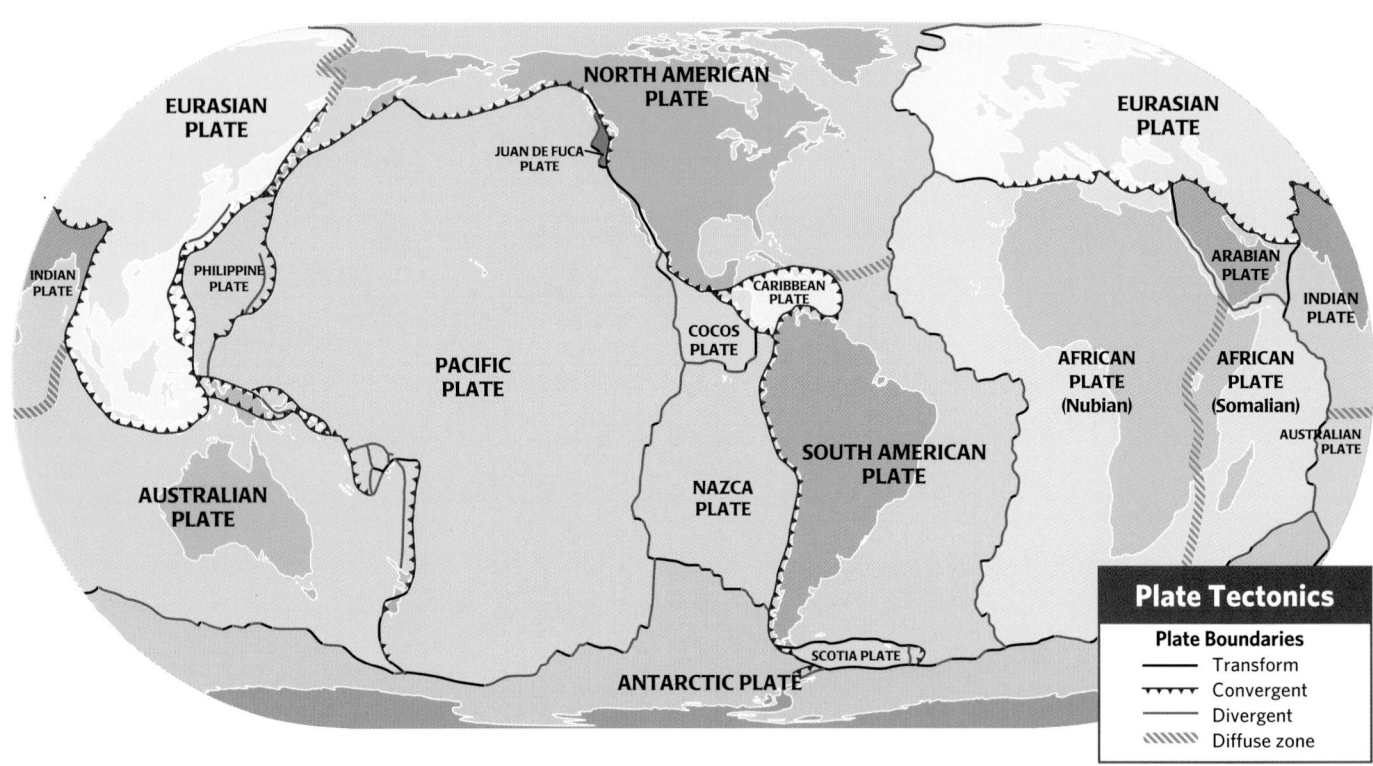

Plate Tectonics

Plate Boundaries

————	Transform
⊤⊤⊤⊤	Convergent
————	Divergent
⧄⧄⧄	Diffuse zone

Transform Plate Boundaries

These plates move side-by-side—sometimes in opposite directions, sometimes in the same direction. This type of plate movement can cause earthquakes.

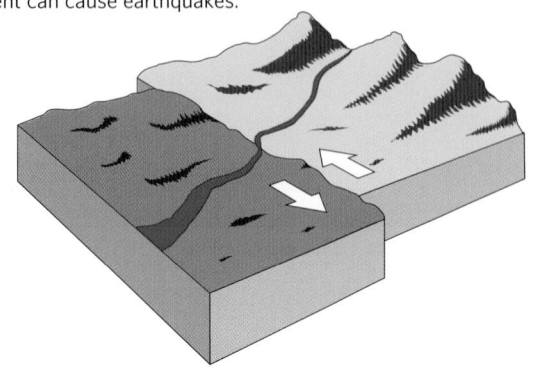

Convergent Plate Boundaries

When one plate moves under another plate—**subduction**—earthquakes and volcanoes can occur. In the long run, the subducted plate will disappear. Convergent plates can be found near South America and the coasts of Asia, and in the western Pacific.

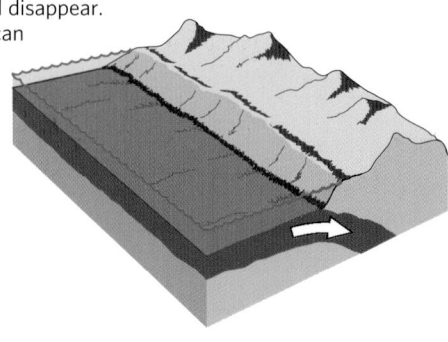

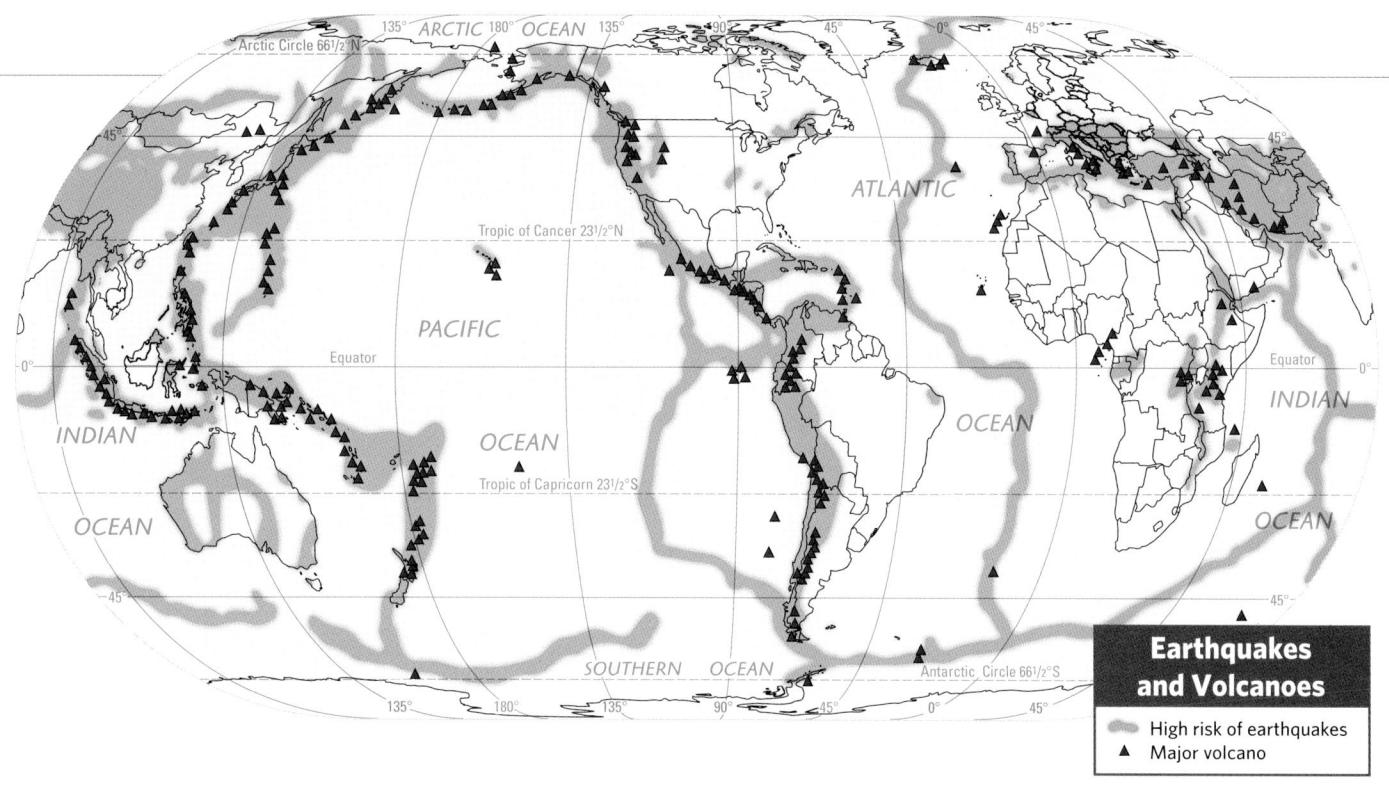

Earthquakes and Volcanoes

◠ High risk of earthquakes
▲ Major volcano

Location, Location

Why does one earthquake with a magnitude of 9.0 cause over 283,000 deaths, while another quake of the same magnitude results in none? It's all in the location. When a quake strikes near a populous area without earthquake-resistant buildings, death rates are high. Depth of the quake and stability of the overlying rock also can affect the death rate.

Divergent Plate Boundaries

These plates move away from each other in opposite directions. The Mid-Atlantic Ridge is on a divergent plate boundary. This movement causes the Atlantic Ocean to widen by about 1.5 miles (2.5 kilometers) every 100,000 years.

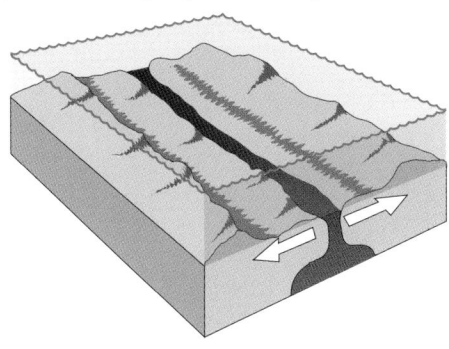

The 2011 volcanic eruption at Puyehue-Cordon Caulle in Chile sent a column of ash more than 8 miles (13 kilometers) into the air. The drifting cloud of ash disrupted air travel across South America, Australia, and New Zealand for several days.

Oceans

Ocean waters cover about 71 percent of Earth's surface. There is only one world ocean, but the continents divide the ocean into five distinct parts—the five oceans named on the map.

- A **continental shelf** is submerged land found just beyond the coastlines of the continents. A shelf may extend 19 to 190 miles (30 to 300 kilometers) from shore.

- **Abyssal plains** are the vast, flat stretches of ocean floor.

- The deepest parts of the ocean are **trenches**, which often lie 2 to 2.5 miles (3.2 to 4.0 kilometers) below the plains.

- The vast majority of sea exploitation—including fishing and gas and oil drilling—occurs on the continental shelf. Coastal areas are in the greatest danger of pollution.

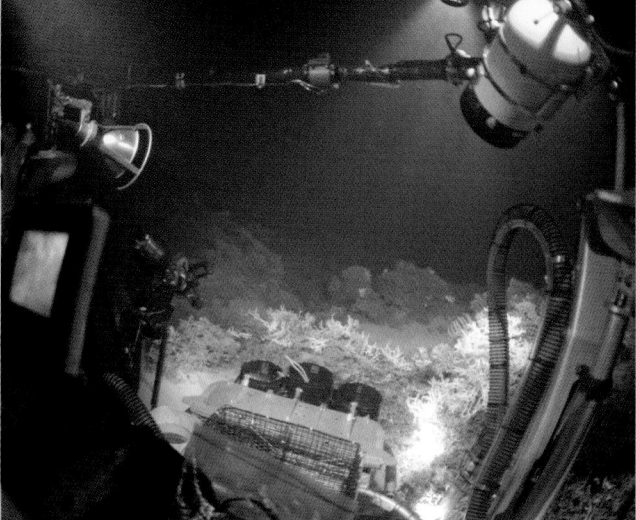

Submersibles and Remotely Operated Vehicles (ROVs) are used to explore the deep sea, the least-explored habitat on Earth. The deepest known area is the Mariana Trench, east of the island of Guam. The trench plummets more than 6.8 miles (11 kilometers) below sea level.

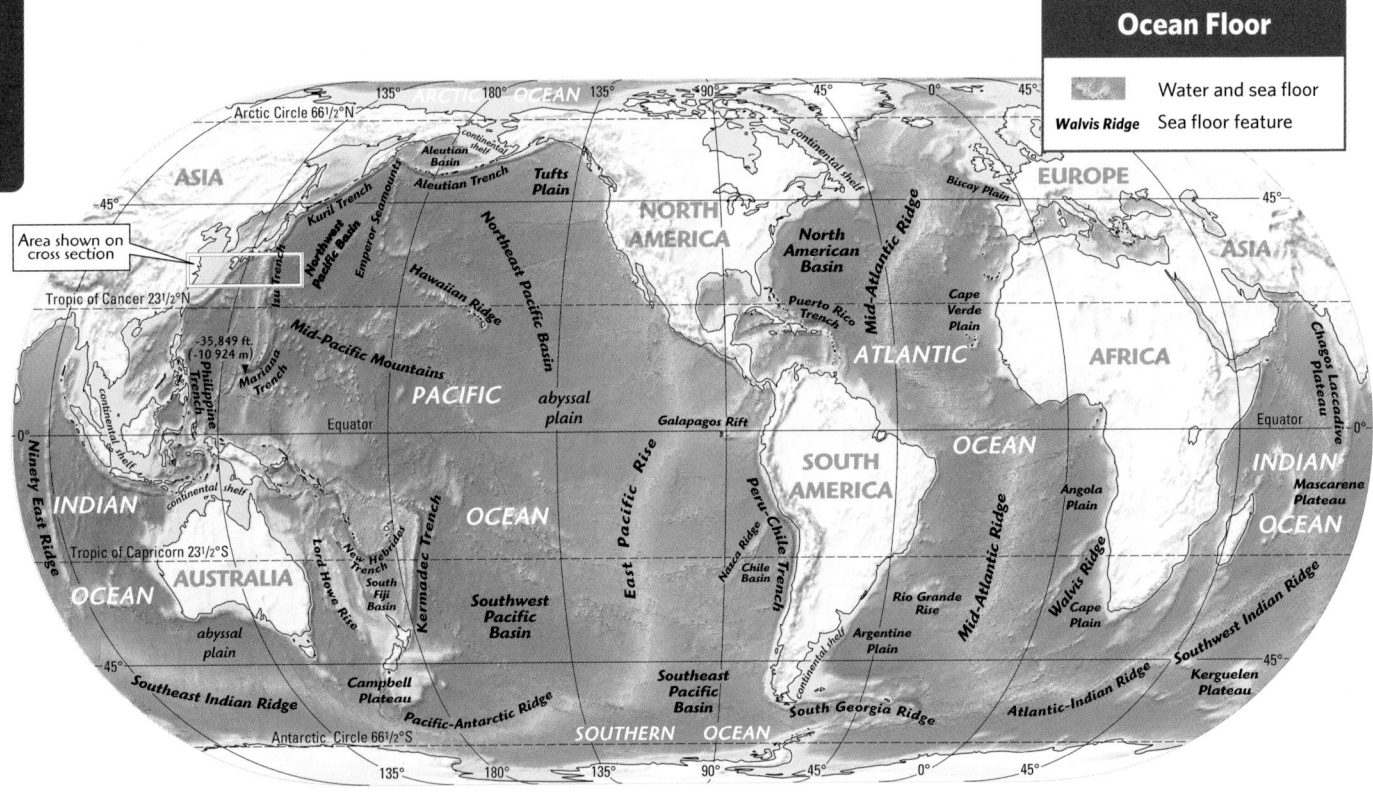

Ocean Floor

	Water and sea floor
Walvis Ridge	Sea floor feature

Cross Section

Vertical exaggeration 40 to 1
Scale at 28°N: 1 in. to 250 mi., 1 cm to 158 km

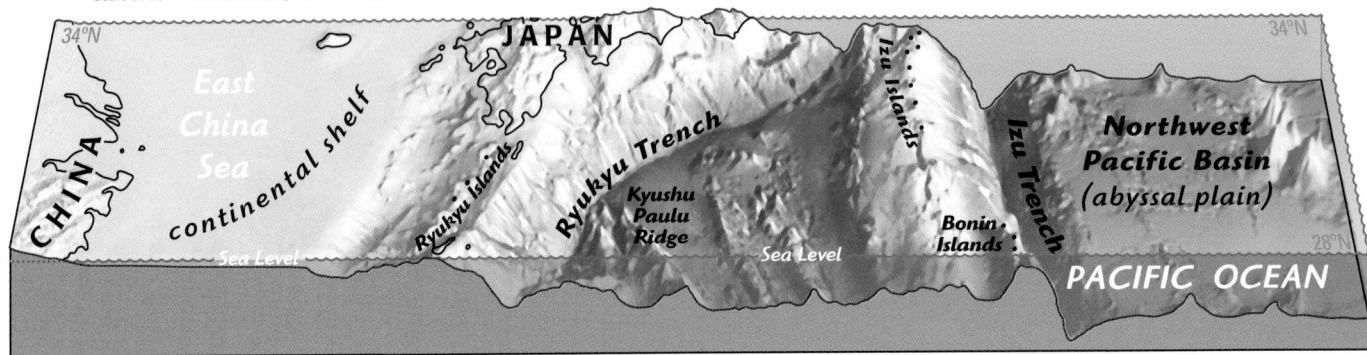

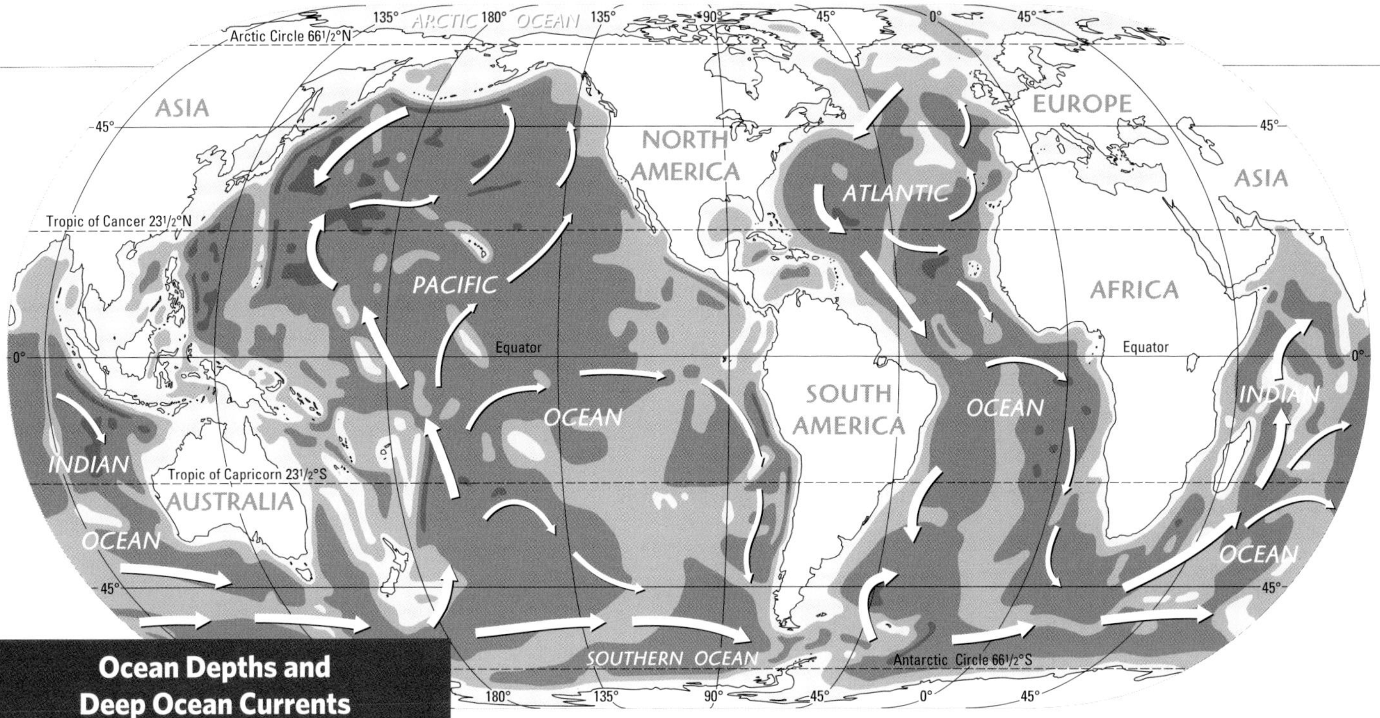

Map 1: Ocean Depths and Deep Ocean Currents

ARCTIC OCEAN

Arctic Circle 66½°N

ASIA

NORTH AMERICA

EUROPE

ASIA

ATLANTIC

Tropic of Cancer 23½°N

AFRICA

PACIFIC

Equator

Equator

OCEAN

SOUTH AMERICA

OCEAN

INDIAN

INDIAN

Tropic of Capricorn 23½°S

AUSTRALIA

OCEAN

OCEAN

SOUTHERN OCEAN

Antarctic Circle 66½°S

Ocean Depths and Deep Ocean Currents

Water Depth in Meters	Water Depth in Feet
0 to 200	0 to 600
200 to 4000	600 to 12,000
4000 to 6000	12,000 to 18,000
More than 6000	More than 18,000

Deep Ocean Currents

Primary flow

Secondary flow

Current Conditions

Deep ocean currents move like a conveyor belt. Heavy, cold, salty water from the northern Atlantic sinks. As the water warms, it moves back up to the surface. If Greenland's ice cap melts too much, it could cause the conveyor belt to shut down.

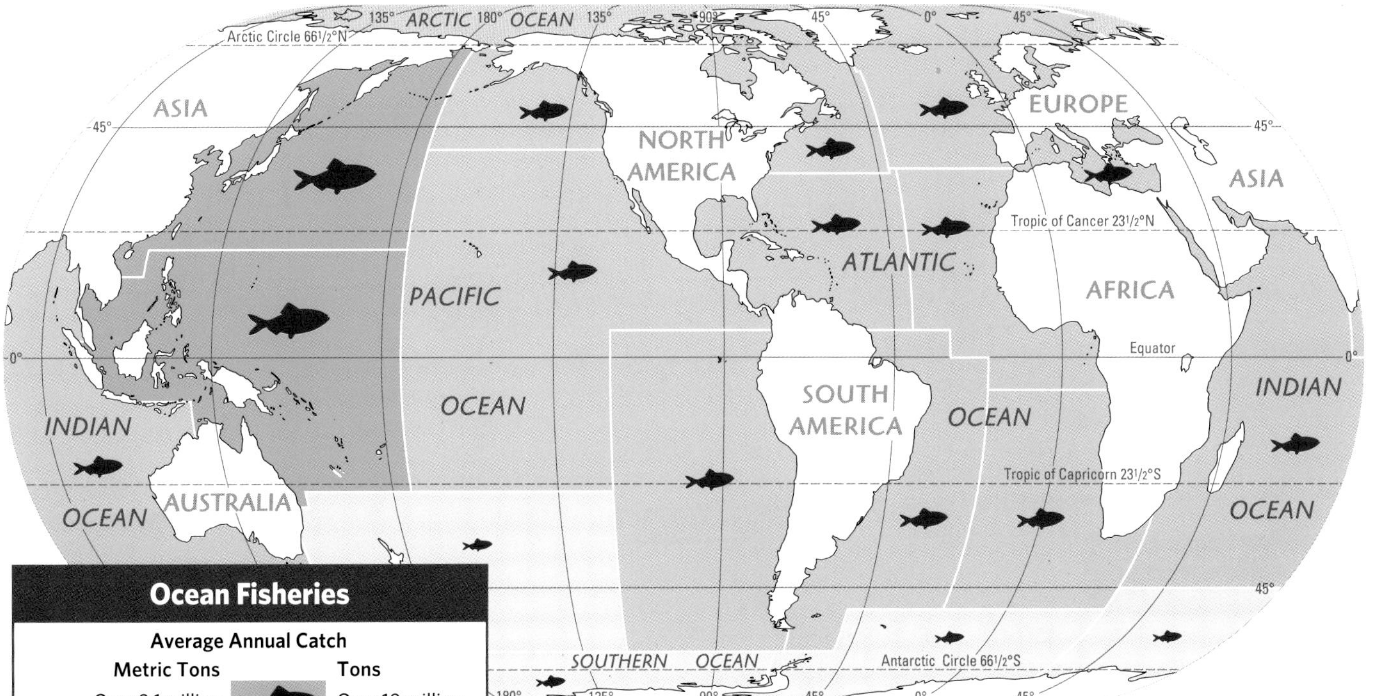

Map 2: Ocean Fisheries

ARCTIC OCEAN

Arctic Circle 66½°N

ASIA

NORTH AMERICA

EUROPE

ASIA

ATLANTIC

Tropic of Cancer 23½°N

AFRICA

PACIFIC

Equator

OCEAN

SOUTH AMERICA

OCEAN

INDIAN

INDIAN

Tropic of Capricorn 23½°S

AUSTRALIA

OCEAN

OCEAN

SOUTHERN OCEAN

Antarctic Circle 66½°S

Ocean Fisheries

Average Annual Catch

Metric Tons		Tons
Over 9.1 million		Over 10 million
910,000 to 9.1 million		1 to 10 million
Under 910,000		Under 1 million
No data		No data

Weather Patterns

Weather is the condition of the atmosphere at a given time and place. Weather involves temperature, precipitation, humidity, wind, and other factors.

- **Temperature** is a measure of how hot or cold the air is near Earth's surface.

- **Precipitation** includes rain, snow, sleet, and hail. Although, on average, 10 inches (25.4 centimeters) of snow equals about 1 inch (2.5 centimeters) of rain, the actual ratio varies. Dry, powdery snow equals less rain than wet, heavy snow.

- **Humidity** is the amount of water vapor in the air, affecting the level of comfort and chance that clouds will form.

- **Seasonal winds** affect weather patterns by moving warm, cold, moist, or dry air to a region. (See the monsoon maps on page 172.)

Salzburg, Austria, is located in the Alps. Its winters are cold, with average temperature in January of 29°F (-2°C). Winters there are snowy and drier than its summers.

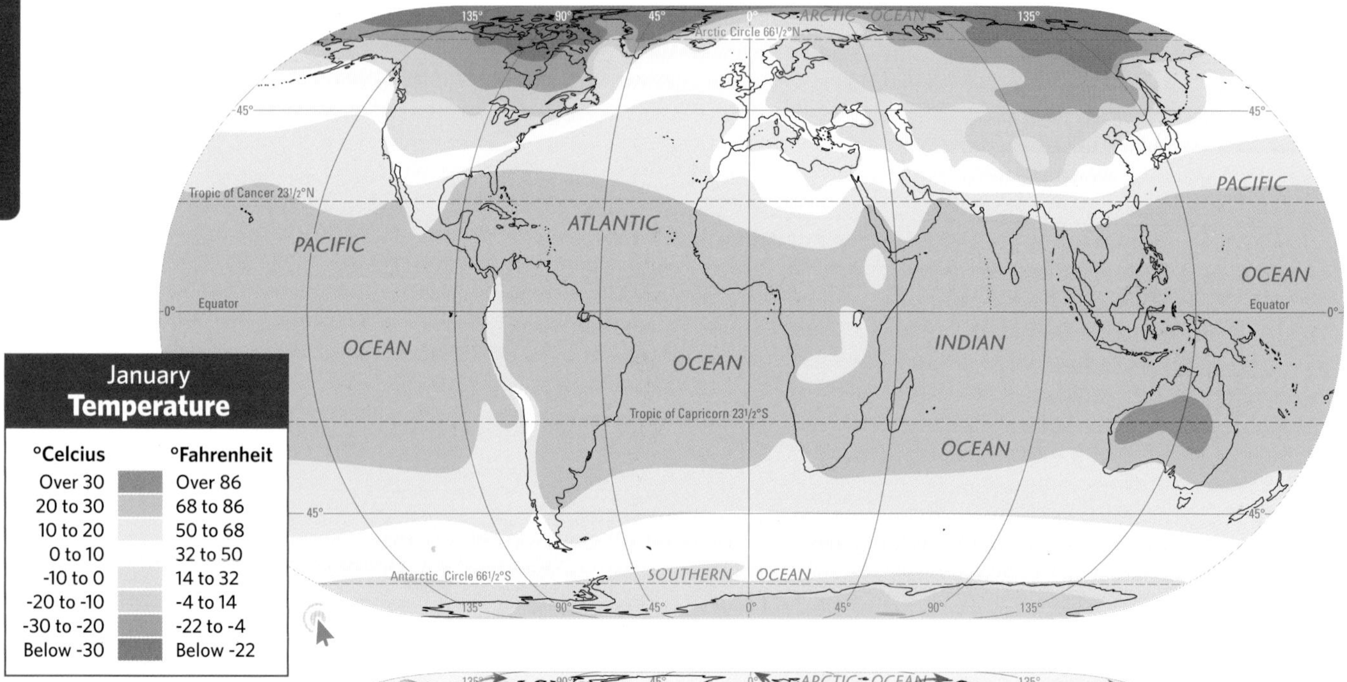

January Temperature

°Celcius		°Fahrenheit
Over 30		Over 86
20 to 30		68 to 86
10 to 20		50 to 68
0 to 10		32 to 50
-10 to 0		14 to 32
-20 to -10		-4 to 14
-30 to -20		-22 to -4
Below -30		Below -22

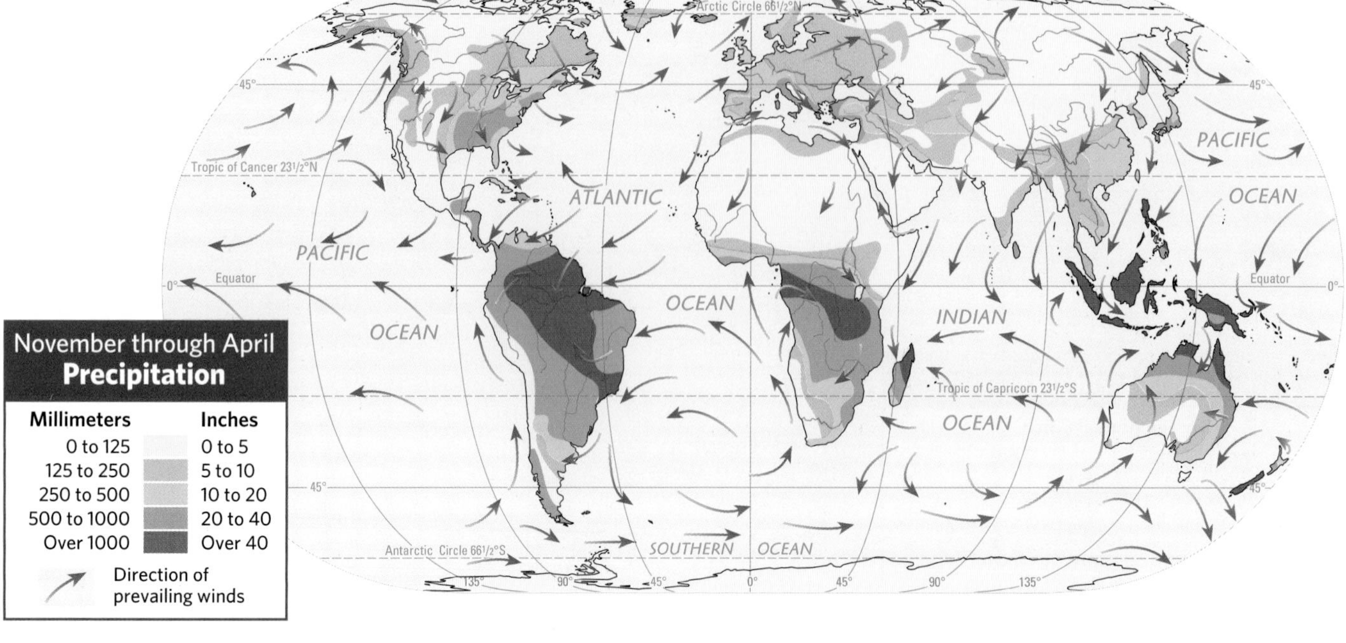

November through April Precipitation

Millimeters		Inches
0 to 125		0 to 5
125 to 250		5 to 10
250 to 500		10 to 20
500 to 1000		20 to 40
Over 1000		Over 40

↗ Direction of prevailing winds

Sun and Seasons

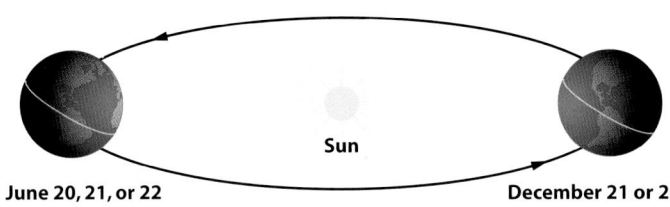

Sun
June 20, 21, or 22
December 21 or 22

The axis of the earth is tilted 23½°. From March through September, the Northern Hemisphere is tilted toward the sun and temperatures rise. The Southern Hemisphere gets warmer from September through March, when it is tilted toward the sun.

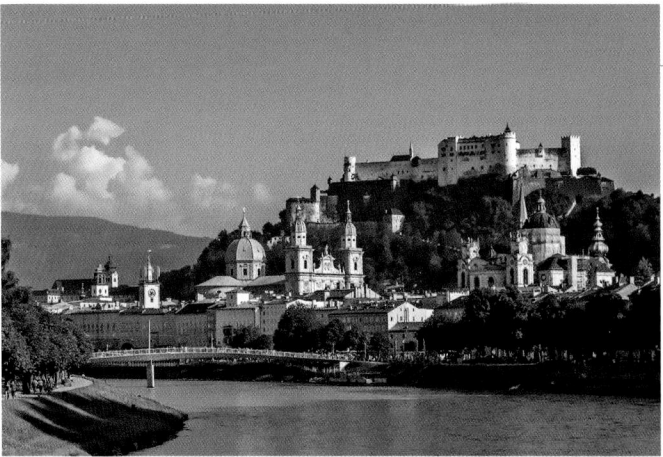

Summers in Salzburg are warm, with an average temperature in July of 64°F (18°C). In summer, the city experiences *Schnürlregen*, a heavy downpour that suddenly appears and then disappears.

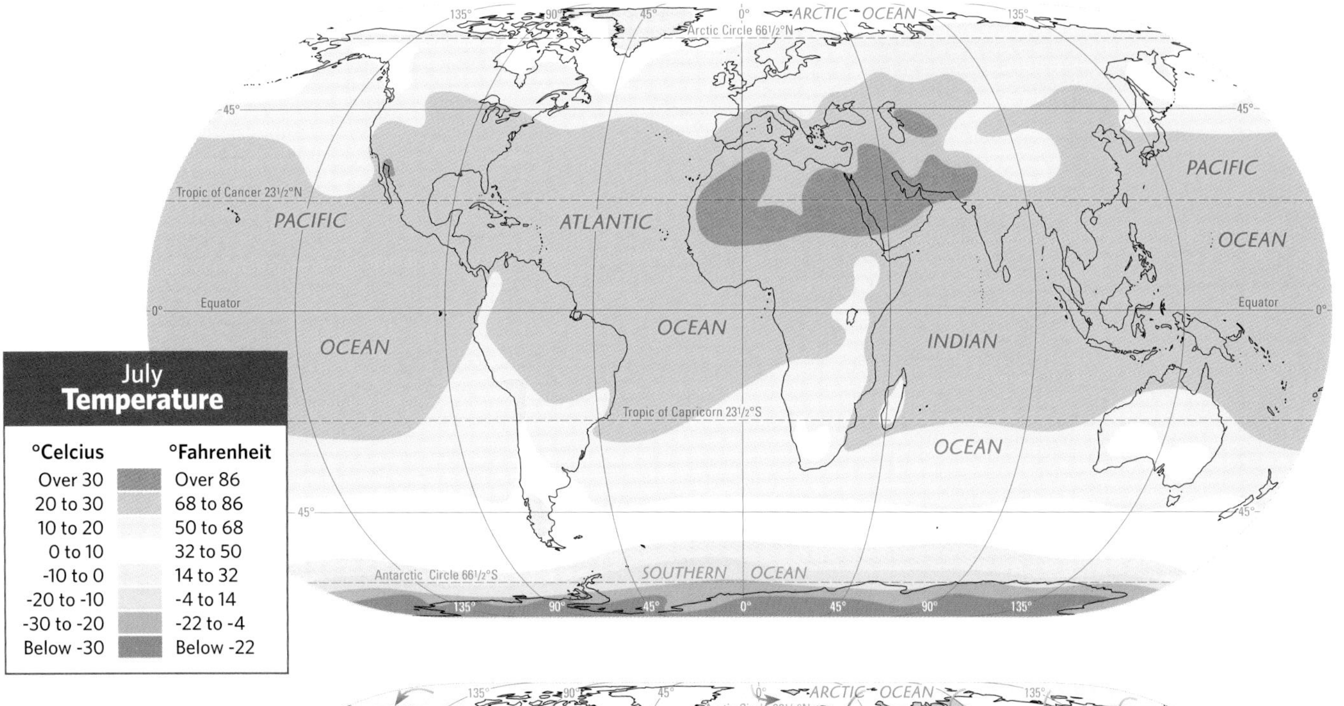

ARCTIC OCEAN
Arctic Circle 66½°N
Tropic of Cancer 23½°N
Equator
Tropic of Capricorn 23½°S
Antarctic Circle 66½°S
PACIFIC OCEAN
ATLANTIC OCEAN
INDIAN OCEAN
SOUTHERN OCEAN
July
Temperature
°Celcius
°Fahrenheit
Over 30
Over 86
20 to 30
68 to 86
10 to 20
50 to 68
0 to 10
32 to 50
-10 to 0
14 to 32
-20 to -10
-4 to 14
-30 to -20
-22 to -4
Below -30
Below -22

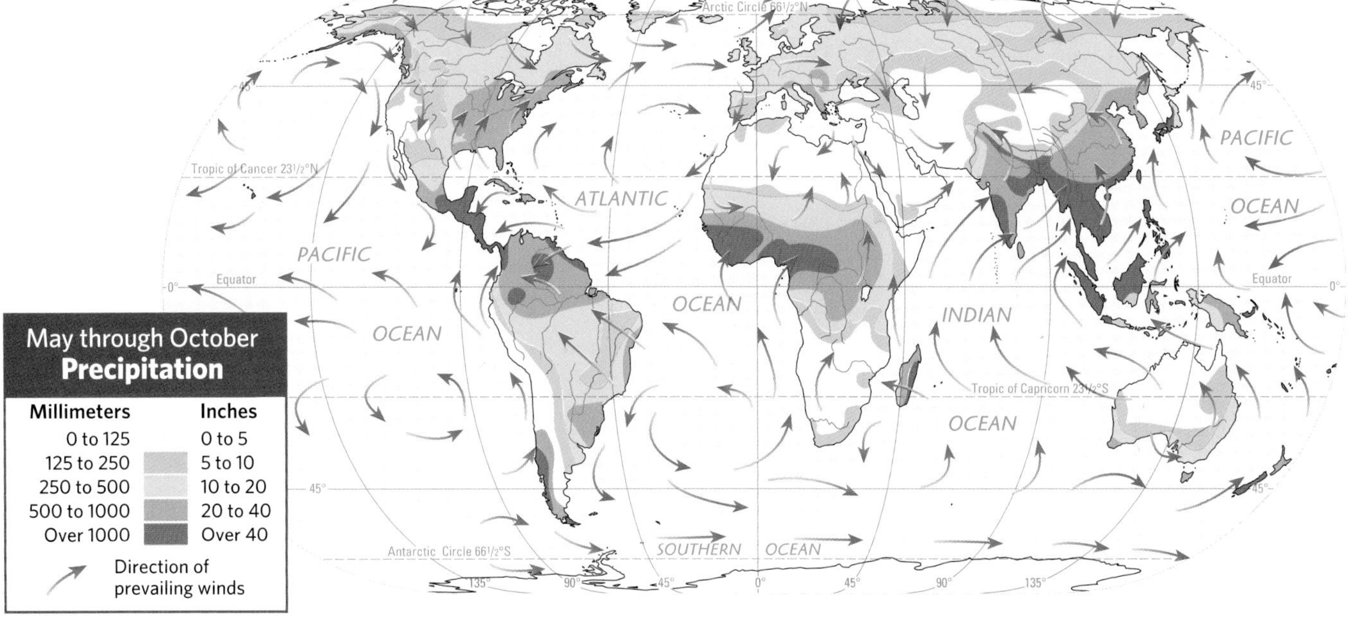

ARCTIC OCEAN
Arctic Circle 66½°N
Tropic of Cancer 23½°N
Equator
Tropic of Capricorn 23½°S
Antarctic Circle 66½°S
PACIFIC OCEAN
ATLANTIC OCEAN
INDIAN OCEAN
SOUTHERN OCEAN
May through October
Precipitation
Millimeters
Inches
0 to 125
0 to 5
125 to 250
5 to 10
250 to 500
10 to 20
500 to 1000
20 to 40
Over 1000
Over 40
Direction of prevailing winds

Climate

While **weather** describes an area's atmosphere at a *specific* time, **climate** describes the usual weather pattern of a region over a *period* of time. Elevation, latitude, distance from oceans, and surface currents help determine a region's climate.

- Temperature and moisture decrease with **elevation**.

- **Latitude** affects temperature. Regions within the **Tropics of Cancer** and **Capricorn** receive direct sunlight and are warmer than polar areas within the **Arctic** and **Antarctic Circles**.

- Earth's rotation and the coasts of the continents drive most **surface currents** in a circular pattern, transferring warm ocean water near the Equator to higher northern and southern latitudes.

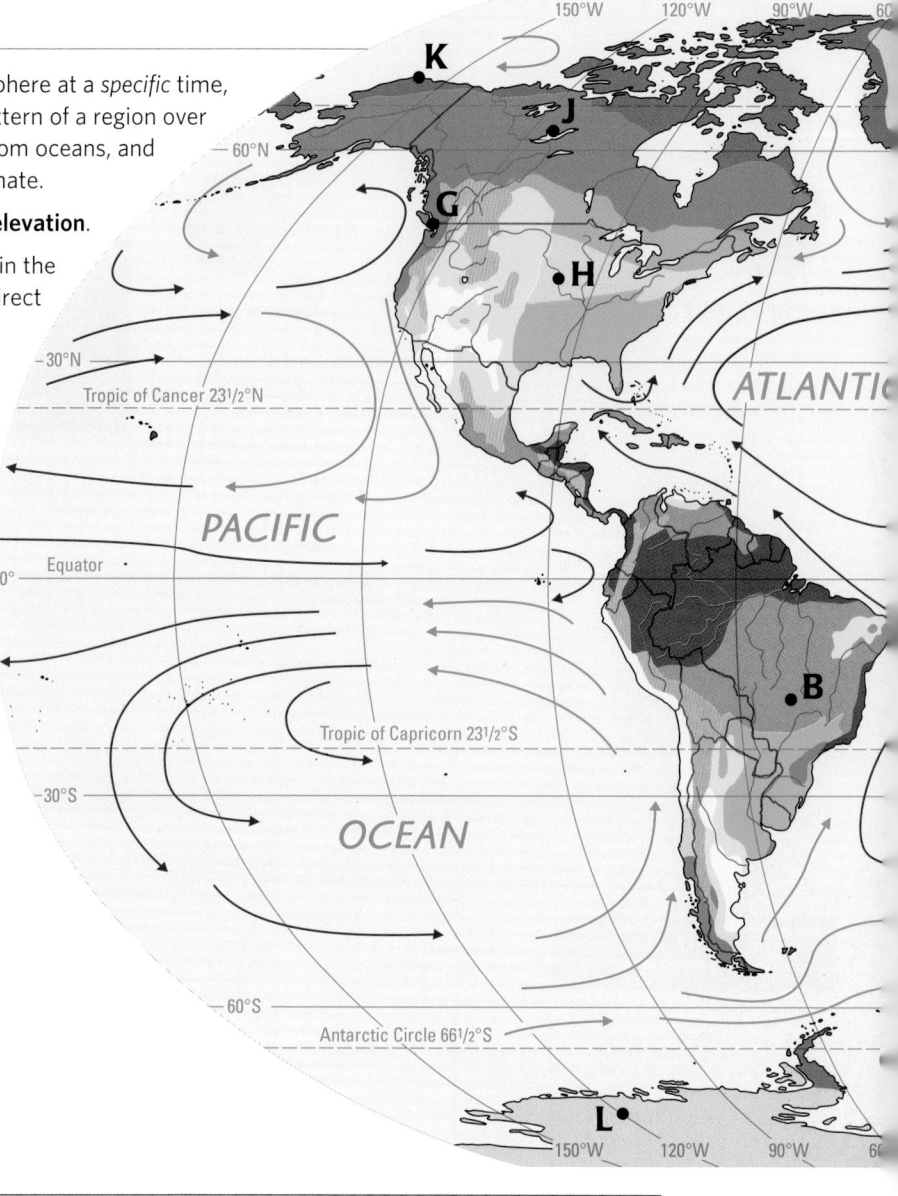

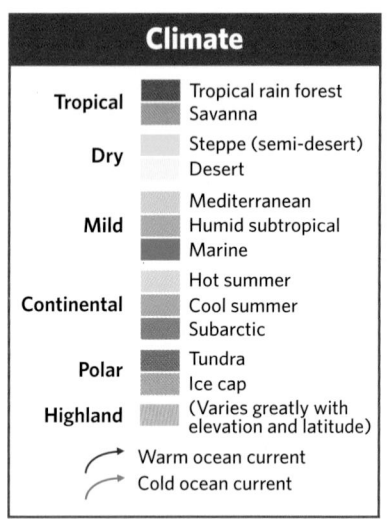

Climate

Tropical		Tropical rain forest
		Savanna
Dry		Steppe (semi-desert)
		Desert
Mild		Mediterranean
		Humid subtropical
		Marine
Continental		Hot summer
		Cool summer
		Subarctic
Polar		Tundra
		Ice cap
Highland		(Varies greatly with elevation and latitude)

→ Warm ocean current
→ Cold ocean current

Climographs

The **climographs** below show location, elevation, average 24-hour temperatures, and average monthly rainfall for several places. Letters refer to locations on the map. Colors indicate climate type. Curved lines show temperatures, while bars represent rainfall.

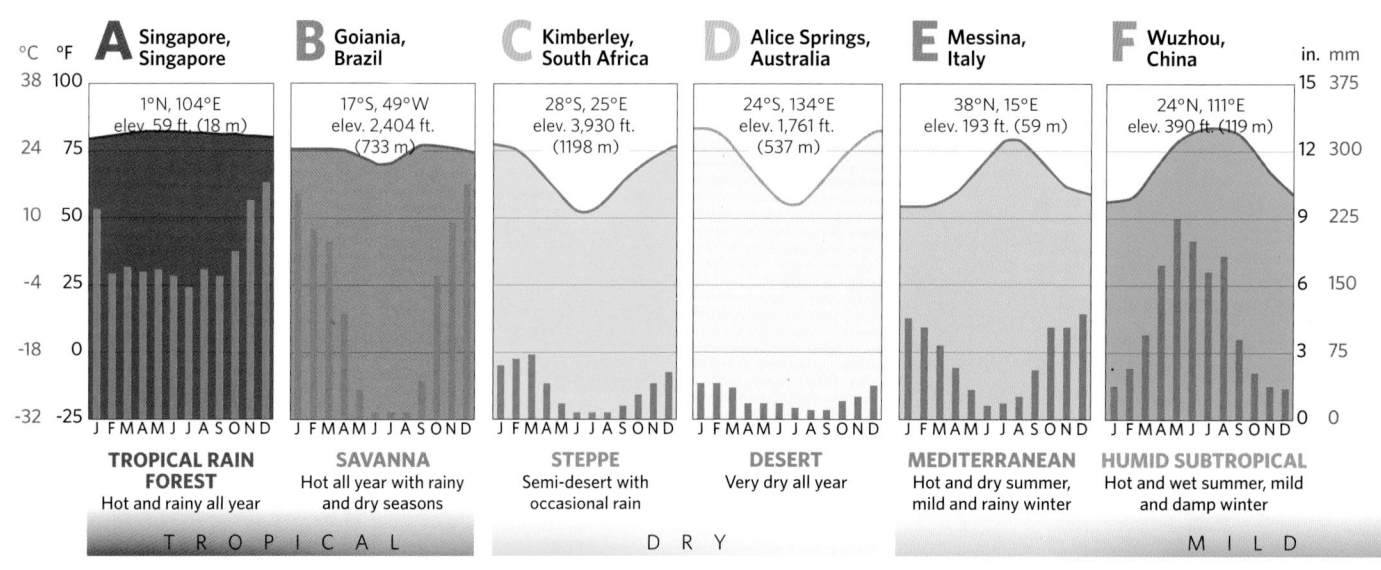

A Singapore, Singapore
1°N, 104°E
elev. 59 ft. (18 m)
TROPICAL RAIN FOREST
Hot and rainy all year

B Goiania, Brazil
17°S, 49°W
elev. 2,404 ft. (733 m)
SAVANNA
Hot all year with rainy and dry seasons

C Kimberley, South Africa
28°S, 25°E
elev. 3,930 ft. (1198 m)
STEPPE
Semi-desert with occasional rain

D Alice Springs, Australia
24°S, 134°E
elev. 1,761 ft. (537 m)
DESERT
Very dry all year

E Messina, Italy
38°N, 15°E
elev. 193 ft. (59 m)
MEDITERRANEAN
Hot and dry summer, mild and rainy winter

F Wuzhou, China
24°N, 111°E
elev. 390 ft. (119 m)
HUMID SUBTROPICAL
Hot and wet summer, mild and damp winter

T R O P I C A L   D R Y   M I L D

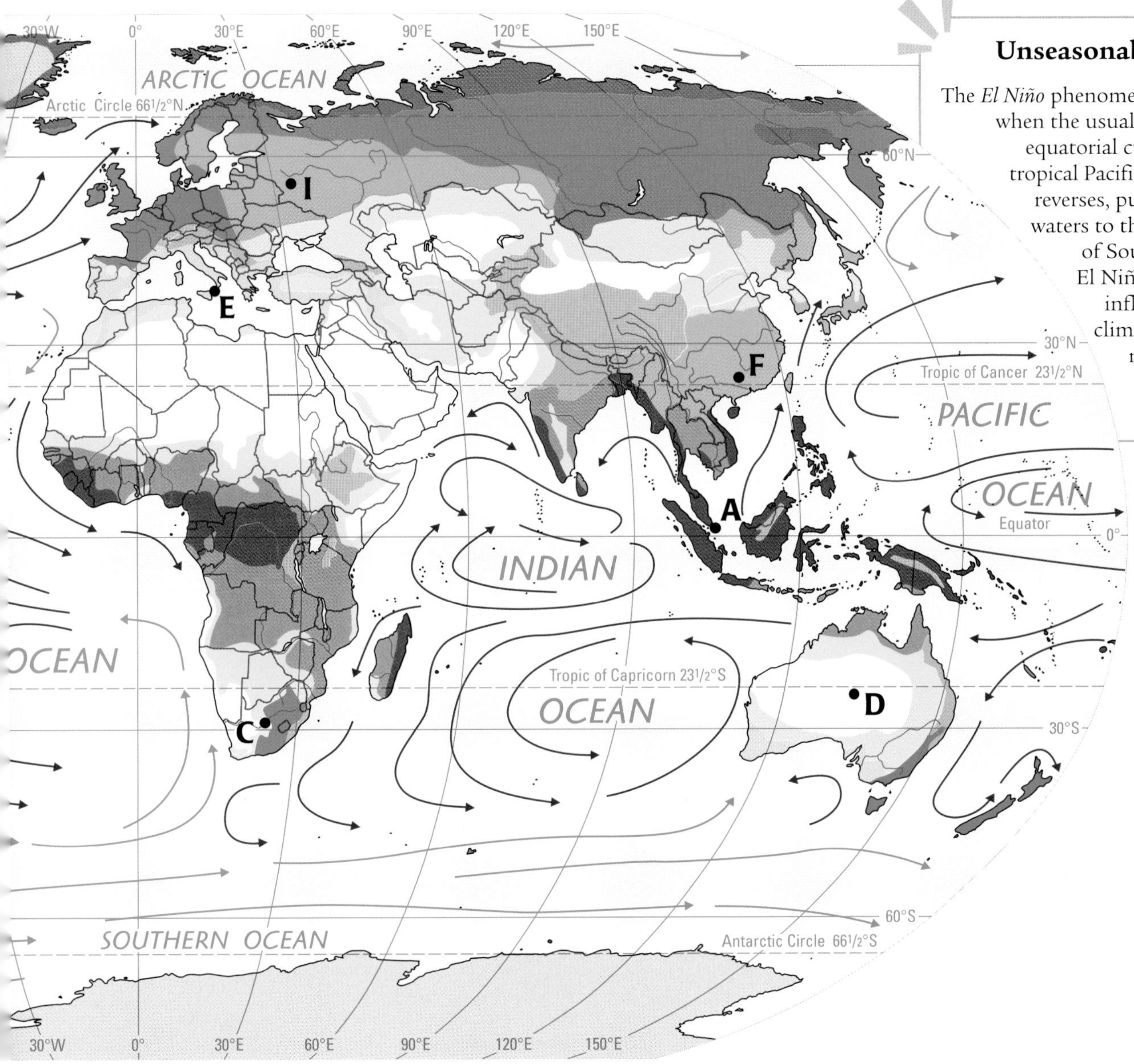

ARCTIC OCEAN

Arctic Circle 66½°N.

60°N

I

E

30°N

Tropic of Cancer 23½°N

F

PACIFIC

A

OCEAN

INDIAN

Equator 0°

C

Tropic of Capricorn 23½°S

OCEAN

D

OCEAN

30°S

SOUTHERN OCEAN

Antarctic Circle 66½°S

60°S

Unseasonably Warm

The *El Niño* phenomenon occcurs when the usual east-to-west equatorial current in the tropical Pacific weakens or reverses, pushing warm waters to the west coast of South America. El Niño events can influence world climate, but they mainly affect regions near the Pacific.

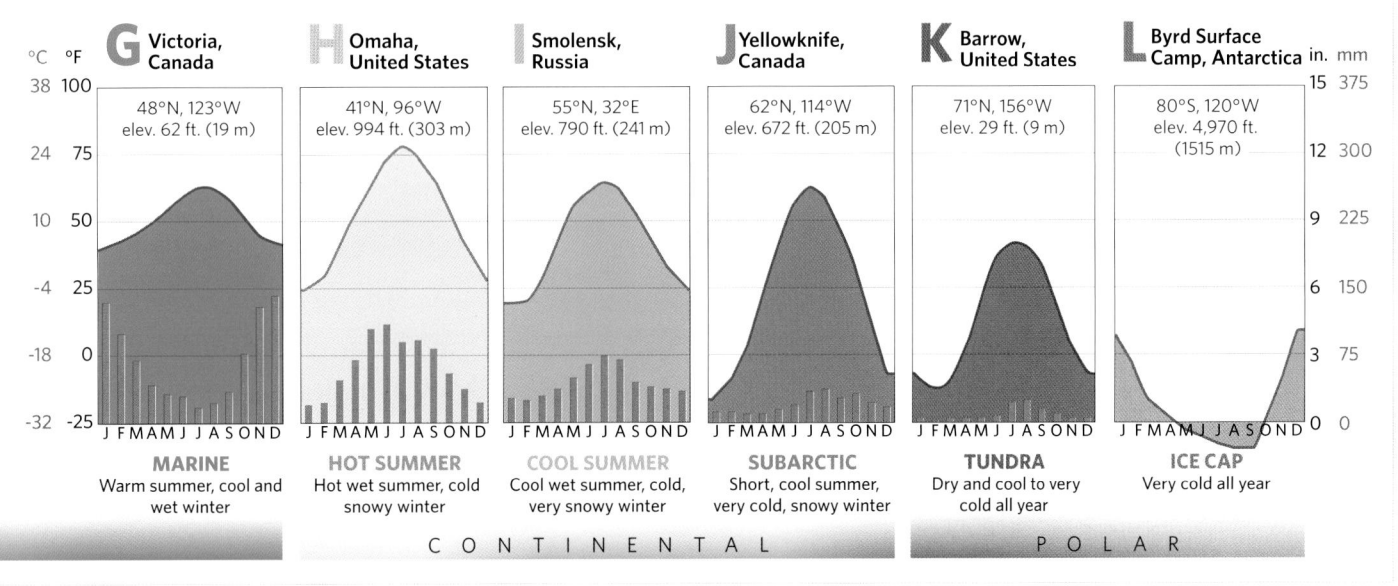

	G Victoria, Canada	**H** Omaha, United States	**I** Smolensk, Russia	**J** Yellowknife, Canada	**K** Barrow, United States	**L** Byrd Surface Camp, Antarctica	in. mm

°C °F

38 100 — 48°N, 123°W elev. 62 ft. (19 m) | 41°N, 96°W elev. 994 ft. (303 m) | 55°N, 32°E elev. 790 ft. (241 m) | 62°N, 114°W elev. 672 ft. (205 m) | 71°N, 156°W elev. 29 ft. (9 m) | 80°S, 120°W elev. 4,970 ft. (1515 m)

15 375

24 75

12 300

10 50

9 225

-4 25

6 150

-18 0

3 75

-32 -25

0 0

J FMAM J J A S O N D (×6)

MARINE
Warm summer, cool and wet winter

HOT SUMMER
Hot wet summer, cold snowy winter

COOL SUMMER
Cool wet summer, cold, very snowy winter

SUBARCTIC
Short, cool summer, very cold, snowy winter

TUNDRA
Dry and cool to very cold all year

ICE CAP
Very cold all year

CONTINENTAL

POLAR

Energy Resources

Oil (petroleum), natural gas, coal, and uranium fill most of the world's energy requirements. All but uranium are **fossil fuels** because they come from prehistoric plants and animals. All four are **consumable**—once used, they cannot be renewed.

- **Coal** is abundant and cheap. Countries use more than 8 billion tons (7.3 billion metric tons) of coal each year. Coal combustion, however, accounts for about one-third of worldwide carbon dioxide emissions.

- **Uranium** is a radioactive metal. Nuclear power plants use this energy source to generate electricity.

- **Renewable energy resources** are an important alternative to fossil fuels. They include hydroelectricity, biomass, and geothermal, ocean thermal, solar, and wind energy.

This solar power plant is in California. It provides electricity 24 hours a day by capturing energy from the sun during the day and converting it into electrical power.

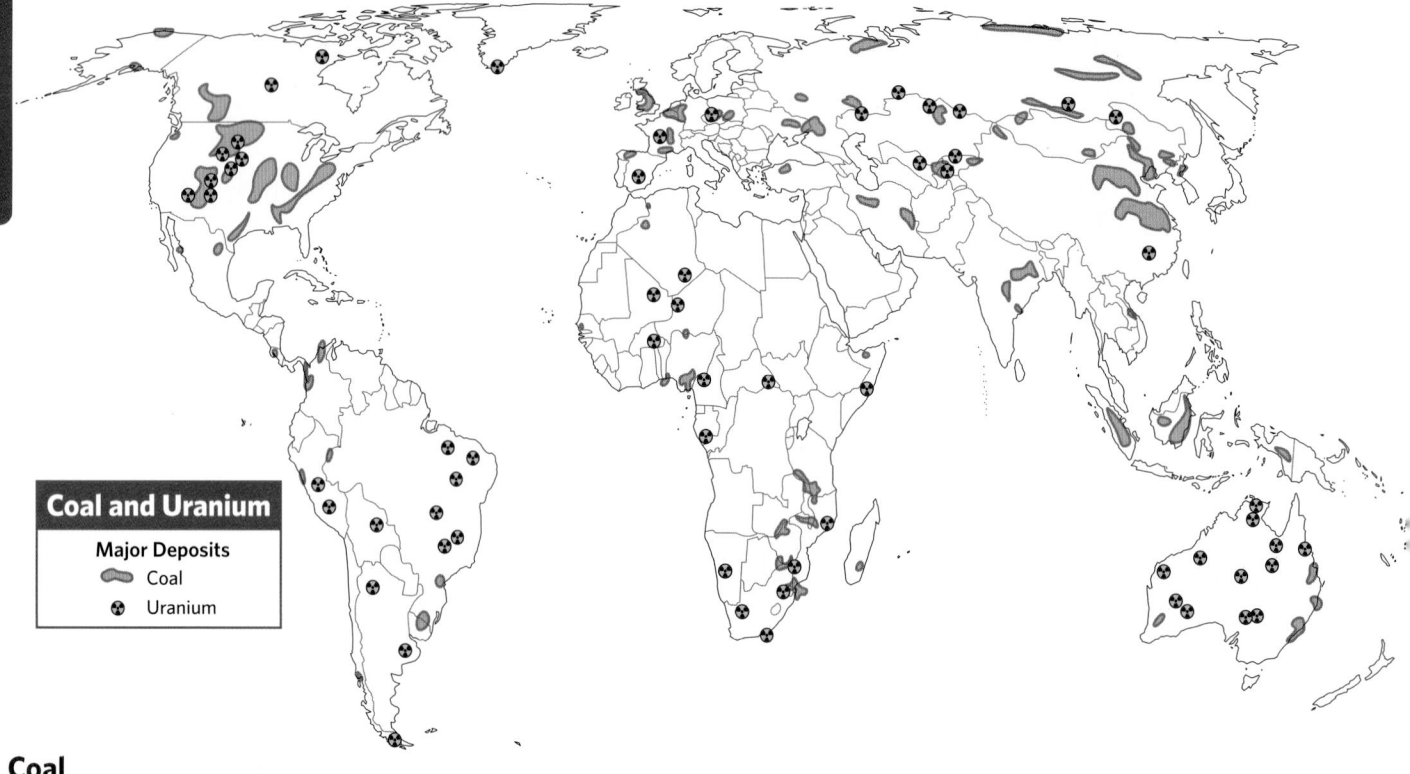

Coal and Uranium

Major Deposits
- Coal
- Uranium

Coal

	Leaders in World **Production**	
48.1%	**China**	
11.1%	**United States**	
7.6%	**India**	
5.8%	**Australia**	
5.7%	**Indonesia**	

	Leaders in World **Consumption**
China	51.3%
United States	10.2%
India	9.5%
Germany	3.0%
Russia	2.7%

Uranium

	Leaders in World **Production**
36.9%	**Kazakhstan**
16.0%	**Canada**
11.3%	**Australia**
7.9%	**Niger**
7.0%	**Namibia**

	Leaders in World **Consumption**
United States	33.6%
France	17.5%
Russia	7.2%
South Korea	6.2%
China	5.5%

Sources of World Energy

Oil is the most-used energy source in the world today. Hydroelectricity is the only major energy source that is renewable. (For more information, see pages 84, 154, and 174–175.)

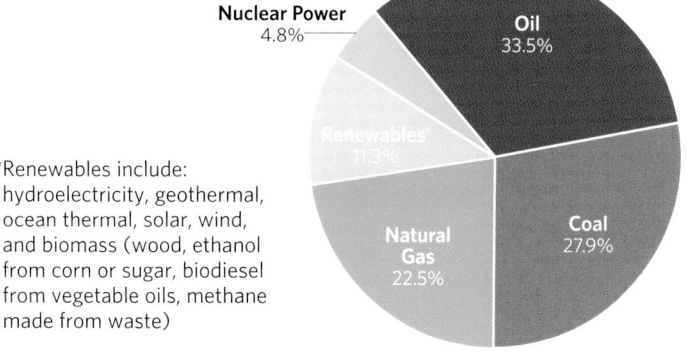

*Renewables include: hydroelectricity, geothermal, ocean thermal, solar, wind, and biomass (wood, ethanol from corn or sugar, biodiesel from vegetable oils, methane made from waste)

Nuclear Power 4.8%
Oil 33.5%
Renewables* 11.3%
Natural Gas 22.5%
Coal 27.9%

Over 85 percent of the electricity in Poland comes from fossil fuels. This particular power plant uses coal.

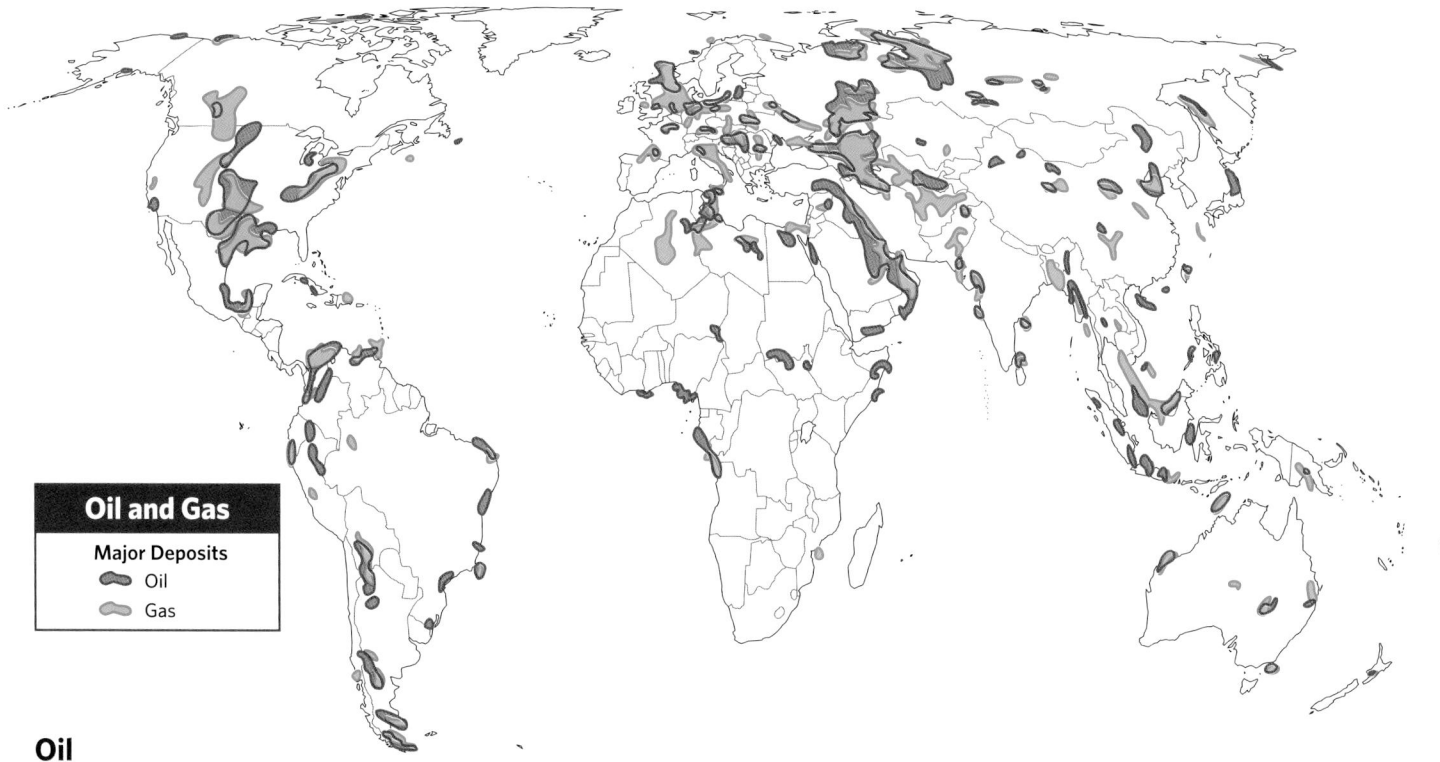

Oil and Gas

Major Deposits
- Oil
- Gas

Oil

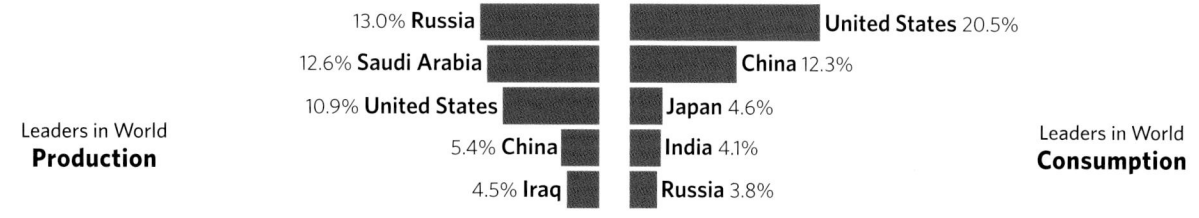

13.0% **Russia**
12.6% **Saudi Arabia**
10.9% **United States**
5.4% **China**
4.5% **Iraq**

Leaders in World **Production**

United States 20.5%
China 12.3%
Japan 4.6%
India 4.1%
Russia 3.8%

Leaders in World **Consumption**

Natural Gas

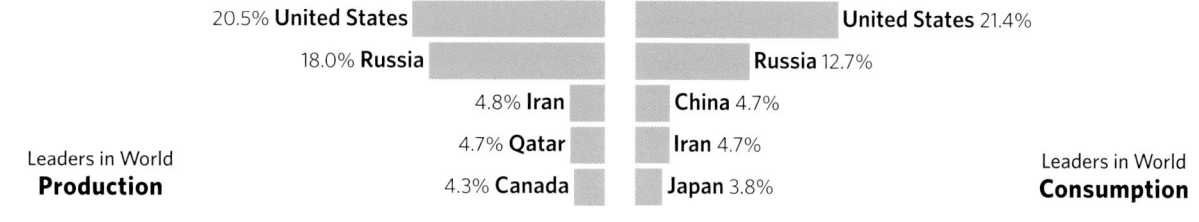

20.5% **United States**
18.0% **Russia**
4.8% **Iran**
4.7% **Qatar**
4.3% **Canada**

Leaders in World **Production**

United States 21.4%
Russia 12.7%
China 4.7%
Iran 4.7%
Japan 3.8%

Leaders in World **Consumption**

Metals

Metals are natural resources whose properties include strength, hardness, and conductivity. Metals such as iron and copper are in products that people use daily.

- **Copper** is responsible for conducting electrical currents in most homes, buildings, motors, and microprocessors.

- **Gold** and **silver** are valuable metals. They are used in dentistry and electronics, as well as in jewelry and coins.

- **Iron** is one of the most abundant and commonly used metals in the world. It is used to produce **steel** and products made from steel, such as cars, bridges, and ships.

- **Nickel, tin,** and **zinc** are often used as coatings to protect steel from rust and corrosion.

South Africa was once the long-standing world leader in gold production, but rising extraction costs and the depletion of existing mines contributed to a sharp drop in production.

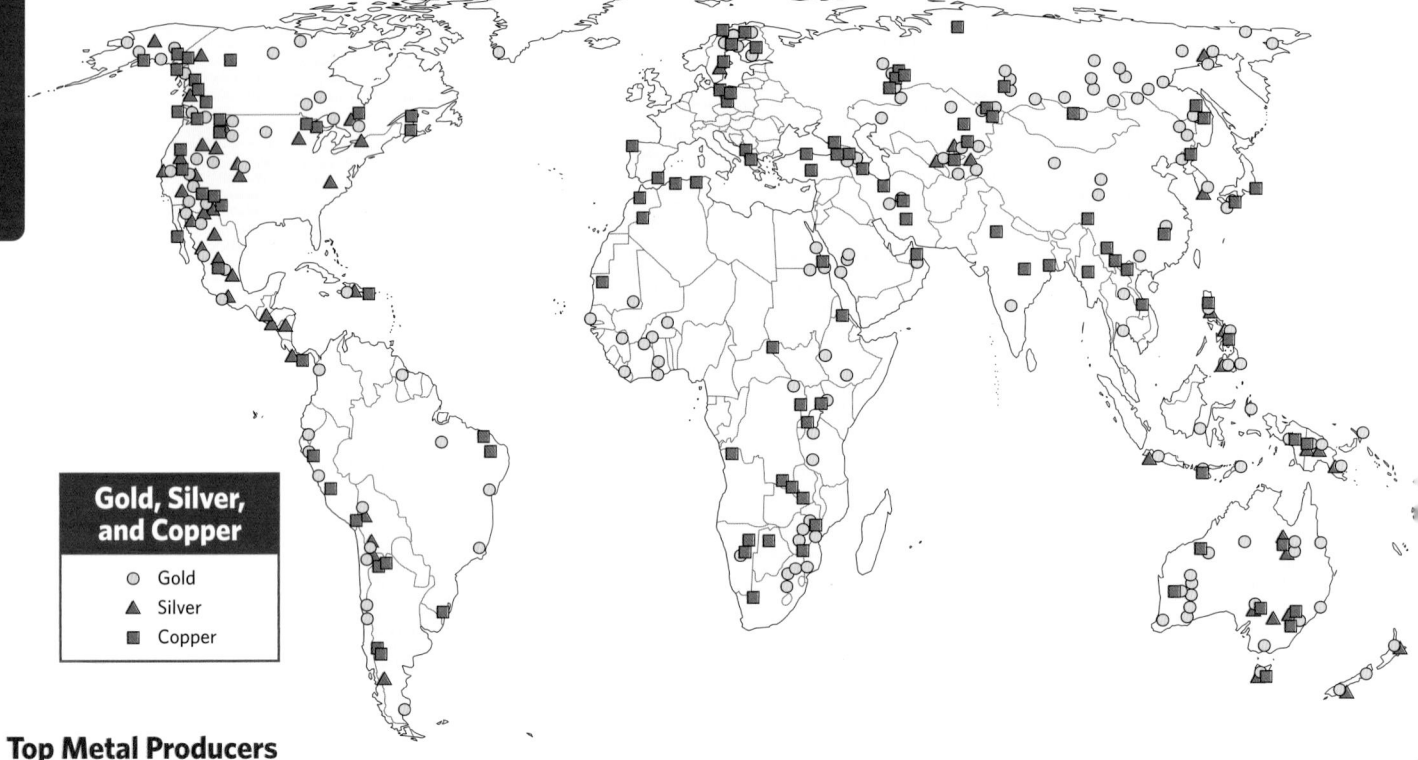

Gold, Silver, and Copper

- ● Gold
- ▲ Silver
- ■ Copper

Top Metal Producers

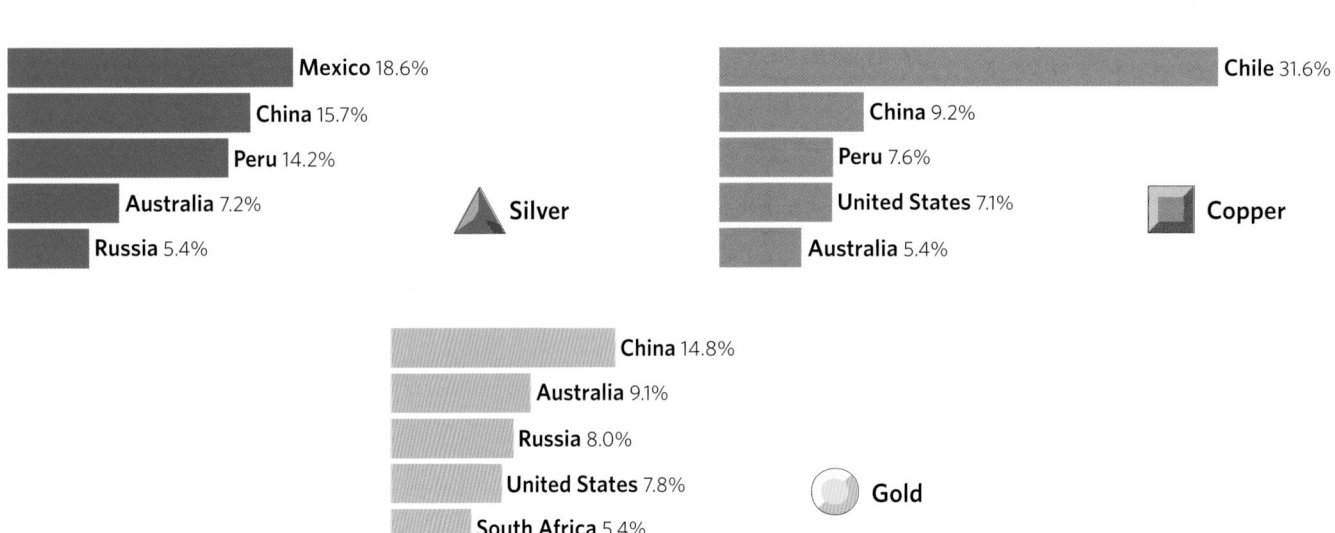

Mexico 18.6%
China 15.7%
Peru 14.2%
Australia 7.2%
Russia 5.4%

▲ **Silver**

Chile 31.6%
China 9.2%
Peru 7.6%
United States 7.1%
Australia 5.4%

■ **Copper**

China 14.8%
Australia 9.1%
Russia 8.0%
United States 7.8%
South Africa 5.4%

● **Gold**

Coal (becomes coke when heated to 2400°F [1300°C])

Limestone

Iron ore

Nickel and chromium added for stainless steel.

Basic oxygen furnace

Blast furnace

Molten iron

Molten steel

Tin added for tin cans.
Zinc added for galvanized steel.

Steel cools

Rolled into sheets

Steel Production

China, Japan, India, and the United States are leaders in steel production worldwide. China has all the raw materials it needs to produce steel. Japan, on the other hand, imports nearly all of its raw materials.

Iron, Nickel, Tin, and Zinc

◇ Iron
◆ Nickel
✚ Tin
✳ Zinc

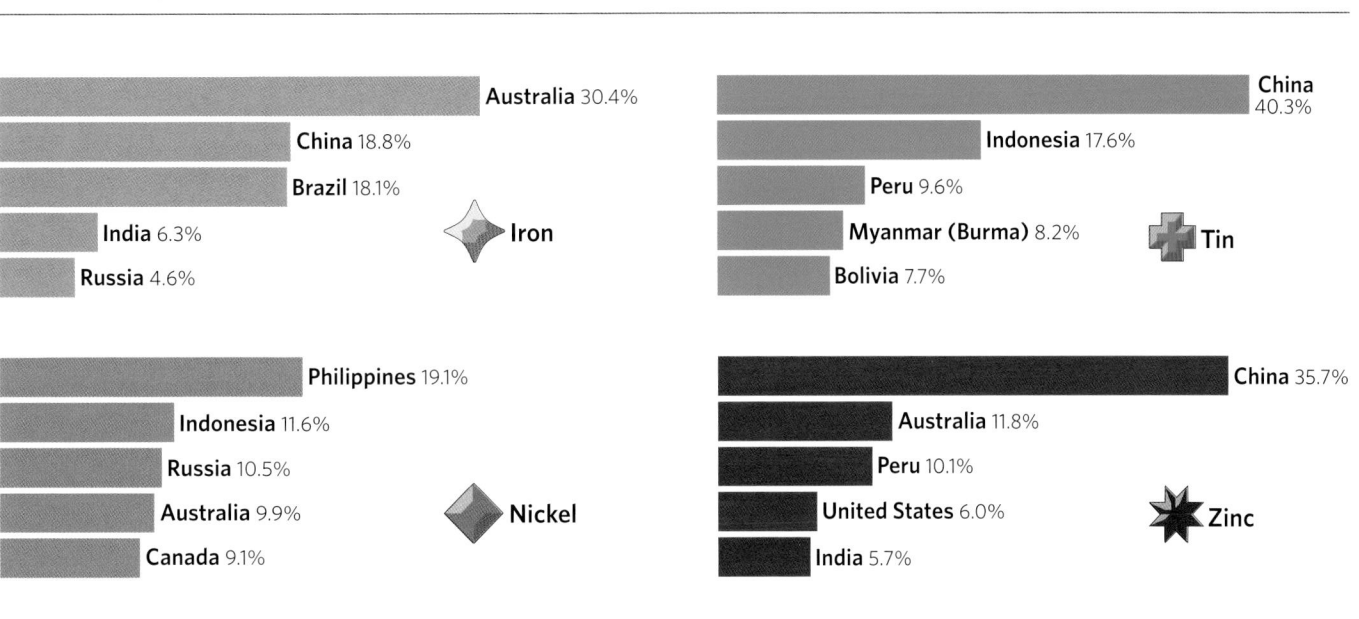

Australia 30.4%
China 18.8%
Brazil 18.1%
India 6.3%
Russia 4.6%

◇ Iron

China 40.3%
Indonesia 17.6%
Peru 9.6%
Myanmar (Burma) 8.2%
Bolivia 7.7%

✚ Tin

Philippines 19.1%
Indonesia 11.6%
Russia 10.5%
Australia 9.9%
Canada 9.1%

◆ Nickel

China 35.7%
Australia 11.8%
Peru 10.1%
United States 6.0%
India 5.7%

✳ Zinc

Using the Land

Land cover, such as desert or cropland, is the most common ground cover found in a given area, though most areas also may contain other types of land cover. **Land use**, such as farming or herding, is the most economically valuable human use of land in a given area, though the area often has other uses as well.

- Land cover often affects the way an area's land can be used.
- At nearly a third of the world's total land cover, **forests** are the most prevalent land cover on Earth.
- **Urban areas** are cities and their surrounding suburbs. Although urban areas are home to about half the world's population, they are the least widespread use of land on Earth.

Tundra

No widespread use

B **Tundra** is used for **nomadic herding** or has **no widespread use** at all. In spring and summer, the frozen soil thaws 1 to 10 feet (0.3 to 3 meters) below the surface, allowing only small plants and low shrubs to grow. This tundra is in northern Canada.

Needleleaf forest

Forestry

A **Needleleaf forests**, as well as **tropical rain forests** and **broadleaf forests**, are used for **forestry**. Only half of the world's original forests remain standing. Canada is home to one-tenth of them.

Cartography 101

How do you map land cover? With a combination of high-tech sources and cartographic techniques. Satellite imagery and scientific analysis provide a detailed picture of the land. Then mapmakers adjust colors and add shading.

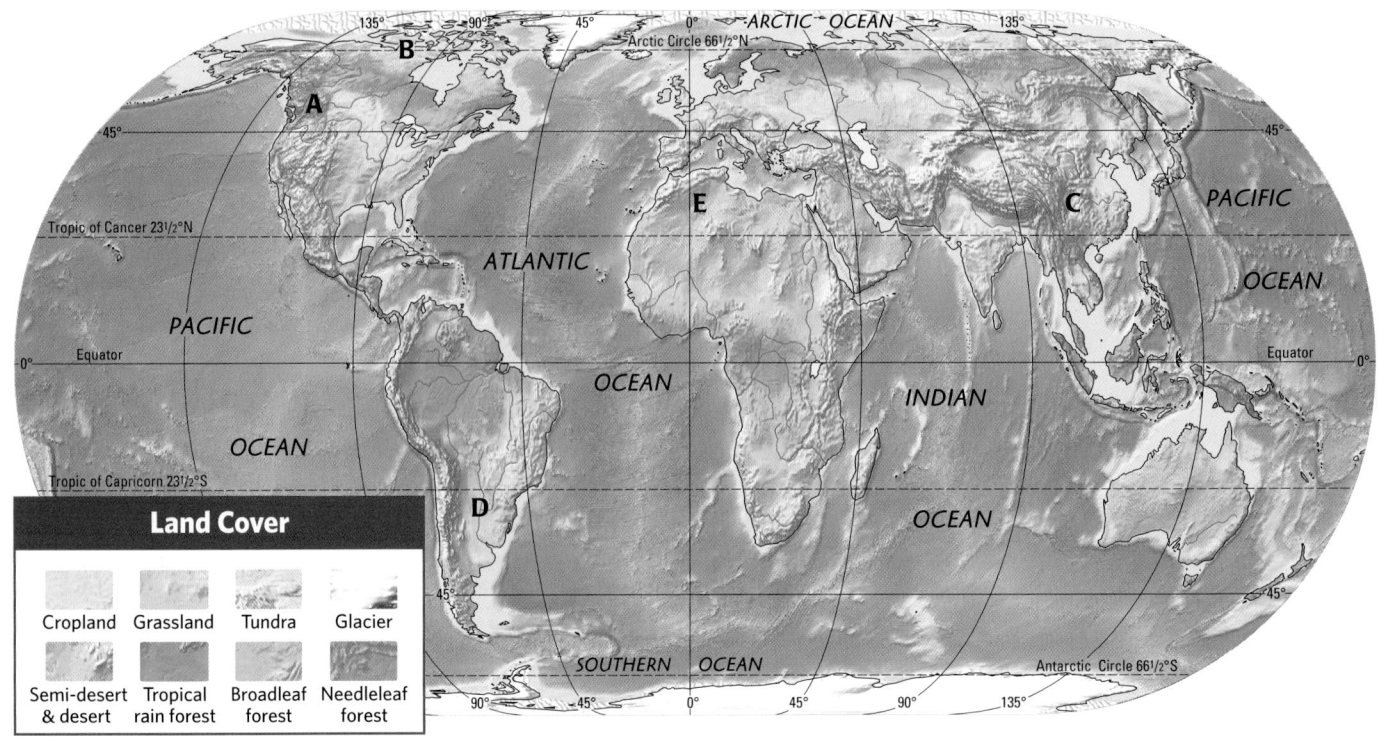

Land Cover

Cropland	Grassland	Tundra	Glacier
Semi-desert & desert	Tropical rain forest	Broadleaf forest	Needleleaf forest

D **Grasslands** are primarily used for **ranching** or **herding**. Ranching often takes place on land too dry to farm. This herd of cattle is grazing on a plain in northern Argentina.

E **Deserts** and **semi-deserts** are typically used for **nomadic herding** or have **no widespread use**. Nomadic herders seasonally move their animals to fresh grazing areas and water. These herders lead camels across the Sahara in Sudan.

C **Cropland** is used for **subsistence farming** or **commercial farming**. Subsistence farmers only are able to raise enough food for their families. Commercial farms raise enough food to sell. These terraced commercial rice fields in China maximize the use of hilly land.

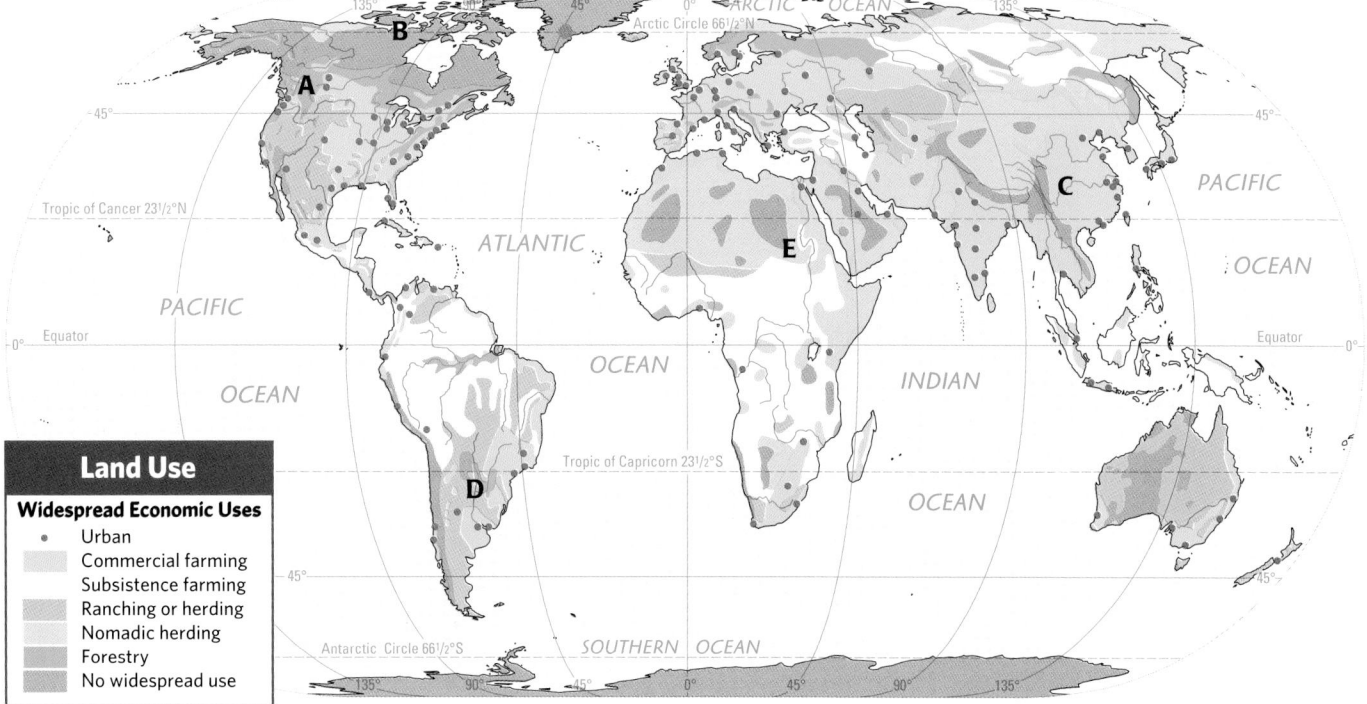

Land Use

Widespread Economic Uses

- • Urban
-   Commercial farming
-   Subsistence farming
-   Ranching or herding
-   Nomadic herding
-   Forestry
-   No widespread use

Environmental Issues

The **environment**, the natural world that we inhabit with all other living things, is affected and often harmed by human activities.

- **Acid rain** is precipitation that contains sulfuric, nitric, or other acids. This precipitation, caused by the burning of fossil fuels, can kill plants and make lakes too acidic for fish.

- **Tropical rain forests** are shrinking at an alarming rate due to logging, mining, and clearing land for agriculture.

- **Global warming** is the increase in the temperature of the earth's atmosphere. Rates of global warming in recent decades are significantly greater than rates of naturally occurring climate change. Scientists have concluded that human activities, such as burning fossil fuels and clearing forests, are the cause.

Wind can carry air pollutants around the globe. Particulate matter in the air can deplete nutrients in soil, make lakes and streams more acidic, and contribute to the effects of acid rain. Acid rain has eroded this statue.

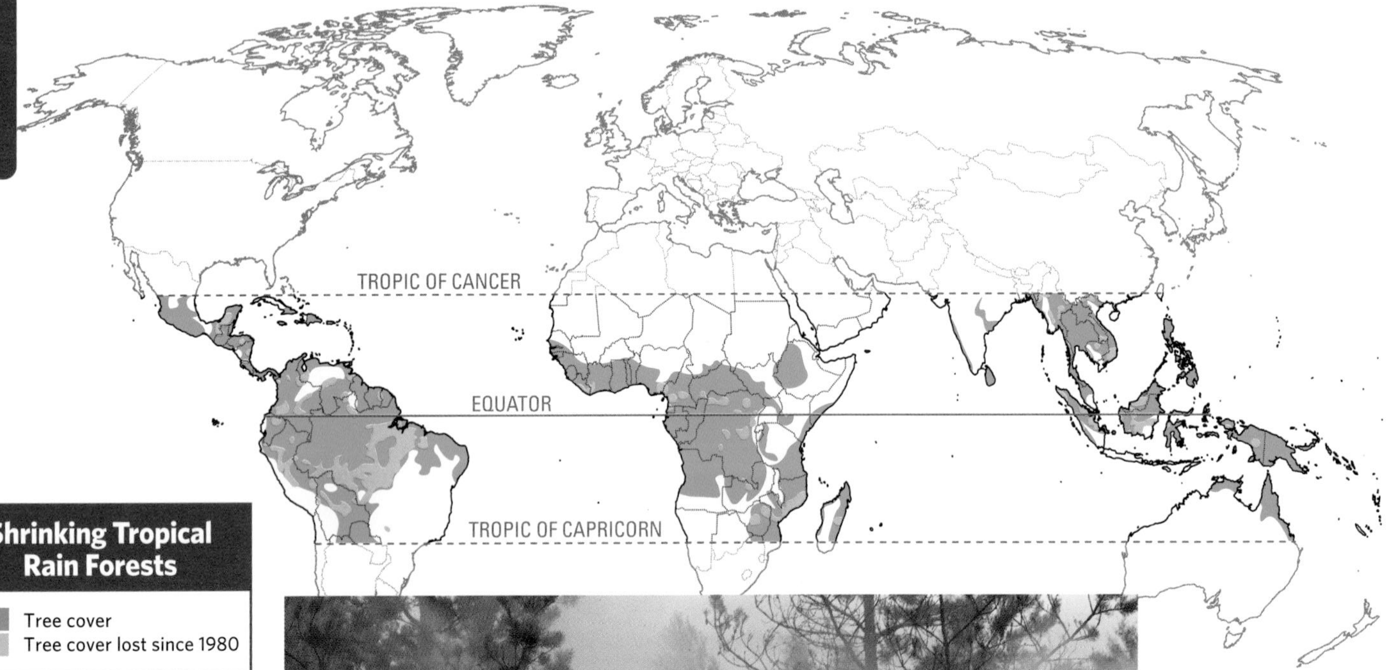

TROPIC OF CANCER

EQUATOR

TROPIC OF CAPRICORN

Shrinking Tropical Rain Forests

Tree cover
Tree cover lost since 1980

Deforestation has reduced tropical rain forests on nearly every continent since 1950. Every year between 29 and 37 million acres of the earth's forests are lost as forest lands are cleared for other uses. (For more information, see page 129.)

In slash-and-burn farming, areas of forests are cut and burned to clear space to grow crops. While this is the most prevalent form of deforestation, it leads to loss of soil fertility.

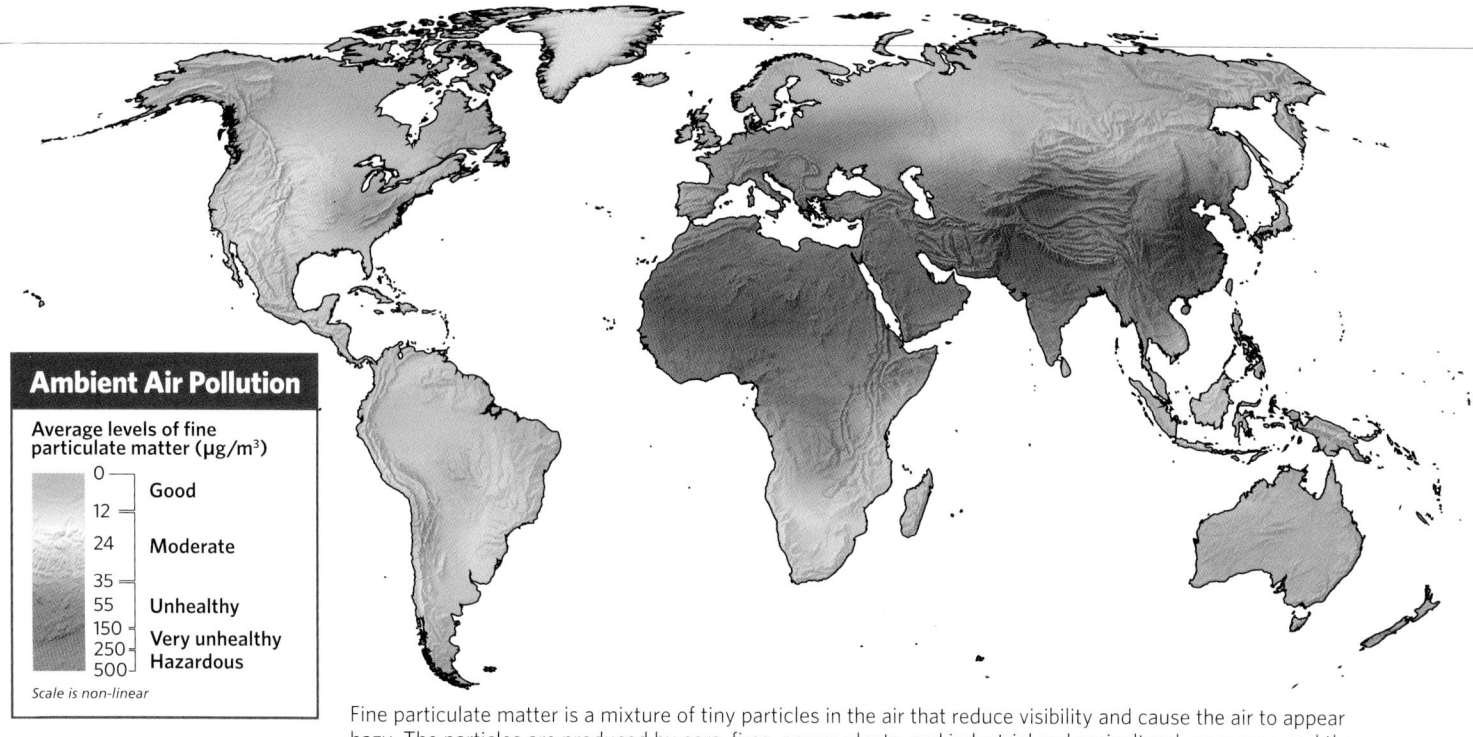

Ambient Air Pollution

Average levels of fine particulate matter (µg/m³)

0	Good
12	
24	Moderate
35	
55	Unhealthy
150	Very unhealthy
250	Hazardous
500	

Scale is non-linear

Fine particulate matter is a mixture of tiny particles in the air that reduce visibility and cause the air to appear hazy. The particles are produced by cars, fires, power plants, and industrial and agricultural processes, and the wind can carry them long distances. Breathing in these particles is dangerous, and they also have a negative effect on the environment. (For more information, see page 162.)

Rising Costs

Tuvalu is a small island country in the western Pacific Ocean near the Equator. As the oceans rise due to climate change, Tuvalu may soon be underwater, forcing its inhabitants to evacuate. By the year 2050, the global economy could lose an estimated US$12 trillion—or 10 percent of global gross domestic product—due to climate change.

Global Warming and Sea Ice

The polar ice cap expands and contracts every year, melting to its smallest size in September, before freezing weather returns. Compare the ice cap in 1979 and 2016. More ice melts now because polar summers are warmer and longer. Melting sea ice does not raise the water level, but melting glaciers do.

September 1979

September 2016

Growing Population

Earth is home to more than 7.3 billion people. Its population continues to grow by about 80 million people per year.

- **Population density** is the average number of people living in a square mile or square kilometer of a region. The world's population density is about 128 people per square mile (49 per square kilometer).

- **Overpopulation** occurs when a population has outgrown an area's resources, such as land and water. Large parts of India, China, and Nigeria are overpopulated.

- **Natural population growth** is calculated by subtracting the total deaths from the total births in an area. It does not include migration to or from the area. The world has a growth rate of 1.1 percent.

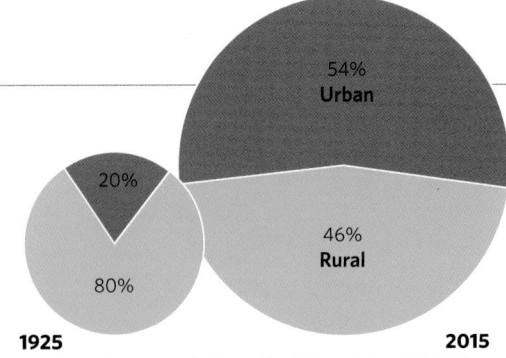

1925
Total Population 1.9 billion

2015
Total Population 7.3 billion

Urbanization

The world's urban population has more than quadrupled in the past 50 years. As farming becomes more efficient, people move to cities in search of jobs. Over half of the world's population now lives in urban areas.

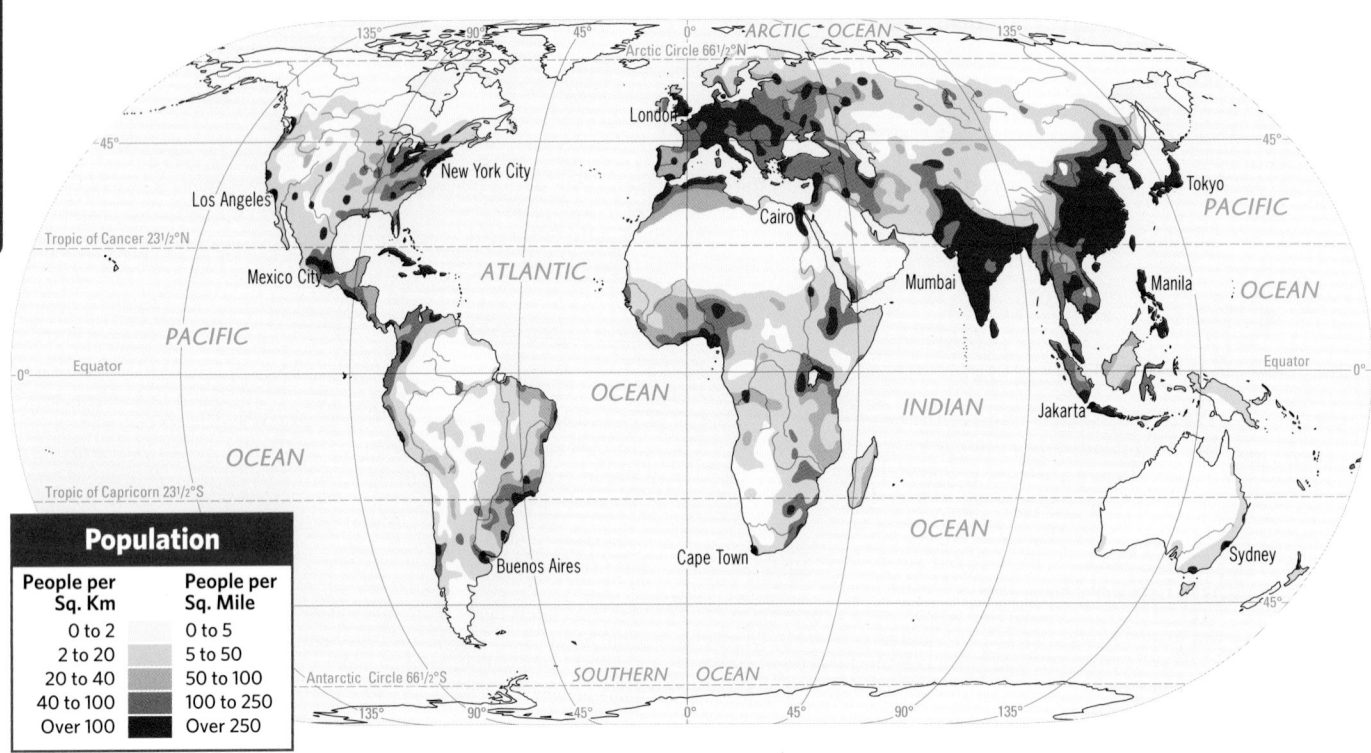

Population

People per Sq. Km	People per Sq. Mile
0 to 2	0 to 5
2 to 20	5 to 50
20 to 40	50 to 100
40 to 100	100 to 250
Over 100	Over 250

Ups and Downs

There is an inverse relationship between prosperity and population. When people have access to quality health care and proper nutrition, they live longer. When women are educated, employed, and can expect that their children will survive childhood, they tend to have fewer children.

Population Pyramids

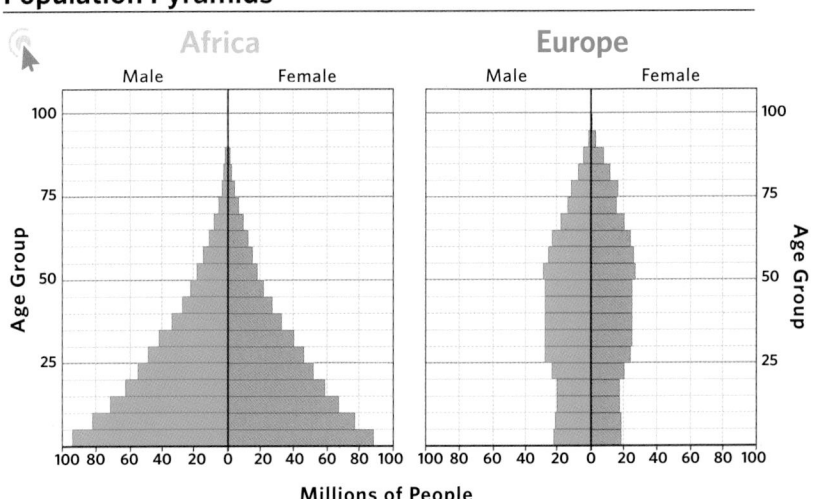

Most of Africa's population is young. This is in stark contrast to the population of Europe, which has over two times as many people over the age of 64 as Africa.

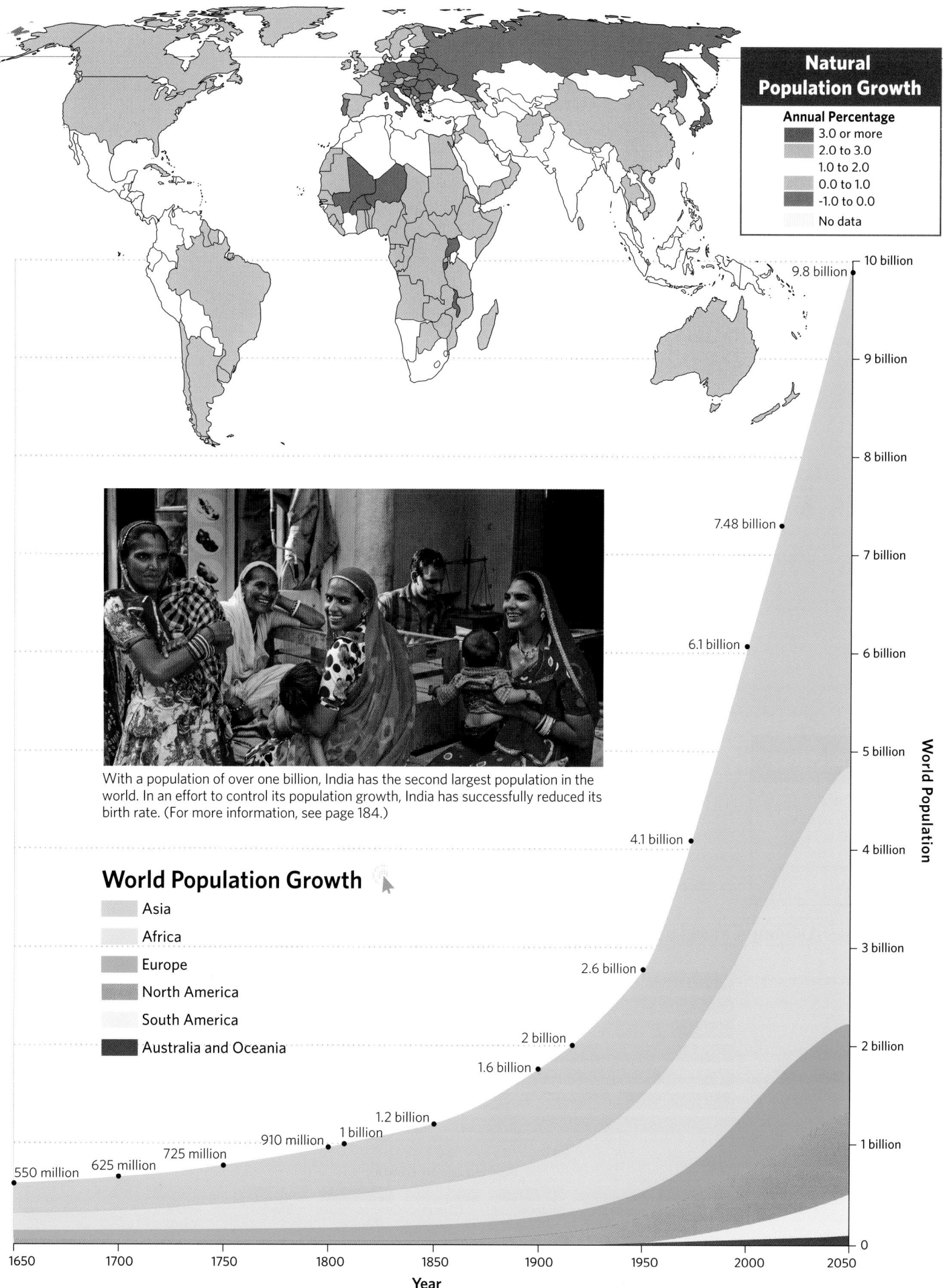

Natural Population Growth

Annual Percentage
- 3.0 or more
- 2.0 to 3.0
- 1.0 to 2.0
- 0.0 to 1.0
- -1.0 to 0.0
- No data

With a population of over one billion, India has the second largest population in the world. In an effort to control its population growth, India has successfully reduced its birth rate. (For more information, see page 184.)

World Population Growth

- Asia
- Africa
- Europe
- North America
- South America
- Australia and Oceania

World Population

- 550 million
- 625 million
- 725 million
- 910 million
- 1 billion
- 1.2 billion
- 1.6 billion
- 2 billion
- 2.6 billion
- 4.1 billion
- 6.1 billion
- 7.48 billion
- 9.8 billion

Year: 1650 1700 1750 1800 1850 1900 1950 2000 2050

Health Concerns

Women collect drinking water from a well in Ethiopia. Access to clean, safe drinking water is limited in the developing world.

Better access to clean water and health care increases life expectancy. However, more than 600 million people lack safe drinking water, and one-third of the world's population has no access to needed medicine.

- **Life expectancy** is the average number of years a person is expected to live. It is based on the death rates of specific age groups in a given population.

- In the developing world, rural water sources are more polluted than urban water sources. Ninety percent of sewage in developing countries is released untreated into rivers, lakes, or the ocean.

- Prevention controls disease. For example, smallpox killed an approximate 300 million people in the twentieth century, but the disease was eradicated by 1979 through a global vaccination program.

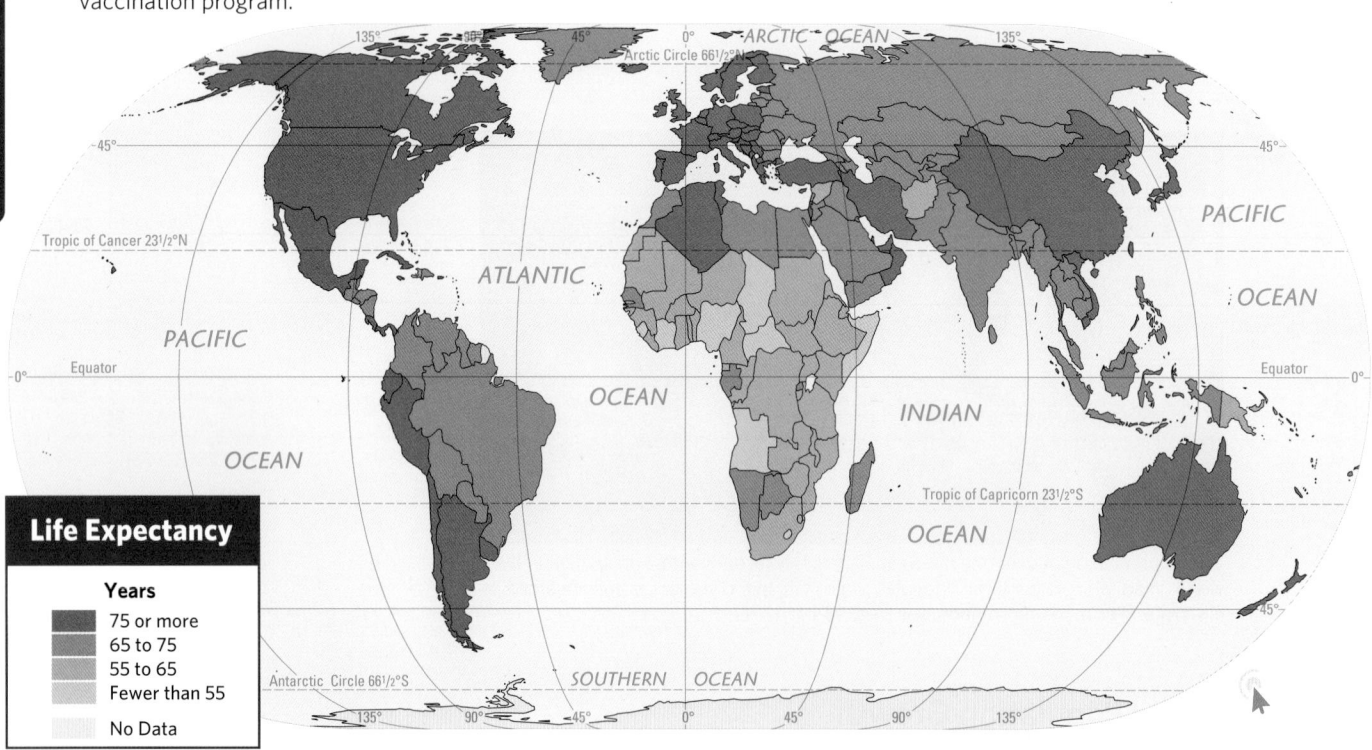

Life Expectancy

Years

- 75 or more
- 65 to 75
- 55 to 65
- Fewer than 55
- No Data

Leading Causes of Death

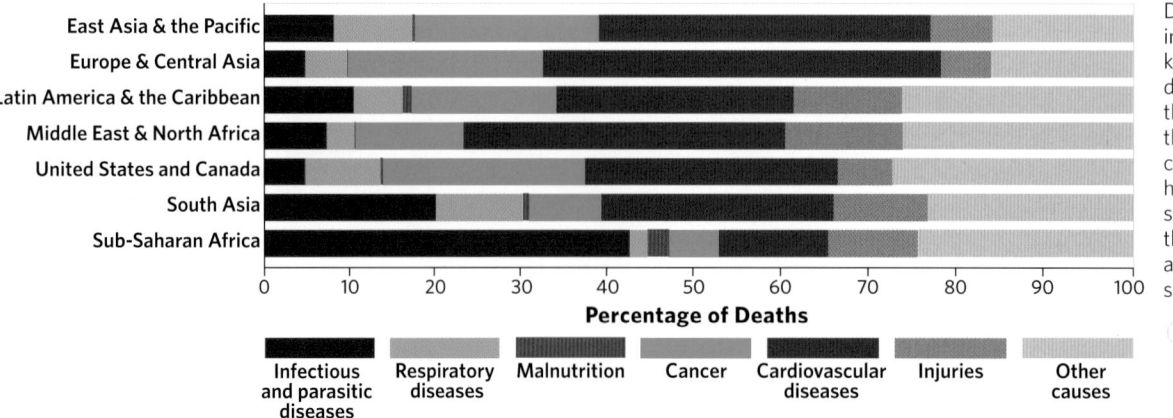

Disease caused by infection and parasites kill more people in developing countries than in other parts of the world. Wealthier countries have better health care systems, so more people die there from diseases associated with aging, such as heart disease.

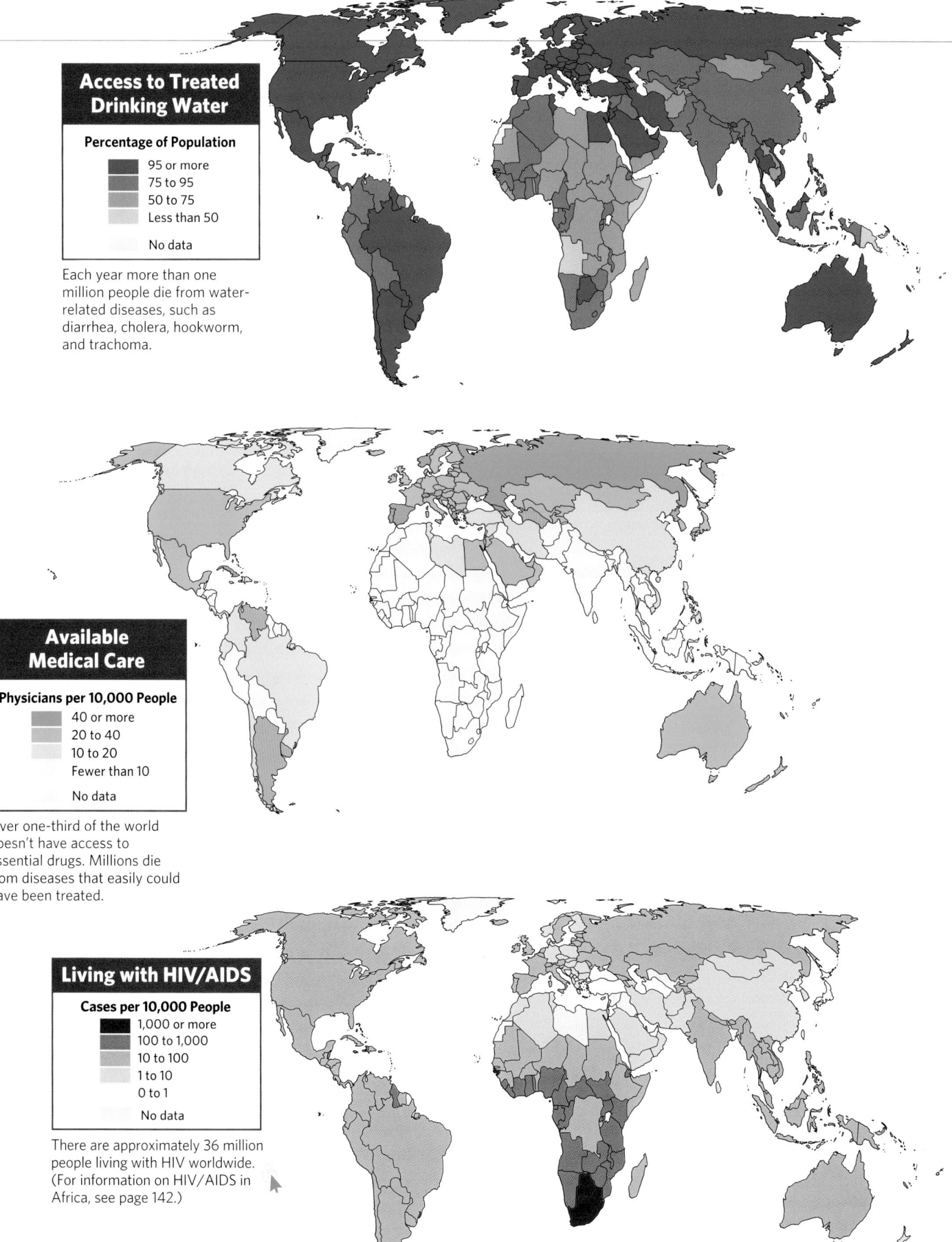

Access to Treated Drinking Water

Percentage of Population

- 95 or more
- 75 to 95
- 50 to 75
- Less than 50

  No data

Each year more than one million people die from water-related diseases, such as diarrhea, cholera, hookworm, and trachoma.

Available Medical Care

Physicians per 10,000 People

- 40 or more
- 20 to 40
- 10 to 20
- Fewer than 10

  No data

Over one-third of the world doesn't have access to essential drugs. Millions die from diseases that easily could have been treated.

Living with HIV/AIDS

Cases per 10,000 People

- 1,000 or more
- 100 to 1,000
- 10 to 100
- 1 to 10
- 0 to 1

  No data

There are approximately 36 million people living with HIV worldwide. (For information on HIV/AIDS in Africa, see page 142.)

Feeding the World

World agriculture is capable of providing everyone on Earth with 2,890 calories a day (more calories than the average 2,100 recommended by the USDA). Even so, 800 million people go to bed hungry every night.

- Labeled as the number one health risk worldwide by the United Nations, world hunger affects one in nine people.

- War, disease, and natural disasters such as drought escalate world hunger by destroying crops and killing heads of households.

- New varieties of crops, such as high-yield rice and wheat and disease-resistant cassava, are helping increase productivity in developing countries.

People line up at a food distribution site in South Sudan. In 2017 the UN declared a famine in South Sudan, where armed conflict and low harvests contributed to extreme food shortages.

Calories and Diet

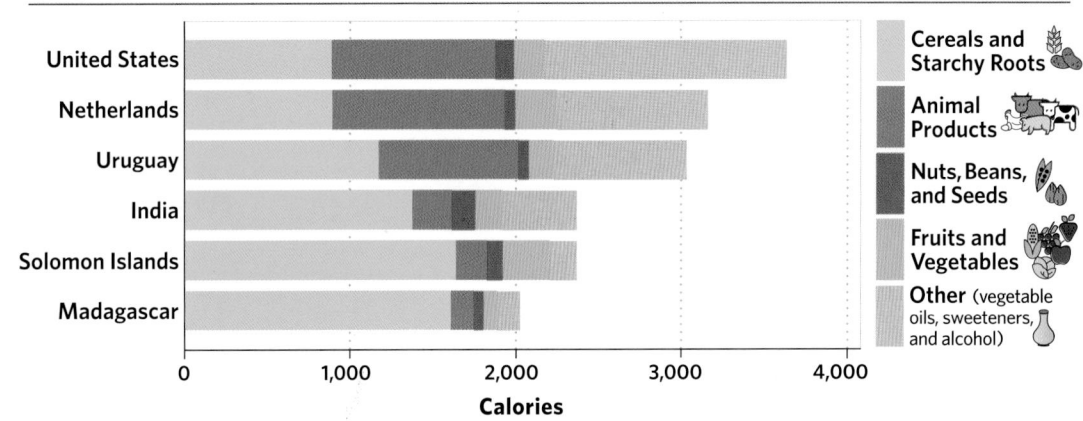

Cereals and Starchy Roots

Animal Products

Nuts, Beans, and Seeds

Fruits and Vegetables

Other (vegetable oils, sweeteners, and alcohol)

When a society gets wealthier, it shifts from a diet of grains to one with more meat, oils, sugars, and alcohol. Calorie consumption also increases.

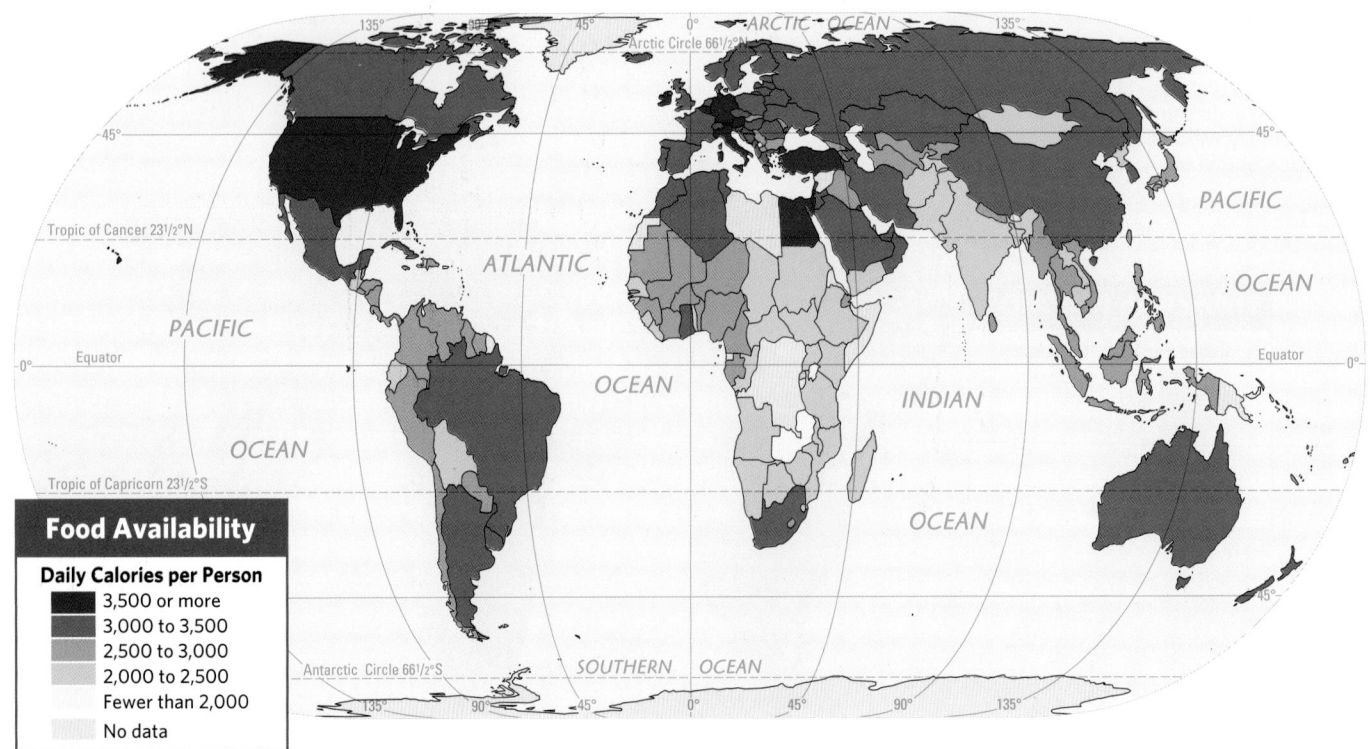

Food Availability

Daily Calories per Person

- 3,500 or more
- 3,000 to 3,500
- 2,500 to 3,000
- 2,000 to 2,500
- Fewer than 2,000
- No data

CANADA
UNITED STATES
MEXICO
VENEZUELA
COLOMBIA
PERU
BRAZIL
ARGENTINA
UNITED KINGDOM
FRANCE
SPAIN
ITALY
GERMANY
UKRAINE
TURKEY
RUSSIA
CHINA
PAKISTAN
IRAN
INDIA
BANGLADESH
SOUTH KOREA
JAPAN
ALGERIA
EGYPT
NIGERIA
ETHIOPIA
SOMALIA
DEM.REP. OF THE CONGO
KENYA
TANZANIA
SOUTH AFRICA
VIETNAM
PHILIPPINES
INDONESIA
AUSTRALIA

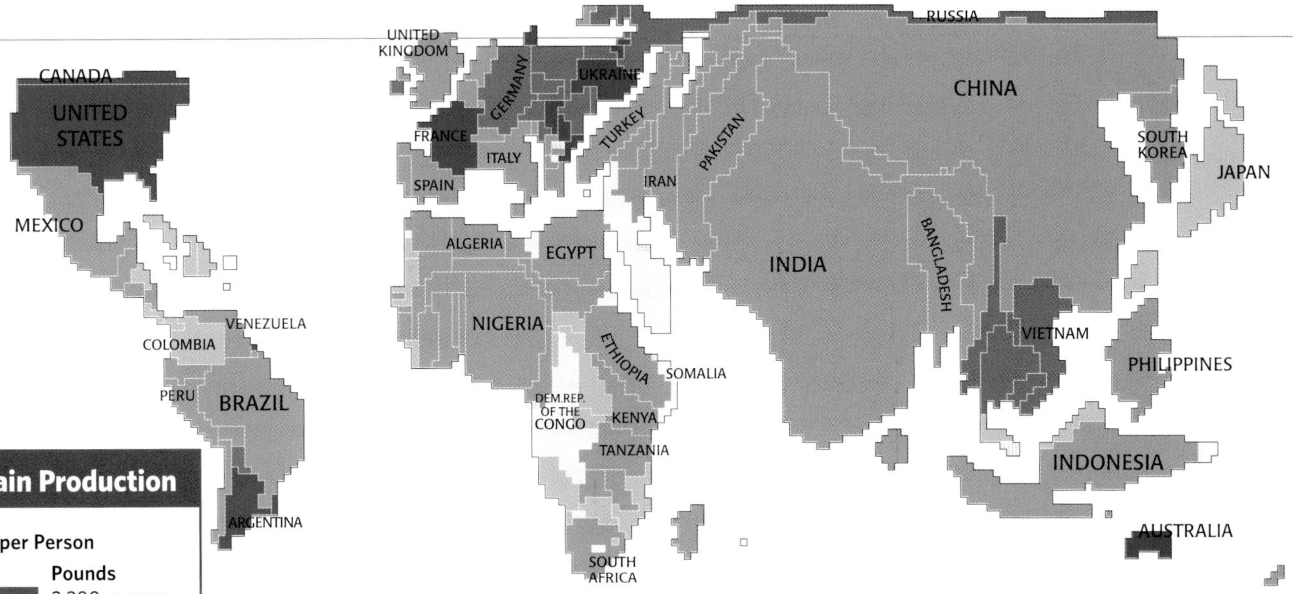

Annual Grain Production

Grain* per Person

Kilograms		Pounds
1000 or more		2,200 or more
500 to 1000		1,100 to 2,200
100 to 500		220 to 1,100
50 to 100		110 to 220
Fewer than 50		Fewer than 110
No data		No data

▫ Represents 1 million people

*Includes corn, rice, wheat, barley, millet, oats, rye, and sorghum

In this cartogram, the size of each country reflects the number of people who live there. Countries with fewer than 500,000 people are not shown.

Starvation vs. Malnutrition

Starvation occurs when a person gets far too little food to eat. On the other hand, ***malnutrition*** occurs when the body lacks certain nutrients or takes in too much unhealthy food. You can eat three meals a day and still be malnourished.

Staple Food Production

Staple foods are the major food sources of particular regions. They are typically energy-rich, inexpensive, and easy to maintain over a long period of time. Most of the world's people rely on grains such as rice, wheat, oats, or millet as their main food sources. In humid tropical and sub-tropical regions, root vegetables such as cassava are staple foods.

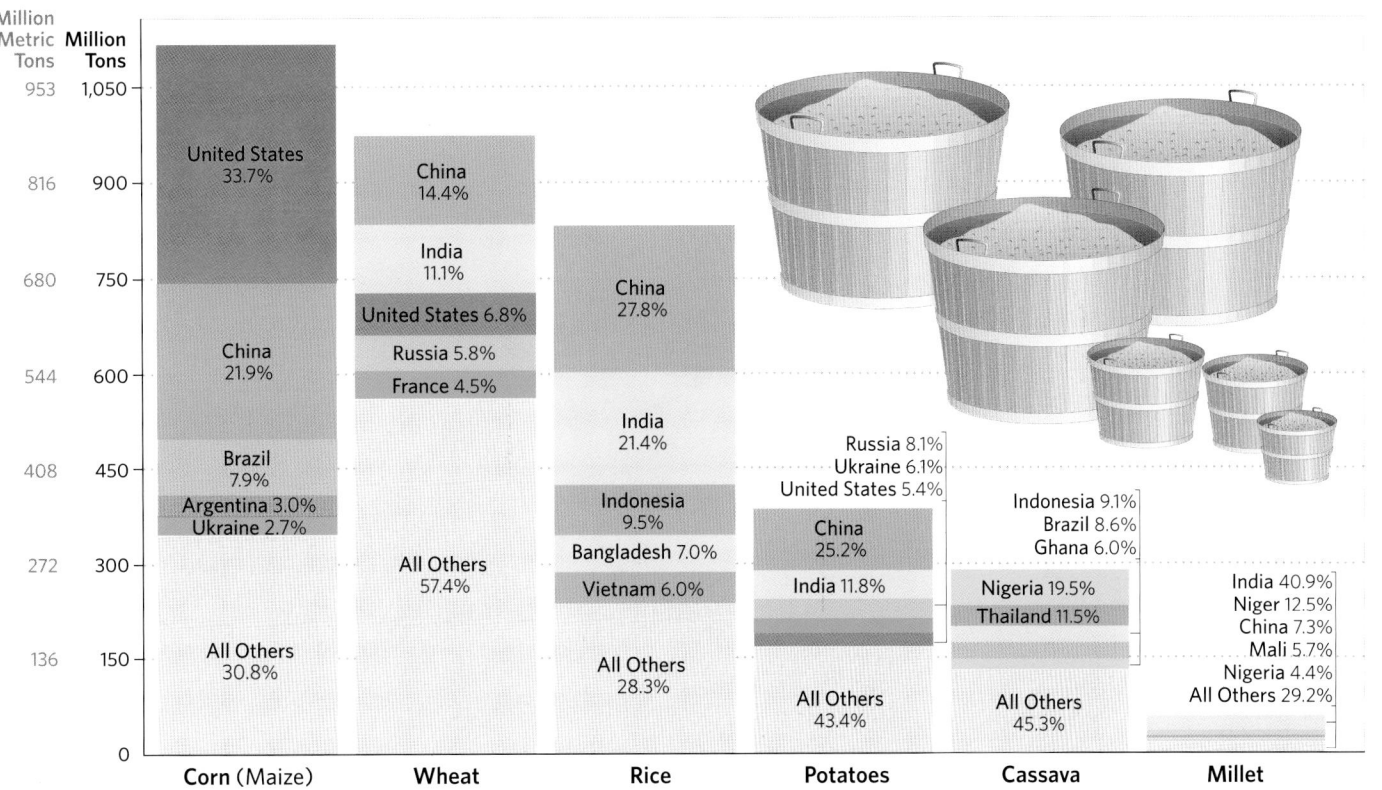

Million Metric Tons
Million Tons
953 1,050
816 900
680 750
544 600
408 450
272 300
136 150
0
United States 33.7%
China 21.9%
Brazil 7.9%
Argentina 3.0%
Ukraine 2.7%
All Others 30.8%
China 14.4%
India 11.1%
United States 6.8%
Russia 5.8%
France 4.5%
All Others 57.4%
China 27.8%
India 21.4%
Indonesia 9.5%
Bangladesh 7.0%
Vietnam 6.0%
All Others 28.3%
Russia 8.1%
Ukraine 6.1%
United States 5.4%
China 25.2%
India 11.8%
All Others 43.4%
Indonesia 9.1%
Brazil 8.6%
Ghana 6.0%
Nigeria 19.5%
Thailand 11.5%
All Others 45.3%
India 40.9%
Niger 12.5%
China 7.3%
Mali 5.7%
Nigeria 4.4%
All Others 29.2%
Corn (Maize)
Wheat
Rice
Potatoes
Cassava
Millet

Rich and Poor

When people cannot afford basic human needs, such as food and housing, they are living in **poverty**. Poverty has different meanings in different parts of the world.

- **Absolute poverty** is poverty that threatens a person's life. In global terms, this is a household earning less than the equivalent of US$1.90 a day. Disease, hunger, and child labor plague people living in absolute poverty.

- **Relative poverty** is having fewer resources than others in a community or country. Countries define their national poverty lines differently.

- In the United States, a person living in poverty earns less than $12,234 a year, or $33.50 a day. According to the U.S. Census Bureau, more than 43 million Americans live below the U.S. poverty line.

In Buenos Aires, Argentina, this shantytown is home to 40,000 poverty-stricken residents. It is separated by railroad tracks from one of the city's wealthiest neighborhoods, visible in the background.

Concentration of Wealth

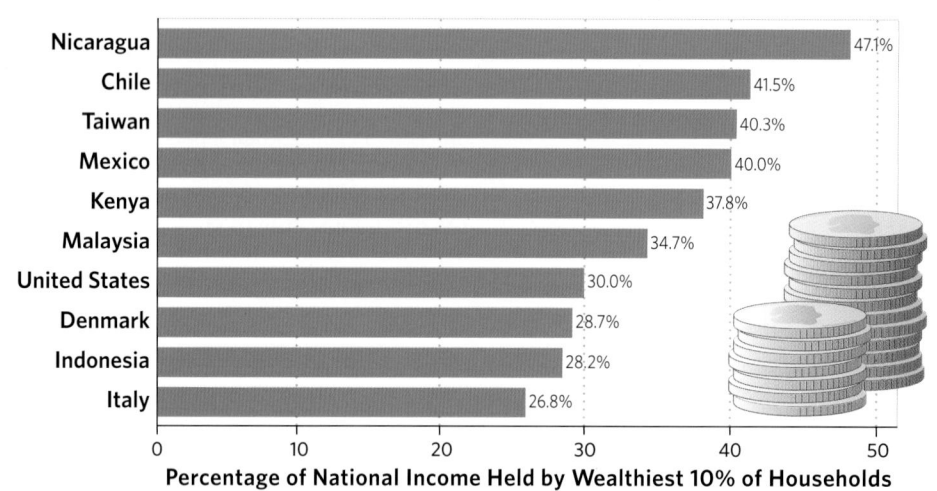

Percentage of National Income Held by Wealthiest 10% of Households

- Nicaragua 47.1%
- Chile 41.5%
- Taiwan 40.3%
- Mexico 40.0%
- Kenya 37.8%
- Malaysia 34.7%
- United States 30.0%
- Denmark 28.7%
- Indonesia 28.2%
- Italy 26.8%

In many countries the largest portion of wealth is controlled by a small portion of the population. This **disparity of income** can lead to social unrest.

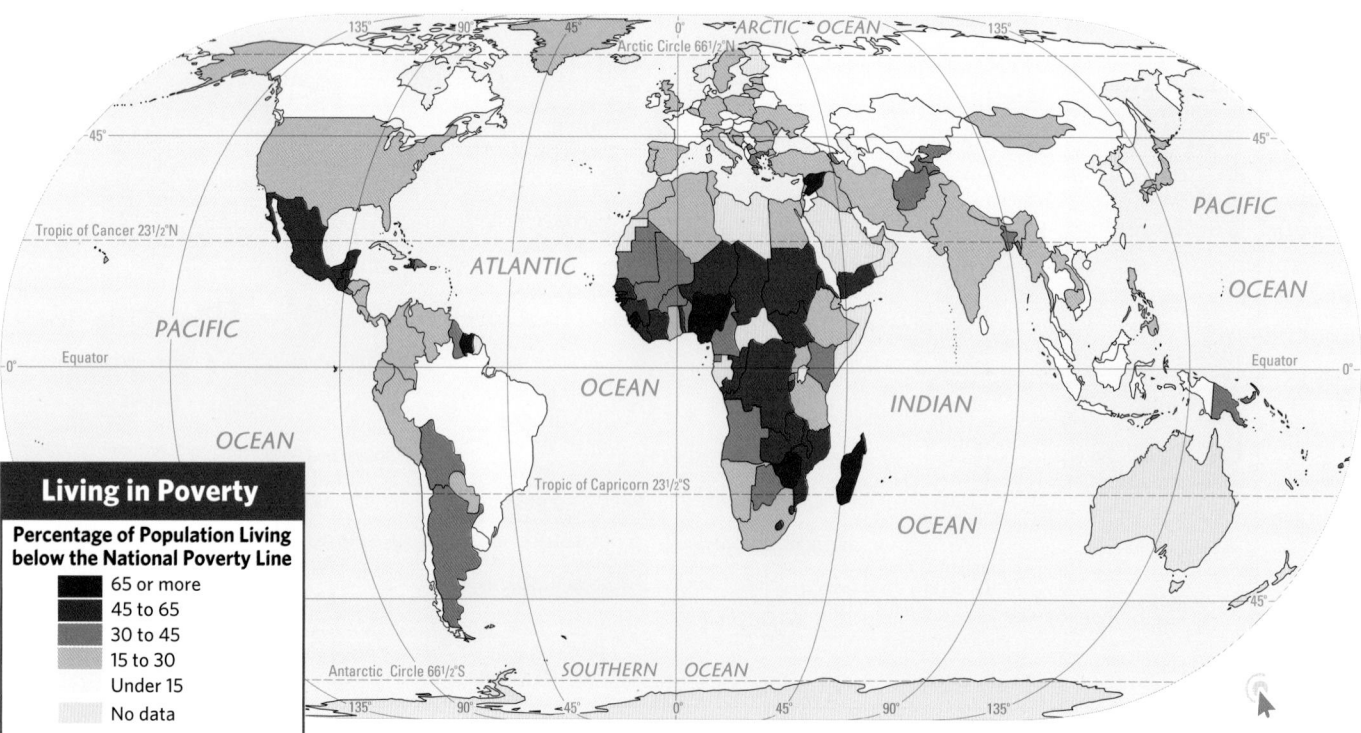

Living in Poverty

Percentage of Population Living below the National Poverty Line

- 65 or more
- 45 to 65
- 30 to 45
- 15 to 30
- Under 15
- No data

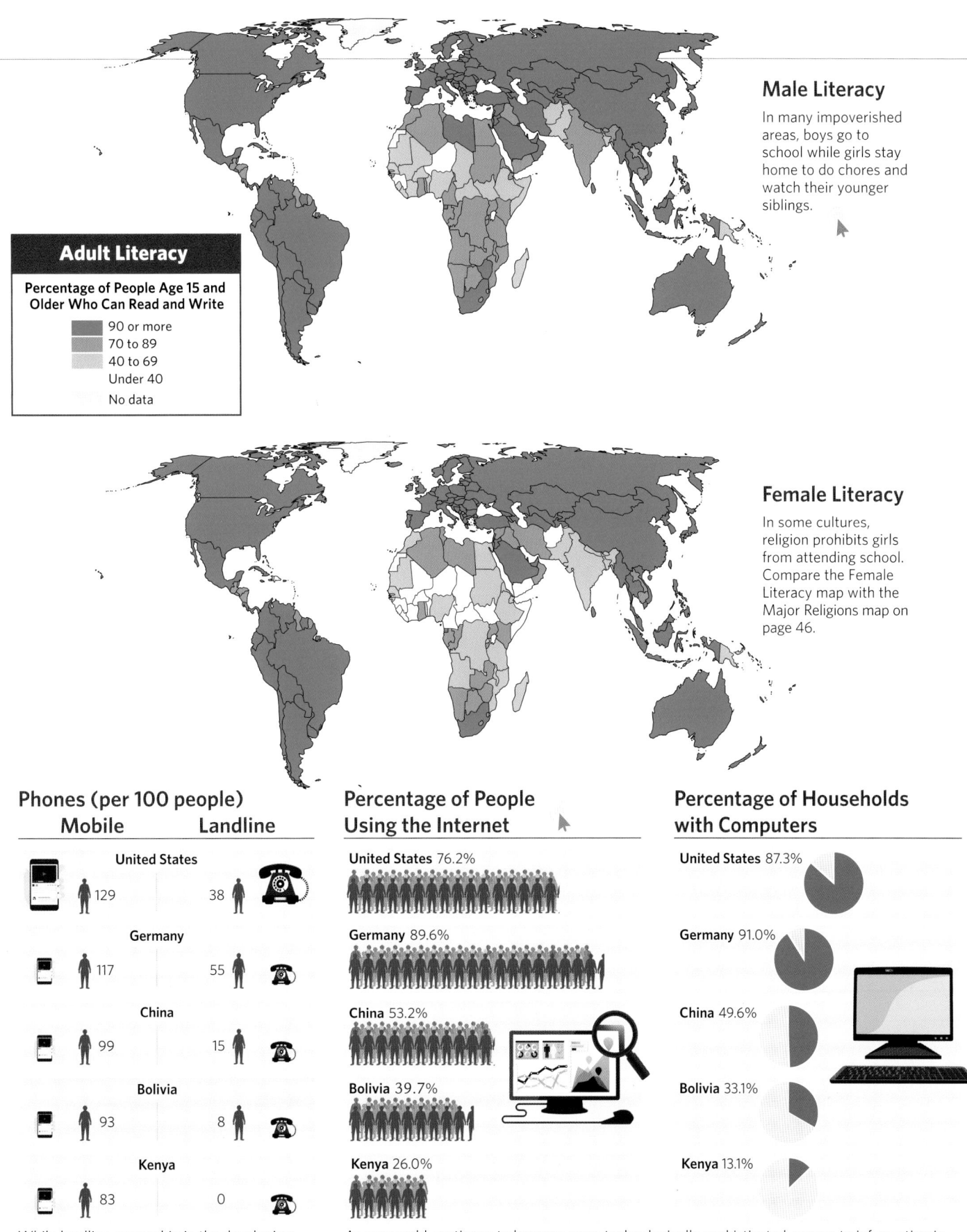

Male Literacy

In many impoverished areas, boys go to school while girls stay home to do chores and watch their younger siblings.

Adult Literacy

Percentage of People Age 15 and Older Who Can Read and Write

- 90 or more
- 70 to 89
- 40 to 69
- Under 40
- No data

Female Literacy

In some cultures, religion prohibits girls from attending school. Compare the Female Literacy map with the Major Religions map on page 46.

Phones (per 100 people)

Mobile		Landline	
United States			
	129	38	
Germany			
	117	55	
China			
	99	15	
Bolivia			
	93	8	
Kenya			
	83	0	

Percentage of People Using the Internet

- **United States** 76.2%
- **Germany** 89.6%
- **China** 53.2%
- **Bolivia** 39.7%
- **Kenya** 26.0%

Percentage of Households with Computers

- **United States** 87.3%
- **Germany** 91.0%
- **China** 49.6%
- **Bolivia** 33.1%
- **Kenya** 13.1%

While landline ownership in the developing world is declining in favor of smartphones, many developing and emerging countries are skipping fixed phones altogether due to a lack of infrastucture for reliable landline connections.

As our world continues to become more technologically sophisticated, access to information is increasingly vital to economic prosperity. As smartphones become more broadly accessible, the percentage of people using the internet can surpass the number of people with computers. An estimated 38 percent of households in the developing world have access to the internet, while only 33 percent have computers.

Global Economy

As products, services, and money circulate around the world at a rapid rate, most countries have become economically interdependent, forming a **global economy**.

- **Gross Domestic Product**, or GDP, is the value of all goods and services produced within a country in a year. The United States accounts for just under a quarter of the world's GDP.

- A **trade deficit** occurs when a country's imports exceed its exports. A **trade surplus** occurs when a country's exports exceed its imports.

- **Free trade** allows people to buy and sell goods across international borders without restrictions. It provides consumers with the cheapest possible goods, but cheaper imports may threaten domestic jobs.

Balance of Trade

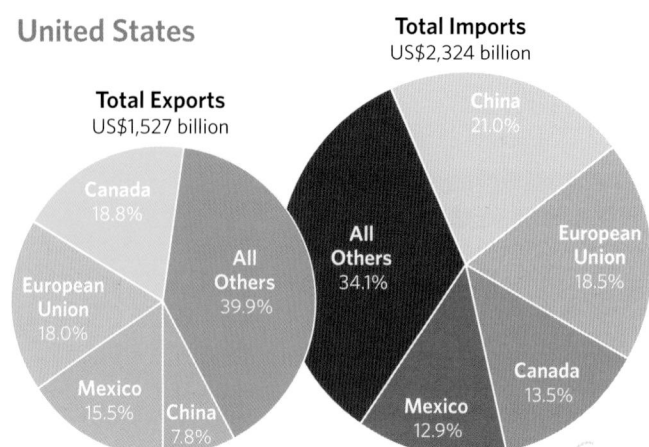

United States

Total Exports
US$1,527 billion

Canada 18.8%
European Union 18.0%
Mexico 15.5%
China 7.8%
All Others 39.9%

Total Imports
US$2,324 billion

China 21.0%
European Union 18.5%
Canada 13.5%
Mexico 12.9%
All Others 34.1%

Balance of trade is the value of a country's exports minus the value of its imports. The United States has four times the trade deficit of any other country in the world.

National Productivity

GDP in US$ Billions
- Over 1,000
- 100 to 1,000
- 10 to 100
- 1 to 10
- Under 1
- No data
- □ Represents 1 million people

Single-Commodity Economies

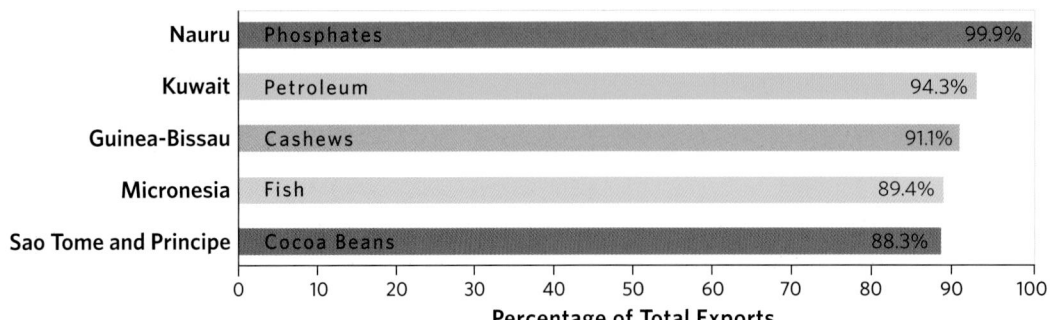

Country	Commodity	Percentage
Nauru	Phosphates	99.9%
Kuwait	Petroleum	94.3%
Guinea-Bissau	Cashews	91.1%
Micronesia	Fish	89.4%
Sao Tome and Principe	Cocoa Beans	88.3%

Percentage of Total Exports

Many countries rely on a single natural resource or crop for 80 percent or more of their exports. These countries run the risk of becoming dependent on other countries for goods and services. Their economies also are vulnerable to sudden changes in international prices and demands for their key commodity.

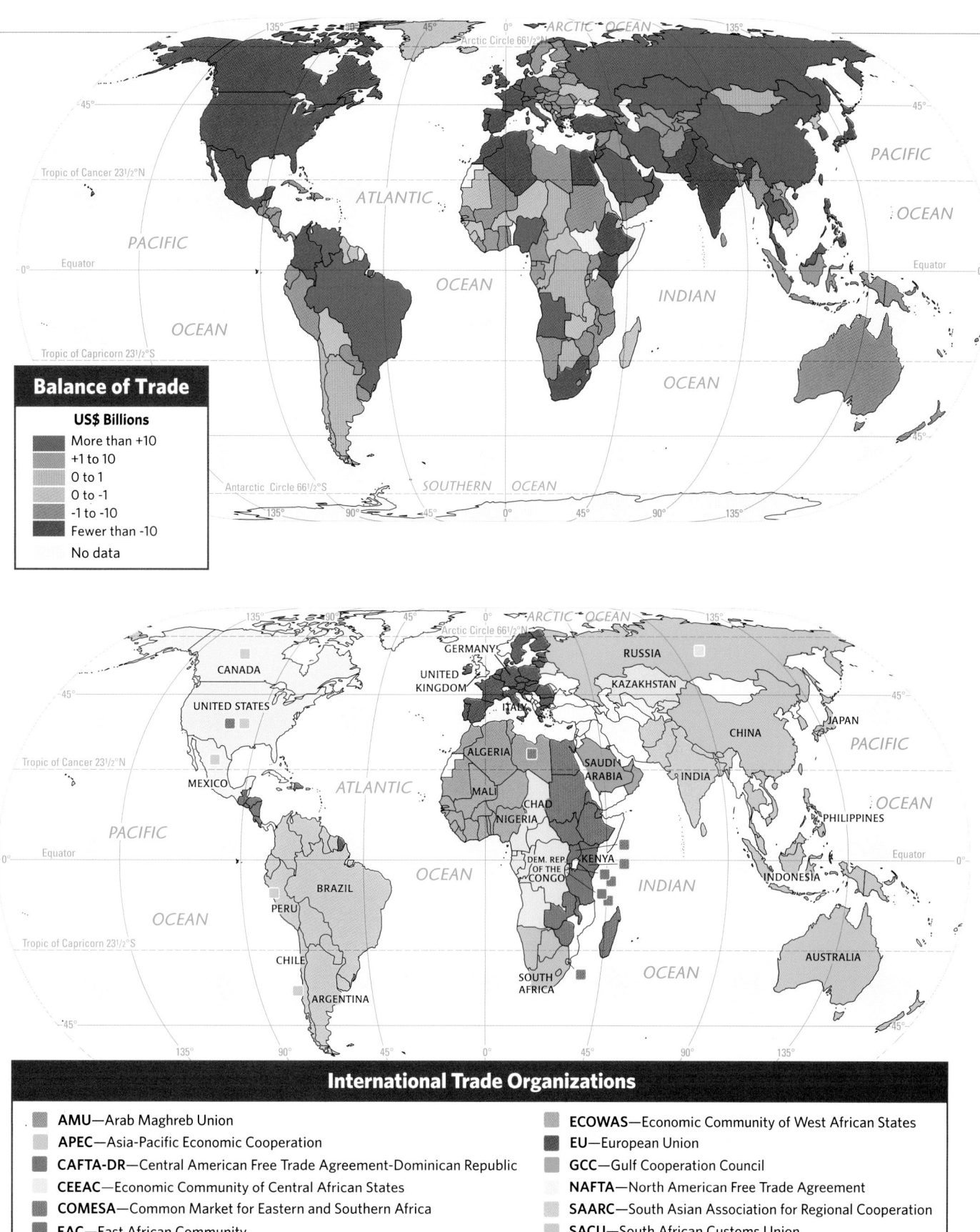

Balance of Trade

US$ Billions

- More than +10
- +1 to 10
- 0 to 1
- 0 to -1
- -1 to -10
- Fewer than -10
- No data

International Trade Organizations

AMU—Arab Maghreb Union
APEC—Asia-Pacific Economic Cooperation
CAFTA-DR—Central American Free Trade Agreement-Dominican Republic
CEEAC—Economic Community of Central African States
COMESA—Common Market for Eastern and Southern Africa
EAC—East African Community
EAEU—Eurasian Economic Union

ECOWAS—Economic Community of West African States
EU—European Union
GCC—Gulf Cooperation Council
NAFTA—North American Free Trade Agreement
SAARC—South Asian Association for Regional Cooperation
SACU—South African Customs Union
UNASUR—Union of South American Nations

Trade organizations are established by agreements between governments to increase free trade. NAFTA and EU are among the wealthiest and most influential trade organizations in the world. (For more information, see pages 57 and 153.)

Cultural Diversity

A nearly 50-foot (15 meter) statue of Buddha sits inside a mandapa, or gathering area, in Wat Si Chun, Sukhothai Province, Thailand. Thailand is 95 percent Buddhist.

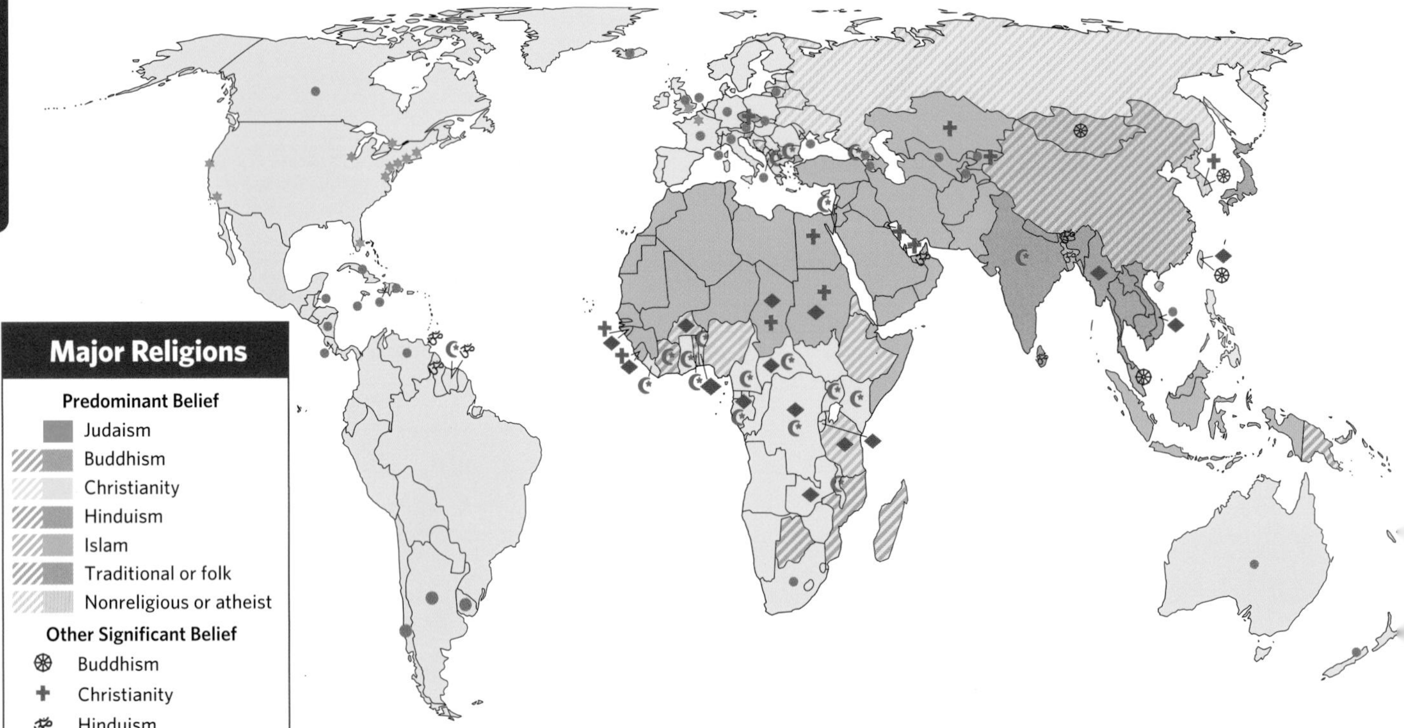

Culture is the way of life of a given human society. Every society in the world has a unique culture.

- Aspects of culture include a society's language, religion, art, customs, ethnicity, institutions, technology, and other traits.

- Countries can have multiple cultures, and cultures can cross national boundaries.

- Language and religion are two distinguishing features of a culture. Thousands of religions are practiced and about 6,000 languages are spoken in the world today.

- **Language families** are groups of related languages that developed slowly over time from a single earlier **parent language**.

Major Religions

Predominant Belief

- Judaism
- Buddhism
- Christianity
- Hinduism
- Islam
- Traditional or folk
- Nonreligious or atheist

Other Significant Belief

- ⊛ Buddhism
- ✝ Christianity
- ॐ Hinduism
- ☪ Islam
- ◆ Traditional or folk
- ● Nonreligious or atheist
- ✳ Urban area with large Jewish population

Major Religions

Each of these religions can be broken down into smaller groups. For example, there are three major groups of Christians: Roman Catholics, Protestants, and Eastern Orthodox. Among Protestants alone, there are hundreds of denominations.

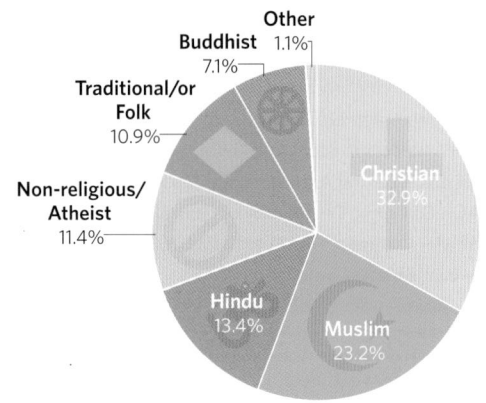

- Other 1.1%
- Buddhist 7.1%
- Traditional/or Folk 10.9%
- Non-religious/Atheist 11.4%
- Christian 32.9%
- Hindu 13.4%
- Muslim 23.2%

Who Are You?

Ethnicity is complex. For example, if your ethnic background is Mexican, you might speak Spanish at home and celebrate *Día de los Muertos* (Day of the Dead). At the same time, you might speak English at school and celebrate American holidays such as the Fourth of July and Thanksgiving.

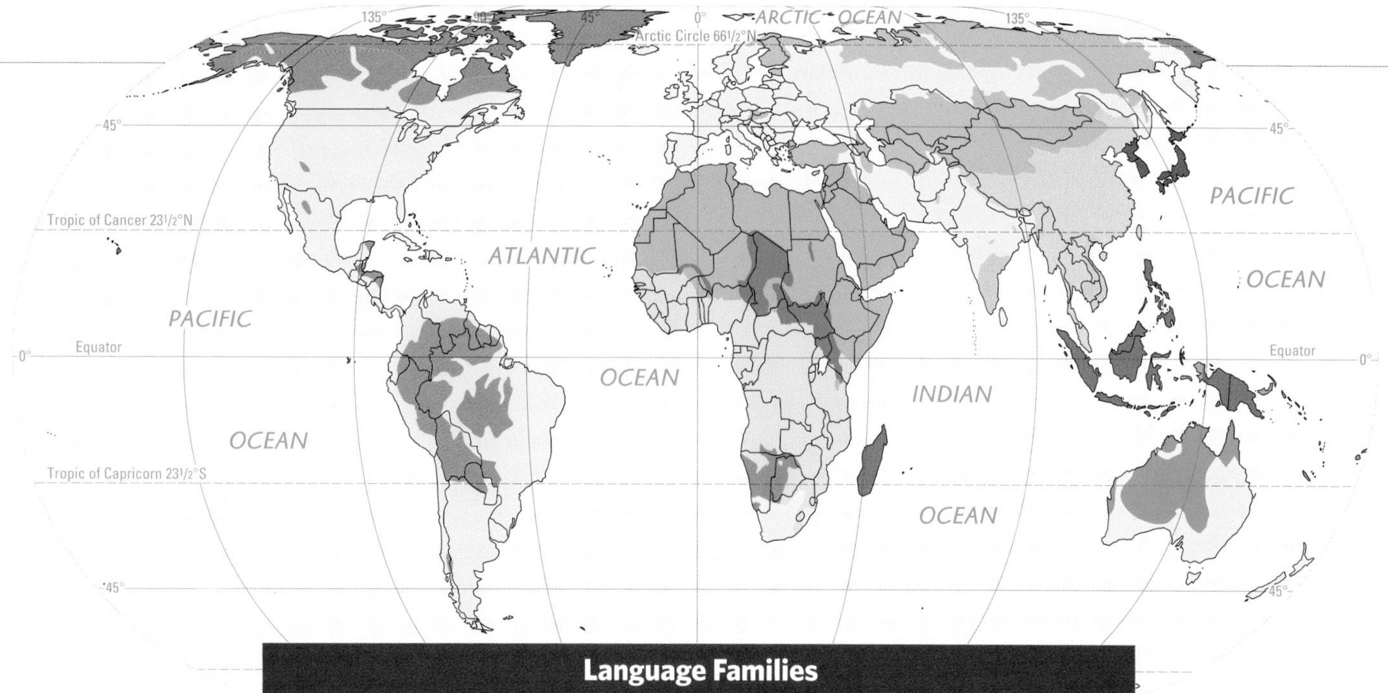

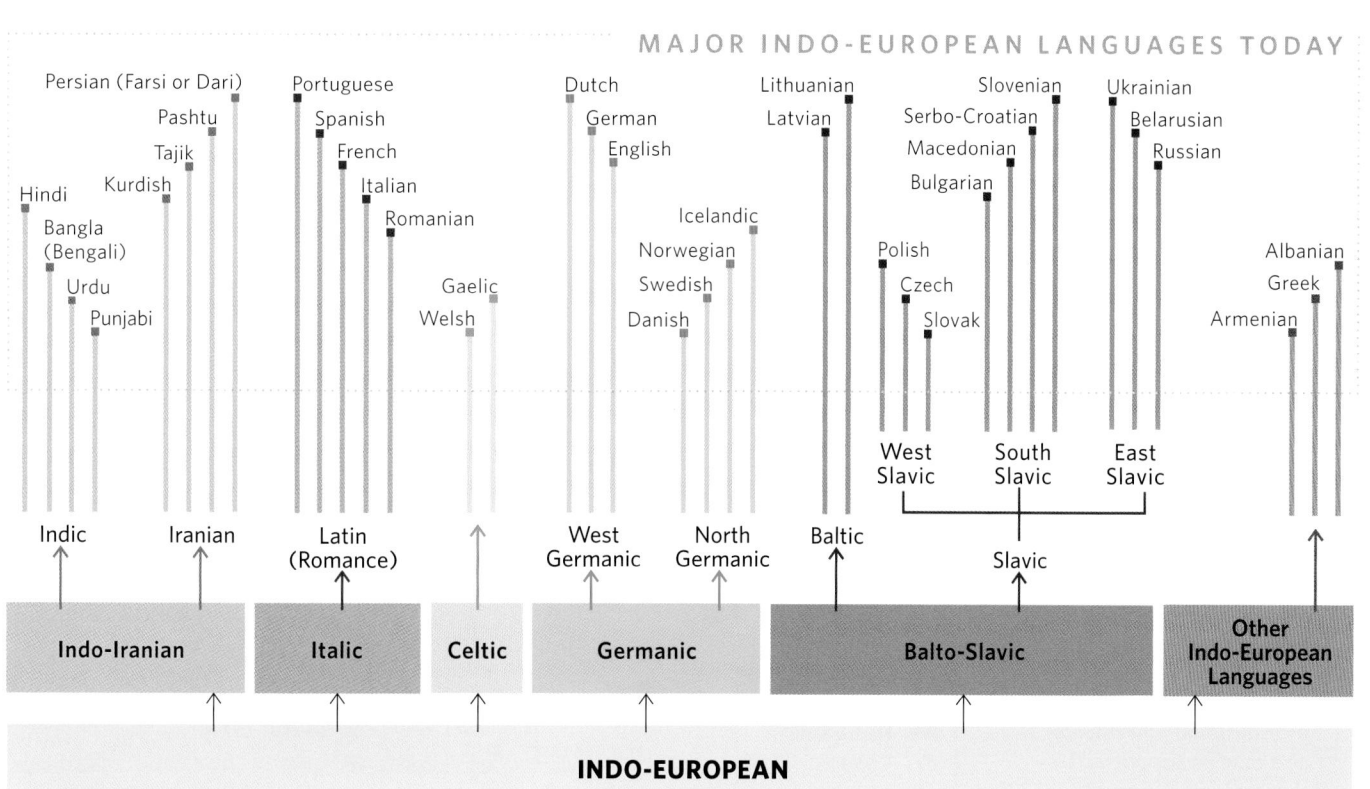

Language Families

- Afro-Asian
- American Indian
- Australian
- Dravidian
- Indo-European
- Inuktitut
- Japanese and Korean
- Khoisan
- Malayo-Polynesian
- Mon-Khmer
- Niger-Congo (Bantu)
- Nilo-Saharan
- Papuan
- Sino Tibetan
- Uralic and Altaic

Unclassifiable

Indo-European Languages

MAJOR INDO-EUROPEAN LANGUAGES TODAY

Indo-Iranian
- Indic: Hindi, Bangla (Bengali), Urdu, Punjabi
- Iranian: Persian (Farsi or Dari), Pashtu, Tajik, Kurdish

Italic
- Latin (Romance): Portuguese, Spanish, French, Italian, Romanian

Celtic: Gaelic, Welsh

Germanic
- West Germanic: Dutch, German, English
- North Germanic: Icelandic, Norwegian, Swedish, Danish

Balto-Slavic
- Baltic: Lithuanian, Latvian
- Slavic:
  - West Slavic: Polish, Czech, Slovak
  - South Slavic: Slovenian, Serbo-Croatian, Macedonian, Bulgarian
  - East Slavic: Ukrainian, Belarusian, Russian

Other Indo-European Languages: Albanian, Greek, Armenian

INDO-EUROPEAN

Indo-European is the most widely spoken language family. About half the people in the world speak languages in this family, which originated in an area that extended from northern India to western Europe.

Human Migration

People have moved to new places throughout history. Today, with improvements in transportation, people can move farther and faster than ever before.

- People often leave their old homes in search of better economic, political, or religious opportunities. These attractions to new homes are called **pull factors**.

- Some people leave their old homes to escape natural disasters, persecution, or war. These are called **push factors**.

- People can move to new locations within their country (**migration**) or move to another country (**immigration**).

With over half of immigrants to Canada entering the country with a college degree, Canada has one of the most successful immigrant populations in the world. It is estimated that immigrants will comprise 25 to 30 percent of Canada's population by 2036.

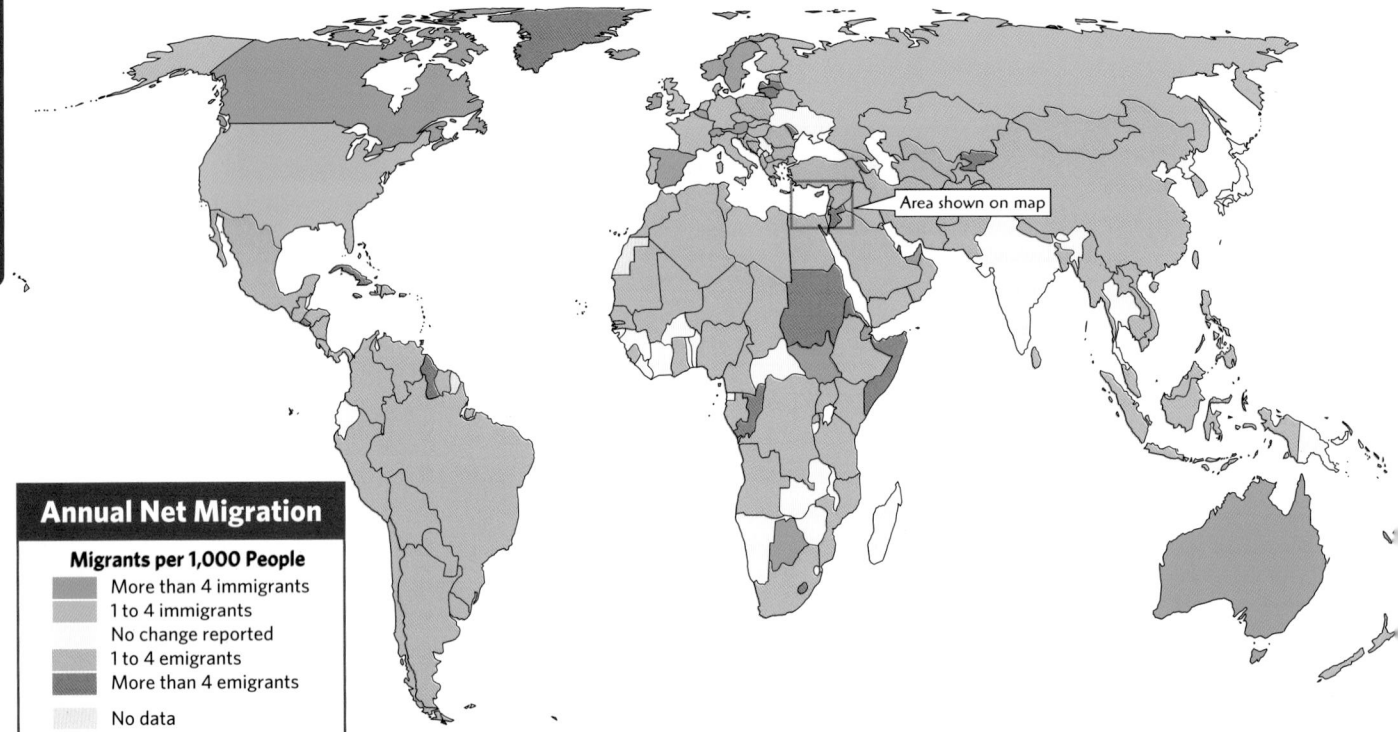

Area shown on map

Annual Net Migration

Migrants per 1,000 People

- More than 4 immigrants
- 1 to 4 immigrants
- No change reported
- 1 to 4 emigrants
- More than 4 emigrants
- No data

Safe Away from Home

People leave their home countries for many reasons. **Refugees** are fleeing for their lives. **Emigrants** leave by their own choice. The difference is very important. Refugees are protected by international agreements and may be supported by the world community. Emigrants do not have these protections.

TURKEY

IRAN

695,000 People*

2,734,000 people

249,000 people

GREECE

CYPRUS

1,030,000 people

6,570,000 people

Mediterranean

LEBANON

SYRIA

Tigris River

Euphrates River

Sea

117,000 people

656,000 people

JORDAN

IRAQ

Syrian Refugees

- Fleeing Syria
- Displaced in Syria
- * To Europe

ISRAEL

SAUDI ARABIA

EGYPT

In 2011, the onset of civil war in Syria initiated a global refugee crisis. To escape the violence and Syria's collapsed infrastructure, at least 12 million people—more than half of Syria's pre-war population—left their homes by the end of 2016. Over 5.5 million people fled the country while an additional 6.5 million were internally displaced.

Internally Displaced People

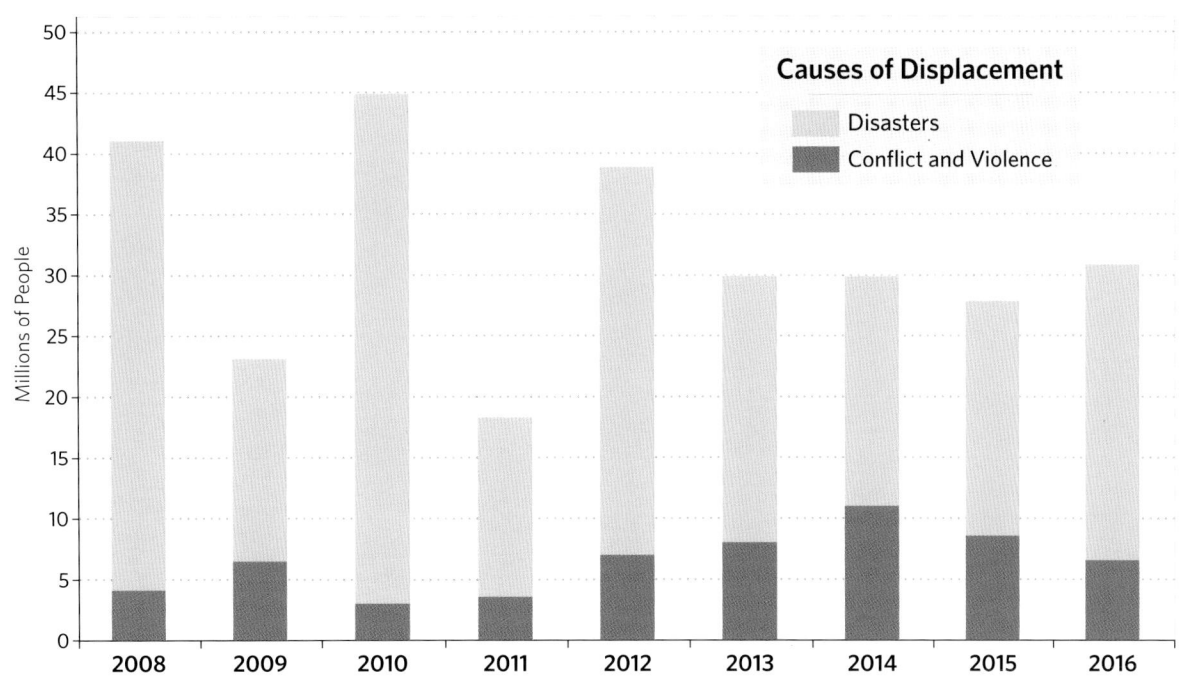

Causes of Displacement
- Disasters
- Conflict and Violence

Destination

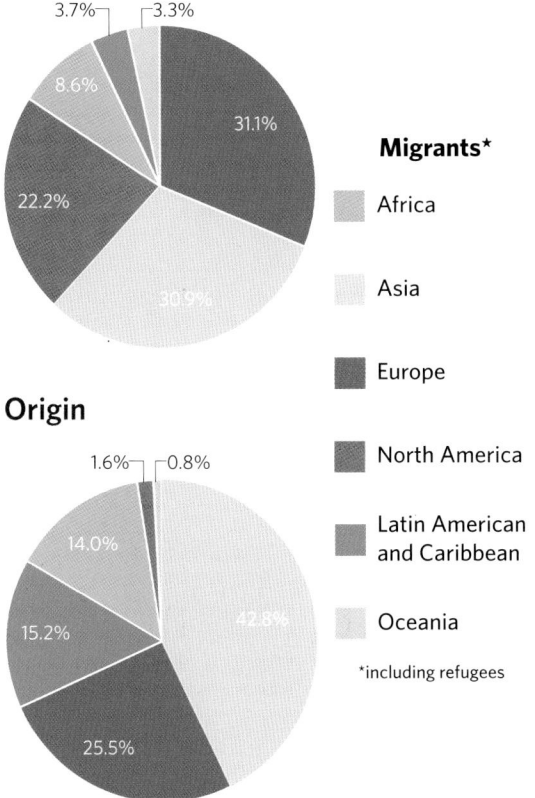

3.7%   3.3%
8.6%
31.1%
22.2%
30.9%

Migrants*

- Africa
- Asia
- Europe
- North America
- Latin American and Caribbean
- Oceania

*including refugees

Origin

1.6%   0.8%
14.0%
15.2%
42.8%
25.5%

Total : 243 million migrants

Forced to Flee

Internally displaced people are people who are forced to leave their homes due to armed conflict, natural disasters, or violations of human rights, but—unlike refugees—choose to stay within their country. The majority of conflict-related displacements occur in sub-Saharan Africa and the Middle East, while disaster-related displacements are more prevalent in East Asia and the Pacific.

Typhoon Haiyan, which made landfall in the Philippines in November 2013, damaged an estimated 1 million houses and displaced approximately 4 million people.

World Extreme Nuuk (Godthab), the smallest capital in the world, is located on the world's largest island, Greenland (Kalaallit Nunaat). A self-governing dependency of Denmark, Greenland is also the largest possession in the world.

North America

North America includes two of the world's largest countries: Canada and the United States. People with ancestors from Europe, Africa, Asia, and the Americas share the plains and mountainous regions of North America.

Physical Features

Highest mountain peak
Denali (Mt. McKinley) 20,310 ft. (6,190 m)

Longest mountain range
Rocky Mountains 3,000 mi. (4,800 km)

Largest island
Greenland (Kalaallit Nunaat) 836,330 sq. mi. (2,166,086 sq. km)

Largest lakes
Lake Superior 31,700 sq. mi. (82,100 sq. km)★
Lake Huron 23,000 sq. mi. (59,600 sq. km)★
Lake Michigan 22,300 sq. mi. (57,800 sq. km)★

Longest rivers
Mississippi-Missouri System 3,741 mi. (6,020 km)★
Mackenzie 2,635 mi. (4,241 km)★

Other key physical features

Canadian Shield	Great Plains
Coastal Plains	Labrador Peninsula
Colorado Plateau	Plateau of Mexico
Florida Peninsula	Yucatan Peninsula
Great Basin	

Cultural Features

Population
577,185,000

Largest countries by area
Canada 3,855,103 sq. mi. (9,984,670 sq. km)★
United States 3,677,649 sq. mi. (9,525,067 sq. km)★

Largest country by population
United States 326,625,791

Most densely populated
Sint Maarten 3,237.2 people per sq. mi. (1,237.7 per sq. km)

Least densely populated
Greenland (Kalaallit Nunaat) 0.1 people per sq. mi. (0.03 per sq. km)

Largest urban areas
Mexico City, Mexico 20,999,000★
New York City, United States 18,593,000★
Los Angeles, United States 12,310,000

★ Among the world's largest. See the inside front cover.

Area Comparison

North America
9,348,000 sq. mi. (24,211,000 sq. km)

Contiguous United States
3,021,295 sq. mi. (7,825,112 sq. km)

Regional Maps of North America

1 Canada pp. 60–61
2 United States pp. 74–75
3 Middle America pp. 106–107

Thematic Maps of North America

● North America; ● Canada; ○ United States; ○ Middle America

Precipitation ● p. 55; ● p. 64; ○ p. 80; ● p.110
Climate ● p. 55; ● p. 64; ○ p. 81; ● p.110
Land Use ● p. 56; ● p. 65; ○ p. 82; ● p.111
Energy Resources and Metals ● p. 56; ● p. 66; ○ pp. 84–85; ● p.112
Trade Organizations ● p. 57
Population ● p. 58; ● p. 67; ○ p. 86; ● p.113
Descendants of Indigenous North Americans ● p. 58

Major Highways and Airports ● p. 66; ○ p. 86
Wetlands ○ p. 80
Tornadoes and Hurricanes ○ p. 81
Agricultural Products ○ p. 83
Volcanoes ● p.109
Latin America ● p.112
Panama Canal ● p.115

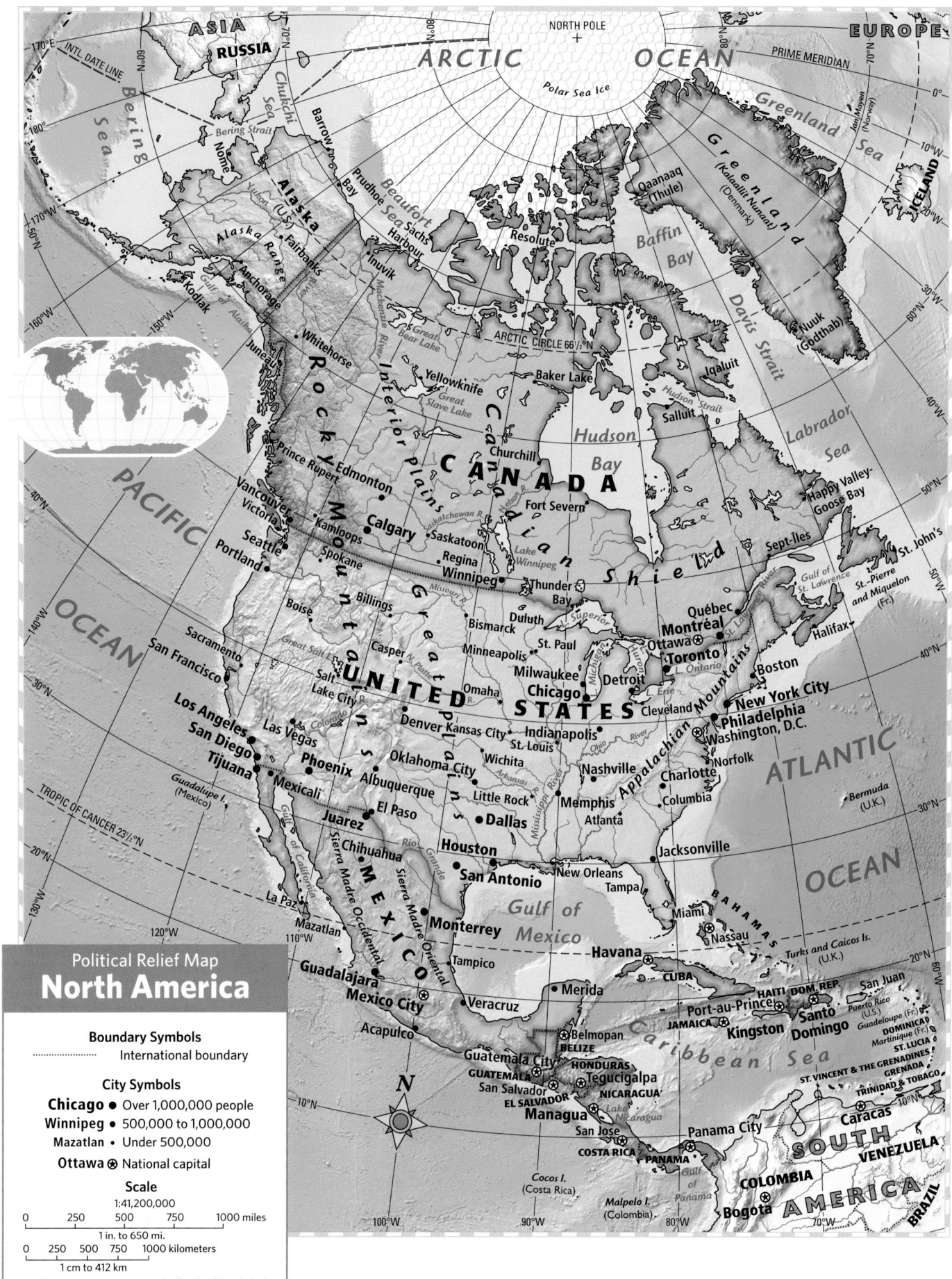

ASIA
RUSSIA
NORTH POLE
ARCTIC OCEAN
EUROPE
PRIME MERIDIAN
Polar Sea Ice
Greenland Sea
Jan Mayen (Norway)
ICELAND

INTL. DATE LINE
Chukchi Sea
Bering Strait
Barrow
Prudhoe Bay
Beaufort Sea
Sachs Harbour
Greenland (Kalaallit Nunaat) (Denmark)
Qaanaaq (Thule)
Baffin Bay
Nome
Alaska (U.S.)
Fairbanks
Inuvik
Resolute
Nuuk (Godthab)
Davis Strait
Kodiak
Anchorage
Gulf of Alaska
Alaska Range
Mackenzie River
ARCTIC CIRCLE 66½°N
Iqaluit

Bering Sea
Juneau
Whitehorse
Rocky Mountains
Interior Plains
Great Bear Lake
Yellowknife
Baker Lake
Hudson Strait
Salluit
Labrador Sea

Prince Rupert
Edmonton
Great Slave Lake
Canadian Shield
Hudson Bay
CANADA
Churchill
Fort Severn
Happy Valley-Goose Bay
Sept-Îles
St. John's

PACIFIC OCEAN
Vancouver
Victoria
Kamloops
Calgary
Saskatoon
Saskatchewan R.
Nelson R.
Lake Winnipeg
Thunder Bay
St-Pierre and Miquelon (Fr.)

Seattle
Spokane
Regina
Winnipeg
Duluth
Québec
Gulf of St. Lawrence
Halifax

Portland
Boise
Billings
Bismarck
Minneapolis
St. Paul
Lake Superior
Montréal
Ottawa
St. Lawrence River
Appalachian Mountains

Sacramento
San Francisco
Great Salt Lake
Casper
N. Platte R.
Missouri R.
Milwaukee
Chicago
Detroit
Lake Michigan
Lake Huron
L. Erie
Toronto
L. Ontario
Boston
New York City

Salt Lake City
UNITED STATES
Great Plains
Omaha
Cleveland
Philadelphia
Washington, D.C.

Los Angeles
San Diego
Las Vegas
Colorado R.
Denver
Kansas City
St. Louis
Indianapolis
Wichita
Nashville
Norfolk
Charlotte
ATLANTIC OCEAN

Tijuana
Phoenix
Albuquerque
Oklahoma City
Little Rock
Memphis
Columbia
Bermuda (U.K.)

Guadalupe I. (Mexico)
Mexicali
Juárez
El Paso
Arkansas
Dallas
Mississippi River
Atlanta
Jacksonville

TROPIC OF CANCER 23½°N
Chihuahua
Rio Grande
Houston
San Antonio
New Orleans
Tampa

Sierra Madre Occidental
Sierra Madre Oriental
MEXICO
Monterrey
Gulf of Mexico
Miami
BAHAMAS

La Paz
Gulf of California
Mazatlán
Tampico
Havana
Nassau

Guadalajara
Mexico City
Veracruz
Mérida
CUBA
Turks and Caicos Is. (U.K.)

Acapulco
Belmopan
BELIZE
Port-au-Prince
HAITI
DOM. REP.
San Juan
Puerto Rico (U.S.)
Guadeloupe (Fr.)

Guatemala City
GUATEMALA
HONDURAS
Tegucigalpa
JAMAICA
Kingston
Santo Domingo
Caribbean Sea
DOMINICA
Martinique (Fr.)
ST. LUCIA

San Salvador
EL SALVADOR
NICARAGUA
Managua
Lake Nicaragua
ST. VINCENT & THE GRENADINES
GRENADA
TRINIDAD & TOBAGO

San José
COSTA RICA
Panama City
PANAMA
Gulf of Panama
Caracas
VENEZUELA

Cocos I. (Costa Rica)
Malpelo I. (Colombia)
Bogotá
COLOMBIA
SOUTH AMERICA
BRAZIL

N

Political Relief Map
North America

Boundary Symbols
·················· International boundary

City Symbols
Chicago ● Over 1,000,000 people
Winnipeg • 500,000 to 1,000,000
Mazatlan · Under 500,000
Ottawa ⊛ National capital

Scale
1:41,200,000

| 0 | 250 | 500 | 750 | 1000 miles |

1 in. to 650 mi.

| 0 | 250 | 500 | 750 | 1000 kilometers |

1 cm to 412 km

Detailed legend on page 8   Lambert Equal Area Projection

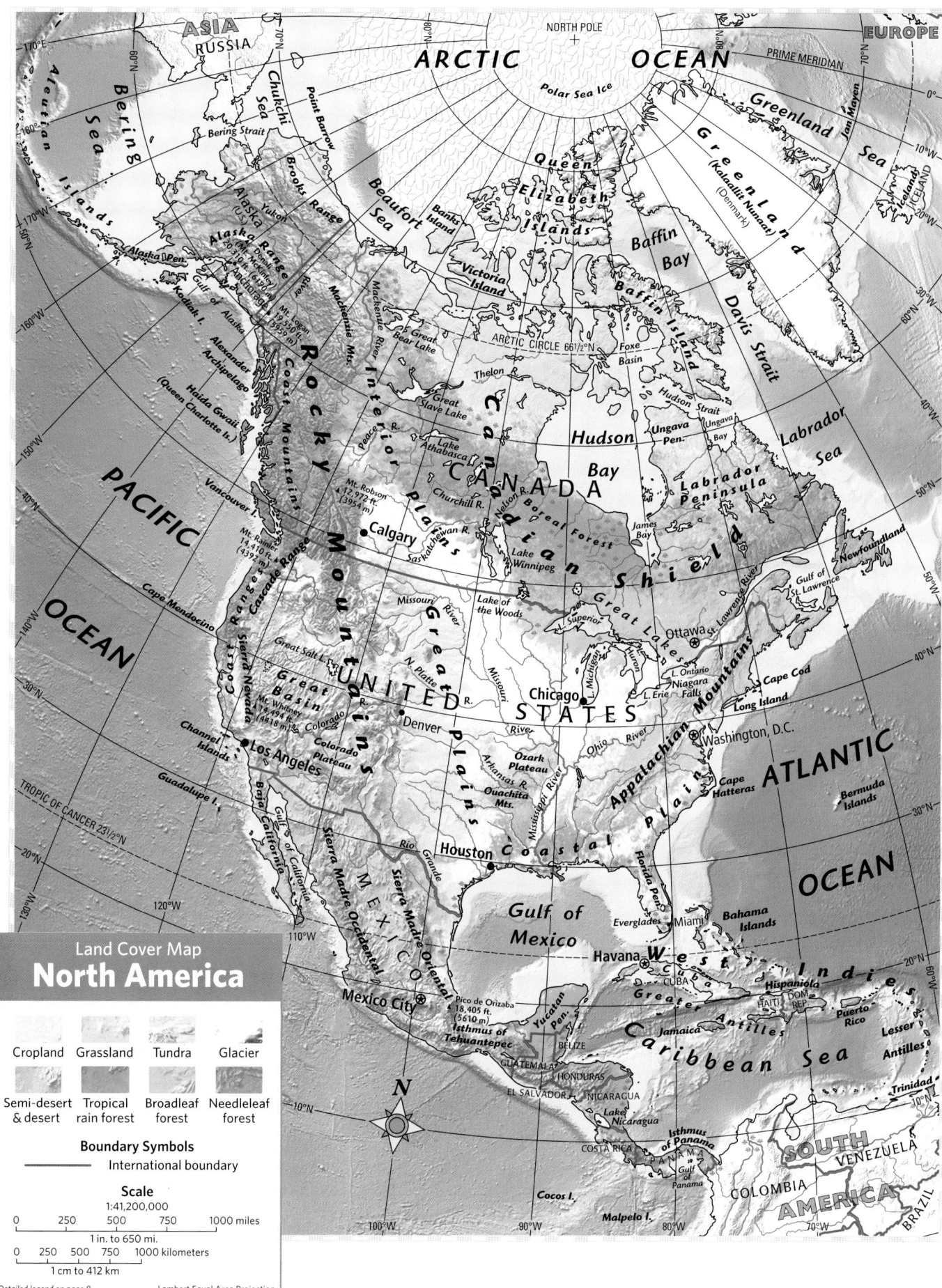

ASIA
RUSSIA
NORTH POLE
ARCTIC   OCEAN
EUROPE
PRIME MERIDIAN
Polar Sea Ice
Greenland
Sea
Jan Mayen
Chukchi
Sea
Point Barrow
Bering Strait
Beaufort
Sea
Banks
Island
Queen
Elizabeth
Islands
Greenland
(Kalaallit Nunaat)
(Denmark)
ICELAND
Bering
Sea
Brooks Range
Yukon
Aleutian Islands
Alaska Pen.
Kodiak I.
Gulf of Alaska
Alaska Range
Mt. McKinley
20,320 ft.
(6194 m)
Mt. Logan
19,550 ft.
(5959 m)
Victoria
Island
Baffin
Bay
Baffin Island
Davis Strait
Alexander
Archipelago
Haida Gwaii
(Queen Charlotte Is.)
Mackenzie Mts.
Mackenzie River
Great
Bear Lake
ARCTIC CIRCLE 66½°N
Foxe
Basin
Thelon R.
Hudson Strait
Ungava
Bay
Ungava
Pen.
Labrador

PACIFIC
Vancouver I.
Mt. Robson
12,972 ft.
(3954 m)
Mt. Rainier
14,410 ft.
(4392 m)
Cape Mendocino
Coast Ranges
Cascade Range
Sierra Nevada
Peace R.
Lake
Athabasca
Churchill R.
Nelson R.
Great
Slave Lake
CANADA
Interior Plains
Rocky   Mountains
Calgary
Saskatchewan R.
Hudson
Bay
Canadian   Shield
Boreal Forest
James
Bay
Labrador
Peninsula
Labrador
Sea
Newfoundland
Gulf of
St. Lawrence

OCEAN
Channel
Islands
Los Angeles
Mc Whitney
14,494 ft.
(4418 m)
Great
Basin
Colorado
Plateau
UNITED   STATES
Great Salt L.
Great   Plains
Missouri
River
N. Platte
Missouri
R.
Colorado   R.
Denver
Lake
Winnipeg
Lake of
the Woods
Superior
Great   Lakes
L. Michigan
L. Huron
Ottawa
St. Lawrence River
L. Ontario
Niagara
Falls
L. Erie
Cape Cod
Long Island
Appalachian   Mountains
Washington, D.C.
Ozark
Plateau
Arkansas R.
Ouachita
Mts.
Ohio   River
Mississippi River
Chicago
ATLANTIC
Cape
Hatteras
Bermuda
Islands

Guadalupe I.
Gulf of California
Baja California
MEXICO
Sierra Madre Occidental
Sierra Madre Oriental
Rio
Grande
Houston
Coastal   Plain
Florida Pen.
Everglades
Miami
Bahama
Islands
OCEAN

TROPIC OF CANCER 23½°N
Mexico City
Pico de Orizaba
18,405 ft.
(5610 m)
Isthmus of
Tehuantepec
Yucatan
Pen.
Gulf   of
Mexico
Havana
West
CUBA
Indies
Greater
Jamaica
Antilles
Hispaniola
HAITI
DOM.
REP.
Puerto
Rico
Lesser
Antilles
N

BELIZE
GUATEMALA
HONDURAS
EL SALVADOR
NICARAGUA
Lake
Nicaragua
Isthmus
of Panama
PANAMA
Gulf of
Panama
COSTA RICA
Caribbean   Sea
Trinidad
SOUTH
VENEZUELA
COLOMBIA
AMERICA
BRAZIL
Cocos I.
Malpelo I.

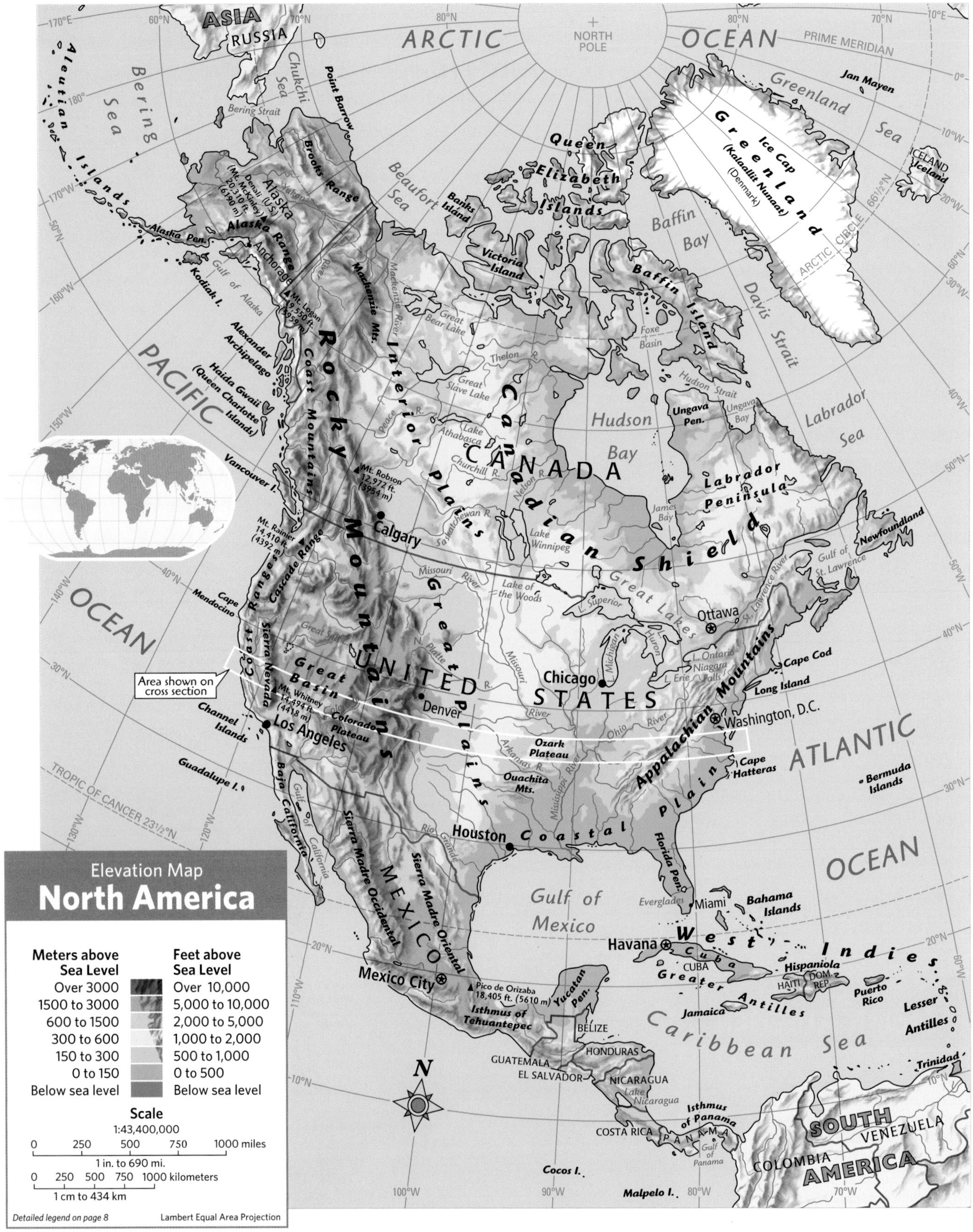

ASIA
RUSSIA
ARCTIC OCEAN
NORTH POLE
PRIME MERIDIAN
Jan Mayen
Greenland Sea
Aleutian Islands
Bering Sea
Chukchi Sea
Bering Strait
Point Barrow
Brooks Range
Beaufort Sea
Queen Elizabeth Islands
Greenland
Ice Cap (Kalaallit Nunaat) (Denmark)
ICELAND Iceland
ARCTIC CIRCLE 66½°N
Alaska Pen.
Alaska
Denali (Mt. McKinley) 20,310 ft. (6190 m)
Alaska Range
Mt. Logan 19,550 ft. (5959 m)
Banks Island
Victoria Island
Baffin Bay
Baffin Island
Davis Strait
Kodiak I.
Gulf of Alaska
Alexander Archipelago
Haida Gwaii (Queen Charlotte Islands)
Mackenzie Mts.
Mackenzie River
Great Bear Lake
Foxe Basin
Hudson Strait
Labrador Sea
PACIFIC OCEAN
Coast Mountains
Rocky Mountains
Interior Plains
Great Slave Lake
Thelon
CANADA
Hudson Bay
Ungava Pen.
Ungava Bay
Vancouver I.
Mt. Robson 12,972 ft. (3954 m)
Peace River
Lake Athabasca
Churchill
Nelson
James Bay
Labrador Peninsula
Canadian Shield
Newfoundland
Gulf of St. Lawrence
Mt. Rainier 14,410 ft. (4392 m)
Calgary
Saskatchewan R.
Lake Winnipeg
Cascade Range
Coast Ranges
Cape Mendocino
Sierra Nevada
Missouri River
Lake Superior
Lake of the Woods
Great Lakes
Great Plains
St. Lawrence River
Ottawa
Area shown on cross section
Great Basin
UNITED STATES
Platte R.
Missouri R.
L. Michigan
L. Huron
L. Ontario
Niagara Falls
L. Erie
Appalachian Mountains
Cape Cod
Long Island
Channel Islands
Los Angeles
Mt. Whitney 14,494 ft. (4418 m)
Colorado Plateau
Denver
Chicago
Ohio River
Washington, D.C.
Guadalupe I.
TROPIC OF CANCER 23½°N
Sierra Nevada
Baja California
Gulf of California
Rio Grande
MEXICO
Sierra Madre Occidental
Houston
Ozark Plateau
Arkansas River
Ouachita Mts.
Mississippi River
Coastal Plain
Florida Pen.
Cape Hatteras
ATLANTIC OCEAN
Bermuda Islands
Gulf of Mexico
Everglades
Miami
Bahama Islands
Havana
CUBA
West Indies
Greater Antilles
Hispaniola
HAITI
DOM. REP.
Puerto Rico
Lesser Antilles
Mexico City
Pico de Orizaba 18,405 ft. (5610 m)
Isthmus of Tehuantepec
Yucatan Pen.
Jamaica
Caribbean Sea
Trinidad
BELIZE
GUATEMALA
EL SALVADOR
HONDURAS
NICARAGUA
Lake Nicaragua
Isthmus of Panama
COSTA RICA
PANAMA
Gulf of Panama
SOUTH AMERICA
VENEZUELA
COLOMBIA
Cocos I.
Malpelo I.

N

Elevation Map
North America

Meters above Sea Level	Feet above Sea Level
Over 3000	Over 10,000
1500 to 3000	5,000 to 10,000
600 to 1500	2,000 to 5,000
300 to 600	1,000 to 2,000
150 to 300	500 to 1,000
0 to 150	0 to 500
Below sea level	Below sea level

Scale
1:43,400,000

0   250   500   750   1000 miles
1 in. to 690 mi.

0   250   500   750   1000 kilometers
1 cm to 434 km

Detailed legend on page 8   Lambert Equal Area Projection

Cross Section
Vertical exaggeration 25 to 1
Scale at 36°N: 1 in. to 400 mi., 1 cm to 253 km

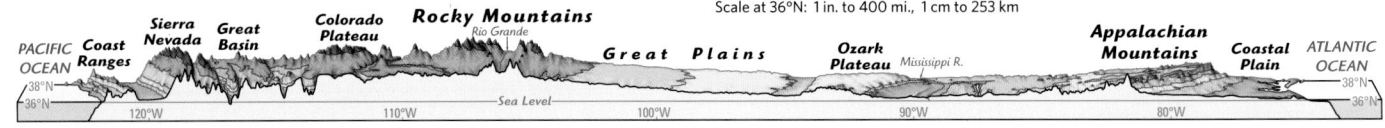

PACIFIC OCEAN | Coast Ranges | Sierra Nevada | Great Basin | Colorado Plateau | Rocky Mountains | Rio Grande | Great Plains | Ozark Plateau | Mississippi R. | Appalachian Mountains | Coastal Plain | ATLANTIC OCEAN

Sea Level
38°N   120°W   110°W   100°W   90°W   80°W   36°N

Rain Shadow Effect

When moist warm air meets a mountain range, it rises, cools, and creates clouds that rain on the **windward** side of the mountain. The air then becomes drier as it descends the opposite **leeward** side of the mountain. Few clouds reach the leeward side, so it is relatively dry. Astoria lies near the Pacific Coast on the windward side of the Cascade Range, while Sunnyside lies on the leeward side.

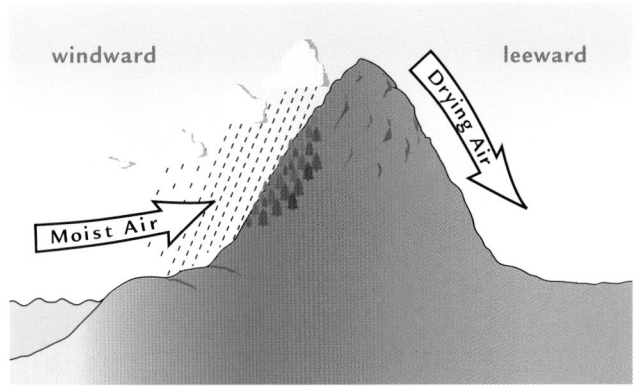

Climographs

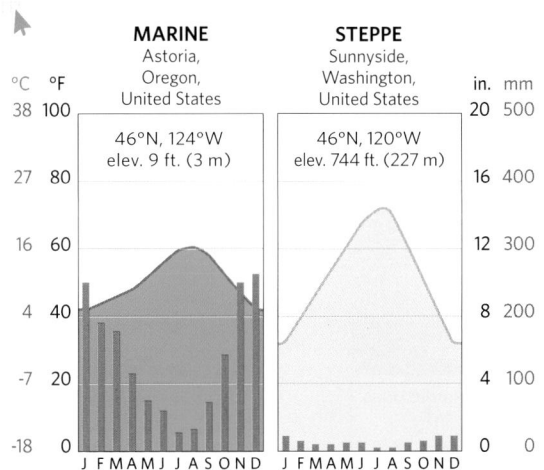

Precipitation

Millimeters per Year	Inches per Year
0 to 250	0 to 10
250 to 500	10 to 20
500 to 1000	20 to 40
1000 to 2000	40 to 80
Over 2000	Over 80

A Smoggy Day

Combine calm winds and a sunny day with nitrogen oxides from car and factory exhaust fumes and volatile organic compounds and you get **smog**. Any city can have smog, but it's especially a problem when smog is trapped by nearby mountains, as in Los Angeles, Denver, and Mexico City.

Climate

Tropical	Tropical rain forest
	Savanna
Dry	Steppe (semi-desert)
	Desert
Mild	Mediterranean
	Humid subtropical
	Marine
Continental	Hot summer
	Cool summer
	Subarctic
Polar	Tundra
	Ice cap
Highland	(Varies greatly with elevation and latitude)

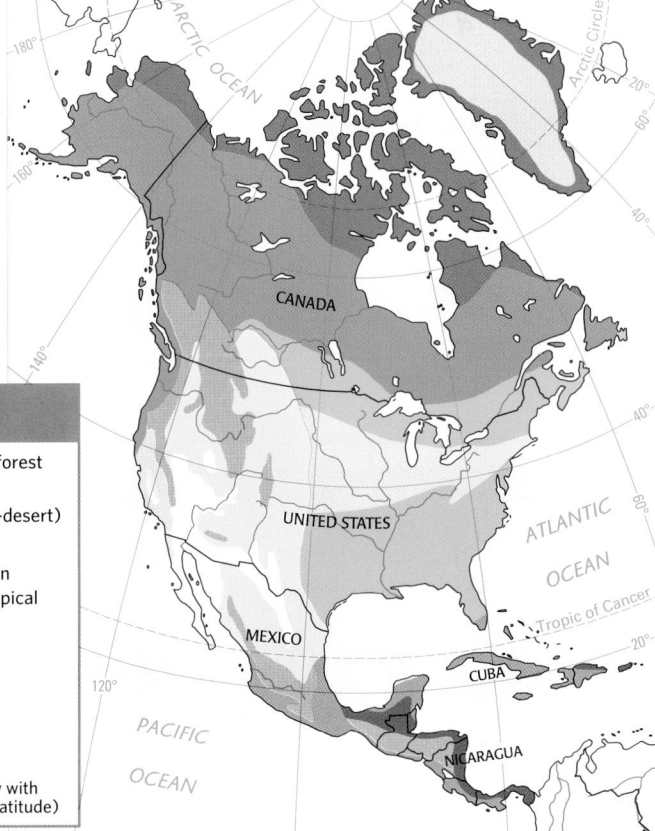

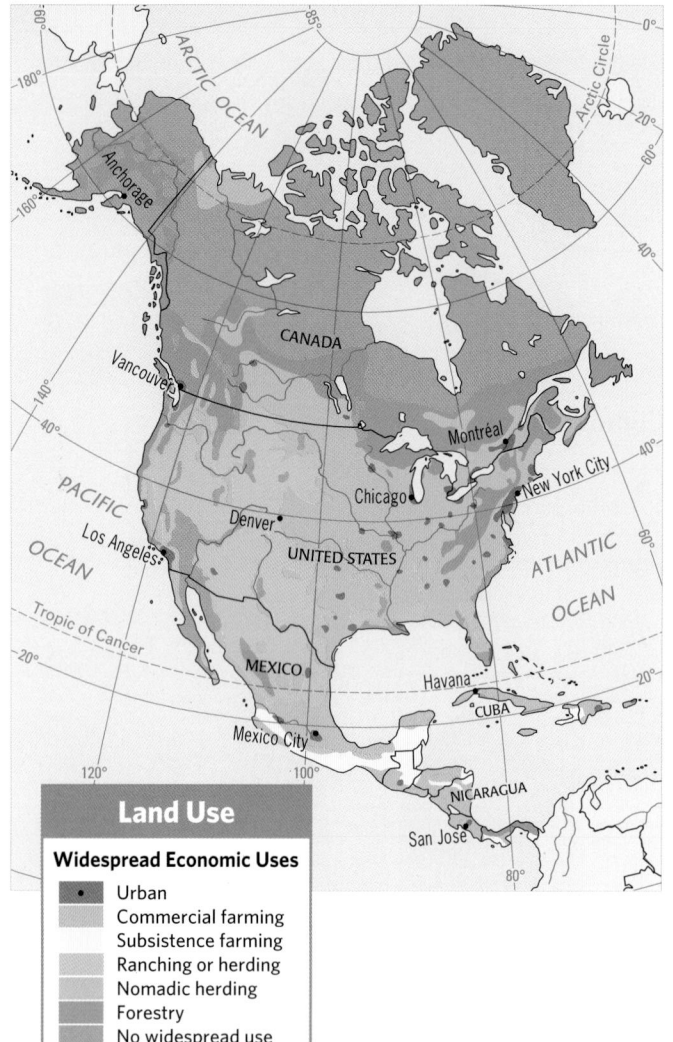

Land Use

Widespread Economic Uses

- Urban
- Commercial farming
- Subsistence farming
- Ranching or herding
- Nomadic herding
- Forestry
- No widespread use

North America is the world's leading corn producer, with the United States, Mexico, and Canada ranking first, seventh, and eleventh in global production. Corn grows on over 90 million acres (140,625 square miles) of land in the United States.

Waves of Grain

North America is one of the world's leading agricultural exporters, shipping corn, soybeans, wheat, and other crops to Europe, Japan, and China. The United States and Canada rank among the top five exporters of wheat, and the United States ranks first in soybean exports.

The 800-mile Trans-Alaska Pipeline System transports oil from northern Alaska to an ice-free port in southern Alaska, where it can be shipped to the contiguous states and eastern Asia. North America is home to three of the world's top ten oil producers—the United States, Mexico, and Canada.

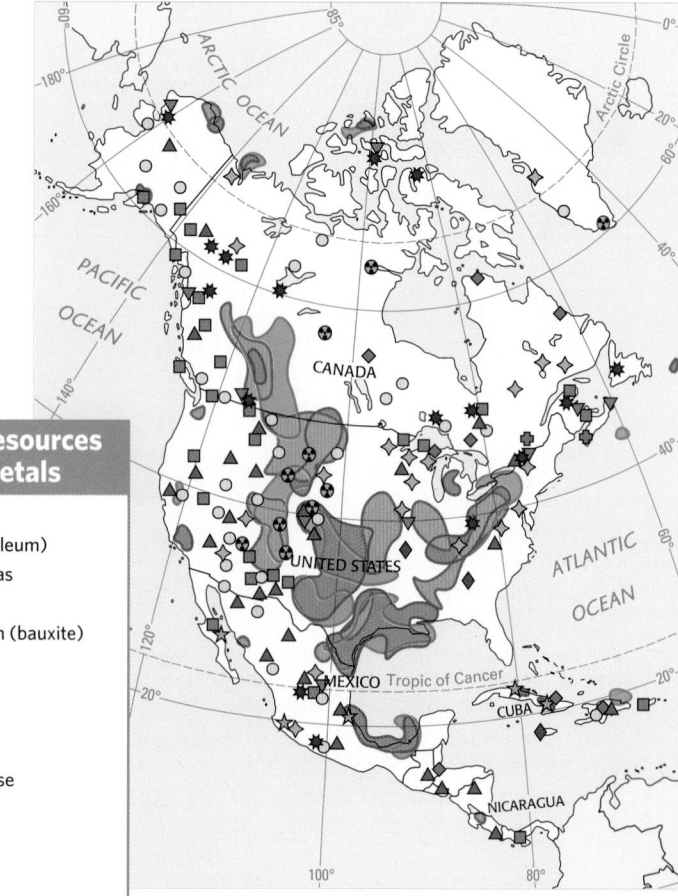

Energy Resources and Metals

- Coal
- Oil (petroleum)
- Natural gas
- ⊗ Uranium
- ◆ Aluminum (bauxite)
- ■ Copper
- ○ Gold
- ◇ Iron
- ▼ Lead
- ★ Manganese
- ◆ Nickel
- ▲ Silver
- ✚ Tin
- ✳ Zinc

North American Trade Organizations

- ■ **CAFTA-DR**—Central American Free Trade Agreement-Dominican Republic
- ■ **CARICOM**—Caribbean Community and Common Market
- ■ **NAFTA**—North American Free Trade Agreement

Trade organizations encourage the buying and selling of foreign goods from member countries by reducing or eliminating tariffs and other restrictions on imports. Trade agreements can increase employment opportunities and economic growth.

Top North American GDPs

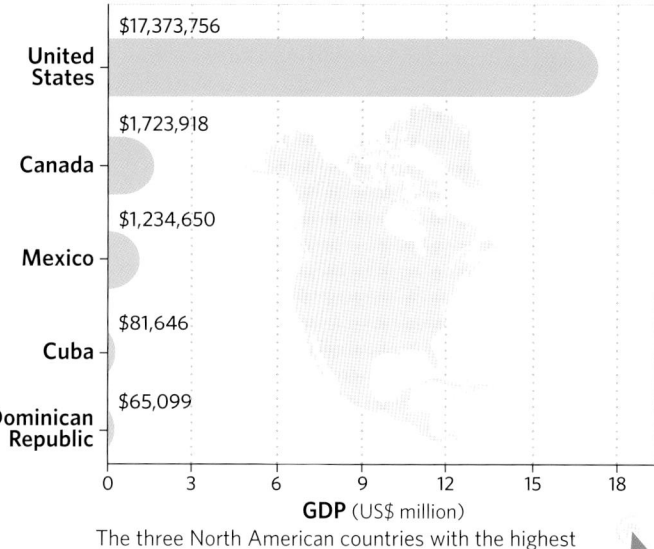

United States	$17,373,756
Canada	$1,723,918
Mexico	$1,234,650
Cuba	$81,646
Dominican Republic	$65,099

GDP (US$ million)

The three North American countries with the highest GDPs benefit from diverse and technologically advanced industries. North American countries with lower GDPs have economies supported mainly by agriculture and tourism.

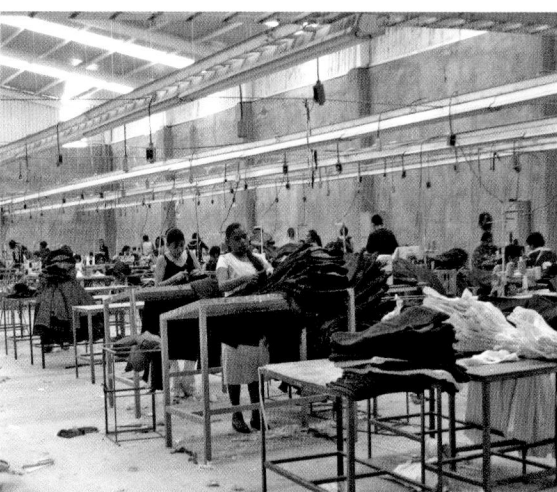

Mostly women work in Mexico's *maquiladoras*, industrial plants owned by foreign corporations. These factories often assemble parts and clothing for American companies. The finished products are usually sold in the United States.

Balance of Trade

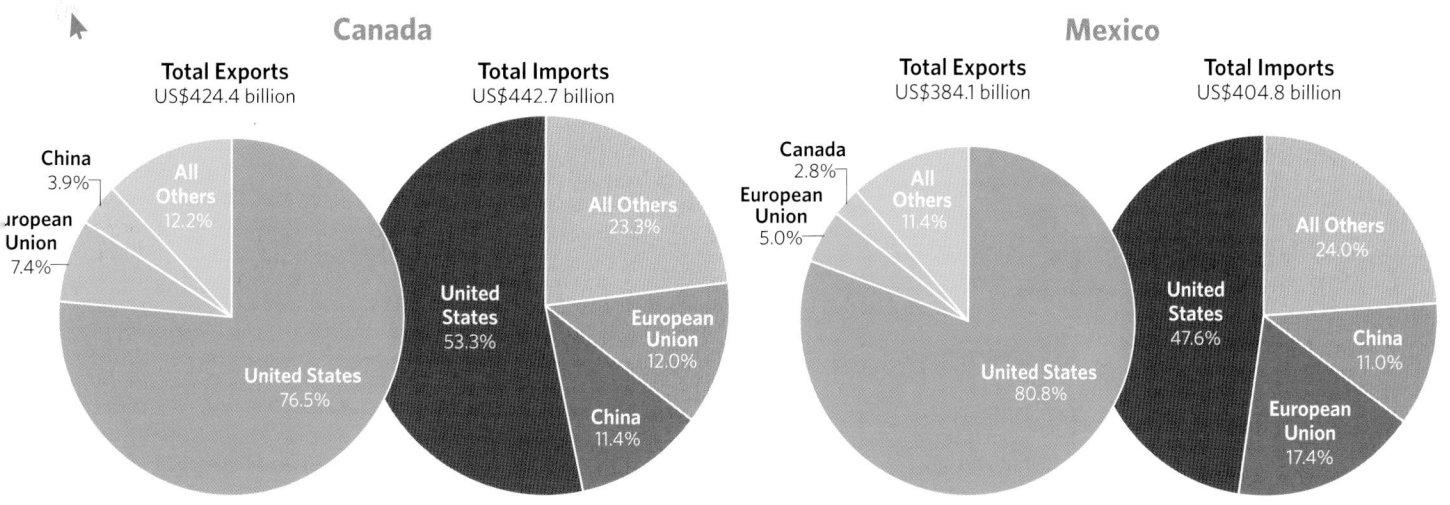

Canada

Total Exports
US$424.4 billion

- China 3.9%
- European Union 7.4%
- All Others 12.2%
- United States 76.5%

Total Imports
US$442.7 billion

- All Others 23.3%
- United States 53.3%
- European Union 12.0%
- China 11.4%

Mexico

Total Exports
US$384.1 billion

- Canada 2.8%
- European Union 5.0%
- All Others 11.4%
- United States 80.8%

Total Imports
US$404.8 billion

- All Others 24.0%
- United States 47.6%
- China 11.0%
- European Union 17.4%

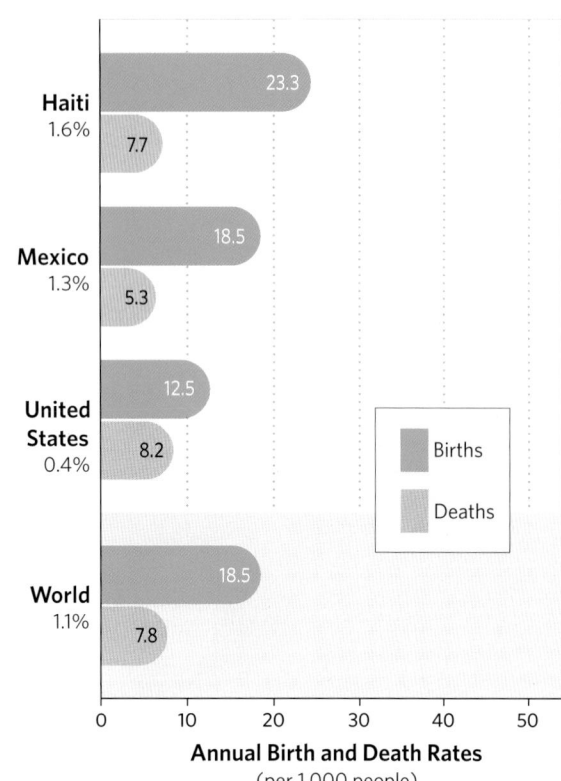

Natural Population Growth

North America

Births

Deaths

Haiti
1.6%
23.3
7.7

Mexico
1.3%
18.5
5.3

United States
0.4%
12.5
8.2

World
1.1%
18.5
7.8

0   10   20   30   40   50

Annual Birth and Death Rates
(per 1,000 people)

Population

People per Sq. Km	People per Sq. Mile
0 to 2	0 to 5
2 to 20	5 to 50
20 to 40	50 to 100
40 to 100	100 to 250
Over 100	Over 250

Inuit live in some of the coldest places on Earth: Alaska, northern Canada, Greenland, and eastern Siberia. Many of these indigenous people still engage in traditional activities, such as hunting and fishing.

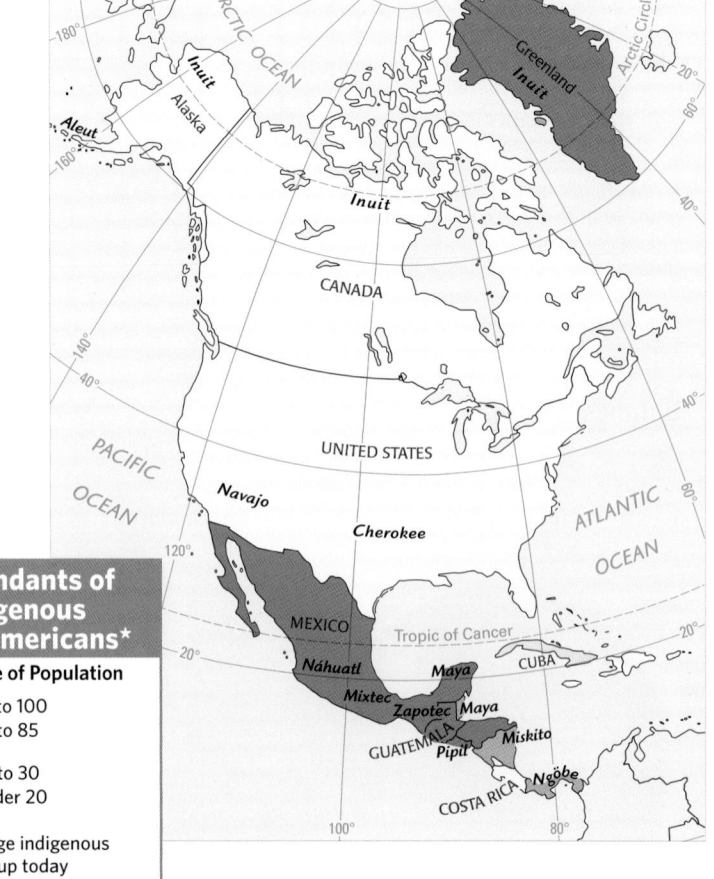

Descendants of Indigenous North Americans*

Percentage of Population

	85 to 100
	70 to 85
	20 to 30
	Under 20

Inuit   Large indigenous group today

*Includes Métis, Mestizo, and Garifuna

ISSUES / TODAY

What impact does immigration have?

Since the 1500s, North America has been a destination for millions of voluntary and involuntary immigrants. The overwhelming majority of North Americans are descendants of immigrants from Europe, Africa, or Asia. Do immigrants have a positive or negative impact on their host countries? There are many perspectives on this issue. Here are two of them.

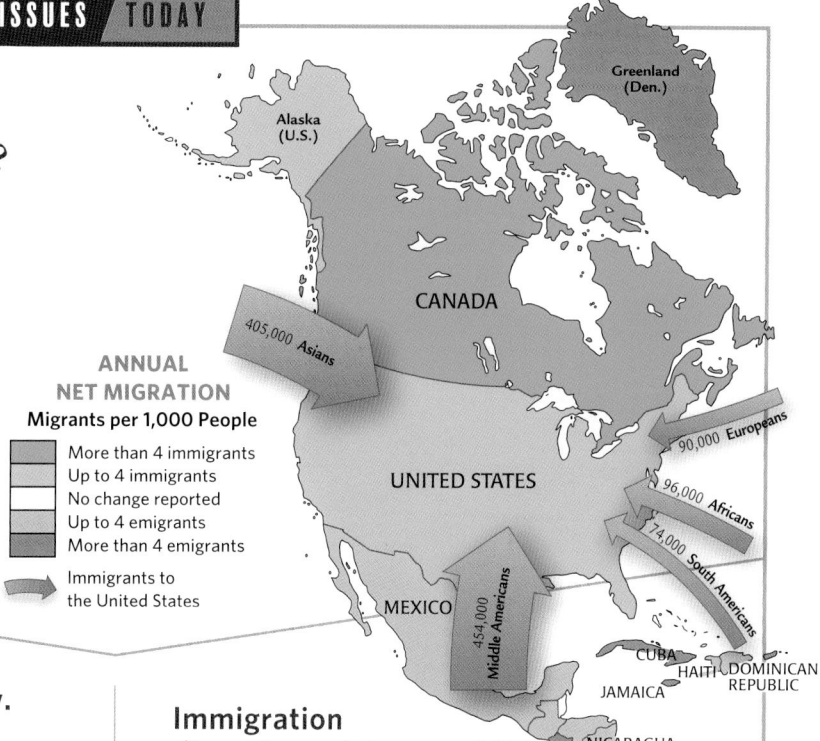

ANNUAL NET MIGRATION
Migrants per 1,000 People

- More than 4 immigrants
- Up to 4 immigrants
- No change reported
- Up to 4 emigrants
- More than 4 emigrants

→ Immigrants to the United States

Immigrants improve a country.

- Immigration expands the economy. About 80 percent of immigrants who arrive in the United States are of an employable age, ready to pay taxes and make purchases.

- The average immigrant in the United States contributes nearly $128,000 more in taxes than he or she consumes in public benefits (measured in 2017 dollars).

- Immigrants are almost twice as likely as the native-born to become entrepreneurs.

- Many immigrants have training that benefits the country. Almost two-thirds of all immigrants to Canada have college degrees.

- Historically, every group of immigrants has integrated with and contributed to the culture at large. Some famous immigrants include physicist Albert Einstein, industrialist and philanthropist Andrew Carnegie, author Isabel Allende, and businessman Elon Musk.

Immigrants in the United States

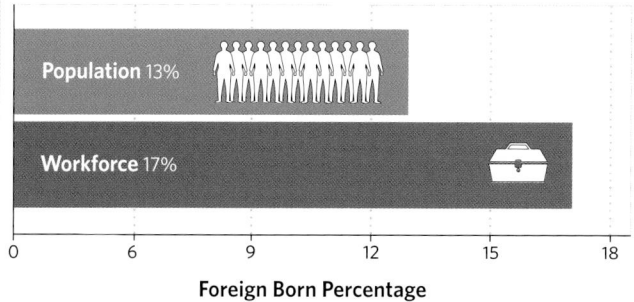

Population 13%

Workforce 17%

0   6   9   12   15   18

Foreign Born Percentage

Immigrants often arrive looking for jobs. They make up a larger percentage of the labor force than of the population.

Immigration disrupts society.

- Some immigrants do not integrate their customs and values with those of their host country.

- Immigrants strain the education system with special needs. Ontario, Canada's most populous province, spends about US$160 million a year on immigrant ESL (English as a Second Language) students.

- Governments try to prevent illegal immigrants from entering their countries. The United States spends about US$19.3 billion annually securing its borders.

- Immigrants drain resources intended for a country's citizens. About 8.1 million foreign-born people in the United States are enrolled in Medicaid, a program that provides health care to low-income individuals.

- Illegal immigrants take jobs from citizens and from immigrants who entered their host countries legally. In the United States, about 8 million workers are illegal immigrants.

The San Ysidro Land Port of Entry, between San Diego, California, and Tijuana, Mexico, is the busiest land border crossing in the Western Hemisphere. About 27 percent of all people in California are immigrants.

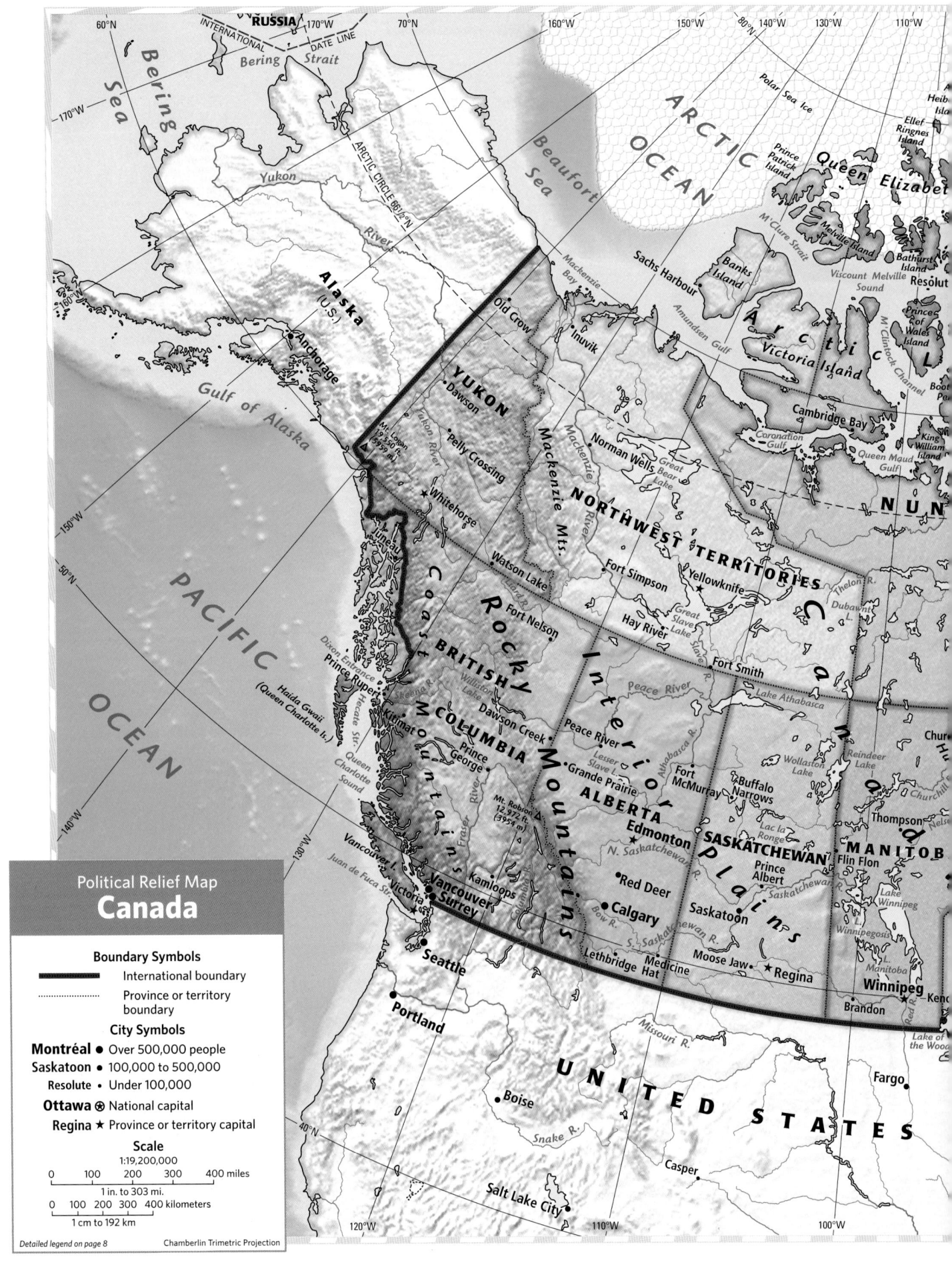

Political Relief Map
Canada

Boundary Symbols

———— International boundary

·············· Province or territory boundary

City Symbols

Montréal ● Over 500,000 people

Saskatoon ● 100,000 to 500,000

Resolute • Under 100,000

Ottawa ⊗ National capital

Regina ★ Province or territory capital

Scale

1:19,200,000

0   100   200   300   400 miles

1 in. to 303 mi.

0   100   200   300   400 kilometers

1 cm to 192 km

Detailed legend on page 8   Chamberlin Trimetric Projection

RUSSIA

INTERNATIONAL DATE LINE

Bering Strait

Bering Sea

Yukon River

ARCTIC CIRCLE 66½°N

Alaska (U.S.)

Anchorage

Gulf of Alaska

PACIFIC OCEAN

ARCTIC OCEAN

Beaufort Sea

Mackenzie Bay

Old Crow

Inuvik

YUKON

Dawson

Pelly Crossing

Mt. Logan 19,550 ft.

Whitehorse

Juneau

Watson Lake

Fort Nelson

Coast Mountains

BRITISH COLUMBIA

Rocky Mountains

Mackenzie Mts.

Norman Wells

Great Bear Lake

NORTHWEST TERRITORIES

Fort Simpson

Yellowknife

Great Slave Lake

Hay River

Fort Smith

Sachs Harbour

Banks Island

Amundsen Gulf

Victoria Island

Coronation Gulf

Cambridge Bay

Queen Maud Gulf

Polar Sea Ice

Prince Patrick Island

Melville Island

Viscount Melville Sound

M'Clure Strait

M'Clintock Channel

King William Island

Queen Elizabeth

Ellef Ringnes Island

Bathurst Island

Resolute

Prince of Wales Island

Heiberg Island

Boot Po

Arctic

Prince of Wales Island

NUN

Dixon Entrance

Prince Rupert

Haida Gwaii (Queen Charlotte Is.)

Hecate Str.

Queen Charlotte Sound

Kitimat

Prince George

Skeena R.

Williston Lake

Dawson Creek

Fraser River

Mt. Robson 12,972 ft. (3954 m)

Peace River

Grande Prairie

ALBERTA

Interior Plains

Peace River

Lesser Slave L.

Slave R.

Lake Athabasca

Fort McMurray

Athabasca R.

Buffalo Narrows

Wollaston Lake

Lac la Ronge

Reindeer Lake

Churchill

Canada

Thelon R.

Dubawnt L.

Edmonton

N. Saskatchewan R.

SASKATCHEWAN

Prince Albert

Saskatchewan R.

MANITOB

Flin Flon

Thompson

Nels

Churchill

Vancouver I.

Victoria

Juan de Fuca Str.

Vancouver

Surrey

Kamloops

Red Deer

Calgary

Bow R.

Lethbridge

Medicine Hat

S. Saskatchewan R.

Saskatoon

Moose Jaw

Regina

Reindeer Lake

Lake Winnipeg

Winnipegosis

Lake Manitoba

Winnipeg

Brandon

Red R.

Kend

Lake of the Woo

Seattle

Portland

Boise

Snake R.

Salt Lake City

Missouri R.

UNITED STATES

Casper

Fargo

120°W

110°W

100°W

60°N

170°W

170°W

160°W

150°W

140°W

130°W

110°W

80°N

50°N

40°N

70°W 60°W 50°W 80°N 40°W 30°W 20°W 70°N 60°N

ICELAND

ARCTIC CIRCLE 66½°N

Ellesmere Island

Kane Basin

Qaanaaq (Thule)

Baffin Bay

G r e e n l a n d
(Kalaallit Nunaat)
(Denmark)

20°W

Devon Island

Lancaster Sound

Clyde River

Baffin Island

Denmark Strait

30°W

of Boothia

Prince Charles I.

Cumberland Sound

Davis Strait

Kugaaruk

Melville Peninsula

Foxe

Nuuk (Godthab)

Foxe Basin

Foxe Peninsula

Iqaluit

Frobisher Bay

Cape Farewell

U T

N

50°N
40°W

Southampton Island

Foxe Channel

Hudson Strait

Cape Chidley

Labrador Sea

ATLANTIC

Chesterfield Inlet

Coats Island

Salluit

Ungava Peninsula

Ungava Bay

OCEAN

Rankin Inlet

Mansel Island

Hudson

R. aux Feuilles

George R.

Kuujjuaq

NEWFOUNDLAND

30°W

Bay

Belcher Islands

Kuujjuarapik

L a b r a d o r   P e n i n s u l a

Smallwood Res.

Churchill R.

Happy Valley-Goose Bay

AND

LABRADOR

40°N

Fort Severn

James Bay

Akimiski I.

Labrador City

Manicouagan Res.

Strait of Belle Isle

Corner Brook

Newfoundland

★ St. John's

Cape Race

Lowlands

Severn R.

Winisk R.

Albany R.

Moosonee

QUÉBEC

S h i e l d

L. Mistassini

Sept-Îles

Anticosti Island

Gulf of
St. Lawrence

St.-Pierre and Miquelon (France)

50°N

O N T A R I O

Val-d'Or

Saguenay

St. Lawrence River

PRINCE EDWARD ISLAND

Charlottetown

Cape Breton Island

40°N

L. Nipigon

Québec

NEW BRUNSWICK
Fredericton

NOVA SCOTIA

Halifax

Sable Island (Nova Scotia)

Thunder Bay

Lake Superior

Sault Ste. Marie Sudbury

L. Nipissing

Gatineau Montréal

Ottawa R.

Saint John

Bay of Fundy

Yarmouth

Cape Sable

neapolis

Georgian Bay

Ottawa

L. Simcoe

Kingston

Boston

Lake Michigan

Toronto

L. Ontario

Mississauga

Hamilton

Buffalo

Niagara Falls

Lake Huron

Chicago

Detroit **Windsor**

Lake Erie

New York City

ssippi R.

90°W 80°W 70°W 60°W

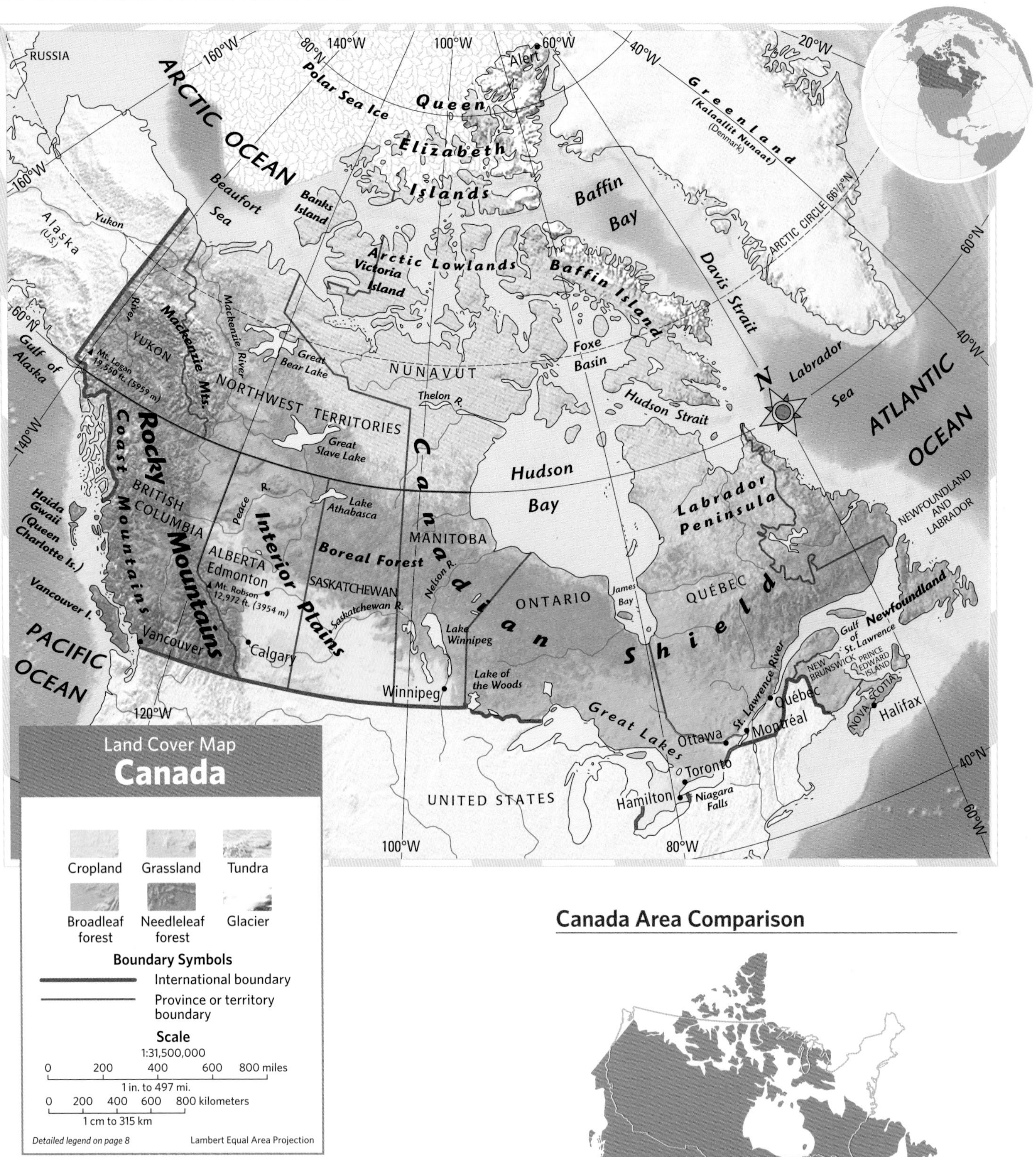

RUSSIA

ARCTIC OCEAN

160°W
140°W
80°N
100°W
60°W
40°W
20°W

Alert

Polar Sea Ice

Queen

Elizabeth

Islands

Baffin

Bay

Greenland
(Kalaallit Nunaat)
(Denmark)

Beaufort
Sea

Banks
Island

ARCTIC CIRCLE 66½°N

Alaska
(US)

Yukon

Arctic Lowlands

Victoria
Island

Baffin Island

Davis Strait

60°N

40°W

Gulf of
Alaska

Mackenzie Mts.

Mt. Logan
19,550 ft. (5959 m)

YUKON

NORTHWEST TERRITORIES

Great
Bear Lake

Mackenzie River

NUNAVUT

Thelon R.

Foxe
Basin

Hudson Strait

Labrador
Sea

N

ATLANTIC
OCEAN

40°W

Coast

Rocky

BRITISH
COLUMBIA

Great
Slave Lake

Hudson

Bay

Labrador
Peninsula

NEWFOUNDLAND
AND
LABRADOR

60°N

Haida
Gwaii
(Queen
Charlotte Is.)

Mountains

Peace R.

Lake
Athabasca

Lake

MANITOBA

James
Bay

QUÉBEC

Mountains

Interior

ALBERTA
Edmonton

Boreal Forest

SASKATCHEWAN

Nelson R.

Newfoundland

Gulf
of
St. Lawrence

Vancouver I.

Mt. Robson
12,972 ft. (3954 m)

Saskatchewan R.

ONTARIO

Shield

St. Lawrence River

NEW
BRUNSWICK
PRINCE
EDWARD
ISLAND

PACIFIC

Vancouver

Plains

Lake
Winnipeg

Canadian

NOVA SCOTIA

Halifax

OCEAN

Calgary

Winnipeg

Lake of
the Woods

Great Lakes

Ottawa
Québec
Montréal

120°W

UNITED STATES

100°W

Toronto

Hamilton

Niagara
Falls

80°W

40°N

60°W

Canada Area Comparison

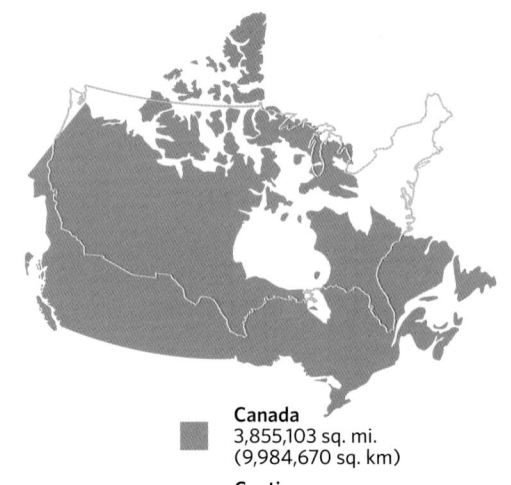

Canada
3,855,103 sq. mi.
(9,984,670 sq. km)

**Contiguous
United States**
3,021,295 sq. mi.
(7,825,112 sq. km)

Hills. Valleys. Canadian Shield?

This vast rocky region covers half of Canada. The Canadian Shield was formed 3 billion years ago. Successive ice ages have stripped away its soil, exposing some of the oldest rocks on Earth. Today most of its surface is gently rolling, although it has hills, mountains, and cliffs in Québec and Labrador.

The Coast Mountains tower over Vancouver, Canada's third largest city. Located near the Pacific Ocean, Vancouver has a relatively mild climate that allows its seaport, Canada's busiest, to remain free of ice year-round.

Elevation Map
Canada

Meters above Sea Level		Feet above Sea Level
Over 3000		Over 10,000
1500 to 3000		5,000 to 10,000
600 to 1500		2,000 to 5,000
300 to 600		1,000 to 2,000
150 to 300		500 to 1,000
0 to 150		0 to 500

Scale
1:31,500,000

0   200   400   600   800 miles
1 in. to 497 mi.

0   200   400   600   800 kilometers
1 cm to 315 km

Detailed legend on page 8   Lambert Equal Area Projection

RUSSIA
160°W
140°W
80°N
100°W
60°W
40°W
Greenland (Kalaallit Nunaat) (Denmark)
ARCTIC CIRCLE 66½°N
160°W
ARCTIC OCEAN
Queen
Elizabeth
Islands
Beaufort Sea
Banks Island
Baffin Bay
Alaska (U.S.)
Yukon
Arctic Lowlands
Victoria Island
Baffin Island
Gulf of Alaska
60°N
YUKON
Mt. Logan 19,550 ft. (5959 m)
Mackenzie Mts.
NORTHWEST TERRITORIES
Great Bear Lake
Mackenzie River
NUNAVUT
Foxe Basin
Thelon
Hudson Strait
140°W
Rocky Mountains
Coast Mountains
BRITISH COLUMBIA
Great Slave Lake
Lake Athabasca
Canadian
Hudson Bay
N
Labrador Sea
ATLANTIC OCEAN
Haida Gwaii (Queen Charlotte Islands)
Peace R.
Labrador Peninsula
NEWFOUNDLAND AND LABRADOR
Area shown on cross section
Vancouver I.
ALBERTA
Edmonton
INTERIOR PLAINS
Interior Plains
Mt. Robson 12,972 ft. (3954 m)
SASKATCHEWAN
MANITOBA
Nelson R.
Saskatchewan R.
Shield
QUÉBEC
Newfoundland
PACIFIC OCEAN
Vancouver
Calgary
ONTARIO
James Bay
Gulf of St. Lawrence
PRINCE EDWARD ISLAND
Winnipeg
Lake Winnipeg
St. Lawrence R.
NEW BRUNSWICK
NOVA SCOTIA
Lake of the Woods
Québec
Montréal
Halifax
Great Lakes
Ottawa
UNITED STATES
Toronto
Hamilton
Niagara Falls
120°W
100°W
80°W
40°N
60°W

Cross Section
Vertical exaggeration 47 to 1
Scale at 50°N: 1 in. to 475 mi., 1 cm to 300 km

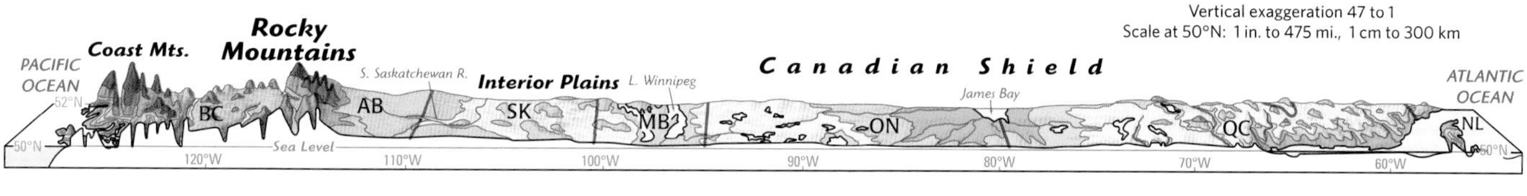

PACIFIC OCEAN
Coast Mts.
Rocky Mountains
S. Saskatchewan R.
Interior Plains
L. Winnipeg
Canadian Shield
James Bay
ATLANTIC OCEAN
52°N
BC
AB
SK
MB
ON
QC
NL
50°N
Sea Level
120°W
110°W
100°W
90°W
80°W
70°W
60°W
50°N

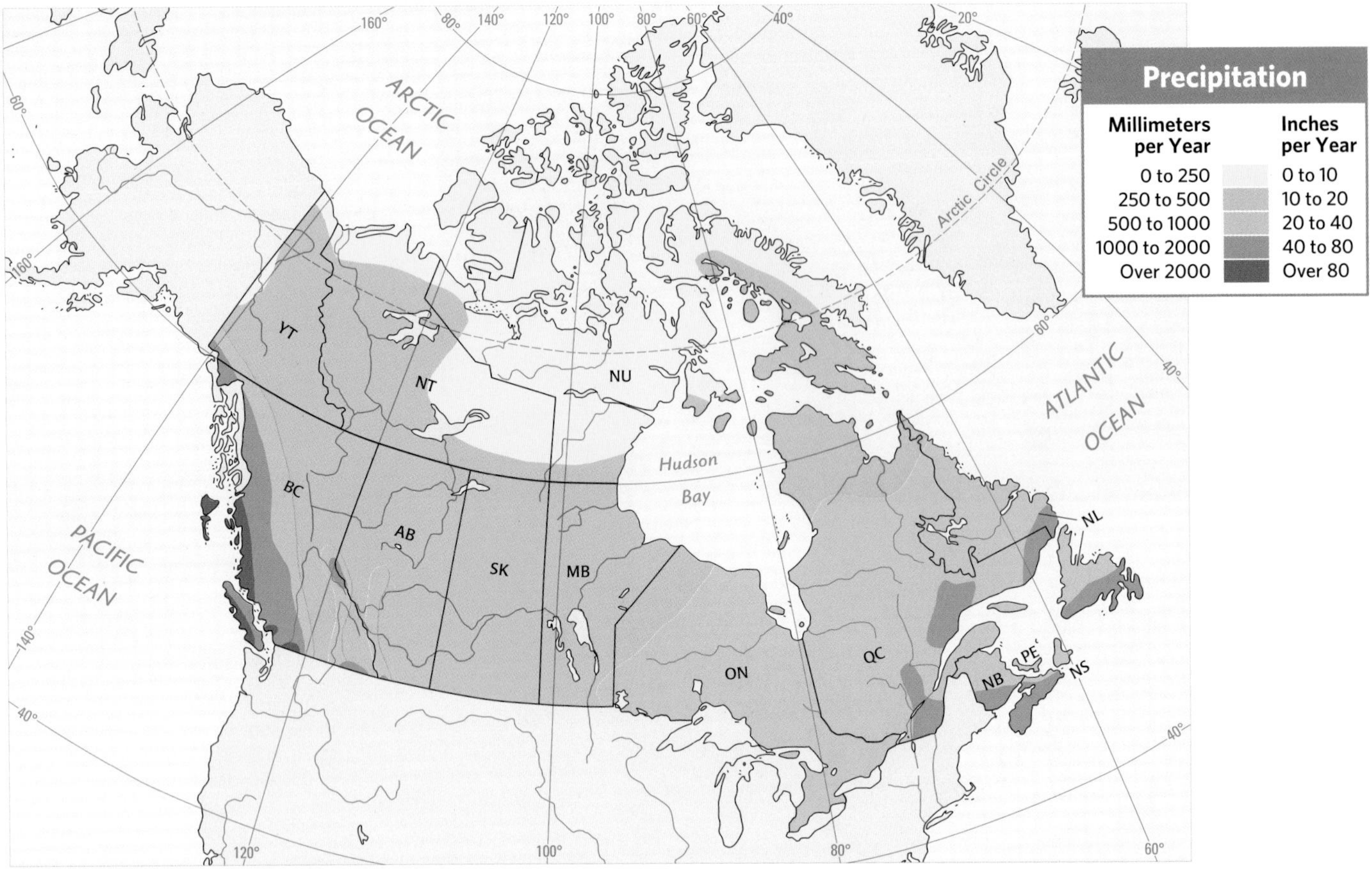
Precipitation
Millimeters per Year
Inches per Year
0 to 250
0 to 10
250 to 500
10 to 20
500 to 1000
20 to 40
1000 to 2000
40 to 80
Over 2000
Over 80
ARCTIC OCEAN
PACIFIC OCEAN
ATLANTIC OCEAN
Hudson Bay
Arctic Circle
YT
NT
NU
BC
AB
SK
MB
ON
QC
NL
NB
PE
NS
160°
140°
120°
100°
80°
60°
40°
20°

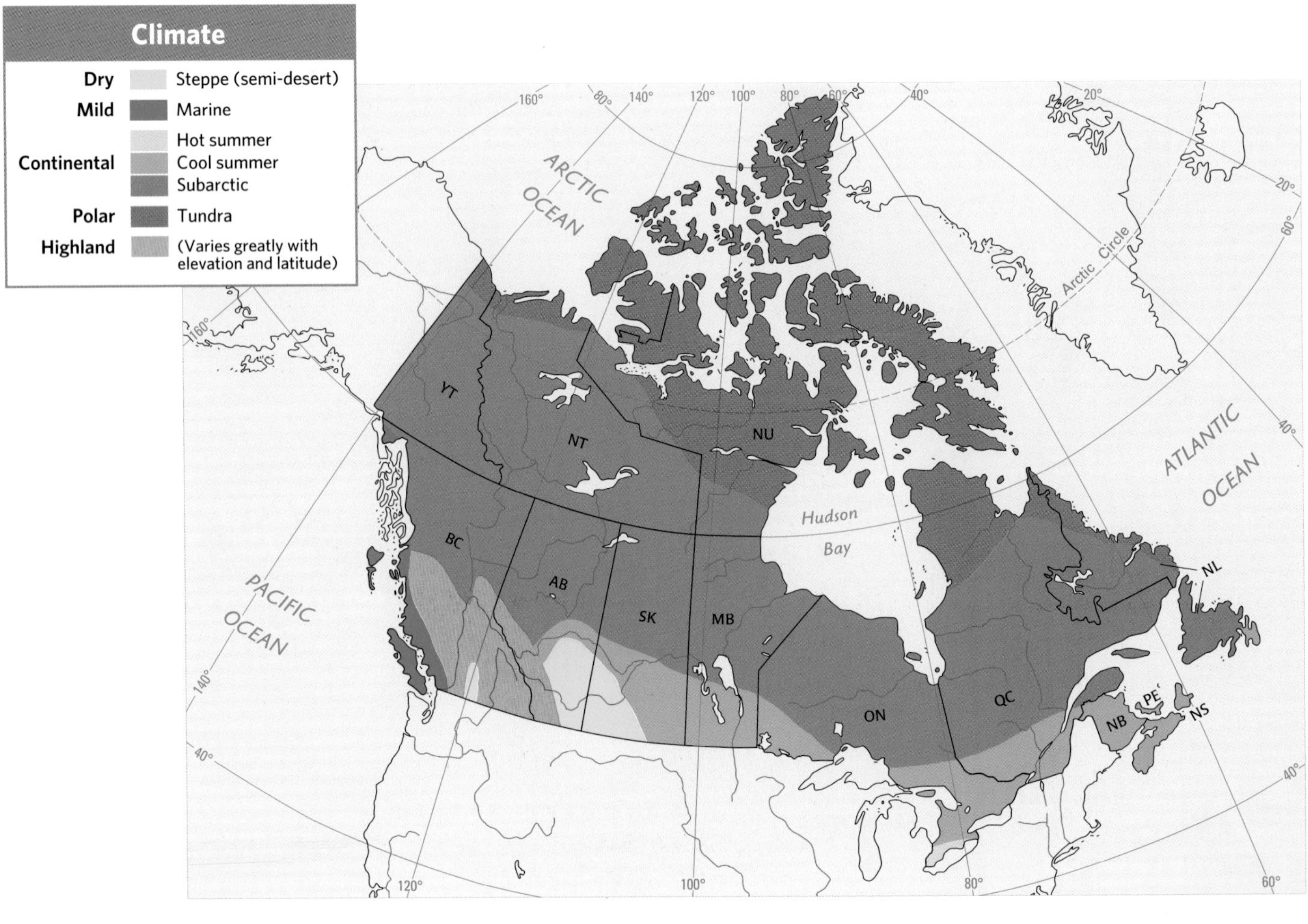
Climate
Dry
Steppe (semi-desert)
Mild
Marine
Continental
Hot summer
Cool summer
Subarctic
Polar
Tundra
Highland
(Varies greatly with elevation and latitude)
ARCTIC OCEAN
PACIFIC OCEAN
ATLANTIC OCEAN
Hudson Bay
Arctic Circle
YT
NT
NU
BC
AB
SK
MB
ON
QC
NL
NB
PE
NS
160°
140°
120°
100°
80°
60°
40°
20°

Canadian Agriculture

Canadian agriculture travels worldwide. Canada exports crops to the United States, Japan, and Mexico. Canola—used in cooking oil, cosmetics, and biodiesel fuel—generates over US$8 billion in export income a year.

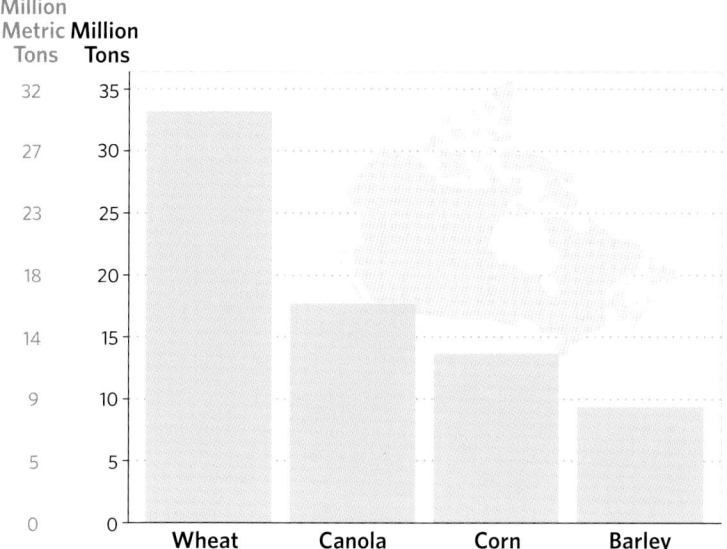

Canada exports over US$4 billion worth of fish and fish products annually. Aquaculture, like these fish farms in Nova Scotia, accounts for about 20 percent of the country's total seafood production. Overfishing in Canadian waters has critically endangered several species of fish.

Forests—Canada's Surplus Crop

Short growing seasons throughout much of Canada make farming difficult, but not forestry. Forests cover nearly 40 percent of the country, giving Canada the third-largest forest in the world. The forest industry contributes approximately US$18 billion to the country's GDP.

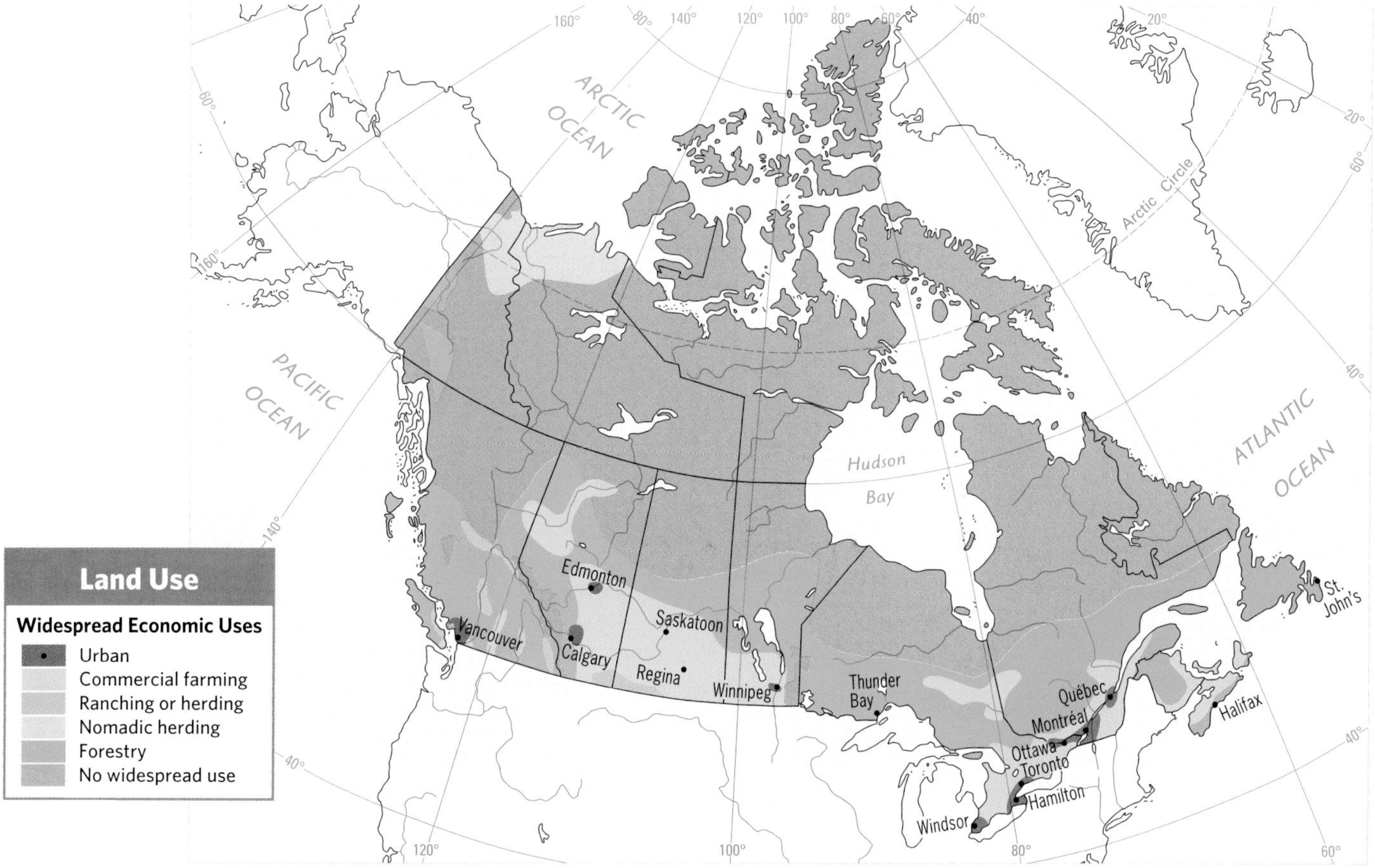

Land Use

Widespread Economic Uses
- Urban
- Commercial farming
- Ranching or herding
- Nomadic herding
- Forestry
- No widespread use

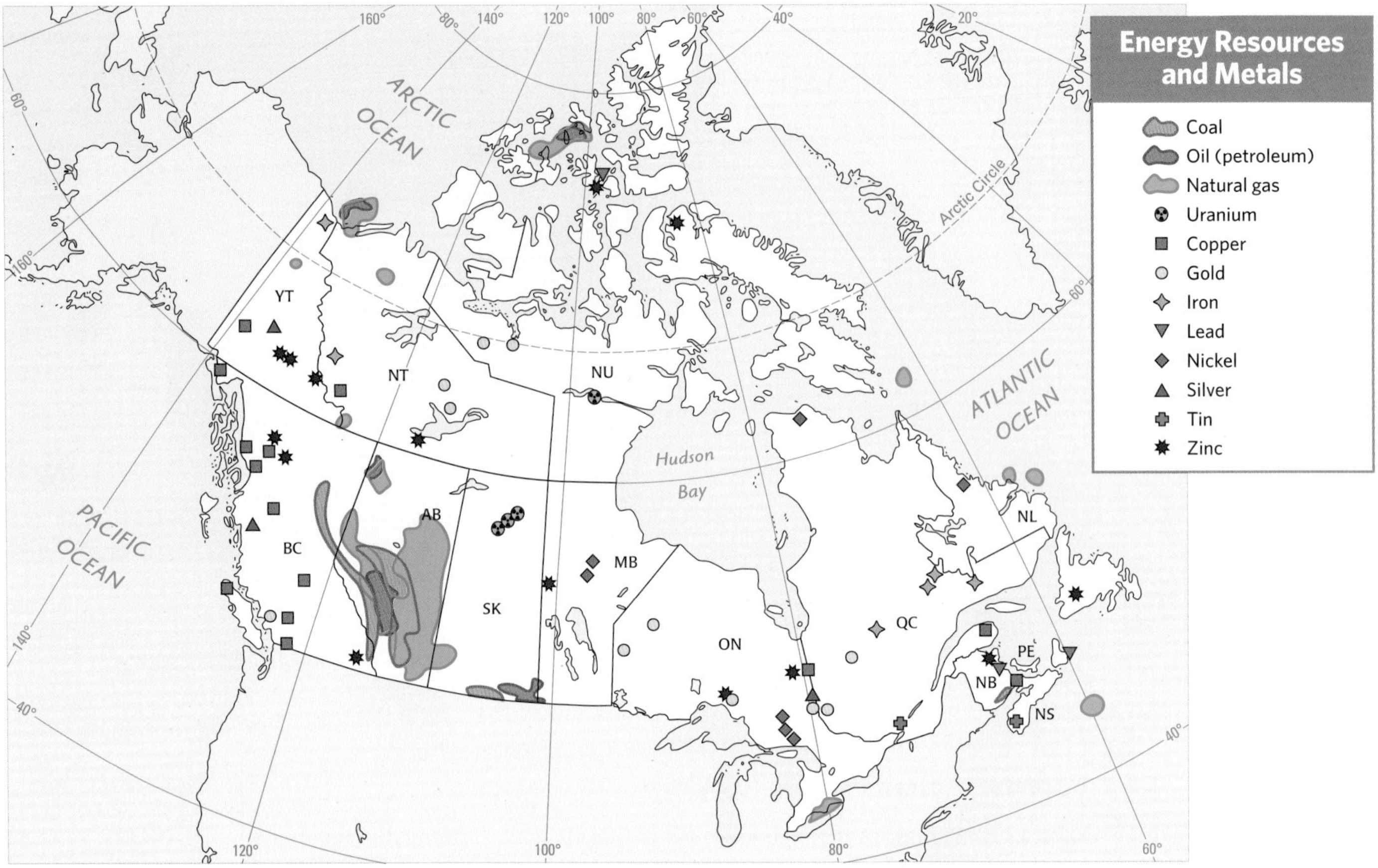

Energy Resources and Metals

- Coal
- Oil (petroleum)
- Natural gas
- ☢ Uranium
- ◼ Copper
- ○ Gold
- ◆ Iron
- ▼ Lead
- ◆ Nickel
- ▲ Silver
- ✚ Tin
- ✳ Zinc

Major Highways and Airports

Canada has more than 500 airports and over 647,600 miles (1.1 million kilometers) of road. The Trans-Canada Highway is the world's longest highway. It connects all 10 Canadian provinces.

Airline Passengers per Year

- ✈ Over 20 million
- ✈ 10 to 20 million
- ✈ 2 to 10 million
- • Other airport
- ～ Trans-Canada and other major highways

Located on the St. Lawrence River, Québec is the oldest city in Canada. The Historic District of Old Québec was named a World Heritage City in 1985.

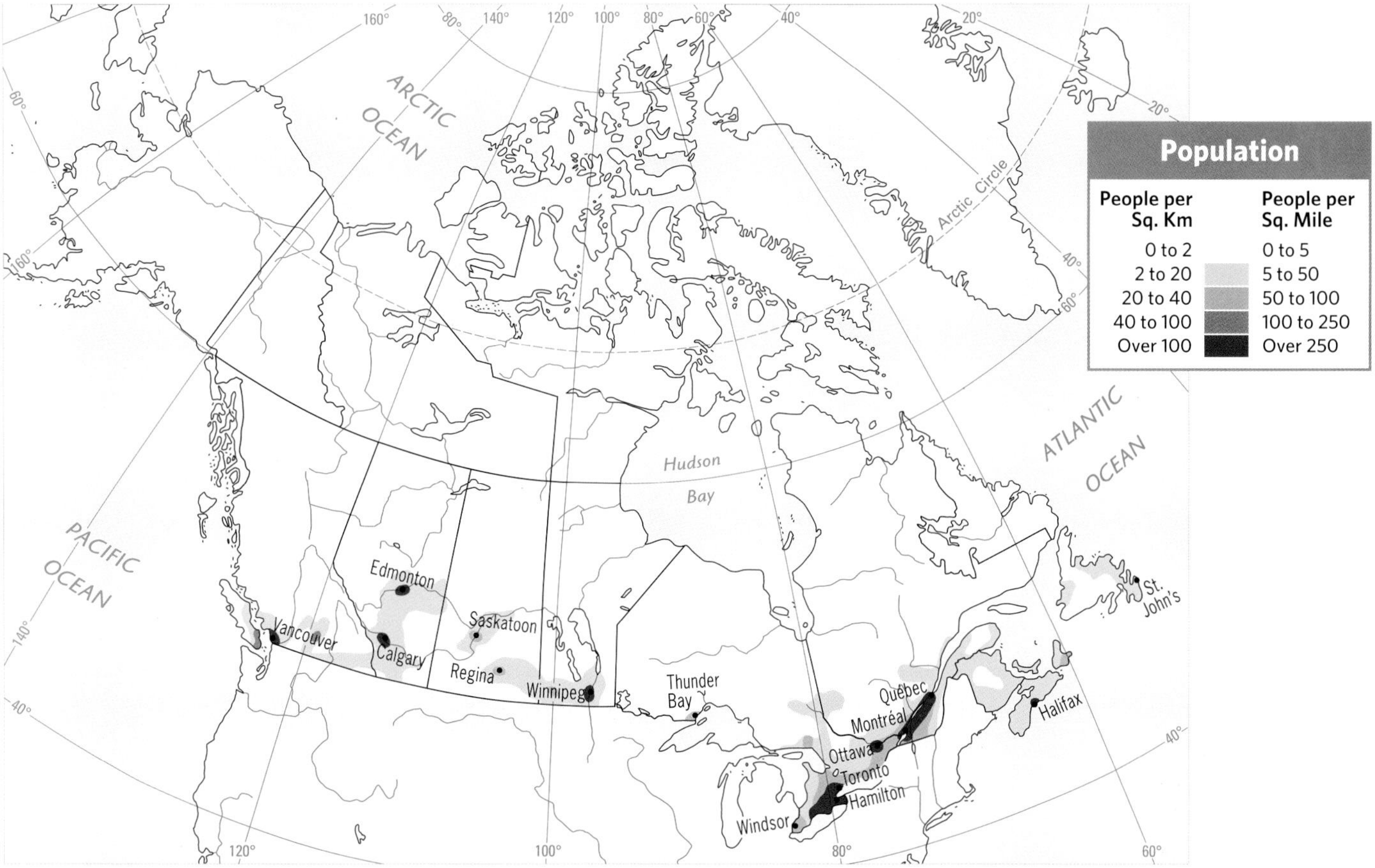

Population

People per Sq. Km	People per Sq. Mile
0 to 2	0 to 5
2 to 20	5 to 50
20 to 40	50 to 100
40 to 100	100 to 250
Over 100	Over 250

ARCTIC OCEAN

Arctic Circle

Hudson Bay

ATLANTIC OCEAN

PACIFIC OCEAN

Edmonton

Vancouver

Calgary

Saskatoon

Regina

Winnipeg

Thunder Bay

Québec

Montréal

Ottawa

Toronto

Hamilton

Windsor

Halifax

St. John's

Ethnic Composition

Canada

British 13.9%

French 6.7%

Italian 4.0%

German 3.7%

Scottish 3.1%

Irish 2.7%

Dutch 1.7%

Ukrainian 1.6%

Polish 1.5%

Chinese 6.2%

East Indian 4.3%

Arab 1.7%

Amerindian 3.4%

Caribbean/ West Indian 1.8%

All Others 43.7%

Languages of Canada

Other Single Languages 7.7%

Multiple Languages 3.5%

Chinese 3.4%

French 20.6%

English 64.8%

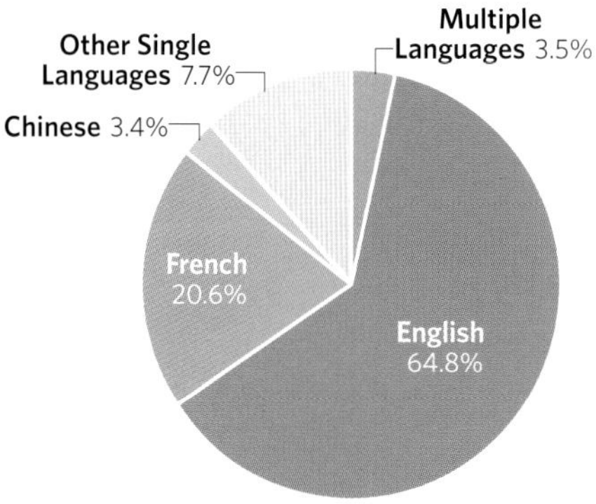

Canada has two official languages: English and French. However, recent immigrants also diversify the country's mix of languages. Compare this graph with the ethnic composition graph above.

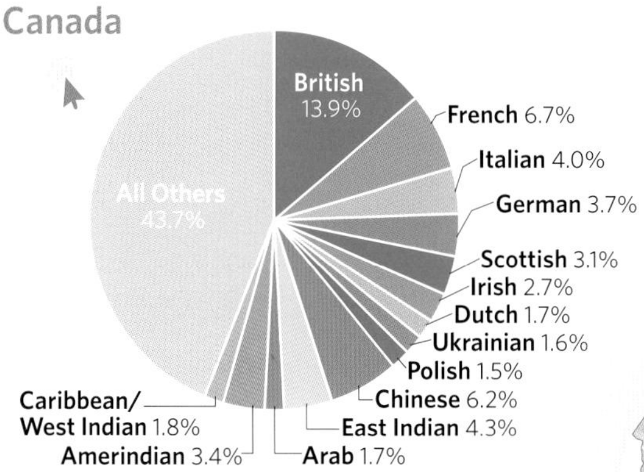

Regional Maps of Canada

1 **Western Canada** pp. 68–69

2 **Central Canada:** *Ontario* p. 70

3 **Central Canada:** *Québec* p. 71

4 **Eastern Canada** p. 72

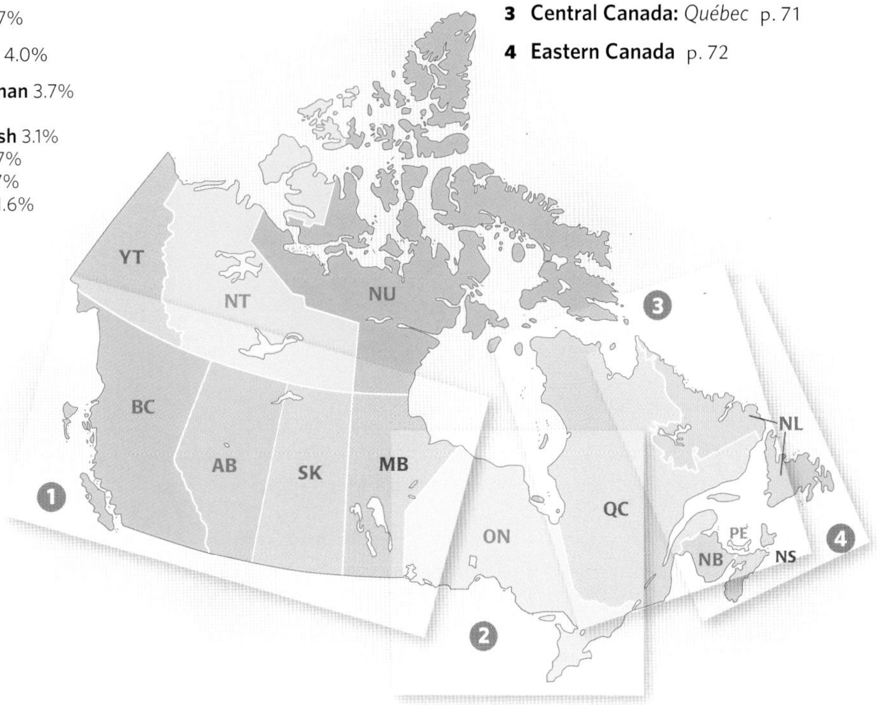

YT

NT

NU

BC

AB

SK

MB

ON

QC

NL

PE

NB

NS

1

2

3

4

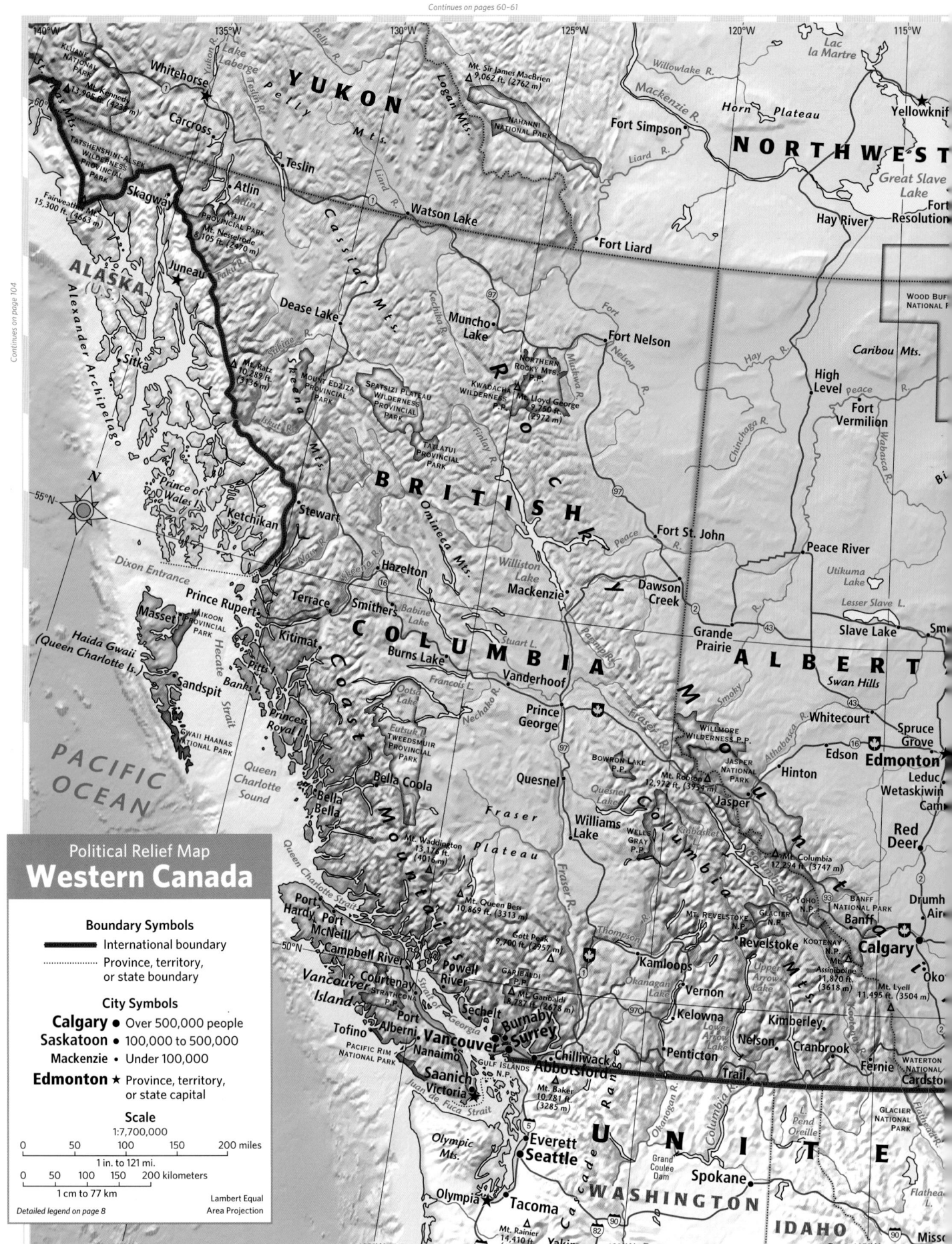

Continues on pages 60–61

Continues on page 104

Political Relief Map
Western Canada

Boundary Symbols
━━━━━ International boundary
············ Province, territory, or state boundary

City Symbols
Calgary ● Over 500,000 people
Saskatoon ● 100,000 to 500,000
Mackenzie • Under 100,000
Edmonton ★ Province, territory, or state capital

Scale
1:7,700,000

0   50   100   150   200 miles

1 in. to 121 mi.

0   50 100 150   200 kilometers

1 cm to 77 km

Detailed legend on page 8

Lambert Equal Area Projection

Continues on pages 100–101

Continues on pages 60–61

110°W
105°W
Dubawnt Lake
100°W
95°W
90°W

Yathkyed Lake
Kaminak Lake

TERRITORIES

Nonacho Lake

Angikuni Lake

NUNAVUT

S. Henik Lake
Nueltin Lake
• Arviat

60°N

Hjalmar Lake
Wholdaia Lake
Snowbird Lake

Ennadai Lake

Kasba Lake

Nejanilini Lake

Caribou River PROVINCIAL WILDERNESS PARK

Button Bay
• Churchill   *Cape Churchill*

Hudson Bay

• Fort Smith

Seal R.

Tadoule Lake

SAND LAKES PROVINCIAL WILDERNESS PARK

Numaykoos Lakes PROVINCIAL WILDERNESS PARK

WAPUSK NATIONAL PARK

Cape Tatnam

• Uranium City   Fond-du-Lac
Lake Athabasca

Black Lake

Fond~du~Lac R.

Churchill R.

• Fort Chepewyan

ATHABASCA SAND DUNES PROVINCIAL WILDERNESS PARK

Macfarlane R.

Wollaston Lake

Northern Indian L.

Hudson Bay Lowlands

Claire

Firebag Hills

Wollaston Lake

Reindeer Lake

Southern Indian Lake

• Gillam

55°N

Athabasca R.

CLEARWATER RIVER PROVINCIAL PARK

Cree Lake

Frobisher Lake

Lynn Lake

Burntwood R.

Nelson R.

Hayes R.

Gods R.

• Fort McMurray

Clearwater

Peter Pond L.

Churchill L.

Granville Lake

• Thompson

Sipiwesk L.

• Buffalo Narrows

Primrose Lake

LAC LA RONGE PROVINCIAL PARK

La Ronge

Lac La Ronge

Churchill R.

Flin Flon

Amisk Lake

MANITOBA

Cross Lake

Molson Lake

Gods Lake

Sandy Lake

Shield

Severn

OPASQUIA P.P.

Cold Lake

Dore L.

SASKATCHEWAN

GRASS RIVER PROVINCIAL PARK

Playgreen Lake

Gunisao R.

Island L.

Cold Lake •

Beaver R.

MEADOW LAKE PROVINCIAL PARK

• Meadow Lake

PRINCE ALBERT NATIONAL PARK

The Pas •

Moose Lake

Cedar L.

• Grand Rapids

ONTARIO

Trout Lake

SLAND NAL PARK

Saskatchewan R.

• Lloydminster

• Prince Albert

Saskatchewan R.

Nipawin •

• Tisdale

Porcupine Hills

Lake Winnipegosis

Lake Winnipeg

Berens R.

ATIKAKI PROV. WILDERNESS PARK

Bloodvein R.

WOODLAND CARIBOU P.P.

• Red Lake

Lac Seul

• Wainwright

North Battleford •

Melfort •

Interior

Battle R.

Martensville •

• Humboldt

Swan River •

DUCK MOUNTAIN PROVINCIAL PARK

HECLA P.P.

Winnipeg R.

NOPIMING P.P.

50°N

Saskatoon •

Assiniboine R.

Lake Manitoba

• Gimli

WHITESHELL P.P.

• Kenora

• Dryden

• Kindersley

Yorkton •
Melville •

DUCK MOUNTAIN PROVINCIAL PARK

Dauphin •

RIDING MOUNTAIN NATIONAL PARK

Russell •

Selkirk •

Lake of the Woods

Lake Diefenbaker

Qu'Appelle R.

★ Regina

Moose Jaw

Winnipeg

Portage la Prairie

• Steinbach

• Fort Frances

• Medicine Hat

Swift Current •

Plains

Coteau du Missouri

Brandon •

Virden •

Winkler •   Emerson

Rainy R.

Rainy Lake

thbridge

• Maple Creek

Cypress Hills

Frenchman R.

• Weyburn

Altona •

Red R.

International Falls

Milk R.

GRASSLANDS NATIONAL PARK

Missouri

Estevan •

Souris R.

Red Lake

MINNESOTA

STATES

• Minot

L. Sakakawea

Grand Forks •

• Great Falls

Missouri R.

Fort Peck L.

Yellowstone R.

NORTH DAKOTA

Fargo •

MONTANA

★ Bismarck

L. Oahe

James R.

Mississippi R.

St. Cloud •

110°W
105°W
100°W
95°W

Continues on page 70

Continues on pages 98–99

Continues on pages 60–61

Political Relief Map
Central Canada
Ontario

Boundary Symbols
━━━━ International boundary
‧‧‧‧‧‧‧‧ Province or state boundary

City Symbols
Mississauga ● Over 500,000 people
Sudbury ● 100,000 to 500,000
Nipigon · Under 100,000
Ottawa ⊗ National capital
Toronto ★ Province or state capital

Scale
1:9,000,000

0   50   100   150   200 miles
1 in. to 142 mi.

0   50   100   150   200 kilometers
1 cm to 90 km

Detailed legend on page 8   Albers Equal Area Projection

Continues on pages 68–69

Continues on pages 92–93

Continues on page 71

Continues on pages 88–89

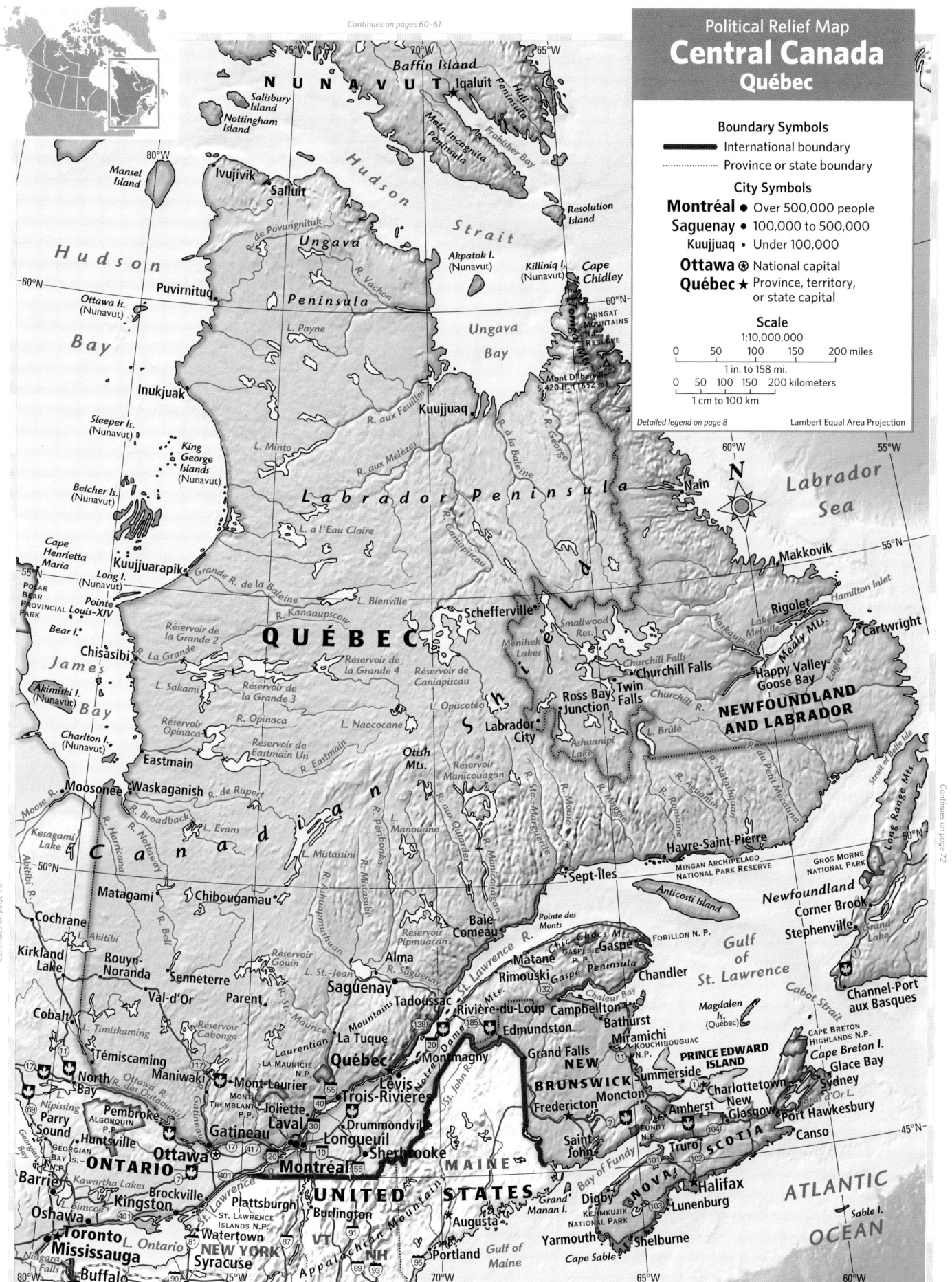

Political Relief Map
Central Canada
Québec

Boundary Symbols
━━━ International boundary
············· Province or state boundary

City Symbols
Montréal ● Over 500,000 people
Saguenay ● 100,000 to 500,000
Kuujjuaq • Under 100,000
Ottawa ⊛ National capital
Québec ★ Province, territory, or state capital

Scale
1:10,000,000
0 50 100 150 200 miles
1 in. to 158 mi.
0 50 100 150 200 kilometers
1 cm to 100 km

Detailed legend on page 8   Lambert Equal Area Projection

Continues on pages 60-61
Continues on page 70
Continues on page 72
Continues on pages 88-89

Continues on pages 60–61

Political Relief Map
Eastern Canada

Boundary Symbols
━━━━━ International boundary
·············· Province or state boundary

City Symbols
Halifax ● Over 100,000 people
Moncton ● 25,000 to 100,000
Makkovik • Under 25,000
St. John's ★ Province capital

Scale
1:8,000,000
0   50   100   150   200 miles
1 in. to 126 mi.
0   50   100   150   200 kilometers
1 cm to 80 km

Detailed legend on page 8   Lambert Equal Area Projection

Killiniq Island (Nunavut)
Cape Chidley
Ungava Bay
TORNGAT MOUNTAINS NATIONAL PARK RESERVE
Torngat Mts.
Mont D'Iberville
5,420 ft. (1652 m)

R. aux Feuilles
R. aux Mélèzes
R. Caniapiscau
R. de la Baleine
R. George
Fraser R.

Kuujjuaq

Labrador Peninsula
QUÉBEC

Labrador Sea

Nain

ATLANTIC OCEAN

Schefferville
Adlatok R.
Makkovik

Réservoir de Caniapiscau
Menihek Lakes
Smallwood Res.
Naskaupi R.
Kanairiktok R.
Rigolet
Hamilton Inlet
Lake Melville
Cartwright
Medly Mts.

Canadian
Lac Opiscotéo
Churchill Falls
Churchill Falls
Ross Bay Junction
Twin Falls
Churchill R.
Happy Valley-Goose Bay
Eagle R.

Shield
Labrador City
Little
Mecatina
L. Brûlé
Lake Ashuanipi
Alexis R.
Port Hope Simpson

NEWFOUNDLAND AND LABRADOR

Otish Mts.
R. aux Outardes
R. Ste-Marguerite
R. Moisie
R. Romaine
R. Natashquan
R. Nabisipi
R. du Petit Mécatina
R. St-Paul
R. St-Augustin
Strait of Belle Isle

Réservoir Manicouagan

St. Anthony

Sept-Îles
Havre-Saint-Pierre
MINGAN ARCHIPELAGO NATIONAL PARK RESERVE

50°N

Long Range Mts.
White Bay

Notre Dame Bay

Baie-Comeau
Pointe des Monts
Anticosti Island
GROS MORNE NATIONAL PARK

St. Lawrence River
Chic-Chocs Mts.
Matane
GASPÉSIE P.P.
FORILLON N.P.
Gaspé
Bay of Islands
Windsor
Gander
Bonavista Bay

Notre Dame Mts.
Rimouski
Gaspé Peninsula
Gulf of St. Lawrence
Corner Brook
Stephenville
Grand Lake
Grand Falls
TERRA NOVA N.P.
Trinity Bay

Campbellton
Chaleur Bay
Chandler
St. George's Bay
Long Range Mts.
Lloyds R.
Newfoundland
Clarenville
Conception Bay
Cape Spear

Edmundston
Bathurst
MOUNT CARLETON P.P.
Magdalen Islands (Québec)
St. John's

St. John R.
Grand Falls
NEW
Miramichi
KOUCHIBOUGUAC N.P.
PRINCE EDWARD ISLAND
CAPE BRETON HIGHLANDS N.P.
Channel-Port aux Basques
Fortune Bay
Placentia
Avalon Peninsula

MAINE (U.S.)
BRUNSWICK
Fredericton
Miramichi R.
Summerside
PRINCE EDWARD ISLAND N.P.
St.-Pierre and Miquelon (France)
Placentia Bay
Cape Race

Moncton
Charlottetown
Northumberland Str.
Sydney
St. Mary's Bay

Saint John
FUNDY N.P.
New Glasgow
Glace Bay
Louisbourg
Cape Breton I.

Truro
Port Hawkesbury
St. Ann's Bay
Bras d'Or L.

KEJIMKUJIK NATIONAL PARK
Digby
NOVA SCOTIA
Canso
Sherbrooke
ATLANTIC OCEAN

Grand Manan Island
Halifax
Bay of Fundy

Gulf of Maine
Yarmouth
Shelburne
Lunenburg
L. Rossignol
Cape Sable
Sable I. (Nova Scotia)

N

Continues on page 71

Continues on pages 88–89

ISSUES / TODAY

How does mining affect the economy?

Canada produces more than 60 minerals and metals. Its petroleum industry is growing rapidly. The mining industry makes important contributions to Canada's economy. However, do the economic benefits of mining outweigh its toll on the environment? There are many perspectives on this issue. Here are two of them.

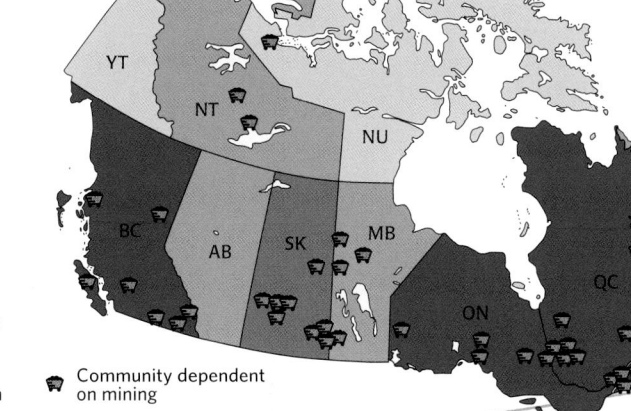

Mining in Canada

Value of Mining (US$)

- More than 5 billion
- 3 to 5 billion
- 1 to 3 billion
- Fewer than 1 billion

⛏ Community dependent on mining

Mining causes profound damage to the environment.

- Mining is very disruptive to the environment. Roughly 135 tons of ore are excavated to extract just one ton of copper, and about 20 tons of mined waste are produced to extract enough gold for one ring.

- Mining not only affects the environment at the site of the mine but also harms the surrounding area through air and ground water pollution.

- Canada has over 10,000 abandoned mines. The government must pay for their rehabilitation to minimize their impact on the environment. For example, the cleanup of one abandoned lead-zinc mine is estimated to cost over half a billion dollars and to take 10 to 15 years to complete.

- The mining and processing of resources pollute more than just the land and water. Compared to gasoline made from conventional crude oil, gasoline made from oil sands produces up to 20 percent more greenhouse gases once accounting for extraction, transporting, refining, and consumption.

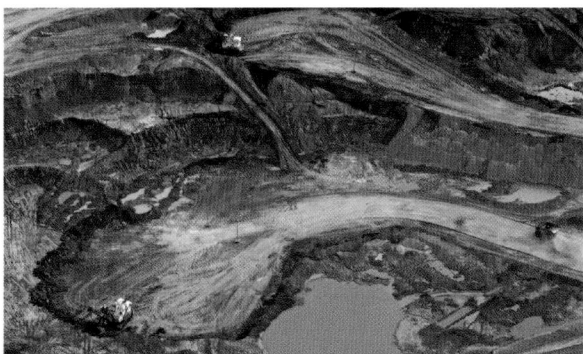

One of Canada's major industries, mining leads to pollution of the air, water, and land. Environmental contamination and pollution from mining threaten wildlife and ecosystems and leaves land barren and uninhabitable.

The benefits of mining outweigh its costs.

- The mining and mineral processing industries are major employers in Canada. These industries employ over 373,000 full-time workers.

- The minerals and metals industry pays some of the highest wages in the Canadian economy, averaging over US$88,000 per year. In comparison, the average annual salary in Canada is just under US$50,000 per year.

- In 2015, mining contributed US$44 billion to Canada's gross domestic product (GDP).

- Mining yields a host of minerals that are essential in many other industries. For example, the energy industry uses 29 different minerals to generate and deliver the energy people depend on every day.

GDP by Sector

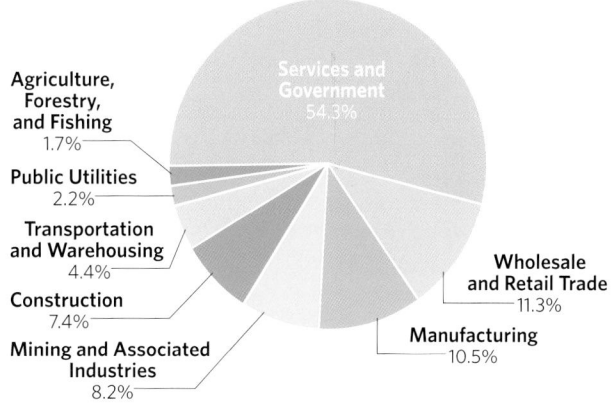

- Agriculture, Forestry, and Fishing 1.7%
- Public Utilities 2.2%
- Transportation and Warehousing 4.4%
- Construction 7.4%
- Mining and Associated Industries 8.2%
- Services and Government 54.3%
- Wholesale and Retail Trade 11.3%
- Manufacturing 10.5%

Manufacturing, construction, transportation, and public utilities also depend on minerals, metals, and oil.

130°W 125°W 120°W 50°N 115°W 110°W 105°W 100°W

Vancouver
Bellingham
Seattle
Olympia
Tacoma
Astoria
Spokane
Franklin D. Roosevelt Lake
Lake Pend Oreille
Coeur d'Alene Lake
Flathead Lake
Milk R.
Lake Manitoba

C A

WASHINGTON
Vancouver
Columbia R.
Portland
Salem
Corvallis
Eugene
Coos Bay
Medford
Bend
Ontario
Klamath Falls
Goose Lake

Moscow
Lewiston
Walla Walla
Pendleton
Baker City
Snake R.
Salmon R.
Missoula
Helena
Butte
Great Falls
Missouri R.
MONTANA
Billings
Yellowstone R.
Fort Peck Lake
Missouri R.
Powder R.

NORTH DAKOTA
Minot
Bismarck
Aberdeen
Lake Sakakawea
Lake Oahe

OREGON
IDAHO
Boise
Idaho Falls
Snake R.
Twin Falls
American Falls Res.
Pocatello
Bear R.
Yellowstone Lake
Bighorn R.
WYOMING
Sheridan
Gillette
Casper
Rock Springs
Pathfinder Res.
Seminoe Res.
Laramie
Cheyenne

SOUTH DAKOTA
Pierre
Rapid City
Lake Francis Case
Niobrara R.

Plateau
Great Salt Lake
Ogden
Salt Lake City
Utah Lake
Provo

NEBRASKA
North Platte
Grand Island
Platte R.
Republican R.
Hastings

PACIFIC
Eureka
Redding
Shasta Lake
Chico
Sacramento R.
Humboldt R.
Elko
Winnemucca
Pyramid Lake
Carson Sink
Reno
Carson City
Lake Tahoe

NEVADA
Great Basin
Sevier Lake

UTAH
Green R.
Sevier R.
Grand Junction
Moab
Colorado R.

Fort Collins
Boulder
Denver
Aurora
Colorado Springs
Greeley
Goodland
Smoky Hill R.

COLORADO
Pueblo
Durango
Arkansas R.
Dodge City

KAN

San Francisco
Oakland
San Jose
Monterey Bay
Monterey
Fresno
CALIFORNIA
Sierra Nevada
San Joaquin R.
Bakersfield
Santa Barbara
Los Angeles
Pasadena
Long Beach
Santa Ana
San Bernardino
Riverside
Salton Sea
San Diego
Tijuana

Las Vegas
Boulder City
Lake Mead
Grand Canyon
Colorado R.
Lake Powell
Little Colorado R.
Flagstaff
Prescott
ARIZONA
Phoenix
Gila R.
Salt R.
Yuma
Tucson
Nogales
Nogales

Farmington
Gallup
Plateau
Santa Fe
Albuquerque
NEW MEXICO
Silver City
Las Cruces
Carlsbad
Roswell
Elephant Butte Res.
Juarez
El Paso

Raton
Canadian R.
Amarillo
Lawton
Red R.
Lubbock
Wichita Falls
Abilene
Brownwood
N. Canadian R.

OK

TEXAS
San Antonio
Del Rio
Rio Grande
Pecos R.
MEXICO
Nuevo Laredo
Laredo
McA
Monterrey

105°W 100°W

160°W 158°W 156°W
HAWAII
22°N
Lihue
Honolulu
Wailuku
Pearl Harbor
Pacific Ocean
20°N
Hilo
Pahala
18°N
1:15,900,000
0 100 mi.
1 in. to 251 mi.
0 100 km
1 cm to 159 km

ARCTIC OCEAN
Barrow
Beaufort Sea
Mackenzie Bay
70°N
Chukchi Sea
Prudhoe Bay
RUSSIA
Brooks Range
Kotzebue
ARCTIC CIRCLE 66½°N
65°N
Bering Strait
Nome
Norton Sound
ALASKA
Fairbanks
Yukon R.
CANADA
60°N
Bethel
Kuskokwim R.
Alaska Range
Anchorage
Valdez
Seward
Bristol Bay
Iliamna Lake
Gulf of Alaska
Juneau
Kodiak
Sitka

1:29,100,000
0 200 mi.
1 in. to 460 mi.
0 200 km
1 cm to 291 km
30°N

Pacific Ocean
INTERNATIONAL DATE LINE
Bering Sea
Aleutian Islands
Unalaska
180° 175°W 170°W 165°W 160°W 155°W 150°W 145°W 140°W 135°W

Juan de Fuca Strait
Puget Sound
Willamette R.
45°N
40°N
35°N
30°N

Political Relief Map
United States

Boundary Symbols

━━━━━ International boundary

·············· State boundary

City Symbols

Los Angeles ● Over 500,000 people

Anchorage ● 100,000 to 500,000

Marquette • Under 100,000

Washington, D.C. ⊗ National capital

Honolulu ★ State capital

Scale

1:12,700,000

| 0 | 100 | 200 | 300 miles |

1 in. to 200 mi.

| 0 | 100 | 200 | 300 kilometers |

1 cm to 127 km

Detailed legend on page 8   Albers Equal Area Projection

130°W 120°W 50°W 115°W 110°W 105°W 100°W

Cape Flattery
Juan de Fuca Strait
Vancouver
Puget Sound
Olympic Mts.
Seattle
Grand Coulee Dam
Lake Pend Oreille
Coeur d'Alene
Flathead Lake
Lake Manitoba
CANADA

WASHINGTON
Columbia R.
Franklin D. Roosevelt Lake
Coast Ranges
Cascade Range
Portland
45°N

Columbia R.
Blue Mts.
Snake R.
Salmon R.
Bitterroot Range
Milk R.
Missouri R.
Fort Peck Lake
Yellowstone R.
Powder R.
Lake Sakakawea
NORTH DAKOTA

OREGON
Columbia Plateau
Salmon River Mts.
IDAHO
ROCKY
MONTANA
Yellowstone R.
Lake Oahe
Great
SOUTH DAKOTA

Goose Lake
American Falls Res.
Yellowstone Lake
Bighorn R.
Bighorn Mts.
Black Hills
Harney Peak 7,242 ft. (2207 m)
Lake Francis Case
40°N
Cape Mendocino

Shasta Lake
Sacramento R.
Pyramid Lake
Humboldt R.
Great Salt Lake
WYOMING
Pathfinder Res.
Seminoe Res.
Niobrara R.
Sand Hills
NEBRASKA

Lake Tahoe
Carson Sink
Basin and Range
Great Basin
Ruby Mts.
Great Salt Lake Desert
Wasatch Range
Great Divide Basin
Plains
Great
S. Platte R.
Platte R.

San Francisco
Coast Ranges
Sierra Nevada
Sacramento Valley
San Joaquin R.
NEVADA
Utah Lake
Sevier Lake
UTAH
Uinta Mts.
Green R.
Colorado R.
Mt. Elbert 14,433 ft. (4399 m)
Denver
Pikes Peak 14,110 ft. (4301 m)
Republican R.
Smoky Hill R.
KA

Monterey Bay
CALIFORNIA
San Joaquin Valley
Mt. Whitney 14,494 ft. (4418 m)
Sevier R.
Lake Powell
Colorado
Plateau
Mountains
Front Range
Park Range
San Juan Mts.
COLORADO
Arkansas R.
35°N

Pt. Conception
Death Valley 282 ft.
Lake Mead
Glen Canyon Dam
Grand Canyon
San Juan R.
Sangre de Cristo Mts.

Mojave Desert
Hoover Dam
Little Colorado R.
Plateau

Los Angeles
Channel Is.
Colorado R.
Parker Dam
ARIZONA
NEW MEXICO
Canadian R.
N. Canadian R.
OK

PACIFIC
Salton Sea
Imperial Valley
Phoenix
Salt R.
Gila R.
Elephant Butte Res.
Rio Grande
Sacramento Mts.
Llano Estacado
Red R.

San Diego
Tijuana
Sonoran Desert
Llano Estacado

OCEAN
30°N

120°W 115°W 110°W
El Paso
Guadalupe Peak 8,749 ft. (2667 m)
Pecos R.
Edwards Plateau
TE

Rio Bravo del Norte
Rio Grande
Davis Mountains
Stockton Plateau
30°N

HAWAII inset:
160°W 158°W 156°W 22°N
Kauai
Niihau
Oahu
HAWAII
Pearl Harbor
Molokai
Maui
PACIFIC OCEAN
Lanai
Kahoolawe
20°N
Hawaii
Mauna Kea 13,796 ft. (4205 m)
18°N
1:15,900,000
0   100 mi.
1 in. to 251 mi.
0   100 km
1 cm to 159 km

ALASKA inset:
Chukchi Sea
Point Barrow
Beaufort Sea
Brooks Range
RUSSIA
Bering Strait
ARCTIC CIRCLE 66½°N
1:29,100,000
0   200 mi.
1 in. to 460 mi.
0   200 km
1 cm to 291 km
Seward Peninsula
Norton Sound
ALASKA
Yukon R.
CANADA
65°N
St. Lawrence I.
Yukon R.
Denali (Mt. McKinley) 20,310 ft. (6190 m)
Tanana R.
Kuskokwim R.
Alaska Range
60°N

Bering Sea
Nunivak I.
Iliamna Lake
Anchorage
Kenai Peninsula
Bristol Bay
Kodiak I.
Gulf of Alaska
Alexander Archipelago

Aleutian Islands
Alaska Peninsula
180° 175°W 170°W 165°W 160°W 155°W 150°W 145°W 140°W 135°W

MEXICO
Monterrey
25°N
105°W 100°W

Land Cover Map
United States

Cropland Grassland Tundra Glacier

Semi-desert Tropical Broadleaf Needleleaf
& desert rain forest forest forest

Boundary Symbols
International boundary
State boundary

Scale
1:12,700,000

0   100   200   300 miles
1 in. to 200 mi.
0   100   200   300 kilometers
1 cm to 127 km

Detailed legend on page 8   Albers Equal Area Projection

Elevation Map
United States

Meters above Sea Level		Feet above Sea Level
Over 3000		Over 10,000
1500 to 3000		5,000 to 10,000
600 to 1500		2,000 to 5,000
300 to 600		1,000 to 2,000
150 to 300		500 to 1,000
0 to 150		0 to 500
Below sea level		Below sea level

Boundary Symbols

International boundary
State boundary

Scale
1:13,900,000

0   100   200   300 miles
1 in. to 220 mi.
0   100   200   300 kilometers
1 cm to 139 km

Detailed legend on page 8   Bonne Projection

HAWAII

Kauai   Niihau   Oahu   Molokai   Lanai   Maui   Kahoolawe   Hawaii

PACIFIC OCEAN

Pearl Harbor

Mauna Kea 13,796 ft. (4205 m)

0   100 mi.
1 in. to 273 mi.
0   100 km
1 cm to 173 km

ALASKA

Point Barrow   Beaufort Sea   Chukchi Sea   Brooks Range   RUSSIA   Bering Strait   Seward Peninsula   Norton Sound   St. Lawrence I.   Nunivak I.   Yukon R.   Kuskokwim R.   Alaska Range   Denali (Mt. McKinley) 20,310 ft. (6190 m)   Tanana R.   CANADA   Anchorage   Iliamna Lake   Kenai Peninsula   Bristol Bay   Gulf of Alaska   Kodiak I.   Alaska Peninsula   Alexander Archipelago   Aleutian Islands   Bering Sea   ARCTIC CIRCLE 66½°N

0   200 mi.
1 in. to 500 mi.
0   200 km
1 cm to 330 km

CANADA

WASHINGTON   Cape Flattery   Juan de Fuca Strait   Olympic Mts.   Puget Sound   Seattle   Mt. Rainier 14,410 ft. (4392 m)   Grand Coulee Dam   Columbia R.   Franklin D. Roosevelt Lake   Coeur d'Alene Lake   Lake Pend Oreille   Flathead Lake

Coast Ranges   Cascade Range   Columbia Plateau   Portland   OREGON   Blue Mts.   Bitterroot Range   IDAHO   Salmon R.   Snake R.   Salmon River Mts.   American Falls Res.

MONTANA   Milk R.   Missouri R.   Fort Peck Lake   Lake Sakakawea   Yellowstone R.   Powder R.   Bighorn Mts.   Bighorn R.

WYOMING   Great Divide Basin   Great Salt Lake Desert   Great Salt Lake   Wasatch Range   Uinta Mts.   Front Range   Park Range   Platte R.   Niobrara R.   Black Hills   Harney Peak 7,242 ft. (2207 m)   North Platte R.

Great Plains

Sacramento Valley   San Francisco   Monterey Bay   Sierra Nevada Range   CALIFORNIA   San Joaquin Valley   Coast Ranges   Pt. Conception   Channel Is.   Los Angeles   San Diego   Tijuana

NEVADA   Basin and Range   Great Basin   Pyramid Lake   Carson Sink   Ruby Mts.   Sevier Lake   UTAH

Mt. Whitney 14,494 ft. (4418 m)   Death Valley 282 ft. (–86 m)   Mojave Desert   Lake Mead   Hoover Dam   Grand Canyon   Colorado R.   Glen Canyon Dam

COLORADO   Mt. Elbert 14,433 ft. (4399 m)   Denver   Pikes Peak 14,110 ft. (4301 m)   Colorado Plateau   Sangre de Cristo Mts.   San Juan Mts.   San Juan R.

Rocky Mountains

ARIZONA   Parker Dam   Salton Sea   Imperial Valley   Phoenix   Salt R.   Gila R.   Sonoran Desert   Elephant Butte Res.

NEW MEXICO   Sacramento Mts.   Llano Estacado   El Paso   Guadalupe Peak 8,749 ft. (2667 m)   Pecos R.   Davis Mountains   Stockton Plateau   Rio Grande   Canadian R.

MEXICO   Rio Bravo del Norte

PACIFIC OCEAN

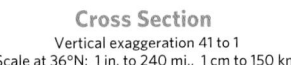

Cross Section
Vertical exaggeration 41 to 1
Scale at 36°N: 1 in. to 240 mi., 1 cm to 150 km

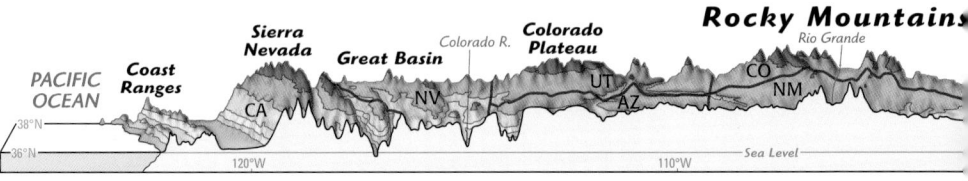

PACIFIC OCEAN   Coast Ranges   Sierra Nevada   Great Basin   Colorado R.   Colorado Plateau   Rocky Mountains   Rio Grande   CA   NV   UT   AZ   CO   NM   Sea Level

Great Plains
Ozark Plateau
Central Lowland
Appalachian Mountains
Atlantic Coastal Plain
ATLANTIC OCEAN

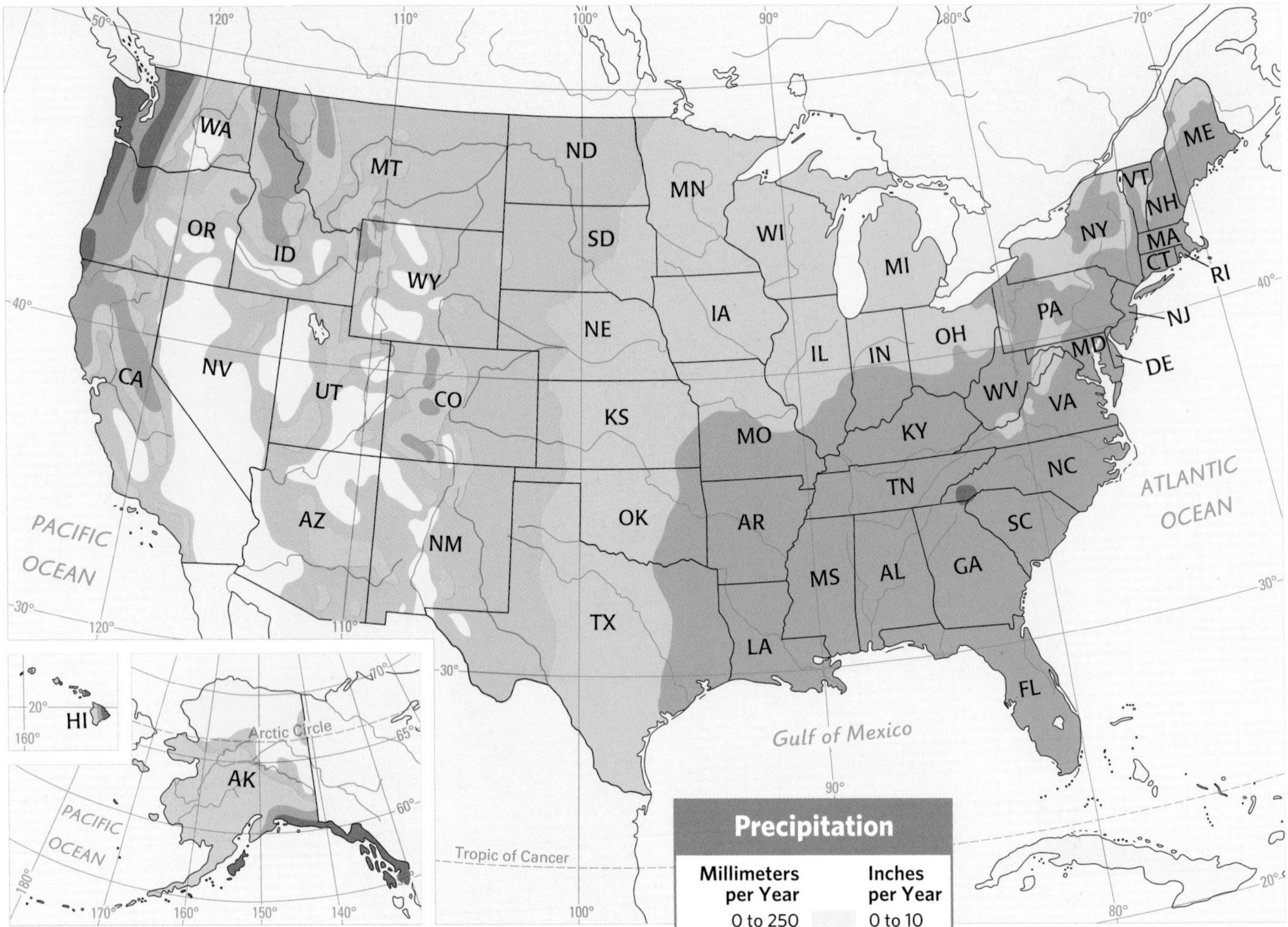

Precipitation	
Millimeters per Year	**Inches per Year**
0 to 250	0 to 10
250 to 500	10 to 20
500 to 1000	20 to 40
1000 to 2000	40 to 80
Over 2000	Over 80

Wetlands

Wetlands play a key role in watershed protection. They provide a barrier against floods and serve as natural filters by trapping pollutants stored in water. They also provide habitat for wildlife.

Predominantly wetland
Small wetlands, some seasonal

In the past 200 years, more than half the wetlands in the United States have been drained, filled, paved, or otherwise altered to develop land to expand cities, towns, and resorts. Part of this coastal marsh in South Carolina was destroyed to make room for a hotel and port.

California has the most extreme fire weather in the United States. Strong desert winds and frequent drought combine to produce major wildfires. Valleys and canyons create natural paths for wildfires.

Tornadoes and Hurricanes

Hurricanes are powerful storms that form over tropical ocean waters and often strike the Atlantic and Gulf coasts. **Tornadoes** are quickly rotating columns of air that form under a thundercloud. Tornadoes can strike in any state, but frequently touch down in a belt known as "Tornado Alley."

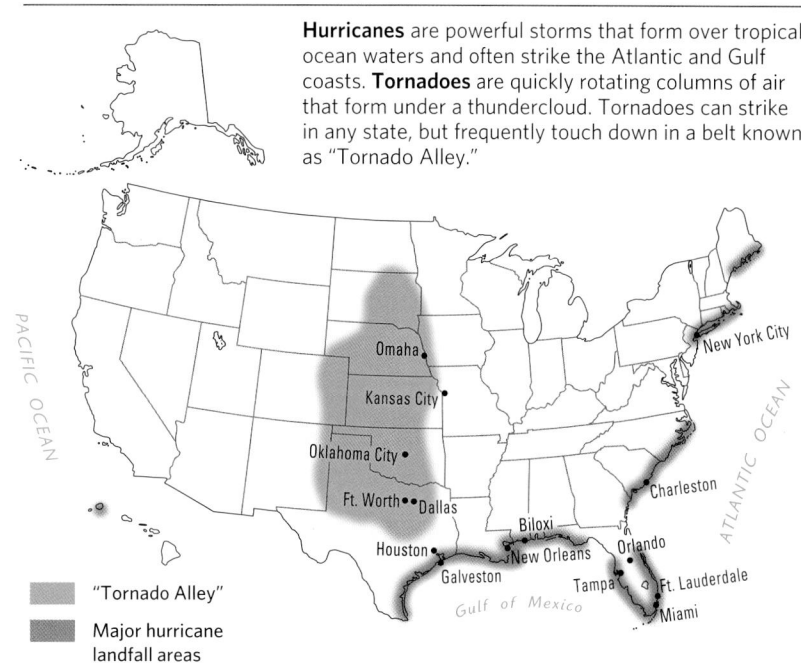

"Tornado Alley"

Major hurricane landfall areas

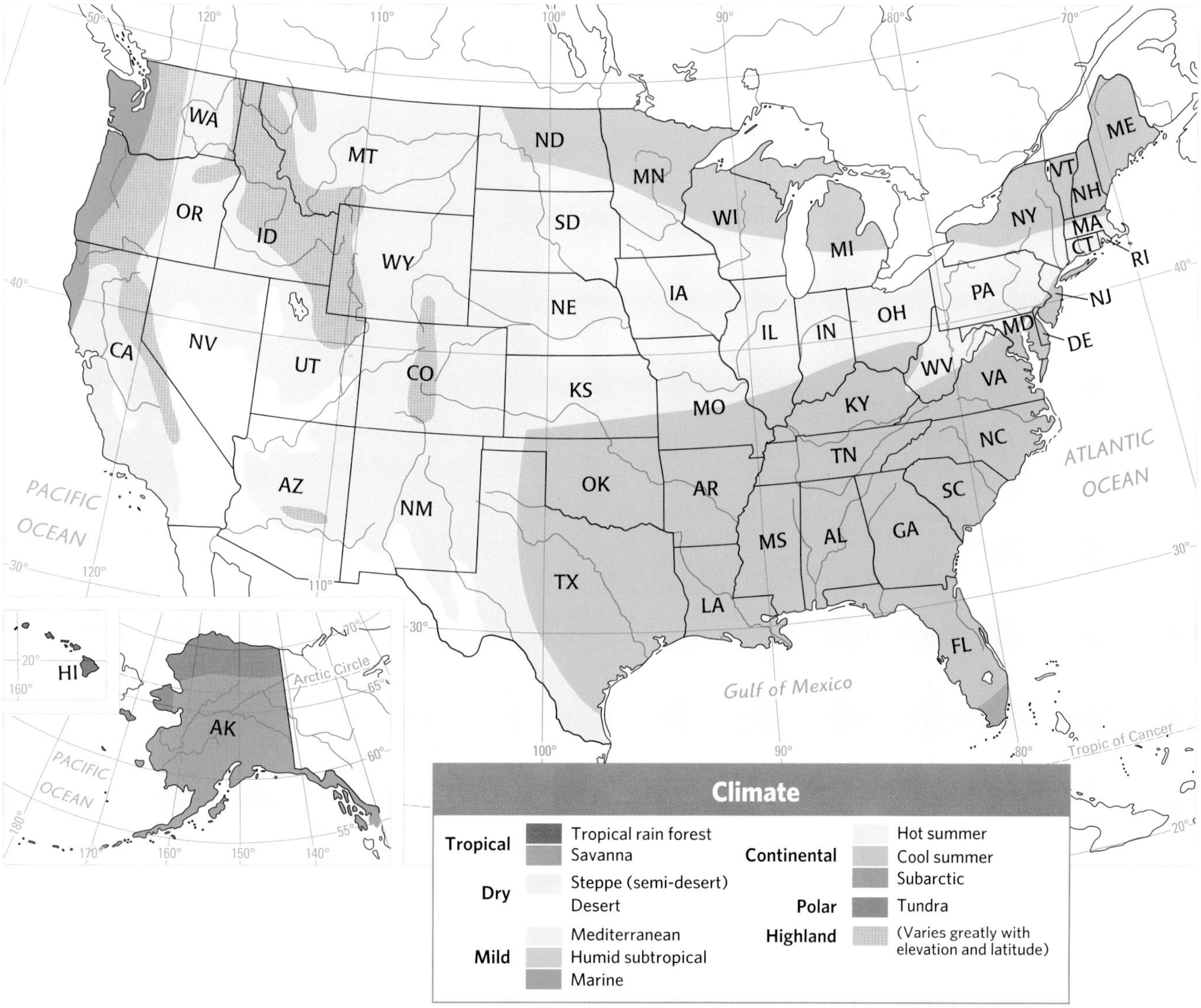

Climate

Tropical		Continental	
	Tropical rain forest		Hot summer
	Savanna		Cool summer
Dry	Steppe (semi-desert)		Subarctic
	Desert	**Polar**	Tundra
	Mediterranean	**Highland**	(Varies greatly with elevation and latitude)
Mild	Humid subtropical		
	Marine		

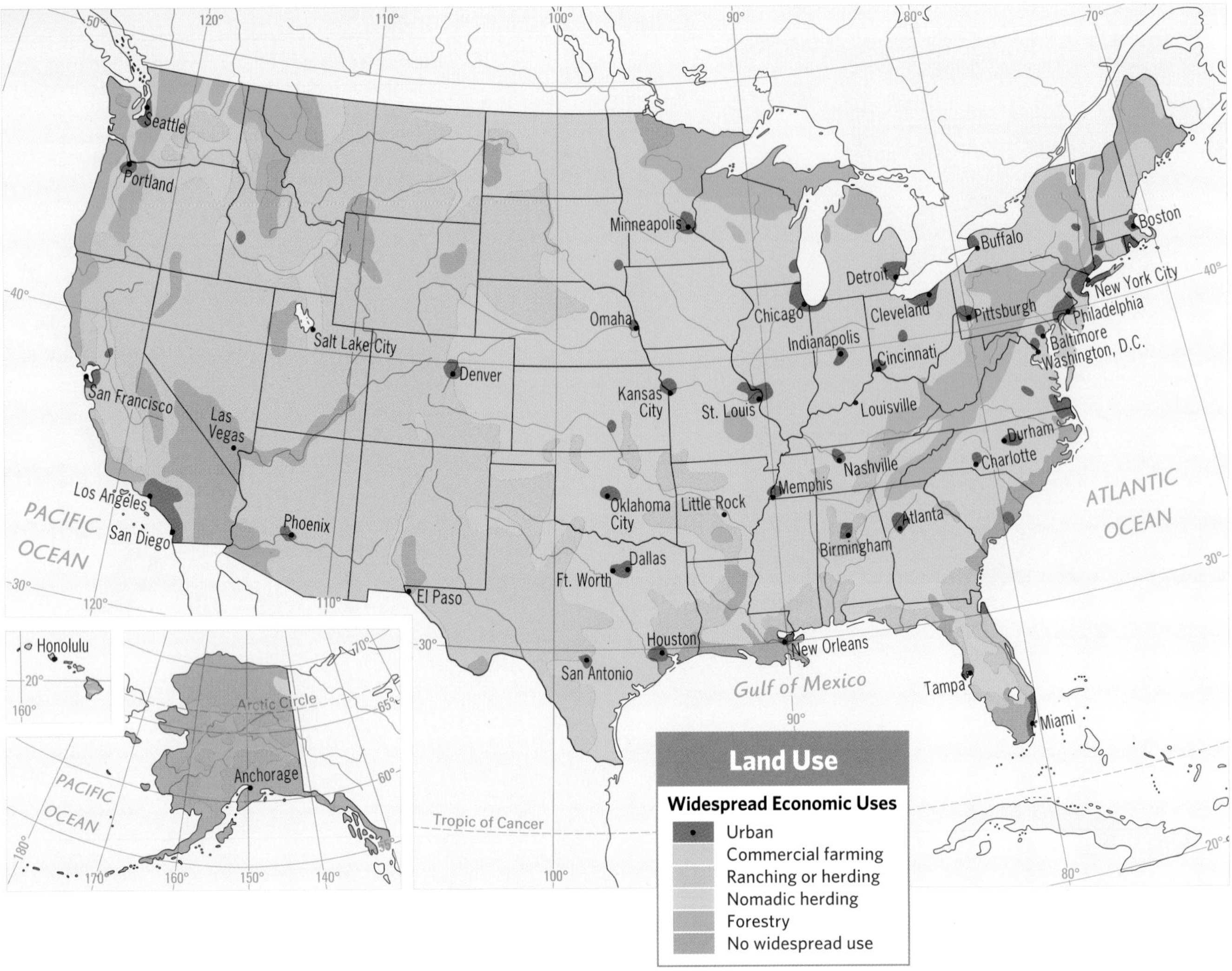

Seattle
Portland
Minneapolis
Detroit
Buffalo
Boston
Salt Lake City
Omaha
Chicago
Cleveland
Pittsburgh
New York City
Denver
Indianapolis
Cincinnati
Philadelphia
Baltimore
Washington, D.C.
San Francisco
Las Vegas
Kansas City
St. Louis
Louisville
Durham
Los Angeles
San Diego
Phoenix
Oklahoma City
Little Rock
Memphis
Nashville
Charlotte
Atlanta
PACIFIC OCEAN
Dallas
Ft. Worth
Birmingham
ATLANTIC OCEAN
El Paso
Houston
New Orleans
San Antonio
Tampa
Gulf of Mexico
Miami
Honolulu
Arctic Circle
Anchorage
PACIFIC OCEAN
Tropic of Cancer

Land Use

Widespread Economic Uses

- Urban
- Commercial farming
- Ranching or herding
- Nomadic herding
- Forestry
- No widespread use

Change in U.S. Farms

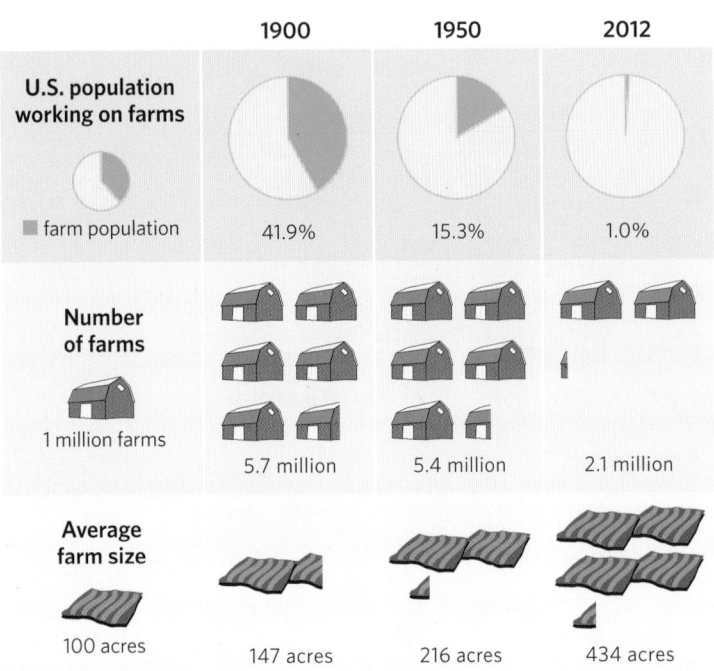

	1900	1950	2012
U.S. population working on farms ▪ farm population	41.9%	15.3%	1.0%
Number of farms 1 million farms	5.7 million	5.4 million	2.1 million
Average farm size 100 acres	147 acres	216 acres	434 acres

Since the turn of the twentieth century, the United States has moved toward fewer, but much larger, farms. The percentage of people directly engaged in farming has also dropped dramatically.

Many farms in the United States use center-pivot irrigation, which creates distinct circular fields that can be seen from above. The efficiency of center-pivot irrigation helps conserve water.

Agricultural Exports

The United States is a leading exporter of corn, wheat, poultry, and other crops. However, agriculture accounts for only 1 percent of our country's gross domestic product.

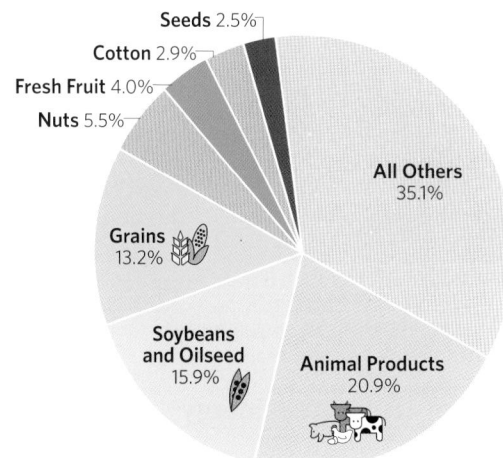

- Seeds 2.5%
- Cotton 2.9%
- Fresh Fruit 4.0%
- Nuts 5.5%
- All Others 35.1%
- Grains 13.2%
- Soybeans and Oilseed 15.9%
- Animal Products 20.9%

Iowa and Illinois are the leading producers of corn and soybeans in the United States. Both crops are used to feed people and animals, and are also used to make many nonfood items. Above, corn is piled into temporary storage as it is harvested from the field.

Still a Nation of Farmers

Agribusiness is one of the most rapidly growing industries in the United States. It includes farms and businesses that produce, process, distribute, transport, and sell farm products. Nearly one out of every ten workers in the United States is employed in agribusiness. About 40 percent of the land in the United States is used for farming.

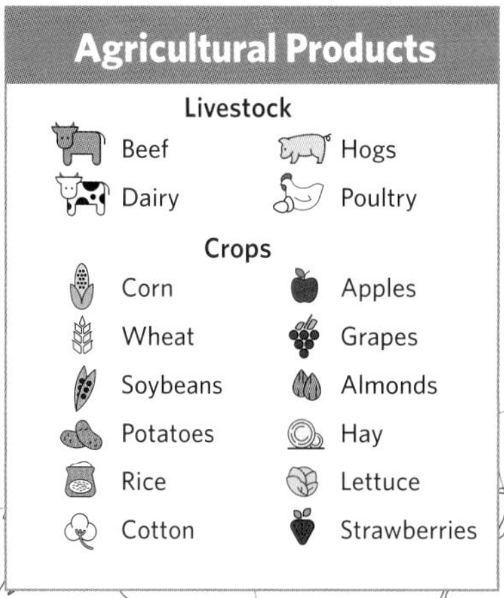

Agricultural Products

Livestock
- Beef
- Hogs
- Dairy
- Poultry

Crops
- Corn
- Apples
- Wheat
- Grapes
- Soybeans
- Almonds
- Potatoes
- Hay
- Rice
- Lettuce
- Cotton
- Strawberries

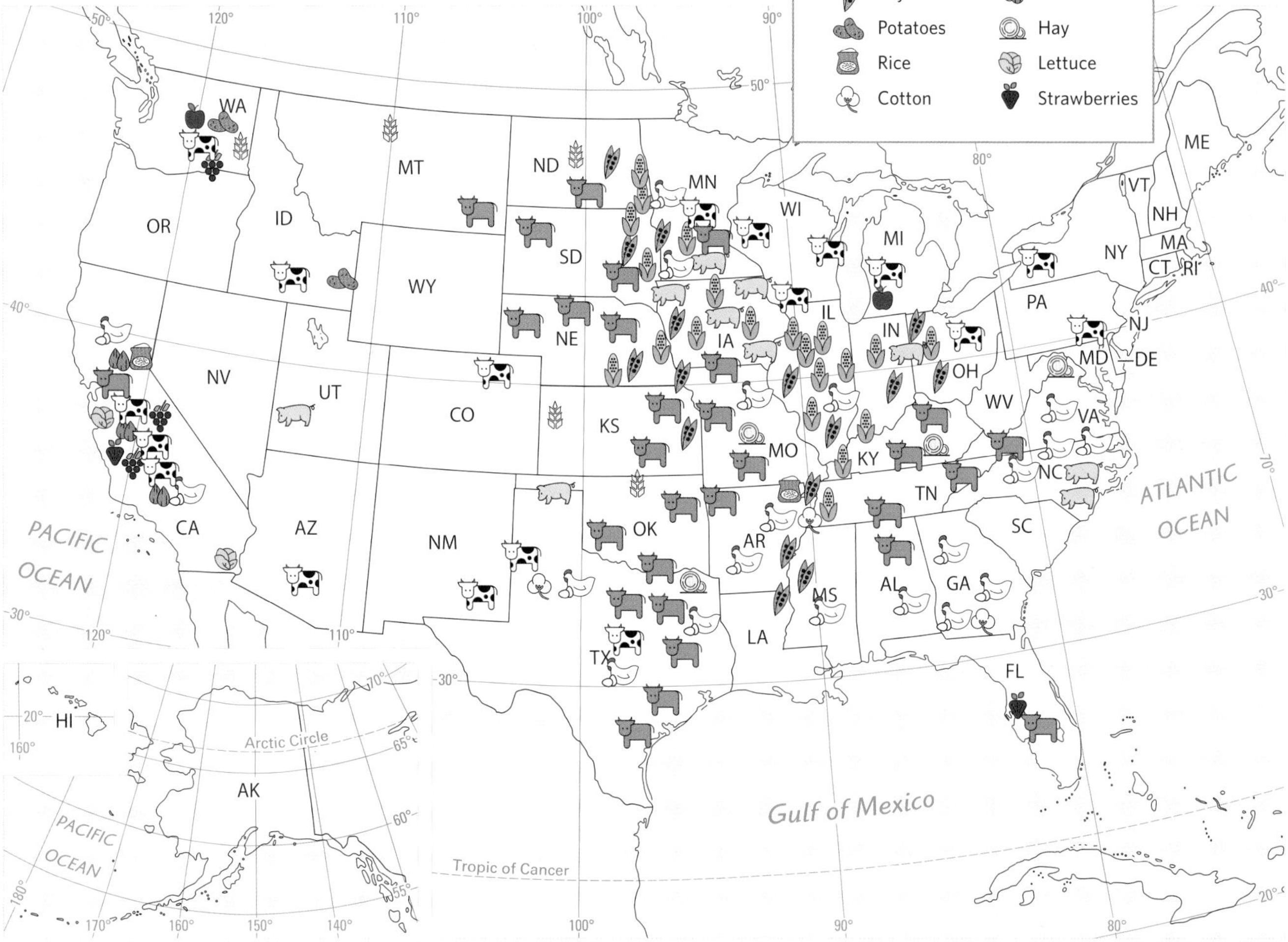

Wind power is a clean energy source that is inexhaustible. However, it is only commercially useful in areas that have strong, steady winds. Only about 2 percent of electric power in the United States is produced by wind.

Times Square in New York City serves as a snapshot of different energy resources and how they are used. Oil is used for transportation, electricity provides power for lights, and heating oil or natural gas supplies heat.

Sources of Consumed Energy

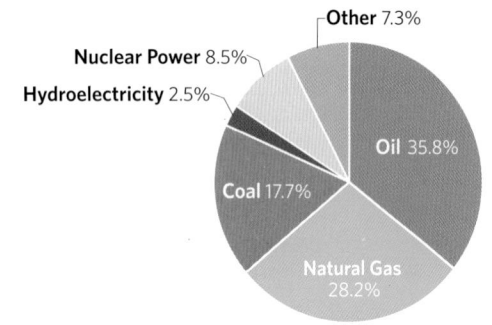

Other 7.3%
Nuclear Power 8.5%
Hydroelectricity 2.5%
Oil 35.8%
Coal 17.7%
Natural Gas 28.2%

Uses of Consumed Energy

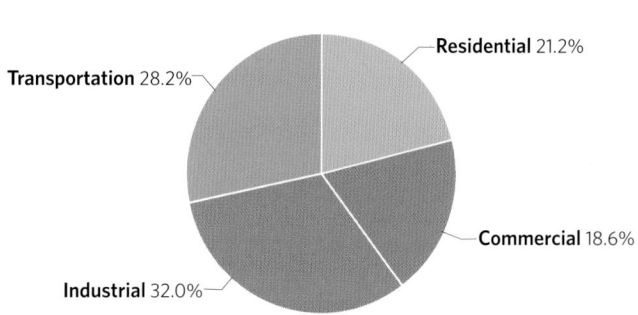

Residential 21.2%
Transportation 28.2%
Commercial 18.6%
Industrial 32.0%

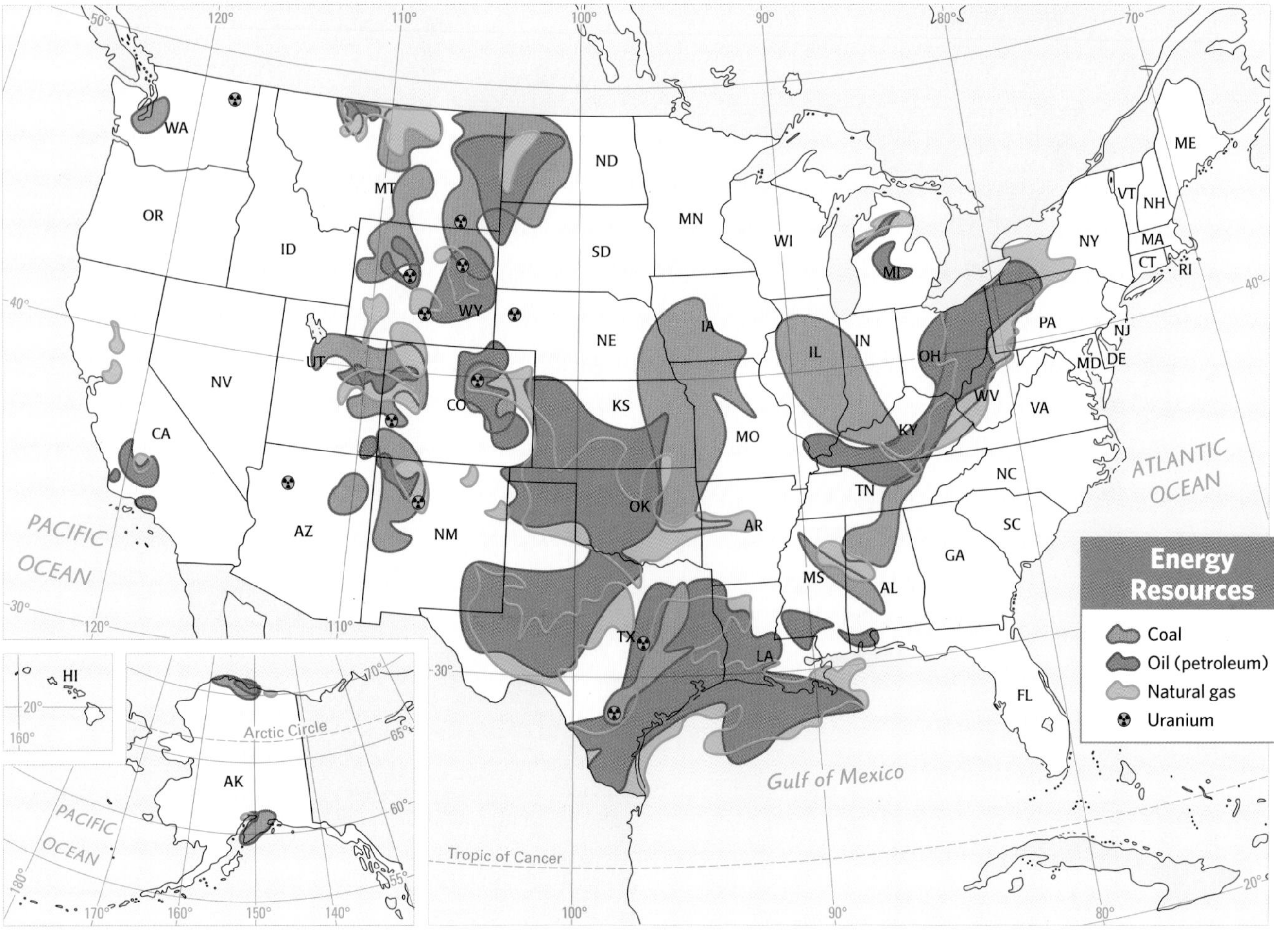

Energy Resources

- Coal
- Oil (petroleum)
- Natural gas
- Uranium

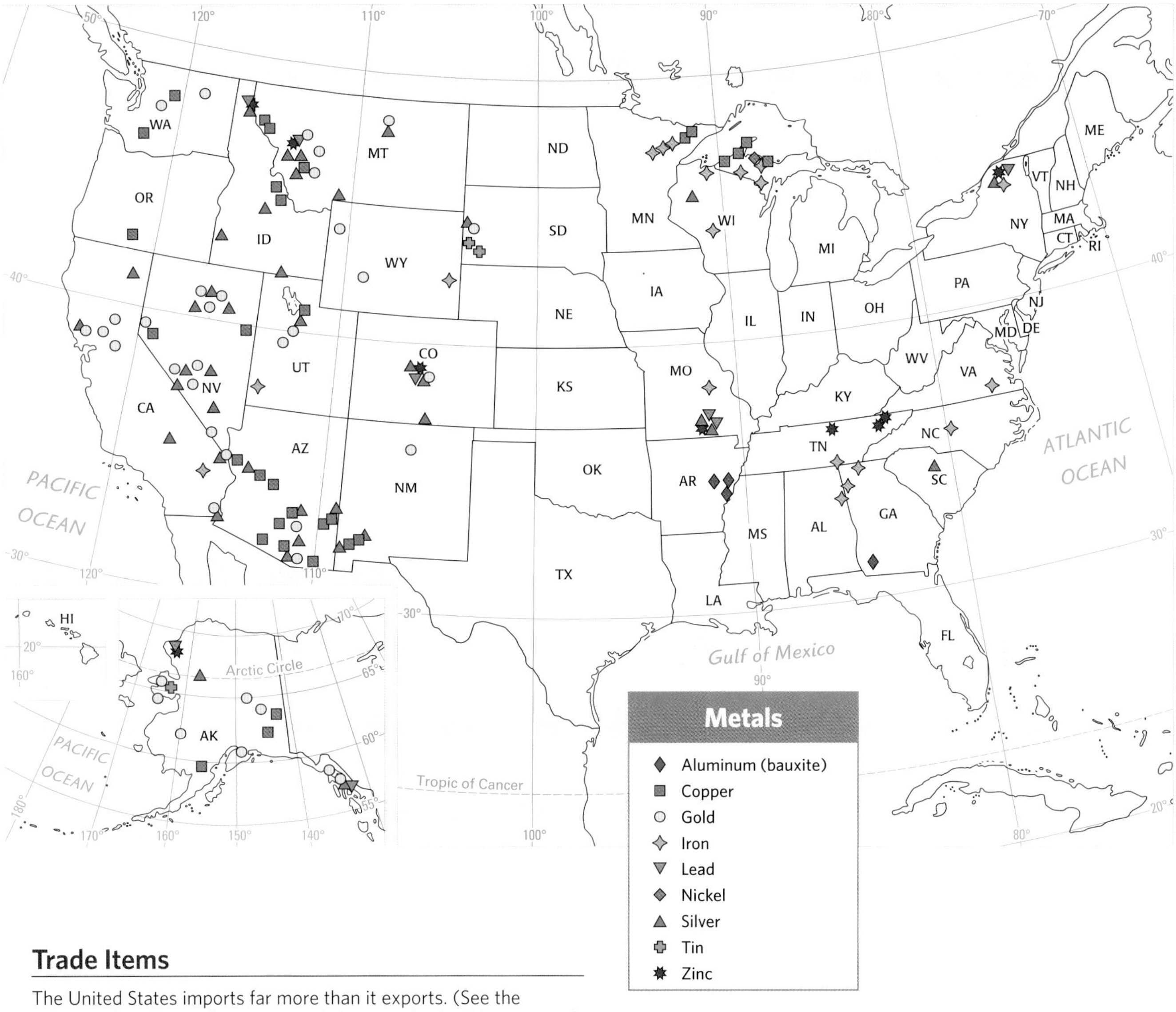

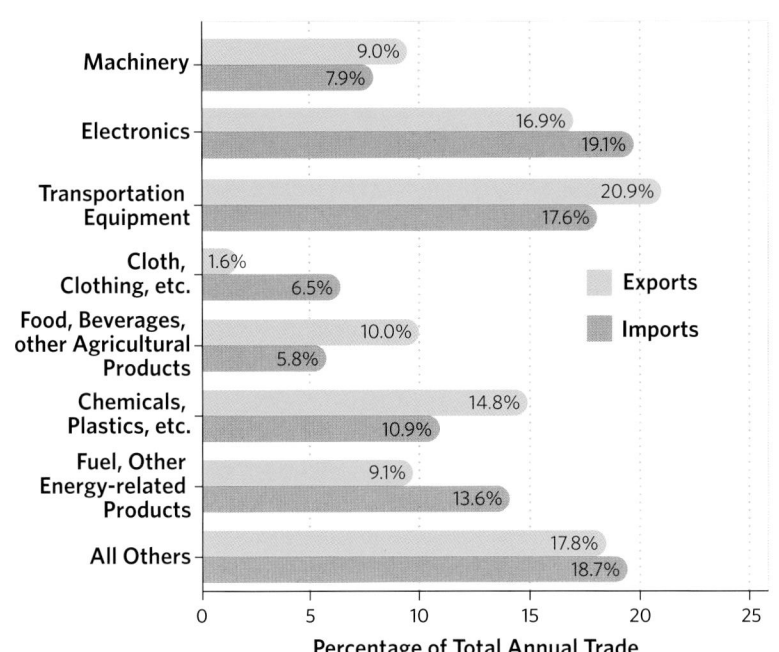

WA
OR
CA
NV
ID
MT
WY
UT
AZ
CO
NM
ND
SD
NE
KS
OK
TX
MN
IA
MO
AR
LA
WI
IL
MI
IN
OH
KY
TN
MS
AL
GA
FL
SC
NC
VA
WV
PA
NY
VT
NH
ME
MA
CT
RI
NJ
DE
MD
HI
AK
Arctic Circle
PACIFIC OCEAN
ATLANTIC OCEAN
Gulf of Mexico
Tropic of Cancer
Metals
Aluminum (bauxite)
Copper
Gold
Iron
Lead
Nickel
Silver
Tin
Zinc

Trade Items

The United States imports far more than it exports. (See the Balance of Trade graph on page 44.) As a result, the 7.9 percent of machinery that is imported is about US$45 billion more than the 9 percent that is exported.

Machinery
9.0%
7.9%
Electronics
16.9%
19.1%
Transportation Equipment
20.9%
17.6%
Cloth, Clothing, etc.
1.6%
6.5%
Food, Beverages, other Agricultural Products
10.0%
5.8%
Chemicals, Plastics, etc.
14.8%
10.9%
Fuel, Other Energy-related Products
9.1%
13.6%
All Others
17.8%
18.7%
Exports
Imports
0
5
10
15
20
25
Percentage of Total Annual Trade

Gross Domestic Product by State

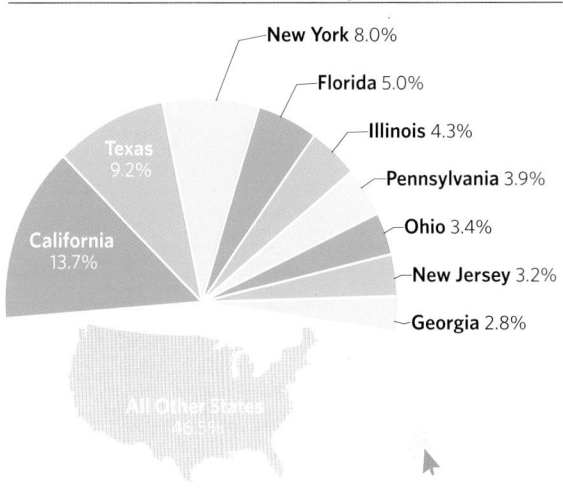

New York 8.0%
Florida 5.0%
Illinois 4.3%
Pennsylvania 3.9%
Ohio 3.4%
New Jersey 3.2%
Georgia 2.8%
Texas 9.2%
California 13.7%
All Other States 45.5%

Nine states in the United States produce more than half of the country's GDP. The GDP of California alone is larger than the GDP of Canada.

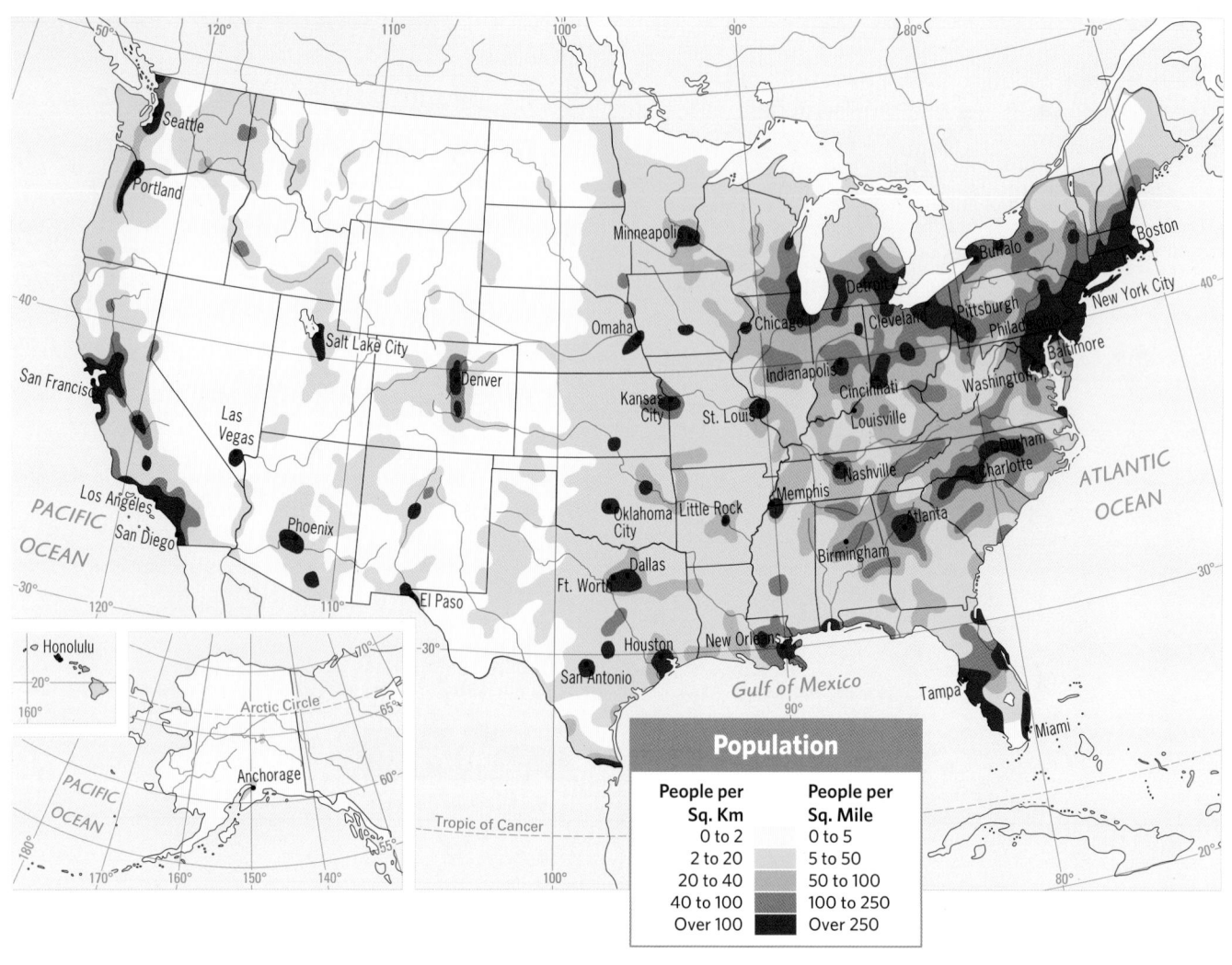

Population

People per Sq. Km	People per Sq. Mile
0 to 2	0 to 5
2 to 20	5 to 50
20 to 40	50 to 100
40 to 100	100 to 250
Over 100	Over 250

Major Highways and Airports

The U.S. highway network consists of over 4 million miles (6.4 million kilometers) of streets and roads. Air travel is the fastest-growing means of transportation in the United States. In 1975, less than 50 percent of all Americans had flown, while today that number has climbed to over 80 percent.

Airline Passengers per Year

- Over 50 million
- 35 to 50 million
- 20 to 35 million
- 10 to 20 million
- Other airport
- Interstate highway

Population in Motion

Domestic migration refers to the movement of people within a country. In the past, the United States' population moved westward. Today the population is shifting from north to south. Between 2010 and 2015 Florida and Texas were the primary destinations for migrants.

Alaska Area Comparison

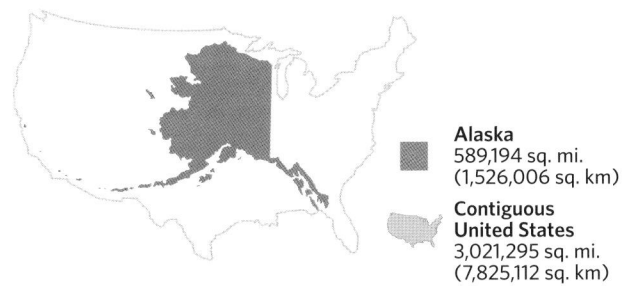

Alaska
589,194 sq. mi.
(1,526,006 sq. km)

Contiguous United States
3,021,295 sq. mi.
(7,825,112 sq. km)

Ethnic Composition

United States

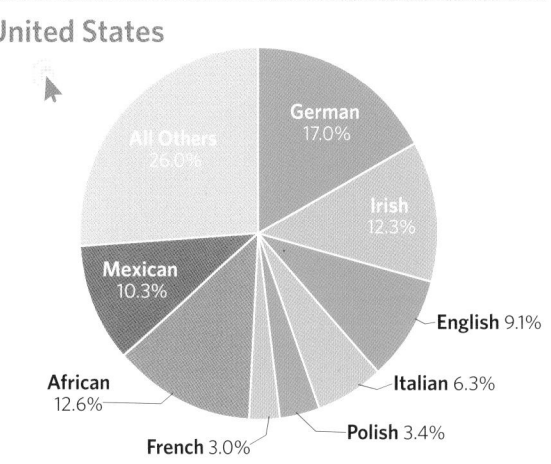

German 17.0%
Irish 12.3%
English 9.1%
Italian 6.3%
Polish 3.4%
French 3.0%
African 12.6%
Mexican 10.3%
All Others 26.0%

Regional Maps of the United States

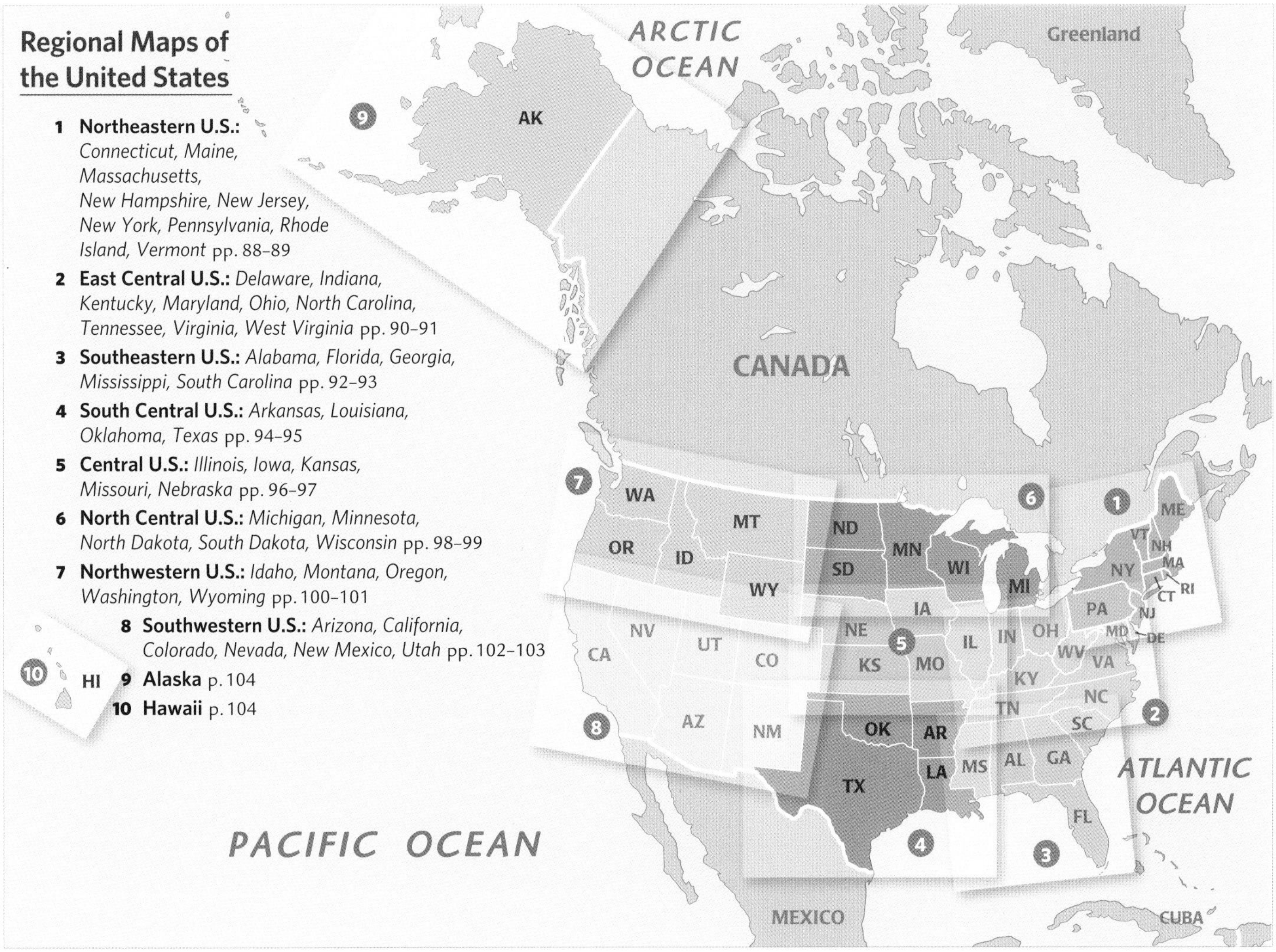

1   **Northeastern U.S.:** *Connecticut, Maine, Massachusetts, New Hampshire, New Jersey, New York, Pennsylvania, Rhode Island, Vermont* pp. 88–89

2   **East Central U.S.:** *Delaware, Indiana, Kentucky, Maryland, Ohio, North Carolina, Tennessee, Virginia, West Virginia* pp. 90–91

3   **Southeastern U.S.:** *Alabama, Florida, Georgia, Mississippi, South Carolina* pp. 92–93

4   **South Central U.S.:** *Arkansas, Louisiana, Oklahoma, Texas* pp. 94–95

5   **Central U.S.:** *Illinois, Iowa, Kansas, Missouri, Nebraska* pp. 96–97

6   **North Central U.S.:** *Michigan, Minnesota, North Dakota, South Dakota, Wisconsin* pp. 98–99

7   **Northwestern U.S.:** *Idaho, Montana, Oregon, Washington, Wyoming* pp. 100–101

8   **Southwestern U.S.:** *Arizona, California, Colorado, Nevada, New Mexico, Utah* pp. 102–103

9   **Alaska** p. 104

10   **Hawaii** p. 104

ARCTIC OCEAN

Greenland

AK

CANADA

WA
MT
ND
MN
OR
ID
SD
WI
MI
WY
IA
NE
IL
IN
OH
PA
NY
ME
VT
NH
MA
CT
RI
NJ
MD
DE
WV
VA
NV
UT
CO
KS
MO
KY
NC
CA
AZ
NM
OK
AR
TN
SC
TX
LA
MS
AL
GA
FL

HI

ATLANTIC OCEAN

PACIFIC OCEAN

MEXICO

CUBA

Continues on page 70

80°W 75°W

Canadian Shield

Sudbury

L. Kempt

Reservoir Cabonga

C A N A D A

Lake Temagami

Lake Kipawa

117

Q U É B E C

Ottawa R.

Lake Nipissing

15

O N T A R I O

Georgian Bay

Gatineau

Gatineau R.

Ottawa

Laval

Montré

Alpena
45°N

Ottawa R.

417

20

St. Lawrence R.

401

Lake Simcoe

Peterborough

Kingston

Thousand Islands

Ogdensburg

Potsdam

Plattsbu

Raquette R.

Mt. Marcy
5,344 ft. △
(1629 m)

Lake Huron

Richmond Hill

Markham

Oshawa

Lake Ontario

Watertown

Adirondack Mountains

Toronto

Mississauga

81

Oswego

Oneida Lake

Rome

Sacandaga Reservoir

Sarato Spring

MI

Guelph

Kitchener

Niagara Falls

Lake Ontario

NEW YORK

Utica

Port Huron

Hamilton

St. Catharines

Niagara Falls

Rochester

Erie Canal

Auburn

Syracuse

Schenectady

69

London

Welland Canal

Tonawanda

90

Skaneateles Lake

Cortland

Cooperstown

Albany

94

Sarnia

402

Cheektowaga

Buffalo

Geneseo

Canandaigua Lake

390

Owasco Lake

Cayuga Lake

Oneonta

88

M

Lake St. Clair

401

Chatham

Lake Erie

Fredonia

Chautauqua Lake

Dansville

Keuka Lake

Seneca Lake

Ithaca

Chemung R.

Binghamton

Susquehanna R.

Catskill Mountains

Erie

Jamestown

Olean

Elmira

Poughkeepsie

Ashtabula

Warren

Allegheny Reservoir

Mansfield

81

L. Candlewo

Newburgh

Sandusky Cleveland

Mentor

90

Genesee R.

87

Lakewood

Euclid

Pymatuning Reservoir

Oil City

PENNSYLVANIA

84

White Plains

Lorain

Parma

Cleveland Heights

79

Allegheny R.

Williamsport

Wilkes-Barre

Pocono Mts.

Kittatinny Mts.

Wallkill R.

Paterson

Elyria

CUYAHOGA VALLEY N.P.

Warren

Clarion

Scranton

80

Yonke

Akron

77

Kent

80

New Castle

80

80

Newark

Barberton

Youngstown

Alliance

Indiana

State College

78

Elizabeth

New York Ci

Wooster

Massillon

Delaware R.

Mansfield

71

Canton

East Liverpool

76

Altoona

Johnstown

Blue Mountain

Allentown

New Brunswick

Perth Amb

Long Bran

Dennison

Weirton

Pittsburgh

Plum

Monroeville

Conemaugh R.

Juniata R.

Easton

Bethlehem

Reading

Steubenville

Bethel Park

Susquehanna R.

Harrisburg

Lancaster

476

95

Trenton

OHIO

Washington

Monongahela R.

W. Branch Susquehanna R.

39

99

Piedmont

Philadelphia

Camden

Asb

Park

Cambridge

70

Wheeling

70

Gettysburg

York

81

Newark

Chester

Wilmington

Pine Barrens

Zanesville

79

Morgantown

Fairmont

68

Cumberland

Hagerstown

MARYLAND

83

Atlantic Coastal Plain

NEW JERSEY

Marietta

Clarksburg

Frederick

70

Towson

95

Vineland

13

Athens

Parkersburg

Ohio R.

Harpers Ferry

Baltimore

Columbia

97

Millville

Atlantic City

Pomeroy

77

WEST VIRGINIA

Elkins

Potomac R.

Silver Spring

95

Washington, D.C.

VIRGINIA

Annapolis

Chesapeake Bay

Dover

Delaware Bay

DE

Cape May

Huttonsville

SHENANDOAH NATIONAL PARK

81

Arlington

Alexandria

66

50

9

80°W 75°W

Continues on pages 98–99

Continues on pages 90–91

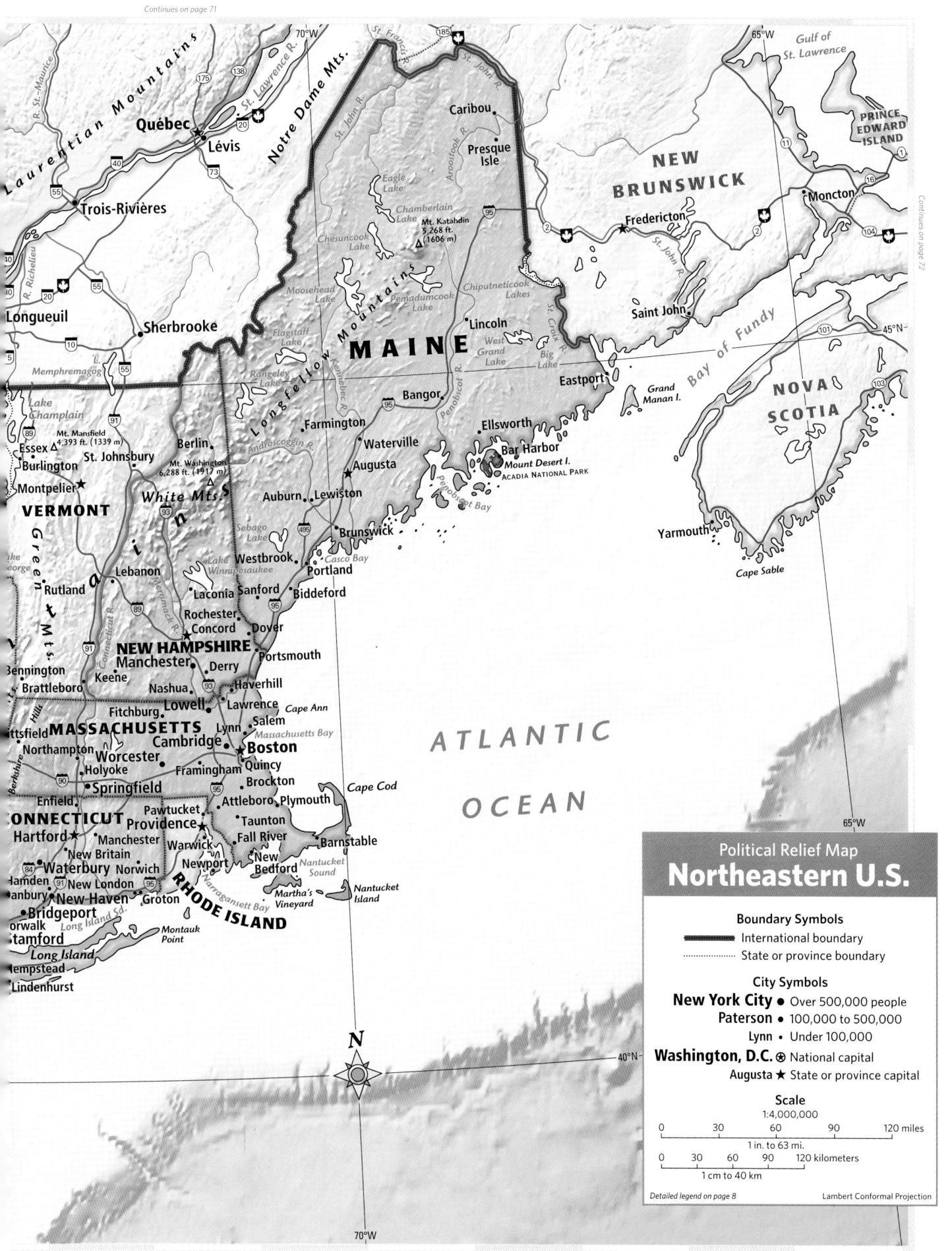

Continues on page 71

Gulf of
St. Lawrence

PRINCE
EDWARD
ISLAND

NEW
BRUNSWICK

Moncton

Fredericton

Saint John

Bay of Fundy

NOVA
SCOTIA

Yarmouth

Cape Sable

Grand
Manan I.

Laurentian Mountains

R. St-Maurice

R. Richelieu

Québec

Lévis

Trois-Rivières

Longueuil

Sherbrooke

Memphremagog

Notre Dame Mts.

St. Lawrence R.

St. Francis

St. John R.

Eagle
Lake

Chamberlain
Lake

Mt. Katahdin
5,268 ft.
△ (1606 m)

Chesuncook
Lake

Moosehead
Lake

Flagstaff
Lake

Rangeley
Lake

Caribou

Presque
Isle

Aroostook R.

Chiputneticook
Lakes

Lincoln

Pemadumcook
Lake

West
Grand
Lake

Big
Lake

St. Croix R.

Eastport

MAINE

Longfellow Mountains

Kennebec R.

Penobscot R.

Androscoggin R.

Farmington

Waterville

Augusta

Bangor

Ellsworth

Bar Harbor
Mount Desert I.
ACADIA NATIONAL PARK

Penobscot Bay

Lake
Champlain

Mt. Mansfield
4,393 ft. (1339 m)

Essex △

Burlington

St. Johnsbury

Montpelier

VERMONT

Berlin

Mt. Washington
6,288 ft. (1917 m) △

White Mts.

Green Mts.

Lake
George

Rutland

Bennington

Brattleboro

Connecticut R.

Merrimack R.

Auburn

Lewiston

Sebago
Lake

Brunswick

Lake
Winnipesaukee

Westbrook
Portland
Casco Bay

Sanford

Biddeford

Laconia

Rochester

Concord

Dover

Lebanon

NEW HAMPSHIRE
Manchester

Derry

Portsmouth

Keene

Nashua

Haverhill

Lawrence

Cape Ann

Lowell

Fitchburg

Salem

Lynn

Massachusetts Bay

ttsfield

MASSACHUSETTS

Northampton

Worcester

Cambridge

Boston

Holyoke

Framingham

Quincy

Springfield

Enfield

Brockton

Attleboro

Plymouth

Cape Cod

Berkshire Hills

Pawtucket

CONNECTICUT

Hartford

Manchester

New Britain

Waterbury

Norwich

Warwick

Providence

Taunton

Fall River

New
Bedford

Barnstable

Nantucket
Sound

Nantucket
Island

Danbury

amden

New London

New Haven

Groton

Bridgeport

orwalk

tamford

Long Island Sd.

Montauk
Point

Long Island

empstead

Lindenhurst

Narragansett Bay

Martha's
Vineyard

RHODE ISLAND

Newport

ATLANTIC

OCEAN

N

40°N

70°W

65°W

45°N

65°W

Continues on page 72

Political Relief Map
Northeastern U.S.

Boundary Symbols

——— International boundary

·············· State or province boundary

City Symbols

New York City ● Over 500,000 people

Paterson • 100,000 to 500,000

Lynn · Under 100,000

Washington, D.C. ⊗ National capital

Augusta ★ State or province capital

Scale

1:4,000,000

| 0 | 30 | 60 | 90 | 120 miles |

1 in. to 63 mi.

| 0 | 30 | 60 | 90 | 120 kilometers |

1 cm to 40 km

Detailed legend on page 8   Lambert Conformal Projection

Continues on pages 98-99

Political Relief Map
East Central U.S.

Boundary Symbols
—— International boundary
········ State boundary

City Symbols
Baltimore ● Over 500,000 people
Knoxville • 100,000 to 500,000
Greensburg • Under 100,000
Washington, D.C. ⊛ National capital
Frankfort ★ State capital

Scale
1:3,800,000

| 0 | 25 | 50 | 75 | 100 miles |

1 in. to 60 mi.

| 0 | 25 | 50 | 75 | 100 kilometers |

1 cm to 38 km

Detailed legend on page 8   Lambert Conformal Projection

Lake Michigan

MICHIGAN

ONTAR (Cana

Chicago
Naperville
Aurora
Hammond
Joliet
East Chicago Gary
Merrillville Valparaiso
Michigan City
South Bend Elkhart Mishawaka
Plymouth
Toledo
Sandusky
Bowling Green
Fremont
Defiance
Findlay
Kankakee
Pontiac
Watseka
Logansport
Fort Wayne
Lima
Mansfie
Marion
West Lafayette
Lafayette
Kokomo Marion
Bellefontaine
Grand Lake
O
Danville
INDIANA
Anderson Muncie
Upper Arlington
Springfield
Columb
Urbana
Champaign Crawfordsville
Indianapolis ★
Richmond
Dayton Huber Heights
Kettering
Lancas
Charleston
Mattoon
Terre Haute
Chillicothe
Middletown
Hamilton
Hillsboro
Bloomington
Monroe Lake
Columbus
Greensburg
Cincinnati
Covington
Jackson
St. Charles
Florissant
St. Louis
East St. Louis
Belleville
ILLINOIS
Effingham
Vincennes
Bedford
Madison
French Lick
Charlestown
New Albany Jeffersonville
Frankfort ★
Georgetown
Portsmouth
Maysville
Iron
Ashlan
Ste. Genevieve
Mount Vernon
Princeton
Louisville
Lexington
Winchester
Morehead
Carbondale
Evansville
Henderson Owensboro
Rough River L.
KENTUCKY
Berea
Manchester
MISSOURI
Cape Girardeau
Wappapello Lake
Madisonville
MAMMOTH CAVE NATIONAL PARK
Somerset
Cumberland Plateau
Poplar Bluff
Sikeston
New Madrid
Cairo
Paducah
Bowling Green
Glasgow
Lake Cumberland
Harlan
Mayfield
Hopkinsville
Middlesboro Cumberland Gap
Kingsp
Fulton
Clarksville
Cherokee Lake
Johns
McKenzie
Dyersburg
Hendersonville
Nashville
Old Hickory L.
Dale Hollow Lake
Oak Ridge
Crossville
Knoxville
Johns
Blytheville
ARKANSAS
Jackson
J. Percy Priest L.
Center Hill L.
Maryville
TENNESSEE
Murfreesboro
McMinnville
GREAT SMOKY MOUNTAINS NATIONAL PARK
Ashev
West Memphis
Bartlett
Columbia
Shelbyville
Watts Bar Lake
Franklin
Memphis
Germantown
Lawrenceburg
Tims Ford L.
Chickamauga Lake
Chattanooga
Cleveland
Corinth
Florence
Huntsville
Dalton
A P P
Tennessee-Tombigbee Waterway
Wilson L.
Wheeler L.
Decatur
Guntersville Lake
Weiss Lake
GEORGIA
Lake Sidney Lanier
Ander
Oxford
Tupelo
MISSISSIPPI
Houston
Hamilton
ALABAMA
Rome
Allatoona Lake
Roswell
Athens
Lewis Smith Lake
Gadsden
Marietta
Smyrna
Stone Mt. △ 1,683 ft. (513 m)

Continues on pages 96-97
Continues on pages 94-95
Continues on pages 92-93

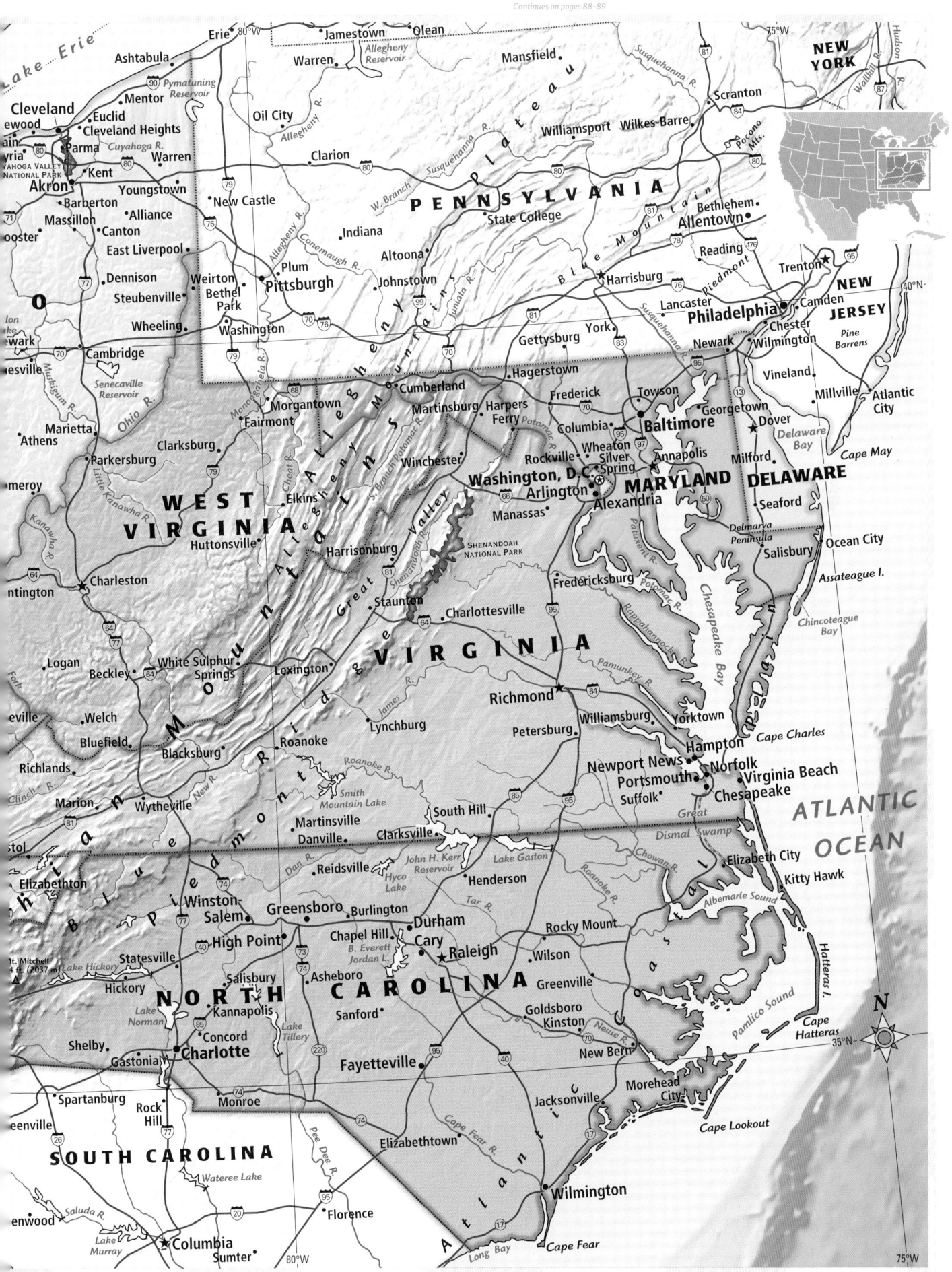

Continues on pages 88–89

Continues on pages 92–93

Continues on pages 94–95
Continues on pages 90–91
Continues on pages 94–95

95°W
35°N
90°W
85°W

OK
North Little Rock
West Memphis
Bartlett
Memphis
TENNESSEE
Chickamauga Lake
Chattanooga
Clevel

HOT SPRINGS N.P.
Hot Springs
Little Rock
Pickwick Lake
Corinth
Lawrenceburg
Florence
Wheeler Lake
Huntsville
Da

ARKANSAS
Ouachita Mts.
Arkabutla Lake
Tennessee-Tombigbee Waterway
Wilson Lake
Decatur
Lewis Smith Lake
Guntersville Lake
75

Pine Bluff
Oxford
Tupelo
Hamilton
Black Warrior R.
65
Allatoona Lake
Rome

Hope
Texarkana
30
Warren
Clarksdale
Houston
Gadsden
Weiss Lake
Marie
Smy

El Dorado
Greenville
Greenwood
Columbus
Birmingham
Bessemer
Hoover
Anniston
Atla

59
Longview Marshall
Bossier City
Yazoo R.
Big Black R.
Tuscaloosa
20
Coosa R.
La Gra

Shreveport
20
Monroe
Tallulah
Yazoo City
MISSISSIPPI
Philadelphia
59
Lake Martin
Montgomery
Auburn
Colum

TEXAS
Red R.
Natchitoches
LOUISIANA
Vicksburg
Jackson
Ross Barnett Reservoir
Meridian
William "Bill" Dannelly Res.
Selma
Phenix City
Walt Geor Rese

Nacogdoches
Toledo Bend Reservoir
Pearl R.
Leaf R.
Tombigbee R.
85

Lufkin
Sam Rayburn Reservoir
Natchez
Laurel
Chickasawhay R.
Jackson
Alabama R.
Troy
Pea R.
Choctawhatchee R.

Alexandria
49
McComb
Hattiesburg
65
Dothan

Gulf
Sabine R.
Coastal
Bogalusa
Baton Rouge
Plain
Pascagoula R.
Brewton
Escambia R.
Lake Seminole

Beaumont
30°N
Lake Charles
Lafayette
12
Biloxi
Gulfport
Mobile
10
Fort Walton Beach
Conecuh R.
Apalachicola R.

Port Arthur
Intracoastal Waterway
New Iberia
10
Kenner
Lake Pontchartrain
Pascagoula
Mobile Bay
Pensacola
Panama City

Metairie New Orleans
Houma
Borgne
Chandeleur Sound
Chandeleur Islands
Apalachicola
Cape San Blas

Atchafalaya Bay
Breton Sound

Terrebonne Bay
Delta of the Mississippi River

Mississippi R.
Arkansas R.
40
530
30
59
55
78
20
55
49

Gulf of Mexico

25°N

90°W
85°W

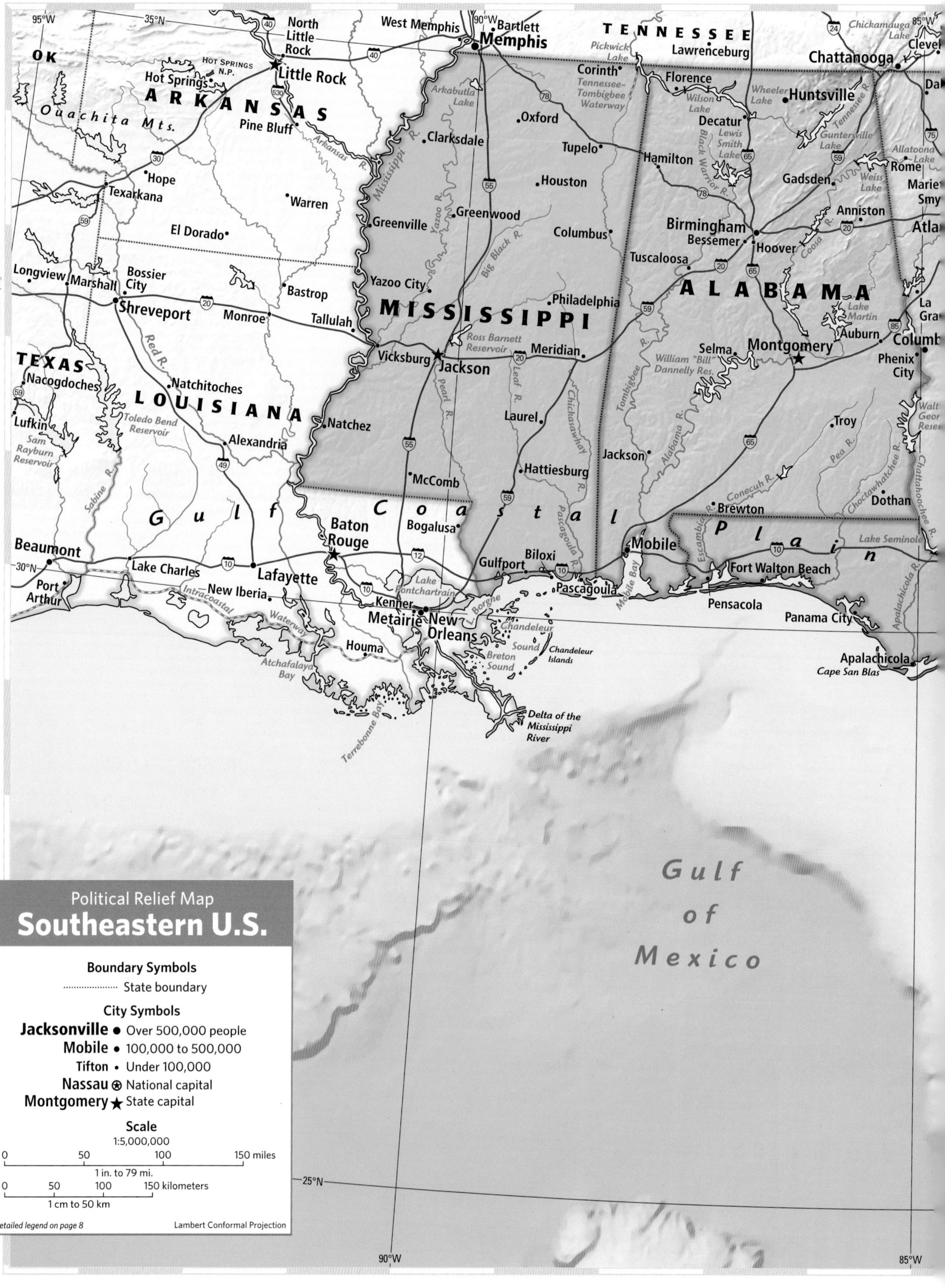

Political Relief Map

Southeastern U.S.

Boundary Symbols

··················· State boundary

City Symbols

Jacksonville ● Over 500,000 people

Mobile ● 100,000 to 500,000

Tifton • Under 100,000

Nassau ⊛ National capital

Montgomery ★ State capital

Scale

1:5,000,000

0   50   150 miles

1 in. to 79 mi.

0   50   100   150 kilometers

1 cm to 50 km

Detailed legend on page 8   Lambert Conformal Projection

Continues on pages 90-91

GREAT SMOKY
MOUNTAINS N.P.
Franklin
Blue Ridge
80°W
220
NORTH CAROLINA
New Bern
35°N
75°W
Gastonia
Charlotte
74
Monroe
Fayetteville
70
85
Rock Hill
Spartanburg
Greenville.
77
Elizabethtown
95
Jacksonville
40
Morehead
City
Anderson
Wateree Lake
17
Athens
Hartwell
Lake
Greenwood
Lake Murray
SOUTH
Columbia
20
CONGAREE N.P.
Sumter
Florence
Wilmington
Stone Mt.
△ 1,683 ft. (513 m)
Decatur
J. Strom Thurmond Res.
(Clarks Hill L.)
CAROLINA
17
Myrtle Beach
Cape Fear
Lake
Oconee
20
Augusta
Orangeburg
26
Lake Marion
Long Bay
GEORGIA
95
Lake
Moultrie
Macon
Ogeechee R.
North Charleston
Warner
Robins
16
Charleston
Mount Pleasant
Dublin
Oconee R.
Flint R.
Ocmulgee R.
Americus
Atlantic
Savannah
Albany
75
Tifton
Altamaha R.
Waycross.
Brunswick
Sea Islands
Thomasville
Valdosta
Okefenokee
Swamp
30°N
Tallahassee
10
St. Johns R.
Jacksonville
95
N
ATLANTIC
palachee
Bay
F
Branford
Gainesville
St. Augustine
Cross City
75
Ocala
L
Suwannee R.
Palatka
Lake George
Ormond Beach
Daytona Beach
Port Orange
O
Sanford
Titusville
OCEAN
Altamonte Springs
Cape Canaveral
Spring Hill.
R
Orlando
Kissimmee
4
Winter
Haven
Melbourne
Clearwater
Tampa
Lakeland
Lake Kissimmee
I
St. Petersburg
95
Fort Pierce
Bradenton
Peace R.
Lake
Istokpoga
D
Port St. Lucie
Sarasota
Arcadia
Punta Gorda
Lake
Okeechobee
West Palm Beach
A
Fort Myers
Caloosahatchee
River
Belle
Glade
Cape Coral
75
Coral Springs
Boca Raton
Pompano Beach
Naples
Big Cypress
Swamp
Davie
Fort Lauderdale
Hollywood
Hialeah
Miami Beach
Everglades
City
Coral Gables
Miami
Homestead
BISCAYNE
NATIONAL
PARK
EVERGLADES
NATIONAL
PARK
Cape Sable
Florida
Bay
25°N
DRY TORTUGAS
NATIONAL PARK
Florida Keys
Straits of Florida
Key West
80°W
220

ATLANTIC
OCEAN

Great Abaco I.

Grand Bahama I.

BAHAMAS

Bimini Is.

Bahama Islands

Eleuthera I.

Nassau
New Providence I.

Andros

Cat I.

Continues on pages 106-107

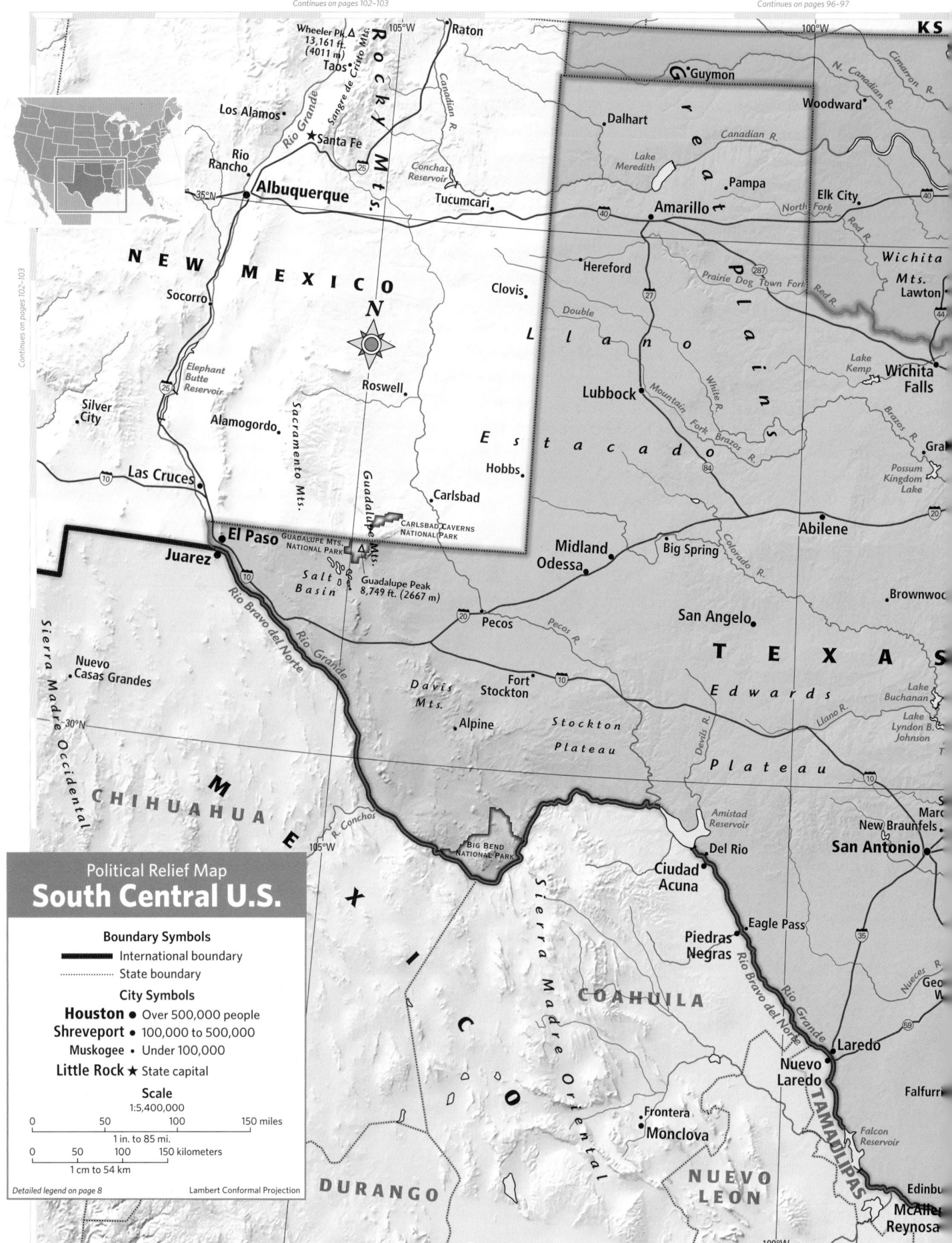

Continues on pages 102–103
Continues on pages 96–97
Continues on pages 102–103

KS

Wheeler Pk. △
13,161 ft.
(4011 m)
Raton

Taos

105°W

Sangre de Cristo Mts.

Rocky Mts.

Canadian R.

Los Alamos

Rio Grande

★ Santa Fe

Rio
Rancho

Conchas
Reservoir

Guymon

Dalhart

Lake
Meredith

Woodward

Canadian R.

Pampa

Elk City

35°N

Albuquerque

Tucumcari

I-25

I-40

Amarillo

North
Fork

Red R.

N E W   M E X I C O

Socorro

Hereford

I-27

Prairie Dog Town Fork

Red R.

Wichita
Mts.
Lawton

I-44

Clovis

Double

White R.

Mountain Fork Brazos R.

Lake
Kemp

Wichita
Falls

Elephant
Butte
Reservoir

I-25

Silver
City

Alamogordo

Sacramento Mts.

L   l   a   n   o

Lubbock

I-84

Brazos R.

Possum
Kingdom
Lake

Gra

E   s   t   a   c   a   d   o

Hobbs

Carlsbad

Abilene

I-20

Las Cruces

I-10

Guadalupe Mts.

CARLSBAD CAVERNS
NATIONAL PARK

El Paso

GUADALUPE MTS.
NATIONAL PARK

Midland
Odessa

Big Spring

Colorado R.

Juarez

I-10

Salt
Basin

Guadalupe Peak
8,749 ft. (2667 m)

△

San Angelo

Brownwoo

Rio Bravo del Norte

Rio Grande

Pecos

I-20

Pecos R.

T   E   X   A   S

Sierra Madre Occidental

Nuevo
Casas Grandes

30°N

Davis
Mts.

Fort
Stockton

I-10

E   d   w   a   r   d   s

Lake
Buchanan

Alpine

Stockton
Plateau

Llano R.

Devils R.

Lake
Lyndon B.
Johnson

P   l   a   t   e   a   u

I-10

New Braunfels

Marc

M   É   X   I   C   O

R. Conchas

BIG BEND
NATIONAL PARK

Amistad
Reservoir

Del Rio

San Antonio

105°W

C H I H U A H U A

Ciudad
Acuna

Sierra Madre Oriental

Eagle Pass

I-35

Piedras
Negras

Rio Bravo del Norte

Rio Grande

Nueces R.

Geo

I-59

C O A H U I L A

Laredo

Nuevo
Laredo

Falfurri

Frontera

Monclova

Falcon
Reservoir

**N U E V O
L E O N**

T A M A U L I P A S

DURANGO

Edinbu

McAlle
Reynosa

100°W

Political Relief Map
South Central U.S.

Boundary Symbols
━━━━━━ International boundary
·············· State boundary

City Symbols

Houston ● Over 500,000 people

Shreveport ● 100,000 to 500,000

Muskogee ● Under 100,000

Little Rock ★ State capital

Scale
1:5,400,000

0   50   100   150 miles

1 in. to 85 mi.

0   50   100   150 kilometers

1 cm to 54 km

Detailed legend on page 8   Lambert Conformal Projection

Continues on page 114

Continues on pages 96-97

Continues on pages 90-91

Continues on pages 92-93

Gulf of Mexico

Continues on pages 98–99

105°W

100°W

Black Hills

Rapid City

WIND CAVE NATIONAL PARK

BADLANDS NATIONAL PARK

Hot Springs

Pierre ★

S O U T H

D A K O T A

White R.

Mitchell

James R.

Lake Francis Case

Sioux Falls

Marsha

Brookings

Big Sioux R.

29

Lewis and Clark Lake

Yankton

Floyd R.

Sioux City

Continues on pages 100–101

WYOMING

20

Chadron

Crawford

Valentine

Niobrara R.

S a n d   H i l l s

O'Neill

20

South Sioux City

29

Norfolk

Elkhorn R.

Alliance

Scottsbluff

N. Platte R.

North Loup R.

Middle Loup R.

Loup R.

N E B R A S K A

Columbus

Fremont

Blair

Omaha

Bellevue

Cheyenne

80

Sidney

Lake McConaughy

South Loup R.

North Platte

Grand Island

Kearney

Platte R.

80

Big Blue R.

Lincoln ★

Greeley

S. Platte R.

76

Imperial

Swanson Reservoir

McCook

Hastings

Republican R.

Beatrice

Aub

40°N

Limon

COLORADO

Goodland

70

Norton

Kirwin Reservoir

Waconda Lake

Concordia

Marysville

Tuttle Creek Lake

Solomon R.

Milford Reservoir

Kansas R.

Manhattan

Topel

Smoky Hill R.

Hays

70

Salina

Abilene

135

Cottonwood R.

Flint Hills

Emporia

John Redmon Reservo

K A N S A S

N

Great Bend

Lamar

Arkansas R.

Garden City

Arkansas R.

Hutchinson

Newton

35

Toronto Reservoir

Dodge City

Pratt

Cheney Reservoir

Wichita

Ninnescah R.

Elk Cit Reservoi

Liberal

Kaw Lake

Ponca City

Bartlesville

Guymon

N. Canadian R.

Cimarron R.

Woodward

Enid

35

O K L A H O M A

Stillwater

Tulsa

T E X A S

Canadian R.

Bro Ar

100°W

Continues on pages 94–95

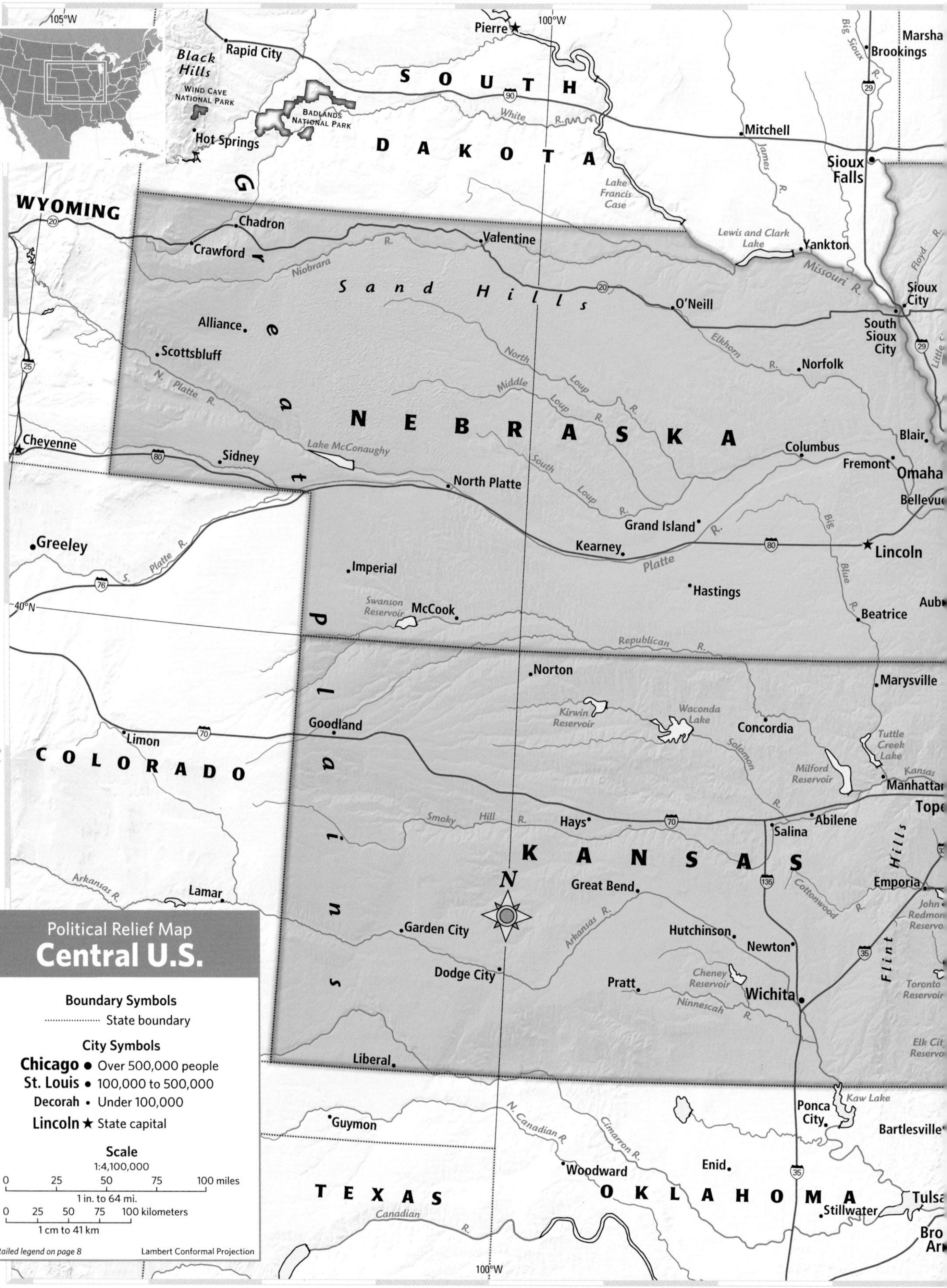

Political Relief Map
Central U.S.

Boundary Symbols
················· State boundary

City Symbols
Chicago ● Over 500,000 people
St. Louis • 100,000 to 500,000
Decorah • Under 100,000
Lincoln ★ State capital

Scale
1:4,100,000

| 0 | 25 | 50 | 75 | 100 miles |

1 in. to 64 mi.

| 0 | 25 | 50 | 75 | 100 kilometers |

1 cm to 41 km

Detailed legend on page 8   Lambert Conformal Projection

Continues on pages 98–99

MINNESOTA

Mankato
Rochester
Winona
Austin
La Crosse

WISCONSIN

Wisconsin Dells
Appleton
Oshkosh
Lake Winnebago
Fond du Lac
Sheboygan

MI

Muskegon
Holland

Madison ★
Janesville

Milwaukee
Racine
Kenosha
Waukegan
Evanston
Chicago

Lake Michigan

St. Joseph
Michigan City

Benton Harbor

Forest City
Mason City
Decorah
Fayette
Turkey R.
Wapsipinicon R.
Upper Iowa R.
Wisconsin R.
Mississippi

Spencer
Storm Lake
Fort Dodge
Cedar Falls
Waterloo
Dubuque
Galena
Freeport
Rockford
Arlington Heights
DeKalb
Elgin
Naperville
Aurora
Hammond
Gary

South Bend

IOWA

Cedar Rapids
Cedar R.
Iowa R.
Marshalltown
Ames
Grinnell
Clinton
Sterling
Rock
La Salle
Fox R.
Joliet
Calumet City
Valparaiso

Denison
Saylorville Reservoir
Des Moines ★
Iowa City
Coralville Res.
Bettendorf
Davenport
Moline
Rock Island

Kankakee R.
Loganspont

Council Bluffs
Des Moines R.
Osceola
Ottumwa
Skunk R.
Burlington
Galesburg
Galesburg
Spoon R.
Peoria
Pontiac
Kankakee
Watseka
West Lafayette
Lafayette

Nishnabotna R.
Rathbun Reservoir
Keokuk
Macomb
Normal
Bloomington

ILLINOIS

Champaign
Urbana
Danville
Crawfordsville

INDIANA

Central
Bethany
Kirksville
Quincy
Springfield ★
Decatur
Charleston
Terre Haute

Nodaway R.
Chariton R.
Hannibal
Jacksonville
Lake Shelbyville
Mattoon
Taylorville
Bloomington

St. Joseph
Chillicothe
Salt R.
Lowland

Atchison
Holt
Mark Twain Lake
Mississippi R.
Illinois R.
Effingham
Little Wabash R.
White R.
Vincennes

Leavenworth
Perry Lake
Kansas City
Independence
Kansas City
Columbia
St. Peters
St. Charles
Alton
Florissant
University City
Carlyle Lake
Wabash R.

Lawrence
Olathe
Lees Summit
St. Louis
East St. Louis
Kirkwood
Belleville
Mount Vernon

Pomona Reservoir
Overland Park
Sedalia
Jefferson City ★
Missouri R.
Rend Lake
Evansville
Henderson
Owensboro

MISSOURI

Lake of the Ozarks
Gasconade R.
Meramec R.
Rolla
Ste. Genevieve
Big Muddy R.
Carbondale
Ohio R.

Fort Scott
Orage R.
Stockton Lake
Pomme de Terre Reservoir
Niangua R.
James R.
Madisonville

Pittsburg
Springfield
Joplin
Ozark Plateau
Current R.
Cape Girardeau
Wappapello Lake
Cairo
Paducah

KENTUCKY

Hopkinsville

Coffeyville
West Plains
Poplar Bluff
Sikeston
New Madrid
Mayfield
Lake Barkley
Clarksville

Table Rock Lake
Bull Shoals Lake
Branson
Norfolk Lake
Dyersburg
Kentucky Lake
Tennessee R.

Lake O' the Cherokees
Springdale
Beaver Lake
Fayetteville

ARKANSAS

Jonesboro
Blytheville

TENNESSEE

Columbia

Muskogee
Boston Mts.
White R.
Jackson

Continues on pages 94–95

Continues on pages 90–91

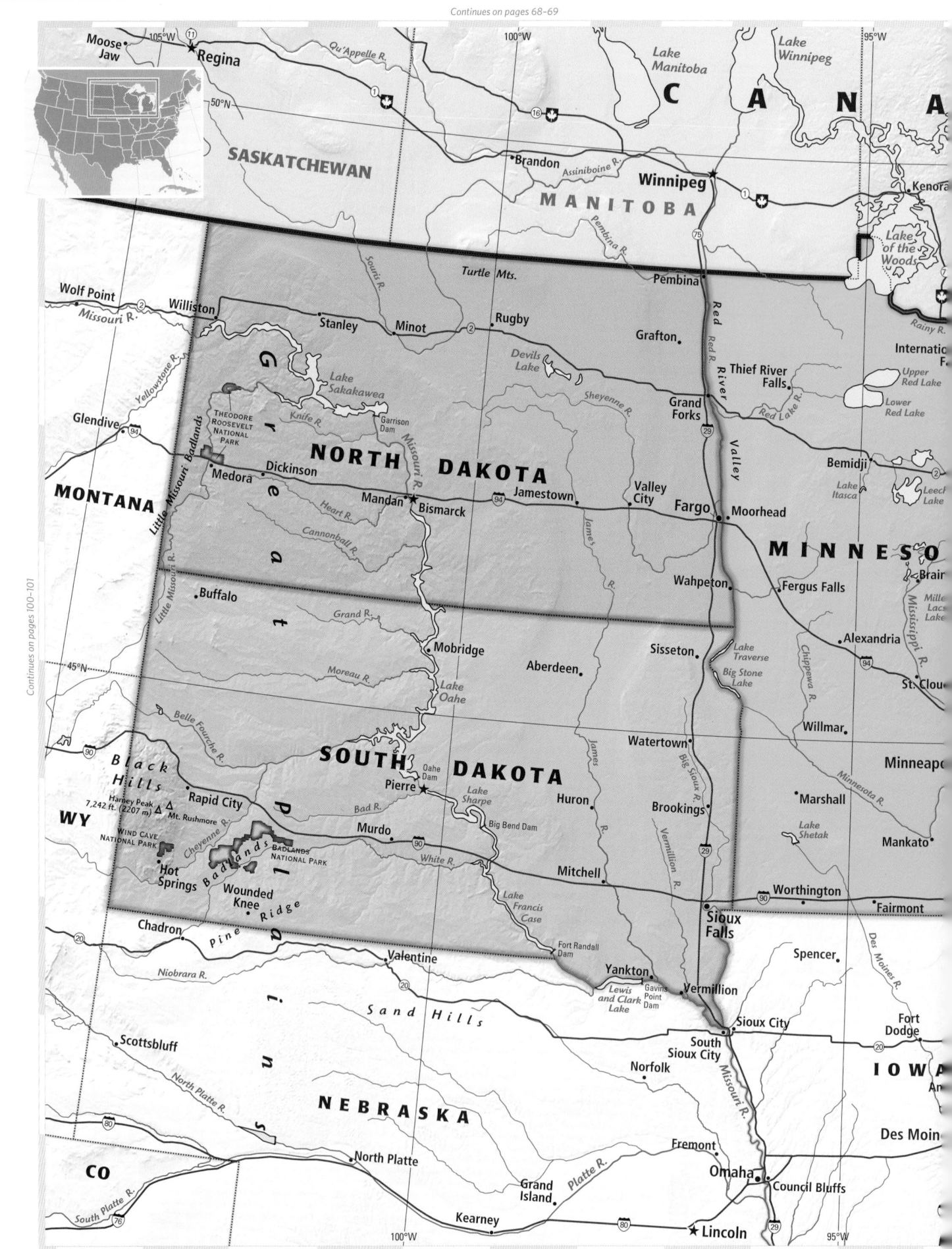

Continues on pages 68–69

Continues on pages 100–101

Continues on page 70

Political Relief Map
North Central U.S.

Boundary Symbols
— International boundary
········· State or province boundary

City Symbols
Detroit ● Over 500,000 people
Green Bay ● 100,000 to 500,000
Bemidji • Under 100,000
Bismarck ★ State or province capital

Scale
1:4,700,000

| 0 | 35 | 70 | 105 | 140 miles |

1 in. to 75 mi.

| 0 | 35 | 70 | 105 | 140 kilometers |

1 cm to 47 km

Detailed legend on page 8   Lambert Conformal Projection

90°W   85°W   50°N   45°N   90°W   85°W

D A A
ONTARIO
Lake Nipigon
Rainy L.
VOYAGEURS NATIONAL PARK
Thunder Bay
Isle Royale
ISLE ROYALE NATIONAL PARK
Lake Superior
Vermillion Lake
Mesabi Range
Ely
Hibbing
St. Louis R.
Duluth
Superior
Ashland
Ironwood
Apostle Islands
Gogebic Range
Houghton
Keweenaw Peninsula
Keweenaw Bay
Marquette
Grand Island
Munising
Whitefish Bay
Sault Ste. Marie
Sault Ste. Marie
North Channel
Manitoulin Island
Drummond Island
M I C H I G A N
Upper Peninsula
Straits of Mackinac
Hayward
Park Falls
Iron River
Menominee Range
Escanaba
Rhinelander
Beaver Island
Charlevoix
Alpena
Lake Huron
Rice Lake
W I S C O N S I N
Flambeau R.
Chippewa R.
Manitou Islands
Traverse City
Door Peninsula
Grand Traverse Bay
Au Sable R.
St. Paul
Bloomington
Eau Claire
Marshfield
Wausau
Stevens Point
Green Bay
Green Bay
Fox R.
Wisconsin R.
Manitowoc
Cadillac
Ludington
Lower Peninsula
Manistee R.
Midland
Bay City
Saginaw
Northfield
Lake City
Rochester
Winona
Tomah
Appleton
Menasha
Neenah
Oshkosh
Lake Winnebago
Fond du Lac
Sheboygan
Muskegon
Muskegon R.
Grand Rapids
Shiawassee R.
Flint
Sarnia
Port Huron
Austin
La Crosse
Driftless Area
Wisconsin Dells
Wisconsin R.
Wauwatosa
Grand Haven
Grand R.
East Lansing
Pontiac
St. Clair R.
Mason City
Madison
Milwaukee
West Allis
Wyoming
Holland
Lansing
Warren
Detroit
Dearborn
Lake St. Clair
Windsor
Mississippi R.
Prairie du Chien
Janesville
Racine
Battle Creek
Jackson
Ann Arbor
Lake Erie
Waterloo
Beloit
Kenosha
Kalamazoo
Portage
Cedar R.
Dubuque
Waukegan
Benton Harbor
St. Joseph R.
Toledo
Cedar Rapids
Rockford
Rock R.
Evanston
St. Joseph
Iowa City
Elgin
Naperville
Aurora
Chicago
Gary
South Bend
Elkhart
Findlay
Davenport
Moline
ILLINOIS
Hammond
Joliet
Rock Island
Illinois R.
Kankakee
INDIANA
Fort Wayne
Lima
OHIO
Ottumwa
Peoria
C e n t r a l   L o w l a n d
Wabash R.
Maumee R.
Lake Michigan

Continues on pages 96–97   Continues on pages 90–91
Continues on page 70

Continues on pages 68–69

Political Relief Map
Northwestern U.S.

Boundary Symbols
— International boundary
···· State or province boundary

City Symbols
Seattle ● Over 500,000 people
Eugene ● 100,000 to 500,000
Bozeman • Under 100,000
Boise ★ State or province capital

Scale
1:5,200,000

| 0 | 40 | 80 | 120 | 160 miles |

1 in. to 82 mi.

| 0 | 40 | 80 | 120 | 160 kilometers |

1 cm to 52 km

Detailed legend on page 8   Lambert Conformal Projection

50°N
125°W   120°W
Kamloops
C   A   N
97
1
5
Kelowna
BRITISH COLUMBIA
Fraser R.
Kootenay Lake
Strait of Georgia
Vancouver Island
Vancouver
Surrey
Bellingham
Mt. Baker
10,778 ft.
(3285 m)
NORTH CASCADES NATIONAL PARK
Ross Lake
Methow R.
Okanogan R.
Pend Oreille R.
Cape Flattery
Juan de Fuca Strait
Victoria
San Juan Is.
Skagit R.
2
Lake Pend Oreille
Port Angeles
OLYMPIC NATIONAL PARK
Hoh R.
Olympic Mts.
Everett
Edmonds
Seattle
Bellevue
Bremerton
Kent
Auburn
Tacoma
Lake Chelan
Okanogan
Franklin D. Roosevelt Lake
Grand Coulee Dam
Spokane
Coeur d' Alen
Quinault R.
Aberdeen
Grays Harbor
Willapa Bay
Chehalis R.
Olympia
Wenatchee
WASHINGTON
Moses Lake
Potholes Reservoir
90
90
Coeur d'Alene Lake
Ellensburg
Mt. Rainier
14,410 ft.
(4392 m)
MT. RAINIER NATIONAL PARK
Yakima
Pullman
Moscow
Cowlitz R.
Longview
Mt. St. Helens
8,365 ft.
(2550 m)
Mt. Adams
12,276 ft.
(3742 m)
Sunnyside
82
Richland
Pasco
Snake R.
Clearwater R.
Lewiston
Astoria
5
Vancouver
Yakima R.
Kennewick
Walla Walla
Clearw Mts
45°N
Tillamook
Portland
Beaverton
Bonneville Dam
Gresham
Mt. Hood
11,239 ft.
(3426 m)
John Day Dam
The Dalles
84
Columbia R.
Pendleton
84
Blue Mts.
Wallowa Mts.
Hell's Canyon
Willamette R.
Salem
Mt. Jefferson
10,497 ft.
(3199 m)
Deschutes R.
John Day R.
Columbia Plate
Powder R.
Newport
Corvallis
Albany
10,047 ft.
(3062 m)
Three Sisters
10,085 ft.
(3074 m)
Cascade
Baker City
Cascade Reservoir
Payette R.
McKenzie R.
Eugene
Springfield
10,358 ft.
(3157 m)
Bend
John Day
Ontario
84
Boise R.
PACIFIC
OCEAN
5
OREGON
Great Sandy Desert
Silvies R.
Caldwell
Bois
Coos Bay
Roseburg
Lake Owyhee
Malheur Lake
Owyhee R.
Nampa
Cape Blanco
Rogue R.
Crater Lake
CRATER LAKE NATIONAL PARK
Harney Basin
Steens Mtn.
Owyhee Mts.
Snake
199
Medford
Upper Klamath Lake
Sprague R.
Klamath Falls
Klamath R.
Goose Lake
Klamath Mts.
REDWOOD NATIONAL PARK
Cascade
Mt. Shasta
14,162 ft.
(4317 m)
G
r
e
a
t
Winnemucca
Humboldt R.
Elk
40°N
Cape Mendocino
Eureka
Trinity R.
Pit R.
LASSEN VOLCANIC NATIONAL PARK
B
a
s
i
n
NEVAD
5
Shasta Lake
Redding
Lassen Pk.
10,457 ft.
(3187 m)
Fel R.
Pyramid Lake
CALIFORNIA
Sacramento R.
80
101
Carson Sink
Reno
125°W
120°W

Continues on pages 102–103

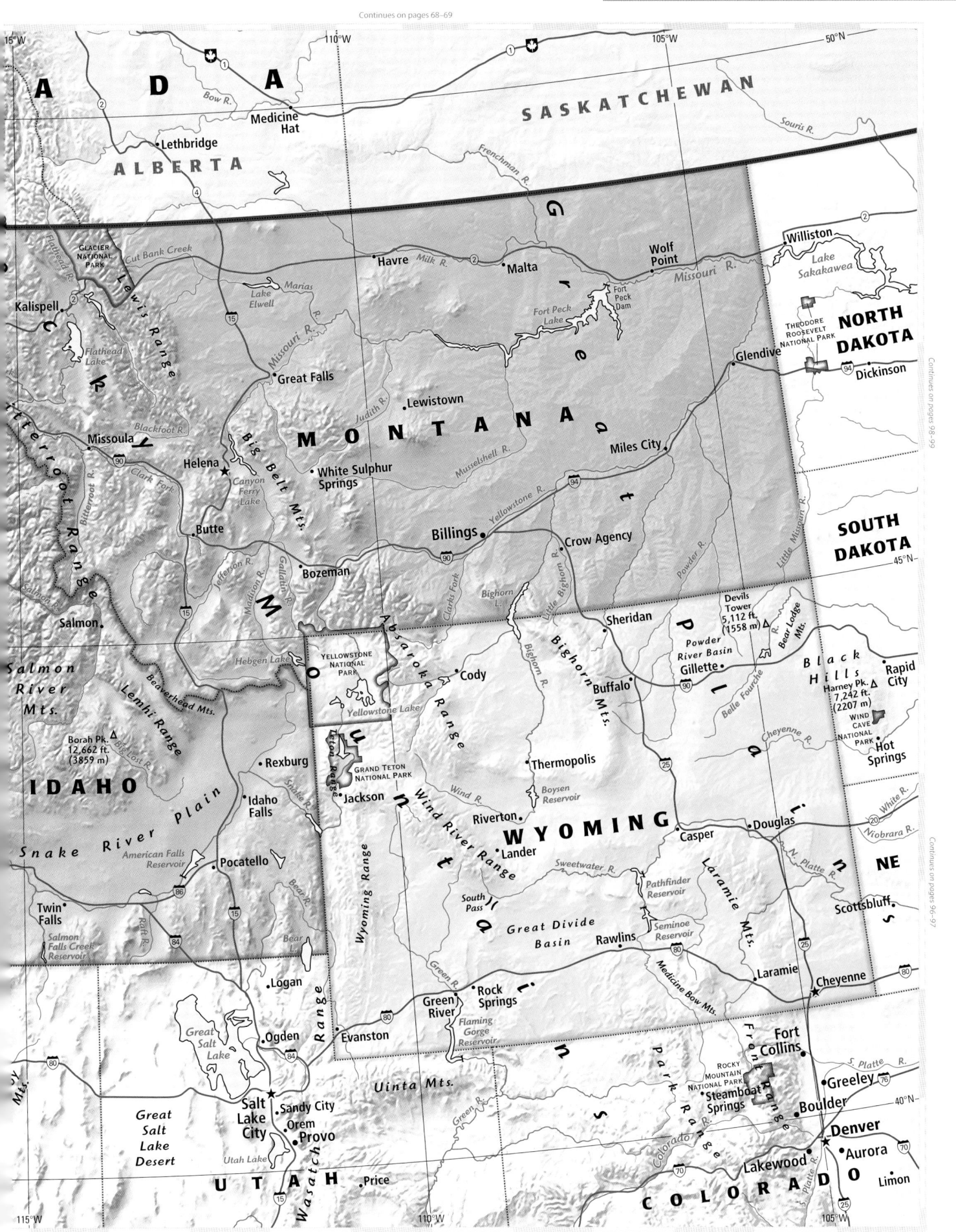

Continues on pages 68–69

CANADA

15°W 110°W 105°W 50°N

SASKATCHEWAN

⚲ 1 ⚲

Bow R.

Medicine
Hat

• Lethbridge

ALBERTA

4

Souris R.

Frenchman R.

GLACIER
NATIONAL
PARK

Cut Bank Creek

Flathead R.

Lewis Range

• Havre   Milk R.   • Malta

2

Missouri R.

Wolf
Point

Fort
Peck
Dam

Fort Peck
Lake

Williston

Lake
Sakakawea

THEODORE
ROOSEVELT
NATIONAL PARK

NORTH
DAKOTA

Kalispell

2

Flathead
Lake

Lake
Elwell

Lake
Marias

Missouri R.

Glendive

94

Dickinson

15

• Great Falls

Judith R.

• Lewistown

Bitterroot Range

Blackfoot R.

M O N T A N A

Little Missouri R.

• Missoula

90

Clark Fork

Helena ★

White Sulphur
Springs

Canyon
Ferry
Lake

Big Belt Mts.

Musselshell R.

• Miles City

SOUTH
DAKOTA

• Butte

Jefferson R.

Gallatin R.

• Bozeman

Madison R.

Billings •

Yellowstone R.

90

Clarks Fork

• Crow Agency

94

Yellowstone R.

45°N

Salmon •

15

Hebgen Lake

YELLOWSTONE
NATIONAL
PARK

Absaroka Range

Bighorn
L.

Little Bighorn R.

Bighorn R.

Sheridan •

Powder R.

Devils
Tower
5,112 ft.
(1558 m) △

Bear Lodge
Mts.

B l a c k

Salmon
River
Mts.

Lemhi Range

Beaverhead Mts.

Yellowstone Lake

• Cody

Powder
River Basin

Gillette •

H i l l s

Harney Pk. △
7,242 ft.
(2207 m)

Rapid
City •

Borah Pk. △
12,662 ft.
(3859 m)

Big Lost R.

Teton Range

GRAND TETON
NATIONAL PARK

Buffalo
Mts.

Buffalo •

90

Belle Fourche

WIND
CAVE
NATIONAL
PARK

I D A H O

Snake   River   Plain

• Rexburg

• Idaho
  Falls

Snake R.

Jackson •

Wind River Range

Thermopolis •

Boysen
Reservoir

Wind R.

25

Cheyenne R.

Hot
Springs •

American Falls
Reservoir

Bear R.

• Pocatello

86

R o c k y

Riverton •

W Y O M I N G

Casper •

Douglas •

N. Platte R.

20

White R.

NE

Niobrara R.

Twin
Falls •

15

84

• Lander

Sweetwater R.

Laramie Mts.

Scottsbluff •

Salmon
Falls Creek
Reservoir

Platte R.

Bear
L.

South
Pass

M o u n t a i n s

Great Divide
Basin

Pathfinder
Reservoir

Seminoe
Reservoir

Rawlins •

Medicine Bow Mts.

80

Laramie •

25

80

Cheyenne ★

• Logan

Green R.

Green
River •

Rock
Springs •

Flaming
Gorge
Reservoir

Fort
Collins •

S. Platte R.

Greeley •

76

80

Great Salt
Lake

84

• Ogden

• Evanston

Wasatch Range

Uinta Mts.

Green R.

ROCKY
MOUNTAIN
NATIONAL PARK

Park Range

Front Range

Steamboat
Springs •

Boulder •

40°N

Great
Salt
Lake
Desert

Salt
Lake
City ★

Sandy City •

Orem •
• Provo

Utah Lake

Colorado R.

Denver ★

Aurora •

Lakewood •

70

70

U T A H

15

Wasatch Range

• Price

110°W

S. Platte R.

25

C O L O R A D O

Limon •

115°W 110°W 105°W

Continues on pages 102–103

Continues on pages 98–99

Continues on pages 96–97

Continues on pages 100–101

Medford
Klamath Falls **OREGON**
Twin Falls
IDAH

125°W
120°W
115°W

84

Klamath Mts.
Klamath R.
Goose Lake

Cascade Range

Mt. Shasta
14,162 ft.
(4317 m)

Cape
Mendocino
Eureka

Pit R.

Lassen Pk.
10,457 ft.
(3187 m)
Trinity R.
Redding
Shasta
Lake
Sacramento R.

LASSEN VOLCANIC
NATIONAL PARK

Winnemucca
Humboldt R.
Elko

Ruby Mts.

Great Salt

REDWOOD
NATIONAL
PARK

80

40°N

Coast Ranges

Chico

Pyramid
Lake

Basin

Great Basi

Ukiah

Clear
Lake

Yuba
City

C A L I F O R N I A

Sierra

Truckee R.

Reno

Carson
Sink

Pt. Arena

101

Santa Rosa
Vacaville
Davis
Napa
Vallejo
San Rafael
Pt. Reyes

Folsom
Lake
Sacramento

Lake
Tahoe

Virginia City
Carson
City

N E V A D A

Ely

Wheeler Peak
13,063 ft.
(3982 m)

GREAT
BASIN
NATIONAL
PARK

San Francisco
Berkeley
Oakland
Daly City
Fremont
San Mateo
Lodi
Stockton

80

99

Carson R.

Range

Tonopah

Sunnyvale
**San
Jose**
Modesto
Turlock
Hetch Hetchy
Aqueduct
Yosemite
Falls
YOSEMITE
NATIONAL
PARK
Mono Lake

PACIFIC

Santa Cruz
Monterey Bay

San Joaquin R.

Merced

Bishop

Salinas

Fresno

KINGS CANYON
NATIONAL PARK

Mt. Whitney
14,494 ft.
(4418 m)

DEATH VALLEY
NATIONAL PARK

Death Valley

Sunrise
Manor

Lake
Mead

OCEAN

Monterey

PINNACLES
NATIONAL
PARK

Visalia

Nevada

SEQUOIA
NATIONAL
PARK

Owens
Lake

−282 ft.
(−86 m)

Las Vegas
Paradise
Henderson
Boulder
City

Hoover
Dam

St.
George

Virgin R.

Ridgecrest

San Luis Obispo

Aqueduct

California

Bakersfield

35°N

Coast

101

Santa Maria

Ranges

San Joaquin Valley

5

99

Tehachapi Mts.
Los Angeles Aqueduct

Mojave

15

Lake
Mohave

Barstow

Desert

40

Kingman

Lancaster

JOSHUA TREE
NATIONAL PARK

Lake Hava
City

Parker
Dam

Lompoc

Santa
Barbara

Pt. Conception
Santa Barbara
Channel

Ventura
Oxnard

Santa
Clarita

Glendale
Pasadena

Los Angeles
Torrance

San
Bernardino

Ontario
Anaheim

Riverside

Lake
Havasu

Colorado R.

Aqueduct

Colorado R.

10

CHANNEL ISLANDS
NATIONAL PARK

Long Beach
Huntington Beach
Santa Ana

405

5

15

Palm
Springs

Indio

Coachella Canal

S o n

Santa
Catalina

Oceanside

Salton
Sea

Imperial

Gila

Channel Islands

San
Clemente

Escondido

Valley
El Centro

D e

San Diego
Chula Vista

Calexico

Yuma

8

Tijuana

20

Mexicali

1D

SONORA

M E

Ensenada

**BAJA
CALIFORNIA**

1

Gulf of California
(Sea of Cortes)

120°W
115°W

Political Relief Map

Southwestern U.S.

Boundary Symbols

────── International boundary

⋯⋯⋯⋯⋯ State boundary

City Symbols

Los Angeles ● Over 500,000 people

Tempe ● 100,000 to 500,000

Aspen • Under 100,000

Santa Fe ★ State capital

Scale
1:5,400,000

| 0 | 50 | | 100 | | 150 miles |

1 in. to 85 mi.

| 0 | 50 | 100 | | 150 kilometers |

1 cm to 54 km

Detailed legend on page 8   Lambert Conformal Projection

N

Continues on page 114

Continues on pages 100–101

110°W
105°W

WYOMING

Bear R.

Great Divide Basin

Pathfinder Reservoir

Seminoe Reservoir

Scottsbluff

North Platte R.

NEBRASKA

Bear Lake

Logan

Rock Springs

Rawlins

North Platte

Sidney

North Platte

Great Salt Lake

Ogden

Evanston

Flaming Gorge Reservoir

Laramie

Cheyenne

Rocky Mountain National Park

Fort Collins

Greeley

40°N

Layton

Bountiful

Salt Lake City

Uinta Mts.

Wasatch Range

Yampa R.

Steamboat Springs

Long Peak 14,265 ft. (4345 m)

Front Range

Longmont

Boulder

South Platte R.

Continues on pages 96–97

Vest Jordan

Sandy City

Orem

Provo

White R.

Arvada

Denver

Aurora

Goodland

Utah Lake

Green R.

Lakewood

Limon

S. Fork Republican R.

Price

Sevier R.

Sevier Bridge Reservoir

Colorado R.

Vail

Sawatch Range

Mt. Elbert 14,433 ft. (4399 m)

Pikes Peak 14,110 ft. (4301 m)

Colorado Springs

N. Fork Smoky Hill R.

KANSAS

UTAH

Sevier Lake

Arches National Park

Grand Junction

Aspen

Black Canyon of the Gunnison National Park

Canyonlands National Park

Moab

Gunnison R.

Pueblo

Arkansas R.

Lamar

Capitol Reef National Park

Henry Mts.

COLORADO

San Rafael R.

Miguel R.

Dolores R.

Great Sand Dunes National Park

Sangre de Cristo Mts.

Purgatoire R.

edar City

Bryce Canyon National Park

San Juan R.

Mesa Verde National Park

San Juan Mts.

Del Norte

Zion National Park

Lake Powell

Durango

Trinidad

OKLAHOMA

Guymon

Glen Canyon Dam

Raton

Wheeler Peak 13,161 ft. (4011 m)

Canadian R.

Dalhart

Grand Canyon National Park

Colorado R.

Black Mesa

Chinle Wash

Farmington

Taos

Lake Meredith

Plateau

Chaco Canyon

Los Alamos

Rio Grande

Conchas Reservoir

Amarillo

Grand Canyon

Little Colorado R.

Oraibi

Santa Fe

Ute Reservoir

Tucumcari

35°N

Humphreys Peak 12,633 ft. (3851 m)

Painted Desert

Window Rock

Gallup

Mt. Taylor 11,301 ft. (3445 m)

Zuni R.

Rio Rancho

Albuquerque

Hereford

Flagstaff

Petrified Forest National Park

Pecos R.

Clovis

Prescott

Mogollon Rim

Verde R.

NEW

Llano

RIZONA

Baldy Peak 11,403 ft. (3476 m)

MEXICO

Estacado

Theodore Roosevelt Lake

Salt R.

Socorro

Roswell

TEXAS

Glendale

Scottsdale

Tempe

Mesa

Chandler

San Carlos Reservoir

Elephant Butte Reservoir

Rio Hondo

Hobbs

Phoenix

a n

Caballo Reservoir

Sacramento Mts.

Lake McMillan

Silver City

Alamogordo

Carlsbad

Odessa

Casa Grande

Gila R.

Las Cruces

Guadalupe Mts.

Carlsbad Caverns National Park

Saguaro National Park

San Pedro R.

Pecos

Pecos R.

r t

Tucson

Salt Basin

Guadalupe Mountains National Park

El Paso

Guadalupe Peak 8,749 ft. (2667 m)

Sierra Vista

Nogales

Douglas

Juarez

Rio Grande

Davis Mts.

Fort Stockton

I C O

Nogales

110°W

CHIHUAHUA

105°W

Continues on page 114

Continues on pages 94–95

Political Relief Map
Alaska

Boundary Symbols

━━━━━ International boundary

·············· Province or territory boundary

City Symbols

Anchorage ● Over 100,000 people

Fairbanks ● 25,000 to 100,000

Valdez • Under 25,000

Juneau ★ State or territory capital

Scale

1:14,500,000

0   100   200   300   400 miles

1 in. to 229 mi.

0   100   200   300   400 kilometers

1 cm to 145 km

Detailed legend on page 8   Lambert Equal Area Projection

ARCTIC OCEAN

Barrow • Point Barrow

Prudhoe Bay

Beaufort Sea

Chukchi Sea

ARCTIC CIRCLE 66½°N

RUSSIA

Kotzebue

Kotzebue Sound

Seward Peninsula

Nome

Norton Sound

Unalakleet

St. Lawrence I.

St. Matthew I.

Nunivak I.

Bering Sea

Pribilof Is.

Umnak I.
Umnak I.

Unalaska
Unalaska I.

Aleutian Islands

Colville R.

Brooks Range

GATES OF THE ARCTIC NATIONAL PARK

KOBUK VALLEY NATIONAL PARK

A L A S K A

Fort Yukon

Yukon R.

Circle

Fairbanks

College

Trans-Alaska Pipeline

Tanana R.

Dawson

65°N

Tok

Porcupine R.

Kuskokwim R.

Yukon R.

Kilbuck Mts.

McGrath

Denali (Mt. McKinley) 20,310 ft. (6190 m)

DENALI NATIONAL PARK ③

Alaska Range

②

④

Willow

①

Bethel

Dillingham

Bristol Bay

Alaska Peninsula

KATMAI NATIONAL PARK

Kodiak

Kodiak I.

LAKE CLARK NATIONAL PARK

Kenai

Soldotna

⑦

Kenai Peninsula

Homer

Seldovia

⑨ Seward

Cook Inlet

Iliamna L.

Anchorage

Valdez

Cordova

Prince William Sound

KENAI FJORDS NATIONAL PARK

Wrangell Mts.

WRANGELL-ST. ELIAS NATIONAL PARK

Mt. St. Elias 18,008 ft. (5489 m)

Yakutat

Mt. Logan 19,550 ft. (5959 m)

①

GLACIER BAY NATIONAL PARK

Gulf of Alaska

Alexander Archipelago

Whitehorse

C A N A D A

Y.T.

B.C.

Rocky Mts.

Haines

Skagway

Juneau

Petersburg

Sitka

Baranof I.

Wrangell

Prince of Wales I.

Craig

Ketchikan

Dixon Entrance

Prince Rupert

Haida Gwaii (Queen Charlotte Is.) (Canada)

Hecate Strait

PACIFIC OCEAN

INTERNATIONAL DATE LINE

Bering Strait

Continues on pages 68–69

Political Relief Map
Hawaii

City Symbols

Honolulu ● Over 100,000 people

Hilo ● 25,000 to 100,000

Lihue • Under 25,000

Honolulu ★ State capital

Scale

1:4,300,000

0   25   50   75   100 miles

1 in. to 67 mi.

0   25   50   75   100 kilometers

1 cm to 43 km

Detailed legend on page 8   Mercator Projection

Niihau

Kauai

Kekaha

Lihue

Kaulakahi Channel

Kauai Channel

HAWAII

Oahu

Waipahu

Kaneohe

Kailua

Honolulu

Pearl Harbor

Kaiwi Channel

Molokai

Kaunakakai

Pailolo Channel

Lanai City

Lanai

Maui

Wailuku

HALEAKALA NATIONAL PARK

Kahoolawe

Alenuihaha Channel

PACIFIC OCEAN

Kamuela

Mauna Kea 13,796 ft. (4205 m)

Hilo

Kailua Kona

Hawaii

Kilauea 4,090 ft. (1247 m)

Mauna Loa 13,677 ft. (4169 m)

HAWAII VOLCANOES NATIONAL PARK

Pahala

How should a country exercise power beyond its borders?

The U.S. military has ground, sea, and air forces spread across the globe to defend its allies and its own interests. As the world's only superpower, the United States often acts alone—*unilateralism*. Some argue that it should work with other countries—*multilateralism*. How should a country respond to world problems? There are many perspectives on this issue. Here are two of them.

World Military Spending

In 2016, the United States spent about US$611 billion on its military.

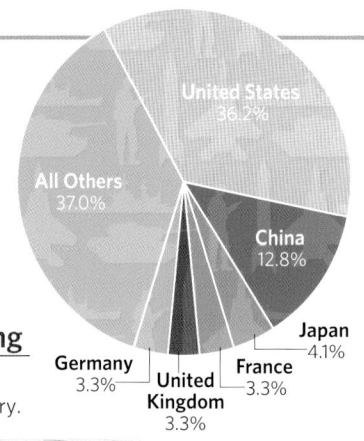

United States 36.2%
All Others 37.0%
China 12.8%
Japan 4.1%
France 3.3%
United Kingdom 3.3%
Germany 3.3%

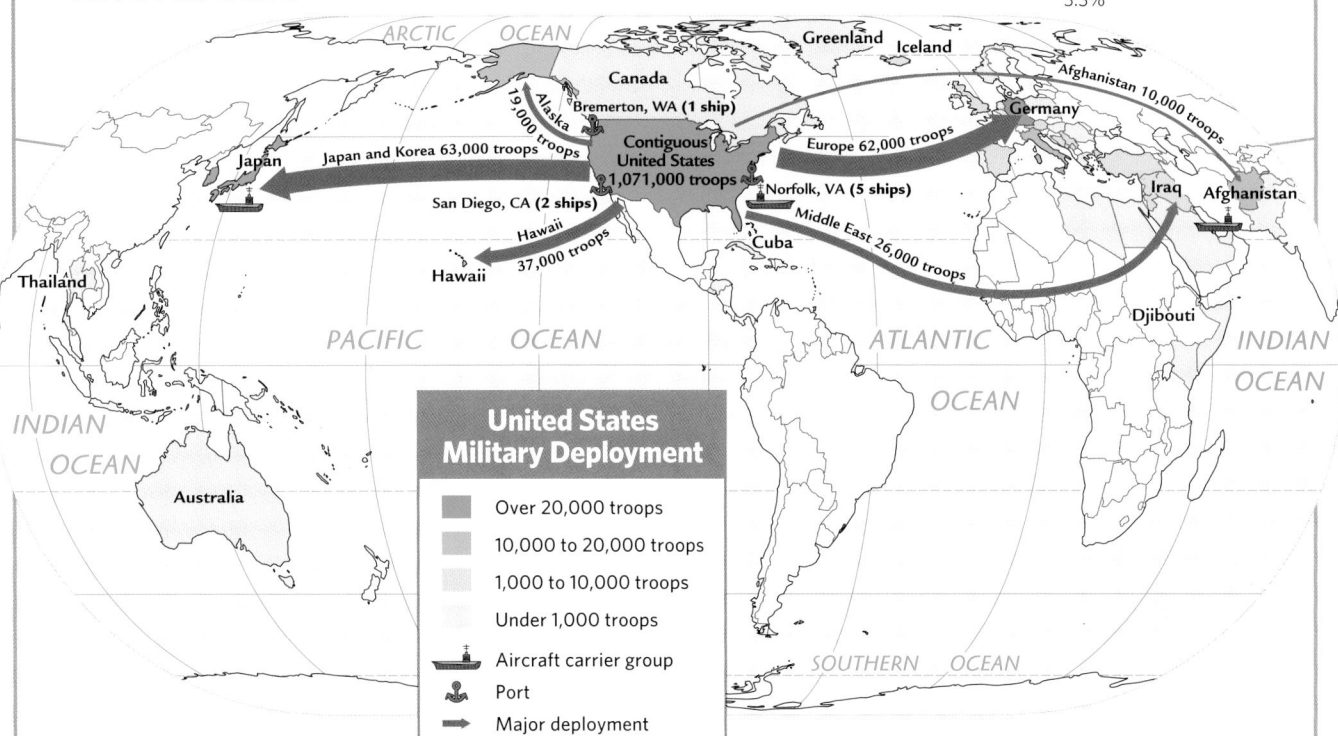

United States Military Deployment

- Over 20,000 troops
- 10,000 to 20,000 troops
- 1,000 to 10,000 troops
- Under 1,000 troops
- Aircraft carrier group
- Port
- Major deployment

Map labels: ARCTIC OCEAN, Greenland, Iceland, Canada, Bremerton, WA (1 ship), Alaska 19,000 troops, Contiguous United States 1,071,000 troops, Japan and Korea 63,000 troops, Japan, San Diego, CA (2 ships), Hawaii 37,000 troops, Hawaii, Thailand, PACIFIC OCEAN, INDIAN OCEAN, Australia, Europe 62,000 troops, Germany, Afghanistan 10,000 troops, Norfolk, VA (5 ships), Cuba, Middle East 26,000 troops, Iraq, Afghanistan, Djibouti, ATLANTIC OCEAN, INDIAN OCEAN, SOUTHERN OCEAN

A country must protect its interests and act alone.

- The attacks on September 11, 2001, proved that Americans are not safe on their own soil. To ensure the safety of American citizens, the United States needs to be able to make decisions swiftly and take action on its own.

- The United States has the largest economy and leads the world in military spending. No other country or group of countries has the resources needed to maintain order on a global scale.

- Coalitions and multilateral organizations take a long time to reach a consensus. By the time everyone agrees on a course of action, the situation is often more difficult to resolve.

- As new multilateral organizations continue to be formed, they dilute the effectiveness of those that already exist.

A country should work cooperatively with other countries.

- Important issues confronting the United States, such as terrorism, are the same issues facing the rest of the world. Only multilateral action can achieve meaningful solutions.

- The United States would benefit from allies sharing the human and financial costs of military action in global conflicts.

- The multilateral peacekeeping efforts of the United Nations cost less annually than what New York City spends on its fire and police departments.

- A "going it alone" attitude isolates the United States from its global neighbors. In the future, when the United States needs help, it may find the world community uncooperative.

- No country or organization is infallible. The built-in checks and balances of multilateral decisions protect the United States and the world.

UNITED STATES

Los Angeles

Memphis

San Diego

Phoenix

Tijuana • Mexicali

NORTH

Salada
Lagoon

Nogales
Nogales

El Paso

Dallas

Juarez

AMERICA

Rio Grande

30°N

Angel de la
Guarda I.

Hermosillo

Yaqui R.

Amistad
Res.

New Orleans

Tiburon I.

Alvaro
Obregon Res.

Conchos R.

Rio Bravo del Norte

Houston

Sebastian
Vizcaino Bay

Gulf
of California
(Sea of Cortes)

Chihuahua

Cedros I.

Point
Eugenia

Ciudad Obregon

Sierra Madre
Occidental

Fuerte R.

Laredo

Nuevo Laredo

Gulf of
Mexico

Baja California

Santa
Margarita I.

San Jose I.

Torreon

Sierra Madre Oriental

Matamoros
Saltillo Monterrey

Brownsville

TROPIC OF CANCER 23½°N

La Paz

MEXICO

Gulf

Madre
Lagoon

Cape San Lucas

Mazatlan

Ciudad Victoria

Coastal Plain

Tampico

Cape Rojo

20°N

Tres Marias Is.

Plateau
of
Mexico

San Luis
Potosi

PACIFIC

Tepic

Leon

Panuco R.

Cancu

Merida

Puerto Vallarta
Cape Corrientes

L. Chapala

Guadalajara

Campeche

Yucatan
Peninsula

Revillagigedo Is.
(Mex.)

Morelia

Paricutin
Volcano
9,213 ft.
(2808 m)

Nezahualcoyotl

Mexico City ⊗ • Puebla

Popocatepetl
17,887 ft.
(5452 m)

Veracruz

Pico de Orizaba
18,405 ft. (5610 m)

Bay of
Campeche

Terminos
Lagoon

Hondo R.

OCEAN

Sierra Madre del Sur

Balsas R.

Villahermosa

El Chichon
3,478 ft. (1060 m)

BELIZE

Che

Belmopa

Acapulco

Oaxaca

Angostura
Res.

Gulf of
Tehuantepec

Sierra Madre

L. Izabal

Tajumulco
13,845 ft.
(4220 m)

GUATEMALA

San Pedro

Gulf

Guatemala City

Teguciga

San Salvador

EL SALVADOR

Gulf of
Fonseca

N

10°N

110°W

100°W

90°W

Political Relief Map
Middle America

Boundary Symbols
.... International boundary

City Symbols
Monterrey ● Over 500,000 people
La Paz • 100,000 to 500,000
Limon • Under 100,000

Mexico City ⊗ National capital

Scale
1:15,300,000

0   100   200   300 miles

1 in. to 242 mi.

0 100 200 300 kilometers

1 cm to 153 km

Detailed legend on page 8   Albers Equal Area Projection

Cocos I.
(Costa Rica

80°W   70°W   60°W

Cape Hatteras

Bermuda
(U.K.)

A T L A N T I C

30°N

O C E A N

Atlanta

L. Okeechobee   Grand
Bahama I.   Great
Abaco I.

Miami   B A H A M A S   TROPIC OF CANCER 23½°N

Florida Keys   Nassau   San Salvador I.
Straits of Florida   Andros I.

Havana   Turks and
Caicos Is.
(U.K.)   20°N

C U B A   Great
Inagua I.

Batabano
Gulf
Isle of Youth   Holguin

Yucatan Channel   Santiago de Cuba   Guantanamo   Windward
Passage   DOMINICAN
REPUBLIC   San
Juan   Virgin Is.
(U.K.)   Anegada Passage   Anguilla
(U.K.)

Cozumel I.   HAITI   Pico Duarte   Ponce   ANTIGUA &
BARBUDA

Cayman Is.
(U.K.)   Jamaica   Port-au-Prince   10,417 ft.
(3175 m)   Santo
Domingo   Mona Passage   Puerto Rico
(U.S.)   Virgin Is.
(U.S.)   ST. KITTS & NEVIS   Montserrat (U.K.)

Montego Bay   Kingston   Guadeloupe
(Fr.)

JAMAICA   Jamaica Channel   DOMINICA

onduras   Martinique
(Fr.)

Honduras   Mont Pelee
4,583 ft.
(1397 m)   ST. LUCIA

Bay Is.   C a r i b b e a n   S e a   BARBADOS

ONDURAS   Caratasca
Lagoon   ST. VINCENT &
THE GRENADINES

Coco R.   Miskito Cays   GRENADA

NICARAGUA   Providencia I.
(Colombia)   Aruba
(Neth.)   Curacao
(Neth.)   Bonaire
(Neth.)   Margarita I.
(Venezuela)   TRINIDAD &
TOBAGO

Point Gallinas   San Andres I.
(Colombia)

Managua   Bluefields   Gulf of
Venezuela   Caracas   Port-of-Spain   10°N

L. Nicaragua   Panama
Canal

Managua   COSTA RICA   Limon   Lake
Maracaibo   V E N E Z U E L A

San Juan R.   Irazu   Mosquito
Gulf   Colon   Gulf of
Darien

San Jose   11,260 ft.
(3432 m)   Orinoco R.

Coronado
Bay   PANAMA   Panama
City

Coiba I.   Gulf of
Panama   S O U T H

A M E R I C A

C O L O M B I A

Bogota   B R A Z I L

80°W   70°W   60°W

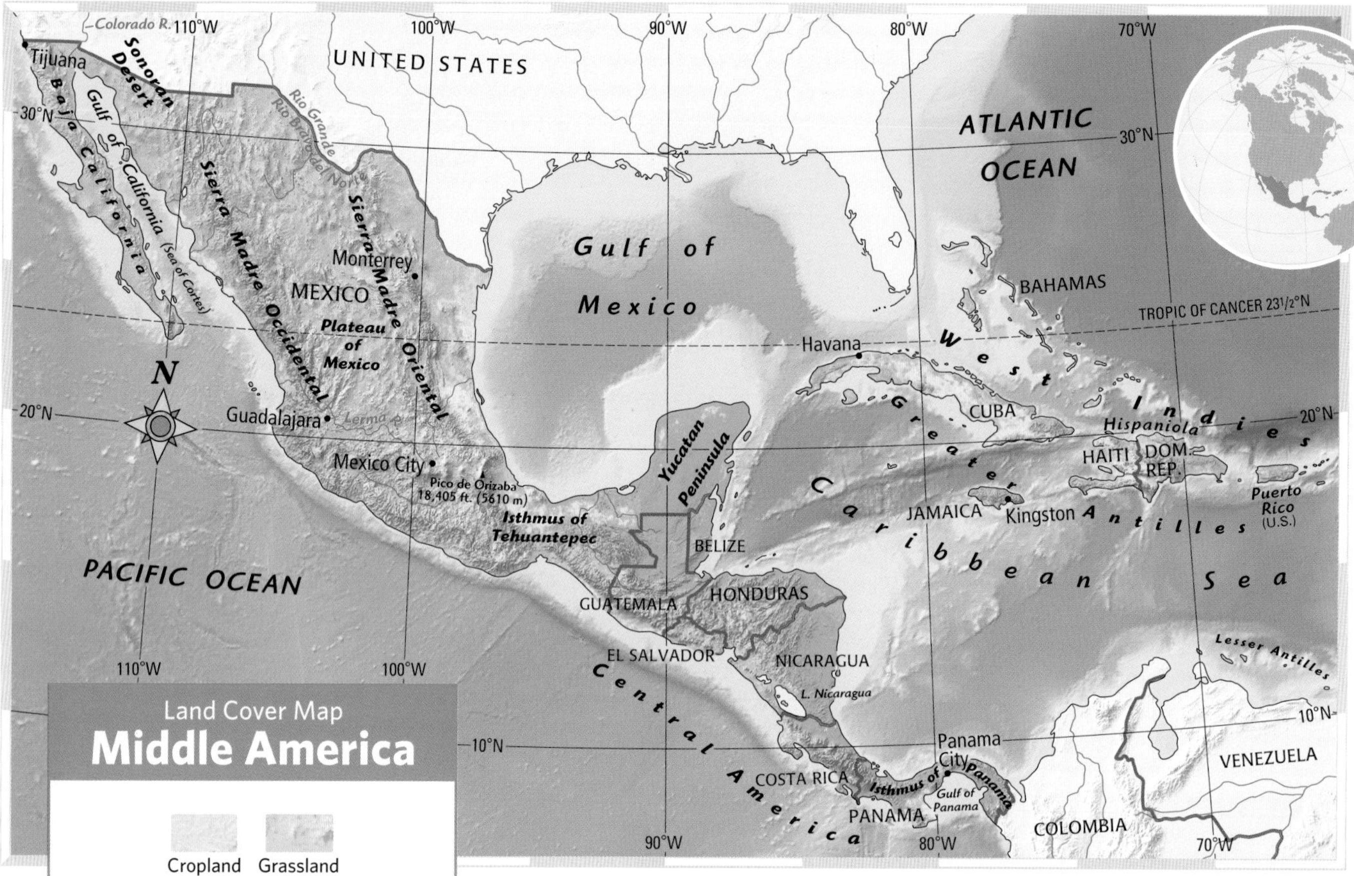

Colorado R. 110°W — 100°W — 90°W — 80°W — 70°W

Tijuana
Sonoran Desert
UNITED STATES
30°N
Gulf of California (Sea of Cortez)
Baja California
Rio Bravo del Norte / Rio Grande
ATLANTIC OCEAN
30°N
Gulf of Mexico
Sierra Madre Occidental
Monterrey
MEXICO
Sierra Madre Oriental
BAHAMAS
TROPIC OF CANCER 23½°N
Plateau of Mexico
Havana
CUBA
West Indies
N
20°N
Guadalajara
Lerma
Mexico City
Pico de Orizaba 18,405 ft. (5610 m)
Isthmus of Tehuantepec
Yucatan Peninsula
HAITI
DOM. REP.
Hispaniola
Puerto Rico (U.S.)
20°N
JAMAICA
Kingston
Greater Antilles
BELIZE
Caribbean Sea
PACIFIC OCEAN
110°W — 100°W
GUATEMALA
HONDURAS
Lesser Antilles
EL SALVADOR
NICARAGUA
L. Nicaragua
Central America
COSTA RICA
Panama City
Isthmus of Panama
Gulf of Panama
PANAMA
VENEZUELA
10°N
90°W
80°W
COLOMBIA
70°W

Land Cover Map
Middle America

Cropland	Grassland
Semi-desert & desert	Tropical rain forest	Broadleaf forest

Boundary Symbols
——— International boundary

Scale
1:28,000,000
0   150   300   450   600 miles
1 in. to 442 mi.
0   150   300   450   600 kilometers
1 cm to 280 km

Detailed legend on page 8   Albers Equal Area Projection

The Sonoran Desert is wetter than most deserts, receiving up to 15 inches (380 millimeters) of rain per year. Its summer rainy season sustains a variety of plants and animals.

Protected areas in Costa Rica account for approximately 25 percent of the country's land area, and ecotourism is a leading sector of Costa Rica's economy. Hanging bridges, like the one above, are used to protect the rain forest floors while tourists admire the landscape. (For more on tropical rain forests, see pages 34 and 129.)

Trickle Down

The Colorado River is the main river in the southwestern United States and northwestern Mexico. Much of the river's water is diverted to Los Angeles. Hydroelectric dams and irrigation for agriculture have also reduced the amount of water reaching the river's delta. Some years, the river never reaches its mouth at the Gulf of California.

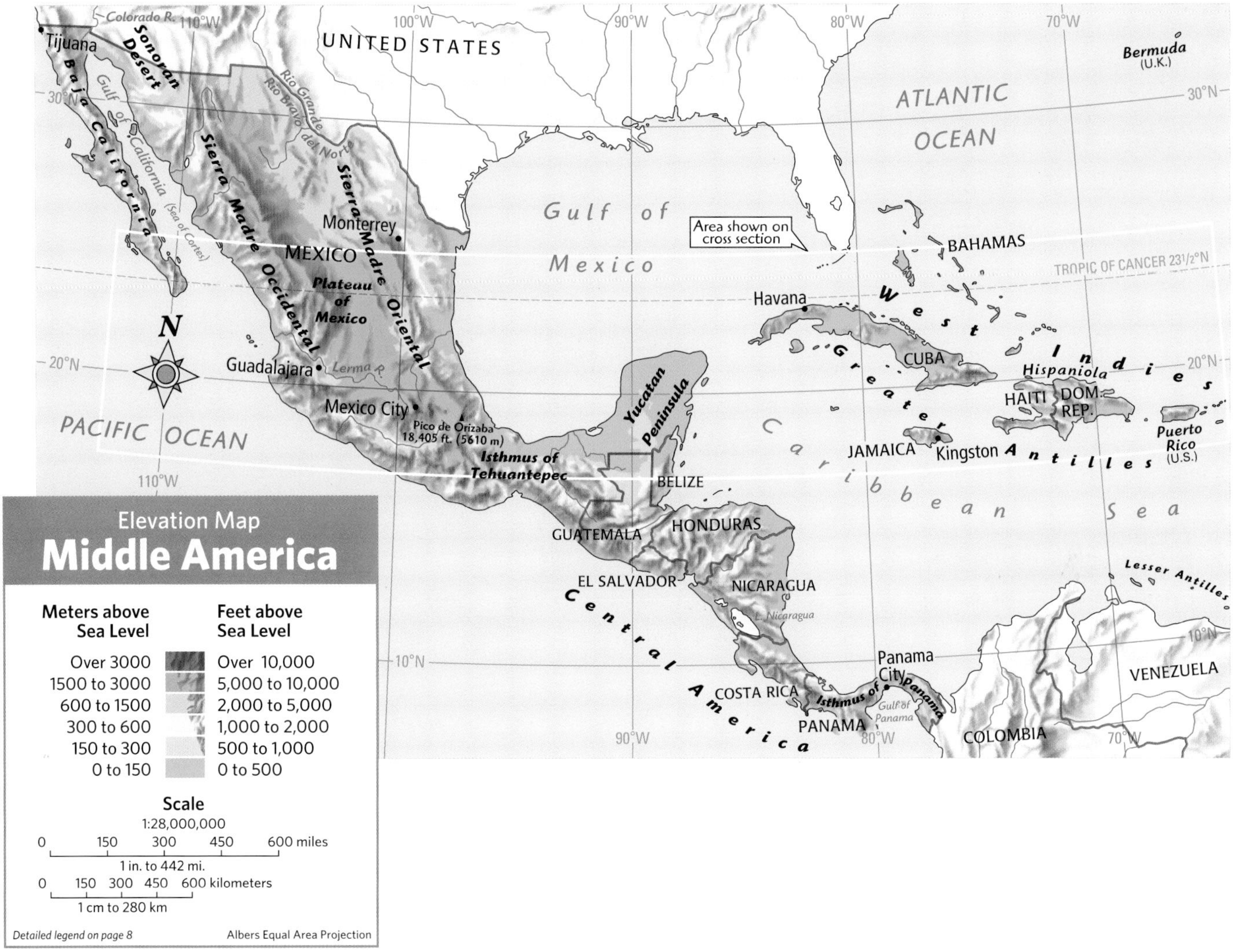
UNITED STATES
Colorado R.
Tijuana
Sonoran Desert
Baja California
Gulf of California (Sea of Cortez)
Rio Grande (Río Bravo del Norte)
Sierra Madre Occidental
Sierra Madre Oriental
Monterrey
MEXICO
Plateau of Mexico
Guadalajara
Lerma R.
Mexico City
Pico de Orizaba 18,405 ft. (5610 m)
Isthmus of Tehuantepec
Yucatan Peninsula
PACIFIC OCEAN
Gulf of Mexico
Area shown on cross section
ATLANTIC OCEAN
Bermuda (U.K.)
BAHAMAS
TROPIC OF CANCER 23½°N
Havana
CUBA
West Indies
Greater Antilles
Hispaniola
HAITI
DOM. REP.
Puerto Rico (U.S.)
JAMAICA
Kingston
Caribbean Sea
BELIZE
GUATEMALA
HONDURAS
EL SALVADOR
NICARAGUA
L. Nicaragua
Central America
COSTA RICA
PANAMA
Panama City
Isthmus of Panama
Gulf of Panama
Lesser Antilles
VENEZUELA
COLOMBIA
110°W
100°W
90°W
80°W
70°W
30°N
20°N
10°N
N
Elevation Map
Middle America
Meters above Sea Level
Feet above Sea Level
Over 3000
Over 10,000
1500 to 3000
5,000 to 10,000
600 to 1500
2,000 to 5,000
300 to 600
1,000 to 2,000
150 to 300
500 to 1,000
0 to 150
0 to 500
Scale
1:28,000,000
0 150 300 450 600 miles
1 in. to 442 mi.
0 150 300 450 600 kilometers
1 cm to 280 km
Detailed legend on page 8
Albers Equal Area Projection

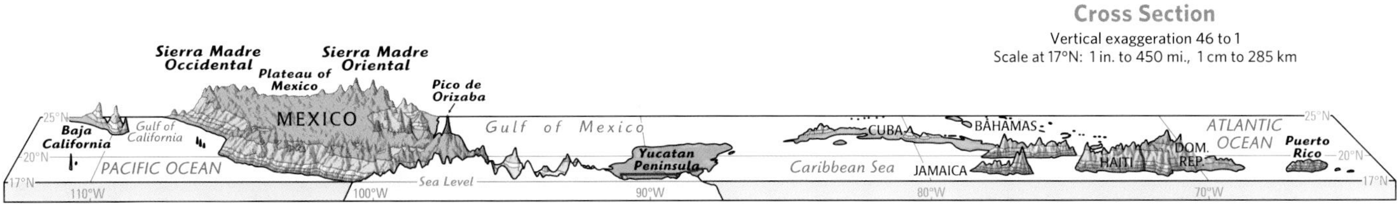
Cross Section
Vertical exaggeration 46 to 1
Scale at 17°N: 1 in. to 450 mi., 1 cm to 285 km
Sierra Madre Occidental
Plateau of Mexico
Sierra Madre Oriental
Pico de Orizaba
Baja California
Gulf of California
MEXICO
PACIFIC OCEAN
Gulf of Mexico
Yucatan Peninsula
Sea Level
CUBA
BAHAMAS
Caribbean Sea
JAMAICA
HAITI
DOM. REP.
ATLANTIC OCEAN
Puerto Rico
25°N
20°N
17°N
110°W
100°W
90°W
80°W
70°W

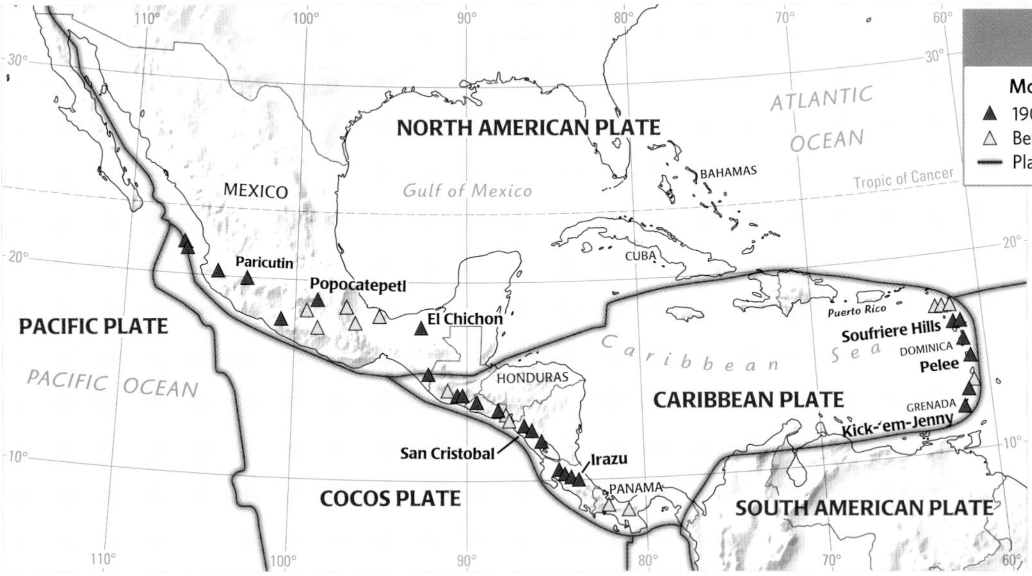
NORTH AMERICAN PLATE
MEXICO
Gulf of Mexico
ATLANTIC OCEAN
BAHAMAS
Tropic of Cancer
CUBA
Paricutin
Popocatepetl
El Chichon
PACIFIC PLATE
PACIFIC OCEAN
HONDURAS
Caribbean Sea
Puerto Rico
Soufriere Hills
DOMINICA
Pelee
CARIBBEAN PLATE
GRENADA
Kick-'em-Jenny
San Cristobal
Irazu
PANAMA
COCOS PLATE
SOUTH AMERICAN PLATE

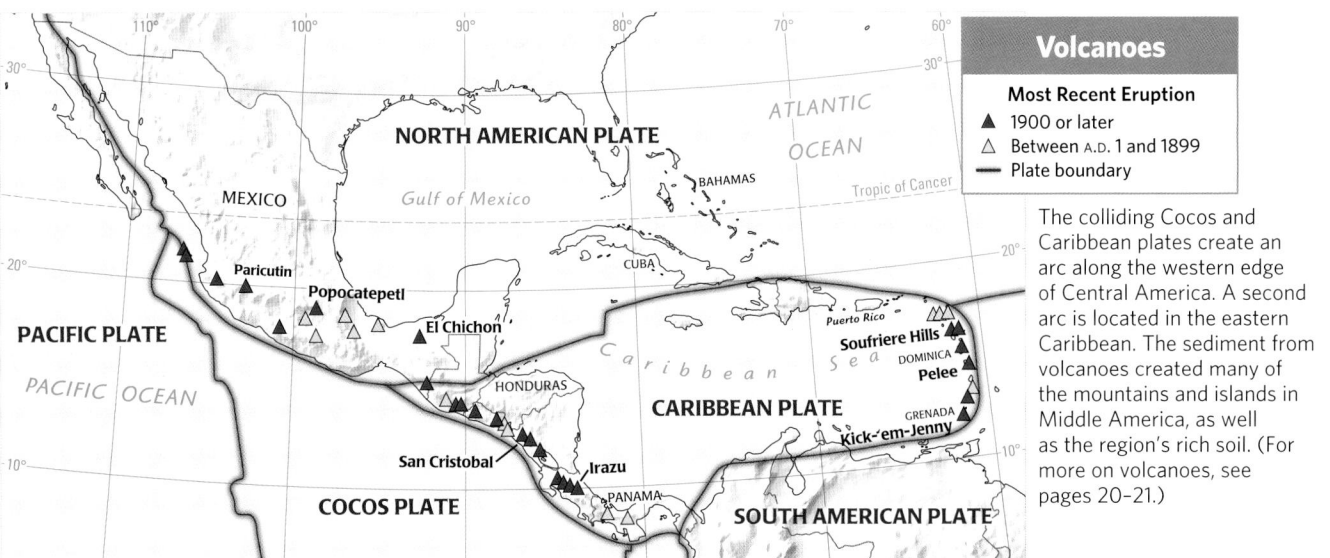

Volcanoes

Most Recent Eruption

- ▲ 1900 or later
- △ Between A.D. 1 and 1899
- — Plate boundary

The colliding Cocos and Caribbean plates create an arc along the western edge of Central America. A second arc is located in the eastern Caribbean. The sediment from volcanoes created many of the mountains and islands in Middle America, as well as the region's rich soil. (For more on volcanoes, see pages 20–21.)

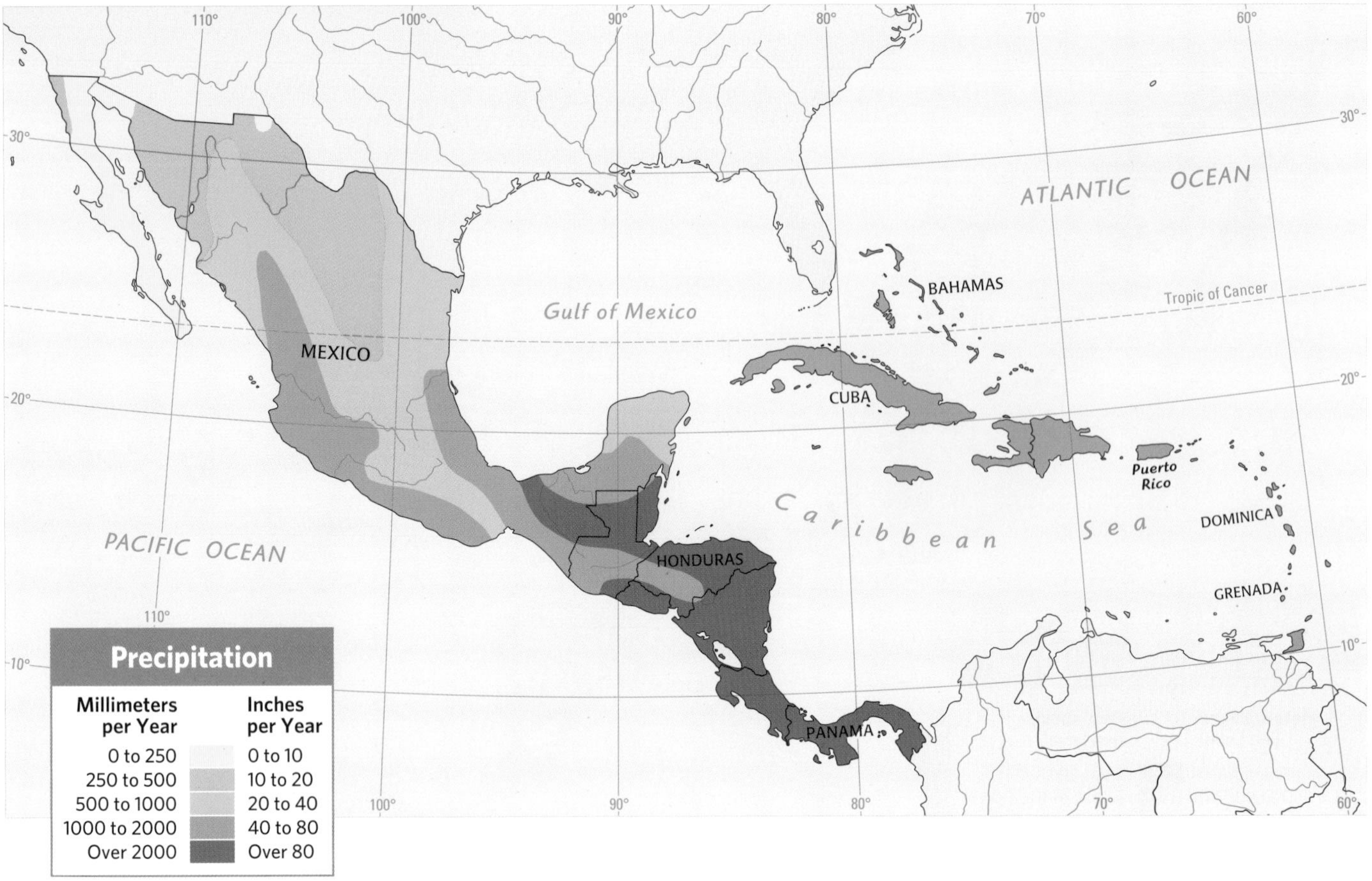

Precipitation
Millimeters per Year
Inches per Year
0 to 250 | 0 to 10
250 to 500 | 10 to 20
500 to 1000 | 20 to 40
1000 to 2000 | 40 to 80
Over 2000 | Over 80
ATLANTIC OCEAN
Gulf of Mexico
PACIFIC OCEAN
Caribbean Sea
Tropic of Cancer
MEXICO
BAHAMAS
CUBA
Puerto Rico
DOMINICA
GRENADA
HONDURAS
PANAMA
110°
100°
90°
80°
70°
60°
30°
20°
10°

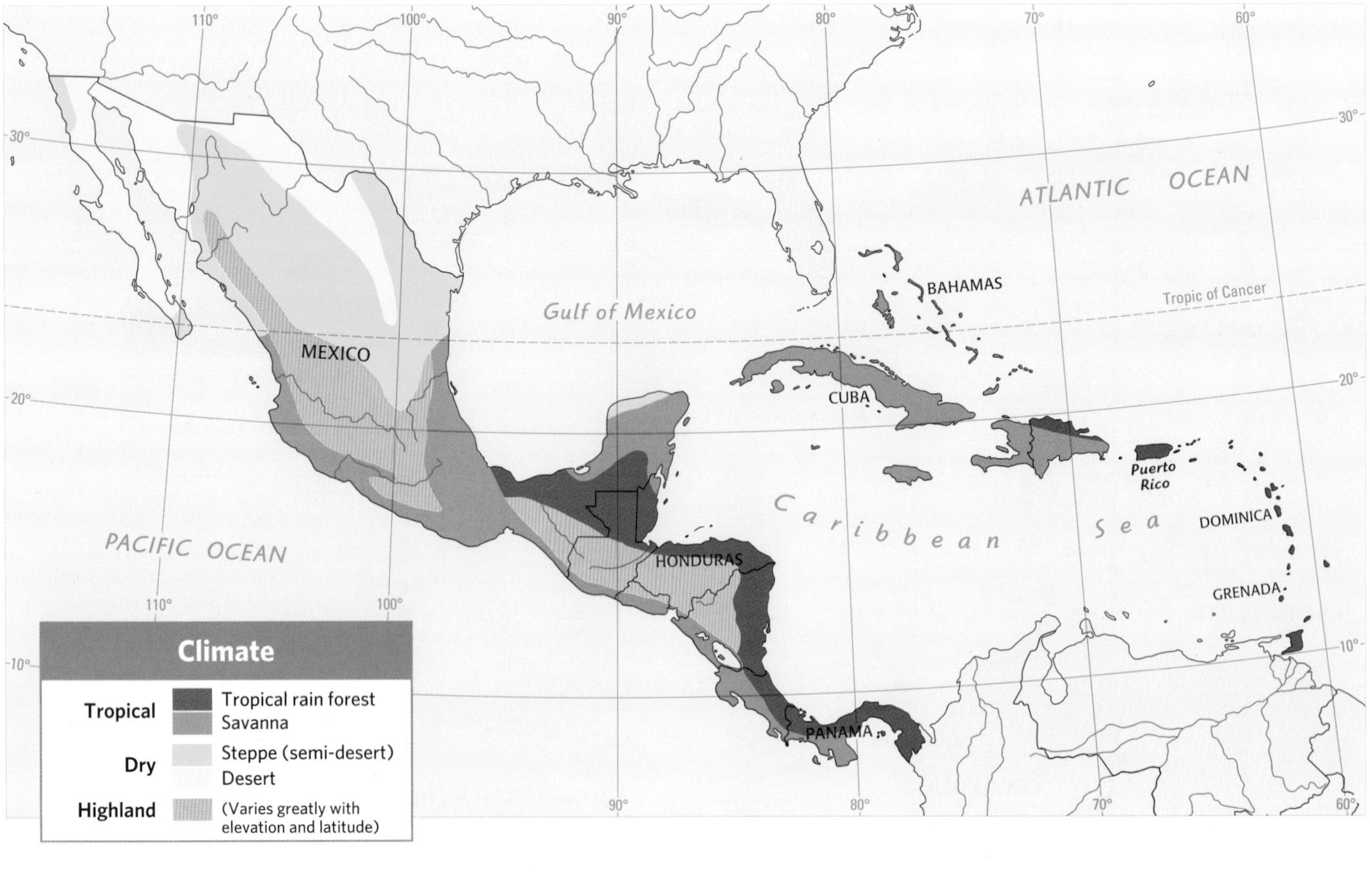

Climate
Tropical
Tropical rain forest
Savanna
Dry
Steppe (semi-desert)
Desert
Highland
(Varies greatly with elevation and latitude)
ATLANTIC OCEAN
Gulf of Mexico
PACIFIC OCEAN
Caribbean Sea
Tropic of Cancer
MEXICO
BAHAMAS
CUBA
Puerto Rico
DOMINICA
GRENADA
HONDURAS
PANAMA
110°
100°
90°
80°
70°
60°
30°
20°
10°

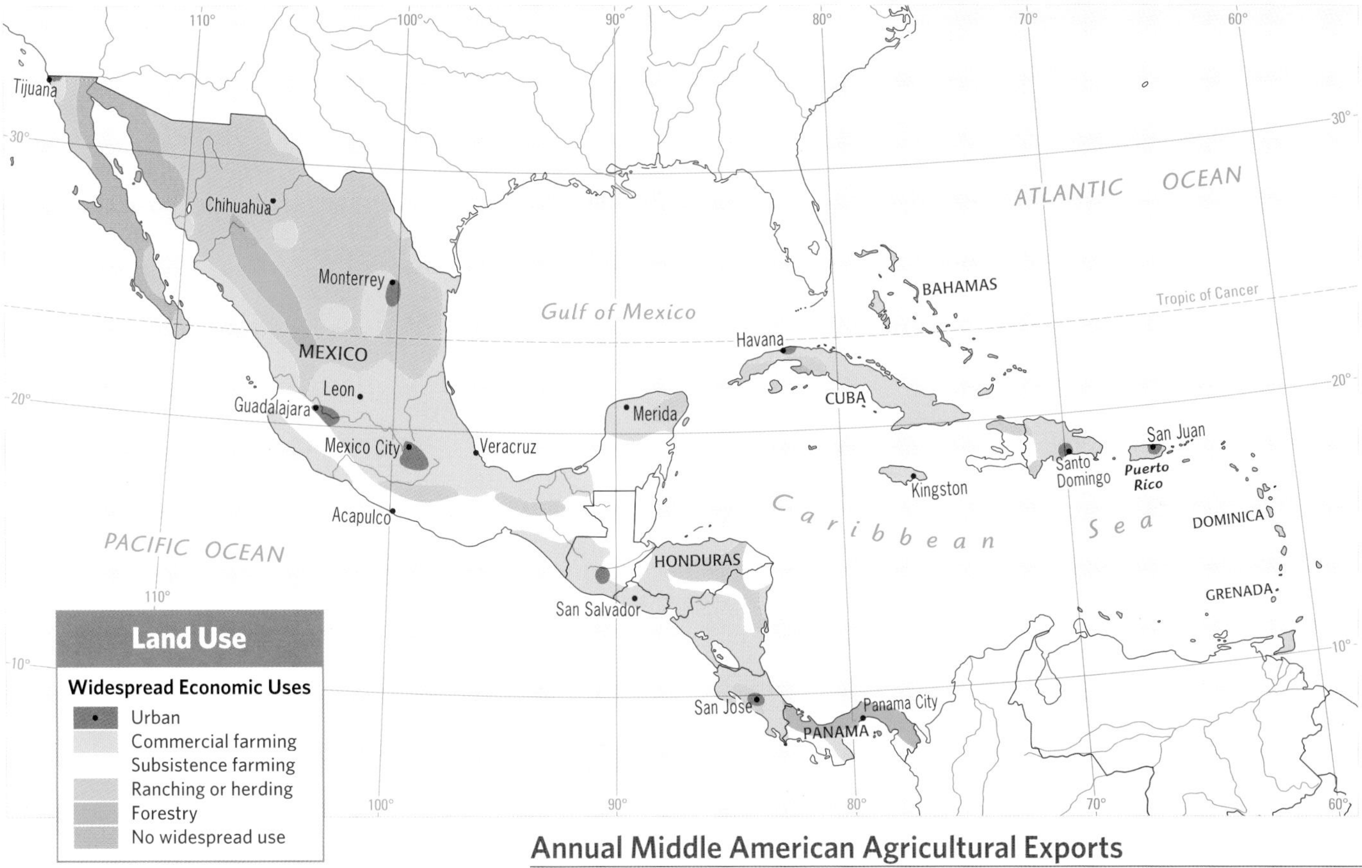

Land Use

Widespread Economic Uses
- Urban
- Commercial farming
- Subsistence farming
- Ranching or herding
- Forestry
- No widespread use

From Bananas to Beaches

Middle American countries were once called **banana republics** because of their heavy reliance on one major export, such as bananas or coffee. Large landowners and foreign fruit companies dominated both politics and the economy. Now tourism provides much of the economic growth for this region. About 75 percent of the GDP in the Bahamas is from tourism.

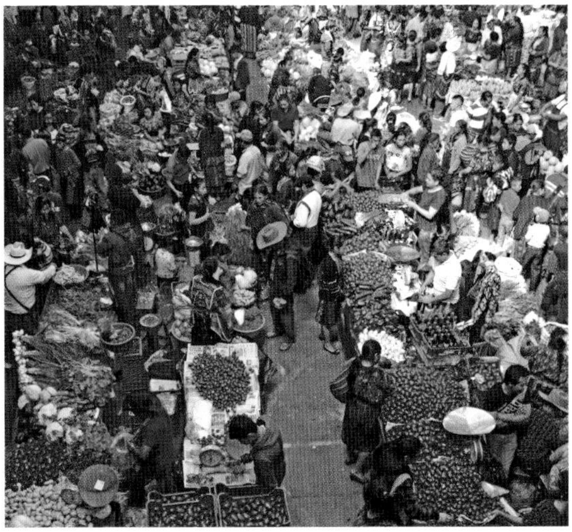

Many Caribbean farmers sell fresh produce, such as plantains, mangoes, and coconuts, at open-air markets like this one in Guatemala.

Annual Middle American Agricultural Exports

Agriculture remains important to Middle America. Fruit and sugarcane are key exports for Mexico and Guatemala. Costa Rica exports approximately 2 million tons of bananas to the United States and other countries each year.

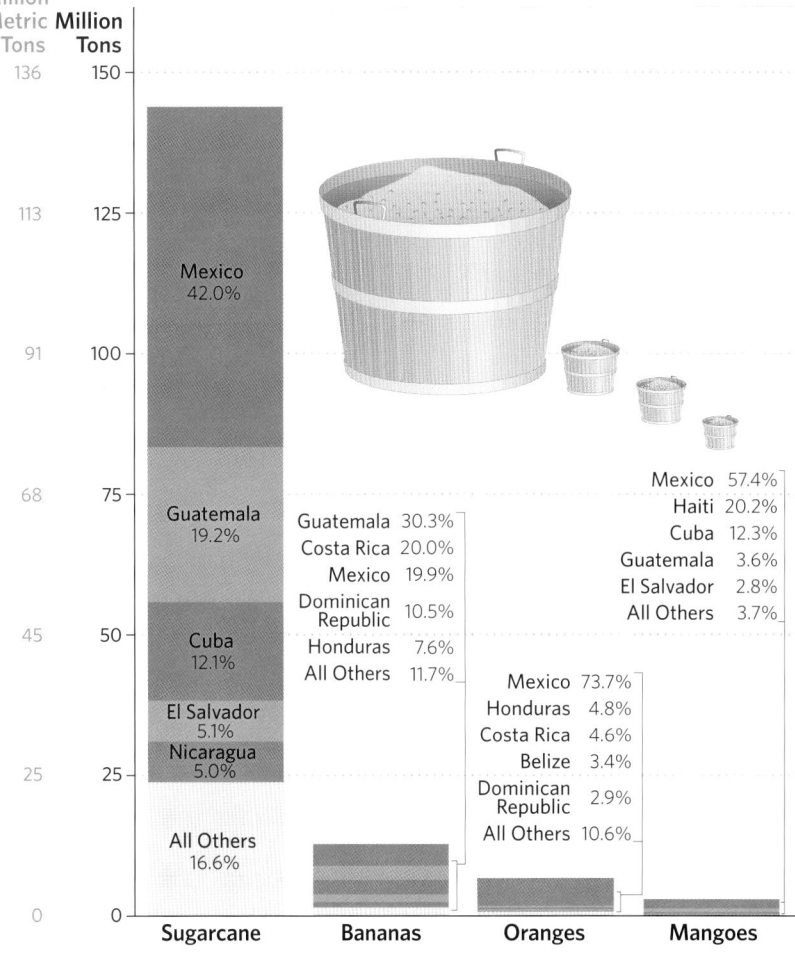

Sugarcane
- Mexico 42.0%
- Guatemala 19.2%
- Cuba 12.1%
- El Salvador 5.1%
- Nicaragua 5.0%
- All Others 16.6%

Bananas
- Guatemala 30.3%
- Costa Rica 20.0%
- Mexico 19.9%
- Dominican Republic 10.5%
- Honduras 7.6%
- All Others 11.7%

Oranges
- Mexico 73.7%
- Honduras 4.8%
- Costa Rica 4.6%
- Belize 3.4%
- Dominican Republic 2.9%
- All Others 10.6%

Mangoes
- Mexico 57.4%
- Haiti 20.2%
- Cuba 12.3%
- Guatemala 3.6%
- El Salvador 2.8%
- All Others 3.7%

Million Metric Tons / Million Tons
136 / 150
113 / 125
91 / 100
68 / 75
45 / 50
/ 25
0 / 0

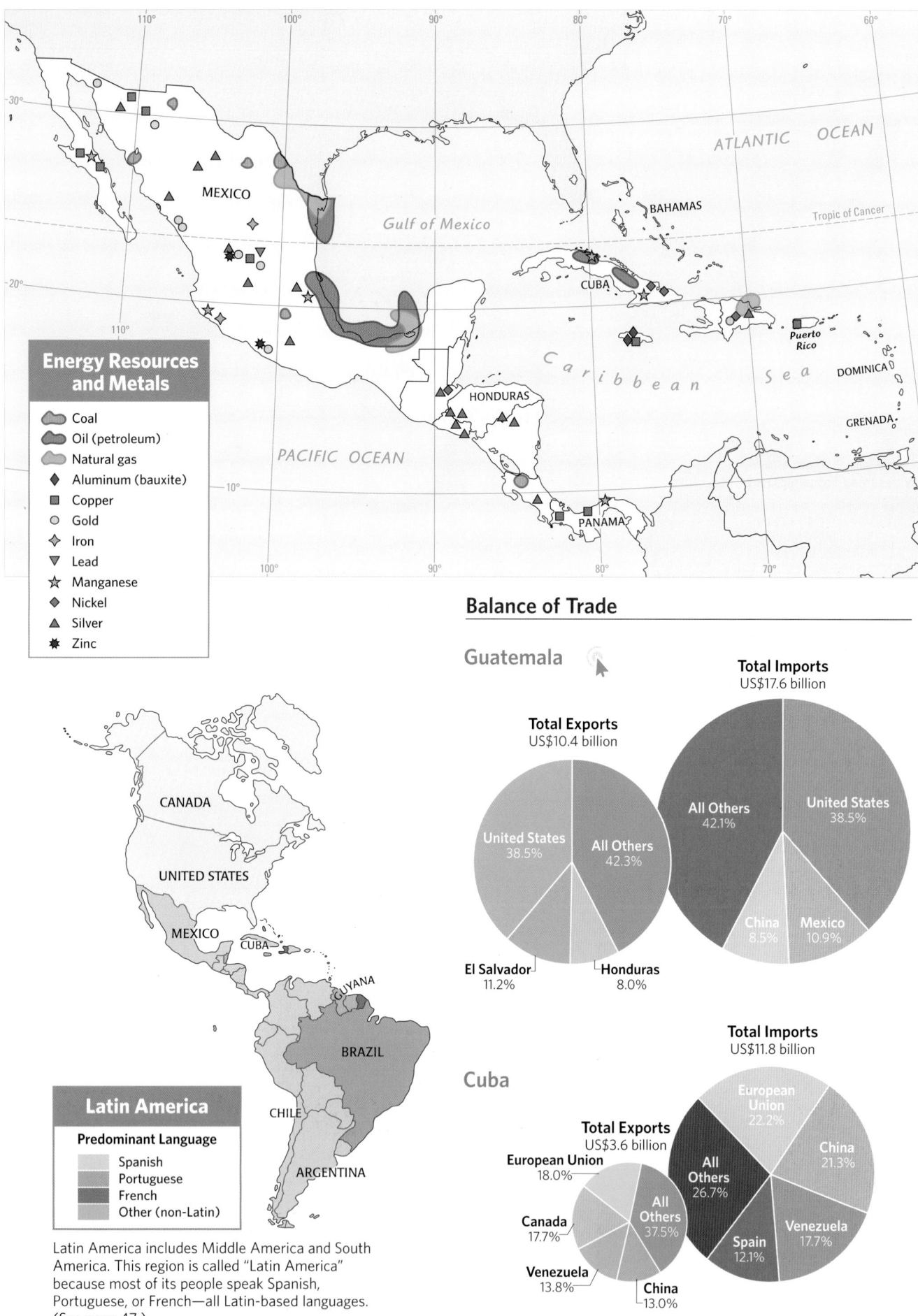

Energy Resources and Metals

- Coal
- Oil (petroleum)
- Natural gas
- ◆ Aluminum (bauxite)
- ■ Copper
- ○ Gold
- ✦ Iron
- ▽ Lead
- ☆ Manganese
- ◆ Nickel
- ▲ Silver
- ✴ Zinc

Latin America

Predominant Language
- Spanish
- Portuguese
- French
- Other (non-Latin)

Latin America includes Middle America and South America. This region is called "Latin America" because most of its people speak Spanish, Portuguese, or French—all Latin-based languages. (See page 47.)

Balance of Trade

Guatemala

Total Exports
US$10.4 billion

- United States 38.5%
- All Others 42.3%
- El Salvador 11.2%
- Honduras 8.0%

Total Imports
US$17.6 billion

- All Others 42.1%
- United States 38.5%
- China 8.5%
- Mexico 10.9%

Cuba

Total Exports
US$3.6 billion

- European Union 18.0%
- Canada 17.7%
- All Others 37.5%
- Venezuela 13.8%
- China 13.0%

Total Imports
US$11.8 billion

- European Union 22.2%
- China 21.3%
- All Others 26.7%
- Venezuela 17.7%
- Spain 12.1%

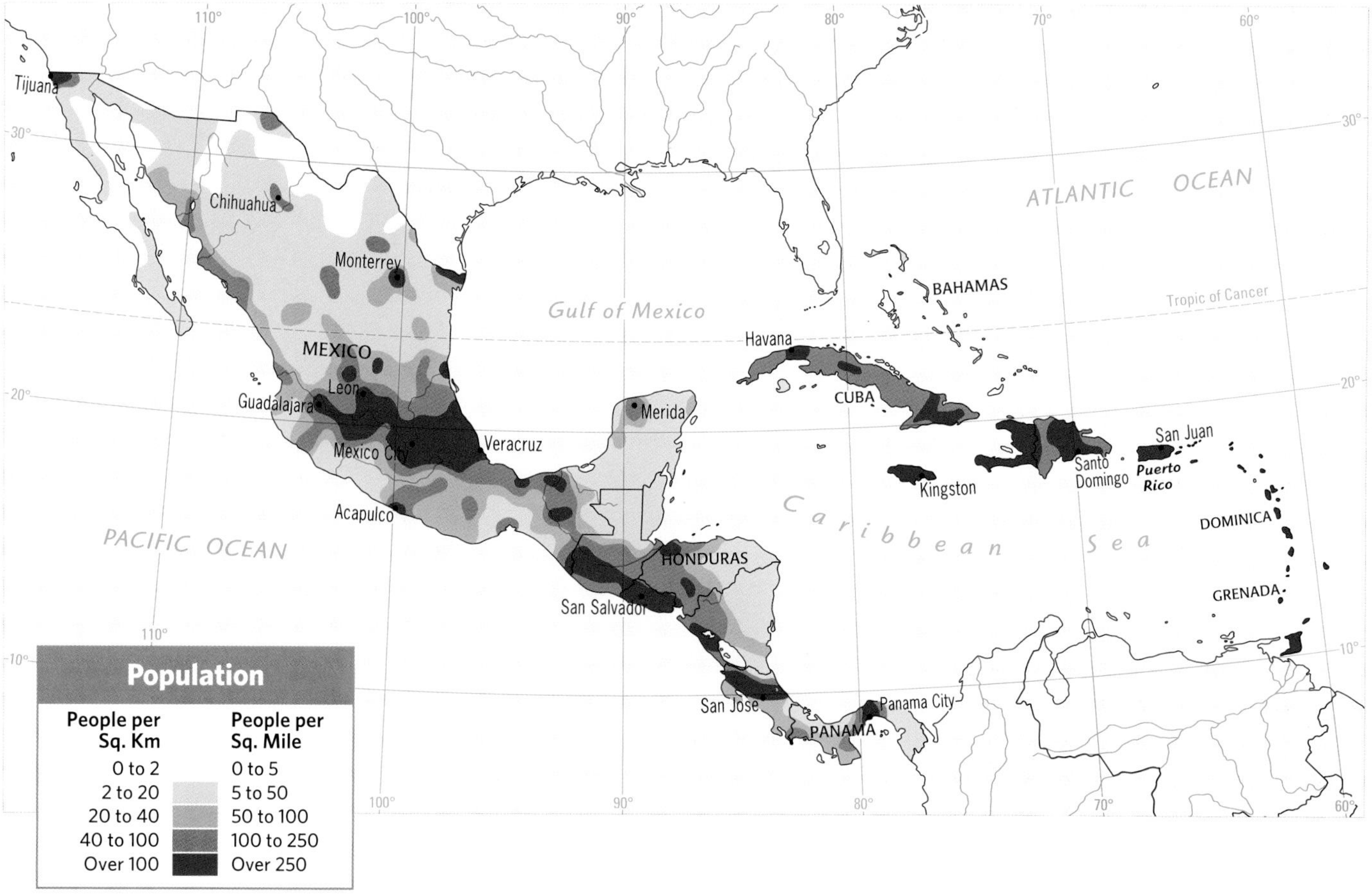

Population

People per Sq. Km	People per Sq. Mile
0 to 2	0 to 5
2 to 20	5 to 50
20 to 40	50 to 100
40 to 100	100 to 250
Over 100	Over 250

The Caribbean Difference

Indigenous West Indians did not survive contact with Europeans. Plantation owners replaced them with African slaves. As a result, the Caribbean is very different from the rest of Middle America. Most West Indians today have African ancestors and many speak French, English, Dutch, or local dialects called patois or creole. In contrast, most people in Mexico and Central America have indigenous ancestors and speak Spanish.

Regional Maps of Middle America

1 **Mexico** p.114

2 **Central America** p.115

3 **Cuba and Its Neighbors** p.116

4 **Puerto Rico and the Lesser Antilles** p.116

Continues on pages 74-75

Los Angeles
San Diego
Tijuana
Ensenada
Mexicali
San Luis Rio Colorado
BAJA CALIFORNIA
Salton Sea
Salada Lagoon
Phoenix
Tucson
Nogales
El Paso
Juarez

NORTH AMERICA
UNITED STATES
Fort Worth
Dallas
Atlanta

Austin
Houston
San Antonio
New Orleans

Gulf Coastal Plain

Gulf of Mexico

Guadalupe I.
Angel de la Guarda I.
Sebastian Vizcaino Bay
Cedros I.
Tiburon I.
SONORA
Hermosillo
Ciudad Obregon
CHIHUAHUA
Chihuahua
Ciudad Acuna
Piedras Negras
COAHUILA
Monclova
Nuevo Laredo
Reynosa
Matamoros

BAJA CALIFORNIA SUR

Gulf of California (Sea of Cortes)

Sierra Madre Occidental

Los Mochis
Gomez Palacio
Lerdo
Torreon
DURANGO
NUEVO LEON
Guadalupe
Monterrey
Saltillo
TAMAULIPAS
Ciudad Victoria

La Paz
Culiacan
SINALOA
Plateau of Mexico
Durango
ZACATECAS
Zacatecas
SAN LUIS POTOSI
Ciudad Madero
Tampico

TROPIC OF CANCER 23½°N
Cape San Lucas
Mazatlan

PACIFIC OCEAN

Tres Marias Is.
NAYARIT
Tepic
Aguascalientes ①
Leon
Irapuato
Zapopan
Guadalajara
Tlaquepaque
JALISCO
Colima
COLIMA
MICHOACAN

San Luis Potosi
Guanajuato ②
Queretaro ③
Pachuca ④
Morelia
Toluca ⑦ ⑥ ⑤
Mexico City
Cuernavaca ⑧
⑨
Puebla
Tehuacan
GUERRERO
Chilpancingo
Acapulco
Oaxaca
OAXACA

Nezahualcoyotl
VERACRUZ
Jalapa
Tlaxcala
Veracruz
Coatzacoalcos
Minatitlan ⑩
Tuxtla Gutierrez
CHIAPAS

Merida
YUCATAN
Cancun
Cozumel I.
Yucatan Peninsula
Campeche
Bay of Campeche
Ciudad del Carmen
CAMPECHE
Villahermosa
San Cristobal de las Casas

QUINTANA ROO
Chetumal
Chetumal Bay

Belmopan
BELIZE
Gulf of Honduras
Bay Is.

Gulf of Tehuantepec
GUATEMALA
Tapachula
Guatemala City
San Salvador
EL SALVADOR

HONDURAS
Tegucigalpa

NICARAGUA
Managua

N

Colorado R.
Rio Grande / Rio Bravo del Norte
Mississippi River
Sonoran Desert
Chihuahuan Desert
Sierra Madre Oriental

TROPIC OF CANCER 23½°N

Continues on page 115

Political Relief Map
Mexico

Boundary Symbols
━━━━━ International boundary
·············· State boundary

City Symbols
Leon ● Over 1,000,000 people
Guadalupe ● 500,000 to 1,000,000
Nogales • Under 500,000
Mexico City ⊗ National capital
Villahermosa ★ State capital

Scale
1:17,700,000
0   125   250   375   500 miles
1 in. to 280 mi.
0   125   250   375   500 kilometers
1 cm to 177 km

Detailed legend on page 8   Albers Equal Area Projection

Mexican States Not Named Above
① AGUASCALIENTES ⑥ FEDERAL DISTRICT
② GUANAJUATO ⑦ MEXICO
③ QUERETARO ⑧ MORELOS
④ HIDALGO ⑨ PUEBLA
⑤ TLAXCALA ⑩ TABASCO

A *quinceañera* is a traditional celebration for 15-year-old girls in Mexico and other Latin American countries, marking their passage into womanhood. The day of the *quinceañera* often begins with a mass and concludes with a formal dinner and dance.

Mexico Area Comparison

■ **Mexico**
758,449 sq. mi.
(1,964,375 sq. km)

Contiguous United States
3,021,295 sq. mi.
(7,825,112 sq. km)

Panama Canal

The Panama Canal is vital to world trade, providing a relatively inexpensive passageway between the Atlantic and Pacific Oceans. Vessels save thousands of miles by traveling through the canal, rather than sailing around South America.

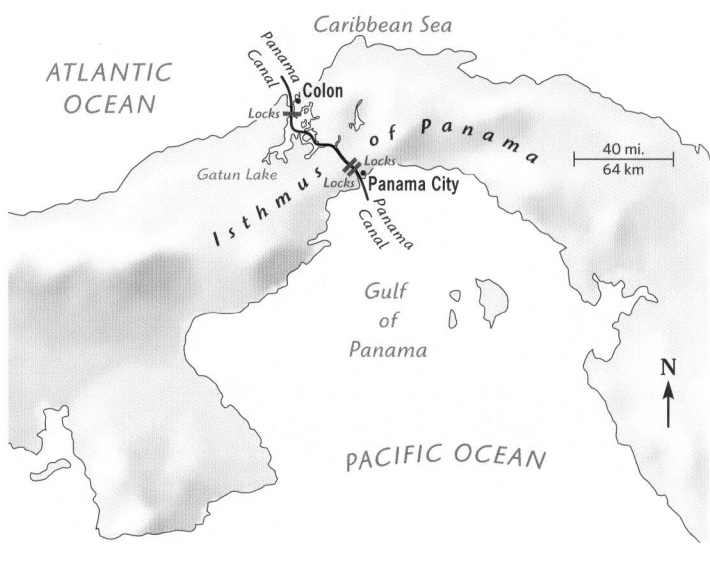

Political Relief Map
Central America

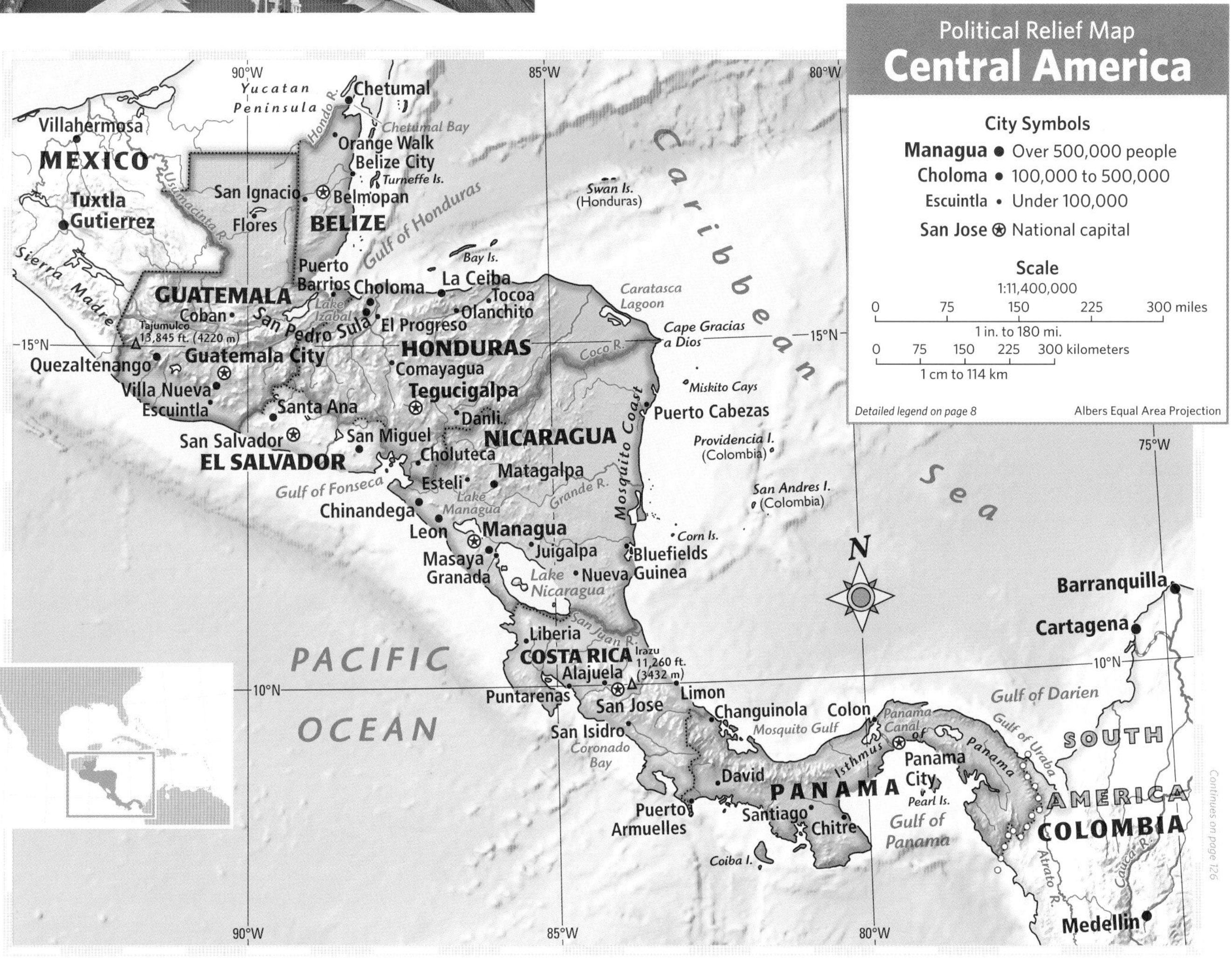

City Symbols

Managua ●	Over 500,000 people
Choloma ●	100,000 to 500,000
Escuintla •	Under 100,000
San Jose ⊛	National capital

Scale

1:11,400,000

0	75	150	225	300 miles

1 in. to 180 mi.

0	75	150	225	300 kilometers

1 cm to 114 km

Detailed legend on page 8   Albers Equal Area Projection

Continues on page 114

Continues on page 126

Continues on page 92-93

Political Relief Map
Cuba and Its Neighbors

City Symbols
Havana ● Over 500,000 people
Port-de-Paix ● 100,000 to 500,000
Punta Cana · Under 100,000
Kingston ⊛ National capital

Scale
1:9,850,000

0　75　150　225 miles
1 in. to 155 mi.

0　75　150　225 kilometers
1 cm to 98 km

Detailed legend on page 8　Albers Equal Area Projection

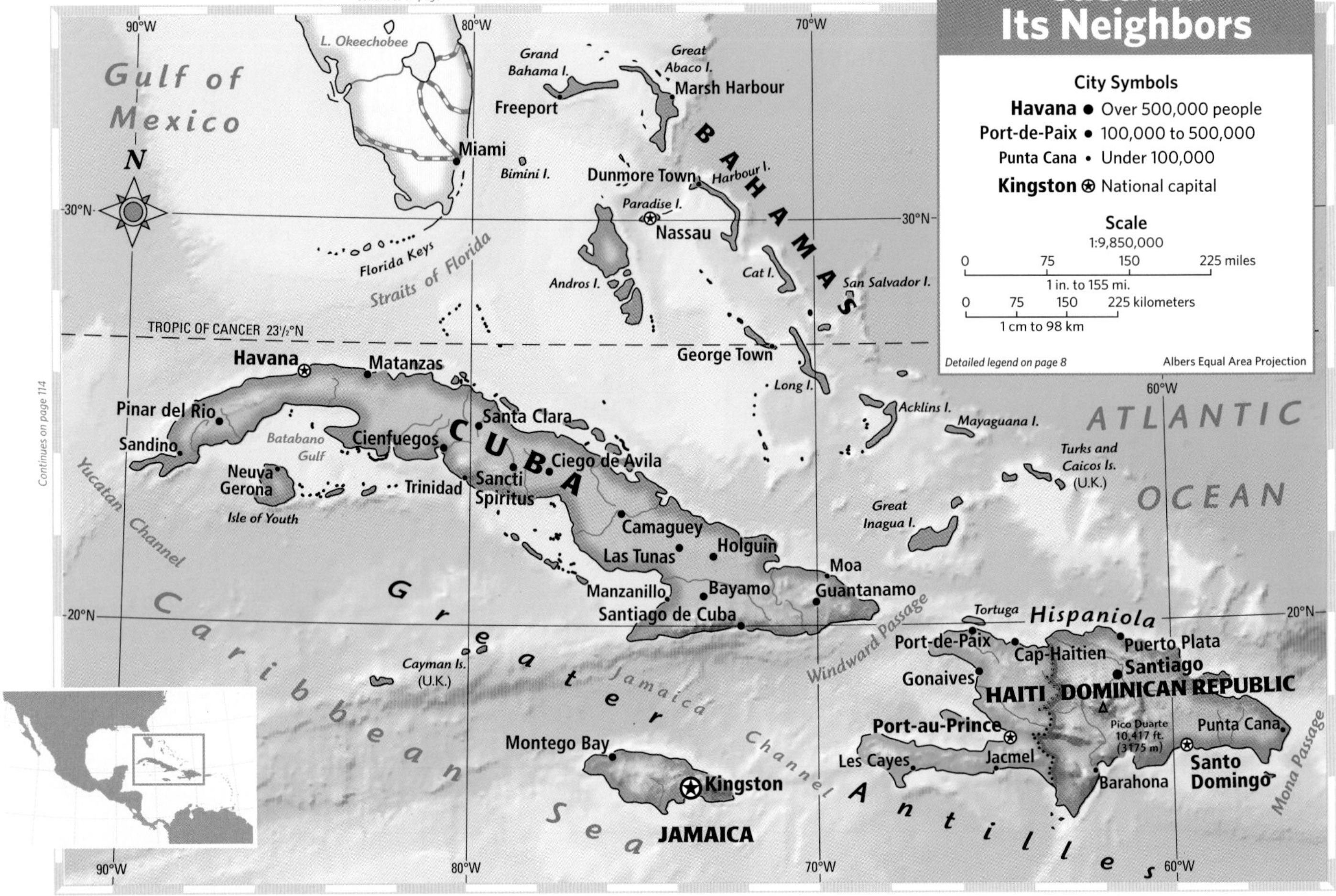

Gulf of Mexico

L. Okeechobee

Continues on page 114

Grand Bahama I.
Great Abaco I.
Marsh Harbour
Freeport
Miami
Bimini I.
Dunmore Town
Harbour I.
Paradise I.
Nassau
BAHAMAS
Florida Keys
Straits of Florida
TROPIC OF CANCER 23½°N
Andros I.
Cat I.
San Salvador I.
George Town
Long I.
Acklins I.
Mayaguana I.

Havana
Matanzas
Pinar del Rio
Santa Clara
Sandino
Batabano Gulf
Cienfuegos
CUBA
Neuva Gerona
Trinidad
Sancti Spiritus
Ciego de Avila
Isle of Youth
Camaguey
Holguin
Las Tunas
Manzanillo
Bayamo
Moa
Santiago de Cuba
Guantanamo

Yucatan Channel

Caribbean Sea

Greater Antilles

Cayman Is. (U.K.)

Jamaica Channel

Montego Bay
Kingston
JAMAICA

ATLANTIC OCEAN

Turks and Caicos Is. (U.K.)
Great Inagua I.
Tortuga
Hispaniola
Port-de-Paix
Cap-Haitien
Puerto Plata
Gonaives
Santiago
HAITI
DOMINICAN REPUBLIC
Windward Passage
Port-au-Prince
Pico Duarte 10,417 ft. (3175 m)
Punta Cana
Les Cayes
Jacmel
Barahona
Santo Domingo
Mona Passage

Continues on page 126

Not Quite Equal

Puerto Rico is a self-governing commonwealth of the United States. Puerto Ricans are U.S. citizens and are subject to most federal laws. Puerto Rico has its own constitution, elects its own governor, and handles its own local affairs like a state. However, Puerto Ricans cannot vote in presidential or congressional elections and do not pay federal taxes.

Political Relief Map
Puerto Rico and the Lesser Antilles

City Symbols
San Juan ● Over 100,000 people
Oranjestad ● 25,000 to 100,000
Basse-Terre · Under 25,000
Roseau ⊛ National capital

Scale
1:12,600,000

0　75　150　225　300 miles
1 in. to 199 mi.

0　75　150　225　300 kilometers
1 cm to 126 km

Detailed legend on page 8　Albers Equal Area Projection

Continues on pages 106-107

ATLANTIC OCEAN
Charlotte Amalie
San Juan
Mayaguez
Mona Passage
Ponce
Mona I.
Puerto Rico (U.S.)
Virgin Is. (U.S.)
St. Croix (U.S.)
Christiansted
Anguilla (U.K.)
St. Martin (France-Neth.)
St. Barthelemy (France)
Anegada Passage
Leeward Islands
ANTIGUA & BARBUDA
Basseterre
ST. KITTS NEVIS
St. John's
Montserrat (U.K.)
Guadeloupe (France)
Basse-Terre
Marie Galante (France)
Aves I. (Ven.)
DOMINICA
Roseau
Caribbean Sea
Mont Pelee 4,583 ft. (1397 m)
Martinique (France)
Fort-de-France
Castries
ST. LUCIA
BARBADOS
Kingstown
ST. VINCENT & THE GRENADINES
Bridgetown
Lesser Antilles
Windward Islands
GRENADA
St. George's
Oranjestad
Aruba (Neth.)
Curacao (Neth.)
Bonaire (Neth.)
Los Roques (Ven.)
Blanquilla I. (Ven.)
Paraguana Peninsula
Willemstad
Orchila I. (Ven.)
TRINIDAD & TOBAGO
Tobago
Margarita I. (Ven.)
Porlamar
Caracas
Tortuga I. (Ven.)
Port-of-Spain
Trinidad
San Fernando
VENEZUELA
SOUTH AMERICA

Continues on page 126

ISSUES / TODAY

Yukateko
(Maya)

MEXICO
Tzotzil   *Tzeltal*   BELIZE
GUATEMALA
Q'eqche
Mam   K'iche   HONDURAS
(Maya)   Kaqchikel
Lenca   *Miskito*
Nahua
EL SALVADOR   NICARAGUA

**Indigenous People of
Tropical North America**

▨ Mainly indigenous population

Mam Large indigenous group today

COSTA RICA

Ngöbe

PANAMA

What rights do indigenous people have?

By the mid-1500s, most of Middle America had fallen under Spanish rule. Agreements between the Spanish king and natives guaranteed indigenous groups ownership of their ancestral lands. Most of these agreements have been ignored. Should indigenous people own this land? There are many perspectives on this issue. Here are two of them.

Indigenous people are entitled to their ancestral land.

- Indigenous people of the past were exploited by colonizing powers. They have a legal claim to ancestral lands that were guaranteed to them in treaties or other binding agreements with Spain and their successor governments.

- Indigenous communities consider their land to be sacred. The dispossession of land would lead to the extinction of indigenous communities, their cultures, and their traditions.

- Indigenous knowledge of plants and their medicinal properties, sustainable agriculture practices, land conservation, and other expertise would disappear along with the people.

- The traditional economy of indigenous people is less destructive to the environment and to natural resources than that of the commercial economy. Giving indigenous people land rights contributes to the preservation of biodiversity and natural resources.

It is impractical to enforce indigenous claims.

- It would be nearly impossible to examine and interpret hundreds of years' worth of incomplete historical documents to determine who has rightful ownership of the land.

- The original treaties were feudal and assumed that all land belonged to the king. Adapting these treaties to modern property laws, which focus on individuals, is almost impossible.

- Few people today live a traditional indigenous lifestyle. However, most people in Central America have descended, at least partly, from indigenous groups. Deciding who receives "ancestral" land would create new conflicts.

- Current landowners should not be punished by having land taken from them for crimes that may or may not have been committed by their ancestors.

Ethnic Composition Guatemala

All Others 0.7%

Mestizo
(European/
Amerindian)
60.0%

Amerindian
(including K'iche
Mayan, Kaqchikel
Mayan, Mam Mayan,
Q'eqchi Mayan)
39.3%

Mestizos in Central America are the result of intermarriage between indigenous people and the Spanish long ago. Over 90 percent of the people in Guatemala, Honduras, and Belize have indigenous ancestry.

For indigenous people, ancestral land represents ties to their ancestors, tradition, and language.

World Extreme: Because of its location along the equatorial buldge, the summit of Mt. Chimborazo in Ecuador—20,702 ft. (6,310 m) above sea level—is the farthest place on the Earth's surface from the Earth's center.

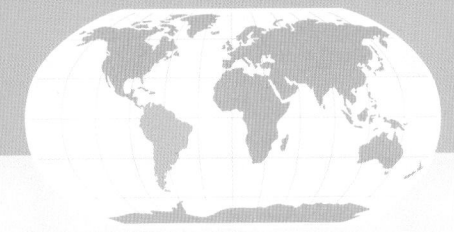

South America

South America is known for its lively and diverse cities, the towering Andes Mountains, and the Amazon rain forest—the largest rain forest in the world.

Physical Features

Highest mountain peak
Aconcagua 22,831 ft. (6,959 m)

Longest mountain range
Andes Mountains 4,500 mi. (7,200 km)

Largest island
Tierra del Fuego 19,280 sq. mi. (49,935 sq. km)

Largest lake
Lake Maracaibo 5,217 sq. mi. (13,412 sq. km)

Highest large lake
Lake Titicaca elev. 12,507 ft. (3,812 km)

Longest rivers
Amazon 4,000 mi. (6,437 km)★
Parana 3,032 mi. (4,880 km)

Other key physical features
Amazon Basin
Brazilian Highlands
Guiana Highlands
Pampas
Patagonia

Cultural Features

Population
420,458,000

Largest countries by area
Brazil 3,287,612 sq. mi. (8,514,877 sq. km)★
Argentina 1,073,400 sq. mi.
(2,780,092 sq. km)★

Largest country by population
Brazil 207,353,391

Most densely populated
Ecuador 164.6 people per sq. mi.
(63.5 per sq. km)

Least densely populated
French Guiana 8.0 people per sq. mi.
(3.1 per sq. km)

Largest urban areas
Sao Paulo, Brazil 21,066,000★
Buenos Aires, Argentina 15,180,000★
Rio de Janeiro, Brazil 12,902,000★

★ Among the world's largest. See the inside front cover.

Area Comparison

South America
6,876,395 sq. mi.
(17,809,780 sq. km)

Contiguous United States
3,021,295 sq. mi.
(7,825,112 sq. km)

Regional Maps of South America

1 Northwestern South America p. 126
2 Southern South America p. 126
3 Brazil and Its Neighbors p. 127

Thematic Maps of South America

Precipitation p. 123
Climate p. 123
Land Use p. 124
Energy Resources and Metals p. 124
Population p. 125
Descendants of Indigenous South Americans p. 125

NORTH
AMERICA

Caribbean Sea

Havana ⊗
CUBA
MEXICO
BELIZE
GUATEMALA
HONDURAS
EL SALVADOR
NICARAGUA
Lake Nicaragua
COSTA RICA
PANAMA
Panama Canal

HAITI DOM. REP.
JAMAICA
Puerto Rico (U.S.)
Anguilla (U.K.)
ST. KITTS NEVIS
ANTIGUA BARBUDA
Guadeloupe (Fr.)
DOMINICA
Martinique (Fr.)
ST. LUCIA
Curacao (Neth.)
ST. VINCENT THE GRENADINES
BARBADOS
GRENADA
TRINIDAD TOBAGO

Cocos I. (Costa Rica)
Malpelo I. (Colombia)

Barranquilla
Maracaibo
Caracas ⊗
Barquisimeto
Lake Maracaibo
Bucaramanga
VENEZUELA
Ciudad Guyana
GUYANA
Georgetown
Paramaribo
SURINAME
Cayenne
French Guiana (Fr.)
Medellin
Bogota ⊗
COLOMBIA
Cali
Angel Falls
Boa Vista
Magdalena R.
Guaviare R.
Orinoco River

Quito ⊗
ECUADOR
Guayaquil
EQUATOR
Galapagos Islands (Ecuador)
Gulf of Guayaquil
Putumayo R.
Amazon
Amazon River
Negro R.
Manaus
Santarem
Macapa
Mouths of the Amazon River
Belem
Sao Luis
Basin
Iquitos
Maranon R.
Amazon
Japura R.
Fernando de Noronha (Brazil)

Piura
Chiclayo
Trujillo
Jurua R.
Purus R.
Madeira R.
Rio Branco
Porto Velho
Topajos R.
Xingu R.
Tapajos R.
Fortaleza
Teresina
Natal
Joao Pessoa
Parnaiba R.
BRAZIL
Paulo Afonso Falls
Recife

ANDES
PERU
Callao
Lima
Huancayo
Cusco
Arequipa
Lake Titicaca
La Paz
BOLIVIA
Santa Cruz
Sucre
Potosi
Mamore R.
Lake Poopo
Cuiaba
Brazilian
Brasilia ⊗
Goiania
Highlands
Montes Claros
Maceio
Aracaju
Feira de Santana
Salvador
Sao Francisco R.
Tres Marias Res.
Uberaba
Belo Horizonte
Vitoria
Campos
Trindade (Brazil)

Iquique
Antofagasta
TROPIC OF CAPRICORN 23½°S
San Felix I. (Chile)
San Ambrosio I. (Chile)
Salta
San Miguel de Tucuman
Santiago del Estero
Asuncion ⊗
PARAGUAY
Campo Grande
Furnas Res.
Parana River
Campinas
Sao Paulo
Santos
Rio de Janeiro
Iguazu Falls
Curitiba
Resistencia
Uruguay R.
Florianopolis
Salado R.
Santa Maria
Porto Alegre
Patos Lagoon

La Serena
CHILE
Cordoba
San Juan
Santa Fe
Salto
URUGUAY
Rosario
Mirim L.
Vina del Mar
Valparaiso
Santiago ⊗
San Luis
Buenos Aires
Montevideo
San Justo
La Plata
Rio de la Plata
Juan Fernandez Is. (Chile)
Salado R.
ARGENTINA
Concepcion
Colorado R.
Bahia Blanca
Mar del Plata
Temuco
Negro R.
Viedma
Blanca Bay

PACIFIC
OCEAN
ATLANTIC
OCEAN

Puerto Montt
Comodoro Rivadavia
Gulf of San Jorge
Gulf of San Matias

SOUTH MOUNTAINS

Rio Gallegos
Strait of Magellan
Falkland Is. (U.K.)
Punta Arenas
Scotia Sea
Drake Passage

ATLANTIC OCEAN
EQUATOR
N

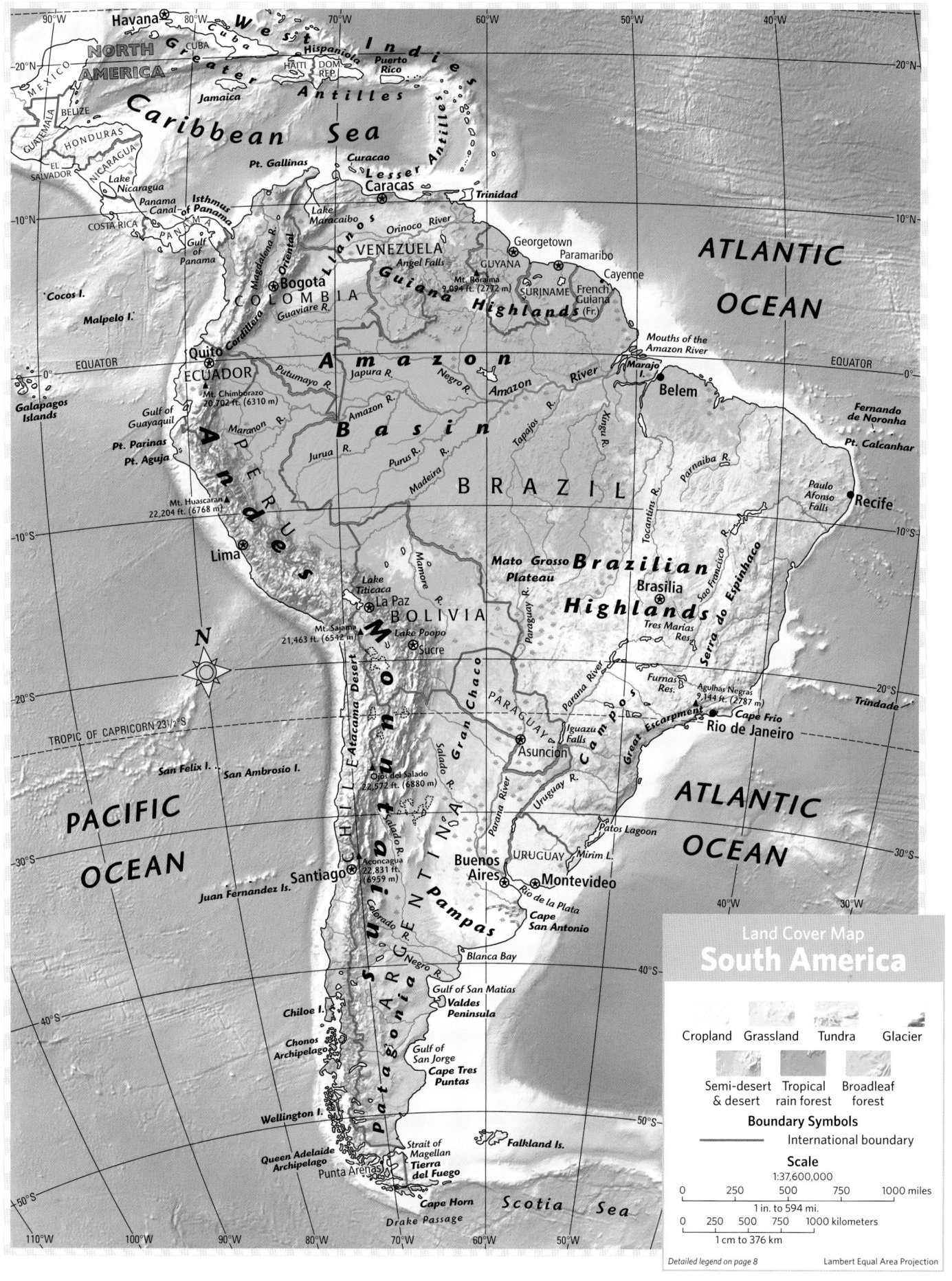

Havana
West
Indies
90°W
80°W
CUBA
70°W
NORTH
AMERICA
CUBA
Hispaniola
Greater
HAITI DOM.
REP.
Puerto
Rico
20°N
MEXICO
Jamaica
Antilles
GUATEMALA
BELIZE
Caribbean
Sea
HONDURAS
Pt. Gallinas
Curacao
Lesser
EL
SALVADOR
NICARAGUA
Lake
Nicaragua
Panama
Isthmus
of Panama
Caracas
Trinidad
10°N
COSTA RICA
PANAMA
Canal
Gulf
of
Panama
Lake
Maracaibo
Llanos
Orinoco River
Georgetown
Paramaribo
ATLANTIC
Cocos I.
VENEZUELA
Angel Falls
GUYANA
Cayenne
Malpelo I.
COLOMBIA
Oriental
Mt. Roraima
9,094 ft. (2772 m)
SURINAME French
Guiana
(Fr.)
OCEAN
Bogota
Guiana Highlands
Guaviare R.
Quito
Cordillera
Amazon
Mouths of the
Amazon River
EQUATOR
ECUADOR
Putumayo R.
Japura R.
Negro R.
Amazon River
Marajo
I.
Belem
0°
Mt. Chimborazo
20,702 ft. (6310 m)
Galapagos
Islands
Gulf of
Guayaquil
Maranon
Amazon R.
B a s i n
Amazon R.
Fernando
de Noronha
Pt. Parinas
A N D E S
Jurua
R.
Purus R.
Madeira R.
Tapajos R.
Xingu R.
Parnaiba R.
Pt. Calcanhar
Pt. Aguja
P E R U
Mt. Huascaran
22,204 ft. (6768 m)
BRAZIL
Paulo
Afonso
Falls
Recife
10°S
Lima
Mamore
Mato Grosso
Plateau
Brazilian
Brasilia
Tocantins R.
Sao Francisco R.
Serra do Espinhaco
Lake
Titicaca
La Paz
BOLIVIA
R.
Highlands
Mt. Sajama
21,463 ft. (6542 m)
M
Lake Poopo
Sucre
Paraguay R.
Tres Marias
Res.
Furnas
Res.
Agulhas Negras
9,144 ft. (2787 m)
Trindade
20°S
A t a c a m a D e s e r t
Gran Chaco
PARAGUAY
Parana River
Campos
Great Escarpment
Cape Frio
Rio de Janeiro
TROPIC OF CAPRICORN 23½°S
Ojos del Salado
22,572 ft. (6880 m)
Salado R.
Iguazu
Falls
San Felix I.
San Ambrosio I.
Asuncion
PACIFIC
Pilcomayo R.
Uruguay R.
ATLANTIC
Aconcagua
22,831 ft. (6959 m)
A R G E N T I N A
Parana River
URUGUAY
Patos Lagoon
OCEAN
Santiago
C H I L E
Colorado R.
Buenos
Aires
Montevideo
OCEAN
30°S
P a m p a s
Rio de la Plata
Negro R.
Cape
San Antonio
40°W
30°W
Blanca Bay
40°S
Gulf of San Matias
Valdes
Peninsula
Chiloe I.
Patagonia
Gulf of
San Jorge
Cape Tres
Puntas
Chonos
Archipelago
Wellington I.
Queen Adelaide
Archipelago
Strait of
Magellan
Falkland Is.
50°S
Punta Arenas
Tierra
del Fuego
Cape Horn
Scotia Sea
Drake Passage
110°W
100°W
90°W
80°W
70°W
60°W
50°W

Land Cover Map
South America

Cropland   Grassland   Tundra   Glacier

Semi-desert   Tropical   Broadleaf
& desert   rain forest   forest

Boundary Symbols
——————   International boundary

Scale
1:37,600,000
0   250   500   750   1000 miles
1 in. to 594 mi.
0   250   500   750   1000 kilometers
1 cm to 376 km

Detailed legend on page 8   Lambert Equal Area Projection

NICARAGUA
Lake Nicaragua
COSTA RICA
Isthmus of Panama
PANAMA
Gulf of Panama
Pt. Gallinas
Caracas
Trinidad
Cocos I.
Malpelo I.
COLOMBIA
Bogota
Cordillera Oriental
Llanos
VENEZUELA
Orinoco River
Angel Falls
Georgetown
Paramaribo
GUYANA
Cayenne
French Guiana (Fr)
SURINAME
Mt. Roraima 9,094 ft (2772 m)
Guiana Highlands
Guaviare R.
ATLANTIC OCEAN
Quito
ECUADOR
Mt. Chimborazo 20,702 ft. (6310 m)
Gulf of Guayaquil
Pt. Parinas
Pt. Aguja
EQUATOR
Putumayo R.
Negro
Amazon
Japura R.
Marañon R.
A m a z o n
B a s i n
B R A Z I L
Mouths of the Amazon River
Marajo I.
Belem
Fernando de Noronha
Pt. Calcanhar
Galapagos Islands
A n d e s
Mt. Huascaran 22,204 ft. (6768 m)
Lima
Jurua
Purus
Madeira R.
Paulo Afonso Falls
Recife
Mato Grosso Plateau
Tapajos R.
Xingu R.
Tocantins R.
Parnaiba R.
São Francisco R.
B r a z i l i a n
H i g h l a n d s
Brasilia
Serra do Espinhaco
La Paz
Lake Titicaca
Mt. Sajama 21,463 ft. (6542 m)
Altiplano
BOLIVIA
Sucre
Mamore R.
Guapore R.
Tres Marias Res.
Furnas Res.
Agulhas Negras 9,144 ft. (2787 m)
Area shown on cross section
M o u n t a i n s
PACIFIC
OCEAN
Atacama Desert
Mt. Sajama
Ojos del Salado 22,572 ft. (6880 m)
Paraguay River
Gran Chaco
PARAGUAY
Pilcomayo R.
Campos
Parana River
Great Escarpment
Cape Frio
Rio de Janeiro
Trindade
TROPIC OF CAPRICORN 23½°S
San Felix I.
San Ambrosio I.
CHILE
Salado R.
Asuncion
Iguazu Falls
Uruguay R.
Juan Fernandez Islands
Aconcagua 22,831 ft. (6959 m)
ARGENTINA
Pampas
URUGUAY
Montevideo
Mirim L.
Patos Lagoon
N
ATLANTIC
OCEAN
Santiago
Salado R.
Buenos Aires
Rio de la Plata
Cape San Antonio
Negro R.
Colorado R.
Blanca Bay
Chiloe I.
Patagonia
Gulf of San Matias
Valdes Peninsula
Chonos Archipelago
Gulf of San Jorge
Cape Tres Puntas
Wellington I.
Queen Adelaide Archipelago
Punta Arenas
Strait of Magellan
Tierra del Fuego
Cape Horn
Drake Passage
Falkland Is.
Scotia Sea
South Georgia I.

Detailed legend on page 8

Elevation Map
South America

Meters above Sea Level		Feet above Sea Level
Over 6000		Over 20,000
3000 to 6000		10,000 to 20,000
1500 to 3000		5,000 to 10,000
600 to 1500		2,000 to 5,000
300 to 600		1,000 to 2,000
150 to 300		500 to 1,000
0 to 150		0 to 500

Scale
1:37,400,000

0 250 500 750 1000 miles

1 in. to 589 mi.

0 250 500 750 1000 kilometers

1 cm to 374 km

Lambert Equal Area Projection

Cross Section
Vertical exaggeration 37 to 1
Scale at 24°S: 1 in. to 315 mi., 1 cm to 200 km

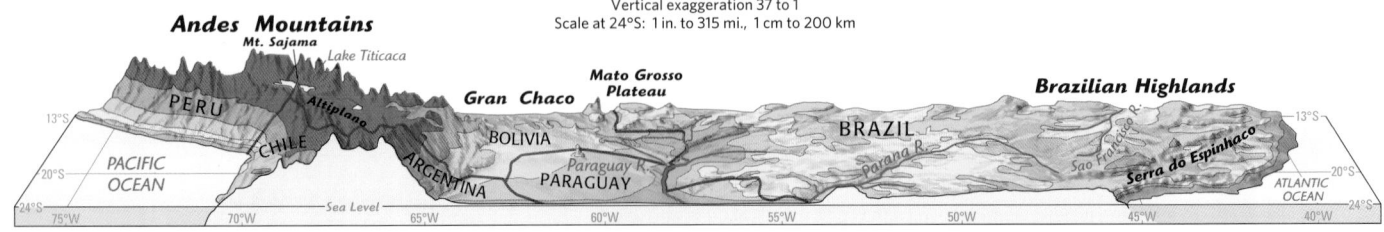

Andes Mountains
Mt. Sajama
Lake Titicaca
PERU
Altiplano
CHILE
Gran Chaco
Mato Grosso Plateau
Brazilian Highlands
BOLIVIA
BRAZIL
Serra do Espinhaco
PACIFIC OCEAN
ARGENTINA
PARAGUAY
Paraguay R.
Parana R.
São Francisco R.
ATLANTIC OCEAN
Sea Level

Altitude Zones in the Andes

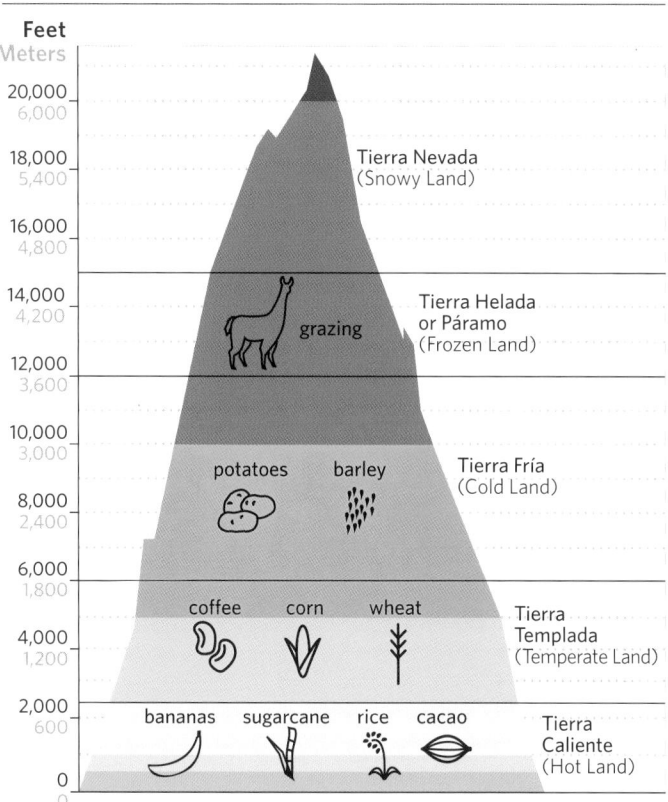

As altitude in the Andes increases, the climate gets colder and drier. For centuries, indigenous people in the region have cultivated crops that grow well at each elevation zone and climate.

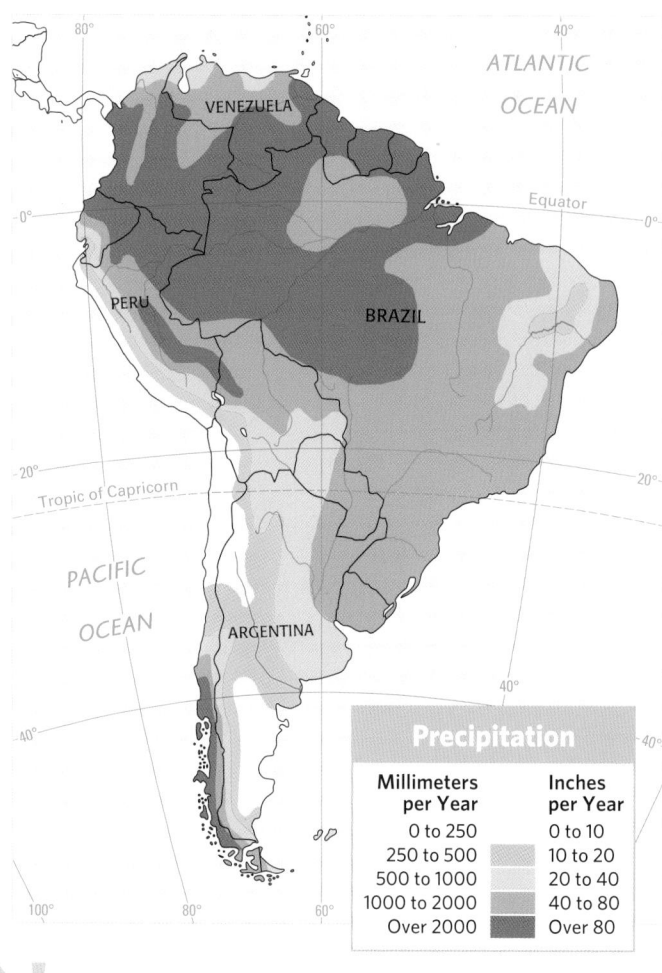

Precipitation	
Millimeters per Year	**Inches per Year**
0 to 250	0 to 10
250 to 500	10 to 20
500 to 1000	20 to 40
1000 to 2000	40 to 80
Over 2000	Over 80

Desert by the Sea

The Atacama Desert along coastal Peru and Chile is among the driest places on Earth. Its dry conditions are caused by the cold Peru Current, which flows north along the western coast of the continent. This surface current cools the air, preventing it from holding much moisture, so very little rain falls in this region.

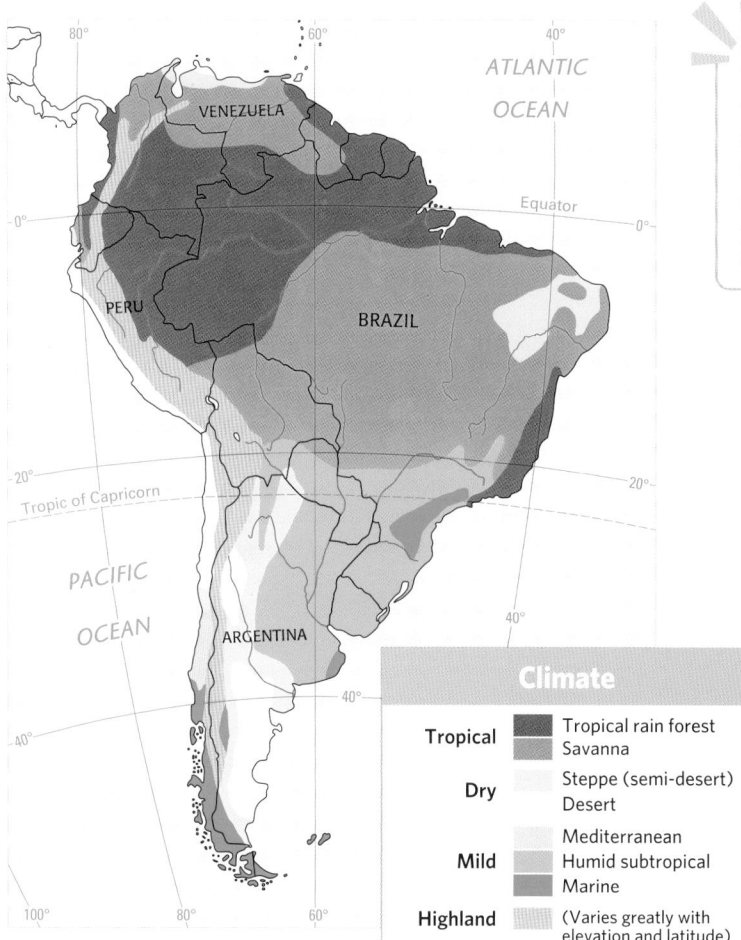

Climate	
Tropical	Tropical rain forest
	Savanna
Dry	Steppe (semi-desert)
	Desert
Mild	Mediterranean
	Humid subtropical
	Marine
Highland	(Varies greatly with elevation and latitude)

Climographs

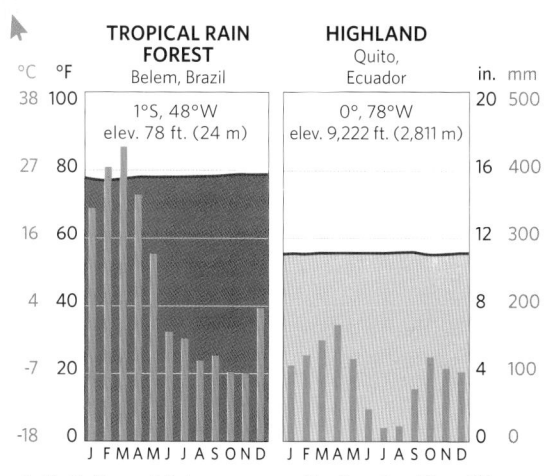

Both Quito and Belem are near the Equator. The difference in their elevations explains why Quito is colder and drier. Air temperature drops about 3.5°F for each rise of 1,000 feet (6.5°C for each 1,000 meters).

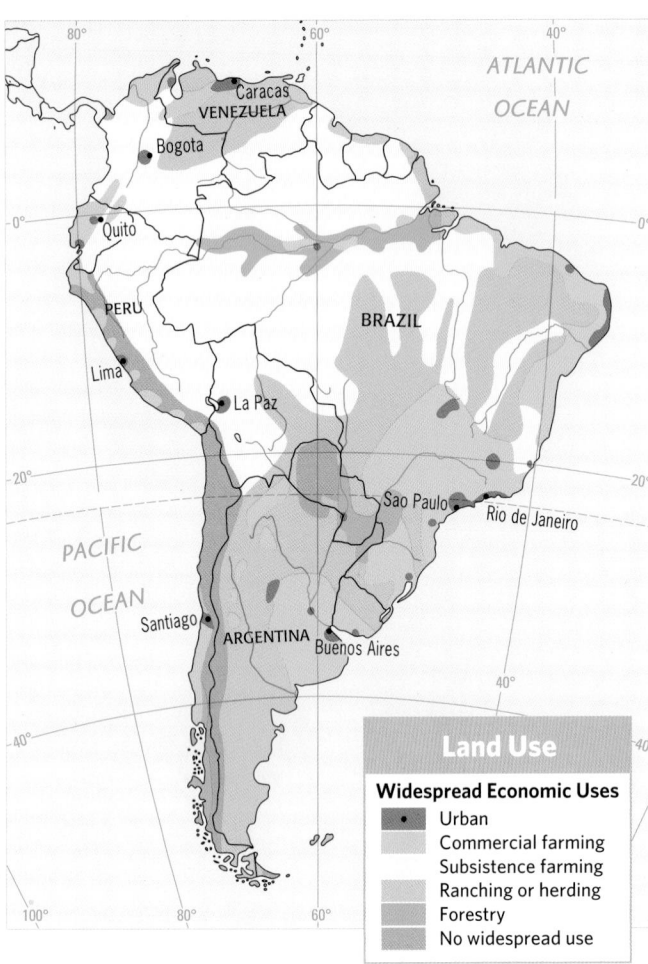

Balance of Trade

Chile

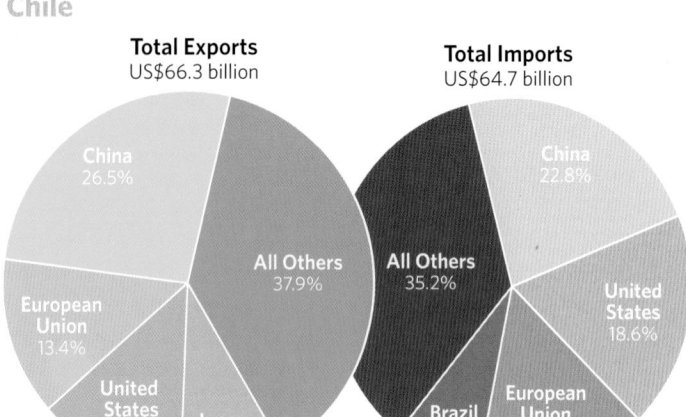

Total Exports
US$66.3 billion

- China 26.5%
- All Others 37.9%
- European Union 13.4%
- United States 13.1%
- Japan 9.1%

Total Imports
US$64.7 billion

- China 22.8%
- All Others 35.2%
- United States 18.6%
- European Union 15.6%
- Brazil 7.8%

Land Use

Widespread Economic Uses

- Urban
- Commercial farming
- Subsistence farming
- Ranching or herding
- Forestry
- No widespread use

Fuel for Thought

During an oil crisis, Brazil found an alternative to gasoline—the biofuel **ethanol**. Made from sugarcane, ethanol is cleaner and cheaper to produce than gasoline. More than half of all registered cars and light trucks in Brazil are flexible-fuel vehicles, which can run on a mixture of gasoline and ethanol.

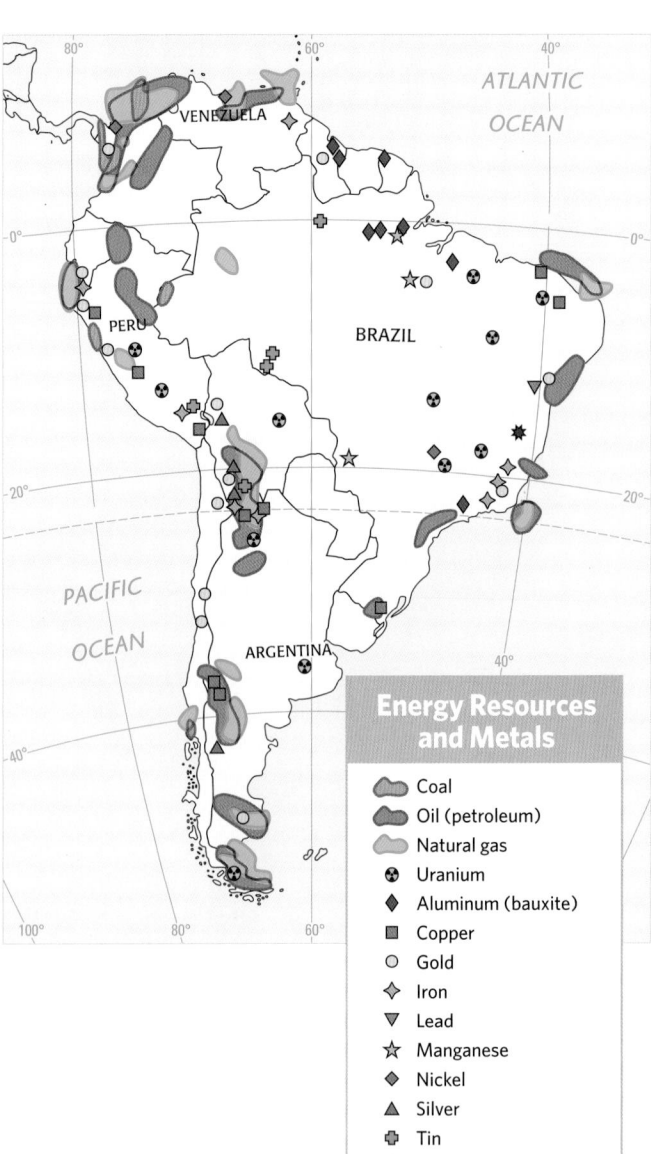

Energy Resources and Metals

- Coal
- Oil (petroleum)
- Natural gas
- ☢ Uranium
- ◆ Aluminum (bauxite)
- ■ Copper
- ○ Gold
- ◇ Iron
- ▽ Lead
- ☆ Manganese
- ◆ Nickel
- ▲ Silver
- ✦ Tin
- ✳ Zinc

Oil tankers are docked at Guaraguao Bay at Puerto La Cruz in northern Venezuela. Venezuela, a founding member of OPEC (see page 174), has the largest oil reserves in the world.

Natural Population Growth

South America

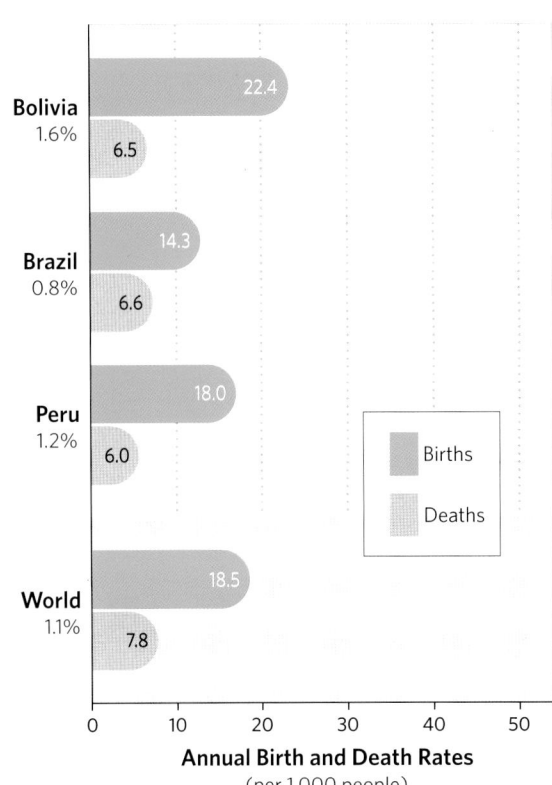

Births

Deaths

Annual Birth and Death Rates
(per 1,000 people)

Bolivia 1.6% — Births 22.4, Deaths 6.5
Brazil 0.8% — Births 14.3, Deaths 6.6
Peru 1.2% — Births 18.0, Deaths 6.0
World 1.1% — Births 18.5, Deaths 7.8

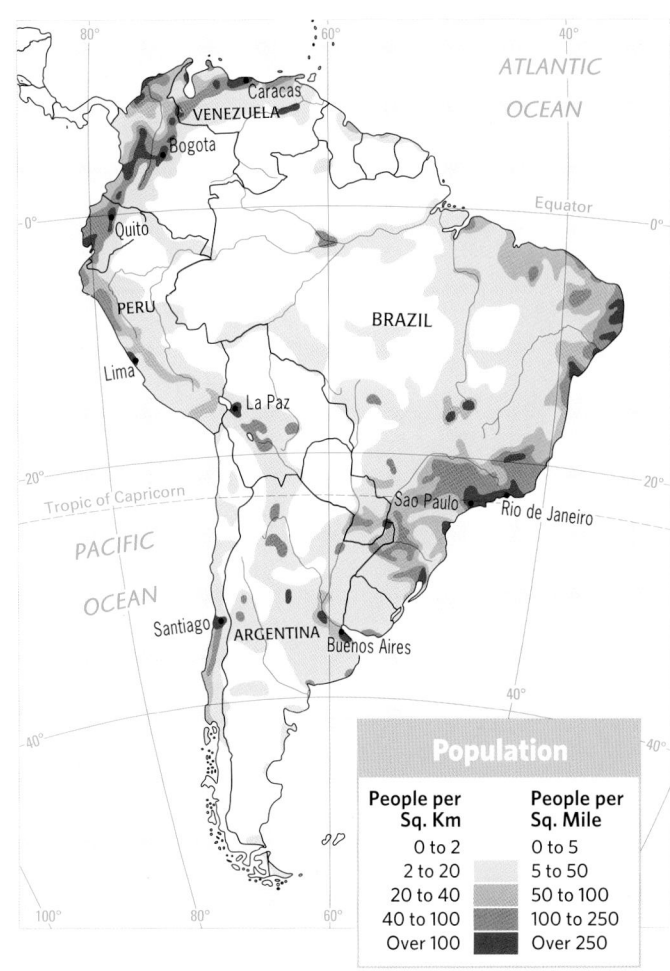

Population

People per Sq. Km	People per Sq. Mile
0 to 2	0 to 5
2 to 20	5 to 50
20 to 40	50 to 100
40 to 100	100 to 250
Over 100	Over 250

Descendants of Indigenous South Americans*

Percentage of Population
- 85 to 100
- 70 to 85
- 50 to 70
- Under 10

Aymara Large indigenous group today

*Includes mestizo

Mixed Roots

Mestizo is Spanish for *mixed*. In Latin America, the term is used to describe a person of mixed European and American Indian parentage. **Mulatto** describes a person of mixed European and African parentage. Over 85 percent of the people in Paraguay are mestizo, while over 35 percent of those in French Guiana are mulatto.

Peru has one of the larger indigenous populations in South America. (For more information, see page 127.) Many Quechua and Aymara still farm and bring goods to market in the highlands.

Continues on pages 106–107

Northwestern South America

Political Relief Map
Northwestern South America

NICARAGUA
Caribbean Sea
DOMINICA
Martinique (France)
ST. LUCIA
ST. VINCENT & THE GRENADINES
GRENADA
BARBADOS
Point Gallinas
Aruba (Neth.)
Curacao (Neth.)
Bonaire (Neth.)
Margarita I. (Ven.)
TRINIDAD & TOBAGO
Santa Marta
Cristobal Colon 18,947 ft. (5775 m)
Barranquilla
Maracaibo
Caracas
Cumana
COSTA RICA
Cartagena
Panama Canal
Barcelona
Maturin
Soledad
Barquisimeto
Valencia
Maracay
San Jose
Panama City
Lake Maracaibo
Pico Bolivar 16,427 ft. (5007 m)
Ciudad Bolivar
Ciudad Guayana
PANAMA
Gulf of Panama
Cucuta
San Cristobal
VENEZUELA
Georgetown
GUYANA
NORTH AMERICA
Bello
Bucaramanga
Mt. Roraima 9,094 ft. (2772 m)
Kaieteur Falls
Medellin
Angel Falls
Guiana Highlands
Malpelo I. (Colombia)
Pereira
Ibague
Bogota
Villavicencio
Boa Vista
Buenaventura
Cali
Neiva
COLOMBIA
EQUATOR
Pasto
Santo Domingo
Quito
Caqueta
Amazon R.
Manta
ECUADOR
Mt. Chimborazo 20,702 ft. (6310 m)
Napo R.
Putumayo R.
Guayaquil
Cuenca
Gulf of Guayaquil
Machala
Iquitos
Maranon R.
Talara
Punta Parinas
Paita
Piura
BRAZIL
Aguja Point
Javari R.
Jurua R.
Chiclayo
Pucallpa
Purus R.
Rio Branco
Trujillo
Chimbote
Mt. Huascaran 22,204 ft. (6768 m)
Huanuco
Madre de Dios R.
PERU
PACIFIC OCEAN
Huancayo
BOLIVIA
Callao
Lima
Ayacucho
Cusco
Ica
Juliaca
Lake Titicaca
La Paz
Arequipa
Altiplano
Tacna

City Symbols

Guayaquil ●	Over 1,000,000 people
Soledad •	500,000 to 1,000,000
Huanuco •	Under 500,000
Caracas ⊗	National capital

Scale
1:26,300,000
0   150   300   600 miles
1 in. to 415 mi.
0 150 300 450 600 kilometers
1 cm to 263 km

Detailed legend on page 8 — Lambert Equal Area Projection

Continues on page 127

Continues on page 127

Southern South America

Political Relief Map
Southern South America

PERU
Cochabamba
Arica
Mt. Sajama 21,463 ft. (6542 m)
Lake Poopo
Sucre
Santa Cruz
Altiplano
Iquique
BOLIVIA
Tarija
TROPIC OF CAPRICORN 23½°S
San Salvador de Jujuy
PARAGUAY
Antofagasta
Salta
Pilcomayo R.
Atacama Desert
San Miguel de Tucuman
Formosa
Asuncion
PACIFIC OCEAN
Copiapo
Ojos del Salado 22,572 ft. (6880 m)
Santiago del Estero
Resistencia
Posadas
Corrientes
Iguazu Falls
BRAZIL
Santa Maria
Gran Chaco
Bermejo R.
Salado R.
La Serena
Coquimbo
Cordoba
Santa Fe
Parana
Concordia
URUGUAY
Aconcagua 22,831 ft. (6959 m)
San Juan
Mendoza
Rosario
Vina del Mar
Valparaiso
San Luis
Uspallata Pass
Rio Cuarto
Montevideo
Santiago
Rancagua
ARGENTINA
Buenos Aires
San Justo
La Plata
Rio de la Plata
Mirim Lake
Talca
Parana R.
Uruguay R.
Pampas
Talcahuano
Concepcion
Salado R.
Bahia Blanca
Mar del Plata
Temuco
Neuquen
Colorado R.
Blanca Bay
Puerto Montt
Chiloe I.
Negro R.
Gulf of San Matias
Corcovado Gulf
Chubut R.
Valdes Peninsula -131 ft. (-40 m)
ATLANTIC OCEAN
Chonos Archipelago
Patagonia
Comodoro Rivadavia
Gulf of San Jorge
Gulf of Penas
Cape Tres Puntas
Laguna del Carbon -344 ft. (-105 m)
Falkland Islands (U.K.)
Queen Adelaide Archipelago
Grande Bay
Strait of Magellan
Punta Arenas
Tierra del Fuego
Staten I.
Beagle Channel
Cape Horn

City Symbols

Cordoba ●	Over 1,000,000 people
Rosario •	500,000 to 1,000,000
Temuco •	Under 500,000
Santiago ⊗	National capital

Scale
1:27,600,000
0   150   300   450   600 miles
1 in. to 436 mi.
0 150 300 450 600 kilometers
1 cm to 276 km

Detailed legend on page 8 — Lambert Equal Area Projection

Continues on page 126

Political Relief Map
Brazil and Its Neighbors

City Symbols

Sao Paulo ● Over 1,000,000 people
Cochabamba ● 500,000 to 1,000,000
Tarija • Under 500,000

Paramaribo ⊛ National capital

Scale
1:26,680,000

0   150   300   450   600 miles

1 in. to 421 mi.

0   150   300   450   600 kilometers

1 cm to 267 km

Detailed legend on page 8   Lambert Equal Area Projection

Ethnic Composition

Peru

All Others 3.7%
Aymara 5.4%
European 12.0%
Quechua 47.0%
Mestizo 31.9%

Brazil

African or African/Amerindian 6.9%
All Others 0.7%
European 48.2%
Mulatto and Mestizo 44.2%

ISSUES / TODAY

What is the best way to develop a nation?

Since independence, South America has had low standards of living compared with Europe, Canada, the United States, and parts of East Asia. Even today South America is growing slower than much of the developing world. Many methods have been tried to improve the economies and standard of living in South America. Here are two of them.

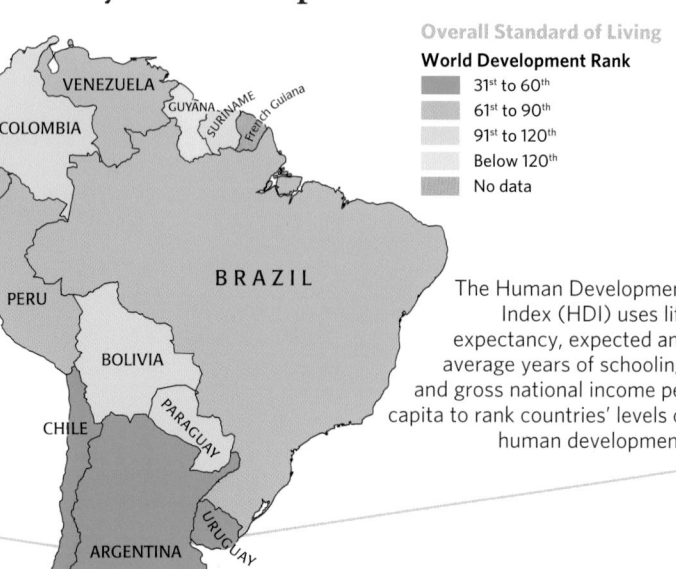

Overall Standard of Living

World Development Rank
- 31st to 60th
- 61st to 90th
- 91st to 120th
- Below 120th
- No data

The Human Development Index (HDI) uses life expectancy, expected and average years of schooling, and gross national income per capita to rank countries' levels of human development.

Development should focus on exports.

- Exports provide a national economy with currency that prevents foreign debt from threatening the economy. This currency can also be used to invest in education, transportation, energy, and health care, improving the lives of everyone in the country.

- Asian economies, such as Japan after World War II, South Korea in the 1970s and 1980s, and China and India from the 1980s into the 2000s, have grown rapidly due to a focus on exports. This growth has improved the lives of hundreds of millions of people across East and South Asia.

- Exported goods and services need to compete in the world economy. As a result, the goods and services produced within the country need to be of high quality and relatively low prices.

- In the 1970s, international lenders encouraged the development of domestic markets in South America, ignoring exports. The results were inefficient industries, inflation, economic stagnation, and social unrest.

Exports as a Percent of GDP

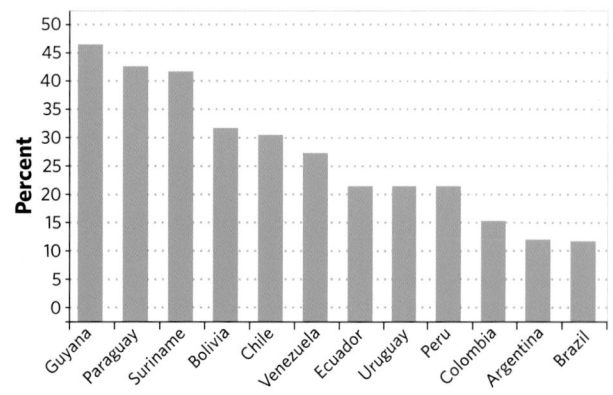

Development should concentrate on improving the lives of the people.

- The focus on exports is a continuation of the old colonial economy that mainly benefits the wealthiest people in the country and foreign investors. Wages for workers are kept low to keep the exports competitive.

- Many exports from South America are natural resources or agricultural goods, which are produced by damaging or destroying the natural environment. These industries have used their wealth and political power to prevent the development of more sustainable industries.

- The modern global economy prevents the policies, including government protection for developing industries, that allowed the East and South Asian economies to develop so rapidly.

- Underdeveloped slums in South America are often breeding grounds for disease. Basic development of sewage and water treatment may not generate profits, but it is better in the long run for the country and the world.

Crowded and underdeveloped slums like this favela in Brazil surround most South American cities.

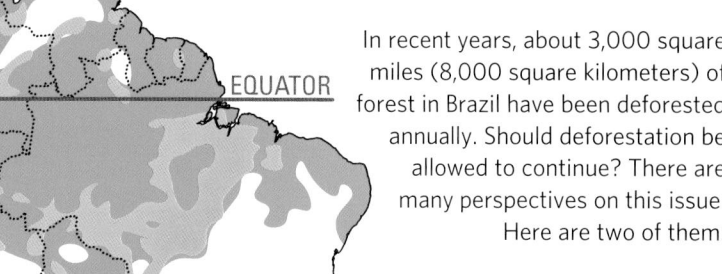

ISSUES / TODAY

What should be done about the rain forest?

The Amazon rain forest, the largest in the world, is shrinking. It contains the widest variety of plant and animal life on Earth and is important to the continent's economy.

EQUATOR

In recent years, about 3,000 square miles (8,000 square kilometers) of forest in Brazil have been deforested annually. Should deforestation be allowed to continue? There are many perspectives on this issue. Here are two of them.

Tropical Rain Forests

◼ Tree cover
◻ Tree cover lost since 1980

TROPIC OF CAPRICORN

Deforestation has a disastrous impact on the environment.

- Trees and plants in the rain forest absorb greenhouse gases. Deforestation, on the other hand, contributes to global warming. Brazil emits more greenhouse gases than any other country in South America.

- About 135 species of plants, animals, and insects disappear every day due to deforestation.

- Deforestation could destroy species with potential cures for diseases. About 25 percent of modern medicines were developed from rain forest plants. Less than 1 percent of rain forest species, however, have been tested for medical value.

- Deforestation displaces the indigenous people who have lived in the rain forest for centuries. Today about 900,000 indigenous people live in Brazil.

- Deforestation accounts for about 15 percent of global carbon emissions.

Carbon Dioxide from Land Use Change

Land Area

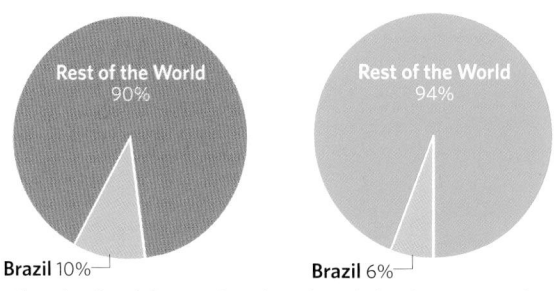

When land is deforested, carbon dioxide levels rise. Brazil contributes a disproportionate share of this pollutant. Carbon dioxide, ozone, and methane are all greenhouse gases that contribute to global warming.

Deforestation is necessary for the economy.

- Brazil has about 865 million acres of unused arable land. Deforestation allows the country to utilize more of its land.

- Deforestation is an indicator of Brazil's economy. When the economy is growing, ranchers expand their pastures, the government builds highways, and deforestation increases.

- Brazil has an external debt of over US$544 billion. Money generated from major exports such as timber and soybeans provides a fast way for Brazil to repay foreign governments and banks.

- Subsistence farmers depend on forest products for their livelihoods.

- Attempts to "save the earth" place an unfair burden on South Americans who could be prohibited from using about half of their own land. Other countries, such as the United States, have already cleared about 90 percent of their original forests.

Brazil's Land Cover

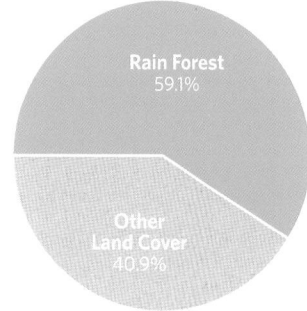

Rain forest in Brazil occupies about 59 percent of Brazil's total land cover. Brazil's Amazon rain forest is the largest in the world.

World Extreme: The Sahara is the largest desert in the world, covering approximately 3.5 million square miles (9 million square kilometers). About 2.5 million people live in the Sahara despite its dry climate. Ninety large oases scattered throughout the Sahara provide water, shelter, and arable land for growing food.

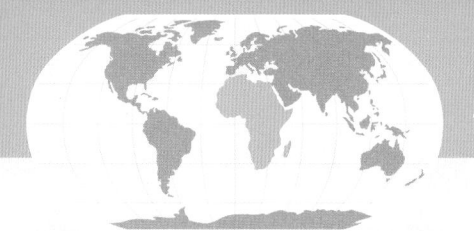

Africa

Africa, located mainly within the tropics, has 54 countries—more than any other continent on Earth. A land of many cultures, Africa is home to hundreds of ethnic groups. The people of Africa speak more than 1,000 languages.

Physical Features

Highest mountain peak
Mt. Kilimanjaro 19,340 ft. (5,895 m)

Longest mountain range
Atlas Mountains 1,500 mi. (2,410 km)

Largest island
Madagascar 226,658 sq. mi. (587,041 sq. km)

Largest lakes
Lake Victoria 26,600 sq. mi. (68,900 sq. km)
Lake Tanganyika 12,600 sq. mi. (32,600 sq. km)

Longest rivers
Nile 4,132 mi. (6,650 km)★
Congo 2,900 mi. (4,700 km)★

Other key physical features

Bie Plateau	Katanga Plateau
Congo Basin	Sahara
Ethiopian Highlands	Sahel
Great Rift Valley	Somali Peninsula

Cultural Features

Population
1,225,081,000

Largest countries by area
Algeria 919,595 sq. mi. (2,381,741 sq. km)
Dem. Rep. of the Congo 905,354 sq. mi. (2,345,858 sq. km)
Sudan 718,723 sq. mi. (1,861,484 sq. km)

Largest country by population
Nigeria 190,632,261

Most densely populated
Mauritius 1,721.3 people per sq. mi. (664.9 per sq. km)

Least densely populated
Western Sahara 6.2 people per sq. mi. (2.4 per sq. km)

Largest urban areas
Cairo, Egypt 18,772,000★
Lagos, Nigeria 13,123,000★
Johannesburg, South Africa 9,399,000

★ Among the world's largest. See the inside front cover.

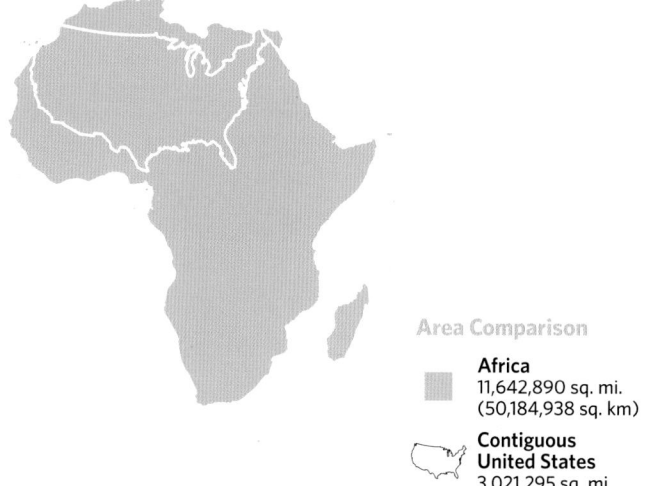

Area Comparison

Africa
11,642,890 sq. mi.
(50,184,938 sq. km)

Contiguous United States
3,021,295 sq. mi.
(7,825,112 sq. km)

Regional Maps of Africa

1 **Northern Africa** pp. 136–137
2 **Western Africa** p. 138
3 **Central Africa** p. 139
4 **Eastern Africa** p. 140
5 **Southern Africa** p. 141

Thematic Maps of Africa

Precipitation p. 135
Climate p. 135
Land Use p. 135
Energy Resources and Metals p. 136
Population p. 137

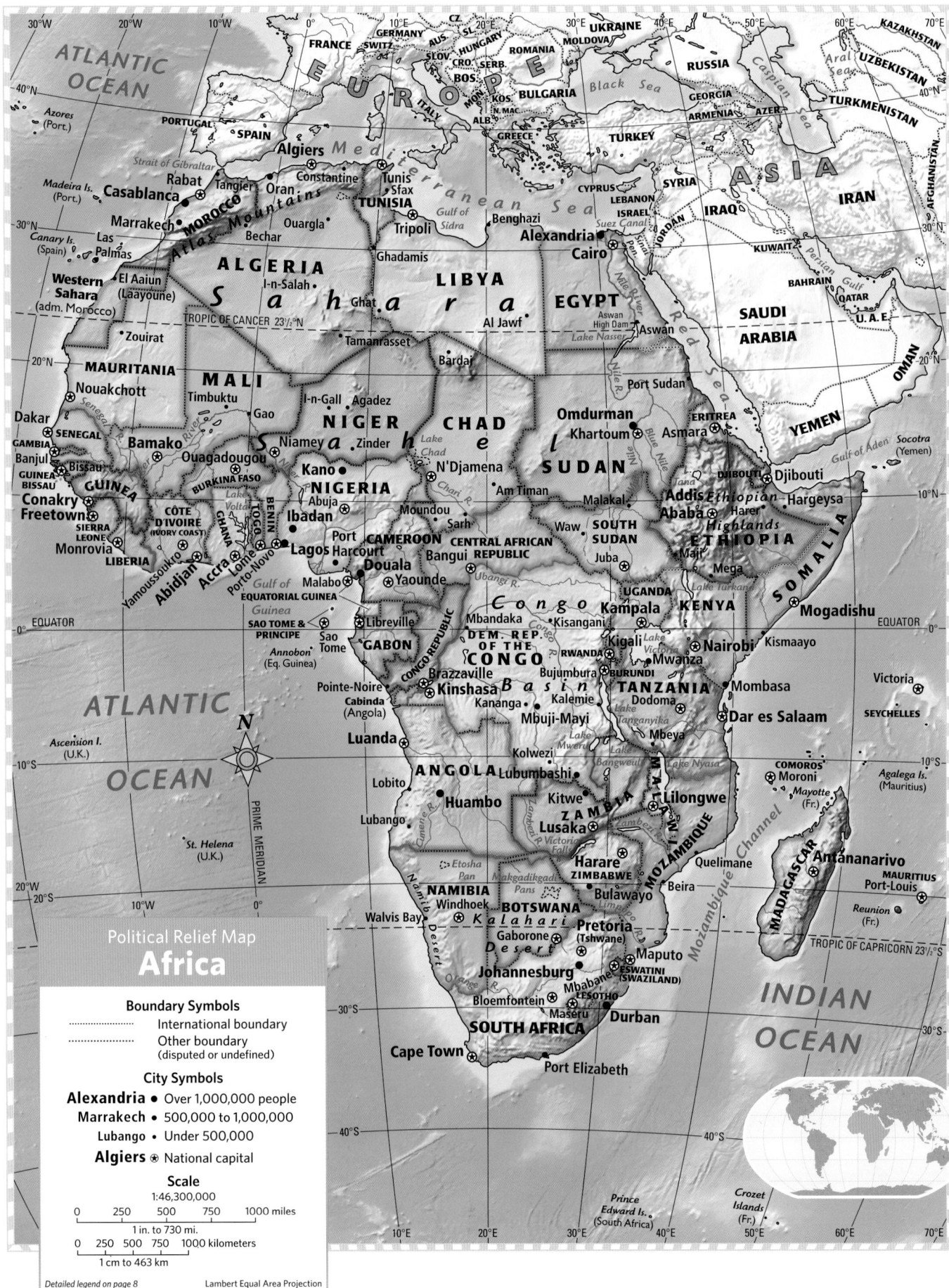

ATLANTIC OCEAN

EUROPE

ASIA

Mediterranean Sea

MOROCCO
ALGERIA
Sahara
LIBYA
EGYPT

WESTERN SAHARA (adm. Morocco)

TROPIC OF CANCER 23½°N

MAURITANIA
MALI
NIGER
CHAD
SUDAN

SENEGAL
GAMBIA
GUINEA-BISSAU
GUINEA
SIERRA LEONE
LIBERIA
CÔTE D'IVOIRE (IVORY COAST)
BURKINA FASO
GHANA
TOGO
BENIN
NIGERIA
CAMEROON
CENTRAL AFRICAN REPUBLIC
SOUTH SUDAN
ETHIOPIA
ERITREA
DJIBOUTI
SOMALIA
UGANDA
KENYA

EQUATOR

EQUATORIAL GUINEA
SAO TOME & PRINCIPE
GABON
CONGO REPUBLIC
DEM. REP. OF THE CONGO
RWANDA
BURUNDI
TANZANIA

Congo Basin

ATLANTIC OCEAN

ANGOLA
ZAMBIA
MALAWI
MOZAMBIQUE
NAMIBIA
BOTSWANA
ZIMBABWE
MADAGASCAR
COMOROS

Kalahari Desert

TROPIC OF CAPRICORN 23½°S

SOUTH AFRICA
ESWATINI (SWAZILAND)
LESOTHO

INDIAN OCEAN

Cities and features:
Azores (Port.), Madeira Is. (Port.), Casablanca, Rabat, Tangier, Oran, Constantine, Algiers, Tunis, Sfax, Tripoli, Benghazi, Alexandria, Cairo, Marrakech, Ouargla, Bechar, Ghadames, Ghat, In-Salah, El Aaiun (Laayoune), Las Palmas, Canary Is. (Spain), Zouirat, Nouakchott, Timbuktu, Gao, I-n-Gall, Agadez, Tamanrasset, Bardai, Al Jawf, Aswan, Aswan High Dam, Lake Nasser, Port Sudan, Omdurman, Khartoum, Asmara, Djibouti, Hargeysa, Dakar, Bamako, Ouagadougou, Niamey, Zinder, Kano, N'Djamena, Am Timan, Moundou, Sarh, Waw, Malakal, Addis Ababa, Harer, Mega, Banjul, Bissau, Conakry, Freetown, Monrovia, Yamoussoukro, Abidjan, Accra, Lome, Porto-Novo, Lagos, Ibadan, Abuja, Port Harcourt, Douala, Malabo, Yaounde, Bangui, Juba, Mogadishu, Kismaayo, Libreville, Sao Tome, Mbandaka, Kisangani, Kampala, Kigali, Nairobi, Mombasa, Mwanza, Brazzaville, Kinshasa, Bujumbura, Dodoma, Dar es Salaam, Pointe-Noire, Cabinda (Angola), Kananga, Kalemie, Mbuji-Mayi, Mbeya, Luanda, Kolwezi, Lubumbashi, Lobito, Huambo, Kitwe, Lilongwe, Lubango, Lusaka, Harare, Quelimane, Beira, Bulawayo, Antananarivo, Port-Louis, Reunion (Fr.), Mayotte (Fr.), Moroni, Windhoek, Walvis Bay, Gaborone, Pretoria (Tshwane), Maputo, Mbabane, Johannesburg, Bloemfontein, Maseru, Durban, Cape Town, Port Elizabeth

Annobon (Eq. Guinea), Ascension I. (U.K.), St. Helena (U.K.), Prince Edward Is. (South Africa), Crozet Islands (Fr.), Agalega Is. (Mauritius), Seychelles, Victoria, MAURITIUS, Socotra (Yemen)

Atlas Mountains, Strait of Gibraltar, Gulf of Sidra, Suez Canal, Nile River, Red Sea, Gulf of Aden, Lake Chad, Chari R., Blue Nile, Lake Tana, Ethiopian Highlands, Ubangi R., Lake Turkana, Lake Victoria, Congo R., Lake Tanganyika, Lake Mweru, Lake Bangweulu, Zambezi R., Lake Nyasa, Victoria Falls, Etosha Pan, Makgadikgadi Pans, Namib Desert, Okavango, Limpopo, Orange R., Mozambique Channel

EUROPE countries: FRANCE, GERMANY, SWITZ., AUS., SLOV., HUNGARY, CZ., SL., ROMANIA, MOLDOVA, UKRAINE, PORTUGAL, SPAIN, ITALY, CRO., BOS., SERB., MON., N. MAC., ALB., GREECE, BULGARIA, TUNISIA

ASIA countries: RUSSIA, GEORGIA, ARMENIA, AZER., TURKEY, CYPRUS, SYRIA, LEBANON, ISRAEL, JORDAN, IRAQ, KUWAIT, SAUDI ARABIA, BAHRAIN, QATAR, U.A.E., OMAN, YEMEN, IRAN, KAZAKHSTAN, UZBEKISTAN, TURKMENISTAN, AFGHANISTAN

Black Sea, Caspian Sea, Aral Sea, Persian Gulf

Political Relief Map
Africa

Boundary Symbols
.... International boundary
.... Other boundary (disputed or undefined)

City Symbols
Alexandria • Over 1,000,000 people
Marrakech • 500,000 to 1,000,000
Lubango • Under 500,000
Algiers ⊛ National capital

Scale
1:46,300,000

0   250   500   750   1000 miles
1 in. to 730 mi.

0   250 500 750 1000 kilometers
1 cm to 463 km

Detailed legend on page 8   Lambert Equal Area Projection

ATLANTIC
OCEAN

Azores

EUROPE

FRANCE
PORTUGAL
SPAIN
Strait of Gibraltar
MOROCCO
Casablanca
Madeira Is.
Canary Is.
Western
Sahara
(adm. Morocco)
Cape
Blanc

GERMANY
SWITZ.
CZ
AUSTRIA
SLOV.
HUNGARY
SL.
ROMANIA
CRO.
SERB.
BOS.
MON.
N.MAC.
ALB.
ITALY
GREECE
BULGARIA

Black Sea

RUSSIA
GEORGIA
ARMENIA
AZER.

Caspian Sea

Aral
Sea
KAZAKHSTAN
UZBEKISTAN
TURKMENISTAN

Algiers Mediterranean Sea
TUNISIA
Tripoli
Gulf of
Sidra

ALGERIA
LIBYA
Shatt al
Jarid

Sahara
TROPIC OF CANCER 23½°N
Ahaggar Mts.
Mt. Tahat.
9,573 ft.
(2918 m)

Libyan Desert

EGYPT
Cairo
Qattara
Depression
-436 ft. (-133 m)
Aswan
High Dam
Lake Nasser

TURKEY
CYPRUS
SYRIA
LEBANON
ISRAEL
JORDAN
Suez Canal

ASIA

IRAQ
KUWAIT

IRAN
AFGHANISTAN

Persian Gulf
BAHRAIN
QATAR
U.A.E.
OMAN

SAUDI
ARABIA

Red Sea

MAURITANIA
MALI
NIGER
CHAD

Tibesti
Mts.
Emi Koussi
11,204 ft.
(3415 m)

Air
Mts.

Sahel
Lake
Chad

Nubian
Desert

Nile River

Khartoum
ERITREA
DJIBOUTI
Gulf of Aden
Cape
Guardafui
Socotra

YEMEN

Cape
Verde
SENEGAL
GAMBIA
GUINEA-
BISSAU
Senegal R.
Niger River
SENEGAL
BURKINA FASO
GUINEA
SIERRA
LEONE
LIBERIA
CÔTE
D'IVOIRE
(IVORY
COAST)
GHANA
Cape Palmas
Lake
Volta
TOGO
BENIN
NIGERIA
Jos
Plateau
Niger R.
Chari R.
SUDAN
SOUTH
SUDAN
Sudd
White Nile
Blue Nile
Ras Dashen
15,158 ft.
(4620 m)
Lake
Tana
Ethiopian
Highlands
ETHIOPIA
SOMALIA
Somali Peninsula

Lagos
Gulf of Guinea
Bioko
EQUATORIAL GUINEA
Príncipe
Sao Tome
Annobon
CAMEROON
Cameroon Mtn.
13,435 ft. (4095 m)
CENTRAL AFRICAN
REPUBLIC
Ubangi R.
Congo
Basin
Congo River
DEM. REP.
OF THE
CONGO
Kasai R.
Congo River
Cabinda
(Angola)
GABON
CONGO REPUBLIC
RWANDA
BURUNDI
UGANDA
Lake
Albert
Lake
Victoria
Margherita
16,762 ft.
(5109 m)
KENYA
Lake
Turkana
Mt. Kenya
17,058 ft. (5199m)
Mogadishu
Nairobi
Mt. Kilimanjaro
19,340 ft. (5895 m)
TANZANIA
Pemba I.
Zanzibar
Dar es
Salaam
Seychelles
Amirante
Is.
Cerf I.
Aldabra Is.
Agalega Is.

EQUATOR

ATLANTIC
OCEAN

Ascension I.

Luanda
Cuanza R.
Cuanza
ANGOLA
Bie
Plateau
Cunene R.
Katanga
Plateau
Lake
Mweru
Lake
Tanganyika
Lake
Bangweulu
ZAMBIA
Zambezi R.
MALAWI
Lake
Nyasa
Comoros
Islands
MADAGASCAR
Mauritius
Reunion
Mascarene Is.

St. Helena

PRIME MERIDIAN

Cape Fria
Etosha
Pan
NAMIBIA
Makgadikgadi
Pans
Namib Desert
Kalahari
Desert
BOTSWANA
Zambezi R.
Victoria
Falls
Kariba L.
ZIMBABWE
Limpopo (R.)
MOZAMBIQUE
Mozambique Channel
Madagascar
TROPIC OF CAPRICORN 23½°S

INDIAN
OCEAN

Orange R.
Pretoria
(Tshwane)
SOUTH
AFRICA
LESOTHO
ESWATINI
(SWAZILAND)
Drakensberg
Cape Town
Cape of
Good Hope
Cape Agulhas

Prince
Edward
Islands
Crozet
Islands

Land Cover Map
Africa

Cropland   Grassland

Semi-desert   Tropical   Broadleaf
& desert   rain forest   forest

Boundary Symbols

——————   International boundary
– – – – – – –   Other boundary
(disputed or undefined)

Scale

1:46,300,000
0   250   500   750   1000 miles
1 in. to 730 mi.
0   250 500 750   1000 kilometers
1 cm to 463 km

Detailed legend on page 8   Lambert Equal Area Projection

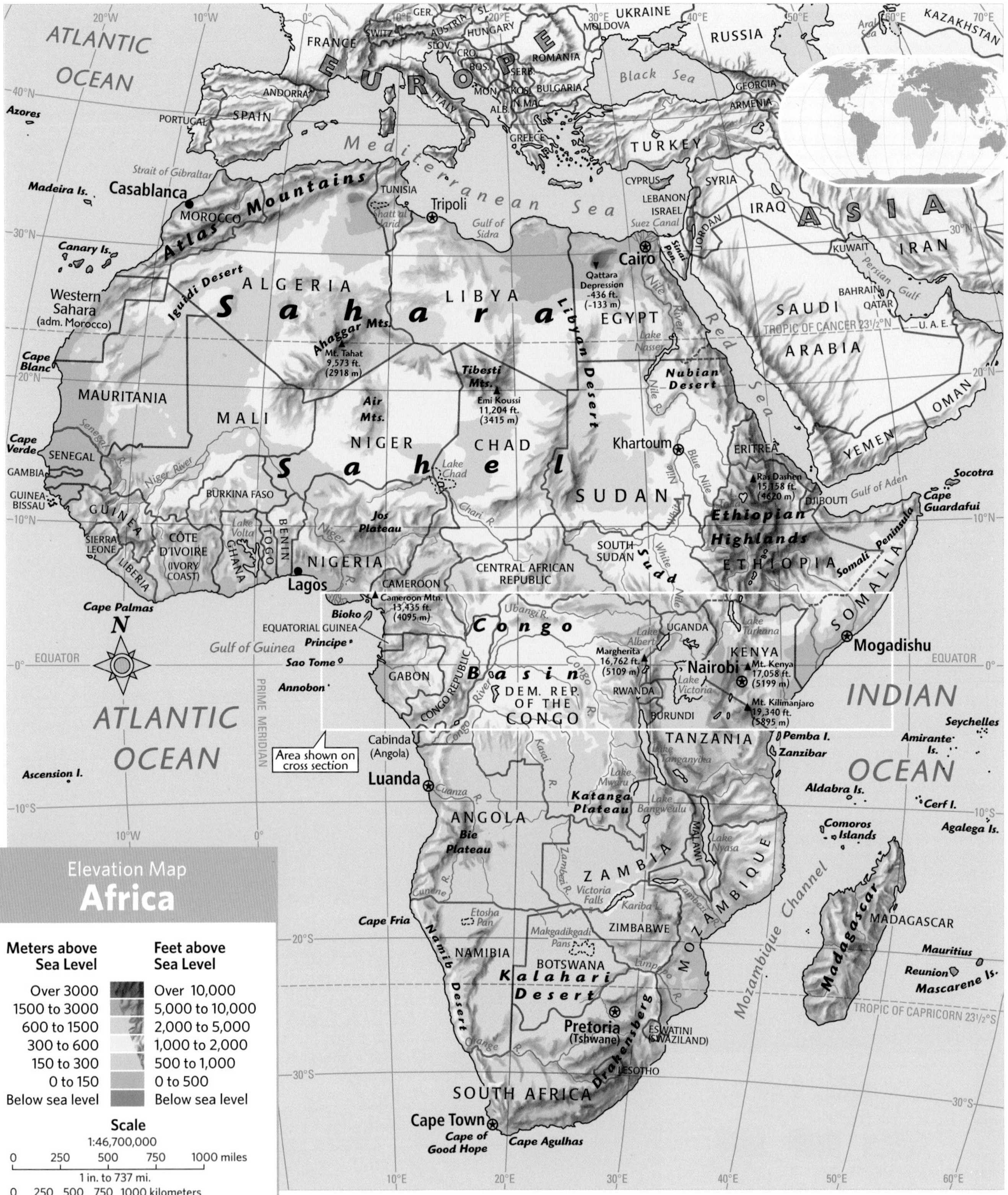

ATLANTIC OCEAN

EUROPE

ASIA

FRANCE
SWITZ. AUSTRIA GER. HUNGARY UKRAINE MOLDOVA RUSSIA
PORTUGAL SPAIN ITALY SLOV. CRO. SERB. ROMANIA GEORGIA KAZAKHSTAN
ANDORRA MON. KOS. N.MAC. BULGARIA ARMENIA
GREECE TURKEY
ALB.

Black Sea

Azores
Madeira Is.
Casablanca
MOROCCO
Canary Is.
Cape Blanc
Western Sahara (adm. Morocco)
MAURITANIA
Cape Verde
SENEGAL
GAMBIA
GUINEA-BISSAU
GUINEA
SIERRA LEONE
LIBERIA
Cape Palmas
CÔTE D'IVOIRE (IVORY COAST)
BURKINA FASO
GHANA
TOGO
BENIN
NIGERIA
Lagos
Gulf of Guinea
EQUATORIAL GUINEA
Bioko
Principe
Sao Tome
Annobon
GABON
CONGO REPUBLIC
CABINDA (Angola)
Luanda

Atlas Mountains
Strait of Gibraltar
Mediterranean Sea
TUNISIA
Tripoli
Gulf of Sidra
ALGERIA
LIBYA
Iguidi Desert
Sahara
Ahaggar Mts.
Mt. Tahat 9,573 ft. (2918 m)
Air Mts.
MALI
NIGER
Sahel
Lake Chad
CHAD
Tibesti Mts.
Emi Koussi 11,204 ft. (3415 m)
Jos Plateau
Lake Volta
Niger River
Senegal R.
Chari R.
CAMEROON
Cameroon Mtn. 13,435 ft. (4095 m)
CENTRAL AFRICAN REPUBLIC
Ubangi R.
Congo River
Congo Basin
DEM. REP. OF THE CONGO
Kasai R.
Cuanza
Cunene

Qattara Depression -436 ft. (-133 m)
Cairo
Sinai Pen.
Suez Canal
EGYPT
Libyan Desert
Nile River
Lake Nasser
Nubian Desert
Red Sea
Khartoum
SUDAN
SOUTH SUDAN
Sudd
White Nile
Blue Nile
ERITREA
Ras Dashen 15,158 ft. (4620 m)
Ethiopian Highlands
ETHIOPIA
DJIBOUTI
Gulf of Aden
Socotra
Cape Guardafui
Somali Peninsula
SOMALIA
Mogadishu
UGANDA
Lake Albert
Lake Turkana
KENYA
Mt. Kenya 17,058 ft. (5199 m)
Margherita 16,762 ft. (5109 m)
Nairobi
RWANDA
Lake Victoria
BURUNDI
Mt. Kilimanjaro 19,340 ft. (5895 m)
TANZANIA
Pemba I.
Zanzibar

UKRAINE
MOLDOVA
RUSSIA
GEORGIA
ARMENIA
AZER.
CYPRUS
SYRIA
LEBANON
ISRAEL
JORDAN
IRAQ
IRAN
KUWAIT
SAUDI ARABIA
BAHRAIN
QATAR
U.A.E.
OMAN
YEMEN
TROPIC OF CANCER 23½°N
Persian Gulf

EQUATOR

INDIAN OCEAN

Seychelles
Amirante Is.
Cerf I.
Aldabra Is.
Agalega Is.
Comoros Islands
MADAGASCAR
Mozambique Channel
MOZAMBIQUE
Mauritius
Reunion
Mascarene Is.
TROPIC OF CAPRICORN 23½°S

Katanga Plateau
Lake Mweru
Lake Bangweulu
Lake Tanganyika
Lake Nyasa
MALAWI
ZAMBIA
Zambezi R.
Victoria Falls
Kariba
ZIMBABWE
Limpopo R.
Makgadikgadi Pans
BOTSWANA
Kalahari Desert
ANGOLA
Bie Plateau
Cape Fria
Etosha Pan
NAMIBIA
Namib Desert
Orange R.
Pretoria (Tshwane)
Drakensberg
ESWATINI (SWAZILAND)
LESOTHO
SOUTH AFRICA
Cape Town
Cape of Good Hope
Cape Agulhas

ATLANTIC OCEAN

Ascension I.

N
Area shown on cross section
PRIME MERIDIAN

Elevation Map
Africa

Meters above Sea Level	Feet above Sea Level
Over 3000	Over 10,000
1500 to 3000	5,000 to 10,000
600 to 1500	2,000 to 5,000
300 to 600	1,000 to 2,000
150 to 300	500 to 1,000
0 to 150	0 to 500
Below sea level	Below sea level

Scale
1:46,700,000

0 250 500 750 1000 miles
1 in. to 737 mi.

0 250 500 750 1000 kilometers
1 cm to 467 km

Detailed legend on page 8   Lambert Equal Area Projection

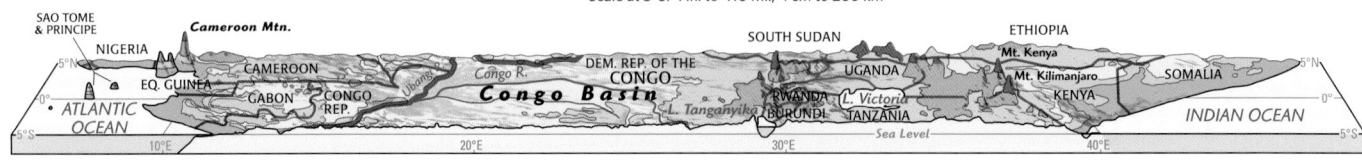

Cross Section
Vertical exaggeration 30 to 1
Scale at 5°S: 1 in. to 410 mi., 1 cm to 260 km

SAO TOME & PRINCIPE
NIGERIA
Cameroon Mtn.
EQ. GUINEA
CAMEROON
GABON
CONGO REP.
Ubangi R.
Congo R.
Congo Basin
DEM. REP. OF THE CONGO
RWANDA
BURUNDI
L. Tanganyika
TANZANIA
L. Victoria
UGANDA
SOUTH SUDAN
KENYA
Mt. Kenya
Mt. Kilimanjaro
ETHIOPIA
SOMALIA
Sea Level
ATLANTIC OCEAN
INDIAN OCEAN

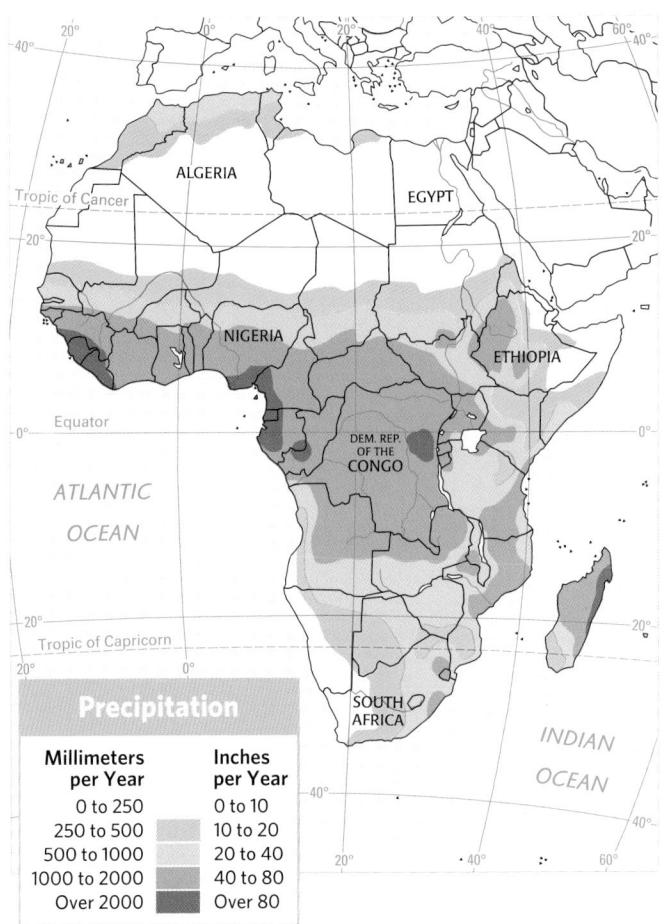

Precipitation

Millimeters per Year	Inches per Year
0 to 250	0 to 10
250 to 500	10 to 20
500 to 1000	20 to 40
1000 to 2000	40 to 80
Over 2000	Over 80

Niger is one of the world's poorest countries, with over 45 percent of its population living on less than US$1.90 a day. Ninety percent of its labor force is involved in agriculture. Unsophisticated farming methods and cycles of drought, however, result in shortages of food.

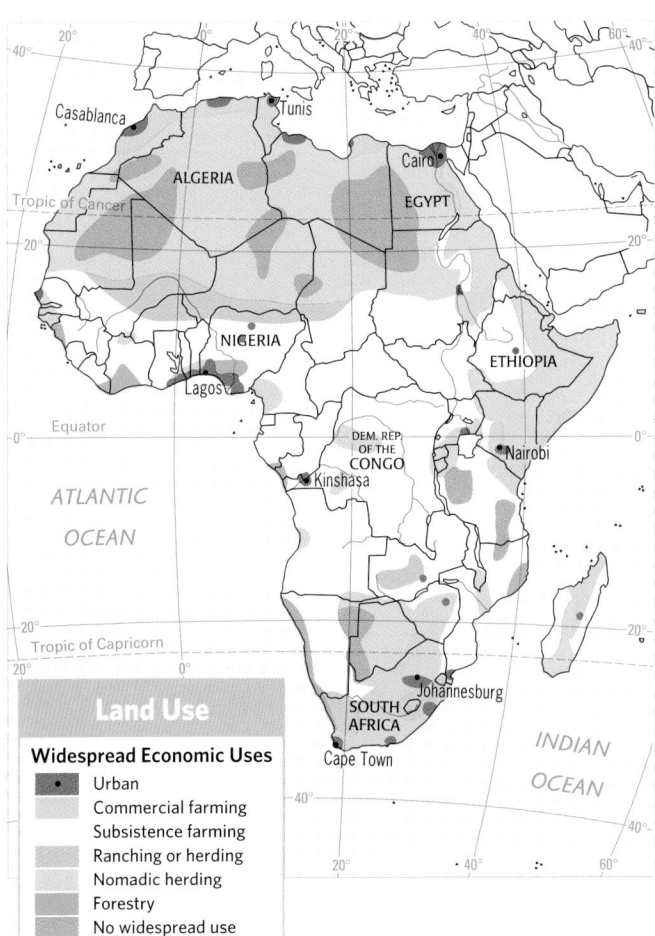

Land Use

Widespread Economic Uses

- Urban
- Commercial farming
- Subsistence farming
- Ranching or herding
- Nomadic herding
- Forestry
- No widespread use

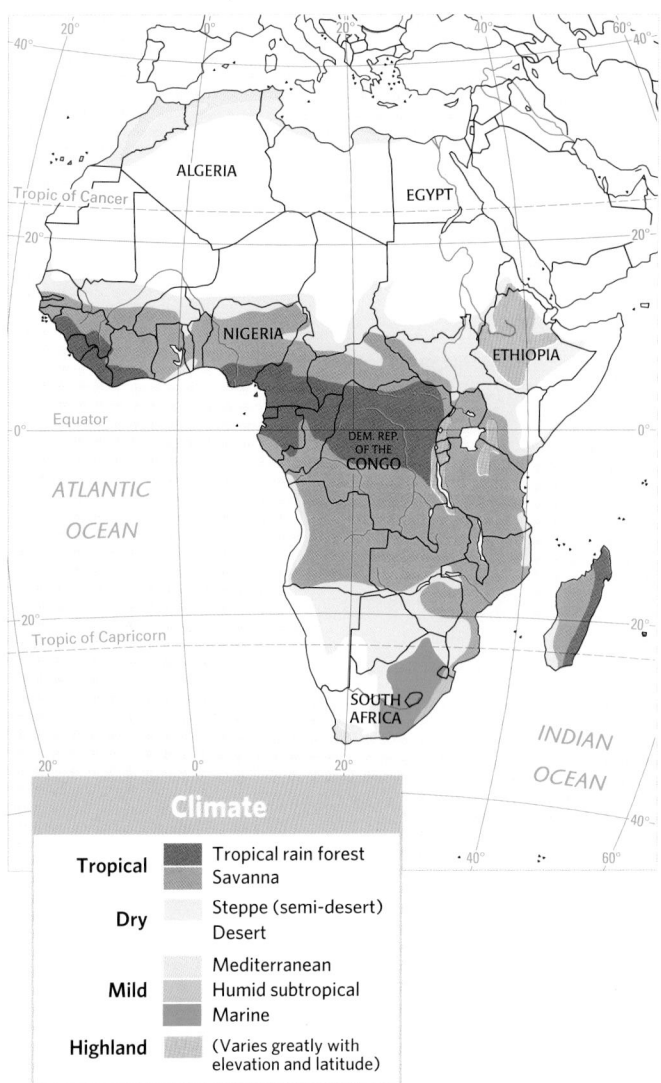

Climate

Tropical		Tropical rain forest
		Savanna
Dry		Steppe (semi-desert)
		Desert
Mild		Mediterranean
		Humid subtropical
		Marine
Highland		(Varies greatly with elevation and latitude)

Energy Resources and Metals

- ⬤ Coal
- ⬤ Oil (petroleum)
- ⬤ Natural gas
- ☢ Uranium
- ◆ Aluminum (bauxite)
- ■ Copper
- ○ Gold
- ✦ Iron
- ▽ Lead
- ★ Manganese
- ◆ Nickel
- ✛ Tin

Balance of Trade

Algeria

Total Exports
US$43.2 billion

- European Union 62.6%
- All Others 23.7%
- United States 9.0%
- Brazil 4.7%

Total Imports
US$52.2 billion

- European Union 49.2%
- All Others 29.8%
- China 16.0%
- United States 5.0%

Egypt

Total Exports
US$23.9 billion

- European Union 28.2%
- All Others 58.6%
- Saudi Arabia 7.5%
- Turkey 5.7%

Total Imports
US$62.8 billion

- European Union 31.8%
- All Others 49.7%
- China 11.9%
- United States 6.

Continues on page 158

Political Relief Map
Northern Africa

City Symbols

Casablanca ● Over 1,000,000 people
Benghazi ● 500,000 to 1,000,000
Qabis · Under 500,000
Cairo ✱ National capital

Scale
1:24,500,000

0   150   300   450   600 miles
1 in. to 387 mi.

0   150   300   450   600 kilometers
1 cm to 245 km

Detailed legend on page 8   Lambert Equal Area Projection

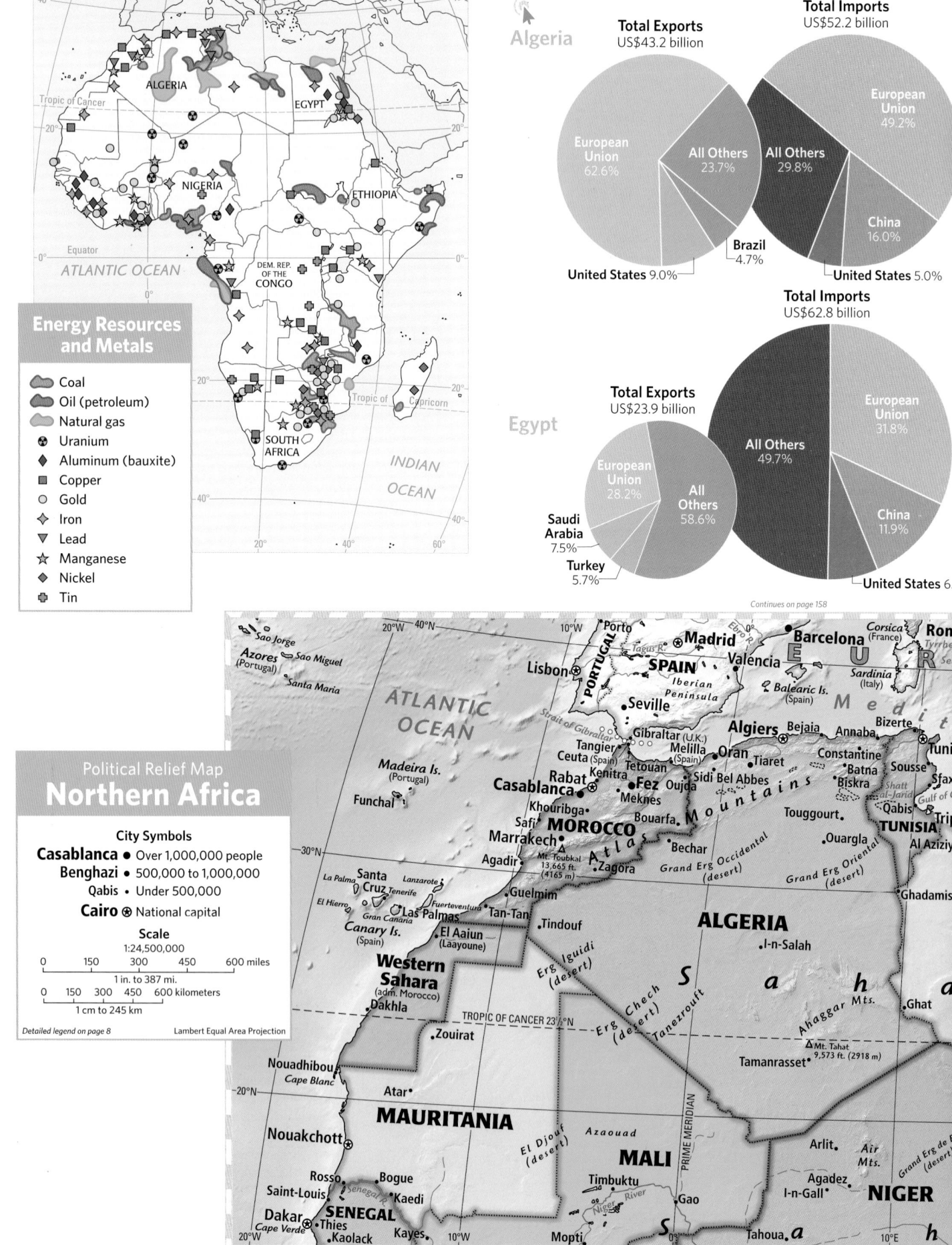

Continues on page 138

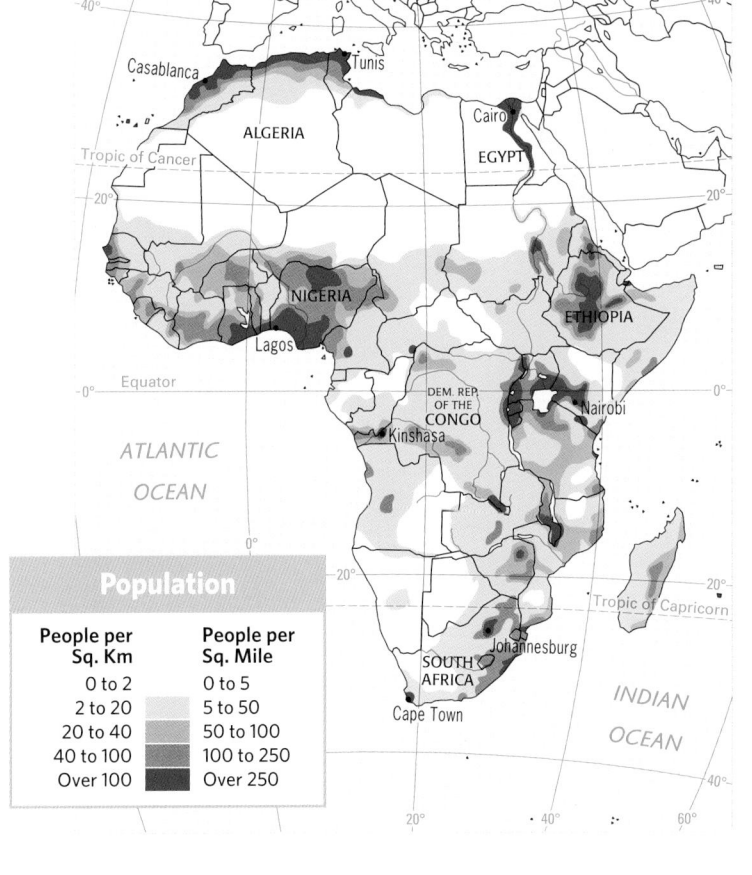

Continues on page 159

Population

People per Sq. Km	People per Sq. Mile
0 to 2	0 to 5
2 to 20	5 to 50
20 to 40	50 to 100
40 to 100	100 to 250
Over 100	Over 250

Natural Population Growth

Africa

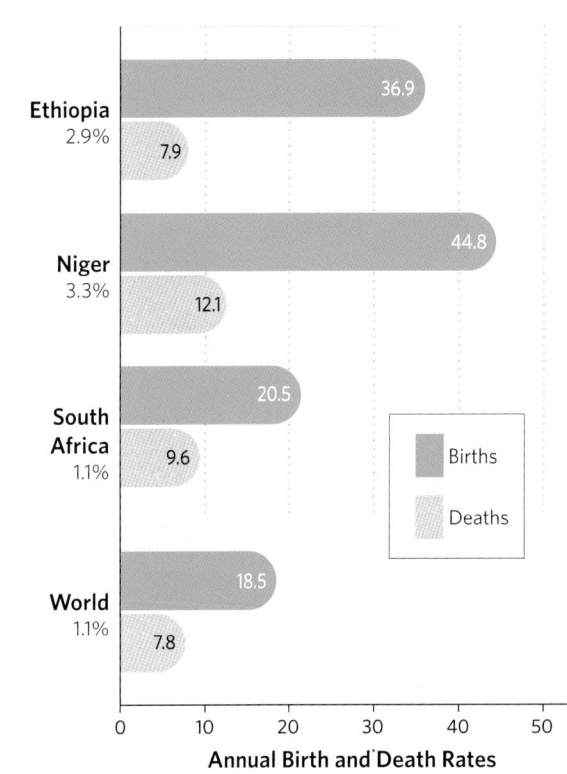

Ethiopia
2.9%
36.9
7.9

Niger
3.3%
44.8
12.1

South Africa
1.1%
20.5
9.6

World
1.1%
18.5
7.8

Births
Deaths

0 10 20 30 40 50

Annual Birth and Death Rates
(per 1,000 people)

Continental Divide

Africa is divided both physically and culturally by the Sahara. Most Africans living north of the Sahara are Arab and Muslim. About 80 percent of all Africans live south of the Sahara. They are more diverse than northern Africans. They belong to 800 ethnic groups and follow Christianity, Islam, or traditional religions.

Continues on page 139   Continues on page 140

Continues on pages 136–137

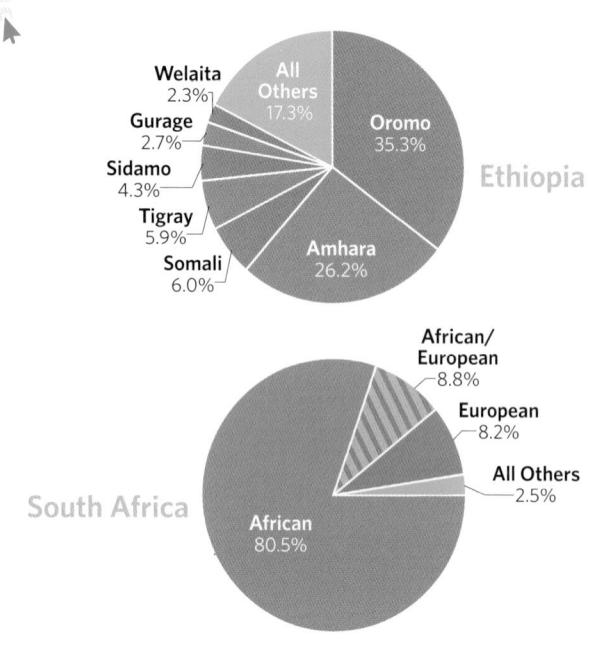

Continues on page 139

Political Relief Map
Western Africa

City Symbols
Lagos ● Over 1,000,000 people
Zaria • 500,000 to 1,000,000
Parakou • Under 500,000

Freetown ⊛ National capital

Scale
1:20,300,000

| 0 | 100 | 200 | 300 | 400 | 500 miles |

1 in. to 320 mi.

| 0 | 100 | 200 | 300 | 400 | 500 kilometers |

1 cm to 203 km

Detailed legend on page 8   Lambert Equal Area Projection

Forced Together

European countries divided Africa among themselves during the late 1800s, drawing arbitrary boundary lines that often put rival ethnic groups in the same country. These divisions have led to bloody conflicts that continue to disrupt Africa today.

Ethnic Composition

Ethiopia

- Oromo 35.3%
- Amhara 26.2%
- All Others 17.3%
- Somali 6.0%
- Tigray 5.9%
- Sidamo 4.3%
- Gurage 2.7%
- Welaita 2.3%

South Africa

- African 80.5%
- African/ European 8.8%
- European 8.2%
- All Others 2.5%

Education is important to economic development, yet 34 million children in sub-Saharan Africa—23 percent of all girls and 19 percent of all boys—do not attend school. Only 72 percent of all men and 54 percent of all women in Africa can read and write.

A refugee camp stretches out near Goma in the Democratic Republic of the Congo. About one third of the world's refugees are African. (For more on refugees, see pages 48-49.)

Political Relief Map
Central Africa

City Symbols

Douala ● Over 1,000,000 people
Lubumbashi • 500,000 to 1,000,000
Bambari • Under 500,000
Brazzaville ⊛ National capital

Scale
1:17,900,000

0   100   200   300   400 miles

1 in. to 282 mi.

0   100   200   300   400 kilometers

1 cm to 179 km

Detailed legend on page 8   Lambert Equal Area Projection

Continues on pages 136-137
Continues on page 140
Continues on page 138
Continues on page 140

NIGER
Lake Chad
20°E
30°E
Abeche
Darfur
Al Fashir
Al Ubayyid
Kusti
Diffa
S a h e l
Jebel Marra
10,131 ft. (3088 m)
CHAD
Nyala
SUDAN
White Nile
Maiduguri
N'Djamena
Maroua
Birao
10°N
10°N
Kaduna
Bauchi
10°E
Mandara Mts.
Garoua
Sarh
Waw
S u d d
Malakal
Abuja
Jos Plateau
Chari R.
Moundou
Sobat R.
Kainji Dam
Ilorin
NIGERIA
Adamoua Plateau
CENTRAL AFRICAN
REPUBLIC
SOUTH
SUDAN
Bahr al Jabal
Ogbomosho
Iwo
Ilesha
Makurdi
Benue R.
Gotel Mts.
Ngaoundere
Bouar
Bambari
Mbomou R.
Juba
Ibadan
Benin City
Enugu
CAMEROON
Bangui
Ubangi R.
Uele R.
Gemena
Isiro
Gulu
Port Harcourt
Aba
Cameroon Mt.
13,435 ft. (4095 m)
Sanaga R.
Douala
Berberati
Congo
Bumba
Lake Albert
Bight of Benin
Niger R.
Niger River Delta
Malabo
Bioko
Edea
Yaounde
Dja R.
C o n g o
Kisangani
Margherita Peak
16,762 ft. (5109 m)
Stanley Falls
UGANDA
Kampala
Gulf of Guinea
EQUATORIAL GUINEA
Bata
Rio Muni
Oyem
Ouesso
Sangha R.
River
B a s i n
Lake Edward
Entebbe
Mbarara
SAO TOME & PRINCIPE
Principe I.
Libreville
Ogooue R.
CONGO
REPUBLIC
Mbandaka
DEMOCRATIC
REPUBLIC
OF THE
CONGO
Nyiragongo
11,400 ft. (3475 m)
Lake Kivu
Kabale
Lake Victoria
Sao Tome
EQUATOR
GABON
Lualaba R.
Kindu
Bukavu
RWANDA
Kigali
Geita
Sao Tome
0°
Port Gentil
Lambarene
Moanda
Franceville
Lake Mai-Ndombe
Uvira
Bujumbura
Annobon (Eq. Guinea)
Mouila
Congo River
Kasai R.
BURUNDI
Kasongo
Kigoma
Ujiji
Mossendjo
Loubomo
Brazzaville
Stanley Pool
Sankuru R.
Lomami R.
Kalemie
Kabalo
TANZANIA
L. Tanganyika
ATLANTIC
OCEAN
Pointe-Noire
Kinshasa
Kwango R.
Kananga
Kamina
Kasanga
Cabinda
(Angola)
Boma
Matadi
Mbuji-Mayi
Kabolo
Mbala
Uige
Mitumba Mts.
Lake Mweru
Kamina
Lake Rukwa
N
Luanda
Malanje
Katanga
Plateau
Kolwezi
Great Rift Valley
Kasama
10°S
Cuanza R.
Likasi
Lubumbashi
10°S
ANGOLA
Bie Plateau
Muchinga Mts.
Lobito
Benguela
Huambo
Kuito
Kitwe
Ndola
ZAMBIA
Kabwe
10°E
20°E
30°E

Continues on page 141

Continues on pages 136-137
Continues on page 178
Continues on page 139
Continues on page 141

LIBYA

Libyan Desert

30°E · Nubian Desert · 40°E · 50°E · 20°N

20°N

SAUDI ARABIA

Rub Al Khali (Empty Quarter)

ASIA

OMAN

3rd Cataract
Dongola
4th Cataract
Port Sudan
Farasan Is.
· Salalah

CHAD

Ennedi Plateau

Marawi
5th Cataract
Atbarah

ERITREA
Keren
Dahlak Arch.
Massawa

YEMEN
Sanaa

Arabian Sea

Sahel
Omdurman
6th Cataract
Khartoum
White Nile Dam
Kassala
Asmara
Al Hudaydah
Al Mukalla

Darfur
· Al Fashir

SUDAN

Wad Medani
Sennar Dam
Sennar
Mekele
Denakil Depression
-381 ft. (-116 m)
Assab
Taizz
Aden
Socotra (Yemen)

△Jebel Marra
10,131 ft. (3088 m)
Al Ubayyid·
Kusti
Ras Dashen
15,158 ft. (4620 m) △
Gonder
Lake Assal
-512 ft. (-156 m)
DJIBOUTI
Boosaaso
Abd al Kuri (Yemen)

·Nyala
Bahir Dar
Dese·
Djibouti
Gulf of Aden
Cape Guardafui (Raas Caseyr)

White Nile
Tississat Falls
Ethiopian
Dire Dawa
Hargeysa
Berbera
Somaliland
Cape Hafun

10°N
·Birao

Sudd
Malakal·
Blue Nile
Sobat R.
Highlands
Addis Ababa·
Nazret
Harer
Burao
Somali Peninsula
Nugaal Valley
10°N

CENTRAL AFRICAN REPUBLIC

Waw·
SOUTH SUDAN
Bahr al Jabal
Jima·
ETHIOPIA
·Awasa
Ogaden
Garoowe

Mbomou R.
Uele R.
Juba⊛
Maji·
Shebele R.
SOMALIA
·Hobyo

Isiro·
Lake Turkana
·Mega
Baidoa·
·Bumba
Moyale·
Jawhar·

Congo R.
Congo
Kisangani·
Margherita Peak
16,762 ft. (5109 m)
Stanley Falls
Lake Albert
·Gulu
UGANDA
Lake Kyoga
Mt. Elgon
△14,178 ft. (4321 m)
KENYA
·Meru
Merca·
Mogadishu

0°
Basin
Lake Edward
Kampala·
Jinja
Eldoret·
EQUATOR
0°

DEM. REP. OF THE CONGO
Kindu·
Entebbe·
Nyiragongo
11,400 ft. (3475 m)△
Lake Kivu
·Mbarara
Kisumu·
Nakuru·
Mt. Kenya
17,058 ft. (5199 m)
Garissa·
Kismaayo·
INDIAN OCEAN

Sankuru R.
RWANDA
Kigali·
Bukavu·
Lake Victoria
Nairobi
·Machakos

Lualaba R.
·Kananga
Bujumbura·
Mwanza·
Serengeti Plain
Mt. Kilimanjaro
19,340 ft. (5895 m)
Malindi·

Lomami R.
BURUNDI
Shinyanga·
·Arusha
Moshi·
Pemba I.

·Mbuji-Mayi
·Kasongo
Kigoma·
Ujiji·
Mombasa·

Kalemie·
Lake Tanganyika
Tabora·
Tanga·

·Kamina
Kabalo·
Dodoma⊛
Morogoro·
Zanzibar
Zanzibar I.

Mitumba Mts.
Katanga Plateau
Lake Mweru
TANZANIA
Dar es Salaam
Mafia I.

·Kamina
Great Rift Valley
Lake Rukwa
·Mbeya
Rufiji R.

10°S
·Kolwezi
Lake Nyasa
Kasama·
Mbala·
Mtwara·
Aldabra Is.
SEYCHELLES
10°S

·Likasi
30°E **ZAMBIA**
Tunduru·
Moroni⊛
COMOROS
50°E

Muchinga Mts.
Mzuzu·
Ruvuma R.
Mayotte (France)

Political Relief Map
Eastern Africa

MALAWI
Lake Nyasa (Lake Malawi)
MOZAMBIQUE
40°E

City Symbols

Omdurman ●	Over 1,000,000 people
Mombasa ●	500,000 to 1,000,000
Tanga ·	Under 500,000
Nairobi ⊛	National capital

Scale
1:19,900,000

0 100 200 300 400 500 miles
1 in. to 314 mi.

0 100 200 300 400 500 kilometers
1 cm to 199 km

Detailed legend on page 8 · Lambert Equal Area Projection

Both Rich and Poor

The world's ten poorest countries are in Africa. More than 40 percent of the population of sub-Saharan Africa survives on less than US$1.90 a day. Although Africa is rich with gold and oil, most mining companies are foreign-owned and they employ few Africans.

Great Rift Valley

The Great Rift Valley stretches 4,500 miles (7,200 kilometers) from Syria in western Asia to Mozambique in southern Africa. The valley is being formed along a fault zone that is developing into a divergent plate boundary (see pages 20–21). In places, it has stretched Africa by up to 60 miles. Lake Tanganyika and Lake Nyasa are just two of the many lakes formed by the rift.

Great Rift Valley

In a dry, mountainous region of northwestern Namibia, the Himba people maintain most of their traditional ways of life. These herders, once threatened by war and drought, now benefit from ecotourism.

Continues on page 139
Continues on page 140

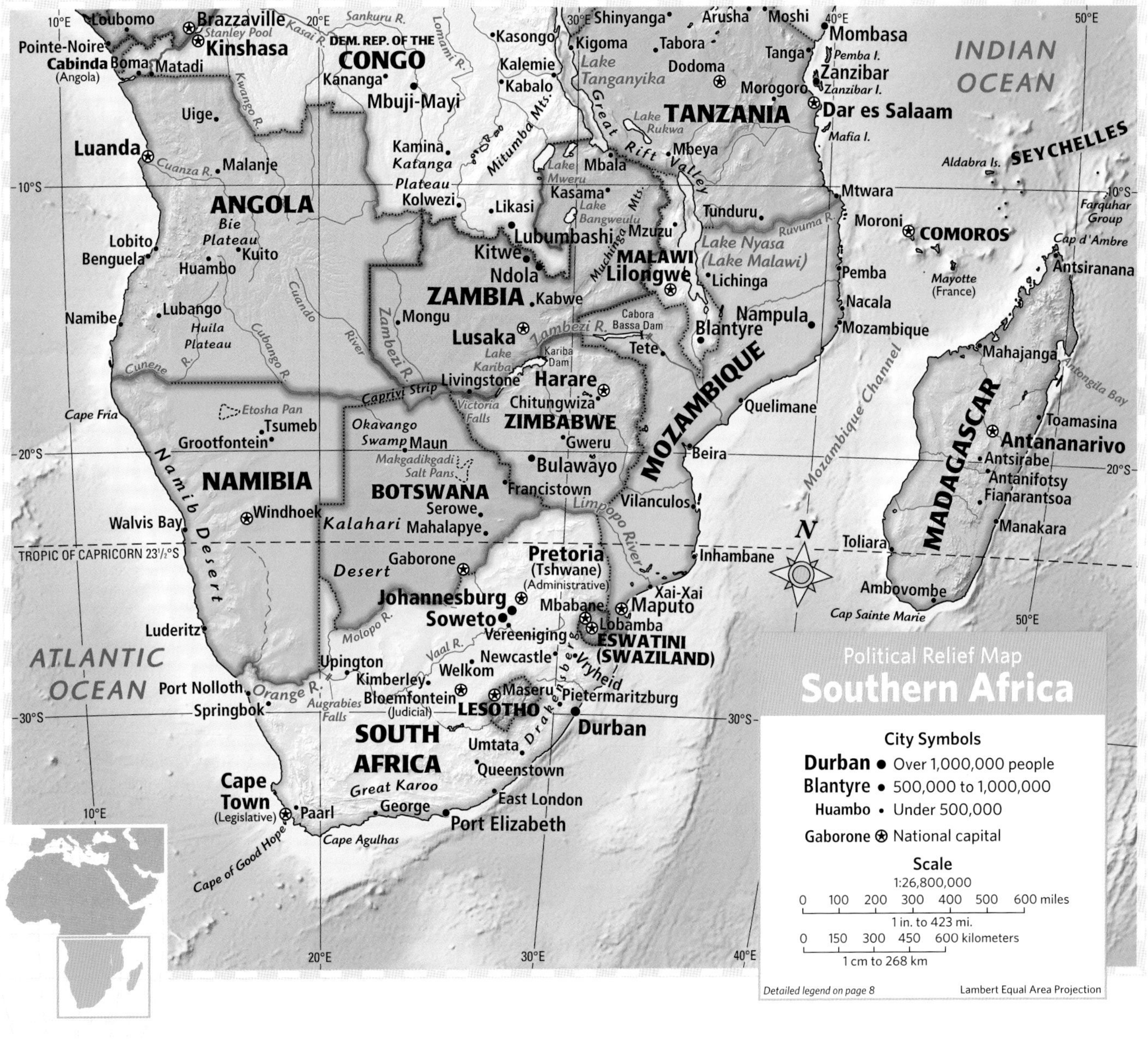

Political Relief Map
Southern Africa

City Symbols

Durban	● Over 1,000,000 people
Blantyre	• 500,000 to 1,000,000
Huambo	• Under 500,000
Gaborone	⊛ National capital

Scale

1:26,800,000

0 100 200 300 400 500 600 miles

1 in. to 423 mi.

0 150 300 450 600 kilometers

1 cm to 268 km

Detailed legend on page 8   Lambert Equal Area Projection

MAP LABELS:

Loubomo, Brazzaville, Pointe-Noire, Cabinda (Angola), Boma, Matadi, Kinshasa, DEM. REP. OF THE CONGO, Kananga, Mbuji-Mayi, Kasongo, Kalemie, Kabalo, Kamina, Katanga Plateau, Kolwezi, Likasi, Lubumbashi, Kitwe, Ndola, ZAMBIA, Kabwe, Mongu, Lusaka, Stanley Pool, Kasai R., Sankuru R., Lomami R., Kwango R., Lake Tanganyika, Shinyanga, Arusha, Moshi, Kigoma, Tabora, Kasongo, Dodoma, Mitumba Mts., Lake Rukwa, TANZANIA, Mbeya, Mbala, Lake Mweru, Kasama, Lake Bangweulu, Mzuzu, Muchinga Mts., Tunduru, Ruvuma R., Lake Nyasa (Lake Malawi), MALAWI, Lilongwe, Lichinga, Mombasa, Pemba I., Tanga, Zanzibar, Zanzibar I., Dar es Salaam, Mafia I., Mtwara, INDIAN OCEAN, Aldabra Is., SEYCHELLES, Farquhar Group, Moroni, COMOROS, Cap d'Ambre, Antsiranana, Mayotte (France), Pemba, Nacala, Mozambique, Nampula, Blantyre, MOZAMBIQUE, Mahajanga, Uige, Luanda, Cuanza R., Malanje, ANGOLA, Bie Plateau, Kuito, Lobito, Benguela, Huambo, Namibe, Lubango, Huila Plateau, Cuando R., Cubango R., Cunene R., Zambezi R., Caprivi Strip, Etosha Pan, Cape Fria, Tsumeb, Grootfontein, Okavango Swamp, Maun, Makgadikgadi Salt Pans, NAMIBIA, Namib Desert, Walvis Bay, Windhoek, Kalahari Desert, BOTSWANA, Serowe, Mahalapye, Gaborone, Cabora Bassa Dam, Tete, Kariba Dam, Lake Kariba, Livingstone, Victoria Falls, Harare, Chitungwiza, ZIMBABWE, Gweru, Bulawayo, Francistown, Limpopo River, Vilanculos, Beira, Quelimane, Mozambique Channel, MADAGASCAR, Toamasina, Antananarivo, Antsirabe, Antanifotsy, Fianarantsoa, Manakara, Antongila Bay, Toliara, Ambovombe, Cap Sainte Marie, Luderitz, ATLANTIC OCEAN, Port Nolloth, Springbok, Upington, Molopo R., Orange R., Augrabies Falls, Vaal R., Kimberley, Welkom, Newcastle, Bloemfontein (Judicial), Maseru, LESOTHO, Drakensberg, Vryheid, Pietermaritzburg, Durban, Pretoria (Tshwane) (Administrative), Johannesburg, Soweto, Vereeniging, Mbabane, Lobamba, ESWATINI (SWAZILAND), Xai-Xai, Maputo, Inhambane, SOUTH AFRICA, Umtata, Queenstown, East London, Port Elizabeth, George, Great Karoo, Cape Town (Legislative), Paarl, Cape of Good Hope, Cape Agulhas, TROPIC OF CAPRICORN 23½°S

How should the AIDS pandemic be controlled?

AIDS (acquired immune deficiency syndrome) is the leading cause of death in Africa. Reaching worldwide pandemic status in the early 1980s, AIDS now kills about 1.1 million people every year. Currently, more than 25 million Africans have HIV (human immunodeficiency virus), the virus that causes AIDS. Approximately 91 percent of children infected with HIV live in Africa. What is the best way to prevent HIV/AIDS? There are many perspectives on this issue. Here are two of them.

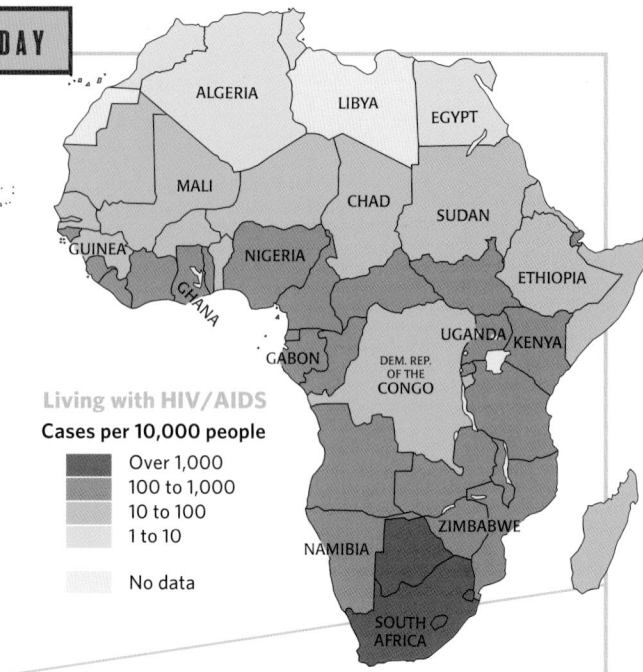

Living with HIV/AIDS

Cases per 10,000 people

- Over 1,000
- 100 to 1,000
- 10 to 100
- 1 to 10

- No data

Education will help control the AIDS pandemic.

- Medical treatment only helps those already infected with HIV. Even with treatment, people can still spread the disease.

- Some people have misconceptions about HIV/AIDS transmission and cures. Once they have a genuine understanding of HIV/AIDS, they can take effective steps to protect themselves, their partners, and their children.

- Education programs for children in South Africa, Zimbabwe, and Malawi teach HIV/AIDS awareness. They enable children and young adults to make more informed decisions.

- In sub-Saharan Africa in 2015, only about one-third of young men and women could correctly identify ways to prevent the spread of HIV/AIDS. Many infections can be prevented if more educational efforts are made to reduce the spread of the disease.

Proper education can reduce the stigma of HIV/AIDS and prevent the disease's spread.

Affordable treatment will help AIDS patients.

- Approximately 20 million people with HIV are not receiving treatment. Affordable treatment would help combat the spread of the disease.

- In 2015, 77 percent of pregnant women with HIV had access to medicine to prevent the transmission of HIV to their offspring.

- The stigma of HIV/AIDS results in a population that fears finding out if they have the disease. Of those with HIV, 40 percent are unaware that they are infected. With treatment available, people are often more willing to get tested.

- Without affordable treatment, AIDS will cripple Africa's already weakened economy. Over 1 million Africans are infected with HIV every year.

- Free antiretroviral drugs reduced AIDS deaths for Brazilians by almost 11 percent since 2003. Such a policy could also prolong the lives of most AIDS patients in Africa.

Population Pyramid Zimbabwe

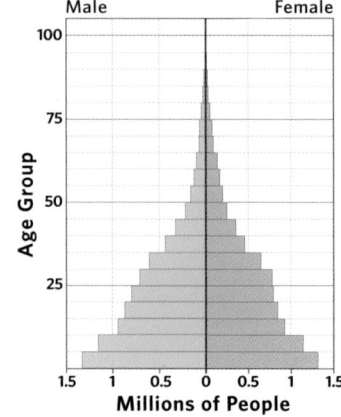

About 1.4 million people in Zimbabwe are living with HIV/AIDS. Zimbabwe has one of the shortest life expectancies in the world—an average of just 58 years.

How should the international community handle refugees?

More people have been forced from their homes in Africa than on any other continent. About 19 million Africans live as refugees. As many as 17 million are internally displaced or live in neighboring countries. The 1951 Refugee Convention and its 1967 Protocol have made the protection of these people an international responsibility. How should the international community handle refugees? There are many perspectives on this issue. Here are two of them.

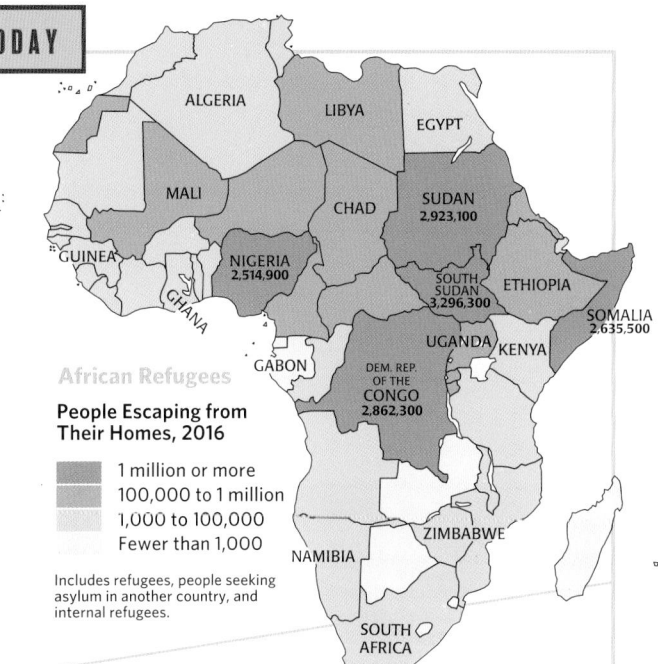

African Refugees

People Escaping from Their Homes, 2016

- 1 million or more
- 100,000 to 1 million
- 1,000 to 100,000
- Fewer than 1,000

Includes refugees, people seeking asylum in another country, and internal refugees.

Refugee agencies should maintain people near their home country.

- Keeping refugees close to their home countries allows them to maintain family and social ties, lessening the sense of isolation experienced by most refugees.

- Refugees living closer to their home are more likely to return home. Once refugees are relocated to a distant country, they rarely can return to their country of origin, even briefly.

- Neighboring countries are far more likely to share similar customs, languages, and lifestyles. As a result, a refugee does not need to face the long process of adjusting to an entirely new country, often without anything in common to its people.

- Distant countries have developed a fear of refugees based on terrorist attacks. This fear disrupts attempts to relocate refugees and can create unwelcoming situations for those that are relocated.

Since 2015 over 1 million refugees and migrants have fled from Africa to Europe across the Mediterranean Sea, and as many as 15,000 have died making the journey.

Refugee agencies should concentrate on relocating people to safe countries.

- Maintaining a large refugee population in camps or other facilities can create tremendous strain on the host countries, many of which are extremely poor themselves. Developing countries host over 80 percent of the world's refugees.

- The wars that cause refugees to flee can spread across borders to neighboring host countries. In 1994, the Rwandan genocide and revolution provoked a refugee crisis that brought down the governments of Burundi and Zaire (now called the Democratic Republic of the Congo) and provoked new wars.

- Security fears in wealthier countries are greatly exaggerated. Refugees are screened more thoroughly than any other group entering a country. Of the 3 million refugees to the United States since 1975, only 20 have been convicted of terrorist planning or attacks.

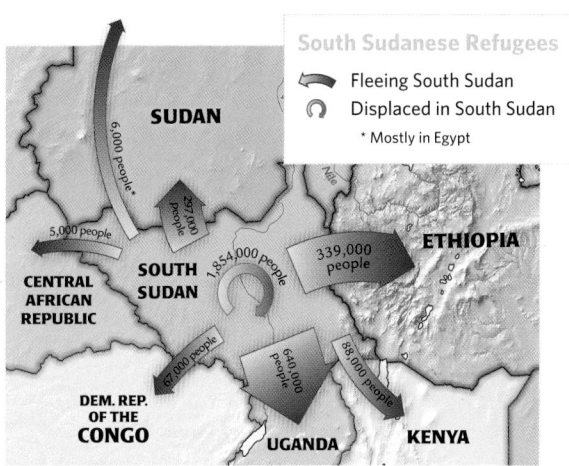

South Sudanese Refugees

- Fleeing South Sudan
- Displaced in South Sudan
- *Mostly in Egypt

South Sudan has suffered continuous war since 1983. Millions have been internally displaced or sought refuge in neighboring countries, all of which are among the poorest on Earth.

World Extreme Vatican City is the world's smallest independent country, with only 109 acres (44 hectares) and a population of fewer than 1,000, but it is home to the world's largest church, St. Peter's Basilica. Vatican City is located entirely within Rome, Italy. It is the headquarters of the Roman Catholic Church.

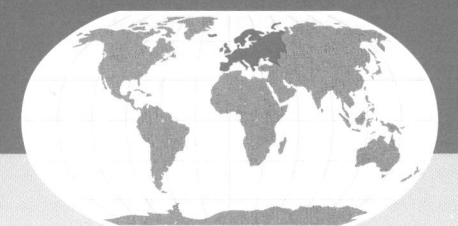

Europe

Europe, which shares a landmass with Asia, is the second most densely populated continent. It is the birthplace of modern industry.

Physical Features

Highest mountain peak
Mt. Elbrus 18,510 ft. (5,642 m)

Longest mountain range
Ural Mountains* 1,500 mi. (2,400 km)

Largest island
Great Britain 88,764 sq. mi. (229,898 sq. km)

Largest lakes
Caspian Sea* 143,300 sq. mi. (371,000 sq. km)★
Lake Ladoga 6,835 sq. mi. (17,703 sq. km)

Longest rivers
Volga 2,193 mi. (3,530 km)
Danube 1,770 mi. (2,850 km)

Other key physical features

Alps	Central Russian Upland
Apennines	Iberian Peninsula
Balkan Peninsula	Northern European Plain
Carpathian Mountains	Pyrenees
Caucasus Mountains*	Scandinavian Peninsula

Cultural Features

Population
741,447,000

Largest country by area
Russia* 6,592,800 sq. mi. (17,075,400 sq. km)★

Largest country by population
Russia* 142,257,519

Most densely populated
Monaco 39,288.5 people per sq. mi. (15,170.7 per sq. km)

Least densely populated
Iceland 8.5 people per sq. mi. (3.3 per sq. km)

Largest urban areas
Istanbul, Turkey 14,164,000★
Moscow, Russia 12,382,000

★ Among the world's largest. See the inside front cover.

*Located in both Europe and Asia.

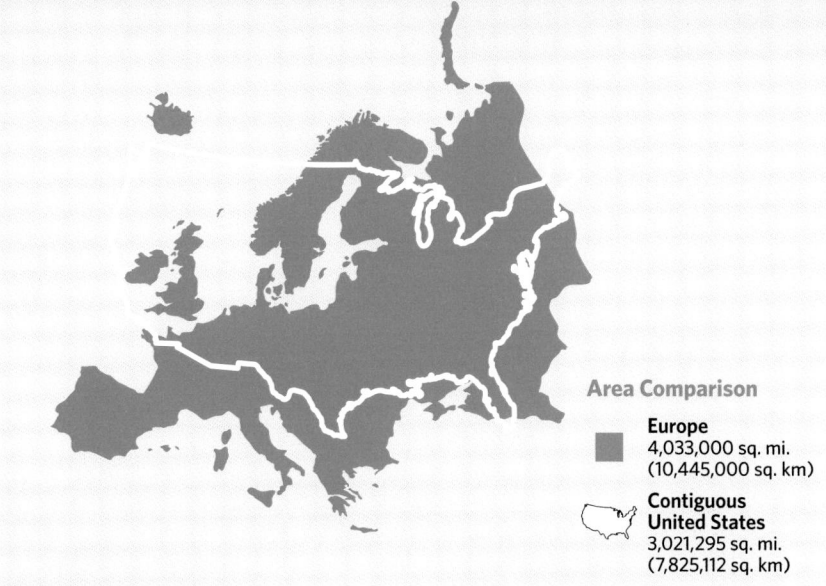

Area Comparison

Europe
4,033,000 sq. mi.
(10,445,000 sq. km)

Contiguous United States
3,021,295 sq. mi.
(7,825,112 sq. km)

Regional Maps of Europe

1 **British Isles** p.156
2 **Northern Europe** p.157
3 **Western Europe** p.158
4 **Central Europe** p.159
5 **Eastern Europe** p.160
6 **The Caucasus** p.161

Thematic Maps of Europe

Reclaimed Land in the Netherlands p.151
Precipitation p.152
Climate p.152
Land Use p.153
European Union p.153
Energy Resources and Metals p.154
Major Highways and Airports p.155
Population p.155
North Atlantic Drift p.156

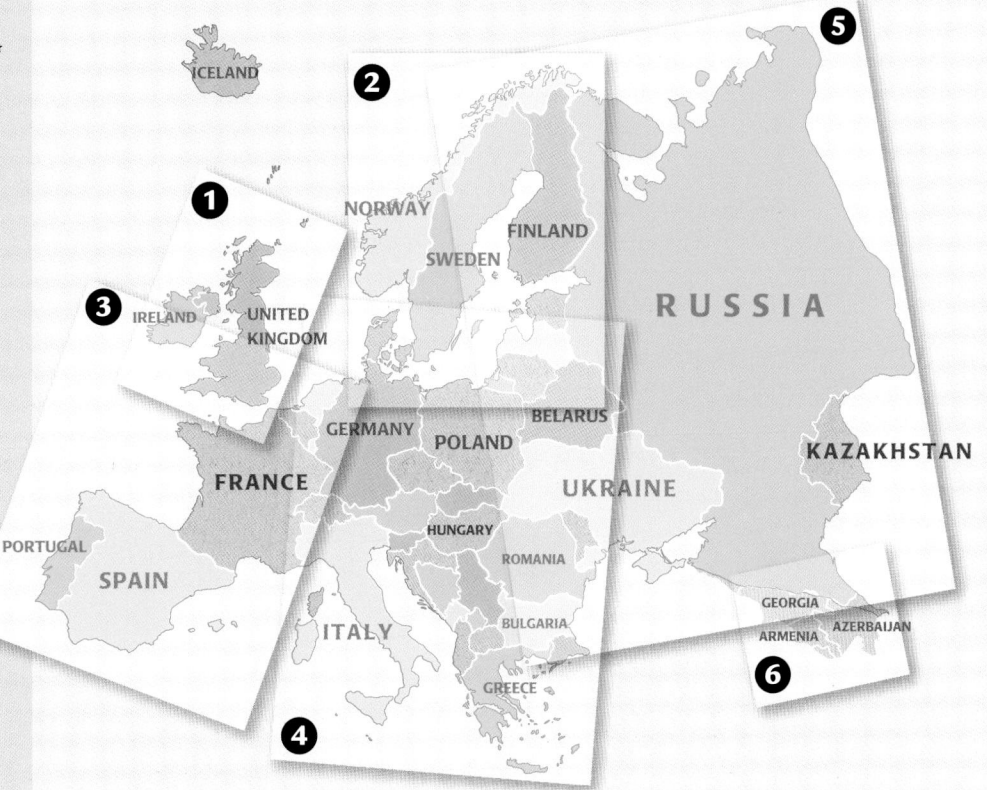

Political Relief Map
Europe

Boundary Symbols

.... International boundary
.... Other boundary
(disputed or undefined)
▣ Small country

City Symbols

Hamburg ● Over 1,000,000 people
Seville ● 500,000 to 1,000,000
Orel ● Under 500,000
Prague ⊛ National capital

Scale
1:17,400,000

0   100   200   300   400 miles
1 in. to 275 mi.
0   100   200   300   400 kilometers
1 cm to 174 km

Detailed legend on page 8   Bonne Projection

40°W   60°N   30°W   20°W   10°W   70°N   0°

Reykjavik
Surtsey I.
Iceland
ICELAND

ARCTIC CIRCLE 66½°N
PRIME MERIDIAN

Norwegian Sea

Trondheims Fiord
Trondheim
NORWAY
Scandinavian Peninsula
SWEDEN
Lillehammer
Bergen
Sogne Fiord
Hardanger Fiord
Bokna Fiord
Oslo
Stavanger
Upp
L. Mälar
Stockho
L. Vänern
Goteborg
Norrkö
L. Vättern

Faroe Islands (Den.)

Shetland Islands (U.K.)
Rockall (U.K.)
Orkney Islands (U.K.)

North Sea

Skagerrak
Kattegat
DENMARK
Århus
Copenhagen
Malmo
Bornholm (Den.)
Balt
Gdans

British Isles
Glasgow
Edinburgh
Great Britain
UNITED KINGDOM
Belfast
Ireland
Dublin
IRELAND
Irish Sea
Liverpool
Cork
Leeds
Manchester
Birmingham
Cardiff
Bristol
Southampton
London
Thames
The Hague
Amsterdam
Rotterdam
NETHERLANDS
Hamburg
Berlin
GERMANY
North
Oder
Poza
POL
Wrocł
Krak

Celtic Sea

English Channel
Channel Is. (U.K.)
Le Havre
Seine
Strait of Dover
Brussels
BELGIUM
Lille
Essen
Bonn
Cologne
LUXEMBOURG
Luxembourg
Frankfurt
Leipzig
Rhine
Elbe
⊛ Prague
CZECH REPUBLIC

ATLANTIC OCEAN

50°N

40°N

20°W

Bay of Biscay

Nantes
Orleans
Loire R.
FRANCE
Paris
Strasbourg
Stuttgart
Danube
Vienna
SLOVAK
Bratisla
Bordeaux
Limoges
Massif Central
Geneva
Bern
SWITZERLAND
LIECH.
Munich
AUSTRIA
Graz
Budapest
HUNGAR
Szege
A Coruña
Porto
Cantabrian Mts.
Bilbao
Douro R.
Iberian
Duero R.
Pyrenees
Toulouse
Lyon
Alps
Milan
Turin
SLOVENIA
Ljubljana
Zagreb
CROATIA
Venice
Po R.
Tiber R.
Belgra
BOSNIA
Sarajevo
Lisbon
PORTUGAL
SPAIN
Madrid
Zaragoza
Tagus R.
ANDORRA
Ebro R.
Gulf of Lion
Marseille
MONACO
Genoa
Ligurian Sea
Apen
Florence
SAN MARINO
VATICAN CITY
Rome
ITALY
MONTENEGRO
Podgorica
KOS
Pri
Skop
Guadiana R.
Peninsula
Seville
Guadalquivir R.
Barcelona
Valencia
Balearic Sea
Palma
Balearic Islands
Bastia
Corsica (Fr.)
Sardinia (Italy)
Adriatic Sea
Naples
Bari
Tirana
ALBANIA
Malaga
Strait of
Gibraltar (U.K.)
Gibraltar
Ceuta (Sp.)
Rabat
Melilla (Sp.)
Algiers
Mediterranean
Cagliari
Tyrrhenian Sea
Palermo
Messina
Sicily
Gulf of Taranto
Ionian Islands
Ionian Sea
Pelopon
MOROCCO
AFRICA
ALGERIA
TUNISIA
Tunis
MALTA
Valletta
Maltese Is.

10°W   30°N   0°   10°E   20°E

OCEAN
Hammerfest
Vardo
Barents Sea
Novaya Zemlya
Kolguyev I.
Narvik
Kiruna
Murmansk
Lapland
Kola Pen.
Pechora R.
Ob River
White Sea
FINLAND
Oulu
Arkhangelsk
Northern Dvina R.
RUSSIA
Ural Mountains
60°N
Gulf of Bothnia
Vaasa
Onega R.
Sukhona R.
Syktyvkar
70°E
Tampere
L. Saimaa
Lake Ladoga
Lake Onega
Kamskoye Res.
Yekaterinburg
Perm
Turku
Helsinki
Gulf of Finland
St. Petersburg
Volga River
Kirov
Izhevsk
Kama R.
Chelyabinsk
70°N
Tallinn
ESTONIA
L. Peipus
Pskov
Rybinsk Res.
Yaroslavl
Gorki Res.
Volga River
Kazan
Ufa
50°N
Riga
LATVIA
Western Dvina
Tver
Nizhniy Novgorod
Oka R.
Kuybyshev Res.
LITHUANIA
Vilnius
Neman R.
Moscow
Smolensk
Tula
Samara
E u r o p e a n   P l a i n
Russia)
Minsk
BELARUS
Bryansk
Orel
Penza
Orenburg
Ural River
Oral
Warsaw
Pripyat
Kursk
Voronezh
Saratov
Volgograd Res.
KAZAKHSTAN
ASIA
Bug R.
Chernobyl
S t e p p e s
Kiev
Kharkiv
Donets R.
Ural River
Aral Sea
Syr Darya
Lviv
UKRAINE
Dnieper R.
Volgograd
Volga River
Astrakhan
Dniester R.
Dnipropetrovsk
Donetsk
Don R.
UZBEKISTAN
MOLDOVA
Chisinau
Rostov-na-Donu
Volga R. Delta
Amu Darya
uj-Napoca
Mures
Prut R.
Odessa
Sea of Azov
Kerch
Krasnodar
ROMANIA
Transylvanian Alps
Crimean Pen.
Novorossiysk
Caspian Sea
TURKMENISTAN
Bucharest
Sevastopol
Yalta
Caucasus Mountains
Grozny
Ashgabat
Danube River
Constanta
GEORGIA
BULGARIA
Black Sea
Tbilisi
Baku
Sofia
Varna
ARMENIA
AZERBAIJAN
Balkan
Plovdiv
Yerevan
NIA
Peninsula
Bosporus
Istanbul
Thessaloniki
Sea of Marmara
Ankara
REECE
Euboea
Dardanelles
Lake Tuz
Lake Van
Lake Urmia
Athens
Cyclades
TURKEY
Tehran
Rhodes
Crete
(Greece)
CYPRUS
Nicosia
SYRIA
IRAQ
IRAN
Cyprus
LEBANON

Land Cover Map
Europe

Cropland Grassland Tundra Glacier

Semi-desert Broadleaf Needleleaf
& desert forest forest

Boundary Symbols

International boundary

Other boundary
(disputed or undefined)

Small country

Scale
1:17,400,000

0 100 200 300 400 miles

1 in. to 275 mi.

0 100 200 300 400 kilometers

1 cm to 174 km

Detailed legend on page 8   Bonne Projection

NC   OCEAN
North Cape
20°E   30°E   40°E   50°E   60°E   70°N   70°N   80°E

Barents Sea   Novaya Zemlya
L.   Kolguyev I.
Inari   Kanin
Pen.   Pechora
Lapland   Kola
Pen.   Pechora
Basin   Mt. Narodnaya
6,217 ft.
(1895 m)   Ob River
Lule R.   White
Sea   Arkhangelsk   Forest   60°N
Gulf of Bothnia   FINLAND   Boreal   Onega R.   R U S S I A
Lake   Northern Dvina R.   U r a l   M o u n t a i n s
Region   Sukhona R.   Kamskoye
Res.   Kama
Saimaa   Lake   Upland   70°E
Åland   Lake   Onega   Kama R.
Is.   Ladoga   Kama R.
Gulf of Finland   St. Petersburg   Vyatka R.
ESTONIA   L.   Rybinsk
Peipus   Res.   E u r o p e a n   Gorki   Kuybyshev
Riga   LATVIA   Res.   Volga River   Res.   50°N
Western   P l a i n
LITHUANIA   Dvina   Moscow   Oka R.   Volga   Ural   River
Neman R.   Central   Oka-Don   Upland
Russia   Russian   Plain   Volgograd
BELARUS   Res.   K A Z A K H S T A N   A S I A
Warsaw   Pripyat Marshes   Upland   S t e p p e s   Aral
Pripyat   Dnieper R.   Ural River   Sea   Syr Darya
Vistula R.   Bug R.   Kiev   Volga River   Caspian
UKRAINE   Lowland   Donets R.   Depression   40°N
Dniester R.   Dnieper R.   Don R.   Volga R. Delta   UZBEKISTAN   Amu Darya
MOLDOVA   Sea   Lowland   60°E
ian Mountains   Mures R.   Odessa   Sea of Azov
Prut R.   Black   Crimean   Caucasus   Mountains   Caspian
OMANIA   Transylvanian Alps   Pen.   Mt. Elbrus   Sea
Bucharest   Black   Sea   18,510 ft.   Baku
Danube   River   (5642 m)   GEORGIA   TURKMENISTAN
BULGARIA   ARMENIA   AZERBAIJAN
Balkan Mts.   Bosporus   Istanbul
lkan   Sea of Marmara   T U R K E Y
ninsula   Olympus   Lake   Lake Urmia
0 ft   Dardanelles   Van   Tehran
7 m)   REECE   Lake Tuz   IRAN
Euboea   SYRIA   IRAQ
Aegean Sea   40°E   50°E
Cyclades
Rhodes   CYPRUS   LEBANON
Crete   Sea   30°E

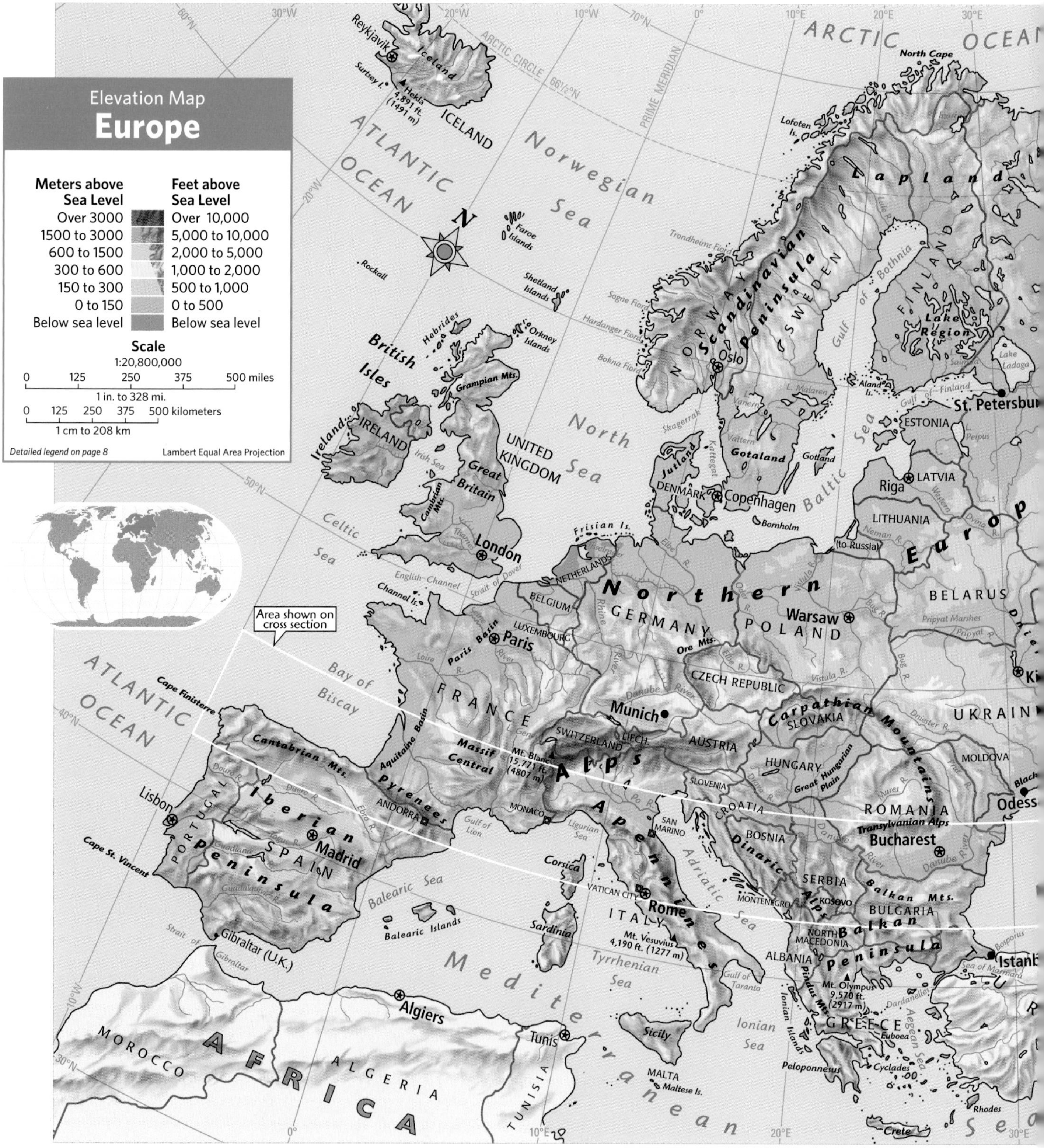

Elevation Map
Europe

Meters above Sea Level	Feet above Sea Level
Over 3000	Over 10,000
1500 to 3000	5,000 to 10,000
600 to 1500	2,000 to 5,000
300 to 600	1,000 to 2,000
150 to 300	500 to 1,000
0 to 150	0 to 500
Below sea level	Below sea level

Scale
1:20,800,000

0   125   250   375   500 miles
1 in. to 328 mi.

0   125   250   375   500 kilometers
1 cm to 208 km

Detailed legend on page 8   Lambert Equal Area Projection

Area shown on cross section

Cross Section
Vertical exaggeration 40 to 1
Scale at 42°N: 1 in. to 291 mi., 1 cm to 184 km

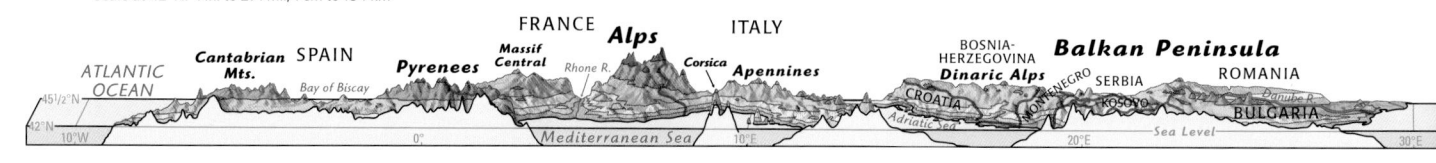

Reclaimed Land in the Netherlands

- ░░ Polder (reclaimed land)
- ⁄⁄ Dam
- ⊣⊢ Canal

Elevation

Land above sea level — sea level
Land below sea level — ocean

About 27 percent of the Netherlands is below sea level. **Polders**, land that has been reclaimed from the sea or marsh, now cover much of this lowland.

Life Beneath the Sea

For centuries, the Dutch have reclaimed land from the North Sea. Dikes hold the sea back, while canals and pumps drain the water. Windmills once powered the pumps, but today they run on diesel and electricity. In 1986, the most recent Dutch province, Flevoland, was created entirely from reclaimed land.

In the central Swiss Alps, green Lauterbrunnen Valley sits 11,000 feet (3,353 meters) below the mountain Jungfrau. Jungfrau has an elevation of 13,641 feet (4,158 meters) and is snow-capped year-round.

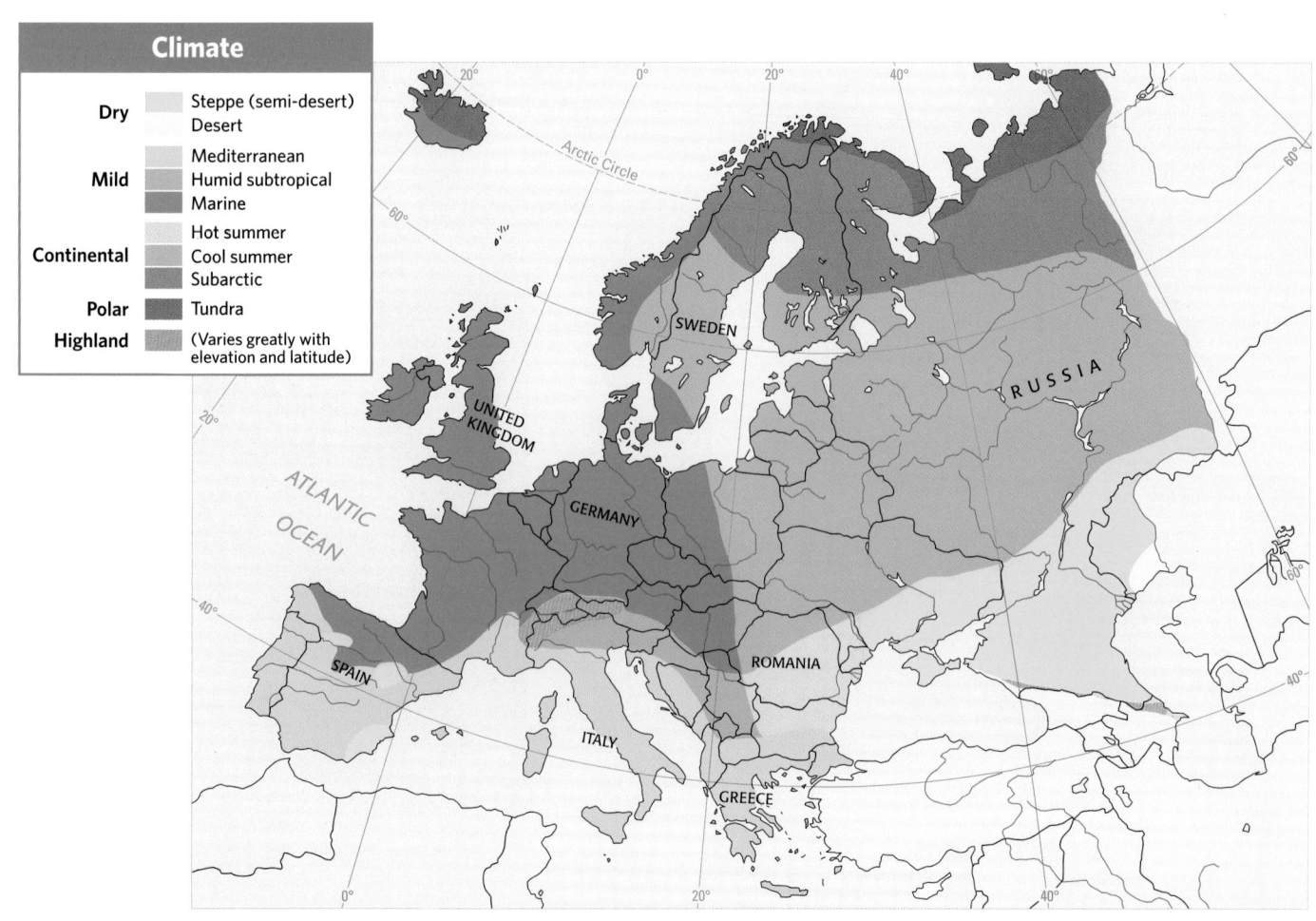

Precipitation

Millimeters per Year	Inches per Year
0 to 250	0 to 10
250 to 500	10 to 20
500 to 1000	20 to 40
1000 to 2000	40 to 80
Over 2000	Over 80

Climate

Dry		Steppe (semi-desert)
		Desert
Mild		Mediterranean
		Humid subtropical
		Marine
Continental		Hot summer
		Cool summer
		Subarctic
Polar		Tundra
Highland		(Varies greatly with elevation and latitude)

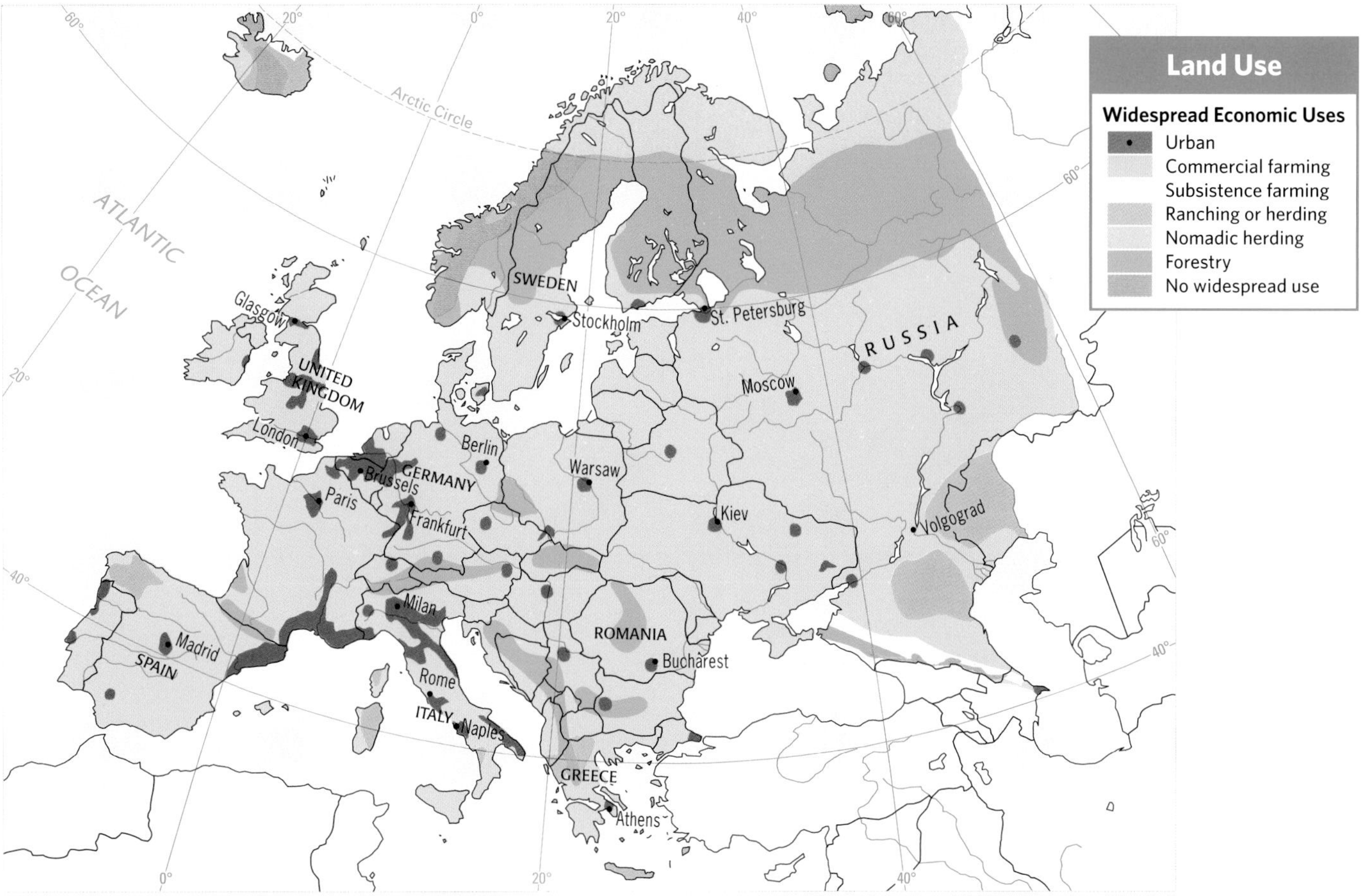

Land Use

Widespread Economic Uses
- Urban
- Commercial farming
- Subsistence farming
- Ranching or herding
- Nomadic herding
- Forestry
- No widespread use

Balance of Trade

European Union

Total Exports
US$2,060 billion

- United States 18.0%
- China 9.0%
- Switzerland 8.6%
- All Others 64.6%

Total Imports
US$2,012 billion

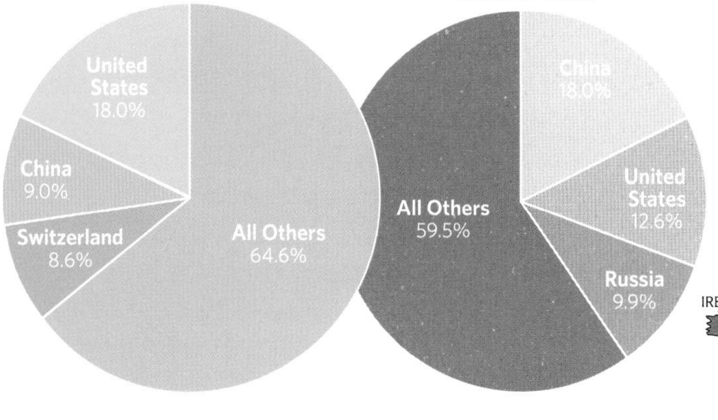

- China 18.0%
- United States 12.6%
- Russia 9.9%
- All Others 59.5%

Member states of the European Union can voluntarily withdraw from the union following the procedure in Article 50 of the Treaty on European Union, which was only introduced in 2009. On March 29, 2017, the United Kingdom became the first member state to invoke Article 50.

European Union

- Member country
- Candidate country
- Former member country

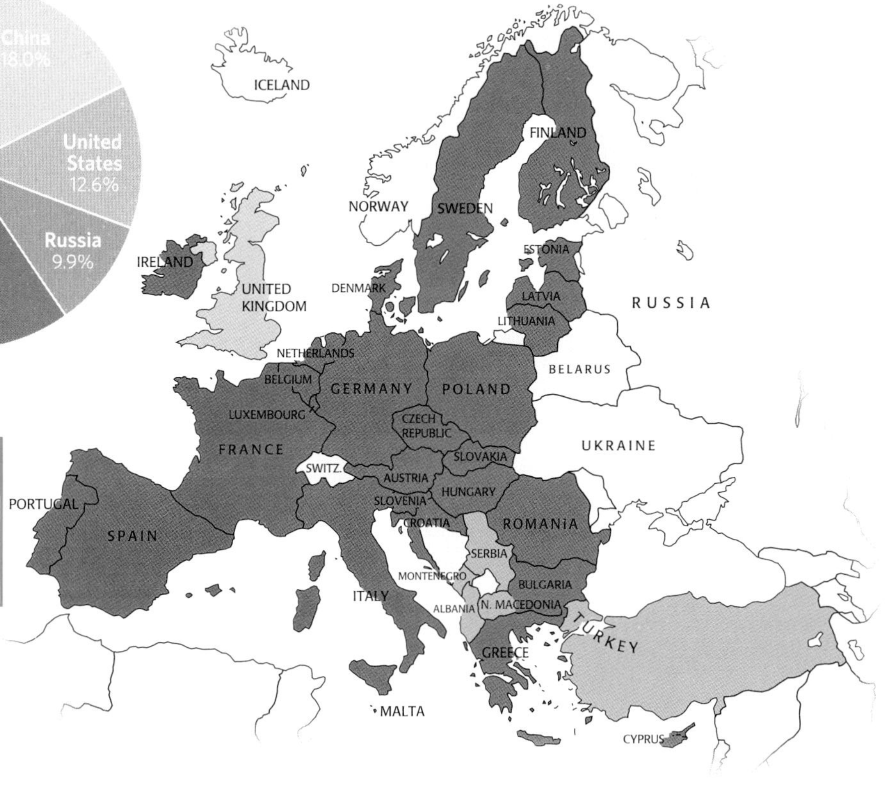

The European Union's single economy insures free trade, as well as democracy and human rights, across much of Europe. Some members also share the same currency, the euro.

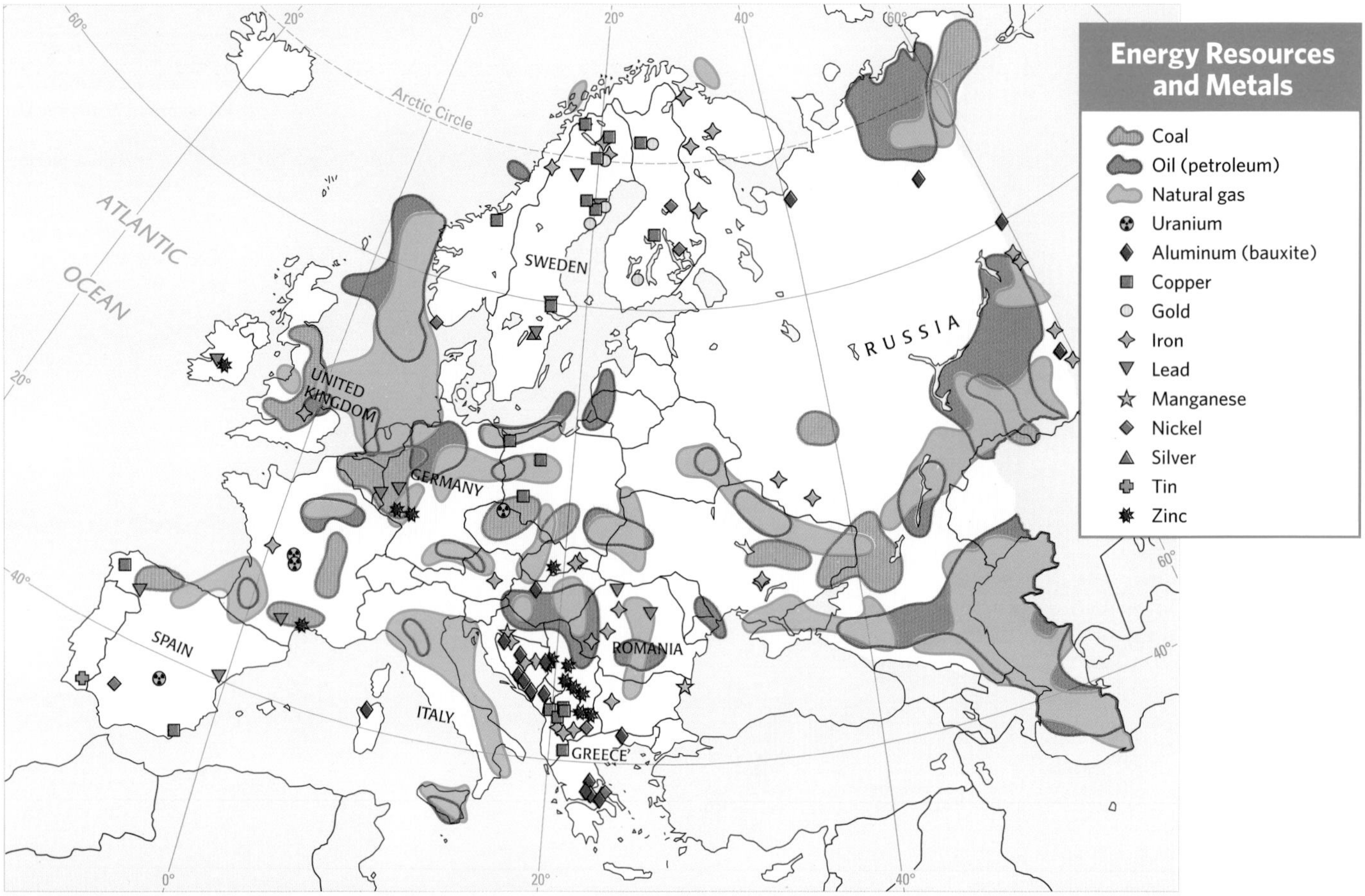

Energy Resources and Metals

- Coal
- Oil (petroleum)
- Natural gas
- Uranium
- Aluminum (bauxite)
- Copper
- Gold
- Iron
- Lead
- Manganese
- Nickel
- Silver
- Tin
- Zinc

Geothermal power, energy from the earth's heat, can generate electricity with little pollution. This geothermal power plant in Iceland is located on a plate boundary, near a volcano. About half of Iceland's energy is geothermal.

Sources of European Electricity

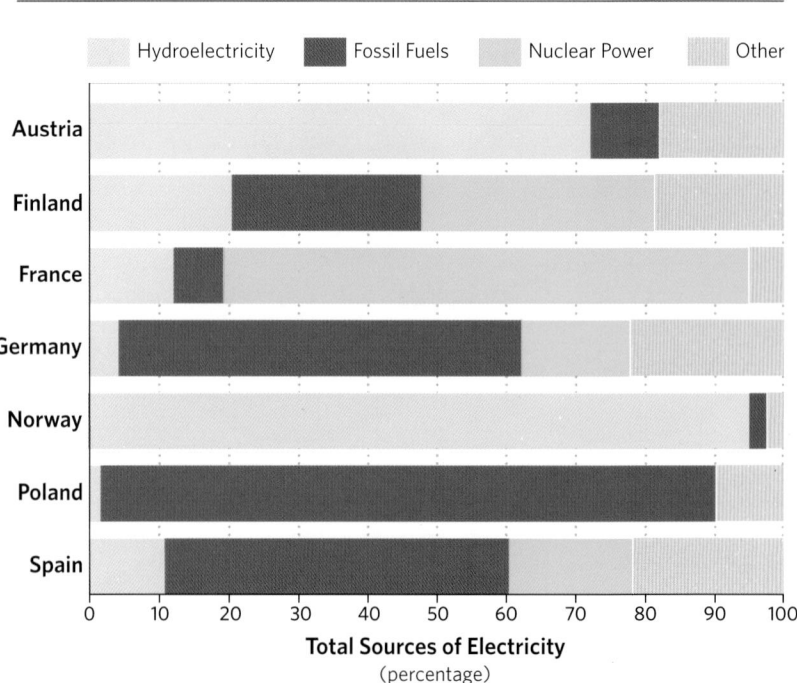

Hydroelectricity　Fossil Fuels　Nuclear Power　Other

Total Sources of Electricity
(percentage)

Due to local resources and government priorities, European countries favor different methods of meeting their energy needs. Even so, most European countries make use of more than one energy source.

Natural Population Growth

Europe

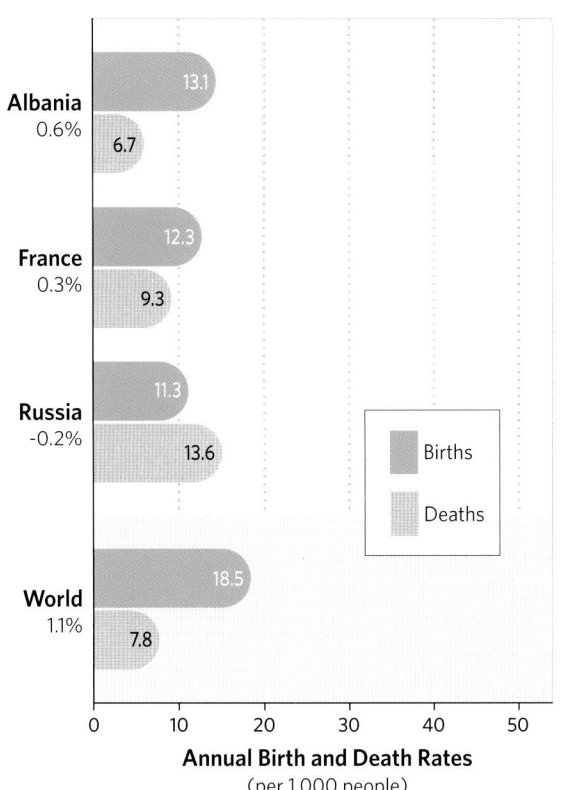

Annual Birth and Death Rates
(per 1,000 people)

- Albania 0.6% — Births 13.1, Deaths 6.7
- France 0.3% — Births 12.3, Deaths 9.3
- Russia -0.2% — Births 11.3, Deaths 13.6
- World 1.1% — Births 18.5, Deaths 7.8

Legend: Births, Deaths

Major Highways and Airports

Europe's highways and airports are concentrated in western Europe, where the population density and wealth are highest. Compare this map with similar maps on pages 66 and 86.

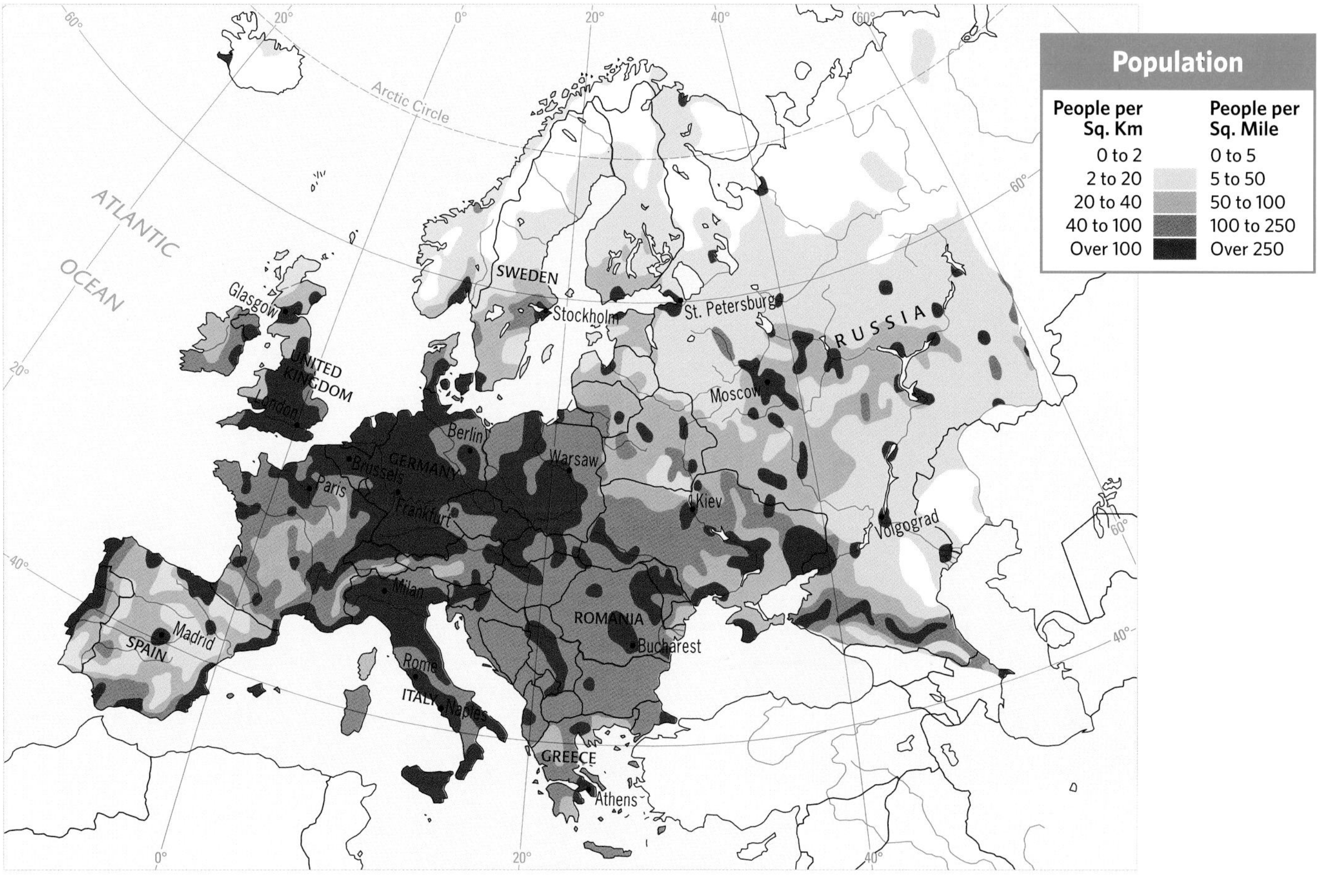

Airline Passengers per Year

- ✈ Over 50 million
- ✈ 35 to 50 million
- ✈ 20 to 35 million
- • Other airport
- ～ Major highway

Population

People per Sq. Km	People per Sq. Mile
0 to 2	0 to 5
2 to 20	5 to 50
20 to 40	50 to 100
40 to 100	100 to 250
Over 100	Over 250

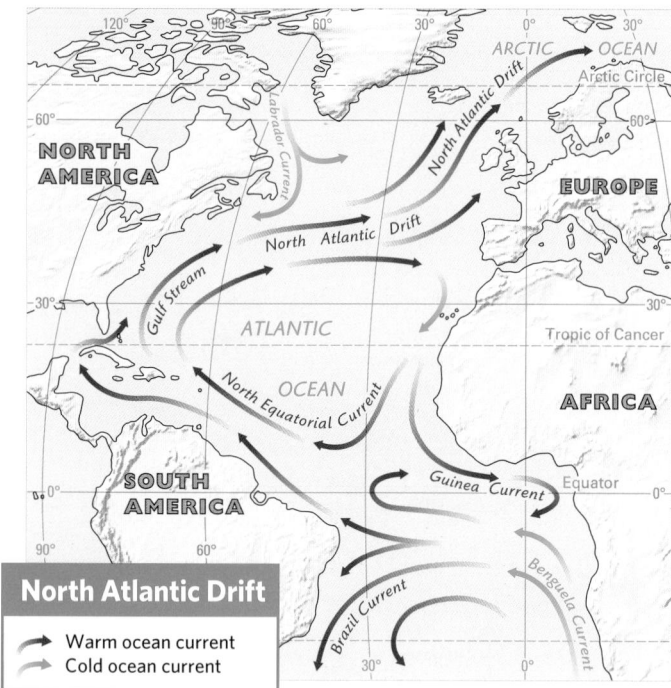

North Atlantic Drift

→ Warm ocean current
→ Cold ocean current

The North Atlantic Drift is responsible for the mild climate of western and northern Europe. It relays the warm currents and winds of the Gulf Stream to the continent. Increasing amounts of cold meltwater from Greenland's ice cap, though, could block its eastward flow.

Climographs

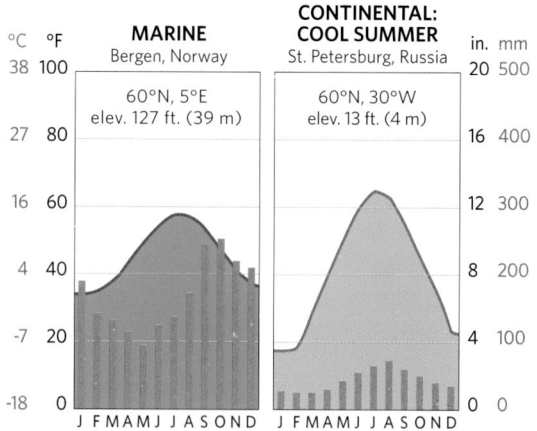

Bergen and St. Petersburg share the same latitude. However, the North Atlantic Drift keeps Bergen, on the Atlantic, warmer overall than St. Petersburg, which is much farther from the ocean.

Political Relief Map
British Isles

City Symbols

London ● Over 1,000,000 people
Sheffield ● 500,000 to 1,000,000
Limerick • Under 500,000

Dublin ⊛ National capital

Scale
1:9,690,000

0   50   100   150   200 miles
1 in. to 153 mi.

0   50 100 150 200 kilometers
1 cm to 97 km

Detailed legend on page 8   Bonne Projection

Ireland, one of the British Isles, is divided between the country of Ireland and the land of Northern Ireland, which is part of the United Kingdom. Here, St. Patrick's Day is celebrated with a parade in Dublin, Ireland.

Continues on page 158

Political Relief Map
Northern Europe

City Symbols

Hamburg ● Over 1,000,000 people
Stockholm ● 500,000 to 1,000,000
Bergen • Under 500,000
Helsinki ⊕ National capital

Scale
1:9,640,000

0   50   100   150   200 miles
1 in. to 152 mi.
0   50   100   150   200 kilometers
1 cm to 96 km

Detailed legend on page 8   Bonne Projection

5°W   0°   5°E   10°E   15°E   20°E   25°E   30°E   35°E

ARCTIC OCEAN

North Cape

Barents Sea

70°N

Hammerfest
Vadso
Varanger Fiord
70°N

Tromso
Pechenga
Severomorsk
Murmansk

Harstad
Lake Inari

Lofoten Is.
Narvik
Lapland
Monchegorsk
Apatity
Kirovsk
Kola Peninsula

Kiruna
Torne R.
Muonio R.

Bodo

Mo i Rana
Lule R.
ARCTIC CIRCLE 66½°N

Rovaniemi
White Sea

65°N
Skelleftea
Kem
65°N
Onega Bay

Norwegian Sea
Trondheim Fiord
Kjolen Mts.
Ume R.
Lulea
Oulu

Molde
Alesund
Trondheim
Scandinavian Peninsula
Ornskoldsvik
Ostersund
Umea
Gulf of Bothnia
Kokkola
FINLAND
Kajaani

NORWAY
Galdhopiggen
8,100 ft. (2469 m) △
Osterdal R.
Sundsvall
Vaasa
Kuopio
Joensuu

Sogne Fiord
Lillehammer
Hamar
SWEDEN
Lake Region
Petrozavodsk

Bergen
60°N
Hardanger Fiord
Gjovik
Klar R.
Gavle
Jyvaskyla
Saimaa
Lake Ladoga

Boknafjord
Drammen
Oslo
Tampere
Pori
Imatra
Vyborg
60°N

Stavanger
Sandnes
Skien
Moss
Fredrikstad
Karlstad
Vasteras
L. Malaren
Uppsala
Aland Is. (Finland)
Hameenlinna
Lahti
Lappeenranta
Kotka
St. Petersburg
Kolpino

Arendal
Larvik
Orebro
Eskilstuna
Stockholm
Turku
Espoo
Helsinki
Narva
RUSSIA

Kristiansand
Lake Vanern
Hiiumaa
Gulf of Finland
Tallinn
Kohtla-Jarve
Velikiy Novgorod

Cape Lindesnes (The Naze)
Skagerrak
Goteborg
Gota Canal
Norrkoping
Linkoping
Saaremaa
ESTONIA
Parnu
Viljandi
Tartu
Lake Peipus
Lake Ilmen
Valdai Hills

North Sea
Kattegat
Lake Vattern
Boras
Jonkoping
Visby
Gotland
Gulf of Riga
Pskov

Aborg
Kungsbacka
Gotaland
Oland
Riga
LATVIA
W. Dvina R.

Randers
Jutland
Arhus
Halmstad
Vaxjo
Kalmar
Liepaja
Jelgava
Rezekne
Daugavpils
Velikiye Luki

DENMARK
Helsingborg
Lund
Malmo
Baltic Sea
Klaipeda
Siauliai
Panevezys
Vitsyebsk

Esbjerg
Kolding
Copenhagen
Odense
Fyn
Sjaelland
Bornholm (Denmark)
LITHUANIA
Kaunas
Vilnius
BELARUS
Smolensk

Kiel Canal
Kiel
Lubeck
Rugen
Rostock
Gdynia
Gdansk
Kaliningrad (to Russia)
Neman R.
Chernyakhovsk
Alytus
Hrodna
Lida
Orsha
Dnieper R.
Mahilyow

Hamburg
Bremen
GERMANY
Elbe R.
Szczecin
POLAND
Northern European Plain
Olsztyin
Minsk

55°N

N

Continues on page 159
Continues on page 160

The Center of Things

The Prime Meridian is the line of longitude at 0°. Unlike the Equator, the Prime Meridian could be located anywhere. An international conference in 1884 decided that the Prime Meridian should pass through the Royal Greenwich Observatory in London (see map at left).

Continues on page 156   Continues on page 157

Political Relief Map
Western Europe

City Symbols

Barcelona ● Over 1,000,000 people
Marseille ● 500,000 to 1,000,000
Porto • Under 500,000
Paris ⊛ National capital

Scale
1:10,400,000

0 50 100 150 200 miles

1 in. to 164 mi.

0 50 100 150 200 kilometers

1 cm to 104 km

Detailed legend on page 8   Bonne Projection

15°W 10°W 5°W 0° 5°E

Galway Dublin Leeds North Sea Frisian Is. Groningen
IRELAND Limerick Liverpool Sheffield NETHERLANDS Bremen
Tralee Birmingham UNITED Leicester Norwich Amsterdam Bielefeld
Waterford Coventry The Hague Utrecht Arnhem Dortmund
Cork KINGDOM Rotterdam Essen
British Cardiff Bristol London Antwerp Dusseldorf
Isles Dover Ghent Brussels Cologne
Celtic Southampton Portsmouth Calais Liege GERMANY
Sea Plymouth Lille BELGIUM Frankfurt
Land's End Amiens LUXEMBOURG Luxembourg Mannheim
English Channel Cherbourg Le Havre St. Quentin Metz Nancy
Channel Is. Rouen Reims Strasbourg
(U.K.) Gulf of Caen Paris Marne River
St. Malo Normandy Seine Versailles Paris Black Forest
Brest St. Malo Chartres Basin Besancon Basel
Brittany Rennes Le Mans Dijon Mulhouse Bern
Angers Orleans SWITZ.
Nantes Tours FRANCE Lake
Geneva
Bay of La Rochelle Vichy Lyon Mt. Blanc Turin
Biscay Limoges Clermont- St. Etienne Grenoble ITALY
Ferrand Massif ALPS
Bordeaux Central Avignon MONACO Riviera
Aquitaine Nimes Aix-en- Nice
Basin Toulouse Montpellier Provence Toulon
A Coruna Gijon Santander San Pau Carcassonne Narbonne Marseille
Cape Finisterre Oviedo Sebastian Gulf of Lion
Vigo Cantabrian Mts. Bilbao Pyrenees ANDORRA
Ourense Leon Vitoria- Andorra Perpignan
ATLANTIC Gasteiz la Vella Catalonia
OCEAN Braga Valladolid Zaragoza Barcelona
Porto Douro R. Duero River Ebro Tarragona
Coimbra Salamanca River Balearic Sea
PORTUGAL Sierra de Minorca
Guadarrama Madrid
Cacares Sierra de SPAIN Valencia Palma
Lisbon Gredos Tagus R. Majorca Balearic Is.
Setubal Guadiana R. Jucar R. (Spain)
Iberian Badajoz Albacete Ibiza Mediterranean
Peninsula Elche Sea
Sierra Morena Alicante
Huelva Guadalquivir R. Murcia
Cordoba
Cape Seville Granada Cartagena Algiers Bejaia
St. Vincent Sierra Nevada Almeria Constantine
Cadiz Malaga ALGERIA
Strait of Gibraltar Gibraltar (U.K.) AFRICA Batna
Tangier Ceuta (Spain) Oran
Tetouan Melilla
MOROCCO (Spain)

50°N 45°N 40°N 35°N

PRIME MERIDIAN

Continues on page 159

Continues on page 136

Ethnic Composition

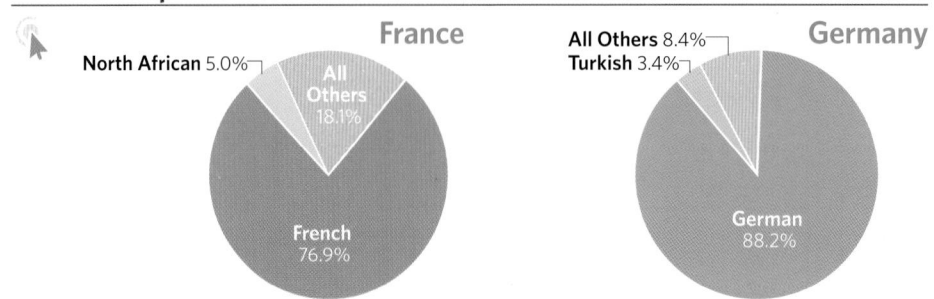

France
North African 5.0%
All Others 18.1%
French 76.9%

Germany
All Others 8.4%
Turkish 3.4%
German 88.2%

Continues on page 157

North
Sea

Skagerrak

Goteborg
Jonkoping
Visby
Gotland

SWEDEN
Gotaland
Kalmar
Oland

Baltic Sea

EST.

Riga
W. Dvina R.
LATVIA

Liepaja
Siauliai
Daugavpils

Kattegat

Alborg
Randers
Arhus
Jutland
DENMARK
Esbjerg
Odense
Copenhagen
Fyn
Staelland
Malmo
Lund
Helsingborg

Bornholm
(Denmark)

Klaipeda

LITHUANIA

Neman R.
Kaunas
(to Russia)
Kaliningrad
Vilnius

BELARUS

Kiel
Kiel Canal
Lubeck
Rostock

Rugen
Gdynia
Gdansk
Gulf of
Gdansk
Elblag

Olsztyn

Hamburg
Bremerhaven
Frisian Is.

NETH.
IJsselmeer
Bremen
Hannover
Amsterdam
The Hague
Bielefeld
Rotterdam
Essen
Munster
Dortmund
Dusseldorf
Aachen
Brussels
Bonn
Cologne
BELGIUM
Wiesbaden
LUXEMBOURG
Luxembourg
Mannheim
Metz
Strasbourg
FRANCE

Brandenburg
Berlin
Potsdam
Magdeburg
Halle
Leipzig
Erfurt
Dresden
Chemitz
Ore Mts.
Braunschweig
Kassel
Weser R.
Elbe R.
Oder R.

Szczecin
Bydgoszcz
Torun

Northern European plain

Warta R.
Poznan
Wloclawek

Bialystok

Vistula R.

POLAND
Warsaw

Kalisz
Lodz
Wroclaw
Radom
Lublin
Kielce
Ostrowiec

Czestochowa
Katowice

Bug R.
Vistula R.

Rzeszow
Krakow

GERMANY
Frankfurt
Bayreuth
Nuremberg
Main R.
Plzen
Bohemia
Elbe R.

Prague
CZECH REPUBLIC
Brno
Ostrava
Moravia

SLOVAKIA
Kosice

UKRAINE

Carpathian Mts.

Stuttgart
Ulm
Bavaria
Augsburg
Black Forest
Danube R.
Linz
Salzburg
Vienna
Innsbruck
AUSTRIA
Klagenfurt
Graz
Bratislava
Gyor
Budapest
HUNGARY
Miskolc
Debrecen
Satu Mare
Oradea
Cluj-Napoca
Iasi
Chisinau
MOL.

Basel
Zurich
Bern
SWITZERLAND
Geneva
Lake Geneva
LIECHTENSTEIN
Bolzano
Trento
A L P S
Jura Mts.
Mt. Blanc
15,771 ft. (4807 m)
Grenoble
Nice
Turin
MONACO
Genoa
Milan
Brescia
Verona
Lake Como
Lake Garda
Padua
Venice
Trieste
Ljubljana
Maribor
SLOVENIA
Rijeka
Drava R.
Pecs
Lake Balaton
Great Hungarian Plain
Danube R.
Szeged
Subotica
Arad
Timisoara
Mures R.
Targu Mures
Brasov
ROMANIA
Galati
Transylvanian Alps
Ploiesti
Braila
Prut R.

La Spezia
Po River
Parma
Modena
Bologna
Ferrara
Rimini
Zadar
Zagreb
Osijek
Novi Sad
Sava R.
Drobeta-Turnu Severin
Pitesti
Bucharest
Craiova
Constanta
Dobrich
Varna

Ligurian Sea
Pisa
Carrara
Florence
Livorno
SAN MARINO
Ancona
CROATIA
Dinaric Alps
Banja Luka
BOSNIA-HERZEGOVINA
Sarajevo
Mostar
Split
SERBIA
Belgrade
Kragujevac
Cacak
Nis
Morava R.
Danube River
Ruse
Olt R.

Corsica
(France)
Bastia
Ajaccio
Elba
(Italy)
VATICAN CITY
Perugia
Tiber R.
Pescara
Dubrovnik
Podgorica
MONTENEGRO
Pristina
KOSOVO
Tetovo
Skopje
NORTH MACEDONIA
Sofia
BULGARIA
Balkan Mts.
Stara Zagora
Sliven
Burgas
Plovdiv
Maritsa R.
Edirne
Istanbul
Black Sea
Balkan Peninsula
Rhodope Mts.

Sardinia
(Italy)
Cagliari
Rome
ITALY
Foggia
Bari
Brindisi
Taranto
ALBANIA
Durres
Tirana
Vlore
Korce
Bitola
Florina
Katerini
Pindus Mts.
Serrai
Kavala
Thessaloniki
Thasos
Samothrace
Gokceada
Thrace
Bursa
Balikesir
Sea of Marmara
Dardanelles
TURKEY
ASIA

Tyrrhenian Sea
MT. Vesuvius
4,190 ft. (1277 m)
Naples
Salerno
Gulf of Taranto
Strait of Otranto
Mt. Olympus
9,570 ft. (2917 m)
Ioannina
Corfu
Larisa
Volos
Limnos
Lesbos
Aegean Sea
Northern Sporades
Euboea Sea
Chios
Izmir
Manisa
Samos

Annaba
Tunis
Pantelleria
(Italy)
Palermo
Messina
Mt. Etna
10,902 ft. (3323 m)
Reggio di Calabria
Catania
Sicily
(Italy)
Cosenza
Catanzaro
Lipari Is.
GREECE
Agrinion
Khalkis
Patrai
Athens
Piraeus
Peloponnesus
Cyclades
Ionian Sea
Ionian Is.
Kalamai
Dodecanese
Rhodes
Rhodes
(Greece)

ALGERIA
AFRICA
Susah
Sfax
TUNISIA
Lampedusa
(Italy)
MALTA
Valletta
Mediterranean Sea
Khania
Iraklion
Crete
(Greece)

Saone R.
Rhine River
Vosges Mts.
Meuse R.
Rhone River

N

Continues on page 158
Continues on page 160
Continues on page 178

Political Relief Map
Central Europe

City Symbols

Milan	●	Over 1,000,000 people
Bremen	●	500,000 to 1,000,000
Salzburg	·	Under 500,000
Warsaw	⊛	National capital

Scale

1:10,900,000

0   75   150   225   300 miles

1 in. to 173 mi.

0   75   150   225   300 kilometers

1 cm to 109 km

Detailed legend on page 8   Bonne Projection

Political Relief Map
Eastern Europe

City Symbols
Kazan ● Over 1,000,000 people
Lviv • 500,000 to 1,000,000
Vologda • Under 500,000
Minsk ⊕ National capital

Scale
1:14,600,000

0   75   150   225   300 miles
1 in. to 230 mi.
0   75   150   225   300 kilometers
1 cm to 146 km

Detailed legend on page 8   Bonne Projection

Continues on page 157
Continues on pages 166–167
Continues on page 159
Continues on page 179
Continues on page 178
Continues on page 161

Vadso
Varanger Fiord
Pechenga
Murmansk
Monchegorsk
Apatity · Kirovsk
Kola Peninsula
Barents Sea
Kolguyev I.
Kanin Pen.
Chesha Bay
Vaigach I.
Salekhard
Ob River
ASIA
Kanin Pen.
ARCTIC CIRCLE 66½°N
Pechora Basin
Pechora
Inta
Ukhta
Mt. Narodnaya 6,217 ft. (1895 m)
Ural Mountains
Zheleznodorozhny
Konzakovski Kamen 5148 ft. (1569 m)
Serov

Kokkola
FINLAND
Kuopio
Jyvaskyla
Lake Region
Tampere
Lahti
Pori
Gulf of Bothnia
Aland Is. (Finland)
Turku
Espoo · Helsinki
Kotka
Vyborg
Lake Ladoga
Petrozavodsk
Lake Onega
Kem
White Sea
Onega Bay
Onega R.
Severodvinsk
Arkhangelsk
Kotlas
Mezen R.
Northern Dvina R.
Pechora R.
Vychegda R.
Syktyvkar
Northern Uvals
Berezniki
Kamskoye Reservoir
Nizhniy Tagil
Perm

Stockholm
Hiiumaa
Tallinn
ESTONIA
Saaremaa
Parnu
Tartu
Gulf of Riga
Baltic Sea
Riga
LATVIA
Liepaja
Klaipeda
Siauliai
LITHUANIA
Daugavpils
Kaliningrad (to Russia)
Kaunas
Neman R.
Vilnius
Hrodna
Bialystok
POLAND
Warsaw
Brest
Lublin
Narva
St. Petersburg
Lake Peipus
Lake Ilmen
Pskov
Velikiy Novgorod
Valdai Hills
Velikiye Luki
Svir R.
Vitsyebsk
Smolensk
Mahilyow
MINSK
BELARUS
Baranavichy
Babruysk
Homyel
Pripyat Marshes
Pinsk
Dnieper R.
Chernobyl

Cherepovets
Vologda
Rybinsk Reservoir
Yaroslavl
Kostroma
Tver
Volga R.
Ivanovo
Gorki Reservoir
Vladimir
Dzerzhinsk
Moscow
Kaluga
Tula
Bryansk
Orel
Central Russian Plain
Lipetsk
Tambov
Oka-Don
Kirov
Kama Upland
Izhevsk
Cheboksary
Nizhniy Novgorod
Kazan
Naberezhnyye Chelny
Ufa
Yekaterinburg
Ural Mountains
Magnitogorsk
Salavat
Ulyanovsk
Kuybyshev Reservoir
Saransk
Penza
Tolyatti
Samara
Volga River
Volga Upland
Orenburg
Orsk
Ryazan
Ural River

RUSSIA

Northern European Plain
Sukhona R.

Chernihiv
Desna R.
Kiev Reservoir
Rivne
Zhytomyr
Lviv
Ternopil
UKRAINE
Vinnytsya
Uzhhorod
Chernivtsi
Carpathian Mountains
Dniester River
Kirovohrad
Pivdenny Buh R.
Cherkasy
Kremenchuk Reservoir
Kremenchuk
Poltava
Kharkiv
Belgorod
Kursk
Voronezh
Don River
Steppes
Upland
Kuzbyshev

Cluj-Napoca
Mures R.
Iasi
Prut R.
MOLDOVA
Chisinau
Tiraspol
ROMANIA
Brasov
Transylvanian Alps
Pitesti
Ploiesti
Galati
Braila
Craiova
Bucharest
Ruse
Danube R.
BULGARIA
Varna
Stara Zagora
Burgas
Balkan Mts.
Plovdiv
Maritsa R.
Rhodope Mts.
Thrace
Istanbul
Sea of Marmara
Izmit
GREECE
Bursa
TURKEY
Zonguldak
Samsun
Pontic Mountains
Trabzon

Kryvyy Rih
Dnieprohes Dam
Dnipropetrovsk
Donetsk
Luhansk
Zaporizhzhya
Taganrog
Mariupol
Rostov-na-Donu
Kakhovka Reservoir
Mykolayiv
Kherson
Odessa
Black Sea Lowland
Crimean Peninsula
Simferopol
Sevastopol
Yalta
Kerch
Strait of Kerch
Novorossiysk
Danube River Delta
Constanta
Sea of Azov
Don R.
Tsimlyansk Reservoir
Volgograd
Volgograd Reservoir
Oral
Aqtobe
KAZAKHSTAN
Atyrau
Astrakhan
Caspian Depression
Caspian Sea
Aqtau
ASIA
Garabogazkol Aylagy
TURKMENISTAN

Black Sea

Krasnodar
Maykop
Kuban R.
Stavropol
Sochi
Abkhazia
Caucasus
Mt. Elbrus 18,510 ft. (5642 m)
Vladikavkaz
South Ossetia
Mountains
Terek R.
Grozny
Chechnya
Makhachkala
Derbent
Batumi
GEORGIA
Tbilisi
ARMENIA
Yerevan
AZERBAIJAN
Baku
Kur R.

N

Russia is the world's largest country—nearly twice the size of Canada. Russia stretches across Europe and Asia from the Baltic Sea to the Pacific Ocean and from the Arctic Ocean to the Black and Caspian Seas. Asian Russia is often called Siberia.

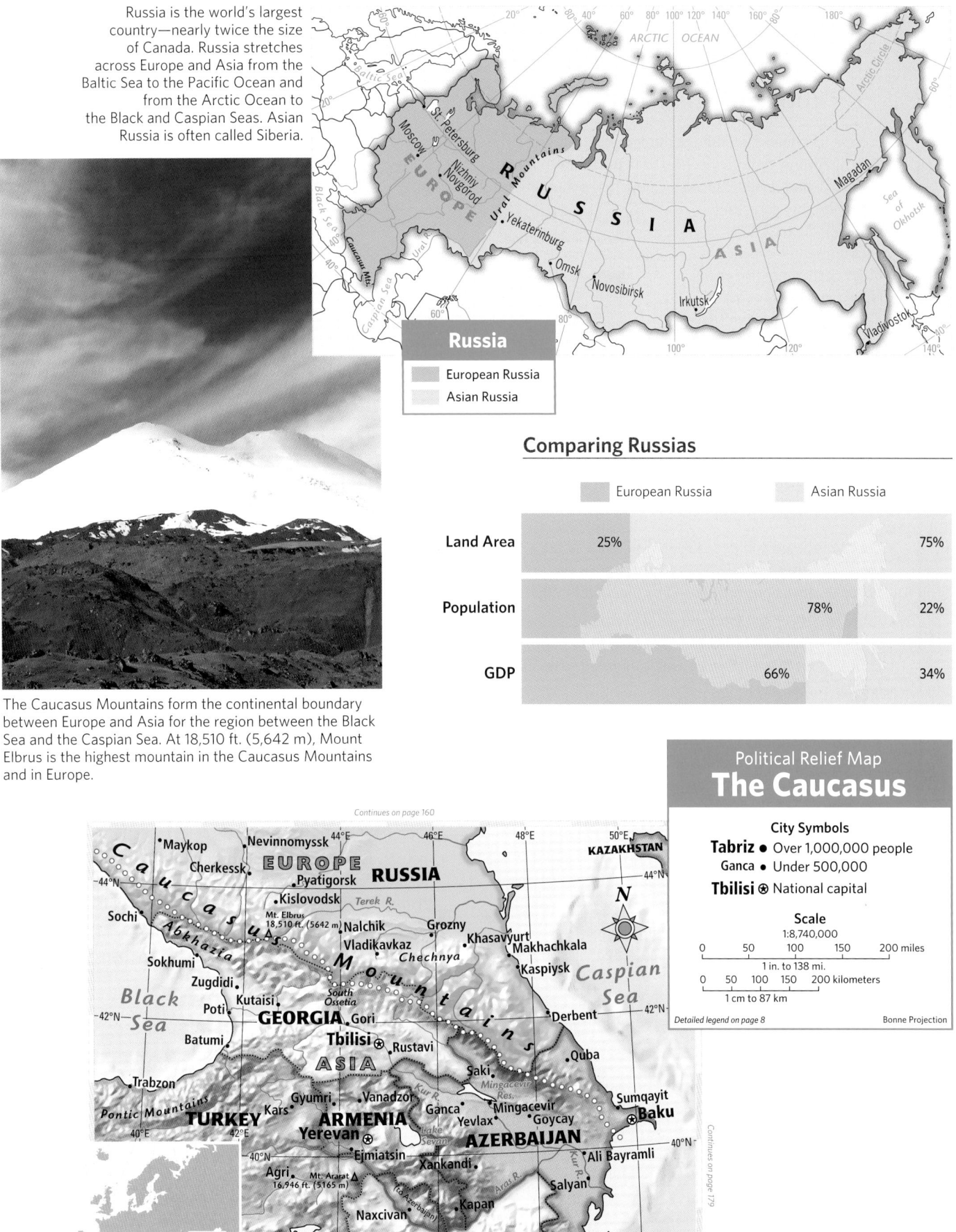

The Caucasus Mountains form the continental boundary between Europe and Asia for the region between the Black Sea and the Caspian Sea. At 18,510 ft. (5,642 m), Mount Elbrus is the highest mountain in the Caucasus Mountains and in Europe.

Russia
- European Russia
- Asian Russia

Comparing Russias

	European Russia	Asian Russia
Land Area	25%	75%
Population	78%	22%
GDP	66%	34%

Political Relief Map
The Caucasus

City Symbols
- **Tabriz** ● Over 1,000,000 people
- Ganca ● Under 500,000
- **Tbilisi** ⊛ National capital

Scale
1:8,740,000
0 50 100 150 200 miles
1 in. to 138 mi.
0 50 100 150 200 kilometers
1 cm to 87 km

Detailed legend on page 8   Bonne Projection

Continues on page 160
Continues on page 179
Continues on page 178

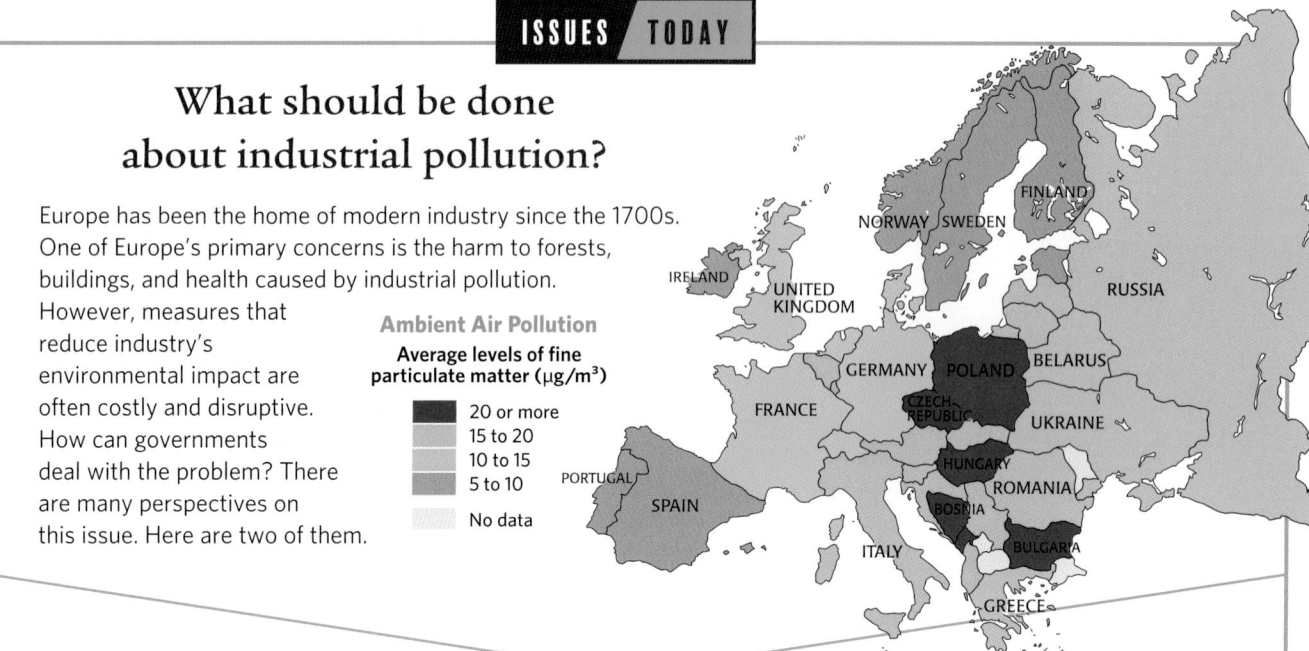

ISSUES / TODAY

What should be done about industrial pollution?

Europe has been the home of modern industry since the 1700s. One of Europe's primary concerns is the harm to forests, buildings, and health caused by industrial pollution. However, measures that reduce industry's environmental impact are often costly and disruptive. How can governments deal with the problem? There are many perspectives on this issue. Here are two of them.

Ambient Air Pollution

Average levels of fine particulate matter (µg/m³)

- 20 or more
- 15 to 20
- 10 to 15
- 5 to 10
- No data

Industry must be regulated to protect the environment.

- Europe is responsible for about 15 percent of the world's greenhouse gas emissions. Twenty percent of Europe's emissions are caused by manufacturing.

- Between 2008 and 2012, the cost of damage to health and the environment from air pollution from the most-polluting facilities in Europe was estimated to be at least US$390 billion.

- Environmental policies have improved air quality throughout Europe. From 1990 to 2015, emissions of sulfur dioxide decreased by 90 percent, non-methane volatile organic compounds by 60 percent, and nitrogen oxides by 50 percent.

- Stricter regulations on emissions of pollutants such as nitrogen oxides and sulfur dioxide in coal-fired power plants alone could save more than 20,000 lives every year.

- A cleaner environment not only benefits future generations, it also improves our current quality of life.

Here, a layer of smog is seen over Paris. About 40 million people in 115 of the European Union's largest cities are exposed to at least one air pollutant that exceeds the World Health Organization's air quality guidelines each year.

Environmental laws must not suppress economic growth.

- If environmental laws force companies to purchase expensive environmental technology, goods become more expensive. This gives goods produced in countries with weaker environmental regulations an advantage.

- Major shifts in environmental policy can seriously disrupt the economy and society. Since regulations often add costs to a company, this can lead to a rise in cost of products and a reduction in sales and employment.

- Europe's steel industry, a major source of industrial pollution, employs about 330,000 people. It produces over 170 million tons of steel each year, valued at more than US$194 billion.

- Industry is no longer the major contributor to air pollution in Europe. Agriculture creates more pollutants than any human source, but it employs substantially fewer people than other major industries.

Sources of Ammonia Pollution

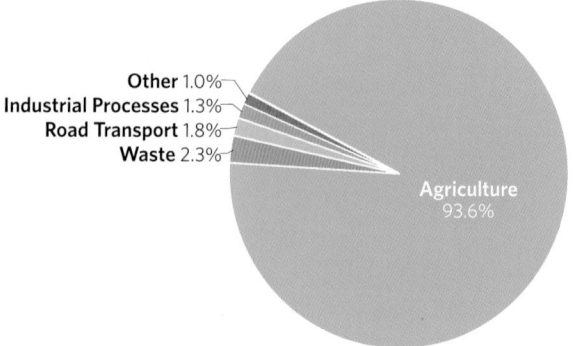

Other 1.0%
Industrial Processes 1.3%
Road Transport 1.8%
Waste 2.3%

Agriculture 93.6%

Agriculture is the biggest contributor to emissions of ammonia. Ammonia leads to acid deposition and eutrophication, which have negative effects on ecosystems and biodiversity.

ISSUES / TODAY

Should international organizations be strengthened?

The European Union (EU) began in 1951 as the European Coal and Steel Community, a six-member international organization that eliminated border restrictions and coordinated regulations in the wake of World War II. The organization now tries to maintain peace, protect human rights, and improve the standard of living throughout Europe. It also has reduced the power of national governments to control their borders and to enact economic and social policies for their own countries. How strong should international organizations be? There are many perspectives on this issue. Here are two of them.

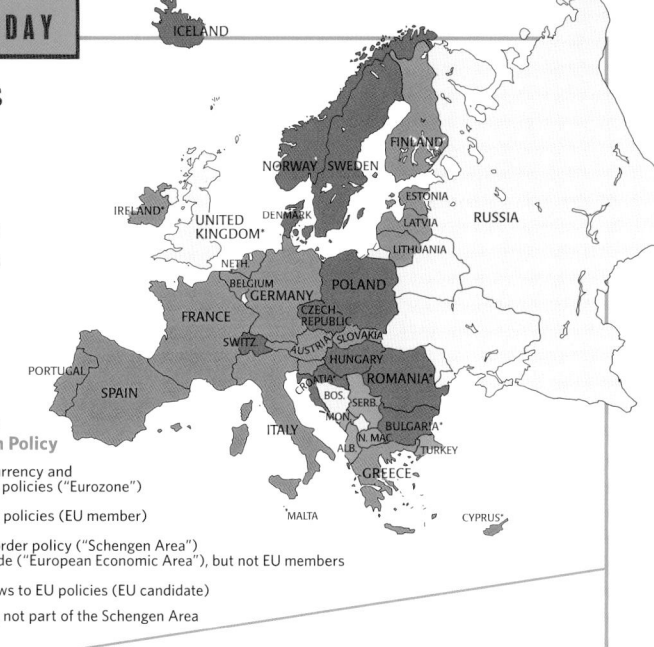

Participation in European Union Policy

- Common currency and all other EU policies ("Eurozone")
- All other EU policies (EU member)
- Common border policy ("Schengen Area") and free trade ("European Economic Area"), but not EU members
- Adapting laws to EU policies (EU candidate)

*EU country not part of the Schengen Area

International organizations threaten national interests.

- International organizations like the European Union tend to develop policies through bureaucratic means. Most EU laws are written by the civil servants of the European Commission and passed without change.

- The European Common Agricultural Policy has long encouraged modernization of European agriculture, potentially threatening traditional farming. Unlike nearly all other economic sectors, agricultural policy is exclusively controlled by the EU rather than in cooperation with national governments.

- The common border and immigration policy effectively prevents countries from being able to address human trafficking, refugees, and other immigration issues without involving the rest of the European Union.

To make debt payments required by the European Central Bank, the Greek government slashed unemployment benefits, pensions, government salaries, and education in the midst of a severe recession. Angry, desperate people rioted to protest the cuts.

International organizations provide peace, stability, and growth.

- European wars between 1910 and 1950 resulted in the deaths of over 50 million people worldwide. The EU and its predecessor organizations reduced distrust and encouraged cooperation to such an extent that there has never been a war between its members.

- International organizations have encouraged economic growth by expanding trade, streamlining regulations, and reducing border restrictions. The result has been a tremendous period of economic growth.

- International organizations protect human rights. Present-day challenges like human trafficking, international terrorism, and climate change cannot be solved using a nation-by-nation approach.

Social Spending per Capita

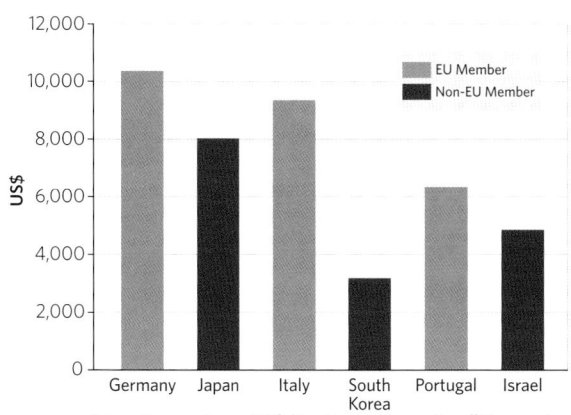

The EU is dedicated to improving standards of living. Supported by the EU's social cohesion fund, national governments insure that the unemployed, sick, elderly, and young have a decent standard of living. As a result, Europeans are more economically secure than people in countries with economies of a similar size.

World Extreme The Dead Sea is located in southwestern Asia between Israel and Jordan. At 1,365 feet (416 meters) below sea level, the Dead Sea coast is the lowest land on Earth. The sea itself is also the world's saltiest body of water, about nine times saltier than the oceans.

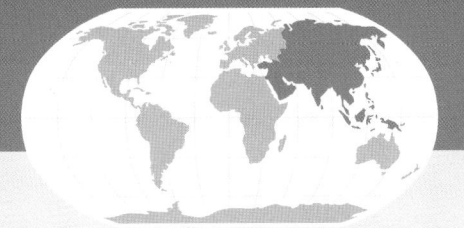

Asia

Asia, which shares a landmass with Europe, is the largest and most populous continent. It is home to over half of the world's population.

Physical Features

Highest mountain peak
Mt. Everest 29,035 ft. (8,850 m)★

Longest mountain ranges
Himalayas 1,500 mi. (2,400 km)
Ural Mountains* 1,500 mi. (2,400 km)

Largest island
Borneo 287,000 sq. mi. (743,330 sq. km)

Largest lakes
Caspian Sea* 143,300 sq. mi. (371,000 sq. km)★
Lake Baikal 12,200 sq. mi. (31,500 sq. km)★

Deepest lake
Lake Baikal 5,315 ft. deep (1,620 m)

Longest rivers
Yangtze 3,915 mi. (6,300 km)★
Yenisey 3,442 mi. (5,540 km)★

Other key physical features
Arabian Peninsula   Plateau of Iran
Central Siberian Plateau   Plateau of Tibet
Indochina Peninsula   West Siberian Plain
Iberian Peninsula

Cultural Features

Population
4,462,677,000

Largest countries by area
Russia* 6,592,800 sq. mi. (17,075,400 sq. km)★
China 3,696,100 sq. mi. (9,572,900 sq. km)★

Largest countries by population
China 1,379,302,771
India 1,281,935,911

Most densely populated
Singapore 21,259.7 people per sq. mi.
(8,201.8 per sq. km)

Least densely populated
Mongolia 5.1 people per sq. mi.
(2.0 per sq. km)

Largest urban areas
Tokyo, Japan 38,001,000★
Delhi, India 25,603,000★
Shanghai, China 23,741,000★

★ Among the world's largest. See the inside front cover.

*Located in both Europe and Asia.

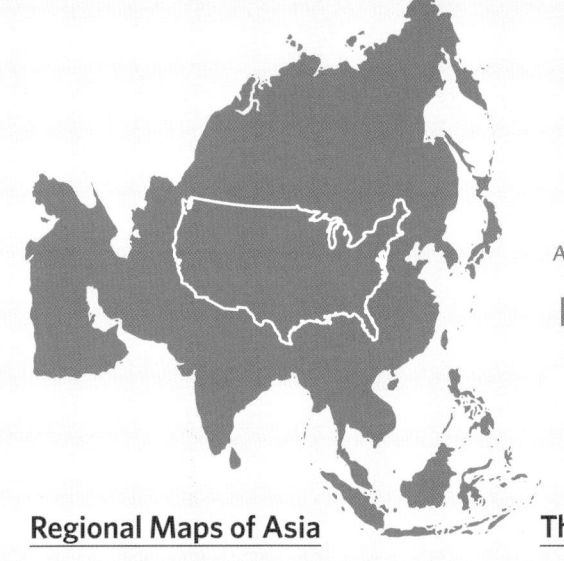

Area Comparison

■ **Asia**
16,992,000 sq. mi.
(44,009,000 sq. km)

Contiguous United States
3,021,295 sq. mi.
(7,825,112 sq. km)

Regional Maps of Asia

1 **Southwestern Asia** p.178
2 **Central Asia** p.179
3 **Southern Asia** p.180
4 **Southeastern Asia** p.181
5 **Eastern Asia** China, Mongolia, and Taiwan p.182
6 **Eastern Asia** Japan and the Koreas p.183

Thematic Maps of Asia

Precipitation p.172
Dry Monsoon; Wet Monsoon p.172
Climate p.173
Land Use p.174
Major Oil Fields p.175
Energy Resources and Metals p.175
Population p.176
Major Religions p.177

NORTH POLE

ATLANTIC OCEAN

Polar Sea Ice

ARCTIC

Svalbard (Norway)

Norwegian Sea

Franz Josef Land (Russia)

Severnaya Zemlya (Russia)

20°W

40°N

50°N

60°N

ARCTIC CIRCLE 66½°N

70°E

80°E

Barents Sea

IRELAND

UNITED KINGDOM

NORWAY

SWEDEN

FINLAND

Novaya Zemlya (Russia)

Kara Sea

Norilsk

Yenisey

10°W

North Sea

DEN.

NETH.

BELGIUM

GERMANY

Baltic Sea

ESTONIA

LATVIA

LITHUANIA

Kaliningrad (Russia)

R U S S I A

Ob River

S I

PORTUGAL

SPAIN

Bay of Biscay

FRANCE

LUX.

E U R O P E

POLAND

BELARUS

Moscow

Nizhniy Novgorod

Yekaterinburg

Omsk

Krasnoyars

Ob River

Lower Tung

MOROCCO

0°

SWITZ.

ITALY

Adriatic Sea

CZ REP.

AUS.

SLOVAKIA

HUNGARY

CRO.

SLOV.

BOS.

UKRAINE

Kharkiv

S t e p p e s

Don R.

Volga R.

Chelyabinsk

Astana (Nur-Sultan)

Novosibirsk

Barnaul

Volga

ALGERIA

30°N

TUNISIA

10°E

MON.

ALB.

MAC.

SERBIA

KOS.

BULGARIA

ROMANIA

MOL.

Black Sea

Caucasus Mts.

Ural

Atyrau

K A Z A K H S T A N

Qaraghandy

Aral Sea

Aral

Lake Zaysan

Altai M

GREECE

TURKEY

Istanbul

Izmir

Anatolia

Ankara

GEORGIA

ARMENIA

AZERBAIJAN

Caspian Sea

Turan Lowland

Syr Darya

Lake Balkhash

Almaty

Urumqi

Ili

LIBYA

EGYPT

Cairo

TROPIC OF CANCER 23½°N

20°N

Nicosia

CYPRUS

LEBANON

Beirut

Jerusalem

ISRAEL

SYRIA

Damascus

Amman

JORDAN

Baghdad

IRAQ

Tabriz

Zagros Mts.

Tehran

Mashhad

TURKMENISTAN

Ashgabat

UZBEKISTAN

Tashkent

Bishkek

KYRGYZSTAN

Tien Shan

Taklimakan Desert

Tarim R.

Shache

CHAD

20°N

Nile River

Red Sea

Tigris R.

Euphrates R.

KUWAIT

Kuwait

IRAN

Esfahan (Isfahan)

Shiraz

TAJIKISTAN

Pamirs

Dushanbe

Kabul

AFGHANISTAN

Herat

Hindu Kush

Plateau of Tibet

Salwe

SUDAN

SAUDI ARABIA

Mecca (Makkah)

Riyadh

BAHRAIN

QATAR

Doha

Persian Gulf

Bandar Abbas

Kandahar

Islamabad

Lahore

PAKISTAN

Delhi

New Delhi

H i m a l a y a s

Lhasa

Thimphu

BHUTAN

NEPAL

Kathmandu

Indus R.

10°N

ERITREA

Arabian Peninsula

UNITED ARAB EMIRATES

Abu Dhabi

Gulf of Oman

Muscat

Karachi

Hyderabad

Kanpur

Ganges R.

Brahmaputra

Dhaka

SOUTH SUDAN

Sanaa

YEMEN

OMAN

Ahmadabad

I N D I A

Kolkata (Calcutta)

BANGLADESH

DEM. REP. OF THE CONGO

UGANDA

ETHIOPIA

AFRICA

Aden

DJIBOUTI

Gulf of Aden

Socotra (Yemen)

Arabian Sea

Narmada R.

Nagpur

Mumbai (Bombay)

Godavari

Deccan Plateau

Hyderabad

KENYA

SOMALIA

0°

Lake Victoria

Mogadishu

Laccadive Is. (India)

Bangalore (Bengaluru)

Chennai (Madras)

Andaman Is. (India)

Bay of Bengal

TANZANIA

EQUATOR

Laccadive Sea

Colombo

SRI LANKA

Nicobar Is. (India)

ZAMBIA

MALAWI

10°S

Dar es Salaam

SEYCHELLES

Male

MALDIVES

I N D I A N

ZIMBABWE

MOZAMBIQUE

COMOROS

MADAGASCAR

Diego Garcia (U.K.)

O C E A N

30°E

40°E

50°E

60°E

70°E

80°E

90°E

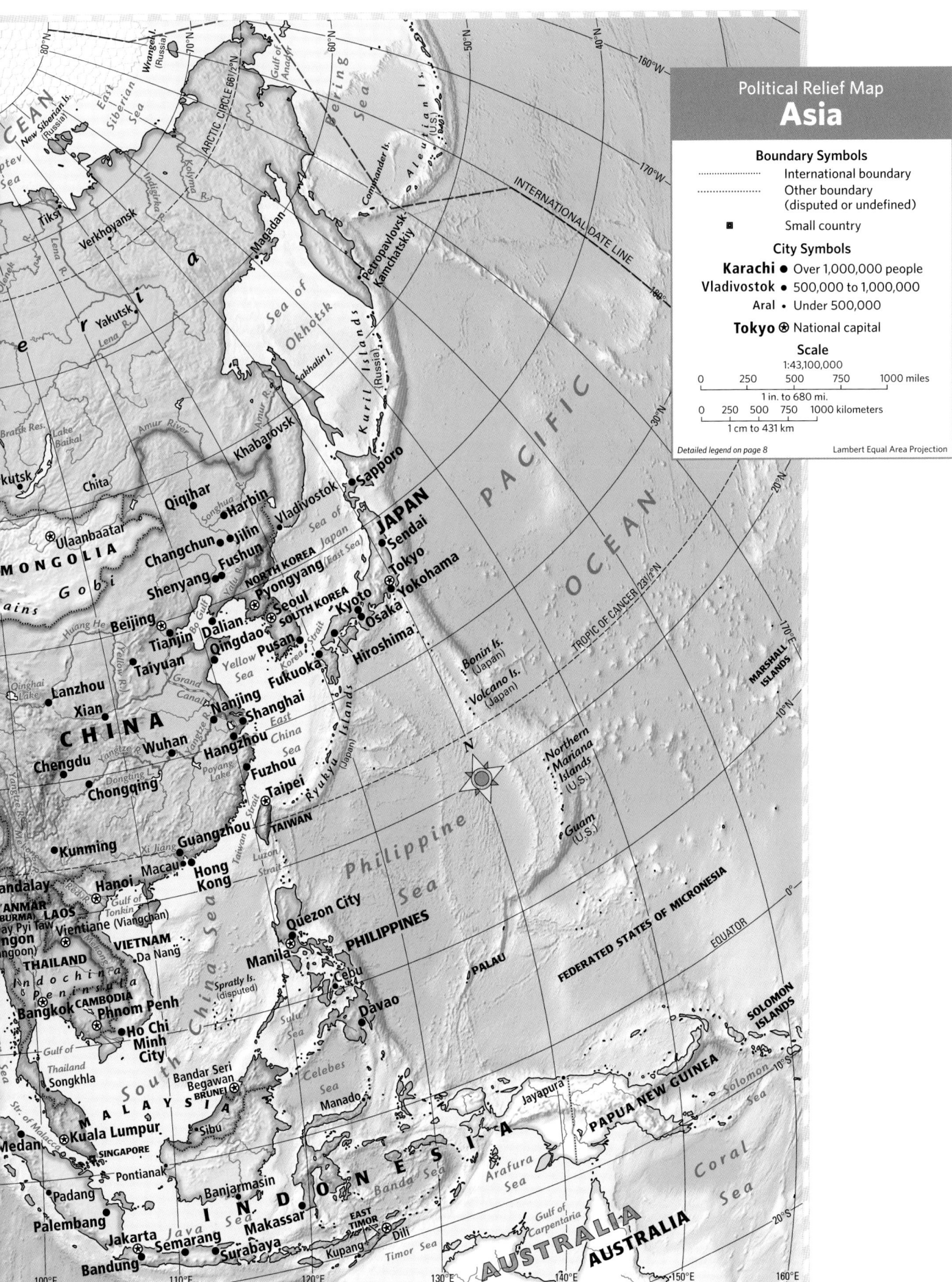

ATLANTIC OCEAN

NORTH POLE

Polar Sea Ice

ARCTIC

Norwegian Sea

Barents Sea

Franz Josef Land

Severne Zem

Novaya Zemlya

Kara Sea

Taymyr Penins.

Svalbard

North Cape

Kolguyev I.

Yamal Pen.

Gydan Pen.

Centr Siberi Plate Tungu

ARCTIC CIRCLE 66½°N

North Sea

IRELAND

UNITED KINGDOM

PORTUGAL

Bay of Biscay

SPAIN

FRANCE

BELGIUM

NETH.

DEN.

NOR-W-A-Y

SWEDEN

FINLAND

Baltic Sea

ESTONIA

LATVIA

LITHUANIA

BELARUS

POLAND

EUROPE

GERMANY

SWITZ.

AUS.

CZ. REP.

SLOVAKIA

HUNGARY

Ob River

West S i b e r i a n Plain

Ob Bay

Ob R.

Yenisey River

RUSSIA

Ural Mountains

Volga R.

Ural R.

Novosibirsk

W. Siberia Borea

PORTUGAL

Strait of Gibraltar

MOROCCO

Mediterranean

ITALY

Adriatic Sea

SLO.

CRO.

BOS.

MONT.

SERBIA

ROMANIA

MOL.

UKRAINE

S t e p p e s

Don R.

Volga R.

Caspian Depression

KAZAKHSTAN

Kazakh Uplands

Irtysh

Lake Zaysan

Altai M

Dzungarian Basin

ALGERIA

TUNISIA

ALB.

MAC.

GREECE

BULGARIA

Black Sea

TURKEY

Ankara

Anatolia

GEORGIA

ARMENIA

AZERBAIJAN

Caucasus Mts.

Caspian Sea

Aral Sea

Syr Darya

UZBEKISTAN

Tashkent

Almaty

Lake Balkhash

KYRGYZSTAN

Tien Shan

Tarim R.

Taklimakan Desert

Kunlun Mountains

LIBYA

TROPIC OF CANCER 23½°N

CYPRUS

LEBANON

ISRAEL

Jerusalem

SYRIA

Euphrates R.

Tigris R.

Zagros Mts.

Elburz Mts.

Tehran

TURKMENISTAN

Kara Kum (desert)

Amu Darya

TAJIKISTAN

Hindu Kush

Pamirs

Mt. Godwin Austen (K2) 28,250 ft. (8611 m)

Plateau of Tibet

EGYPT

Nile River

Sinai Pen.

JORDAN

IRAQ

KUWAIT

Plateau of Iran

IRAN

AFGHANISTAN

Mt. Everest 29,035 ft. (8850 m)

NEPAL

Salwe

CHAD

SUDAN

Red Sea

An Nafud (desert)

SAUDI ARABIA

BAHRAIN

Persian Gulf

QATAR

UNITED ARAB EMIRATES

Gulf of Oman

PAKISTAN

Indus R.

Great Indian Desert

Ganges Plain

Ganges R.

Himalayas

BHUTAN

Brahmapu

SOUTH SUDAN

ERITREA

Mecca (Makkah)

Arabian Peninsula

Empty Quarter

YEMEN

OMAN

Karachi

INDIA

Narmada R.

Kolkata (Calcutta)

BANGLADESH

DEM. REP. OF THE CONGO

UGANDA

ETHIOPIA

DJIBOUTI

Gulf of Aden

Socotra

Arabian Sea

Mumbai (Bombay)

Godavari

Deccan Plateau

Western Ghats

Eastern Ghats

AFRICA

KENYA

SOMALIA

Laccadive Islands

Andaman Islands

Bay of Bengal

Lake Victoria

TANZANIA

Maldive

Laccadive Sea

Sri Lanka

SRI LANKA

Nicobar Islands

ZAMBIA

MALAWI

Maldive Islands

EQUATOR

INDIAN OCEAN

ZIMBABW

MOZAMBIQUE

MADAGASCAR

Comoros Is.

Amirante Isles

Seychelles

Diego Garcia

20°W

10°W

0°

10°W

20°N

20°S

10°N

0°

10°S

30°E

40°E

50°E

60°E

70°E

80°E

90°E

40°N

50°N

60°N

70°N

80°N

30°N

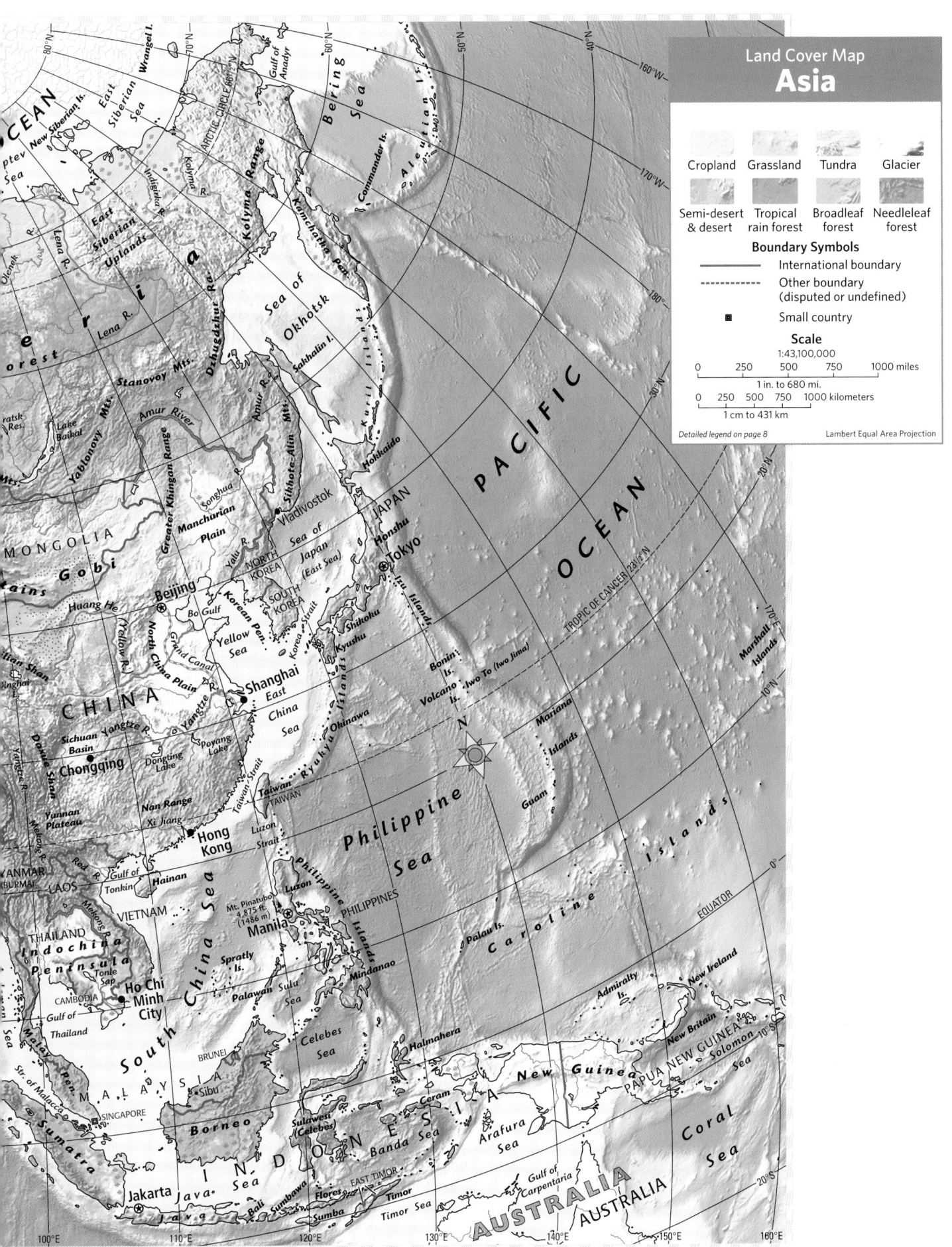

Land Cover Map
Asia

Cropland   Grassland   Tundra   Glacier

Semi-desert   Tropical   Broadleaf   Needleleaf
& desert   rain forest   forest   forest

Boundary Symbols

———————   International boundary

------------   Other boundary
(disputed or undefined)

▣   Small country

Scale
1:43,100,000

| 0 | 250 | 500 | 750 | 1000 miles |

1 in. to 680 mi.

| 0 | 250 | 500 | 750 | 1000 kilometers |

1 cm to 431 km

Detailed legend on page 8   Lambert Equal Area Projection

OCEAN

New Siberian Is.

East
Siberian
Sea

Wrangel I.

Ptev
Sea

Olenek

Lena R.

East
Siberian
Uplands

Indigirka R.

Kolyma R.

Kolyma Ra.

Gulf of
Anadyr

Bering
Sea

Aleutian Is.

Commander Is.

ARCTIC CIRCLE 66½°N

S i b e r i a

forest

Mts.

ratsk.
Res.

Lake
Baikal

Stanovoy Mts.

Yablonovy Mts.

Amur River

Amur R.

Dzhugdzhur Ra.

Stanovoy Mts.

Sea of
Okhotsk

Sakhalin I.

Kamchatka Pen.

Kuril Islands

Greater Khingan Range

Songhua R.

Manchurian
Plain

Sikhote-Alin Mts.

Vladivostok

Sea of
Japan
(East Sea)

Hokkaido

MONGOLIA

Gobi

tains

Mts.

Huang He
(Yellow R.)

Beijing

Bo Gulf

NORTH
KOREA

Yalu R.

Korean Pen.

SOUTH
KOREA

Yellow
Sea

Korean Strait

Korea Strait

JAPAN

Honshu

Tokyo

Shikoku

Kyushu

Izu Islands

PACIFIC

OCEAN

TROPIC OF CANCER 23½°N

Bonin
Is.

Volcano
Is.

Iwo To (Iwo Jima)

Mariana

Islands

Guam

Marshall
Islands

ilian Shan

linghai

CHINA

North China Plain

Grand Canal

Yangtze R.

Shanghai

East
China
Sea

Sichuan
Basin

Daba Shan

Chongqing

Yangtze R.

Dongting
Lake

Poyang
Lake

Nan Range

Yunnan
Plateau

Xi Jiang

Hong
Kong

Luzon
Strait

Taiwan Strait

TAIWAN

Ryukyu Islands

Okinawa

Philippine
Islands

Philippine
Sea

N

Caroline

Islands

YANMAR
(BURMA)

Red R.

Gulf of
Tonkin

Hainan

LAOS

VIETNAM

Mekong R.

Mielong R.

THAILAND

Indochina

Peninsula

Tonle
Sap

CAMBODIA

Gulf of
Thailand

Ho Chi
Minh
City

Mt. Pinatubo
4,875 ft.
(1486 m)

Manila

Luzon

PHILIPPINES

Mindanao

Palau Is.

Admiralty
Is.

New Ireland

New Britain

Spratly
Is.

Palawan

Sulu
Sea

South China Sea

Celebes
Sea

BRUNEI

Halmahera

New Guinea

PAPUA NEW GUINEA

Solomon
Sea

Malay Pen.

Str. of Malacca

SINGAPORE

MALAYSIA

Sibu

Borneo

Sulawesi
(Celebes)

Banda Sea

Ceram Sea

Arafura
Sea

Admiralty
Is.

EQUATOR

Sumatra

Jakarta

Java

Java Sea

I N D O N E S I A

Bali

Sumbawa

Flores

Sumba

EAST TIMOR

Timor

Timor Sea

Gulf of
Carpentaria

AUSTRALIA

AUSTRALIA

Coral
Sea

Elevation Map
Asia

Meters above Sea Level	Feet above Sea Level
Over 6000	Over 20,000
3000 to 6000	10,000 to 20,000
1500 to 3000	5,000 to 10,000
600 to 1500	2,000 to 5,000
300 to 600	1,000 to 2,000
150 to 300	500 to 1,000
0 to 150	0 to 500
Below sea level	Below sea level

Scale
1:51,000,000

0 300 600 900 1200 miles
1 in. to 805 mi.
0 300 600 900 1200 kilometers
1 cm to 510 km

Detailed legend on page 8   Lambert Equal Area Projection

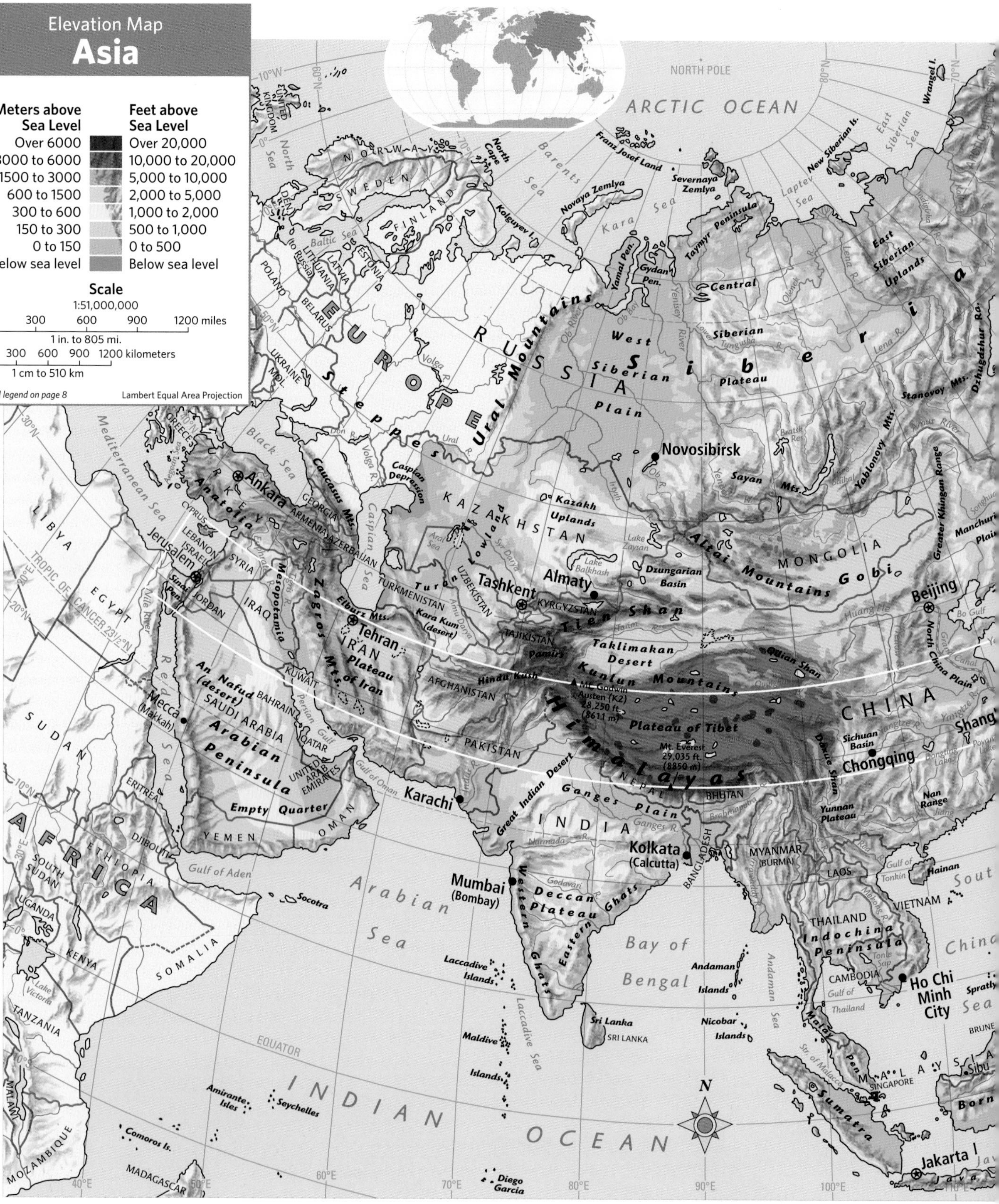

Cross Section
Vertical exaggeration 64 to 1
Scale at 28°N: 1 in. to 708 mi., 1 cm to 448 km

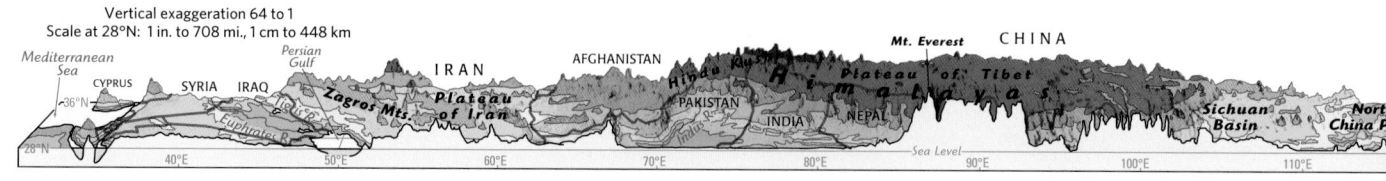

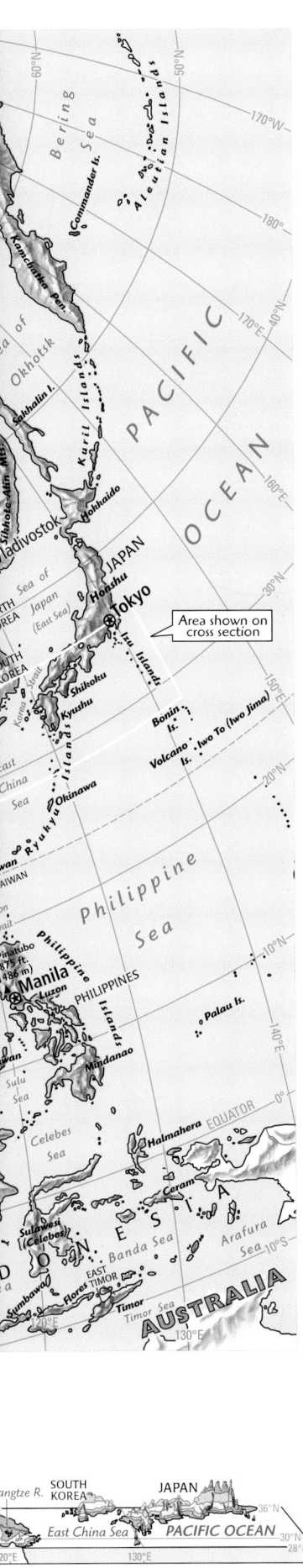

The Himalayas are the highest mountain range in the world. At an elevation of about 11,300 feet (3,400 meters), this village in Nepal is surrounded by many of the world's highest peaks.

Plate Movement and the Himalayas

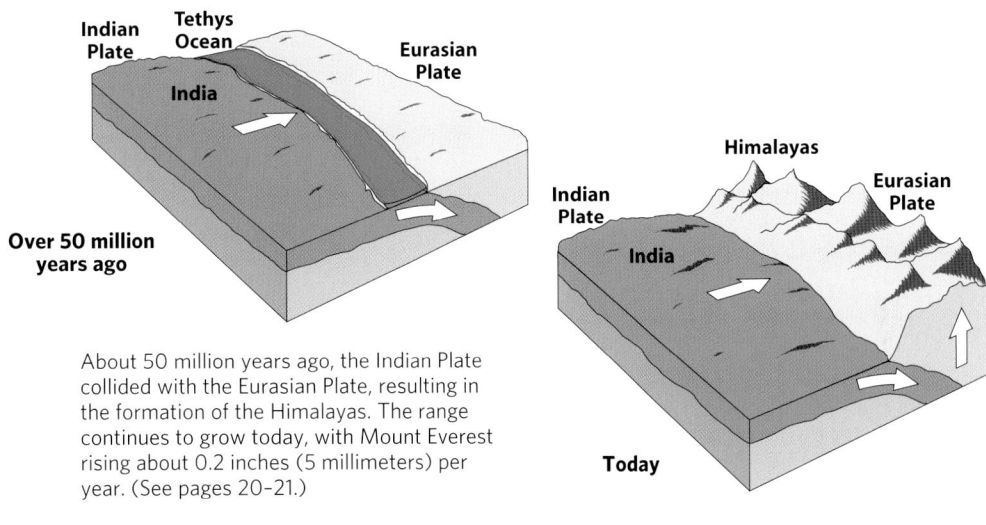

Over 50 million years ago

Today

About 50 million years ago, the Indian Plate collided with the Eurasian Plate, resulting in the formation of the Himalayas. The range continues to grow today, with Mount Everest rising about 0.2 inches (5 millimeters) per year. (See pages 20–21.)

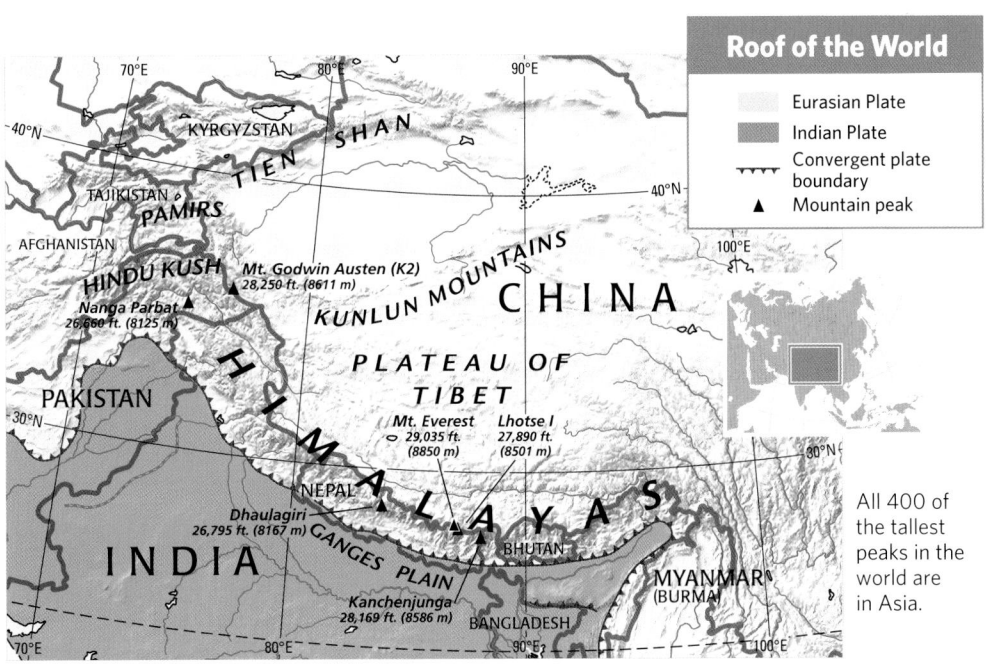

Roof of the World

- Eurasian Plate
- Indian Plate
- ⌄⌄⌄ Convergent plate boundary
- ▲ Mountain peak

All 400 of the tallest peaks in the world are in Asia.

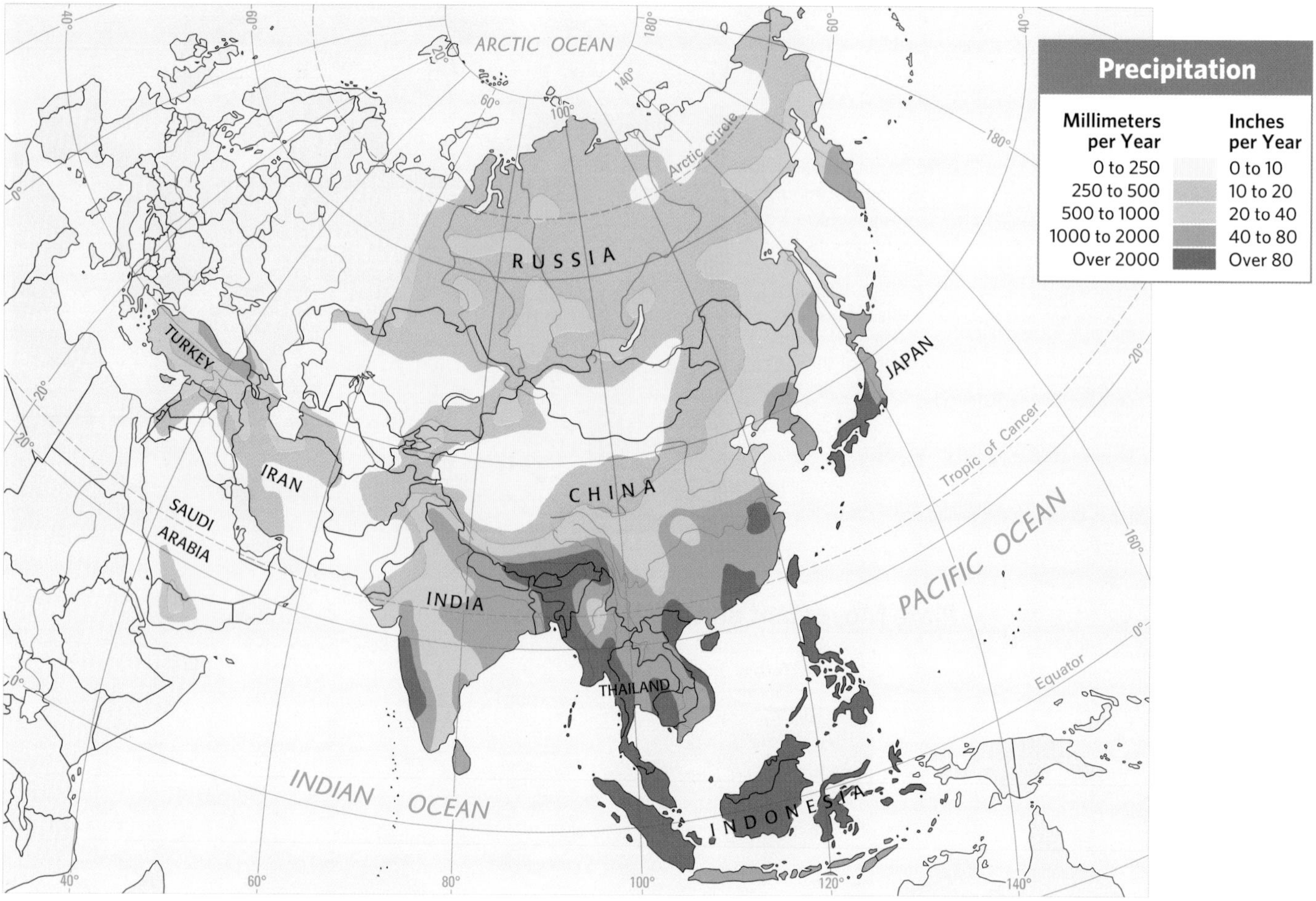

Precipitation

Millimeters per Year	Inches per Year
0 to 250	0 to 10
250 to 500	10 to 20
500 to 1000	20 to 40
1000 to 2000	40 to 80
Over 2000	Over 80

The Dry Continent

More than half of Asia receives 20 inches (500 millimeters) or less of precipitation per year. Asian deserts include the An Nafud and Empty Quarter on the Arabian Peninsula, as well as the Kara Kum Desert, Great Indian Desert, Taklimakan Desert, and Gobi. Even Siberia's tundra has been called the "cold desert."

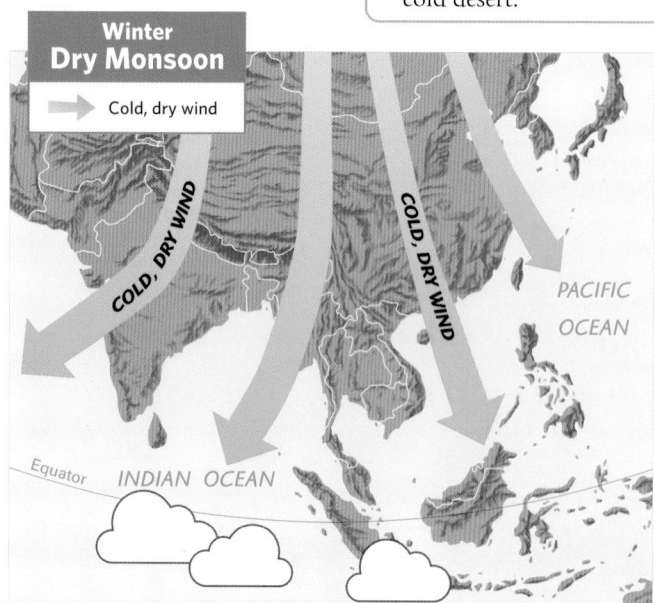

Winter Dry Monsoon

→ Cold, dry wind

The climate of southeastern Asia and India is greatly influenced by large-scale seasonal wind systems called **monsoons**. In winter, dry winds generated over the cold surface of the land blow toward the warmer oceans and keep clouds away.

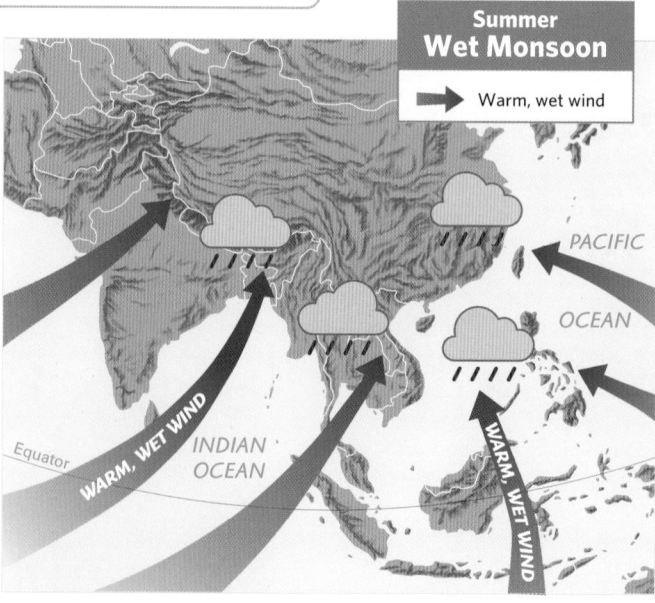

Summer Wet Monsoon

→ Warm, wet wind

In summer, the monsoon changes from dry to wet as the winds reverse direction. Cooler air over the oceans rushes toward warm land, bringing massive amounts of moisture that produce rain. The region's growing season occurs with the wet monsoon.

The map shows the climate regions of Asia.

Climate

Tropical	Tropical rain forest
	Savanna
Dry	Steppe (semi-desert)
	Desert
Mild	Mediterranean
	Humid subtropical
Continental	Hot summer
	Cool summer
	Subarctic
Polar	Tundra
Highland	(Varies greatly with elevation and latitude)

Si-brrr-ia

In Russia, snow and ice cover Siberia for half the year, and the temperature can drop as low as −90°F (−68°C). Verkhoyansk, a town in northeastern Siberia near the Arctic Circle, is the world's coldest continuously inhabited settlement. Without a nearby ocean to moderate its climate, Verkhoyansk can have annual high and low temperatures 140°F (80°C) apart.

During the wet monsoons, intense rainfall can flood city streets, as it has here in India. In July of 2005, 37 inches (940 millimeters) of rain fell on Mumbai in just 24 hours.

Climographs

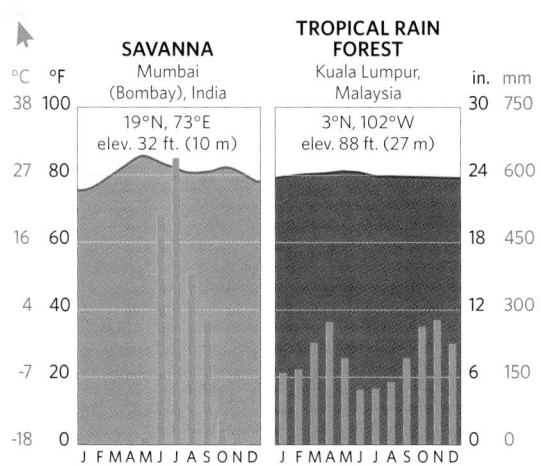

SAVANNA
Mumbai (Bombay), India
19°N, 73°E
elev. 32 ft. (10 m)

TROPICAL RAIN FOREST
Kuala Lumpur, Malaysia
3°N, 102°W
elev. 88 ft. (27 m)

While Mumbai and Kuala Lumpur each receive over 80 inches (2,000 millimeters) of precipitation per year, their rain patterns are very different. Kuala Lumpur receives significant amounts of rain each month, while Mumbai receives most of its rain during the summer monsoon.

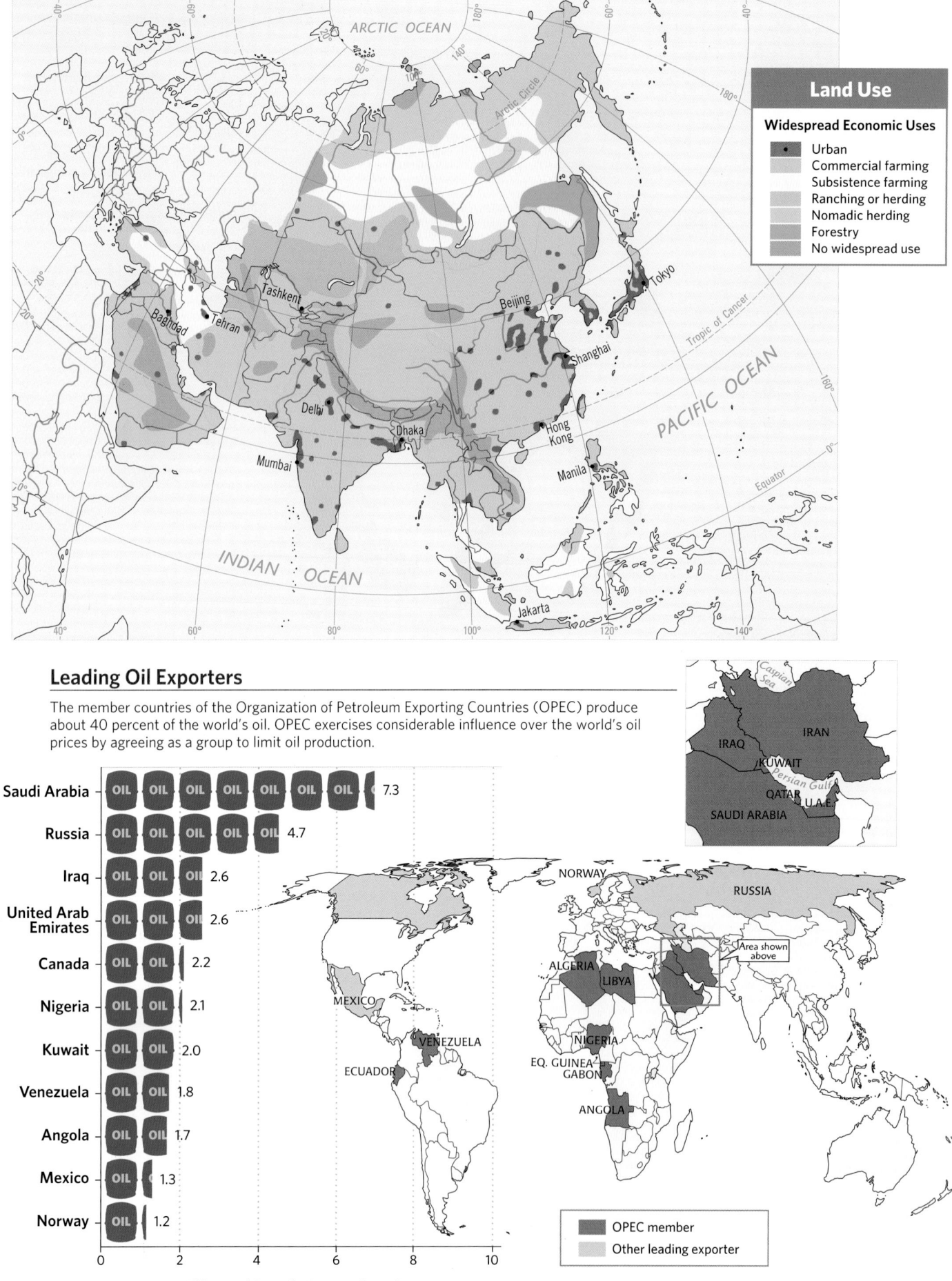

Land Use

Widespread Economic Uses
- Urban
- Commercial farming
- Subsistence farming
- Ranching or herding
- Nomadic herding
- Forestry
- No widespread use

Leading Oil Exporters

The member countries of the Organization of Petroleum Exporting Countries (OPEC) produce about 40 percent of the world's oil. OPEC exercises considerable influence over the world's oil prices by agreeing as a group to limit oil production.

Saudi Arabia — 7.3
Russia — 4.7
Iraq — 2.6
United Arab Emirates — 2.6
Canada — 2.2
Nigeria — 2.1
Kuwait — 2.0
Venezuela — 1.8
Angola — 1.7
Mexico — 1.3
Norway — 1.2

0   2   4   6   8   10

Millions of Barrels Exported per Day

- OPEC member
- Other leading exporter

UKRAINE
MOLDOVA
ROMANIA
SERBIA
BULGARIA
RUSSIA
KAZAKHSTAN
UZBEKISTAN
Black Sea
GEORGIA
ARMENIA
AZERBAIJAN
Caspian Sea
TURKMENISTAN
TURKEY
Mediterranean Sea
SYRIA
IRAQ
IRAN
KUWAIT
Persian Gulf
EGYPT
SAUDI ARABIA
QATAR
U.A.E.
Red Sea
OMAN
YEMEN
Arabian Sea
20°
30°
40°
50°
60°
Major Oil Fields
Working oil field
Known oil deposit

Balance of Trade

Qatar

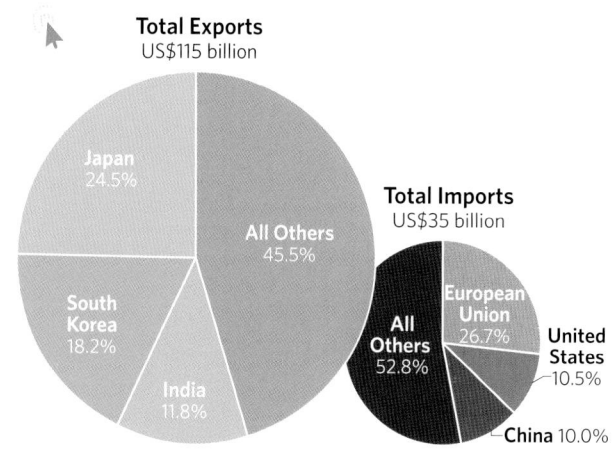

Total Exports
US$115 billion
Japan 24.5%
All Others 45.5%
South Korea 18.2%
India 11.8%
Total Imports
US$35 billion
European Union 26.7%
United States 10.5%
China 10.0%
All Others 52.8%

Over half of the world's proven oil reserves are located in southwestern Asia. As global oil resources continue to be depleted, southwestern Asia continues to be important for meeting the world's energy needs.

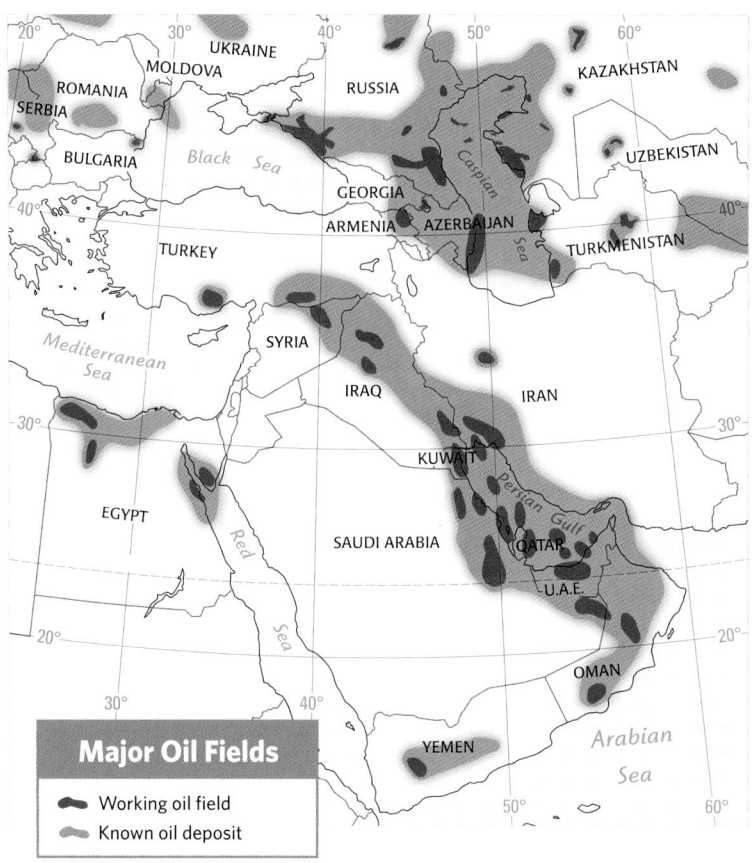

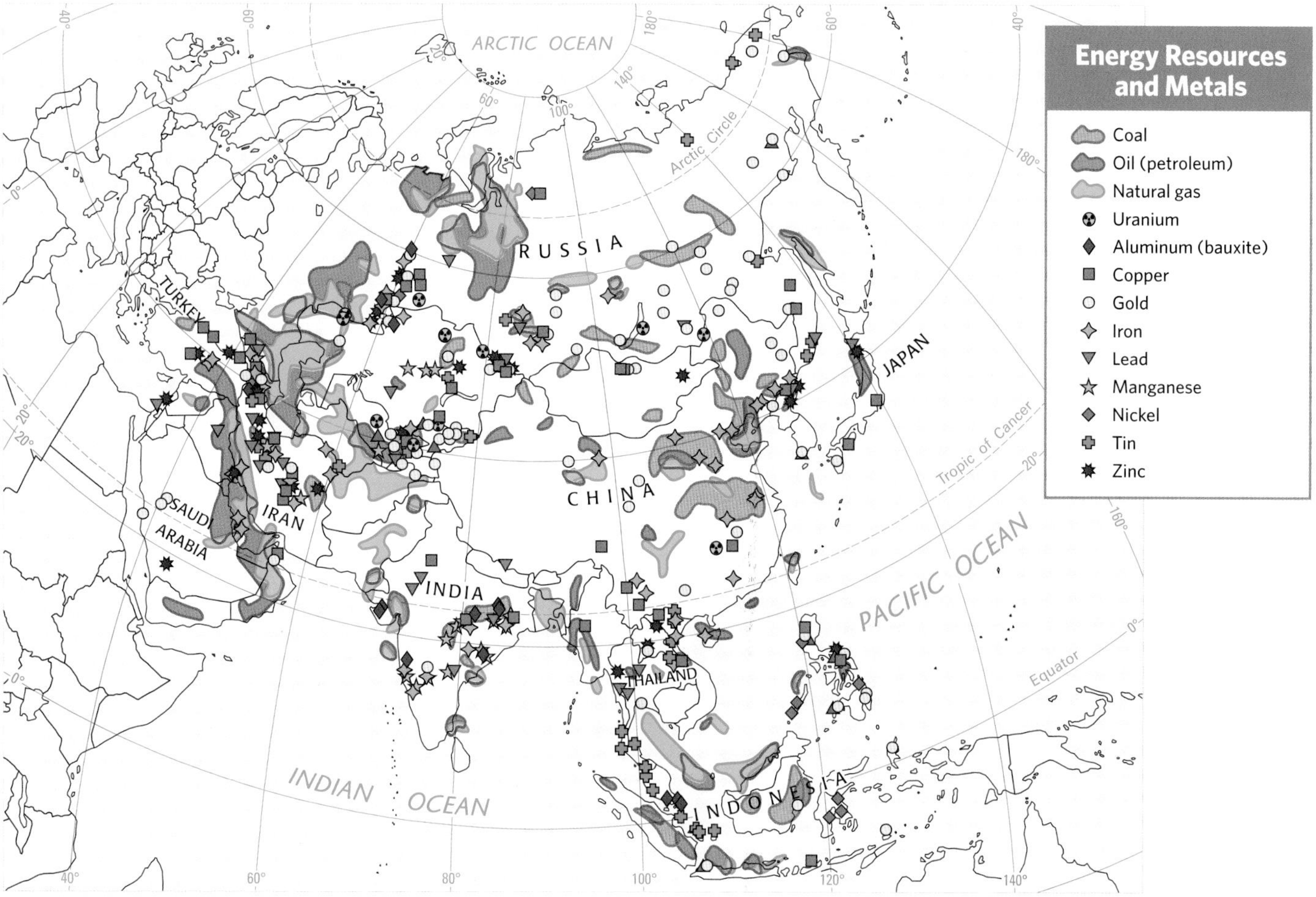

ARCTIC OCEAN
Arctic Circle
RUSSIA
TURKEY
SAUDI ARABIA
IRAN
CHINA
JAPAN
INDIA
THAILAND
INDONESIA
Tropic of Cancer
PACIFIC OCEAN
Equator
INDIAN OCEAN
40°
60°
80°
100°
120°
140°
160°
180°
Energy Resources and Metals
Coal
Oil (petroleum)
Natural gas
Uranium
Aluminum (bauxite)
Copper
Gold
Iron
Lead
Manganese
Nickel
Tin
Zinc

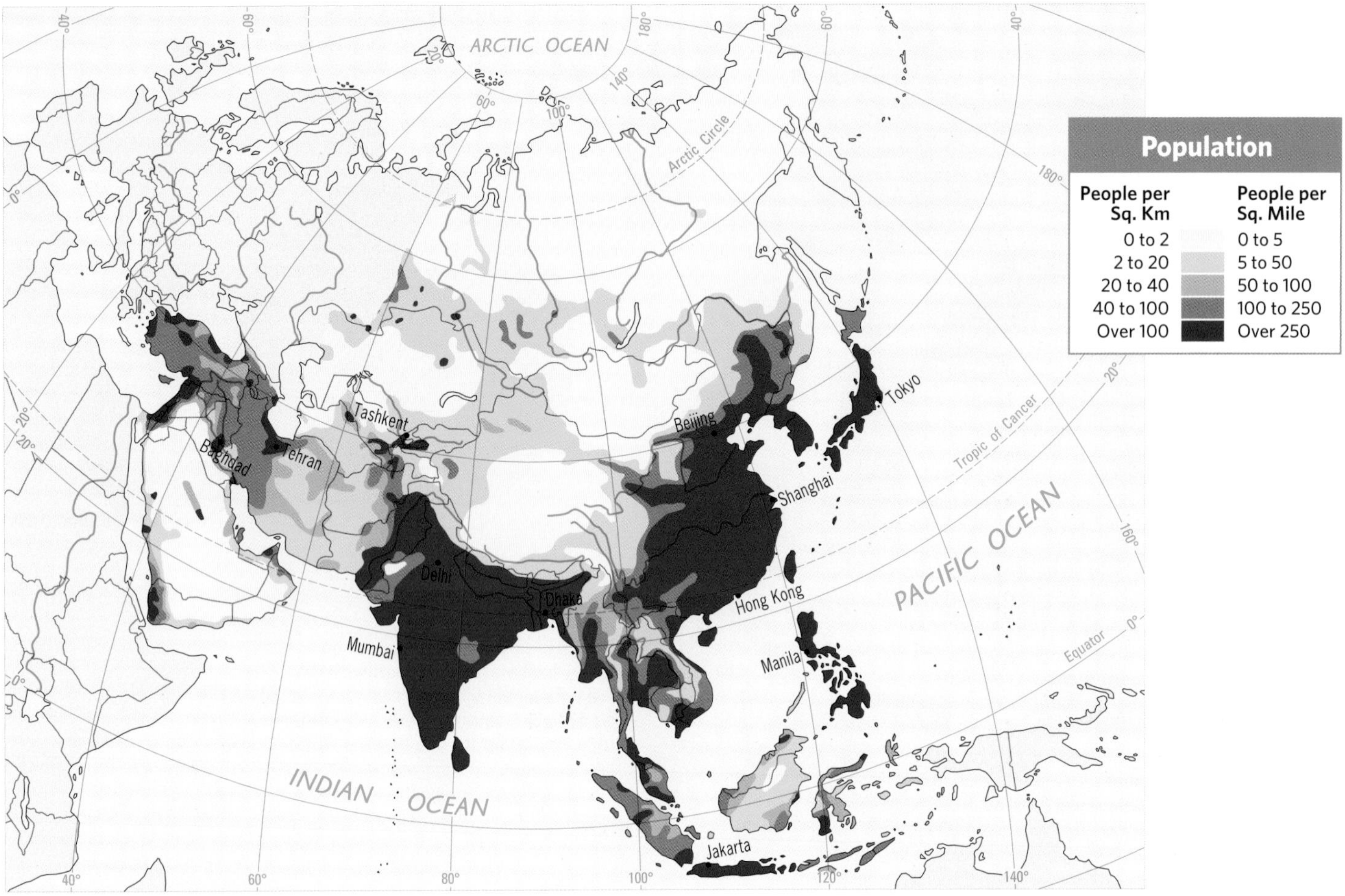

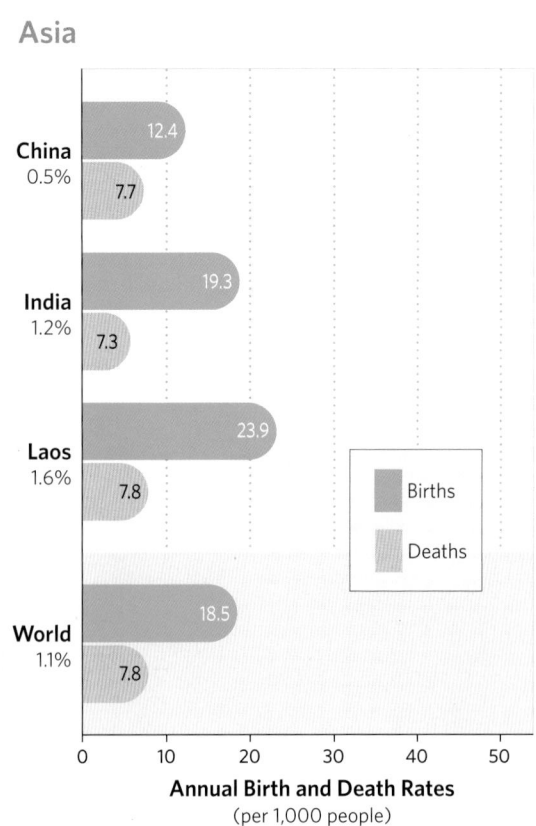

ARCTIC OCEAN
Arctic Circle
Population
People per Sq. Km
People per Sq. Mile
0 to 2
0 to 5
2 to 20
5 to 50
20 to 40
50 to 100
40 to 100
100 to 250
Over 100
Over 250
Tokyo
Beijing
Tashkent
Baghdad
Tehran
Tropic of Cancer
Shanghai
PACIFIC OCEAN
Delhi
Dhaka
Hong Kong
Mumbai
Manila
Equator
INDIAN OCEAN
Jakarta
40°
60°
80°
100°
120°
140°
160°
180°
20°
0°

Say It in Mandarin

Ni hao is a Mandarin greeting spoken by over a billion people in China, Taiwan, and other countries. Mandarin, one of the most spoken languages in the world, is a Sino-Tibetan language. (See page 47.)

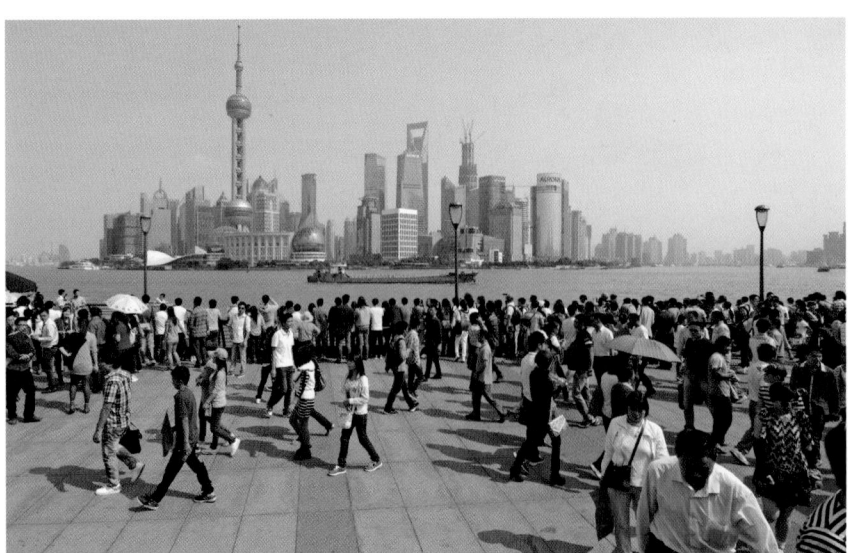

With over 20 million people, Shanghai is the most populous city in China. This waterfront area is a popular destination in the city center.

Natural Population Growth

Asia
China
0.5%
12.4
7.7
India
1.2%
19.3
7.3
Laos
1.6%
23.9
7.8
World
1.1%
18.5
7.8
Births
Deaths
0
10
20
30
40
50
Annual Birth and Death Rates
(per 1,000 people)

World Population

Six countries in Asia—China, India, Indonesia, Pakistan, Bangladesh, and Japan—are home to about half of the world's population. The nearly three and a half billion people living in these countries, however, occupy less than 11 percent of the world's land area.

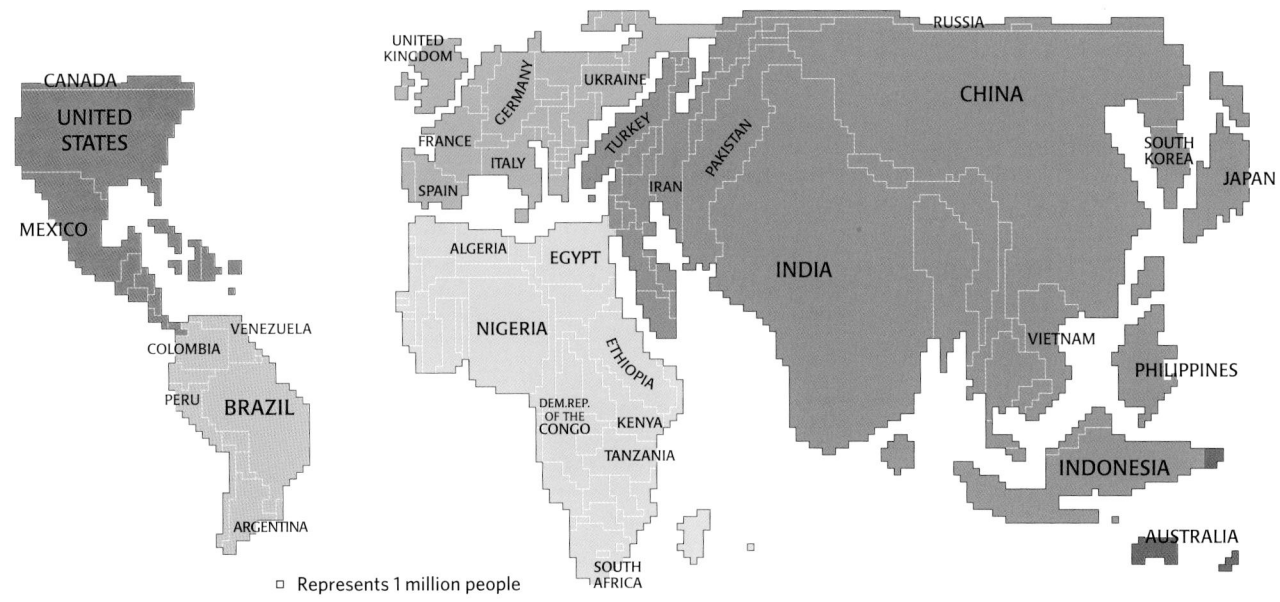

□ Represents 1 million people

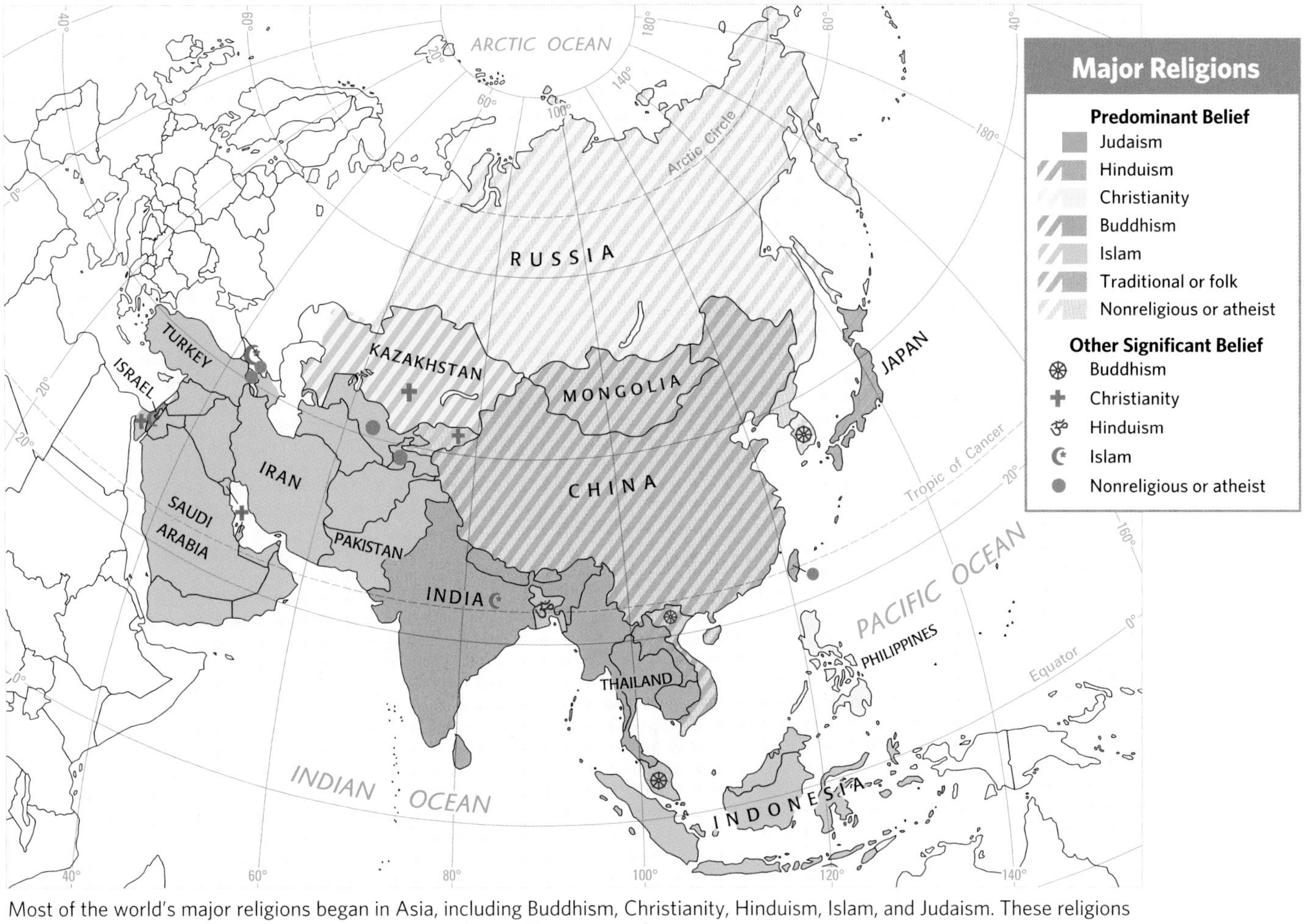

Major Religions

Predominant Belief
- Judaism
- Hinduism
- Christianity
- Buddhism
- Islam
- Traditional or folk
- Nonreligious or atheist

Other Significant Belief
- ✳ Buddhism
- ✝ Christianity
- ৩ Hinduism
- ☾ Islam
- ● Nonreligious or atheist

Most of the world's major religions began in Asia, including Buddhism, Christianity, Hinduism, Islam, and Judaism. These religions are practiced by over 70 percent of the world's population. (See page 46.)

Continues on page 160
Continues on page 179
Continues on page 159
Continues on page 180
Continues on pages 136–137
Continues on page 140

Main Map

BULGARIA
EUROPE
Black Sea
Sochi
Sokhumi
Caucasus Mountains
RUSSIA
Vladikavkaz
KAZAKHSTAN
Turan Lowland
Amu Darya
UZBEKISTAN
Edirne
30°E
Bosporus
Sea of Marmara
Istanbul
Bursa
Balikesir
Ankara
Kirikkale
Samsun
Trabzon
Batumi
Tbilisi
GEORGIA
Kelkit R.
ARMENIA
AZERBAIJAN
Sumqayit
Baku
50°E
Turkmenbat
Kara Kum Canal
Ashgabat
60°E
Buxoro
TURKMENISTAN
Balkanabat
Kara Kum (desert)
40°N
Koroglu Mts.
Erzincan
Pontic Mountains
Eskisehir
Lake Sevan
Yerevan
Mt. Ararat 16,946 ft. (5165 m)
(to Azer.)
Khvoy
Tabriz
Lake Urmia
Rasht
Amol
Sari
Gorgan
Neyshabur
Mashhad
Kopet Dag Mts.
Atrak R.
Mary
Murgab R.
Herat
Hariri R.
Izmir
Aydin
Isparta
Konya
Kayseri
Maras
Malatya
Diyarbakir
Van
Lake Van
Kurdistan
Qazvin
Elburz Mountains
Mt. Damavand 18,386 ft. (5604 m)
Karaj
Tehran
IRAN
Qom
AFGHANISTAN
40°N
Antalya
Mersin
Adana
Gaziantep
Mosul
Arbil
Sulaymaniyah
Kermanshah
Arak
Esfahan (Isfahan)
Plateau of Iran
Dasht-e Kavir (desert)
Dasht-e Lut (desert)
Saberi Lake
Farah R.
Helmand R.
Rhodes (Greece)
TURKEY
Taurus Mountains
Antakya (Antioch)
(1974 cease-fire line)
Aleppo
SYRIA
Kirkuk
Diyala R.
Samarra
Baghdad
Fallujah
Al Kut
Yazd
Kerman
Sistan Marsh
Crete (Greece)
CYPRUS
Nicosia
Homs
LEBANON
Beirut
Damascus
Golan Heights
Tharthar Lake
Syrian
Karbala
IRAQ
Euphrates
Tigris
Mesopotamia
Zagros Mountains
Ahvaz
Zahedan
PAKISTAN
30°N
Mediterranean Sea
ISRAEL
Jerusalem
Gaza
Amman
JORDAN
Desert
An Nafud (desert)
Nasiriyah
Basra
Kuwait
Shiraz
Kerman
Baluchistan
Alexandria
Nile River Delta
Ismailia
Suez Canal
Dead Sea −1,365 ft. (−416 m)
Arar
Sakakah
KUWAIT
Hafar al Batin
Persian
Gulf
Mand R.
Halil R.
Kul R.
Murian Lake
Dasht-e...
Giza
Cairo
Al Fayyum
Bani Suwayf
Sinai Peninsula
Al Aqabah
Gulf of Aqaba
Gulf of Suez
Tabuk
Hail
Al Hasa
Ad Dammam
BAHRAIN
Manama
QATAR
Doha
Dubai
Abu Dhabi
Bandar Abbas
Qeshm I.
Strait of Hormuz (to Oman)
Gulf of Oman
Al Minya
EGYPT
Suhaj
Qina
Arabian Desert
Buraydah
Al Mubarraz
Riyadh
Gulf of Bahrain
UNITED ARAB EMIRATES
Suhar
As-Sib
Muscat
Akhdar Mts.
Ras al Hadd
AFRICA
Nile R.
Hejaz
Medina
Yanbu
Najd
Al Kharj
Mecca (Makkah)
TROPIC OF CANCER 23½°N
SAUDI ARABIA
Rub al Khali (Empty Quarter)
OMAN
Umm as Samim
Masira I.
Gulf of Masira
20°N
Jiddah
At Taif
Red Sea
Port Sudan
Nubian Desert
(adm. boundary)
(treaty boundary)
Tihamah
SUDAN
Khamis Mushayt
Najran
Farasan Is.
Dahlak Archipelago
Mt. Hadur Shuayb 12,336 ft. (3760 m)
Asmara
ERITREA
Sanaa
Dhamar
YEMEN
Wadi al Masilah
Al Mukalla
Arabian Sea
Kuria Muria Is.
Salalah
N
30°E
20°N
Al Hudaydah
Ibb
Taizz
Aden
Gulf of Aden
Abd al Kuri (Yemen)
Socotra (Yemen)
Cape Guardafui (Raas Caseyr)
Mekele
ETHIOPIA
DJIBOUTI
Djibouti
Berbera
SOMALIA
60°E
10°N
Lake Abbe
Dire Dawa
40°E
50°E

Inset Map (Eastern Mediterranean)

CYPRUS
Limassol
Tartus
36°E
Homs
Tripoli
LEBANON
34°N
Beirut
Zahlah
Sidon
Tyre
SYRIA
Damascus
Al Qunatirah
Golan Heights (adm. by Israel)
Haifa
Sea of Galilee
As Suwayda
Nazareth
Irbid
Dara
Mediterranean Sea
N
Tel Aviv
Nablus
West Bank (adm. by Israel and Palestinian Authority)
Jordan R.
32°N
Ramallah
Amman
Gaza (adm. by Palestinian Authority)
Jerusalem
Jericho
Madaba
Hebron
Dead Sea −1,365 ft. (−416 m)
Gaza
Beersheba
ISRAEL
JORDAN
EGYPT
Negev (desert)
Maan
Great Rift Valley
30°N
Sinai Peninsula
Al Jafr
34°E
0 25 50 miles
Elat
Al Aqabah
Gulf of Aqaba
SAUDI ARABIA
36°E

Control Issues

In 1948 the West Bank and Gaza Strip became "temporary" homes to thousands of Arabs who had once lived in British Palestine. Today, the West Bank and Gaza are not officially part of any country. Some sections are run by local Palestinian Arabs and others by the Israeli Army.

Political Relief Map
Southwestern Asia

City Symbols

Jiddah ● Over 1,000,000 people
Kirkuk ● 500,000 to 1,000,000
Taizz • Under 500,000
Tehran ⊗ National capital

Scale

1:20,400,000

0 100 200 300 400 500 miles

1 in. to 322 mi.

0 100 200 300 400 500 kilometers

1 cm to 204 km

Detailed legend on page 8

Lambert Conformal Projection

Continues on page 160
Continues on pages 166–167
Continues on page 160
Continues on page 182
Continues on page 161

Ulyanovsk · Kurgan · Omsk · Novosibirsk · Prokopyevsk · Novokuznetsk
Penza · Ufa · Chelyabinsk · Petropavl · Barnaul · Biysk
RUSSIA · Samara · Magnitogorsk · Qostanay · Kokshetau · Pavlodar · Rubtsovsk
Saratov · EUROPE · Orenburg · Astana (Nur-Sultan) · Semey · Oskemen
Volga River · Oral · Orsk · Arqalyq · Qaraghandy · Lake Zaysan
Aqtobe · Steppe · Qaraghandy · Kazakh Uplands · Tarbagatay Mts.
Volgograd · Ural River · KAZAKHSTAN · Karamay · Dzungarian Basin
Caspian Depression · Atyrau · Kulsary · Zhezqazghan · Aral · Balqash · Taldyqorghan
Astrakhan · Aral Sea · Lake Balkhash
Makhachkala · Ust-Urt Plateau · Aqtau · Muynak · Qyzylorda · Syr Darya · Almaty
Caspian Sea · Turan Lowland · Kyzyl Kum (desert) · Taraz · Bishkek · Karakol
AZERBAIJAN · Garabogazkol Aylagy · Qunghirot · Nukus · UZBEKISTAN · Shymkent · KYRGYZSTAN · Aksu
Baku · Dasoguz · Urganch · Tashkent · Namangan · Tien Shan · CHINA · Taklimakan Desert
Turkmenbashy · Gazojak · Nawoiy · Jizzakh · Khujand · Andijon · Oqon · Osh · Kashi
Balkanabat · TURKMENISTAN · Buxoro · Samarqand · Dushanbe · TAJIKISTAN
Gumdag · Kara Kum (desert) · Turkmenbat · Qarshi · Qurghonteppa · Kulob · Pamirs
Gyzylarbat · Buzmeyin · Ashgabat · Kerki · Termiz · Hindu Kush
Rasht · Tejen · Mary · Bayramaly · Yolotan · Amu Darya
Tehran · Elburz Mountains · Mashhad · Mazar-e Sharif · PAKISTAN
Hamadan · Mt. Damavand 18,386 ft. (5604 m) · AFGHANISTAN · Khyber Pass
Semnan · IRAN · Kabul

Continues on page 178
Continues on page 180

Political Relief Map
Central Asia

City Symbols
Almaty ● Over 1,000,000 people
Barnaul ● 500,000 to 1,000,000
Atyrau · Under 500,000
Tashkent ⊗ National capital

Scale
1:17,700,000

| 0 | 100 | 200 | 300 | 400 miles |

1 in. to 280 mi.

| 0 | 100 | 200 | 300 | 400 kilometers |

1 cm to 177 km

Detailed legend on page 8   Lambert Equal Area Projection

Aral Sea

The Amu Darya drains into the Aral Sea. Beginning in 1956, water from the river was diverted to irrigate cotton fields in the desert of what now is Turkmenistan. Once the fourth largest lake in the world, the Aral Sea is now about one-fifth of its former size. Today the port of Muynak is 90 miles (150 kilometers) from the shore of the Aral Sea.

1976

2014

To celebrate Diwali, the Hindu festival of lights, a girl in India creates a rangoli. Rangoli is an art form made with materials such as flower petals or colored flour. Diwali is usually held in October or November.

Uniquely Indian

The Indian subcontinent is separated from the rest of Asia by the Himalayas. While the subcontinent was not completely cut off from the rest of the continent, it did develop its own unique culture. The subcontinent includes Pakistan, India, Nepal, Bhutan, Bangladesh, and Sri Lanka.

Political Relief Map
Southern Asia

City Symbols

Mumbai ●	Over 3,000,000 people
Rawalpindi ●	1,000,000 to 3,000,000
Khulna •	Under 1,000,000
Dhaka ⊛	National capital

Scale
1:22,200,000

0   150   300   450   600 miles

1 in. to 351 mi.

0   150   300   450   600 kilometers

1 cm to 222 km

Detailed legend on page 8   Lambert Equal Area Projection

Continues on page 179
Continues on page 178
Continues on page 182
Continues on page 181

TURKMENISTAN
UZBEKISTAN   TAJIKISTAN
Ashgabat   Mary   Kashi
Mashhad   Andkhvoy   Dushanbe   Shache   Taklimakan Desert
Termiz   Pamirs
Torbat-e Heydariyeh   Mazar-e Sharif   Meymaneh   Hindu Kush   Shache
Herat   Kuh-e-Fuladi 16,873 ft. (5143 m)   Karakoram Range   Mt. Godwin Austen (K2) 28,250 ft. (8611 m)
Birjand   Ghurian   Kabul   Khyber Pass   Karakoram Pass
AFGHANISTAN   Jalalabad   Srinagar   Himalayas
Farah   Peshawar   Kashmir
Zabol   Rawalpindi   Islamabad
Zaranj   Sialkot   Plateau of Tibet   CHINA
Kandahar   Gujranwala   Tibet   Lhasa
Zahedan   Lashkargah   Faisalabad   Amritsar   Brahmaputra R.
Dalbandin   Quetta   Lahore   Jalandhar
Baluchistan   Multan   Ludhiana   Chandigarh   Mt. Everest 29,035 ft. (8850 m)
PAKISTAN   Delhi   Meerut   NEPAL   Kathmandu   Thimphu
Central Makran Range   Sukkur   New Delhi   Bareilly   BHUTAN   Guwahati
Turbat   Larkana   Jaipur   Agra   Lucknow   Plain   Myitkyina
Gwadar   Hyderabad   Jodhpur   Ganges   Ghaghara R.   Ganges R.   Imphal
Karachi   Kota   Gwalior   Kanpur   Patna
TROPIC OF CANCER 23½°N   Udaipur   Allahabad   Bhagalpur   BANGLADESH
Gulf of Kutch   Sagar   Varanasi   Asansol   Dhaka
Jamnagar   Ahmadabad   Jhansi   Ranchi   Haora   Chittagong
Rajkot   Vadodara   Bhopal   Jabalpur   Jamshedpur   Kolkata (Calcutta)   Namtu
Surat   Indore   INDIA   Hirakud Res.   Khulna   Mandalay
Narmada R.   Nagpur   Raipur   Mouths of the Ganges   MYANMAR (BURMA)
Nasik   Cuttack   Thayetmyo   Nay Pyi Taw
Gulf of Khambhat   Aurangabad   Godavari R.   Myanaung
Thane   Kalyan   Vishakhapatnam   Bay of Bengal   Yangon (Rangoon)
Mumbai (Bombay)   Pune   Hyderabad   Pathein   Mawlamyine
Arabian Sea   Sholapur   Vijayawada   Mouths of the Irrawaddy   Gulf of Martaban
Krishna R.   Deccan Plateau   Eastern Ghats
Hubli-Dharwad   Coromandel Coast
Western Ghats   Bangalore (Bengaluru)   Chennai (Madras)
Malabar Coast   Cauvery R.   Andaman Is. (India)
Mangalore   Mysore   Port Blair
Laccadive Is. (India)   Cauvery Falls   Andaman Sea
Kozhikode (Calicut)   Coimbatore
Kochi (Cochin)   Madurai   Jaffna
Thiruvnanthapuram (Trivandrum)   Palk Strait
Gulf of Mannar   SRI LANKA   Kandy   Nicobar Is. (India)
MALDIVES   Cape Comorin   Colombo   Sri Jayewardenepura Kotte   Banda Aceh
INDIAN   OCEAN   Sumatra   INDONESIA

IRAN

N

Continues on page 182

Political Relief Map
Southeastern Asia

City Symbols
Guangzhou ● Over 3,000,000 people
Medan ● 1,000,000 to 3,000,000
Ipoh · Under 1,000,000
Bangkok ⊗ National capital

Scale
1:21,100,000
0   100   200   300   400   500 miles
1 in. to 335 mi.
0 100 200 300 400 500 kilometers
1 cm to 211 km

Detailed legend on page 8   Lambert Equal Area Projection

Himalayas
BHUTAN
Brahmaputra R.
Guwahati
·INDIA
Imphal
Chittagong
·Namtu
·Mandalay
MYANMAR
(BURMA)
Nay Pyi Taw ⊗
Thayetmyo
Myanaung
Yangon
(Rangoon)
Bago
Pathein
Pagoda
Point
Mouths of the
Irrawaddy
Gulf of
Martaban
Mawlamyine
Andaman Is.
(India)
Port Blair
Andaman
Sea
Mergui
Archipelago
Nicobar Is.
(India)
Surat Thani
Songkhla
Banda Aceh
George Town
Ipoh
Medan
INDONESIA
Pematangsiantar
Simeulue
Nias
INDIAN
OCEAN
EQUATOR

Myitkyina
Chindwin R.
Irrawaddy R.
Panzihua
Yunnan Plateau
Kunming
CHINA
TROPIC OF CANCER 23½°N
Dien Bien
Phu
Louangphrabang
LAOS
Chiang
Rai
Chiang Mai
Vientiane
(Viangchan)
Udon Thani
THAILAND
Khon
Kaen
Mawlamyine
Thon
Buri
Nakhon
Ratchasima
Bangkok
Isthmus
of Kra
Gulf
of
Thailand
Malay
Peninsula
Kuala
Terengganu
M
Natuna
Besar Is.
(Indonesia)
Kuantan
Kiang
Kuala Lumpur
Putrajaya
Johor Baharu
☐ SINGAPORE
Pekanbaru
Sumatra
Strait of Malacca

Guiyang
Nanchang
Nanning
Wuzhou
Guangzhou
Shantou
Macau
Hong
Kong
Hanoi
Haiphong
Nam Dinh
Haikou
Gulf of
Tonkin
Hainan
Vinh
Hue
Da Nang
VIETNAM
Savannakhet
Mun R.
Indochina Peninsula
Plateau of
Kontum
Qui Nhon
CAMBODIA
Kracheh
Phnom Penh
Tonle
Sap
Khone
Falls
Bien Hoa
Nha Trang
Ho Chi Minh City
Long Xuyen
Can
Tho
Mouths of
the Mekong
Con Son Is.
Point
Bai Bung
Chao Phraya
Chi
Mekong
Annamite Mts.
Salween R.
Ping R.
Black R.
Red R.
Hongshui R.
Xi Jiang

Paracel Is.
(disputed)
South
China
Sea
Spratly Is.
(disputed)
N

Escarpada Point
120°E
Luzon
Mt. Pinatubo
4,875 ft. (1486 m)
Quezon
City
Manila ⊗
Mindoro
Philippine
Sea
PHILIPPINES
Panay
Iloilo
Bacolod
Cebu
Samar
Negros
Puerto Princesa
Palawan
Butuan
Sulu Sea
Pagadian
Mindanao
Davao
General Santos
Balabac Strait
Kinabalu
13,455 ft.
(4101 m)
Kota Kinabalu
Sandakan
Bandar Seri Begawan
BRUNEI
Celebes
Sea
Tarakan
Sibu Sarawak
Kuching
Borneo
INDONESIA
Kayan R.
Rajang R.
Kapuas R.
Strait of
Makassar
Sulawesi
(Celebes)
Manado
Molucca Sea

Scale at Equator
1:31,800,000
0   250 mi.
1 in. to 502 mi.
0   250 km
1 cm to 318 km
Miller Projection
N

Banda Aceh
Medan
Simeulue I.
Nias
Pekanbaru
Batu Is.
Mentawai Is.
Padang
Sumatra
Jambi
Palembang
Dempo △
10,364 ft. (3159 m)
Enggano I.
INDIAN
OCEAN
Christmas I.
(Australia)
Ipoh
Kuala
Lumpur
Natuna
Besar Is.
(Indonesia)
M A L A Y S I A
☐ SINGAPORE
EQUATOR
Bangka
Belitung
Bandar Seri Begawan
BRUNEI
Sibu
Kuching
Borneo
Pontianak
Samarinda
Balikpapan
Banjarmasin
Kalimantan
Greater Sunda Is.
Java Sea
Jakarta
Semarang
Bandung
Slamet
11,247 ft.
(3428 m)
Semeru
12,060 ft.
(3676 m)
Java
Malang
Surabaya
Makassar
Kota Kinabalu
Sandakan
PHILIPPINES
Talaud Is.
(Indonesia)
Celebes
Sea
Morotai I.
Manado
Molucca
Palu
Sula Is.
Sulawesi
(Celebes)
Buru I.
Ambon
Banda
Sea
I N D O N E S I A
Ceram
Ceram Sea
Halmahera
Waigeo I.
Morotai I.
Molucca Islands
Fakfak
Jaya Peak △
16,503 ft.
(5030 m)
New Guinea
Sorong
Manokwari
Biak I.
Jayapura
PAPUA
NEW
GUINEA
Flores Sea
Flores
Mt. Tambora
9,350 ft. (2850 m)
Bali
Lombok
Sumba
Sumbawa
Lesser Sunda Is.
Kupang
Timor
Wetar
Moa
Dili
EAST TIMOR
Tanimbar Is.
Aru
Is.
Dolak I.
Merauke
Arafura Sea
Timor Sea

Continues on page 180

Continues on pages 188–189

Continues on page 195

Balance of Trade

China

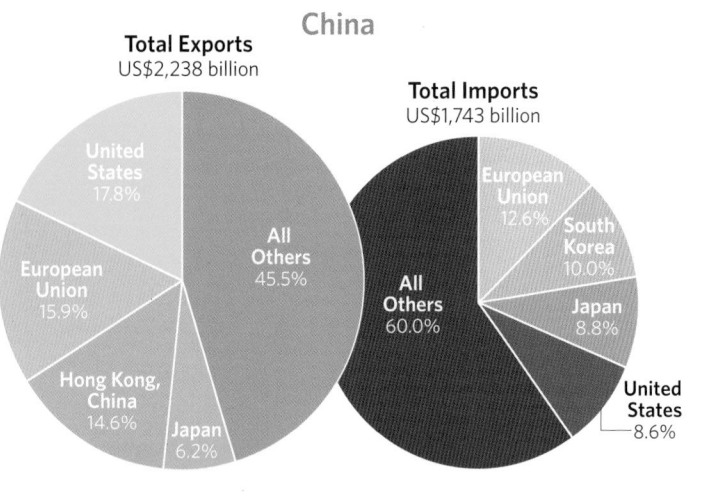

Total Exports
US$2,238 billion

- United States 17.8%
- European Union 15.9%
- Hong Kong, China 14.6%
- Japan 6.2%
- All Others 45.5%

Total Imports
US$1,743 billion

- European Union 12.6%
- South Korea 10.0%
- Japan 8.8%
- United States 8.6%
- All Others 60.0%

Top Asian GDPs

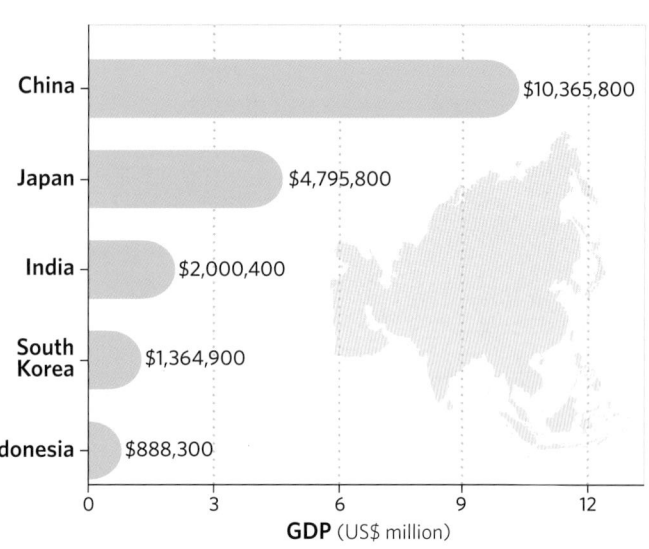

Country	GDP (US$ million)
China	$10,365,800
Japan	$4,795,800
India	$2,000,400
South Korea	$1,364,900
Indonesia	$888,300

GDP (US$ million)

Many of the world's largest economies are located in Asia. Some—such as South Korea and Japan—are **mature** with high standards of living and moderate growth, while others—such as India and China—are **emerging** with moderate to low standards of living and high growth.

Political Relief Map
Eastern Asia
China, Mongolia, and Taiwan

City Symbols

- **Shenyang** ● Over 3,000,000 people
- **Kaohsiung** ● 1,000,000 to 3,000,000
- Uliastay • Under 1,000,000
- **Beijing** ⊛ National capital

Scale
1:30,700,000

0 200 400 600 800 miles
1 in. to 489 mi.

0 200 400 600 800 kilometers
1 cm to 307 km

Detailed legend on page 8   Lambert Equal Area Projection

Continues on pages 166–167

Continues on page 179

Continues on page 180

Continues on page 183

Continues on pages 166–167

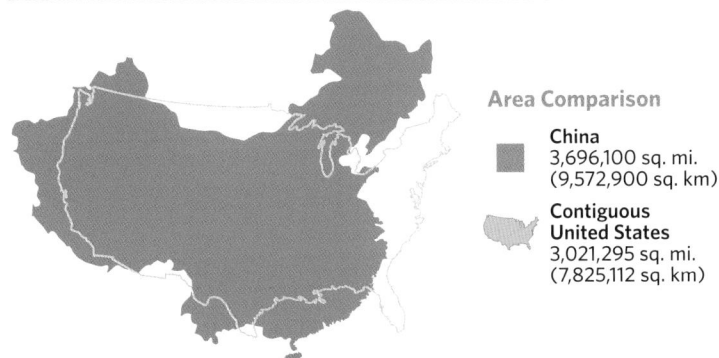

Continues on page 182

Continues on page 181

Political Relief Map
Eastern Asia
Japan and the Koreas

City Symbols

Pusan ● Over 3,000,000 people
Osaka ● 1,000,000 to 3,000,000
Chongjin • Under 1,000,000
Tokyo ⊗ National capital

Scale
1:15,400,000

| 0 | 100 | 200 | 300 miles |

1 in. to 243 mi.

| 0 | 100 | 200 | 300 kilometers |

1 cm to 154 km

Detailed legend on page 8   Bonne Projection

China Area Comparison

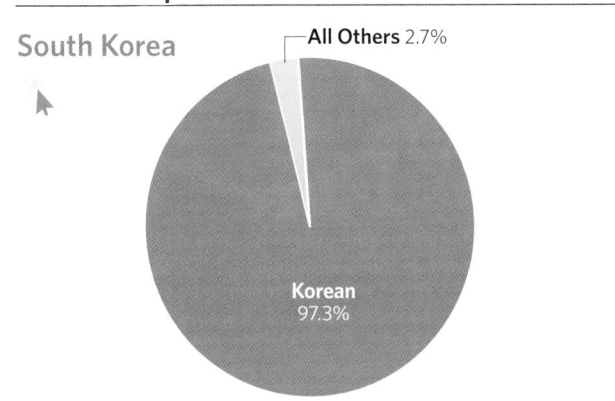

Area Comparison

China
3,696,100 sq. mi.
(9,572,900 sq. km)

**Contiguous
United States**
3,021,295 sq. mi.
(7,825,112 sq. km)

Ethnic Composition

South Korea

All Others 2.7%

Korean
97.3%

The Japanese have one of the world's highest levels of personal income. This busy street crossing is in the Shibuya district of Tokyo, a popular destination for shopping.

How can population growth be controlled?

Asia, the most populated continent on Earth, is home to more than half of the world's people. Its population is projected to reach 5.2 billion by 2050. Unfortunately, Asia's population places a major strain on economic development and the environment. High population density has resulted in a loss of cropland and an increase in waste and pollution. Overpopulation also has reduced access to such basics as food, water, and health care. Should Asian countries carry out policies to regulate population growth? There are many perspectives on this issue. Here are two of them.

Annual Birth Rates
Per 1,000 People

- 35 or more
- 25 to 35
- 15 to 25
- Fewer than 15

Government policy can greatly reduce birth rates.

- In most developing countries, people are encouraged to have many children. Legal and political pressures are needed to counteract these long-standing customs.

- China's planned birth policy (known in the West as the "one-child" policy) used political sanctions to curtail its rapidly increasing population. From 1979 to 2015, the policy prevented an estimated 400 million births.

- Today, over 80 percent of all married women in China use contraception, compared to 33 percent in other developing countries.

- When China's one-child policy was relaxed in 2015, births were expected to increase by 3 million annually. However births only increased 1.3 million in 2016.

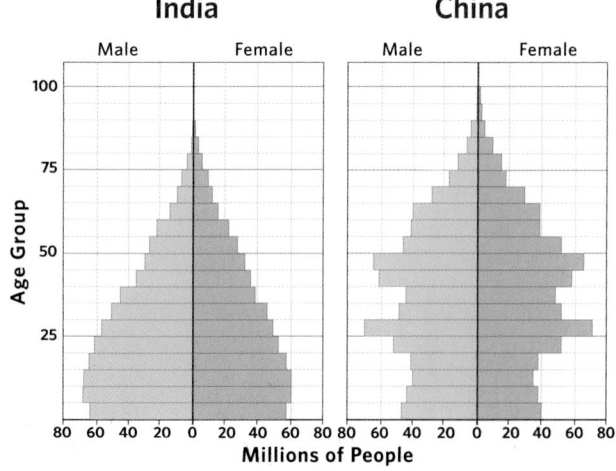

In both China and India, sons traditionally are valued more than daughters. Female infanticide and selective abortion are not uncommon.

Education will control population growth.

- The ability to "found a family" is a basic human right, declared by the United Nations. Education respects that right by allowing people to make their own choices.

- Education helps people make informed choices about their own reproductive health and their children's health.

- High birth rates often compensate for high infant mortality. Reproductive education results in healthier women and healthier babies. With more survivors, parents do not feel the need to have more children.

- India was the first developing country to sponsor a family planning program. Since the 1960s, its annual birth rate has dropped from 35 births to 19 births per 1,000 people.

Family planning and family welfare programs have slowed the rate of population growth in India. Beginning in 1952, family planning has educated women about contraceptive use and raising healthy children. Today, 60 percent of women in India use contraceptives, compared to only 13 percent in 1970.

What should be done about the rapid growth of cities?

In 2007, the world's urban population exceeded the rural population for the first time in human history. Industralization in Europe, North America, and Japan led to the growth of cities between 1850 and 1950. Economic development since 1950 has led to a massive increase in the size of cities in Asia. Many of these cities suffer from poor sanitation, pollution, and severely strained transportation infrastructures. How should governments deal with the rapid growth of cities? There are many perspectives on this issue. Here are two of them.

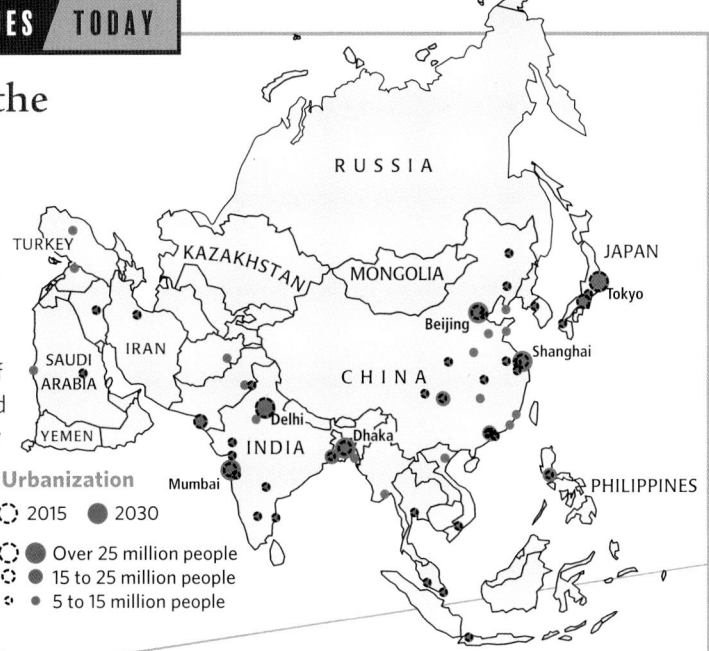

Urbanization
- ◯ 2015 ● 2030
- ◯ ● Over 25 million people
- ◌ ● 15 to 25 million people
- ⁙ ● 5 to 15 million people

Governments should expand services to cope with the rising urban population.

- Housing for the poorest people in huge cities is often primitive and lacks the most basic comforts. Deaths from accidents, like fires and building collapses, are common. Modern buildings and building inspections could easily solve these problems.

- Without clean water, sanitation, and medical care, the population is increasingly at risk for widespread epidemics. In densely populated cities, these epidemics can spread rapidly through the entire urban area.

- Poor services threaten the economic health of the urban area. Poor transportation prevents people from getting to their jobs, inadequate policing places people and businesses at risk, and poor education reduces the quality of the workforce.

Fastest Growing Asian Cities

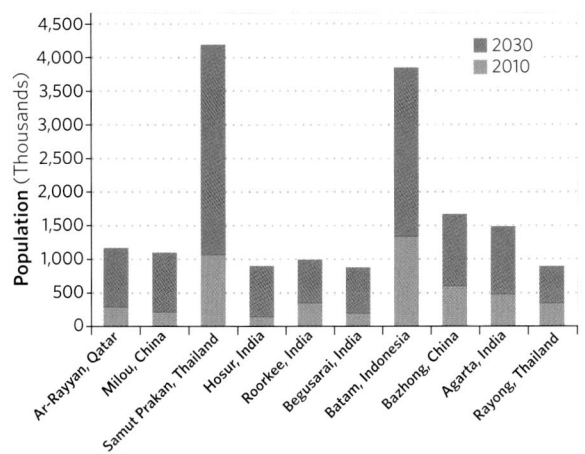

Within twenty years, these cities will have doubled or tripled in size. Infrastructure, health services, and housing must also increase.

Governments should invest in smaller cities and rural communities.

- Modern communications, transportation, and energy infrastructure no longer need to be concentrated to be efficient. As a result, concentrating the population to provide jobs and services is no longer necessary.

- Developing less densely populated areas will allow for more deliberate urban planning. Rather than "playing catch-up," governments can develop city services that meet the needs of the population.

- Europe and the United States slowed the growth of their largest cities by encouraging growth in other regions. A megacity is an urban area with a population of over 10 million. The United States has two megacities, and Europe has three. China, which is only slightly larger in area than the United States, has six. India, roughly a third the size of the United States, has five.

These Beijing residents use masks to protect themselves from the hazardous smog in the air. As more and more people move to the cities, air quality drops dramatically.

World Extreme The Great Barrier Reef is the largest coral reef system in the world. It consists of more than 2,000 individual reefs and extends about 1,240 miles (2,000 kilometers) along the northeast coast of Australia.

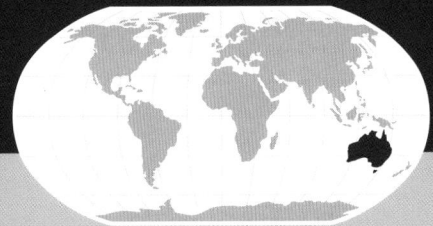

Australia & Oceania

Australia and Oceania—the central and south Pacific—are famous for their thousands of beautiful tropical islands and for their diverse cultures and languages. Unique plants and animals can be found throughout the isolated islands of the region.

Physical Features

Highest mountain peak
Jaya Peak 16,503 ft. (5,030 m)

Longest mountain range
Great Dividing Range 2,300 mi. (3,700 km)

Largest islands
New Guinea 342,000 sq. mi. (885,780 sq. km)
South Island (New Zealand) 58,385 sq. mi. (151,215 sq. km)

Largest lake
Kati Thanda-Lake Eyre* 3,700 sq. mi. (9,583 sq. km)

Longest rivers
Murray 1,200 mi. (1,930 km)
Darling* 1,160 mi. (1,879 km)

Major archipelagos
Hawaiian Islands
New Hebrides
Tuamotu Archipelago

Other key physical features
Great Artesian Basin
Kimberley Plateau
Nullarbor Plain
Western Plateau

Cultural Features

Population
40,117,000

Largest country by area
Australia 2,969,976 sq. mi. (7,692,202 sq. km)★

Largest country by population
Australia 23,232,413

Most densely populated
Nauru 1,205.3 people per sq. mi. (459.1 per sq. km)

Least densely populated
Australia 7.8 people per sq. mi. (3.0 per sq. km)

Largest urban areas
Sydney, Australia 4,505,000
Melbourne, Australia 4,203,000

★ Among the world's largest. See the inside front cover.

*Seasonal

Area Comparison

■ **Australia**
2,969,978 sq. mi.
(7,692,208 sq. km)

Contiguous United States
3,021,295 sq. mi.
(7,825,112 sq. km)

Regional Maps of Australia and Oceania

1 **Australia** p.195
2 **New Zealand** p.195

Thematic Maps of Australia and Oceania

Precipitation p.192
Climate p.192
Land Use p.193
Energy Resources and Metals p.193
Population p.194
Indigenous People p.194

Chengdu
Nanjing
Shanghai
JAPAN
Wuhan
CHINA
Chongqing
Changsha
Nanchang
ASIA
Fuzhou
PACIFIC OCEAN
Nanning
Guangzhou
Taipei
East China Sea
Okinawa
Bonin Islands (Japan)
Minami Tori Shima (Japan)
Macau
Hong Kong
TAIWAN
Kaohsiung
Ryukyu Islands (Japan)
Daito Islands (Japan)
Iwo To (Iwo Jima) (Japan)
Volcano Islands (Japan)
Wake (U.S.)
TROPIC OF CANCER 23½°N
Hanoi
LAOS
Vientiane (Viangchan)
Hainan
Luzon Strait
Babuyan Is.
Okino Tori Shima (Japan)
Farallon de Pajaros
Asuncion I.
Maug Is.
THAILAND
Da Nang
Luzon
Agrihan I.
Pagan I.
Alamagan I.
Guguan I.
Northern Mariana Islands (U.S.)
VIETNAM
Baguio
Quezon City
Philippine Sea
Anatahan I.
Farallon de Medinilla
Saipan I.
Marshall Islands
CAMBODIA
Manila
PHILIPPINES
Tinian I.
Rota I.
Saipan
Taongi Atoll
Phnom Penh
Ho Chi Minh City
Palawan
Cebu
Guam (U.S.)
Hagatna (Agana)
Enewetak Atoll
Bikini Atoll
Ratak Chain
Ulithi Atoll
FEDERATED STATES OF MICRONESIA
Mindanao
Davao
Babelthuap
Koror
Yap Is.
Ngulu Atoll
Sorol Atoll
Namonuito Atoll
Hall Islands
Oroluk Atoll
Ujelang Atoll
Kwajalein Atoll
Kota Kinabalu
Sandakan
Melekeok
Ifalik Atoll
Pulusuk Atoll
Chuuk (Truk) Islands
Pohnpei Islands
Palikir
Majuro Atoll
Majuro
Bandar Seri Begawan
BRUNEI
Sonsorol Is.
Ralik Chain
Kuala Lumpur
MALAYSIA
Sibu
PALAU
Mortlock Islands
Ngatik Atoll
Kosrae I.
Jaluit Atoll
SINGAPORE
EQUATOR
Kapingamarangi Atoll
Samarinda
Manado
Pontianak
Borneo
Banjarmasin
Palu
Sulawesi (Celebes)
Molucca Sea
Sorong
Ninigo Group
Admiralty Is.
Manus I.
St. Matthias Group
Lyra Reef
New Hanover
Yaren District (unofficial)
Palembang
INDONESIA
Buru I.
Ambon
Jayapura
Wewak
Bismarck Archipelago
New Ireland
NAURU
Jakarta
Bandung
Semarang
Surabaya
Makassar
Ceram
Ceram Sea
Banda Sea
Tanimbar Is.
Aru Is.
New Guinea
PAPUA NEW GUINEA
Madang
Bismarck Sea
Rabaul
New Britain
Buka I.
Bougainville
Solomon
Ontong Java Atoll
SOLOMON ISLANDS
Java Sea
Flores Sea
Malang
Bali
Lombok
Sumbawa
Sumba
Kupang
Flores
Dili
EAST TIMOR
Dolak I.
Merauke
Lae
Port Moresby
Gulf of Papua
Woodlark I.
Fergusson I.
New Georgia Group
Santa Isabel
Honiara
Malaita I.
Guadalcanal
San Cristobal
Rennell I.
Indispensable Reefs
Reef Islands
Duff Islands
Santa Cruz Islands
Nendo I.
Vanikolo Is.
Christmas I. (Australia)
Timor
Arafura Sea
Torres Strait
Cape York
Louisiade Archipelago
INDIAN OCEAN
Timor Sea
Browse I.
Darwin
Kuri Bay
Katherine
Gulf of Carpentaria
Groote Eylandt
Wellesley Is.
Great Barrier Reef
Coral Sea
Torres Islands
Banks Islands
Maewo I.
Pentecost I.
Ambrym I.
Broome
Great Sandy Desert
Lake Argyle
Mitchell R.
Cairns
VANUATU
Espiritu Santo
Malakula I.
Epi I.
Port-Vi Efate I.
Erromar
Eighty Mile Beach
Port Hedland
Fitzroy R.
Fortescue R.
Townsville
Mackay
Great Dividing Range
Chesterfield Isles
New Hebrides
Tanna
North West Cape
TROPIC OF CAPRICORN 23½°S
Western
Macdonnell Ranges
Alice Springs
Plateau
Rockhampton
New Caledonia (France)
New Caledonia
Noumea
Ouvea Atoll
Lifou I.
Loyalty Is.
Mare I.
Isle of Pines
Walpole
AUSTRALIA
Gibson Desert
AUSTRALIA
Great Artesian Basin
Bundaberg
Geraldton
Great Victoria Desert
Kati Thanda-Lake Eyre
-52 ft. (-16 m)
Toowoomba
Brisbane
Gold Coast
Norfolk I. (Australia)
Kalgoorlie
Woomera
Darling R.
Tamworth
Coffs Harbor
Perth
Mandurah
Bunbury
Cape Leeuwin
Great Australian Bight
Whyalla
Murray R.
Lord Howe I. (Australia)
Newcastle
Gosford
Sydney
Albany
Spencer Gulf
Mildura
Albury
Canberra
Tasman Sea
Adelaide
Kangaroo I.
Ballarat
Australian Alps
Geelong
Melbourne
INDIAN OCEAN
Bass Strait
NEW ZEALAND
Launceston
Tasmania
Hobart
South Island
Milford Sound
Dune

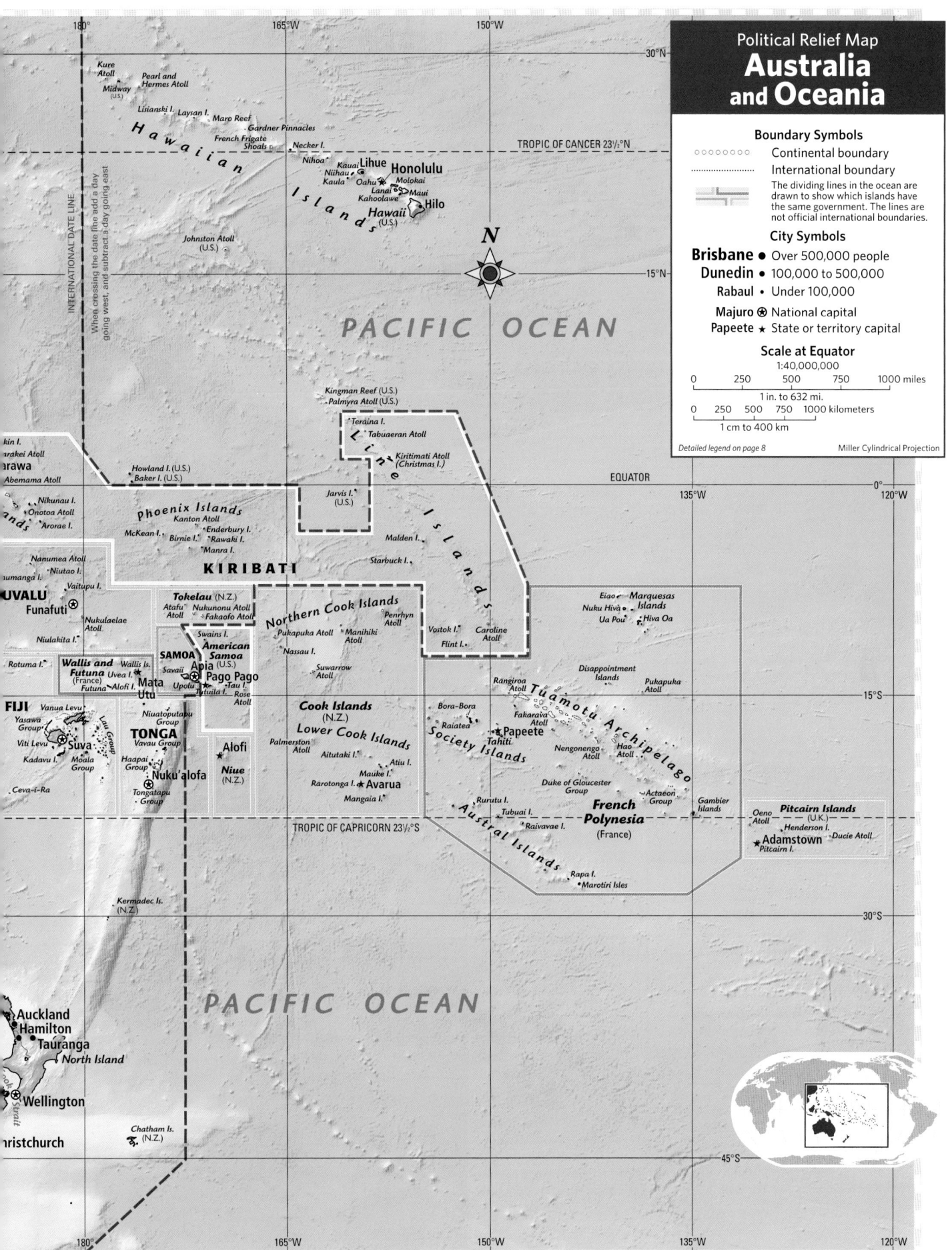

Boundary Symbols

○○○○○○○○ Continental boundary

.... International boundary

The dividing lines in the ocean are drawn to show which islands have the same government. The lines are not official international boundaries.

City Symbols

Brisbane ● Over 500,000 people

Dunedin ● 100,000 to 500,000

Rabaul • Under 100,000

Majuro ⊗ National capital

Papeete ★ State or territory capital

Scale at Equator

1:40,000,000

0   250   500   750   1000 miles

1 in. to 632 mi.

0   250 500 750 1000 kilometers

1 cm to 400 km

Detailed legend on page 8   Miller Cylindrical Projection

PACIFIC OCEAN

INTERNATIONAL DATE LINE

When crossing the date line add a day going west, and subtract a day going east

TROPIC OF CANCER 23½°N

30°N

15°N

Kure Atoll

Midway (U.S.)

Pearl and Hermes Atoll

Lisianski I. Laysan I.

Maro Reef

Gardner Pinnacles

French Frigate Shoals

Necker I.

Nihoa I.

Kauai Lihue

Niihau Oahu **Honolulu**

Kaula Molokai

Lanai Maui

Kahoolawe

Hawaii **Hilo**

(U.S.)

Hawaiian Islands

Johnston Atoll (U.S.)

Kingman Reef (U.S.)

Palmyra Atoll (U.S.)

Teraina I.

Tabuaeran Atoll

Kiritimati Atoll (Christmas I.)

Line Islands

Jarvis I. (U.S.)

EQUATOR   135°W   0°   120°W

...kin I.

...arakei Atoll

...arawa

Abemama Atoll

Nikunau I.

Onotoa Atoll

Arorae I.

Phoenix Islands

Kanton Atoll

McKean I. Birnie I. Enderbury I.

Rawaki I.

Manra I.

Malden I.

Starbuck I.

KIRIBATI

Nanumea Atoll

Niutao I.

...umanga I.

Vaitupu I.

UVALU

Funafuti ⊗

Nukulaelae Atoll

Niulakita I.

Rotuma I.

TUVALU

Tokelau (N.Z.)

Atafu I. Nukunonu Atoll

Fakaofo Atoll

Swains I.

Northern Cook Islands

Pukapuka Atoll Manihiki Atoll

Penrhyn Atoll

Nassau I.

Suwarrow Atoll

Vostok I.

Flint I.

Caroline Atoll

Eiao Marquesas Islands

Nuku Hiva Ua Pou Hiva Oa

Disappointment Islands

Pukapuka Atoll

SAMOA *American Samoa*

Savaii *Apia* ⊗ (U.S.)

Upolu **Pago Pago**

Tau I.

Tutuila I. Rose Atoll

Rangiroa Atoll

Tuamotu Archipelago

Fakarava Atoll

Bora-Bora

Raiatea

Society Islands **Papeete** ★

Tahiti

Nengonengo Atoll

Hao Atoll

Wallis and Futuna (France)

Wallis Is. Uvea I.

Futuna Alofi I.

Mata Utu

FIJI

Vanua Levu

Yasawa Group

Viti Levu **Suva**

Kadavu I.

Moala Group

Ceva-i-Ra

Niuatoputapu Group

TONGA

Vavau Group

Haapai Group

Nuku'alofa

Tongatapu Group

Cook Islands (N.Z.)

Lower Cook Islands

Palmerston Atoll

Aitutaki I.

Atiu I.

Mauke I.

Rarotonga I. **Avarua**

Mangaia I.

Alofi ★

Niue (N.Z.)

Duke of Gloucester Group

Rurutu I.

Tubuai I.

Raivavae I.

Austral Islands

French Polynesia (France)

Actaeon Group

Gambier Islands

Oeno Atoll

Pitcairn Islands (U.K.)

Henderson I.

Adamstown ★

Pitcairn I.

Ducie Atoll

TROPIC OF CAPRICORN 23½°S   15°S

Rapa I.

Marotiri Isles

Kermadec Is. (N.Z.)

30°S

PACIFIC OCEAN

Auckland

Hamilton

Tauranga

North Island

Wellington

...ristchurch

Chatham Is. (N.Z.)

...lk Strait

45°S

180°   165°W   150°W   135°W   120°W

N

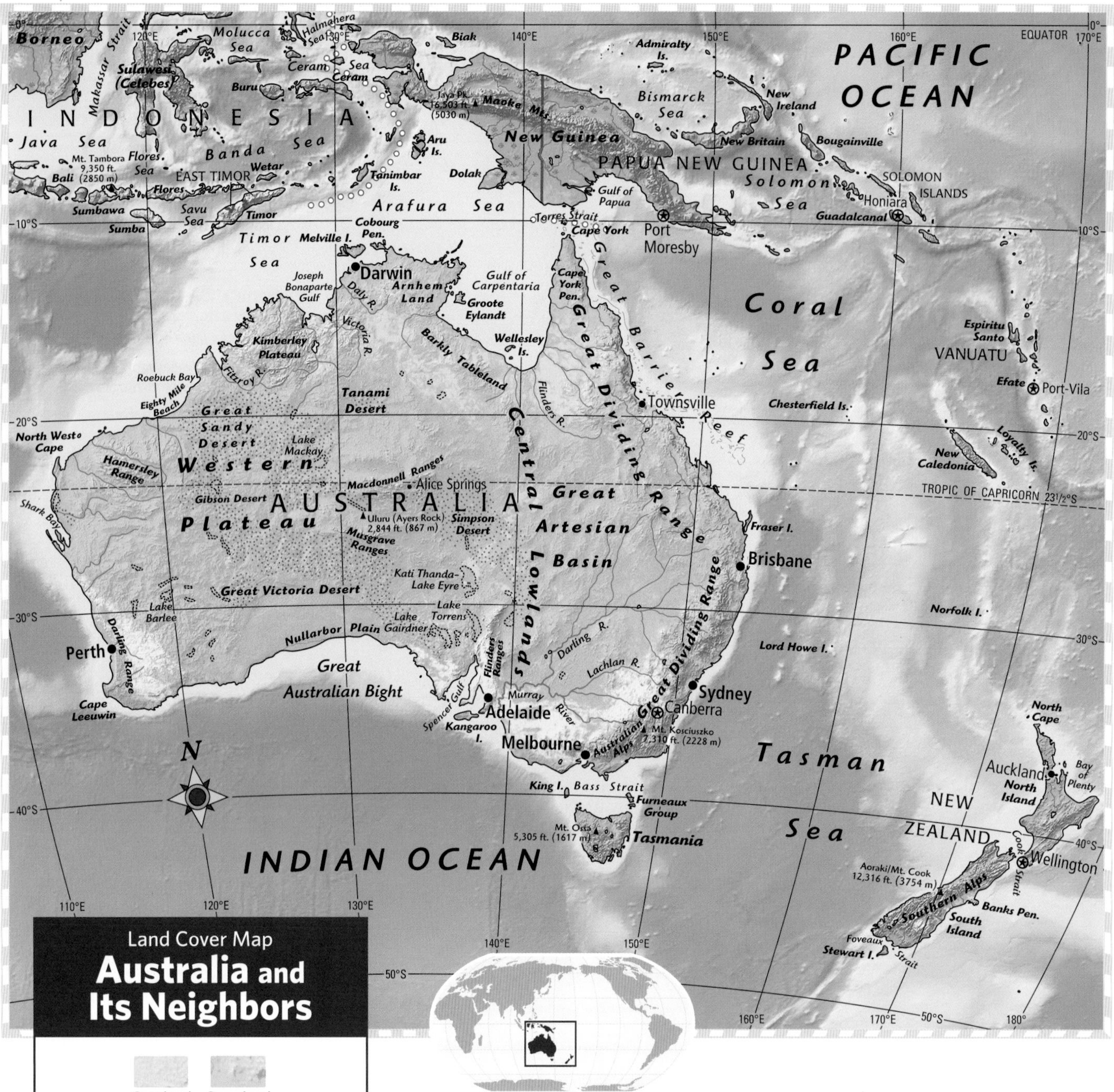

Borneo
Makassar Strait
Molucca Sea
Halmahera
Sea
Ceram Sea
Biak
Admiralty Is.
PACIFIC OCEAN
EQUATOR
Sulawesi (Celebes)
Buru
Ceram
Bismarck Sea
New Ireland
New Britain
Bougainville
SOLOMON ISLANDS
INDONESIA
Java Sea
Mt. Tambora 9,350 ft. (2850 m)
Flores
Banda Sea
Aru Is.
Java Pk. (5,030 ft.) (5030 m)
Maoke Mts.
New Guinea
PAPUA NEW GUINEA
Solomon Sea
Honiara
Bali
Flores
Sea
Tanimbar Is.
Dolak
Gulf of Papua
Guadalcanal
Sumbawa
Savu Sea
Timor
Arafura Sea
Sumba
Timor Sea
Torres Strait
Cape York
Port Moresby
Coral Sea
VANUATU
Espiritu Santo
Melville I.
Cobourg Pen.
Darwin
Joseph Bonaparte Gulf
Arnhem Land
Groote Eylandt
Gulf of Carpentaria
Cape York Pen.
Great Barrier Reef
Efate
Port-Vila
Daly R.
Victoria R.
Kimberley Plateau
Wellesley Is.
Loyalty Is.
Roebuck Bay
Fitzroy R.
Barkly Tableland
Flinders R.
Townsville
Chesterfield Is.
New Caledonia
North West Cape
Eighty Mile Beach
Great Sandy Desert
Tanami Desert
Hamersley Range
Lake Mackay
Western
Macdonnell Ranges
Alice Springs
Great
TROPIC OF CAPRICORN 23½°S
Shark Bay
Gibson Desert
AUSTRALIA
Plateau
Uluru (Ayers Rock) 2,844 ft. (867 m)
Simpson Desert
Artesian
Fraser I.
Brisbane
Musgrave Ranges
Basin
Great Victoria Desert
Kati Thanda–Lake Eyre
Lake Barlee
Lake Torrens
Norfolk I.
Perth
Darling Range
Nullarbor Plain
Lake Gairdner
Flinders Ranges
Darling R.
Lachlan R.
Lord Howe I.
Great Australian Bight
Spencer Gulf
Murray River
Great Dividing Range
Sydney
Canberra
Cape Leeuwin
Adelaide
Kangaroo I.
Melbourne
Australian Alps
Mt. Kosciuszko 7,310 ft. (2228 m)
Tasman Sea
Auckland
North Cape
Bay of Plenty
N
King I.
Bass Strait
Furneaux Group
NEW ZEALAND
North Island
INDIAN OCEAN
Mt. Ossa 5,305 ft. (1617 m)
Tasmania
Sea
Wellington
Cook Strait
Aoraki/Mt. Cook 12,316 ft. (3754 m)
Southern Alps
South Island
Banks Pen.
Foveaux Strait
Stewart I.

The vast, sparsely populated Australian **outback** covers 80 percent of the continent. The outback consists mostly of large deserts and is known for its unusual wildlife. Here, kangaroos are seen in front of one of the many large termite mounds that punctuate the landscape.

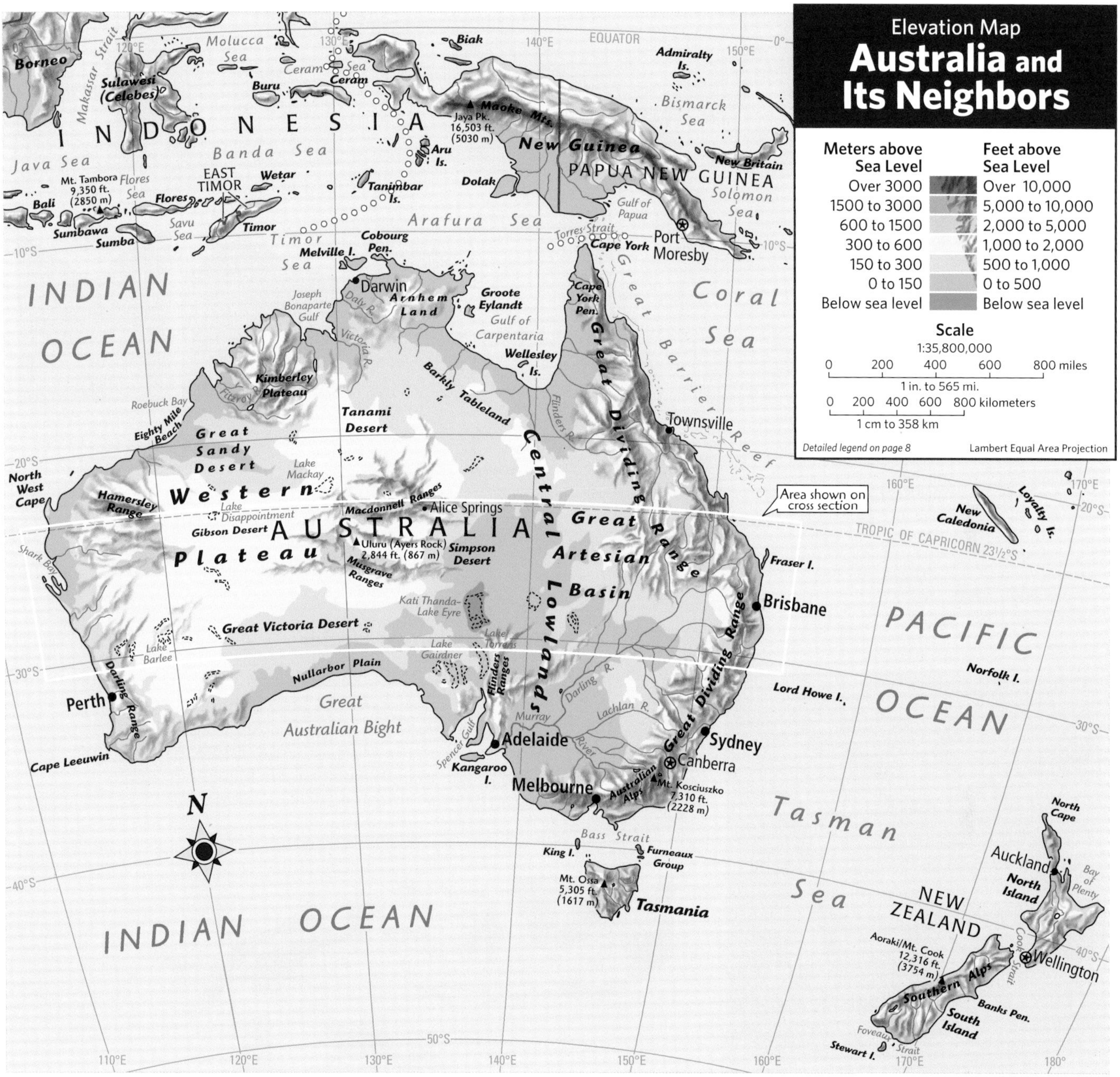

Elevation Map
Australia and Its Neighbors

Meters above Sea Level	Feet above Sea Level
Over 3000	Over 10,000
1500 to 3000	5,000 to 10,000
600 to 1500	2,000 to 5,000
300 to 600	1,000 to 2,000
150 to 300	500 to 1,000
0 to 150	0 to 500
Below sea level	Below sea level

Scale
1:35,800,000

0   200   400   600   800 miles
1 in. to 565 mi.

0   200   400   600   800 kilometers
1 cm to 358 km

Detailed legend on page 8   Lambert Equal Area Projection

Map labels:

Borneo · Makassar Strait · Sulawesi (Celebes) · Molucca Sea · Ceram Sea · Ceram · Buru · Biak · Admiralty Is. · Bismarck Sea · New Britain · EQUATOR

INDONESIA · Banda Sea · Java Sea · Mt. Tambora 9,350 ft. (2850 m) · Flores Sea · Flores · EAST TIMOR · Wetar · Tanimbar Is. · Dolak · Aru Is. · Jaya Pk. 16,503 ft. (5030 m) · Maoke Mts. · New Guinea · PAPUA NEW GUINEA · Solomon Sea · Gulf of Papua · Port Moresby

Bali · Sumbawa · Sumba · Savu Sea · Timor · Timor Sea · Arafura Sea · Torres Strait · Cape York

INDIAN OCEAN · Cobourg Pen. · Melville I. · Arnhem Land · Groote Eylandt · Gulf of Carpentaria · Wellesley Is. · Cape York Pen. · Coral Sea · Great Barrier Reef

Joseph Bonaparte Gulf · Darwin · Daly R. · Victoria R. · Roebuck Bay · Kimberley Plateau · Barkly Tableland · Flinders R. · Great Dividing Range

Eighty Mile Beach · Great Sandy Desert · Tanami Desert · Townsville

North West Cape · Hamersley Range · Western AUSTRALIA Plateau · Lake Mackay · Macdonnell Ranges · Alice Springs · Great Artesian Basin

Shark Bay · Lake Disappointment · Gibson Desert · Uluru (Ayers Rock) 2,844 ft. (867 m) · Simpson Desert · Musgrave Ranges · Central Lowlands

New Caledonia · Loyalty Is. · TROPIC OF CAPRICORN 23½°S · Fraser I.

Great Victoria Desert · Kati Thanda–Lake Eyre · Lake Torrens · Brisbane · PACIFIC OCEAN

Lake Barlee · Lake Gairdner · Flinders Ranges · Darling R. · Norfolk I.

Perth · Darling Range · Nullarbor Plain · Great Australian Bight · Murray River · Lachlan R. · Lord Howe I. · Sydney

Cape Leeuwin · Spencer Gulf · Adelaide · Canberra · Australian Alps · Mt. Kosciuszko 7,310 ft. (2228 m)

Kangaroo I. · Melbourne · Tasman Sea

N

Bass Strait · King I. · Furneaux Group · North Cape · Auckland · North Island · Bay of Plenty

Mt. Ossa 5,305 ft. (1617 m) · Tasmania · NEW ZEALAND · Cook Strait · Wellington

INDIAN OCEAN · Aoraki/Mt. Cook 12,316 ft. (3754 m) · Southern Alps · Banks Pen. · South Island · Foveaux Strait · Stewart I.

Area shown on cross section

Cross Section

Vertical exaggeration 78 to 1
Scale at 24°S: 1 in. to 470 mi., 1 cm to 298 km

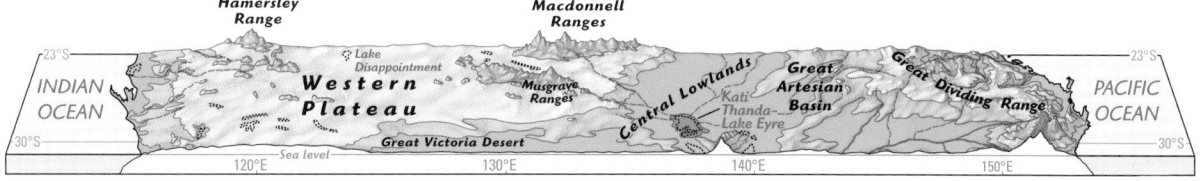

INDIAN OCEAN · Hamersley Range · Lake Disappointment · Western Plateau · Musgrave Ranges · Macdonnell Ranges · Great Victoria Desert · Central Lowlands · Kati Thanda–Lake Eyre · Great Artesian Basin · Great Dividing Range · PACIFIC OCEAN · Sea level

---

Drawing Lines

Alfred Russel Wallace, a British naturalist, discovered that animals in Indonesia are divided into two groups of species. He drew a line that runs through the Maskassar Strait (between Borneo and Sulawesi) and matches the geological history of the region. Species to the west of the **Wallace Line** are related to the animals of Asia, while those east of the line are relatives of Australian animals.

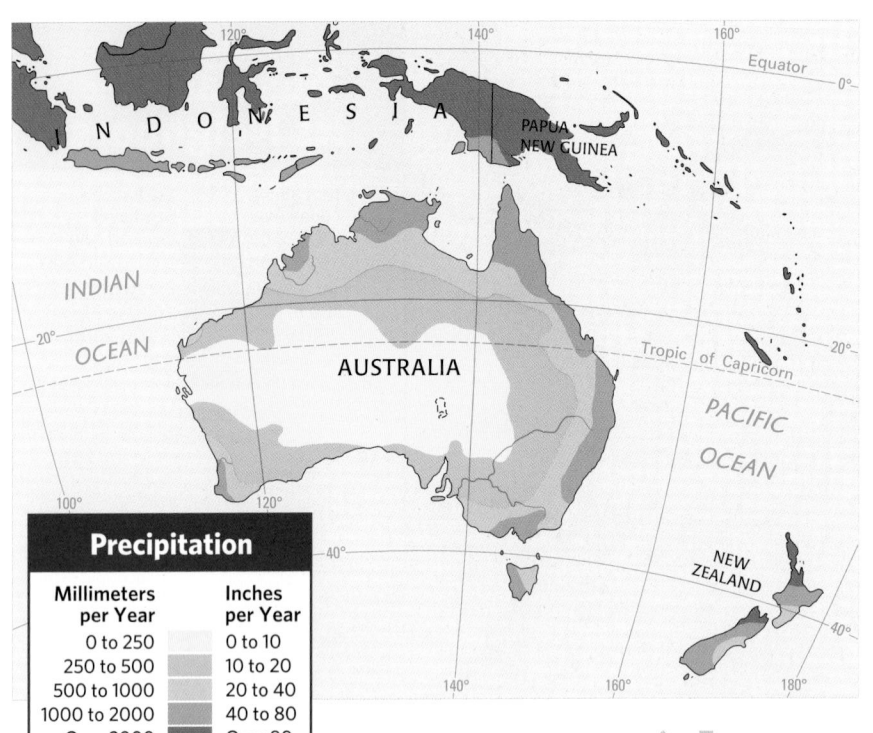

Precipitation

Millimeters per Year	Inches per Year
0 to 250	0 to 10
250 to 500	10 to 20
500 to 1000	20 to 40
1000 to 2000	40 to 80
Over 2000	Over 80

Climographs

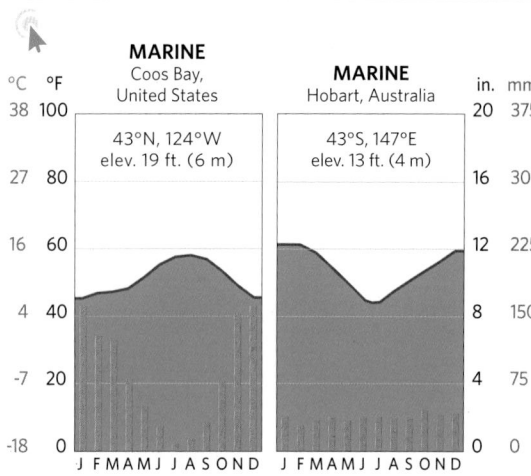

MARINE
Coos Bay, United States
43°N, 124°W
elev. 19 ft. (6 m)

MARINE
Hobart, Australia
43°S, 147°E
elev. 13 ft. (4 m)

There is a six-month difference in seasons between Coos Bay and Hobart. This is because the Southern Hemisphere experiences winter when the Northern Hemisphere has summer. (For more information, see page 25.)

Stations Down Under

In Australia and New Zealand, large cattle or sheep ranches are called **stations**. Cattle stations are usually much larger than sheep stations. Anna Creek in South Australia, Australia's largest cattle station, covers about 9,400 square miles (24,000 square kilometers) and is larger than the state of New Hampshire.

Tropical rain forests, such as this one in Papua New Guinea, exist only in regions that have high temperatures and high precipitation year-round. Tropical rain forests are the most biologically diverse ecosystems in the world. (For more information, see pages 34 and 129.)

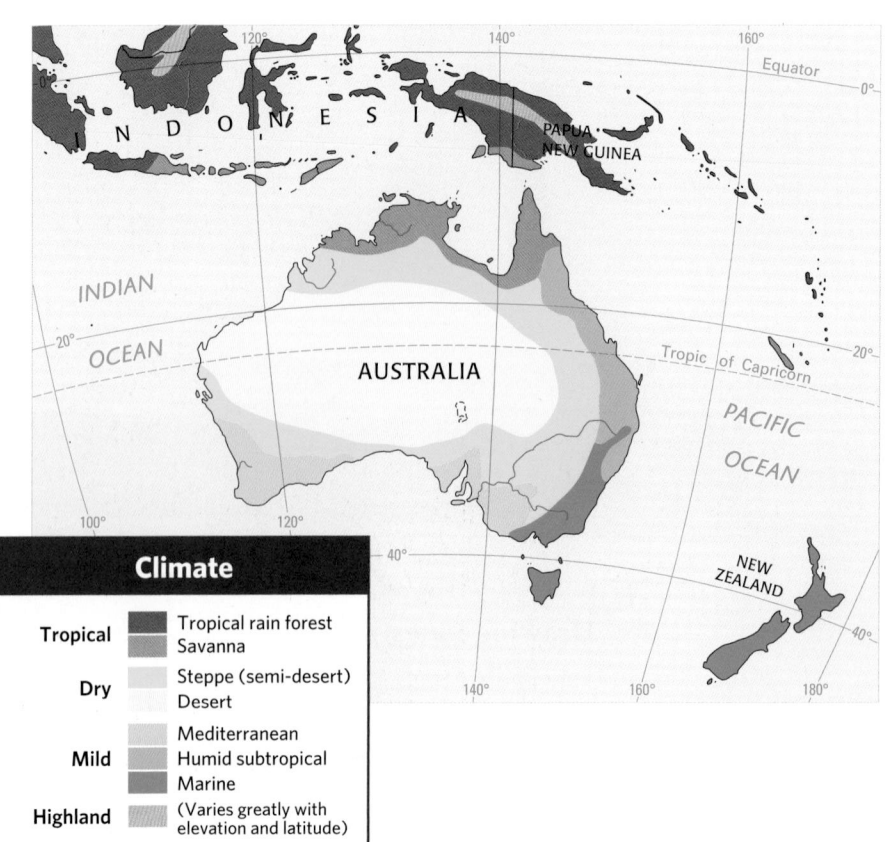

Climate

Tropical	Tropical rain forest
	Savanna
Dry	Steppe (semi-desert)
	Desert
Mild	Mediterranean
	Humid subtropical
	Marine
Highland	(Varies greatly with elevation and latitude)

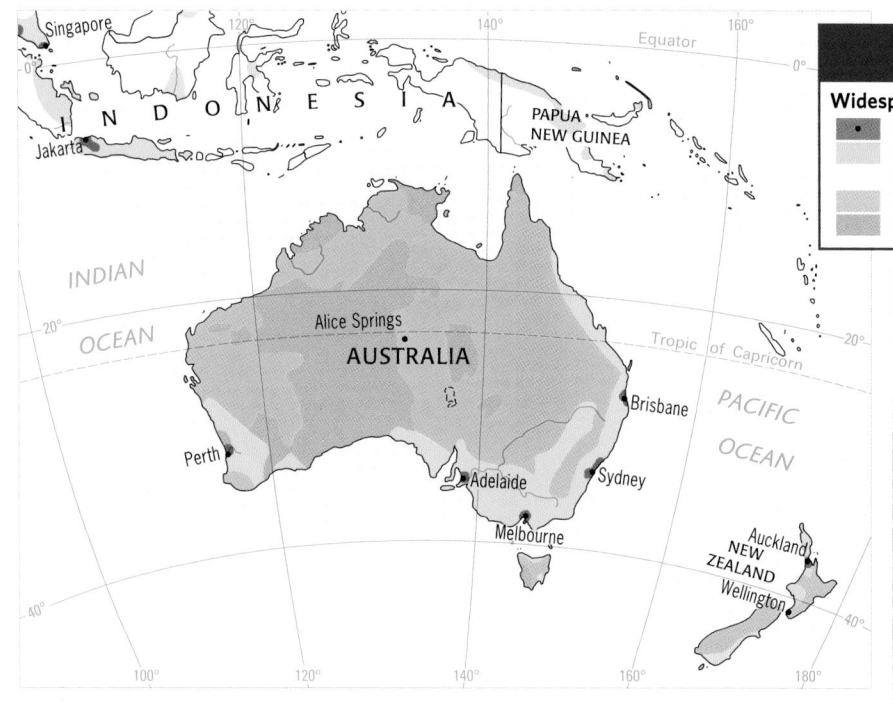

Land Use

Widespread Economic Uses
- Urban
- Commercial farming
- Subsistence farming
- Ranching or herding
- No widespread use

Winemaking is a rapidly growing industry in Australia. The South Australia region, where this Barossa Valley vineyard is located, produces about 40 percent of the wine in the country.

Balance of Trade

Australia

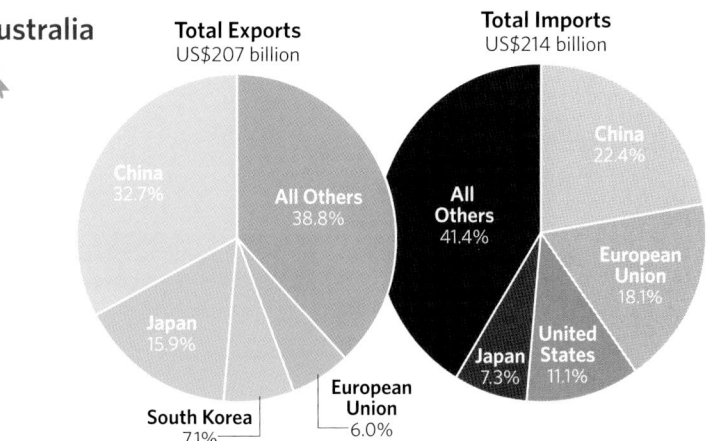

Total Exports
US$207 billion

- China 32.7%
- All Others 38.8%
- Japan 15.9%
- South Korea 7.1%
- European Union 6.0%

Total Imports
US$214 billion

- China 22.4%
- All Others 41.4%
- European Union 18.1%
- United States 11.1%
- Japan 7.3%

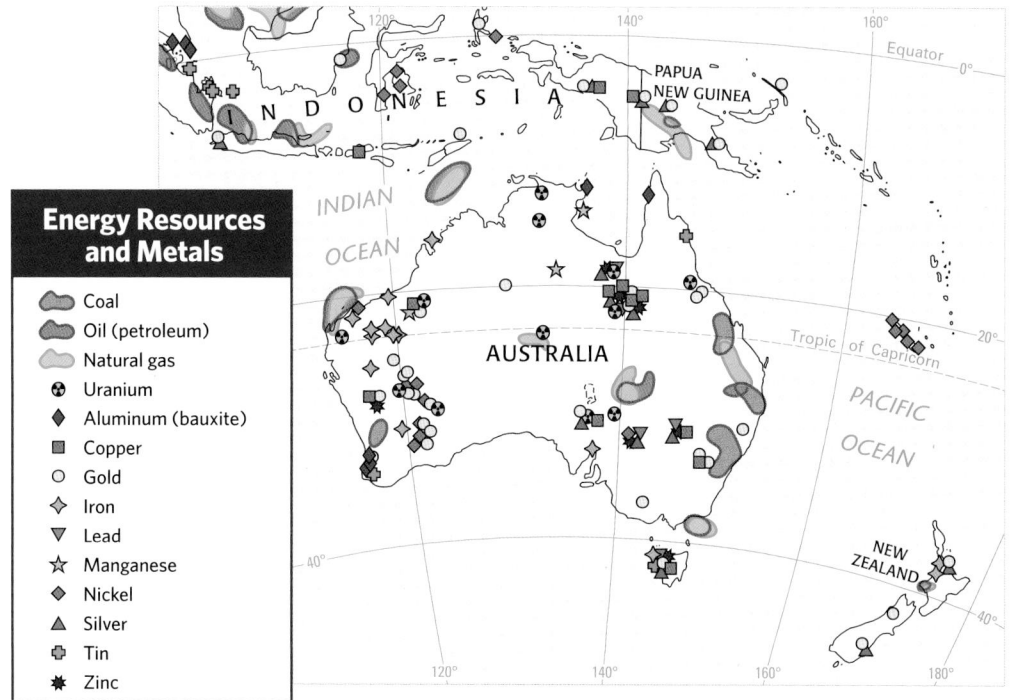

Energy Resources and Metals

- Coal
- Oil (petroleum)
- Natural gas
- ☢ Uranium
- ◆ Aluminum (bauxite)
- ■ Copper
- ○ Gold
- ✦ Iron
- ▽ Lead
- ☆ Manganese
- ◆ Nickel
- ▲ Silver
- ✚ Tin
- ✸ Zinc

Population

People per Sq. Km	People per Sq. Mile
0 to 2	0 to 5
2 to 20	5 to 50
20 to 40	50 to 100
40 to 100	100 to 250
Over 100	Over 250

Members of New Zealand's international rugby team, the All Blacks, perform a traditional Maori war chant at the start of each game. Several members of the team are Maori.

Ethnic Composition

New Zealand

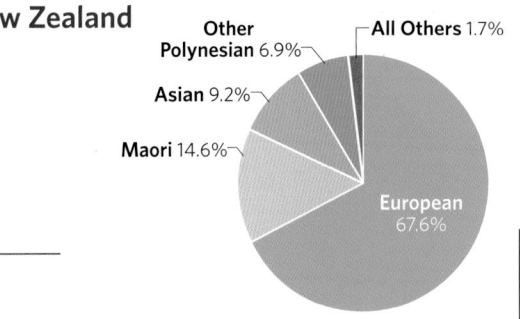

Other Polynesian 6.9%
All Others 1.7%
Asian 9.2%
Maori 14.6%
European 67.6%

Natural Population Growth

Australia and Oceania

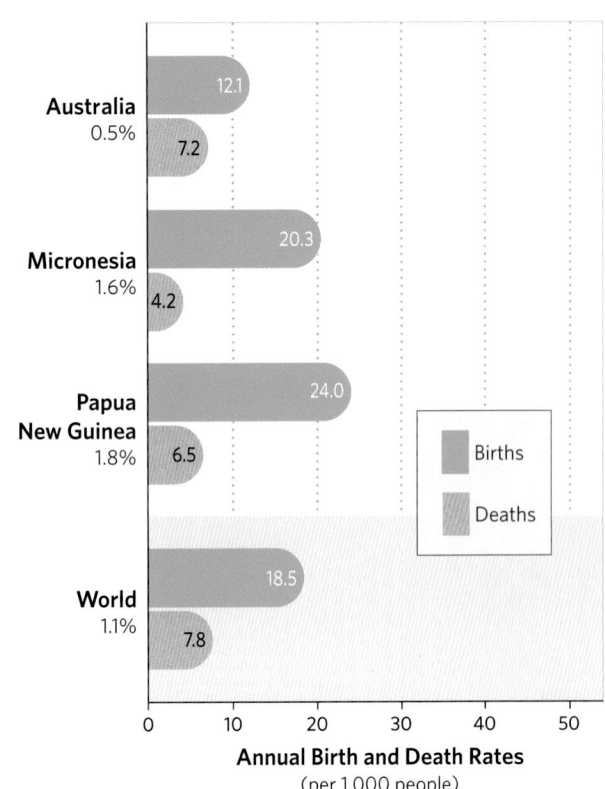

Australia 0.5% — 12.1 / 7.2
Micronesia 1.6% — 20.3 / 4.2
Papua New Guinea 1.8% — 24.0 / 6.5
World 1.1% — 18.5 / 7.8

Births
Deaths

Annual Birth and Death Rates
(per 1,000 people)

Indigenous People

MICRONESIANS Major group
Hawaiians Smaller group

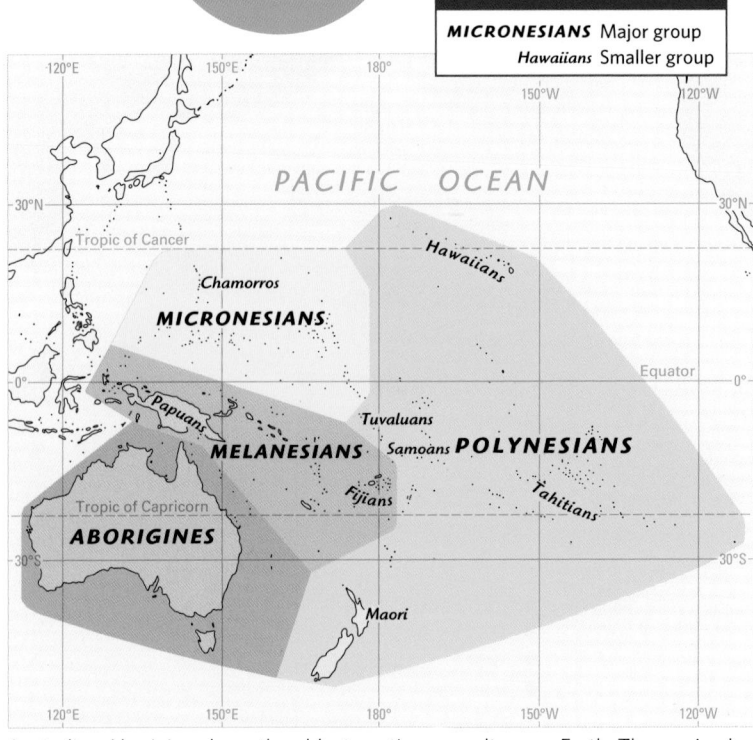

Australian Aborigines have the oldest continuous culture on Earth. They arrived in Australia at least 50,000 years ago. Papuans occupied New Guinea about 40,000 years ago. However, some distant islands in Oceania were occupied much later. For example, Hawaii was first settled 2,000 years ago.

Continues on page 181

Political Relief Map
Australia

Boundary Symbols
------------ State or territory boundary

City Symbols
Sydney ● Over 500,000 people
Cairns ● 100,000 to 500,000
Bunbury • Under 100,000
Canberra ⊛ National capital
Perth ★ State or territory capital

Scale
1:33,600,000

0   200   400   600   800 miles
1 in. to 531 mi.
0   200   400   600   800 kilometers
1 cm to 336 km

Detailed legend on page 8   Lambert Equal Area Projection

Map labels (Australia)

INDIAN OCEAN
INDONESIA — Kupang — Timor
Sumba — Savu Sea
Arafura Sea — Torres Strait
Port Moresby — PAPUA NEW GUINEA
Cape York — Coral Sea
Melville I. — Cobourg Pen.
Bathurst I. — Darwin
Ashmore Is. — Joseph Bonaparte Gulf
Cartier I. — Arnhem Land — Katherine
Browse I. — Wyndham — Lake Argyle
Kuri Bay — Kimberley Plateau
Adele I. — Derby — Fitzroy R.
Broome — Eighty Mile Beach
Groote Eylandt — Wellesley Is.
Gulf of Carpentaria — Cape York Pen.
Great Barrier Reef
Cooktown — Cairns — Townsville — Bowen
Coral Sea Is. Territory (Australia)
Barkly Tableland — Mitchell R. — Flinders R.
Mount Isa — Mackay
Tennant Creek — Tanami Desert
NORTHERN TERRITORY
Macdonnell Ranges — Alice Springs
Uluru (Ayers Rock) 2,844 ft. (867 m)
Simpson Desert
QUEENSLAND — Emerald — Rockhampton — Gladstone
Great Artesian Basin — Roma — Toowoomba
Bundaberg — Fraser I. — Maryborough
Brisbane — Gold Coast — Lismore — Coffs Harbour
Karratha — Port Hedland — Hamersley Range
Barrow I. — North West Cape
Great Sandy Desert — Western — Lake Mackay
TROPIC OF CAPRICORN 23½°S
Gibson Desert — Plateau
WESTERN AUSTRALIA
Shark Bay — Carnarvon
Geraldton
Lake Barlee — Kalgoorlie — Merredin
Great Victoria Desert
Musgrave Ranges — Kati Thanda–Lake Eyre -52 ft. (-16 m)
SOUTH AUSTRALIA
Lake Torrens — Lake Gairdner
Woomera — Broken Hill
Darling R. — Tamworth — Port Macquarie
Perth — Fremantle — Mandurah — Bunbury
Darling Range
Nullarbor Plain — Esperance — Albany
110°E Cape Leeuwin
Great Australian Bight
Port Augusta — Whyalla — Flinders Ranges
Spencer Gulf — Salisbury
Port Lincoln — Adelaide — Mildura
Kangaroo Island
NEW SOUTH WALES
Orange — Wagga Wagga — Albury
Newcastle — Gosford — Sydney
Wollongong — Canberra
AUSTRALIAN CAPITAL TERRITORY
Lord Howe Island
Tasman Sea
Murray R. — Lachlan R.
Mount Gambier — VICTORIA — Ballarat
Australian Alps — Mt. Kosciuszko 7,310 ft. (2228 m)
Geelong — Melbourne — King I.
Bass Strait — Furneaux Group
Devonport — Launceston
Mt. Ossa 5,305 ft. (1617 m) — TASMANIA — Hobart
Tasmania
INDIAN OCEAN
10°S — 20°S — 30°S — 40°S
110°E — 120°E — 130°E — 140°E — 150°E — 160°E

Political Relief Map
New Zealand

City Symbols
Auckland ● Over 100,000 people
Westport • Under 100,000
Wellington ⊛ National capital

Scale
1:19,000,000

0   100   200   300   400 miles
1 in. to 300 mi.
0   100   200   300   400 kilometers
1 cm to 190 km

Detailed legend on page 8   Miller Projection

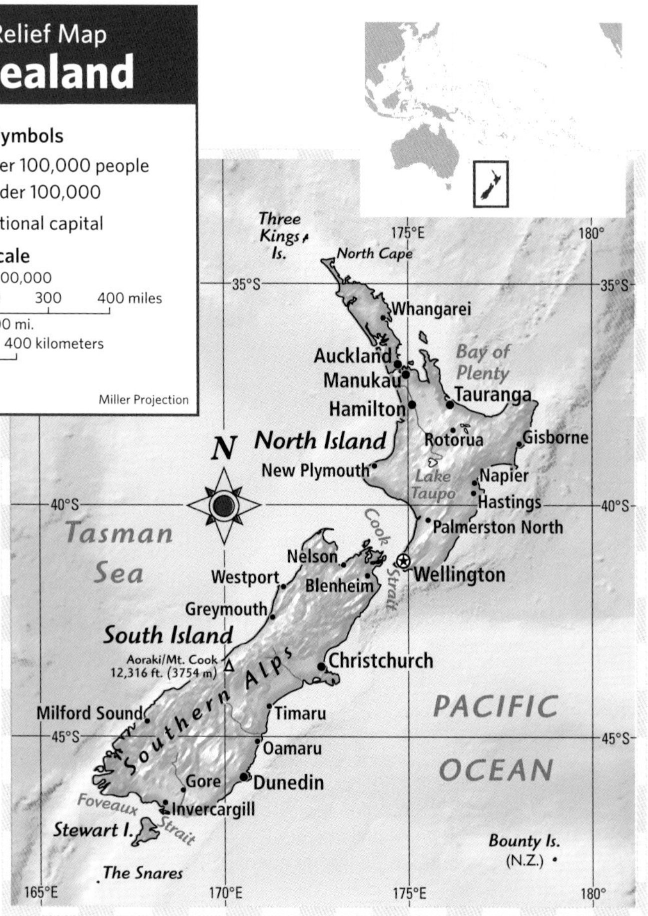

Map labels (New Zealand)

Three Kings Is. — North Cape
Whangarei
Auckland — Manukau — Hamilton
Bay of Plenty — Tauranga
North Island — Rotorua — Gisborne
New Plymouth — Lake Taupo — Napier — Hastings
Tasman Sea — Palmerston North
Nelson — Cook Strait — Wellington
Westport — Blenheim
Greymouth — Southern Alps
South Island
Aoraki/Mt. Cook 12,316 ft. (3754 m)
Milford Sound — Timaru — Christchurch
Oamaru
Gore — Dunedin
Foveaux Strait — Invercargill
Stewart I.
PACIFIC OCEAN
The Snares — Bounty Is. (N.Z.)
35°S — 40°S — 45°S
165°E — 170°E — 175°E — 180°E

Students learn to surf on Manly Beach in Sydney. Water sports such as surfing are popular in Australia, where most people live near the ocean. Surfing originated in Hawaii, in northeastern Oceania, before the fifteenth century.

ISSUES / TODAY

What should be done about introduced species?

Introduced species are living things brought to non-native environments. When these species breed quickly and have few or no natural enemies, they can become invasive. They compete with native species for food and other resources. Do introduced species damage native ecosystems, or are they important resources? There are many perspectives on this issue. Here are two of them.

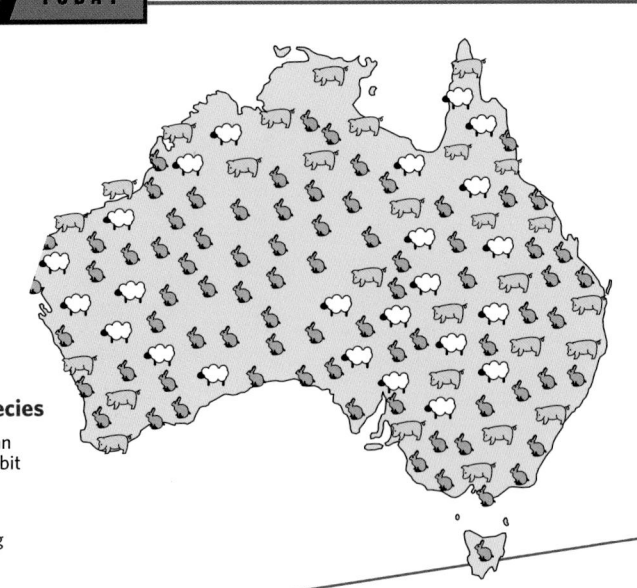

Range of Introduced Species

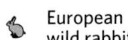 European wild rabbit

 Sheep

 Feral pig

All new species must be kept out.

- Because the continent of Australia shares no point of contact with any other land mass, native species have evolved over millions of years in isolation. Any introduction of new species has the potential to be catastrophically disruptive.

- It is nearly impossible to predict when introduced species will harm the environment. For example, the cane toad was introduced to Australia to control the cane beetle population. However, the cane toad population exploded, threatening many native species.

- Measures to control invasive species, such as chemicals and traps, often harm native species as well.

- Invasive species of plants cost Australia over US$3 billion annually in lost production and in control management. Invasive species of pest animals, such as wild rabbits and feral foxes, cost Australia over US$800 million a year.

Invasive animals eat plants and other animals, dig tunnels, and foul water. Feral pigs, for example, are responsible for killing lambs, competing with livestock for pastures, and spreading diseases to humans and other animals. There are an estimated 24 million feral pigs in Australia.

Not all introduced species are bad.

- Australia is one of the most biologically diverse places on Earth, but native species on the continent were never domesticated. As a result, all domesticated species currently found in Australia—including key crops, livestock, and pets—were introduced from abroad.

- European settlers introduced a host of economically important species to Australia, including wheat, sheep, cattle, and grapes.

- Today, agriculture is an important contributor to the Australian economy. Agriculture and its closely related industries generate over US$125 billion each year and employ over 1.5 million people.

- Introduced species can be used against each other to limit damage to the environment and to native species. Goats consume blackberries and other highly invasive weeds, cats and foxes help control the rabbit population, and cats eat pests such as mice and rats.

Wool and Wheat Exports

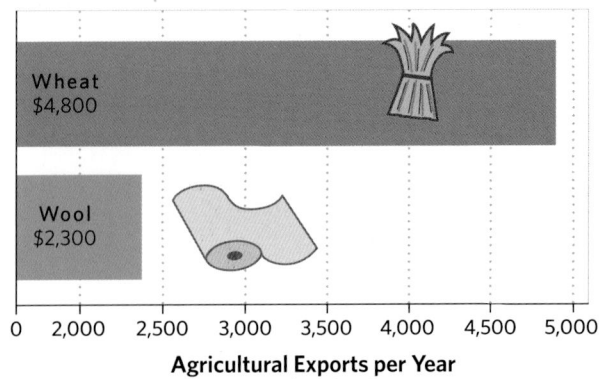

Wheat $4,800

Wool $2,300

0   2,000   2,500   3,000   3,500   4,000   4,500   5,000

Agricultural Exports per Year
(US$ million)

Australia is the world's leading producer of wool. Sheep were first brought to the continent in 1788 by the British.

How should rising sea levels be addressed?

As global temperatures increase, sea levels rise as a result of ice melting and warmer oceans expanding. High oceans can erode coastlines, especially in areas of low elevation. In some cases entire low islands such as the coral atolls of the Pacific Ocean could disappear completely into the ocean. Hundreds of thousands of people could lose their homes on Pacific islands as agricultural land and fresh water are tainted by sea water. How should rising sea levels be addressed? There are many perspectives on these issues. Here are two of them.

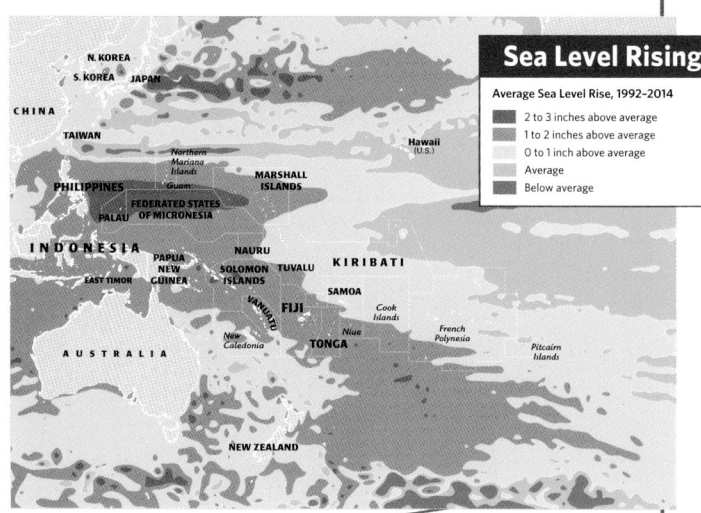

Sea Level Rising

Average Sea Level Rise, 1992–2014

- 2 to 3 inches above average
- 1 to 2 inches above average
- 0 to 1 inch above average
- Average
- Below average

Areas most at risk should be protected.

- Various projects, including protecting coastlines by planting trees or building sea walls, can protect populated areas and agricultural lands.

- Large-scale evacuations would violate international human rights accords and create thousands of refugees. These "climate refugees" would find themselves in unfamiliar environments and cultures with few economic or cultural resources to support themselves.

- The climate change that threatens the islands does not stem from the Pacific islanders' behavior but from economic growth in other parts of the world. These areas, including Europe, North America, and Asia, should help the people who are paying the price for their economic growth.

- The people of the islands have a close cultural connection to their homelands. They deserve to be allowed to continue to live there.

Global Average Sea Level

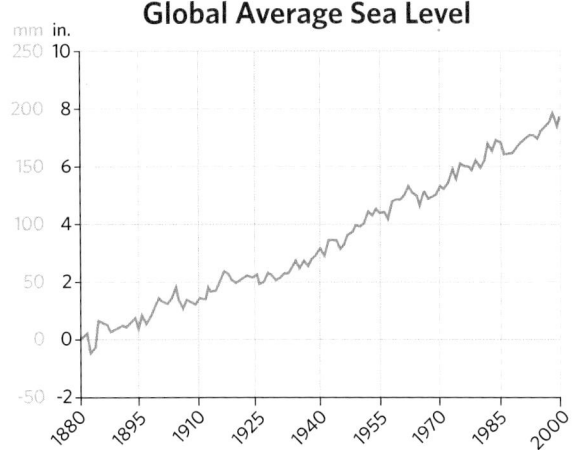

Global sea levels have been rising since the 1800s. Although nine inches may not seem like a large amount, many inhabited areas are only a few feet above sea level.

The international community should fight the causes of sea level rise.

- Rising sea levels are part of a large set of problems caused by greenhouse gas emissions. Simply focusing on protecting the Pacific islands ignores the much greater problem.

- Greenhouse gas emissions do more than simply raise temperatures and cause sea levels to rise. Climate change affects hurricanes for the worse, which could overwhelm even the most advanced coastal protections.

- Dissolved greenhouse gases cause the acidity of the ocean to rise, which, combined with increased temperature, kills coral. Coral reefs are critical to the ecosystems and economies of many islands and protect the islands from waves.

- Without broader efforts to reduce the causes of sea level rise, artificial protections will need to be constantly maintained, repaired, and increased. At the same time, wealthier nations will need to spend more to protect their own much larger populations. At some point, wealthy nations are likely to abandon efforts to protect Pacific islands and their populations.

Tarawa Atoll is the capital of Kiribati and is home to half of the country's population. Its highest elevation is only 10 feet (3 meters) above sea level. Rising sea levels erode the island's beaches and contaminate fresh groundwater with salt

World Extreme While water comprises most of the Arctic, Antarctica is a continental landmass. The ice and snow that cover 98 percent of Antarctica's land account for 70 percent of the world's fresh water. Despite its high water content, Antarctica's low annual precipitation makes it a desert.

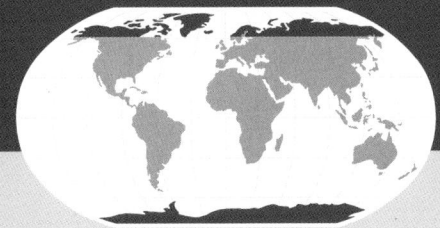

Antarctica ...

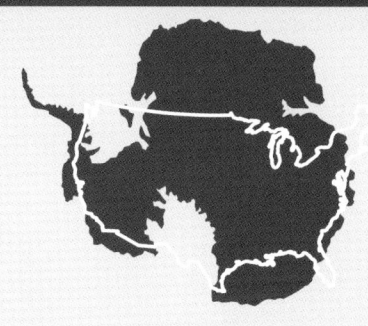

Antarctica is a single continent located almost entirely south of the Antarctic Circle. It is the world's coldest region. There are no countries in Antarctica.

Antarctica's Features

Highest mountain peak
Vinson Massif 16,864 ft. (5,140 m)

Longest mountain range
Transantarctic Mountains 1,900 mi. (3,000 km)

Largest ocean
Southern Ocean 7,848,000 sq. mi. (20,327,000 sq. km)

Other key features
Bentley Subglacial Trench
8,383 ft. below sea level (2,555 m)
Antarctic Peninsula
Polar Plateau

Largest research station
McMurdo (U.S.) temporary population:
180 people (winter), 1,000 people (summer)

Area Comparison

Antarctica
5,400,000 sq. mi.
(14,000,000 sq. km)

Contiguous United States
3,021,295 sq. mi.
(7,825,112 sq. km)

Regional Maps of Antarctica

1 **Antarctica** p. 200

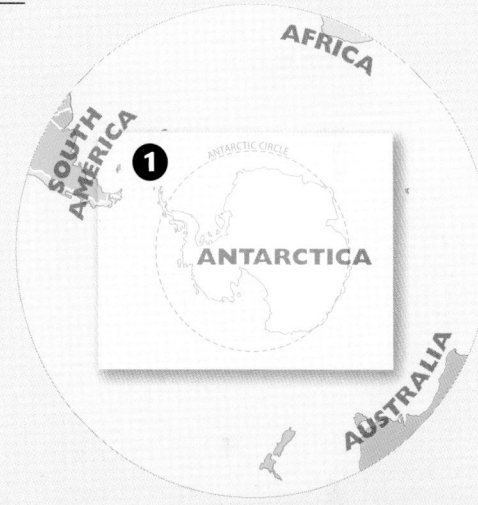

... and the Arctic

The Arctic includes the islands, northern areas of three continents, and sea ice north of the Arctic Circle. Most of the area north of the Arctic Circle is water, not land.

The Arctic's Features

Largest island
Greenland 836,330 sq. mi. (2,166,066 sq. km)

Largest ocean
Arctic Ocean 5,427,000 sq. mi. (14,056,000 sq. km)

Largest city
Murmansk, Russia 299,148 people

Regional Maps of the Arctic

1 **Arctic** p. 201

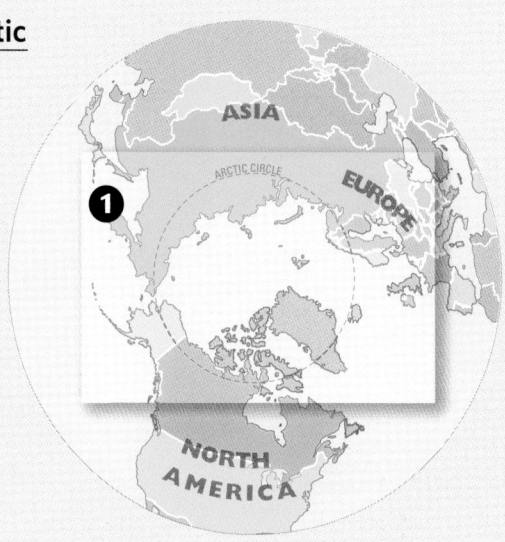

Climographs

Antarctica's average elevation is 7,500 feet (2,300 meters), while most of the Arctic is at or near sea level. Antarctica is much colder due to its higher elevation. The world's coldest recorded temperature, -128.6°F (-89.2°C), was measured at Vostok.

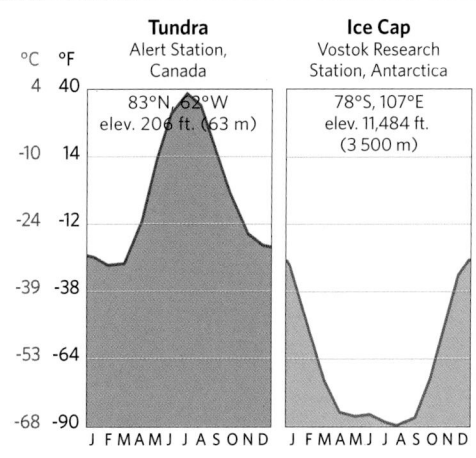

Tundra
Alert Station, Canada

83°N, 62°W
elev. 206 ft. (63 m)

Ice Cap
Vostok Research Station, Antarctica

78°S, 107°E
elev. 11,484 ft.
(3 500 m)

°C	°F
4	40
-10	14
-24	-12
-39	-38
-53	-64
-68	-90

J F M A M J J A S O N D   J F M A M J J A S O N D

Calving is the fracturing of large pieces of ice off the edge of a glacier as it reaches the sea. These chunks become icebergs.

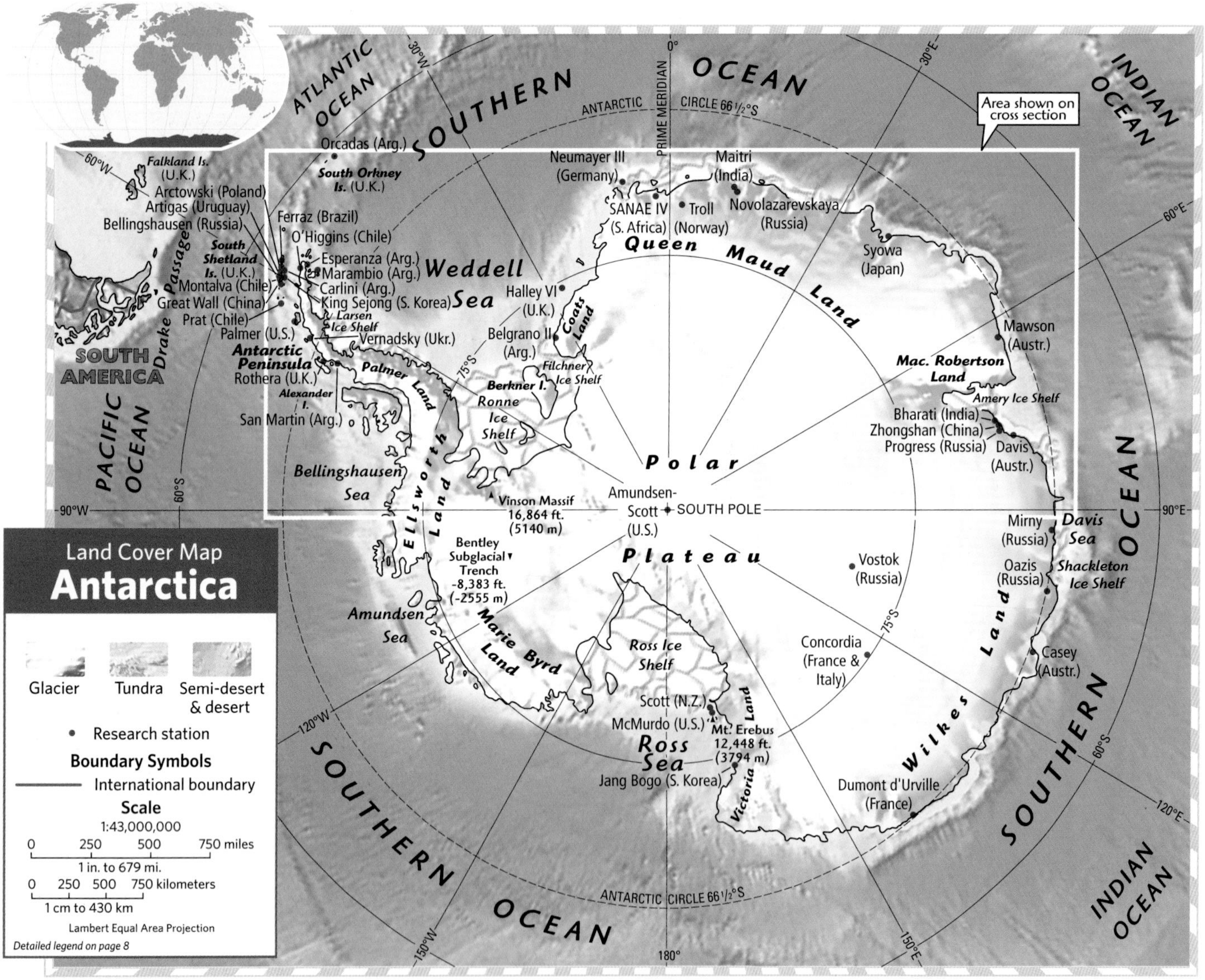

Land Cover Map
Antarctica

Area shown on cross section

Legend
Glacier   Tundra   Semi-desert & desert

• Research station

Boundary Symbols
—— International boundary

Scale
1:43,000,000

0   250   500   750 miles
1 in. to 679 mi.

0   250   500   750 kilometers
1 cm to 430 km

Lambert Equal Area Projection

Detailed legend on page 8

Map labels

ATLANTIC OCEAN
SOUTHERN OCEAN
INDIAN OCEAN
PACIFIC OCEAN

ANTARCTIC CIRCLE 66½°S
PRIME MERIDIAN

Orcadas (Arg.)
Neumayer III (Germany)
Maitri (India)
Falkland Is. (U.K.)
South Orkney Is. (U.K.)
Arctowski (Poland)
Artigas (Uruguay)
Bellingshausen (Russia)
Ferraz (Brazil)
O'Higgins (Chile)
SANAE IV (S. Africa)
Troll (Norway)
Novolazarevskaya (Russia)
Esperanza (Arg.)
Marambio (Arg.)
Carlini (Arg.)
King Sejong (S. Korea)
Weddell Sea
Halley VI (U.K.)
Queen Maud Land
Syowa (Japan)
South Shetland Is. (U.K.)
Montalva (Chile)
Great Wall (China)
Prat (Chile)
Palmer (U.S.)
Larsen Ice Shelf
Vernadsky (Ukr.)
Coats Land
Belgrano II (Arg.)
Mawson (Austr.)
Antarctic Peninsula
Rothera (U.K.)
Alexander I.
San Martin (Arg.)
Palmer Land
Filchner Ice Shelf
Berkner I.
Ronne Ice Shelf
Mac. Robertson Land
Amery Ice Shelf
Bharati (India)
Zhongshan (China)
Progress (Russia)
Davis (Austr.)
Bellingshausen Sea
Ellsworth Land
Vinson Massif 16,864 ft. (5140 m)
Amundsen-Scott (U.S.) SOUTH POLE
Polar Plateau
Bentley Subglacial Trench -8,383 ft. (-2555 m)
Mirny (Russia)
Davis Sea
Amundsen Sea
Marie Byrd Land
Ross Ice Shelf
Vostok (Russia)
Oazis (Russia)
Shackleton Ice Shelf
Concordia (France & Italy)
Casey (Austr.)
Scott (N.Z.)
McMurdo (U.S.)
Mt. Erebus 12,448 ft. (3794 m)
Ross Sea
Victoria Land
Jang Bogo (S. Korea)
Wilkes Land
Dumont d'Urville (France)
SOUTHERN OCEAN
INDIAN OCEAN
Drake Passage
SOUTH AMERICA
ANTARCTIC CIRCLE 66½°S

Cross Section
Vertical exaggeration 37 to 1
Scale at 90°E/W: 1 in. to 690 mi., 1 cm to 437 km

The ice cap on the Polar Plateau is up to 2½ miles (4 km) thick.

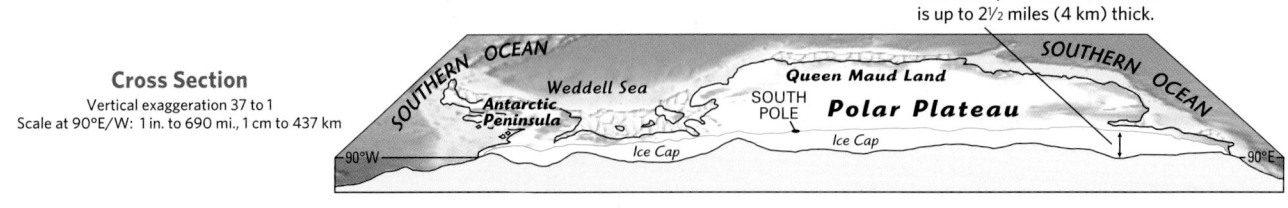

SOUTHERN OCEAN
Weddell Sea
Antarctic Peninsula
SOUTH POLE
Queen Maud Land
Polar Plateau
SOUTHERN OCEAN
Ice Cap
90°W
90°E

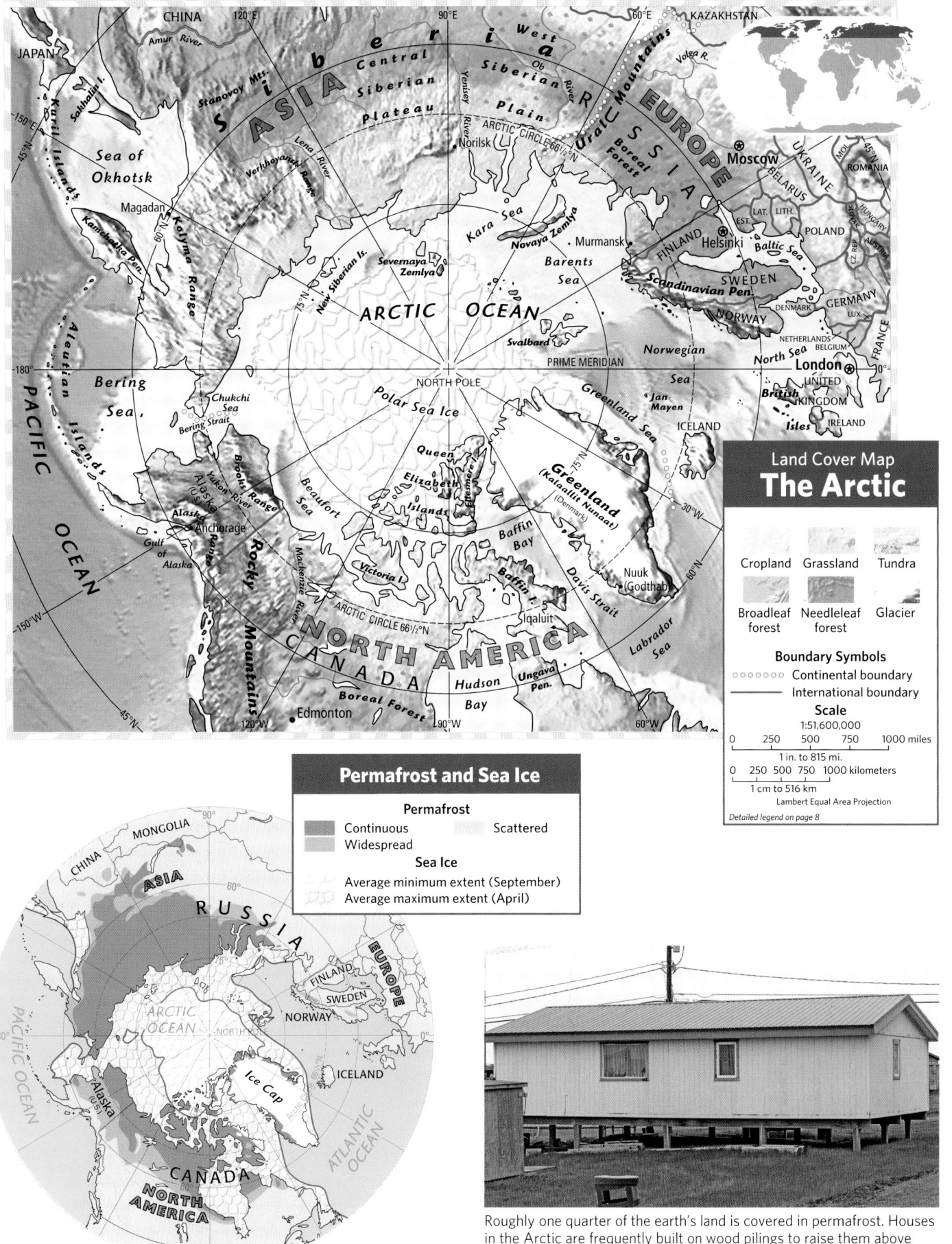

CHINA 120°E 90°E 60°E KAZAKHSTAN

JAPAN

Amur River

West
Siberian
Plain

Central
Siberian
Plateau

Stanovoy Mts.

Sakhalin I.

Kuril Islands

Sea of
Okhotsk

Magadan

Kamchatka Pen.

Kolyma Range

Verkhoyansk Range

Lena River

Yenisey River

Ob River

Volga R.

Ural Mountains

ARCTIC CIRCLE 66½°N

Norilsk

Boreal Forest

RUSSIA

EUROPE

Moscow

UKRAINE

BELARUS

MOL.

ROMANIA

LAT. LITH.

POLAND

HUNGARY

AUSTRIA

CZ. REP.

GERMANY

LUX.

FRANCE

Kara Sea

Novaya Zemlya

Murmansk

Barents
Sea

FINLAND

Helsinki

Baltic Sea

SWEDEN

Scandinavian Pen.

NORWAY

DENMARK

NETHERLANDS

BELGIUM

Severnaya
Zemlya

ARCTIC OCEAN

New Siberian Is.

75°N

Svalbard

Norwegian
Sea

North Sea

London

UNITED
KINGDOM

British
Isles

IRELAND

PRIME MERIDIAN

0°

NORTH POLE

Polar Sea Ice

Greenland Sea

Jan
Mayen

ICELAND

30°W

Chukchi
Sea

Bering
Strait

Bering
Sea

Beaufort
Sea

Brooks Range

Alaska (U.S.)

Anchorage

Gulf
of
Alaska

Yukon River

Queen
Elizabeth
Islands

Ellesmere I.

Greenland
(Kalaallit Nunaat)
(Denmark)

60°N

Baffin
Bay

Nuuk
(Godthab)

Aleutian
Islands

PACIFIC

OCEAN

Victoria I.

Mackenzie River

Rocky Mountains

Baffin I.

Davis Strait

Iqaluit

Labrador
Sea

NORTH AMERICA

CANADA

ARCTIC CIRCLE 66½°N

Hudson
Bay

Ungava
Pen.

Boreal Forest

Edmonton

120°W 90°W 60°W 45°N

Land Cover Map
The Arctic

Cropland	Grassland	Tundra
Broadleaf forest	Needleleaf forest	Glacier

Boundary Symbols
○○○○○○○ Continental boundary
——— International boundary

Scale
1:51,600,000

0   250   500   750   1000 miles
1 in. to 815 mi.

0   250 500 750 1000 kilometers
1 cm to 516 km

Lambert Equal Area Projection
Detailed legend on page 8

Permafrost and Sea Ice

Permafrost
Continuous   Scattered
Widespread

Sea Ice
Average minimum extent (September)
Average maximum extent (April)

MONGOLIA 90°

CHINA

ASIA

RUSSIA

60°

EUROPE

FINLAND

SWEDEN

NORWAY

ARCTIC
OCEAN

NORTH
POLE

ICELAND

Ice Cap

PACIFIC OCEAN

180°

Alaska
(U.S.)

ATLANTIC
OCEAN

CANADA

NORTH
AMERICA

90°

Roughly one quarter of the earth's land is covered in permafrost. Houses in the Arctic are frequently built on wood pilings to raise them above the frozen soil. Without the pilings, heat from a house can melt the permafrost and cause the foundation to sink.

Country Tables

COUNTRY, Dependency *Official Name (if different)*	CAPITAL(S) (Island location)	PRINCIPAL LANGUAGES OFFICIAL and other languages	AREA mi²/km²	POPULATION	POPULATION DENSITY per mi²/km²	NATURAL POP. GROWTH % gain	LIFE EXPECTANCY Male Female	
Africa (For country locations, see page 132.)								
ALGERIA *People's Democratic Republic of Algeria*	Algiers	ARABIC, BERBER (Tamazight), French	919,595 2,381,741	40,969,443	44.6 17.2	1.79	75.5	78.2
ANGOLA *Republic of Angola*	Luanda	PORTUGUESE, Ovimbundu (Umbundu), Mbundu, Kongo	481,354 1,246,700	29,310,273	60.9 23.5	3.5	54.8	57.2
BENIN *Republic of Benin*	Porto-Novo, Cotonou	FRENCH, Fon, Yoruba (Nago), Adja	44,310 114,763	11,038,805	249.1 96.2	2.71	60.5	63.3
BOTSWANA *Republic of Botswana*	Gaborone	ENGLISH, Tswana	224,607 581,730	2,214,858	9.9 3.8	1.25	56.3	52.6
BURKINA FASO	Ouagadougou	FRENCH, Moore (Mossi), Fula (Fulani)	104,543 270,764	20,107,509	192.3 74.3	3.0	53.4	57.6
BURUNDI *Republic of Burundi*	Bujumbura, Gitega	RUNDI, FRENCH, Hutu	10,747 27,834	11,466,756	1,067.0 412.0	3.25	58.8	62.3
CAMEROON *Republic of Cameroon*	Yaounde	ENGLISH, FRENCH, Fang, Bamileke, Duala, Fula (Fulani), Tikar	183,920 476,350	24,994,885	135.9 52.5	2.58	57.1	59.9
CAPE VERDE (Cabo Verde) *Republic of Cabo Verde*	Praia (on Santiago)	PORTUGUESE, Crioulo (Portuguese Creole)	1,557 4,033	560,899	360.2 139.1	1.4	69.8	74.5
CENTRAL AFRICAN REPUBLIC	Bangui	SANGO, FRENCH, Gbaya (Baya), Banda	240,324 622,436	5,625,118	23.4 9.0	2.11	51.0	53.7
CHAD *Republic of Chad*	N'Djamena	FRENCH, ARABIC, Sara, Mayo-Kebbi	495,755 1,284,000	12,075,985	24.4 9.4	2.18	49.0	51.5
COMOROS *Union of the Comoros*	Moroni (on Grande Comore)	COMORIAN, FRENCH, ARABIC	719 1,862	808,080	1,123.9 434.0	1.89	61.9	66.6
CONGO REPUBLIC *Republic of the Congo*	Brazzaville	FRENCH, Monokutuba, Lingala, Kongo	132,047 342,000	4,954,674	37.5 14.5	2.49	55.8	58.9
CÔTE D'IVOIRE (Ivory Coast) *Republic of Côte d'Ivoire*	Yamoussoukro, Abidjan	FRENCH, Akan, Gur, Malinke, Kru	124,503 322,462	24,184,810	194.3 75.0	1.83	58.1	60.6
DEMOCRATIC REPUBLIC OF THE CONGO	Kinshasa	FRENCH, Lingala, Swahili, Kongo, Luba	905,568 2,345,410	83,301,151	92.0 35.5	2.39	57.5	59.9
DJIBOUTI *Republic of Djibouti*	Djibouti	FRENCH, ARABIC, Somali, Afar	8,956 23,200	865,267	96.6 37.3	1.59	60.7	65.8
EGYPT *Arab Republic of Egypt*	Cairo	ARABIC	384,791 996,603	97,041,072	252.2 97.4	2.5	71.4	74.2
EQUATORIAL GUINEA *Republic of Equatorial Guinea*	Malabo	SPANISH, FRENCH, Fang	10,831 28,051	778,358	71.9 27.7	2.44	63.1	65.4
ERITREA *State of Eritrea*	Asmara	Tigrinya, Tigre	46,760 121,100	5,918,919	126.6 48.9	2.24	62.4	67.5
ESWATINI (Swaziland) *Kingdom of Eswatini*	Mbabane, Lobamba	SWAZI, ENGLISH	6,704 17,364	1,467,152	218.8 84.5	1.08	52.2	51.0
ETHIOPIA *Federal Democratic Republic of Ethiopia*	Addis Ababa	Oromo (Oromifa), Amharic	410,678 1,063,652	105,350,020	256.5 99.0	2.88	59.8	64.7
GABON *Gabonese Republic*	Libreville	FRENCH, Fang	103,347 267,667	1,772,255	17.1 6.6	2.12	51.6	52.5
GAMBIA *Republic of The Gambia*	Banjul	ENGLISH, Malinke, Fula (Fulani), Wolof	4,491 11,632	2,051,363	456.8 176.4	2.24	62.5	67.3
GHANA *Republic of Ghana*	Accra	ENGLISH, Hausa, Akan	92,098 238,533	27,499,924	298.6 115.3	2.35	64.1	69.1
GUINEA *Republic of Guinea*	Conakry	FRENCH, Fula (Fulani), Malinke, Susu	95,926 245,857	12,413,867	129.4 50.5	2.61	59.0	62.2
GUINEA-BISSAU *Republic of Guinea-Bissau*	Bissau	PORTUGUESE, Crioulo (Portuguese Creole), Balante, Fula (Fulani)	13,948 36,125	1,792,338	128.5 49.6	1.86	48.6	52.7
KENYA *Republic of Kenya*	Nairobi	SWAHILI, ENGLISH, Kikuyu, Luhya, Luo	224,961 582,646	47,615,739	211.7 81.7	1.72	62.6	65.5
LESOTHO *Kingdom of Lesotho*	Maseru	SOTHO, ENGLISH, Zulu	11,720 30,355	1,958,042	167.1 64.5	0.96	52.9	53.1
LIBERIA *Republic of Liberia*	Monrovia	ENGLISH, Krio (English Creole), Kpelle, Bassa	37,420 96,917	4,689,021	125.3 48.4	3.07	57.3	60.8
LIBYA *State of Libya*	Tripoli	ARABIC, Berber	647,184 1,676,198	6,653,210	10.3 4.0	1.39	74.7	78.3
MADAGASCAR *Republic of Madagascar*	Antananarivo	MALAGASY, FRENCH	226,756 578,295	25,054,161	110.5 43.3	2.51	64.4	67.4
MALAWI *Republic of Malawi*	Lilongwe	ENGLISH, Chewa, Lomwe, Yao	45,747 118,484	19,196,246	419.6 162.0	3.31	59.2	63.2

COUNTRY, Dependency: all independent countries, as well as selected dependencies; includes both conventional and official forms of country names. **CAPITALS:** all national capitals, with island location when applicable. **PRINCIPAL LANGUAGE(S):** all official languages, as well as primary languages spoken by a substantial proportion of the population. **POPULATION DENSITY:** computed as population divided by area; given per square mile and per square kilometer. **NATURAL POP. GROWTH:** annual population increase; does not include population change due to immigration or emigration. **LIFE EXPECTANCY:** average length of life in years at birth; given for males and females.

COUNTRY, Dependency *Official Name (if different)*	CAPITAL(S) (Island location)	PRINCIPAL LANGUAGES OFFICIAL and other languages	AREA mi²/km²	POPULATION	POPULATION DENSITY per mi²/km²	NATURAL POP. GROWTH % gain	LIFE EXPECTANCY Male	Female
MALI *Republic of Mali*	Bamako	FRENCH, Bambara	482,077 1,248,574	17,885,245	37.1 14.3	3.41	53.9	57.7
MAURITANIA *Islamic Republic of Mauritania*	Nouakchott	ARABIC, Hassaniya Arabic	397,956 1,030,700	3,758,571	9.4 3.6	2.25	60.7	65.4
MAURITIUS *Republic of Mauritius*	Port Louis	ENGLISH, French, Creole, Bhojpuri	788 2,040	1,356,388	1,721.3 664.9	0.59	72.2	79.2
MOROCCO *Kingdom of Morocco*	Rabat	ARABIC, BERBER (Tamazight), French	169,827 439,850	33,986,655	200.1 77.3	1.28	73.8	80.1
MOZAMBIQUE *Republic of Mozambique*	Maputo	PORTUGUESE, Makua	308,642 799,380	26,573,706	86.1 33.2	2.65	52.6	54.1
NAMIBIA *Republic of Namibia*	Windhoek	ENGLISH, Ovambo, Nama, Kavango, Afrikaans	318,772 825,615	2,484,780	7.8 3.0	1.94	62.1	65.1
NIGER *Republic of Niger*	Niamey	FRENCH, Hausa, Songhai, Zerma	489,191 1,267,000	19,245,344	39.3 15.2	3.24	54.3	56.8
NIGERIA *Federal Republic of Nigeria*	Abuja	ENGLISH, Hausa, Yoruba, Igbo (Ibo), Fula (Fulani)	356,669 923,768	190,632,261	534.5 206.4	2.45	52.4	54.5
RWANDA *Republic of Rwanda*	Kigali	RWANDA, FRENCH, ENGLISH	10,185 26,379	11,901,484	1,168.5 451.2	2.43	58.5	61.7
SAO TOME AND PRINCIPE *Democratic Republic of Sao Tome and Principe*	Sao Tome	PORTUGUESE, Crioulo (Portuguese Creole)	386 1,001	201,025	520.8 200.8	2.56	63.6	66.3
SENEGAL *Republic of Senegal*	Dakar	FRENCH, Wolof, Fula (Fulani)-Tukulor	75,955 196,722	14,668,522	193.1 74.6	2.53	59.7	63.8
SEYCHELLES *Republic of Seychelles*	Victoria (on Mahe)	French, English, Seselwa (French Creole)	175 453	93,920	536.7 207.3	0.67	70.2	79.4
SIERRA LEONE *Republic of Sierra Leone*	Freetown	ENGLISH, Krio (English Creole), Mende, Temne	27,699 71,740	6,163,195	222.5 85.9	2.59	55.6	60.9
SOMALIA *Federal Republic of Somalia*	Mogadishu	SOMALI, ARABIC	246,201 637,657	11,031,386	44.8 17.3	2.65	50.3	54.5
SOUTH AFRICA *Republic of South Africa*	Pretoria (Tshwane), Cape Town, Bloemfontein	ZULU, XHOSA, AFRIKAANS, SOTHO, TSWANA, ENGLISH, TSONGA, VENDA, SWATI, NDEBELE, PEDI	471,359 1,220,813	54,841,552	116.3 44.9	1.08	61.6	64.6
SOUTH SUDAN *Republic of South Sudan*	Juba	ENGLISH, Arabic, Juba Arabic, Dinka, Nver, Zande, Bari, Shiluk	248,777 644,330	13,026,129	52.4 20.2	2.78	no data	no data
SUDAN *Republic of the Sudan*	Khartoum	ARABIC, ENGLISH, Nubian languages, Beja	712,280 1,844,797	37,345,935	52.4 20.2	2.06	62.0	66.3
TANZANIA *United Republic of Tanzania*	Dar es Salaam, Dodoma	SWAHILI, ENGLISH, Nyamwesi (Sukuma)	365,759 947,303	53,950,935	147.5 57.0	2.8	60.8	63.6
TOGO *Togolese Republic*	Lome	FRENCH, Ewe, Kabre	21,853 56,600	7,965,055	364.5 140.7	2.64	62.3	67.7
TUNISIA *Republic of Tunisia*	Tunis	ARABIC, French	63,170 163,610	11,403,800	180.5 69.7	1.19	74.0	78.4
UGANDA *Republic of Uganda*	Kampala	ENGLISH, SWAHILI, Ganda (Luganda)	93,263 241,551	39,570,125	424.3 163.8	3.27	54.0	56.9
Western Sahara *(adm. Morocco)*	El Aauin (Laayoune)	Arabic	97,344 252,120	603,253	6.2 2.4	2.12	60.7	65.4
ZAMBIA *Republic of Zambia*	Lusaka	ENGLISH, Bemba, Nyanja, Tonga	290,585 752,612	15,972,000	55.0 21.2	2.93	50.8	54.1
ZIMBABWE *Republic of Zimbabwe*	Harare	ENGLISH, Shona, Ndebele	150,872 390,757	13,805,084	91.5 35.3	2.4	57.3	58.7

Asia (For country locations, see pages 166–167.)

COUNTRY, Dependency *Official Name (if different)*	CAPITAL(S) (Island location)	PRINCIPAL LANGUAGES OFFICIAL and other languages	AREA mi²/km²	POPULATION	POPULATION DENSITY per mi²/km²	NATURAL POP. GROWTH % gain	LIFE EXPECTANCY Male	Female
AFGHANISTAN *Islamic Republic of Afghanistan*	Kabul	PASHTO, DARI (Persian), Tajik, Hazara, Uzbek	252,072 652,864	34,124,811	135.4 52.3	2.45	49.9	52.7
ARMENIA *Republic of Armenia*	Yerevan	ARMENIAN	11,484 29,743	3,045,191	265.2 102.4	0.35	71.4	78.3
AZERBAIJAN *Republic of Azerbaijan*	Baku	AZERBAIJANI (Azeri)	33,436 86,600	9,961,396	297.9 115.0	0.87	69.5	75.8
BAHRAIN *Kingdom of Bahrain*	Manama	ARABIC	297 770	1,410,942	4,750.6 1,832.4	1.05	76.7	81.1
BANGLADESH *People's Republic of Bangladesh*	Dhaka	BANGLA (Bengali)	56,977 147,570	157,826,578	2,770.0 1,069.5	1.34	71.0	75.4
BHUTAN *Kingdom of Bhutan*	Thimphu	DZONGKHA, Nepali (Hindi)	14,824 38,394	758,288	51.2 19.8	1.08	69.1	71.1
BRUNEI *Brunei Darussalam*	Bandar Seri Begawan	MALAY, English, Chinese	2,226 5,765	443,593	199.3 76.9	1.34	74.8	79.6
CAMBODIA *Kingdom of Cambodia*	Phnom Penh	KHMER	69,898 181,035	16,204,486	231.8 89.5	1.55	62.0	67.1
CHINA *People's Republic of China*	Beijing	MANDARIN, Chinese (Han), Wu, Cantonese (Yue)	3,696,100 9,572,900	1,379,302,771	373.2 144.1	0.45	73.5	77.9
CYPRUS *Republic of Cyprus*	Nicosia	GREEK, TURKISH	3,572 9,251	1,221,549	342.0 132.0	0.45	75.8	81.6

COUNTRY, Dependency *Official Name (if different)*	CAPITAL(S) (Island location)	PRINCIPAL LANGUAGES OFFICIAL and other languages	AREA mi²/km²	POPULATION	POPULATION DENSITY per mi²/km²	NATURAL POP. GROWTH % gain	LIFE EXPECTANCY Male	Female
EAST TIMOR *Democratic Republic of Timor-Leste*	Dili	Tetum (Tetun), Portuguese	5,773 14,954	1,291,358	223.7 86.4	2.75	66.5	69.7
GEORGIA	Tbilisi	GEORGIAN, Russian, Armenian	26,911 69,700	4,926,330	183.1 70.7	0.14	72.1	80.6
INDIA *Republic of India*	New Delhi	HINDI, ENGLISH, Bangla (Bengali), Telugu, Marathi, Tamil, Urdu, Gujarati	1,222,550 3,166,391	1,281,935,911	1,048.6 404.9	1.17	67.3	69.8
INDONESIA *Republic of Indonesia*	Jakarta (on Java)	INDONESIAN (Malay), Javanese, Sundanese	737,815 1,910,931	260,580,739	353.2 136.4	0.97	70.1	75.5
IRAN *Islamic Republic of Iran*	Tehran	FARSI (Persian), Azerbaijani (Azeri)	628,872 1,628,771	82,021,564	130.4 50.4	1.26	69.8	73.1
IRAQ *Republic of Iraq*	Baghdad	ARABIC, KURDISH	167,618 434,128	39,192,111	233.8 90.3	2.66	72.6	77.2
ISRAEL *State of Israel*	Jerusalem	HEBREW, ARABIC	8,357 21,643	8,299,706	993.1 383.5	1.29	80.6	84.4
JAPAN	Tokyo (on Honshu)	JAPANESE	145,898 377,873	126,451,398	866.7 334.6	-0.21	81.7	88.5
JORDAN *Hashemite Kingdom of Jordan*	Amman	ARABIC	34,284 88,794	10,248,069	298.9 115.4	2.05	73.2	76.1
KAZAKHSTAN *Republic of Kazakhstan*	Astana (Nur-Sultan)	KAZAKH, Russian	1,052,089 2,724,900	18,556,698	17.6 6.8	1.0	65.5	75.7
KUWAIT *State of Kuwait*	Kuwait	ARABIC	6,880 17,818	2,875,422	417.9 161.4	1.7	76.6	79.4
KYRGYZSTAN *Kyrgyz Republic*	Bishkek	KYRGYZ, RUSSIAN, Uzbek	77,199 199,945	5,789,122	75.0 29.0	1.56	66.5	75.1
LAOS *Lao People's Democratic Republic*	Vientiane (Viangchan)	LAO-LUM (Lao), Lao-Theung	91,429 236,800	7,126,706	77.9 30.1	1.62	62.2	66.4
LEBANON *Lebanese Republic*	Beirut	ARABIC, French	4,036 10,452	6,229,794	1,543.6 596.0	0.93	76.3	78.9
MALAYSIA	Kuala Lumpur	MALAY, English	127,526 330,290	31,381,992	246.1 95.0	1.4	72.2	78.0
MALDIVES *Republic of Maldives*	Male (on Male)	DIVEHI (Maldivian)	115 298	392,709	3,414.9 1,317.8	1.21	73.3	78.0
MONGOLIA	Ulaanbaatar	KHALKHA (Mongolian)	603,926 1,564,160	3,068,243	5.1 2.0	1.26	65.4	74.1
MYANMAR (Burma) *Union of Myanmar*	Nay Pyi Taw, Yangon (Rangoon)	BURMESE	261,228 676,577	55,123,814	211.0 81.5	1.07	64.2	69.2
NEPAL *Federal Democratic Republic of Nepal*	Kathmandu	NEPALI, English	56,827 147,181	29,384,297	517.1 199.6	1.39	70.1	71.3
NORTH KOREA *Democratic People's Republic of Korea*	Pyongyang	KOREAN	47,399 112,762	25,248,140	532.7 223.9	0.53	66.6	74.5
OMAN *Sultanate of Oman*	Muscat	ARABIC	119,500 309,500	3,424,386	28.7 11.1	2.07	73.5	77.5
PAKISTAN *Islamic Republic of Pakistan*	Islamabad	URDU, Punjabi, Pashto, Sindhi, English, Saraiki	340,499 881,889	204,924,861	601.8 232.4	1.56	65.8	69.8
PHILIPPINES *Republic of the Philippines*	Manila (on Luzon)	PILIPINO, ENGLISH, Cebuano	115,831 300,000	104,256,076	900.1 347.5	1.76	65.7	72.9
QATAR *State of Qatar*	Doha	ARABIC	4,481 11,607	2,314,307	516.5 199.4	0.81	76.7	80.8
SAUDI ARABIA *Kingdom of Saudi Arabia*	Riyadh	ARABIC	830,000 2,149,690	28,571,770	34.4 13.3	1.49	73.2	77.4
SINGAPORE *Republic of Singapore*	Singapore	MANDARIN, ENGLISH, MALAY, TAMIL, Chinese	277 718	5,888,926	21,259.7 8,201.8	0.51	82.3	87.8
SOUTH KOREA *Republic of Korea*	Seoul	KOREAN	38,486 99,678	51,181,299	1,329.9 513.5	0.23	79.3	85.8
SRI LANKA *Democratic Socialist Republic of Sri Lanka*	Colombo, Sri Jayewardenepura Kotte	SINHALA, TAMIL	25,332 65,610	22,409,381	884.6 341.6	0.9	73.3	80.4
SYRIA *Syrian Arab Republic*	Damascus	ARABIC	71,498 185,180	18,028,549	252.2 97.4	1.72	72.5	77.4
TAIWAN *Republic of China on Taiwan*	Taipei	MANDARIN, Min, Hakka	13,973 36,190	23,508,428	1,682.4 649.6	0.09	77.0	83.5
TAJIKISTAN *Republic of Tajikistan*	Dushanbe	TAJIK, Uzbek	55,251 143,100	8,468,555	153.3 59.2	1.73	64.6	71.0
THAILAND *Kingdom of Thailand*	Bangkok	THAI (Siamese), Lao, Chinese	198,117 513,120	68,414,135	345.3 133.3	0.3	71.5	78.0
TURKEY *Republic of Turkey*	Ankara	TURKISH, Kurdish	303,224 785,347	80,845,215	266.6 102.9	0.97	72.5	77.3
TURKMENISTAN	Ashgabat	TURKMEN	189,657 491,210	5,351,277	28.2 10.9	1.3	67.1	73.3
UNITED ARAB EMIRATES	Abu Dhabi	ARABIC	32,280 83,600	6,072,475	188.1 72.6	1.32	74.8	80.2

COUNTRY, Dependency *Official Name (if different)*	CAPITAL(S) (Island location)	PRINCIPAL LANGUAGES OFFICIAL and other languages	AREA mi²/km²	POPULATION	POPULATION DENSITY per mi²/km²	NATURAL POP. GROWTH % gain	LIFE EXPECTANCY Male Female	
UZBEKISTAN *Republic of Uzbekistan*	Tashkent	UZBEK	172,742 447,400	29,748,859	172.2 66.5	1.15	70.7	77.0
VIETNAM *Socialist Republic of Vietnam*	Hanoi	VIETNAMESE	127,882 331,212	96,160,163	751.9 290.3	0.96	70.9	76.2
YEMEN *Republic of Yemen*	Sanaa	ARABIC	203,891 528,076	28,036,829	137.5 53.1	2.24	63.4	67.8

Australia and Oceania (For country locations, see pages 188–189.)

AUSTRALIA *Commonwealth of Australia*	Canberra	ENGLISH	2,969,976 7,692,202	23,232,413	7.8 3.0	0.48	79.8	84.8
FIJI *Republic of Fiji*	Suva (on Viti Levu)	ENGLISH, Fijian, Hindi	7,055 18,272	920,938	130.5 50.4	1.25	70.0	75.5
French Polynesia (Fr.)	Papeete (on Tahiti)	FRENCH. TAHITIAN, Polynesian languages	1,609 4,167	287,881	178.9 69.1	0.96	74.9	79.6
KIRIBATI *Republic of Kiribati*	Tarawa (on Tarawa)	ENGLISH, Kiribati	313 811	108,145	345.5 133.3	1.42	63.7	68.8
MARSHALL ISLANDS *Republic of the* *Marshall Islands*	Majuro (on Majuro)	MARSHALLESE, ENGLISH	70 181	74,539	1,064.8 411.8	2.02	70.9	75.4
MICRONESIA *Federated States* *of Micronesia*	Palikir (on Pohnpei)	Chuukese/Mortlockese, Pohnpeian	271 701	104,196	384.5 148.6	1.58	70.8	75.0
NAURU *Republic of Nauru*	Yaren District (unofficial)	English, Nauruan	8 21	9,642	1,205.3 459.1	1.81	63.0	70.5
New Caledonia (Fr.) *Territory of New Caledonia* *and Dependencies*	Noumea	FRENCH, Melanesian and Polynesian languages	7,172 18,575	279,070	38.9 15.0	0.93	73.7	81.9
NEW ZEALAND	Wellington (on North Island)	ENGLISH, MAORI	104,515 270,692	4,510,327	43.2 16.7	0.57	79.1	83.3
PALAU *Republic of Palau*	Melekeok (on Babelthuap)	PALAUAN, ENGLISH	188 488	21,431	114.0 43.9	0.32	69.9	76.5
PAPUA NEW GUINEA *Independent State of* *Papua New Guinea*	Port Moresby (on New Guinea)	ENGLISH, Tok Pisin (English Creole), Papuan and Melanesian languages	178,704 462,840	6,909,701	38.7 14.9	1.71	65.0	69.5
SAMOA *Independent State of Samoa*	Apia (on Upolu)	SAMOAN, ENGLISH	1,075 2,785	200,108	186.1 71.9	1.51	70.8	76.8
SOLOMON ISLANDS	Honiara (on Guadacanal)	ENGLISH, Melanesian languages	10,954 28,370	647,581	59.1 22.8	2.11	72.7	78.1
TONGA *Kingdom of Tonga*	Nuku'alofa (on Tongatapu)	TONGAN, ENGLISH	289 748	106,479	368.4 142.4	1.73	74.7	77.8
TUVALU	Funafuti (on Funafuti)	Tuvaluan	10 26	11,052	1,105.2 425.1	1.52	64.3	68.8
VANUATU *Republic of Vanuatu*	Port-Vila (on Efate)	BISLAMA (English Creole), ENGLISH, FRENCH	4,707 12,190	282,814	60.1 23.2	2.0	71.8	75.1

Europe (For country locations, see pages 146-147.)

ALBANIA *Republic of Albania*	Tirana	ALBANIAN	11,082 28,703	3,047,987	275.0 106.2	0.64	75.7	81.2
ANDORRA *Principality of Andorra*	Andorra la Vella	CATALAN, Spanish	180 468	85,702	476.1 183.1	0.02	80.6	85.1
AUSTRIA *Republic of Austria*	Vienna	GERMAN	32,386 83,879	8,754,413	270.3 104.4	-0.01	78.9	84.3
BELARUS *Republic of Belarus*	Minsk	BELARUSIAN, RUSSIAN	80,153 207,595	9,549,747	119.1 46.0	-0.29	67.2	78.6
BELGIUM *Kingdom of Belgium*	Brussels	DUTCH, FRENCH, GERMAN	11,787 30,528	11,491,346	974.9 376.4	0.16	78.4	83.7
BOSNIA AND **HERZEGOVINA**	Sarajevo	BOSNIAN, SERBIAN, CROATIAN	19,772 51,209	3,856,181	195.0 75.3	-0.12	73.7	80.0
BULGARIA *Republic of Bulgaria*	Sofia	BULGARIAN	42,858 111,002	7,101,510	165.7 64.0	-0.58	71.2	78.0
CROATIA *Republic of Croatia*	Zagreb	SERBO-CROATIAN (Croatian)	21,851 56,594	4,292,095	196.4 75.8	-0.33	72.7	79.2
CZECH REPUBLIC	Prague	CZECH, Moravian	30,450 78,865	10,674,723	350.6 135.4	-0.12	75.7	81.8
DENMARK *Kingdom of Denmark*	Copenhagen	DANISH	16,570 42,916	5,605,948	338.3 130.6	0.02	77.0	82.0
ESTONIA *Republic of Estonia*	Tallinn	ESTONIAN, Russian	17,462 45,227	1,251,581	71.7 27.7	-0.25	71.9	81.7
FINLAND *Republic of Finland*	Helsinki	Finnish, Swedish	150,928 390,903	5,518,371	36.6 14.1	0.07	77.9	84.0
FRANCE *French Republic*	Paris	FRENCH	210,026 543,965	62,814,233	299.1 115.5	0.29	78.7	85.1
GERMANY *Federal Republic of Germany*	Berlin	GERMAN	137,879 357,104	80,594,017	584.5 225.7	-0.31	78.4	83.1
GREECE *Hellenic Republic*	Athens	GREEK	50,949 131,957	10,768,477	211.4 81.6	-0.29	77.9	83.3

COUNTRY, Dependency *Official Name (if different)*	CAPITAL(S) (Island location)	PRINCIPAL LANGUAGES OFFICIAL and other languages	AREA mi²/km²	POPULATION	POPULATION DENSITY per mi²/km²	NATURAL POP. GROWTH % gain	LIFE EXPECTANCY Male Female	
HUNGARY	Budapest	HUNGARIAN	35,919 93,030	9,850,845	274.3 105.9	-0.38	72.2	79.8
ICELAND *Republic of Iceland*	Reykjavik	ICELANDIC	39,777 103,022	339,747	8.5 3.3	0.73	80.9	85.3
IRELAND	Dublin	ENGLISH, IRISH	27,133 70,273	5,011,102	184.7 71.3	0.75	78.5	83.2
ITALY *Italian Republic*	Rome	ITALIAN	116,346 301,336	62,137,802	534.1 206.2	-0.18	79.6	85.0
KOSOVO *Republic of Kosovo*	Pristina	ALBANIAN, SERBIAN Bosnian, Turkish	4,212 10,908	1,895,250	450.0 173.7	no data	no data	no data
LATVIA *Republic of Latvia*	Riga	LATVIAN, Russian	24,938 64,589	1,944,643	78.0 30.1	-0.48	69.9	79.3
LIECHTENSTEIN *Principality of Liechtenstein*	Vaduz	GERMAN	62 160	38,244	616.8 239.0	0.3	79.7	84.6
LITHUANIA *Republic of Lithuania*	Vilnius	LITHUANIAN	25,212 65,300	2,823,859	112.0 43.2	-0.47	69.5	80.6
LUXEMBOURG *Grand Duchy of Luxembourg*	Luxembourg	Luxemburgian, Portuguese	999 2,586	594,130	594.7 229.7	0.42	79.8	84.9
MALTA *Republic of Malta*	Valletta	MALTESE, ENGLISH	122 315	416,338	3,412.6 1,321.7	0.07	78.0	82.8
MOLDOVA *Republic of Moldova*	Chisinau	ROMANIAN (Moldovan), Russian	13,067 33,843	3,474,121	265.9 102.7	-0.11	66.9	74.8
MONACO *Principality of Monaco*	Monaco	FRENCH, Italian, Monegasque	1 2	30,645	39,288.5 15,170.8	-0.32	85.6	93.5
MONTENEGRO	Podgorica	MONTENEGRIN	5,333 13,812	642,550	120.5 46.5	0.03	no data	no data
NETHERLANDS *Kingdom of the Netherlands*	Amsterdam, The Hague	DUTCH	16,158 41,850	17,084,719	1,057.4 408.2	0.2	79.2	83.6
NORTH MACEDONIA *Republic of North Macedonia*	Skopje	MACEDONIAN, Albanian	9,928 25,713	2,103,721	211.9 81.8	0.22	73.6	79.0
NORWAY *Kingdom of Norway*	Oslo	NORWEGIAN	148,718 385,178	5,320,045	35.8 13.8	0.41	79.8	83.9
POLAND *Republic of Poland*	Warsaw	POLISH	120,726 312,679	38,476,269	318.7 123.1	-0.09	73.7	81.7
PORTUGAL *Portuguese Republic*	Lisbon	PORTUGUESE	35,603 92,212	10,839,514	304.5 117.5	-0.21	76.1	82.8
ROMANIA	Bucharest	ROMANIAN	92,043 238,391	21,529,967	233.9 90.3	-0.31	71.7	78.8
RUSSIA *Russian Federation*	Moscow	RUSSIAN	6,601,700 17,098,200	142,257,519	21.5 8.3	-0.25	65.0	76.8
SAN MARINO *Republic of San Marino*	San Marino	ITALIAN (Romagnolo)	24 61	33,537	1,397.4 549.8	-0.01	80.7	86.1
SERBIA *Republic of Serbia*	Belgrade	SERBO-CROATIAN (Serbian)	29,922 77,498	7,111,024	237.7 91.8	-0.46	72.6	78.5
SLOVAKIA *Slovak Republic*	Bratislava	SLOVAK	18,932 49,043	5,445,829	287.7 111.0	-0.02	73.5	80.9
SLOVENIA *Republic of Slovenia*	Ljubljana	SLOVENE	7,827 20,273	1,972,126	252.0 97.3	-0.34	74.6	82.0
SPAIN *Kingdom of Spain*	Madrid	CASTILIAN SPANISH, Catalan, Galician	195,364 505,990	48,958,159	250.6 96.8	0.01	78.7	84.9
SWEDEN *Kingdom of Sweden*	Stockholm	SWEDISH	172,750 447,420	9,960,487	57.7 22.3	0.27	80.2	84.1
SWITZERLAND *Swiss Confederation*	Bern, Lausanne	GERMAN, FRENCH, ITALIAN	15,940 41,258	8,236,303	516.7 199.6	0.22	80.3	85.0
UKRAINE	Kiev	UKRAINIAN, Russian	233,062 603,628	44,033,874	188.9 72.9	-0.41	67.1	76.9
UNITED KINGDOM *United Kingdom of Great Britain and Northern Ireland*	London (on Great Britain)	ENGLISH	93,628 242,495	64,769,452	691.8 267.1	0.27	78.5	83.0
VATICAN CITY *The Holy See (State of the Vatican City)*	Vatican City	Italian, Latin, French	0 0	1,000	5,882.4 2,272.7	no data	no data	no data
North America (For country locations, see page 52.)								
ANTIGUA AND BARBUDA	Saint John's (Antigua)	ENGLISH, Antiguan creole	171 442	94,731	554.0 214.3	1	74.4	78.8
Aruba (Neth.)	Oranjestad	DUTCH, Papiamento	75 193	115,120	1,534.9 596.5	0.4	73.7	79.9
BAHAMAS *Commonwealth of the Bahamas*	Nassau (on New Providence)	ENGLISH, English Creole	5,382 13,939	329,988	61.3 23.7	0.81	70.0	74.8
BARBADOS	Bridgetown	ENGLISH, Bajan (English Creole)	166 430	292,336	1,761.1 679.9	0.31	73.0	77.7
BELIZE	Belmopan	ENGLISH, English Creole, Spanish	8,867 22,965	360,346	40.6 15.7	1.8	67.2	70.4
CANADA	Ottawa	ENGLISH, FRENCH	3,855,103 9,984,670	35,623,680	9.2 3.6	0.16	79.2	84.6

COUNTRY, Dependency *Official Name (if different)*	CAPITAL(S) (Island location)	PRINCIPAL LANGUAGES OFFICIAL and other languages	AREA mi²/km²	POPULATION	POPULATION DENSITY per mi²/km²	NATURAL POP. GROWTH % gain	LIFE EXPECTANCY Male Female	
COSTA RICA *Republic of Costa Rica*	San José	SPANISH	19,730 51,100	4,930,258	249.9 96.5	1.08	75.9	81.4
CUBA *Republic of Cuba*	Havana	SPANISH	42,426 109,884	11,147,407	262.7 101.4	0.2	76.4	81.1
Curacao (Neth.)	Willemstad	DUTCH, PAPIAMENTO, ENGLISH	171 444	149,648	875.1 337.0	0.53	76.0	80.7
DOMINICA *Commonwealth of Dominica*	Roseau	ENGLISH, English Creole, French Creole	290 751	73,897	254.8 98.4	0.72	74.0	80.1
DOMINICAN REPUBLIC	Santo Domingo	SPANISH	18,653 48,311	10,734,247	575.5 222.2	1.37	75.9	80.5
EL SALVADOR *Republic of El Salvador*	San Salvador	SPANISH	8,124 21,040	6,172,011	759.7 293.3	1.04	71.4	78.1
Greenland (Kalaallit Nunaat) (Den.)	Nuuk (Godthab)	GREENLANDIC, DANISH	836,330 2,166,086	57,713	0.1 0.0	0.57	69.7	75.2
GRENADA	Saint George's	ENGLISH, English Creole	133 344	111,724	840.0 324.8	0.73	71.7	77.1
GUATEMALA *Republic of Guatemala*	Guatemala City	SPANISH, Quiche, Cakchiquel, Kekchi, Mam	42,042 108,889	15,460,732	367.7 142.0	1.94	70.3	74.4
HAITI *Republic of Haiti*	Port-au-Prince	HAITIAN (French Creole), FRENCH	10,695 27,700	10,646,714	995.5 384.4	1.54	61.2	66.4
HONDURAS *Republic of Honduras*	Tegucigalpa	SPANISH	43,433 112,429	9,038,741	208.1 80.4	1.71	69.5	72.8
JAMAICA	Kingston	ENGLISH, English Creole	4,244 10,991	2,990,561	704.7 272.1	1.11	72.0	75.3
MEXICO *United Mexican States*	Mexico City	SPANISH, Aztec (Nahuatl), Yucatec (Mayan)	758,450 1,964,375	124,574,795	164.2 63.4	1.3	73.1	78.8
NICARAGUA *Republic of Nicaragua*	Managua	SPANISH	50,337 130,373	6,025,951	119.7 46.2	1.26	71.1	75.5
PANAMA *Republic of Panama*	Panama City	SPANISH, English Creole	28,640 74,177	3,753,142	131.0 50.6	1.3	75.8	81.6
Puerto Rico (U.S.) *Commonwealth of Puerto Rico*	San Juan	SPANISH, ENGLISH	3,424 8,868	3,351,827	978.9 378.0	-0.05	75.1	83.1
SAINT KITTS AND NEVIS *Federation of St. Kitts (Christopher) and Nevis*	Basseterre (on St. Kitts)	ENGLISH, English Creole	104 269	52,715	506.9 196.0	0.61	73.3	78.2
SAINT LUCIA	Castries	ENGLISH, English-French Creole	238 617	164,994	693.3 267.4	0.56	75.0	80.7
SAINT VINCENT AND THE GRENADINES	Kingstown (on St. Vincent)	ENGLISH, English Creole	150 389	102,089	680.6 262.4	0.59	73.3	77.4
Sint Maarten (Neth.)	Philipsburg	DUTCH, ENGLISH, Papiamento	13 34	42,083	3,237.2 1,237.7	0.79	75.8	80.6
TRINIDAD AND TOBAGO *Republic of Trinidad and Tobago*	Port-of-Spain (on Trinidad)	ENGLISH, Trinidad English	1,980 5,127	1,218,208	615.3 237.6	0.39	69.9	75.9
UNITED STATES *United States of America*	Washington, D.C.	English, Spanish	3,677,649 9,525,067	326,625,791	88.8 34.3	0.43	77.5	82.1

South America (For country locations, see page 120.)

ARGENTINA *Argentine Republic*	Buenos Aires	SPANISH	1,073,520 2,780,400	44,293,293	41.3 15.9	0.92	74.0	80.4
BOLIVIA *Plurinational State of Bolivia*	La Paz, Sucre	SPANISH, QUECHUA, AYMARA	424,165 1,098,581	11,138,234	26.3 10.1	1.56	66.4	72.1
BRAZIL *Federative Republic of Brazil*	Brasilia	PORTUGUESE	3,287,956 8,515,767	207,353,391	63.1 24.3	0.74	70.2	77.5
CHILE *Republic of Chile*	Santiago	SPANISH, Araucanian (Mapuche)	291,930 756,096	17,789,267	60.9 23.5	0.74	75.7	81.9
COLOMBIA *Republic of Colombia*	Bogota	SPANISH	440,831 1,141,748	47,698,524	108.2 41.8	1.06	72.6	79.0
ECUADOR *Republic of Ecuador*	Quito	SPANISH, Quechuan	98,985 256,370	16,290,913	164.6 63.5	1.28	73.8	79.9
French Guiana (Fr.) *Territorial Collectivity of French Guiana*	Cayenne	FRENCH, French Creole	32,253 83,534	257,000	8.0 3.1	no data	no data	no data
GUYANA *Cooperative Republic of Guyana*	Georgetown	ENGLISH, English Creole	83,012 214,999	737,718	8.9 3.4	0.8	65.4	71.5
PARAGUAY *Republic of Paraguay*	Asuncion	GUARANI, SPANISH	157,048 406,752	6,943,739	44.2 17.1	1.18	74.5	80.0
PERU *Republic of Peru*	Lima	SPANISH, QUECHUA, AYMARA	496,225 1,285,216	31,036,656	62.5 24.1	1.17	71.7	75.9
SURINAME *Republic of Suriname*	Paramaribo	DUTCH, English Creole	63,251 163,820	591,919	9.4 3.6	0.97	69.8	74.8
URUGUAY *Oriental Republic of Uruguay*	Montevideo	SPANISH	68,679 177,879	3,360,148	48.9 18.9	0.36	74.1	80.5
VENEZUELA *Bolivarian Republic of Venezuela*	Caracas	SPANISH	353,841 916,445	31,304,016	88.5 34.2	1.35	72.7	78.9

Glossary

acid rain Rain or snow that carries acids formed from chemical pollutants in the atmosphere.

Antarctic Circle Imaginary line of latitude located at 66½°S, approximately 1,630 miles (2620 kilometers) from the South Pole.

Arctic Circle Imaginary line of latitude located at 66½°N, approximately 1,630 miles (2620 kilometers) from the North Pole.

ANTARCTIC CIRCLE (66 ½°S)   ARCTIC CIRCLE (66 ½°N)

atoll Low, ring-shaped island formed by coral reefs.

balance of trade Difference between the value of a country's exports and the value of its imports, commonly measured in U.S. dollars. A country that exports more than it imports has a positive balance of trade, or *trade surplus*. A country that imports more than it exports has a negative balance of trade, or *trade deficit*.

basin 1. Area drained by a river and its branches. 2. Area surrounded by higher land.

biofuel Renewable alternative fuel that is made from recently living plant or animal material.

broadleaf forest Forest whose trees have broad leaves. In places with cold winters, broad leaves change color and fall off each autumn.

cartogram Special map that shows countries at equal scale—not by area but by another attribute, such as population.

climate Pattern of weather conditions for a place or region in a typical year. Climate is affected by latitude, elevation, topography, ocean currents, and wind.

climograph Graph showing annual patterns of temperature and precipitation for a specified place.

combustion Burning or other process that produces heat and light.

commercial farming Growing crops or raising livestock, largely for sale to others.

cropland Region used mainly to grow crops.

culture Beliefs, practices, and customs of a group of people.

deforestation Removal of all trees from a vast area of forest.

desert Dry region receiving little or no precipitation and with little or no vegetation.

dispossession Seizure of land from a person or group.

elevation Height above sea level.

emigration Movement of people away from their native country or region to a new home elsewhere. The people moving away are called *emigrants*.

Equator Imaginary line that divides the earth into the Northern and Southern Hemispheres. All points along the Equator have a latitude of 0°.

ethanol Alternative energy source made from plants, often corn or sugarcane.

ethnicity Group identity based on ancestral homeland, language, religion, and/or race.

European Union (EU) Group of European countries whose main goal is to establish themselves, for trading purposes, as a single market. (See map on page 153.)

export Sale of goods to a foreign country.

fault Boundary between plates of the earth's crust. An area where this boundary is indistinct is a *fault zone*.

feral Regarding a domesticated animal that has returned to the wild or one of its descendants.

forestry Use of forests for lumber, paper, and other products.

fossil fuels Natural fuels that were formed from the remains of plants and animals over millions of years. Principal fossil fuels are petroleum, natural gas, and coal.

free trade System of buying and selling of goods across international borders without restrictions.

glacier Large body of ice formed from a long-lasting accumulation of snow on mountains and in polar regions.

global warming Increase in worldwide air temperature, thought to be caused by pollution and the greenhouse effect.

grassland Region where grass grows, sometimes mixed with scattered trees and shrubs. Grasslands are often used for grazing.

greenhouse effect Trapping of solar radiation in the atmosphere due to high concentrations of gases that absorb heat, such as carbon dioxide, methane, and water vapor.

Greenwich Mean Time (GMT) Time of day along the Prime Meridian, also called Universal Time or Zulu Time. All other time zones are identified in hours before or after GMT.

gross domestic product (GDP) Annual value of all goods and services produced within a country's borders. GDP includes production by foreign-owned facilities.

immigration Movement of people into a new country of residence. The people moving in are called *immigrants*.

import Purchase of goods produced in a foreign country.

indigenous Native to a particular region. Indigenous peoples are related to the earliest known inhabitants of a region.

International Date Line Imaginary line located along and near 180° longitude that divides calendar days. Places west of the line are 24 hours ahead of places east of the line.

land cover Vegetation, deserts, and glaciers covering the earth's surface.

land use Principal economic activity in an area. It is not the only activity, but it is the most significant or widespread.

landform Natural feature of the landscape, such as a mountain, plain, or island.

latitude Distance from the Equator measured in degrees. Lines of latitude, or *parallels*, are numbered north and south from the Equator and appear on maps as east-west lines.

life expectancy Average number of years that people born today may expect to live based on the prevailing death rates for that population. Life expectancy reflects the group's general health and welfare.

literacy Ability to both read and write. The percentage of literate people is a good indicator of a country's educational level; literacy standards vary by country.

longitude Distance from the Prime Meridian measured in degrees. Lines of longitude, or *meridians*, are numbered east and west from the Prime Meridian and appear on maps as north-south lines.

map projection Any system for drawing lines of latitude, lines of longitude, and earth features on a map. Projections are never completely accurate, distorting either sizes or shapes of the earth's land and water features.

metal Element that reflects light, conducts electricity and heat, and can be manipulated into new shapes. Metal and metal-bearing ores are mined at and below the earth's surface.

migration Mass movement from one region or country to another.

national poverty line Poverty as defined by a government for an entire country. National poverty lines are a measure of *relative poverty*.

natural population growth (NPG) Annual difference between the number of births and the number of deaths in a country or region; does not include change due to population movement.

needleleaf forest Forest of needleleaf trees, such as pines and other evergreens.

nomadic herding Raising herds of animals, moving them in a yearly cycle from one seasonal source of food and water to the next.

Oceania Collective name for islands of the central and southern Pacific Ocean, usually including New Zealand and sometimes also including Australia.

Organization of Petroleum Exporting Countries (OPEC) Association of countries that control most of the world's known oil reserves. (See maps on page 174.)

pandemic Disease spread over a wide geographic area.

permafrost Ground that is frozen most or all of the year.

plain Broad area of land that is gently rolling or almost flat.

plate Any of the sections of the earth's crust that float above the molten interior of the planet. Lighter and thicker areas of the plates form the continents, while denser and thinner areas form ocean floors.

plateau Elevated plain, usually with at least one steeply dropping or rising side; tableland.

population density The number of people living in a given area such as a square mile or square kilometer.

poverty Inability to acquire basic human needs, such as food and housing. In global terms, poverty is defined as living on the equivalent of less than US$1 a day.

precipitation Water from the atmosphere that accumulates on the earth's surface as rain, snow, hail, sleet, or dew.

Prime Meridian Imaginary line of longitude, the 0° meridian, which passes through Greenwich, United Kingdom.

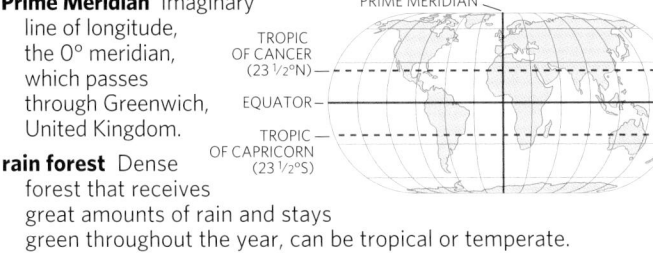

rain forest Dense forest that receives great amounts of rain and stays green throughout the year, can be tropical or temperate.

ranching and herding Raising herds of livestock on large, open ranches. The livestock graze or feed on the natural grasses growing there.

region Large area that is different from the areas around it. A region can be defined by a single feature or by several features, either physical or cultural.

renewable energy resource Power source that can be grown, such as firewood, or that cannot by used up, such as wind.

rural Relating to the countryside, as opposed to cities.

Sahel Narrow, semi-arid region south of Africa's Sahara that extends east-west between Somalia and Senegal.

scale Relationship between an actual distance on the earth and the same distance as shown on a map.

semi-desert Region covered by scattered vegetation but too dry for crops without irrigation. Also called *semi-arid.*

staple food Foodstuff that constitutes a major part of the diet for a region's population.

subsistence farming Agriculture that produces only enough for the needs of a farmer and his or her family, with little or nothing left to sell.

surface current Continuous flow of water at or near the surface of an ocean.

territory 1. Part of a country that does not have the rights of a state or province. **2.** Any large region, often with poorly defined boundaries.

thermal energy Energy derived from a heat source, usually natural, to create electricity.

time zone Region that shares the same time of day, usually one hour earlier than the zone to the west. Time zones are roughly centered on lines of longitude 15° apart.

trade organization Group established by an agreement between governments to promote trade. Examples include EU and OPEC.

Tropic of Cancer Imaginary line of latitude located at 23½°N. It marks the northern boundary of the tropics.

Tropic of Capricorn Imaginary line of latitude located at 23½°S. It marks the southern boundary of the tropics.

tropical rain forest Dense forest in or near the tropics that receives great amounts of rain and stays green year round.

tundra 1. Polar or mountainous area with no glaciers but too cold for trees to grow. **2.** Small plants that grow close to the ground in places that are cool or cold most of the year.

urban Relating to cities and their surrounding suburbs, the opposite of rural.

urbanization Change at a place as it grows into a city or is absorbed by an expanding city nearby.

vertical exaggeration 1. Increase in the height of a cross section or other diagram on order to show landforms more clearly. **2.** Ratio of vertical scale to horizontal scale. If vertical exaggeration is 32:1, one vertical mile appears 32 times larger than one horizontal mile.

weather Temperature, rainfall, and other conditions of the atmosphere over a short time in one place.

wetland Transition zone between land and water where the water level remains near or above the ground's surface for most of the year. Wetlands include swamps, marshes, and bogs.

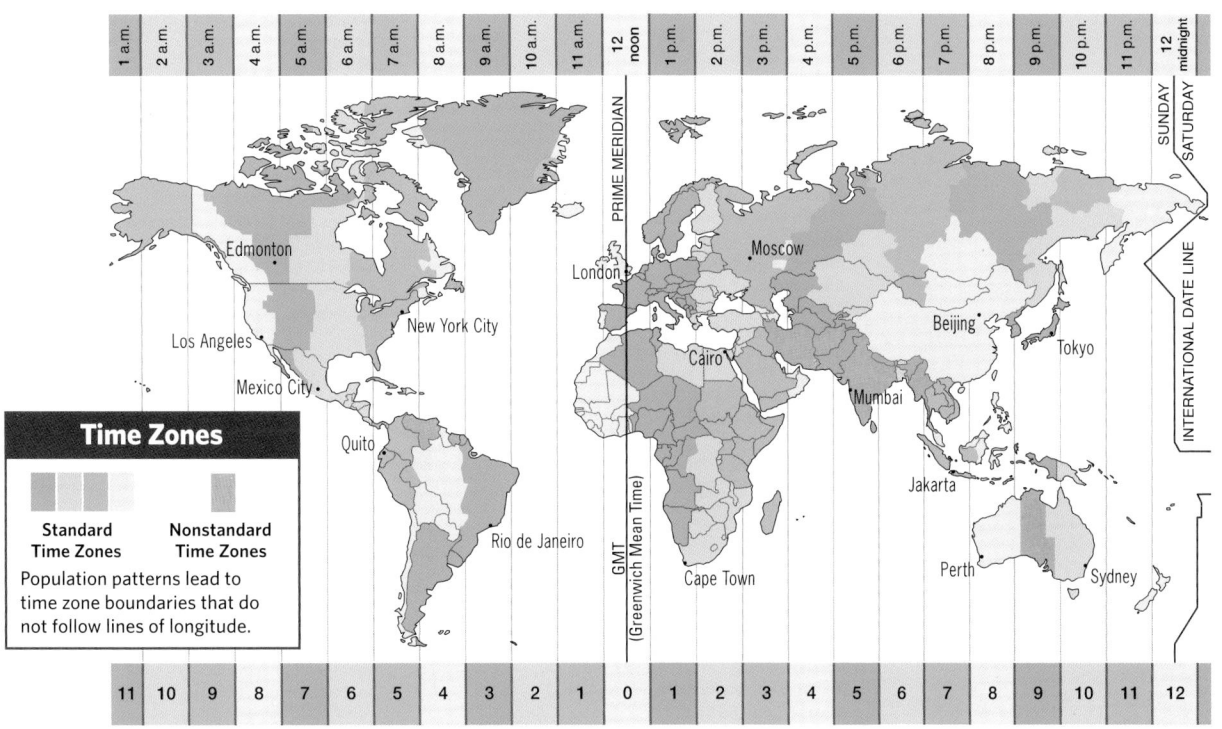

Subtract time zone number from GMT to obtain local time.

Add time zone number to GMT to obtain local time.

Index

The index lists all the place names that appear in the atlas. Entries for physical features are alphabetized by the proper part of their names, not by the descriptive part. For example, Lake Superior is listed as **Superior, L.** Entries for cities, however, are alphabetized by the first word in their names. So the city of Lake Charles is listed as **Lake Charles**. Similarly, foreign names, such as Rio Grande, are alphabetized by the first word in the name. Names beginning with St. are spelled **Saint** in the index. Abbreviations used in the index and in other parts of the atlas are listed on page 240.

Name (Pronunciation), Description (Lat., Long.) Page

A

A Coruna, Spain (43°N, 8°W) 158
Aachen (AH kuhn), Germany (51°N, 6°E) 159
Aba (ah BAH), Nigeria (5°N, 7°E) 138
Abbe, L., Africa (11°N, 41°E) 178
Abd al Kuri, island in Arabian Sea (12°N, 51°E) 178
Abeche, Chad (14°N, 21°E) 139
Abemama Atoll, Pacific O. (0°N, 174°E) 189
Aberdeen, Scotland (57°N, 2°W) 156
Aberdeen, SD (46°N, 99°W) 98
Aberdeen, WA (47°N, 124°W) 100
Aberystwyth (ab uh RIS twith), Wales (52°N, 4°W) 156
Abidjan (ab ih JAHN), Côte d'Ivoire (5°N, 4°W) 138
Abilene (AB uh leen), KS (39°N, 97°W) 96
Abilene, TX (32°N, 100°W) 94
Abitibi, L. (ab uh TIHB ee), Canada (49°N, 80°W) 70
Abitibi R., ON (51°N, 81°W) 70
Abkhazia, region of Georgia (43°N, 41°E) 161
Absaroka Range (ab SAHR uh kuh), WY (44°N, 110°W) 101
Abu Dhabi (ahb oo DAHB ee), U.A.E. (24°N, 55°E) 178
Abuja (ah BOO juh), Nigeria (9°N, 8°E) 138
Abuna R. (ah boo NAH), South America (10°S, 67°W) 126
Acadia N.P. (uh KAY dee uh), ME (44°N, 68°W) 89
Acapulco (ah kah POOL koh), Mexico (17°N, 100°W) 114
Accra, Ghana (6°N, 0°) 138
Aconcagua (ah kawng KAH gwah), mt. in South America (33°S, 70°W) 126
Actaeon Group, Pacific O. (21°S, 137°W) 189
Ad Dammam, Saudi Arabia (27°N, 50°E) 178
Adamaoua Plateau (ah duh MAH wuh), Africa (8°N, 15°E) 139
Adams, Mt., WA (46°N, 121°W) 100
Adamstown, Pitcairn Is. (25°S, 130°W) 189
Adana, Turkey (37°N, 35°E) 178
Addis Ababa (AD ihs AB uh buh), Ethiopia (9°N, 39°E) 140
Adelaide (AD uh layd), Australia (35°S, 138°E) 195
Adele I., Indian O. (15°S, 123°E) 195
Aden (AHD uhn), Yemen (13°N, 45°E) 178
Aden, Gulf of, Arabian Sea (13°N, 48°E) 178
Adirondack Mts., NY (44°N, 74°W) 79
Adlatok R., NL (55°N, 61°W) 72
Admiralty I., Papua New Guinea (2°S, 147°E) 188
Adriatic Sea, Europe (44°N, 13°E) 159
Aegean Sea, Mediterranean Sea (38°N, 25°E) 159
Afghanistan, country in Asia (34°N, 65°E) 180
Africa, continent 133
African (Nubian) Plate, Atlantic O. and Africa 20
African (Somalian) Plate, Indian O. and Africa 20
Agadez, Niger (17°N, 8°E) 138
Agadir, Morocco (31°N, 10°W) 136
Agalega Is., Indian O. (10°S, 57°E) 132
Agra, India (27°N, 78°E) 180
Agri, Turkey (40°N, 43°E) 161
Agrihan I., Pacific O. (19°N, 146°E) 188
Agrinion (ah GREEN yawn), Greece (39°N, 21°E) 159
Aguanish, R., QC (51°N, 63°W) 71
Aguascalientes (ah wuh skahl YEN tuhs), Mexico (22°N, 102°W) 114
Aguascalientes, state in Mexico (22°N, 102°W) 114
Aguja, Point (ah GOO hah), Peru (6°S, 81°W) 126
Agulhas, Cape (uh GUHL uhs), South Africa (35°S, 20°E) 141
Agulhas Negras, mt. in Brazil (22°S, 46°W) 127
Ahaggar Mts., Africa (25°N, 5°E) 134
Ahmadabad, India (23°N, 73°E) 180
Ahvaz, Iran (31°N, 49°E) 178
Air Mts., Niger (18°N, 8°E) 134
Airdrie, AB (50°N, 114°W) 68

Name (Pronunciation), Description (Lat., Long.) Page

Aitutaki I. (eye too TAH kee), Pacific O. (19°S, 162°W) 189
Aix-en-Provence (ayk sahn pruh VAHNS), France (44°N, 5°E) 158
Ajaccio (ah YAHCH oh), France (42°N, 9°E) 159
Ajdabiya, Libya (31°N, 20°E) 137
Akhdar Mts., Oman (24°N, 57°W) 178
Akimiski I., James Bay (53°N, 80°W) 61
Akita (ah KEET uh), Japan (40°N, 140°E) 183
Akosambo Dam, Africa (6°N, 0°) 138
Akpatok I. (AK puh tok), Hudson Str. (61°N, 67°W) 71
Akron, OH (41°N, 81°W) 91
Aksu (ahk SOO), China (41°N, 80°E) 182
Al Aqabah, Jordan (30°N, 35°E) 178
Al Aziziyah (al az ee ZEE yuh), Libya (33°N, 13°E) 136
Al Fashir (al FAH shuhr), Sudan (14°N, 25°E) 140
Al Fayyum (al fay YOOM), Egypt (29°N, 31°E) 137
Al Hudaydah, Yemen (15°N, 43°E) 178
Al Jafr, Jordan (30°N, 36°E) 178
Al Jawf, Libya (24°N, 23°E) 137
Al Kharijah, Egypt (25°N, 30°E) 137
Al Kharj, Saudi Arabia (24°N, 47°E) 178
Al Kut, Iraq (33°N, 46°E) 178
Al Marj, Libya (33°N, 21°E) 137
Al Minya, Egypt (28°N, 31°E) 137
Al Mubarraz, Saudi Arabia (23°N, 46°E) 178
Al Mukalla, Yemen (14°N, 49°E) 178
Al Qunatirah, Syria (33°N, 36°E) 178
Al Ubayyid, Sudan (13°N, 30°E) 140
Alabama, state in U.S. (33°N, 87°W) 92
Alabama R., AL (32°N, 88°W) 92
Alajuela (ah lah HWA lah), Costa Rica (10°N, 84°W) 115
Alamagan I., Pacific O. (18°N, 147°E) 188
Alamogordo (al uh muh GAWRD oh), NM (33°N, 106°W) 103
Aland Is., Finland (60°N, 21°E) 157
Alaska, state of U.S. (65°N, 155°W) 104
Alaska, Gulf of, Pacific O. (59°N, 145°W) 104
Alaska Pen., AK (55°N, 164°W) 104
Alaska Range, AK (63°N, 150°W) 104
Albacete, Spain (39°N, 2°W) 158
Albania, country in Europe (41°N, 20°E) 159
Albany, Australia (35°S, 118°E) 195
Albany, GA (32°N, 84°W) 93
Albany, NY (43°N, 74°W) 88
Albany, OR (45°N, 123°W) 100
Albany R., ON (51°N, 85°W) 70
Albemarle Sound, NC (36°N, 76°W) 91
Albert, L., Africa (2°N, 31°E) 140
Alberta, prov. in Canada (57°N, 115°W) 68–69
Alborg (AWL bawrg), Denmark (57°N, 10°E) 157
Albuquerque (AL buh kur kee), NM (35°N, 107°W) 103
Albury, Australia (36°S, 147°E) 195
Aldabra Is., Indian O. (9°S, 46°E) 133
Alenuihaha Channel (ahl uh noo ee HAH hah), HI (20°N, 156°W) 104
Aleppo, Syria (36°N, 37°E) 178
Alert Station, NU (83°N, 62°W) 62
Alesund (O leh son), Norway (62°N, 6°E) 157
Aleutian Basin, Pacific O. (60°N, 180°) 22
Aleutian Is. (uh LOO shuhn), Bering Sea (52°N, 180°) 104
Aleutian Trench, Pacific O. (50°N, 165°W) 22
Alexander Arch., Gulf of Alaska (57°N, 135°W) 104
Alexander I., Antarctica (70°S, 70°W) 200
Alexandria, Egypt (31°N, 30°E) 137
Alexandria, LA (32°N, 93°W) 95
Alexandria, MN (46°N, 95°W) 98
Alexandria, VA (39°N, 77°W) 91
Alexandrina, L., Australia (36°S, 139°E) 195
Alexis R., NL (53°N, 52°W) 72
Algeria, country in Africa (28°N, 3°E) 136

Name (Pronunciation), Description (Lat., Long.) Page

Algiers (al JEERS), Algeria (37°N, 3°E) 136
Algonquin P.P., ON (46°N, 78°W) 70
Ali Bayramli, Azerbaijan (40°N, 49°E) 161
Alicante, Spain (38°N, 1°W) 158
Alice Springs, Australia (24°S, 134°E) 195
Allahabad (al uh huh BAD), India (26°N, 82°E) 180
Allatoona L., GA (34°N, 85°W) 92
Allegheny Mts. (al uh GAY nee), U.S. (38°N, 80°W) 91
Allegheny Plateau, U.S. (39°N, 80°W) 91
Allegheny Res., U.S. (42°N, 79°W) 88
Allegheny R., PA (41°N, 80°W) 88
Allentown, PA (41°N, 75°W) 88
Alliance, NE (42°N, 103°W) 96
Alliance, OH (41°N, 81°W) 91
Allier R. (al YAY), France (46°N, 3°E) 158
Alma, QC (48°N, 72°W) 71
Almaty, Kazakhstan (43°N, 77°E) 179
Almeria (ahl may RE ah), Spain (37°N, 2°W) 158
Alofi, Niue (20°S, 170°W) 189
Alofi I., Pacific O. (15°S, 178°W) 189
Alpena, MI (45°N, 83°W) 99
Alpine, TX (30°N, 104°W) 94
Alps, mt. range in Europe (45°N, 10°E) 150
Altai Mts. (AL ty), Asia (49°N, 90°E) 182
Altamaha R., GA (32°N, 82°W) 93
Altamonte Springs (al tuh MAHNT), FL (29°N, 81°W) 93
Altiplano, plateau in Bolivia (19°S, 68°W) 127
Alton, IL (39°N, 90°W) 97
Altona, MB (49°N, 98°W) 69
Altoona, PA (40°N, 78°W) 88
Altun Mts. (ahl toon), China (40°N, 90°E) 182
Alvaro Obregon Res., Mexico (28°N, 110°W) 106
Alvorada, Brazil (12°S, 49°W) 127
Alytus (ah LEE toos), Lithuania (54°N, 24°E) 157
Am Timan, Chad (11°N, 20°E) 132
Amarillo, TX (35°N, 102°W) 94
Amazon Basin, South America (5°S, 65°W) 122
Amazon, Mouths of the, Brazil (0°, 50°W) 127
Amazon R., South America (5°S, 60°W) 127
Ambon, Indonesia (4°S, 128°E) 181
Ambovombe, Madagascar (24°S, 47°E) 141
Ambrym I., Pacific O. (16°S, 168°E) 188
American Falls Res., ID (43°N, 113°W) 101
American Samoa, poss. of U.S. (14°S, 170°W) 189
Americus, GA (32° 84°W) 93
Amery Ice Shelf, Antarctica (70°S, 70°E) 200
Ames, IA (42°N, 94°W) 97
Amherst, NS (46°N, 64°W) 72
Amiens (AM ee uhnz), France (50°N, 2°E) 158
Amirante Is. (AM uh rant), Indian O. (5°S, 53°E) 133
Amisk L., SK (55°N, 102°W) 69
Amistad Res., Mexico and U.S. (30°N, 101°W) 94
Amman, Jordan (32°N, 36°E) 178
Amol, Iran (36°N, 53°E) 178
Amritsar (uhm RIHT suhr), India (32°N, 75°E) 180
Amsterdam, Netherlands (53°N, 5°E) 158
Amsterdam I., Indian O. (38°S, 78°E) 15
Amu Darya (ahm oo DAHR yuh), r. in Asia (40°N, 63°E) 179
Amundsen Gulf, Beaufort Sea (71°N, 125°W) 60
Amundsen-Scott Station, Antarctica (90°S) 200
Amundsen Sea, Antarctica (70°S, 110°W) 200
Amur R. (ah MOOR), Asia (55°N, 125°E) 170
An Nafud (an nuh FOOD), desert in Saudi Arabia (28°N, 40°E) 178
Anadyr, Gulf of, Bering Sea (65°N, 178°W) 169
Anaheim (AN uh hym), CA (34°N, 118°W) 102
Anapolis, Brazil (16°S, 49°W) 127
Anatahan I., Pacific O. (16°N, 147°E) 188
Anatolia (an uh TOH lee uh), region of Turkey (38°N, 30°E) 178
Anatom I., Pacific O. (20°S, 170°E) 188

Name (Pronunciation), Description (Lat., Long.) Page

Anchorage, AK (61°N, 150°W) 104
Ancona (ang KOH nuh), Italy (44°N, 14°E) 159
Andaman Is., Bay of Bengal (12°N, 93°E) 180
Andaman Sea, Indian O. (12°N, 96°E) 180
Anderson, IN (40°N, 86°W) 90
Anderson, SC (35°N, 83°W) 93
Andes Mts. South America (5°S, 75°W) 122
Andijon, Uzbekistan (41°N, 72°E) 179
Andkhvoy, Afghanistan (36°N, 65°E) 180
Andorra, country in Europe (43°N, 2°E) 158
Andorra la Vella (an DAWR uh lah VEL ah), Andorra (43°N, 2°E) 158
Andros I., Atlantic O. (24°N, 78°W) 93
Androscoggin R., ME (44°N, 71°W) 89
Anegada Passage, Caribbean Sea (18°N, 64°W) 116
Angel de la Guarda I., Gulf of California (29°N, 113°W) 114
Angel Falls, waterfall in Venezuela (6°N, 63°W) 126
Angers (ahn ZHAY), France (47°N, 1°W) 158
Angikuni L., NU (62°N, 100°W) 69
Angola, country in Africa (12°S, 17°E) 141
Angola Plain, Atlantic O. (10°S, 5°E) 22
Anguilla (ang GWIL uh), island in Caribbean Sea (18°N, 63°W) 116
Anju (AHN joo), N. Korea (40°N, 126°E) 183
Ankara, Turkey (40°N, 33°E) 178
Ann, Cape, MA (43°N, 71°W) 89
Ann Arbor, MI (42°N, 84°W) 99
Annaba (an NAHB uh), Algeria (37°N, 8°E) 136
Annamite Mts., Asia (17°N, 106°E) 181
Annapolis, MD (39°N, 76°W) 91
Anniston, AL (34°N, 86°W) 92
Annobon, island in Atlantic O. (2°S, 6°E) 139
Anshan, China (41°N, 123°E) 182
Antakya, Turkey (36°N, 36°E) 178
Antalya (ant uhl YAH), Turkey (37°N, 31°E) 178
Antalya, Gulf of, Turkey (37°N, 31°E) 178
Antananarivo (ahn tuh nah nuh REE voh), Madagascar (19°S, 47°E) 141
Antanifotsy, Madagascar (20°S, 48°E) 141
Antarctic Pen., Antarctica (66°S, 60°W) 200
Antarctic Plate, Southern O. and Antarctica 20
Antarctica, continent 200
Anticosti I., QC (49°N, 62°W) 71
Antigua and Barbuda, country in Caribbean Sea (18°N, 62°W) 116
Antioch, alternative name for Antakya, Turkey (36°N, 36°E) 178
Antofagasta, Chile (24°S, 70°W) 126
Antongila Bay, Madagascar (16°S, 50°E) 141
Antsirabe, Madagascar (20°S, 47°E) 141
Antsiranana, Madagascar (12°S, 49°E) 141
Antwerp, Belgium (51°N, 4°E) 158
Aomori (OW muh ree), Japan (41°N, 141°E) 183
Aoraki/Mt. Cook, New Zealand (44°S, 170°E) 195
Apalachee Bay, FL (30°N, 85°W) 93
Apalachicola (ap uh lach uh KOHL uh), FL (30°N, 85°W) 92
Apalachicola R., FL (30°N, 85°W) 92
Apatity, Russia (67°N, 34°E) 157
Apennines, mt. range in Italy (43°N, 13°E) 159
Apia, Samoa (14°S, 172°W) 189
Apostle Is. (uh pahs uhl), L. Superior (47°N, 91°W) 99
Appalachian Mts., U.S. (35°N, 80°W) 79
Appleton, WI (44°N, 88°W) 99
Aqaba, Gulf of, Red Sea (29°N, 35°E) 178
Aqtau, Kazakhstan (44°N, 51°E) 179
Aqtobe, Kazakhstan (50°N, 57°E) 179
Aquitaine Basin, France (44°N, 1°W) 158
Arabian Desert, Egypt (26°N, 34°E) 137
Arabian Pen., Asia (20°N, 45°E) 178
Arabian Plate, Arabian Pen. 20
Arabian Sea, Indian O. (15°N, 65°E) 166
Aracaju (ar uh kuh ZHOO), Brazil (11°S, 37°W) 127
Arad, Romania (46°N, 21°E) 159
Arafura Sea (ar uh FOOR uh), Indian O. (10°S, 135°E) 190
Araguaia R. (ah rah GWAH yah), Brazil (9°S, 50°W) 127
Arak, Iran (34°N, 50°E) 178
Aral, Kazakhstan (47°N, 62°E) 179
Aral Sea (AR uhl), Asia (45°N, 60°E) 179
Arapiraca, Brazil (9°S, 37°W) 127
Arar, Saudi Arabia (31°N, 42°E) 178
Ararat, Mt., Turkey (40°N, 44°E) 178
Aras R., Asia (39°N, 47°E) 161
Arawa, Papua New Guinea (6°S, 156°E) 188
Arbil, Iraq (36°N, 44°E) 178
Arbuckle Mts., OK (34°N, 97°W) 95
Arcadia, FL (27°N, 84°W) 93
Arches N.P., UT (39°N, 110°W) 103
Arctic Lowlands, Canada (71°N, 100°W) 62
Arctic Ocean 14-15
Arctic, The, region of Europe, Asia, and North America 201
Ardabil, Iran (38°N, 48°E) 161
Ardmore, OK (34°N, 97°W) 95
Arena, Point, CA (39°N, 124°W) 102
Arendal (AH rehn dahl), Norway (58°N, 9°E) 157
Arequipa (ar uh KEE pah), Peru (16°S, 72°W) 126
Argentina, country in South America (35°S, 65°W) 126
Argentine Plain, Atlantic O. (40°S, 60°W) 22
Argun R. (ar GOON), Asia (50°N, 119°E) 182
Argyle, L., Australia (16°S, 129°E) 195
Arhus (AWR hoos), Denmark (56°N, 10°E) 157
Arica (uh REE kuh), Chile (19°S, 70°W) 126
Aripuana R. (ar uhp wuh NA), Brazil (5°S, 60°W) 127
Arizona, state in U.S. (34°N, 114°W) 102-103
Arkabutla L. (ahr kuh BUHT lay), MS (35°N, 90°W) 92
Arkansas, state in U.S. (35°N, 94°W) 95
Arkansas R., U.S. (35°N, 100°W) 78-79
Arkhangelsk (ur KAHN gihlsk), Russia (65°N, 41°E) 160
Arlington, TX (33°N, 97°W) 95
Arlington, VA (39°N, 77°W) 91
Arlington Heights, IL (42°N, 88°W) 97
Arlit, Niger (19°N, 8°E) 138
Armenia, country in Asia (40°N, 45°E) 161
Armstrong, ON (50°N, 89°W) 70
Arnhem (AHRN hem), Netherlands (52°N, 6°W) 158
Arnhem Land, Australia (13°S, 134°E) 190
Aroostook R. (uh ROOS tuhk), ME (47°N, 68°W) 89
Arorae I., Pacific O. (3°S, 177°E) 189
Arqalyq, Kazakhstan (51°N, 68°E) 179
Aru Is., Arafura Sea (6°S, 134°E) 181
Aruba, overseas part of Neth. (12°N, 70°W) 116
Arusha (uh ROOSH uh), Tanzania (3°S, 37°E) 140
Arvada, CO (40°N, 105°W) 103
Arviat, NU (62°N, 94°W) 69
As-Sib, Oman (24°N, 58°E) 178
As Suwayda, Syria (33°N, 37°E) 178
Asahi, Mt. (ah sah hee), Japan (44°N, 143°E) 183
Asahikawa (ah sah hee KAH wuh), Japan (44°N, 142°E) 183
Asansol (AHS uhn sohl), India (24°N, 87°E) 180
Asbury Park, NJ (40°N, 74°W) 88
Ascension I. (uh SEHN shuhn), island in Atlantic O. (8°S, 14°W) 132
Asheboro, NC (36°N, 80°W) 91
Asheville, NC (36°N, 83°W) 90-91
Asheweig R., ON (54°N, 87°W) 70
Ashgabat, Turkmenistan (38°N, 58°E) 179
Ashland, KY (38°N, 83°W) 90
Ashland, WI (47°N, 91°W) 99
Ashmore Is., Indian O. (12°S, 123°E) 195
Ashtabula (ash tuh byoo luh), OH (42°N, 81°W) 91
Ashuanipi, L. (ash wuh nihp ee), NL (52°N, 67°W) 72
Ashuapmushuan R. (uh shah muhsh WAHN), QC (49°N, 73°W) 71
Asia, continent 168-169
Asir, region of Saudi Arabia (18°N, 42°E) 178
Asmara, Eritrea (15°N, 39°E) 140
Aspen, CO (39°N, 107°W) 103
Assab, Eritrea (13°N, 44°E) 140
Assal, L., Africa (12°N, 42°E) 140
Assateague I. (as uh TEEG), Atlantic O. (38°N, 75°W) 91
Assiniboine, Mt. (uh SIHN uh boyn), BC (51°N, 116°W) 68
Assiniboine R., Canada (52°N, 102°W) 69
Astana, Kazakhstan (51°N, 71°E) 179
Astoria, OR (46°N, 124°W) 100
Astrakhan, Russia (46°N, 48°E) 160
Asuncion (ah SOON see awn), Paraguay (25°S, 57°W) 127
Asuncion I., Pacific O. (20°N, 145°E) 188
Aswan, Egypt (24°N, 33°E) 137
Aswan High Dam, Egypt (24°N, 33°E) 137
Asyut (as ee YOOT), Egypt (27°N, 31°E) 137
At Taif (at TAY if), Saudi Arabia (21°N, 41°E) 178
Atacama Desert, South America (23°S, 69°W) 126
Atafu Atoll, Pacific O. (9°S, 173°W) 189
Atar, Mauritania (21°N, 13°W) 136
Atbara R., Africa (17°N, 35°E) 140
Atbarah, Sudan (18°N, 33°E) 140
Atchafalaya Bay (uh CHAF uh LY uh), LA (30°N, 92°W) 95
Atchafalaya R. , LA (31°N, 92°W) 95
Atchison, KS (40°N, 95°W) 97
Athabasca, L., Canada (60°N, 109°W) 69
Athabasca R., Canada (55°N, 115°W) 68-69
Athabasca Sand Dunes P.P., SK (57°N, 109°W) 69
Athens, GA (34°N, 83°W) 93
Athens, Greece (38°N, 24°E) 159
Athens, OH (39°N, 82°W) 91
Atikaki P.W.P., MB (51°N, 90°W) 69
Atikokan, ON (49°N, 92°W) 70
Atiu I., Pacific O. (20°S, 158°W) 189
Atlanta, GA (34°N, 84°W) 92-93
Atlantic City, NJ (39°N, 75°W) 88
Atlantic Coastal Plain, U.S. (32°N, 81°W) 79
Atlantic-Indian Ridge, Atlantic and Indian O. (55°S, 20°W) 22
Atlantic Ocean 14-15
Atlas Mts., Africa (32°N, 6°W) 136
Atlin, BC (59°N, 135°W) 68
Atlin, L., BC (60°N, 133°W) 68
Atlin P.P., BC (59°N, 135°W) 68
Atol das Rocas, Brazil (4°N, 43°W) 127
Atrak R., Asia (38°N, 57°E) 178
Atrato R. (ah TRAH toh), Columbia (7°N, 77°W) 126
Attawapiskat (at uh wuh PIHS kuht), ON (53°N, 82°W) 70
Attawapiskat R., ON (53°N, 86°W) 70
Attleboro, MA (42°N, 71°W) 89
Atyrau, Kazakhstan (47°N, 52°E) 179
Au Sable R. (oh SAY buhl), MI (45°N, 84°W) 99
Au Sable R., NY (44°N, 74°W) 88
Auburn (AW buhrn), AL (33°N, 85°W) 92
Auburn, ME (44°N, 70°W) 89
Auburn, NE (40°N, 96°W) 97
Auburn, NY (43°N, 77°W) 88
Auburn, WA (47°N, 122°W) 100
Auckland (AWK luhnd), N.Z. (37°S, 175°E) 195
Auckland Is., Indian Ocean (51°S, 167°E) 15
Auglaize R. (oh GLAYZ), OH (41°N, 84°W) 90
Augrabies Falls, waterfall in South Africa (29°S, 20°E) 141
Augsburg (awgz buhrg), Germany (48°N, 11°E) 159
Augusta, GA (33°N, 82°W) 93
Augusta, ME (44°N, 70°W) 89
Aurangabad (ow RUNG uh bahd), India (20°N, 76°E) 180
Aurora, CO (40°N, 105°W) 103
Aurora, IL (42°N, 88°W) 97
Austin, MN (44°N, 93°W) 99
Austin, TX (30°N, 98°W) 95
Austral Islands, Pacific O. (25°S, 148°W) 189
Australia, country and continent 190, 195
Australian Alps, Australia (37°S, 148°E) 190
Australian Capital Terr., Australia (36°S, 149°E) 195
Australian Plate, Australia and Indian O. 20
Austria, country in Europe (47°N, 14°E) 159
Avalon Pen., NL (47°N, 53°W) 72
Avarua, Cook Islands (21°S, 160°W) 189
Aves I., Caribbean Sea (16°N, 64°W) 116
Avignon (ah vee NYAWN), France (44°N, 5°E) 158
Awasa, Ethiopia (7°N, 39°E) 140
Axel Heiberg I., Arctic O. (80°N, 92°W) 60
Aydin, Turkey (38°N, 28°E) 178
Ayers Rock, alternative name for Uluru (25°S, 131°E) 190
Ayr, Scotland (55°N, 5°W) 156
Azaouad, region of Mali (18°N, 3°W) 138

Name (Pronunciation), Description (Lat., Long.) Page

Azerbaijan, country in Europe and Asia (41°N, 48°E) 161
Azores, islands in Atlantic O. (38°N, 25°W) 133
Azov, Sea of, Europe (46°N, 37°E) 160

B

B. Everett Jordan L., NC (36°N, 79°W) 91
Bab el Mandeb, strait between Africa and Asia (13°N, 43°E) 140
Babelthuap, island in Pacific O. (8°N, 135°E) 188
Babine L. (BAH been), BC (55°N, 126°W) 68
Babruysk, Belarus (53°N, 29°E) 160
Babuyan Is. (bab BOO yahn), Luzon Strait (20°N, 123°E) 188
Bacolod (bah KOH lod), Philippines (11°N, 123°E) 181
Bad R., SD (44°N, 101°W) 98
Badajoz (bah dhah HOHTH), Spain (39°N, 7°W) 158
Badlands N.P., SD (44°N, 102°W) 98
Badlands, eroded landscape, SD (44°N, 103°W) 98
Baffin Bay, Arctic O. (74°N, 65°W) 61
Baffin I., NU (70°N, 72°W) 71
Baghdad, Iraq (33°N, 44°E) 178
Bago, Myanmar (17°N, 97°E) 181
Baguio (BAHG yo), Philippines (16°N, 121°E) 188
Bahama Is., Atlantic O. (24°N, 76°W) 93
Bahamas, country in Atlantic O. (24°N, 76°W) 93
Bahia Blanca (bu hee uh BLANG kuh), Argentina (39°S, 62°W) 126
Bahir Dar, Ethiopia (12°N, 37°E) 140
Bahr al Jabal, r. in Africa (5°N, 32°E) 140
Bahrain, country in Asia (27°N, 51°E) 178
Bahrain, Gulf of, Arabian Sea (26°N, 51°E) 178
Bai Bung, Pt., Vietnam (8°N, 105°E) 181
Baidoa, Somalia (4°N, 45°E) 140
Baie-Comeau (bay KOH moh), QC (49°N, 68°W) 71
Baikal, L., Russia (52°N, 105°E) 167
Baja California (BAH hah), peninsula in Mexico (30°N, 115°W) 114
Baja California, state in Mexico (30°N, 117°W) 114
Baja California Sur, state in Mexico (26°N, 114°W) 114
Baker City, OR (45°N, 118°W) 100
Baker I., poss. of U.S. (1°N, 176°W) 189
Baker, Mt., WA (49°N, 122°W) 100
Bakersfield, CA (35°N, 119°W) 102
Baku, Azerbaijan (40°N, 50°E) 161
Balabac Strait (buh LAHB ahk), Borneo and Palawan (8°N, 117°E) 181
Balbina Res., Brazil (2°S, 60°W) 127
Baldy Peak, AZ (34°N, 110°W) 103
Balearic Is., Mediterranean Sea (39°N, 3°E) 158
Balearic Sea, Europe (40°N, 2°E) 158
Baleine, Grande R. de la, QC (55°N, 77°W) 71
Bali, island in Flores Sea (8°S, 105°E) 181
Balikesir, Turkey (40°N, 28°E) 178
Balkan Mts., Europe (43°N, 24°E) 159
Balkan Pen., Europe (42°N, 25°E) 159
Balkanabat, Turkmenistan (40°N, 54°E) 179
Balkhash, L., Kazakhstan (47°N, 75°E) 179
Ballarat, Australia (38°S, 144°E) 195
Balqash, Kazakhstan (47°N, 75°E) 179
Balsas R., Mexico (18°N, 100°W) 106
Baltic Sea, Europe (55°N, 18°E) 157
Baltimore, MD (39°N, 77°W) 91
Baluchistan (buh loo chih STAN), region of Pakistan and Iran (28°N, 63°E) 180
Bamako, Mali (13°N, 8°W) 138
Bambari, Central African Republic (6°N, 21°E) 139
Bamenda, Cameroon (6°N, 10°E) 139
Banaba I., (bah NAH bah) Pacific O. (1°S, 170°E) 188
Bancroft, ON (45°N, 78°W) 70
Banda Aceh, Indonesia (5°N, 95°E) 181
Banda Sea, Indian O. (5°S, 128°E) 181
Bandar Abbas, Iran (27°N, 56°E) 178
Bandar Seri Begawan, Brunei (5°N, 115°E) 181
Bandung, Indonesia (7°S, 108°E) 181
Banff, AB (51°N, 115°W) 68
Banff N.P. (bamf), AB (51°N, 116°W) 68
Bangalore, India (13°N, 78°E) 180
Bangka, island in Karimata Strait (2°S, 106°E) 181
Bangkok, Thailand (14°N, 100°E) 181
Bangladesh, country in Asia (24°N, 90°E) 180
Bangor, ME (45°N, 69°W) 89
Bangui (bahng GEE), Central African Republic (4°N, 19°E) 139
Bangweulu, L. (bang wee OO loo), Zambia (11°S, 30°E) 141
Bani R., Mali (13°N, 6°W) 138
Bani Suwayf, Egypt (29°N, 31°E) 178
Banja Luka (bahn yuh LOO kuh), Bos. (45°N, 17°E) 159
Banjarmasin (bahn jur MAH sihn), Indonesia (3°S, 114°E) 181
Banjul (BAHN jool), Gambia (13°N, 17°W) 138
Banks I., Arctic O. (73°N, 120°W) 60
Banks I., Hecate Strait (53°N, 130°W) 68
Banks Is., Pacific O. (14°S, 168°E) 188
Banks Pen., New Zealand (44°S, 173°E) 190
Baotou (bow toh), China (40°N, 110°E) 182
Bar Harbor, ME (44°N, 68°W) 89
Baranavichy (BAH rah noh vee cheh), Belarus (53°N, 26°E) 160
Baranof I., Gulf of Alaska (57°N, 135°W) 104
Barbados (bahr BAY dohz), country in Caribbean Sea (14°N, 59°W) 116
Barberton, OH (41°N, 82°W) 91
Barcelona (bahr suh LOH nuh), Spain (41°N, 2°E) 158
Barcelona, Venezuela (10°N, 65°W) 126
Bardai (bahr DY), Chad (22°N, 17°E) 137
Bareilly (buh RAY lee), India (28°N, 79°E) 180
Barents Sea (BAK uhnts), Arctic O. (70°N, 40°E) 149
Bari, Italy (41°N, 17°E) 159
Barkley, L., U.S. (37°N, 88°W) 91
Barkly Tableland, plateau in Australia (16°S, 134°E) 190
Barlee, L., Australia (31°S, 121°E) 190
Barnaul (bahr nuh OOL), Russia (53°N, 83°E) 179
Barnstable, MA (42°N, 70°W) 89
Barquisimeto (bahr kee see MAY toh), Venezuela (10°N, 69°W) 126
Barranquilla (bahr uhn KEE uh), Colombia (11°N, 75°W) 126
Barrie, ON (44°N, 80°W) 70
Barrow, AK (71°N, 156°E) 104
Barrow I., Indian O. (21°S, 115°E) 195
Barrow, Point, AK (71°N, 156°W) 104
Barrow R., Ireland (52°N, 7°W) 156
Barstow (BAHR stoh), CA (35°N, 117°W) 102
Bartholomew Bayou, r. in U.S. (33°N, 92°W) 95
Bartlesville, OK (37°N, 96°W) 95
Bartlett, TN (37°N, 90°W) 90
Basel (BAHZ uhl), Switzerland (48°N, 8°E) 159
Basin and Range, U.S. (40°N, 118°W) 102
Baskatong Res., QC (47°N, 76°W) 70
Basra, Iraq (31°N, 48°E) 178
Bass Strait, Australia and Tasmania (40°S, 145°E) 190
Basse-Terre, Guadeloupe (16°N, 62°W) 116
Basseterre, St. Kitts and Nevis (17°N, 63°W) 116
Bastia, France (43°N, 9°E) 159
Bastrop, LA (33°N, 92°W) 95
Bata, Equatorial Guinea (2°N, 10°E) 139
Batabano Gulf (baht uh buh NOH), Caribbean Sea (22°N, 83°W) 89
Bath, England (51°N, 2°W) 156
Bathurst, NB (48°N, 66°W) 72
Bathurst I., Arctic O. (76°N, 100°W) 60
Bathurst I., Timor Sea (11°S, 130°E) 195
Batna, Algeria (36°N, 6°E) 136
Baton Rouge (BAT uhn ROOZH), LA (31°N, 91°W) 95
Battle Creek, MI (42°N, 85°W) 99
Battle R., AB (52°N, 110°W) 68–69
Batu Is., Indonesia (0°, 99°E) 181
Batumi, Georgia (41°N, 42°E) 161
Bauchi (bow chee), Nigeria (10°N, 10°E) 138
Baura, Brazil (22°S, 49°W) 127
Bavaria, state in Germany (49°N, 11°E) 159
Bawku, Ghana (11°N, 0°) 138
Bay City, MI (44°N, 84°W) 99
Bay Islands, Honduras (16°N, 87°W) 115
Bayou d'Arbonne L. (BY yoo dahr BON), LA (33°N, 92°W) 95
Bayramaly, Turkmenistan (38°N, 62°E) 179
Bayreuth (by ROYT), Germany (50°N, 12°E) 159
Baytown, TX (30°N, 95°W) 95
Beagle Channel, South America (56°S, 66°W) 126
Bear I., James Bay (54°N, 81°W) 70
Bear L., U.S. (42°N, 111°W) 101
Bear Lodge Mts., WY (45°N, 104°W) 101
Bear R., ID (43°N, 112°W) 101
Beatrice (bee AH trus), NE (40°N, 97°W) 96
Beaufort Sea, Arctic O. (72°N, 135°W) 60
Beaumont (BOH mont), TX (30°N, 94°W) 95
Beaver I., L. Michigan (46°N, 86°W) 99
Beaver L., AR (36°N, 94°W) 95
Beaver R., Canada (54°N, 111°W) 69
Beaverhead Mts., ID (44°N, 113°W) 101
Beaverton, OR (45°N, 123°W) 100
Bechar (bay SHAHR), Algeria (32°N, 2°W) 132
Beckley, WV (38°N, 81°W) 91
Bedford, IN (39°N, 87°W) 90
Beersheba, Israel (31°N, 35°E) 178
Beijing (bay JIHNG), China (40°N, 116°E) 182
Beira (BAY ruh), Mozambique (20°S, 35°E) 141
Beirut (bay ROOT), Lebanon (33°N, 36°E) 178
Bejaia, Algeria (37°N, 5°E) 136
Belarus (BEHL ah ruhs), country in Europe (52°N, 27°E) 160
Belcher Is., Hudson Bay (56°N, 79°W) 71
Belem (buh LEM), Brazil (1°S, 48°W) 127
Belep Is., Pacific O. (20°S, 164°E) 188
Belfast, Northern Ireland (55°N, 6°W) 156
Belgium (BEL jum), country in Europe (51°N, 5°E) 158
Belgorod (BYEHL guh rut), Russia (51°N, 37°E) 160
Belgrade, Serbia (45°N, 21°E) 159
Belgrano II, Antarctica (78°N, 31°W) 200
Belize (buh LEEZ), country in Central America (17°N, 89°W) 115
Belize City, Belize (18°N, 88°W) 115
Bell R., QC (50°N, 78°W) 71
Bella Bella, BC (52°N, 128°W) 68
Bella Coola, BC (52°N, 127°W) 68
Belle Fourche R., U.S. (44°N, 105°W) 101
Belle Glade, FL (27°N, 81°W) 93
Belle Isle, Strait of, Canada (52°N, 57°W) 72
Bellefontaine (behl FOWNT uhn), OH (40°N, 84°W) 90
Belleville, IL (39°N, 90°W) 97
Belleville, ON (44°N, 77°W) 70
Bellevue (BEHL vyoo), NE (41°N, 96°W) 96
Bellevue, WA (48°N, 122°W) 100
Bellingham, WA (49°N, 123°W) 100
Bellingshausen Sea (BEH lingz HOWZ ehn), Antarctica (68°S, 85°W) 200
Bello, Colombia (6°N, 76°W) 126
Belmopan (bel moh PAN), Belize (17°N, 89°W) 115
Belo Horizonte (BAY loh hawr uh ZAHN tee), Brazil (20°S, 44°W) 127
Beloit (buh LOYT), WI (43°N, 89°W) 99
Bemidji (buh MIJ ee), MN (47°N, 95°W) 98
Ben Nevis, mt. in Scotland (57°N, 5°W) 156
Bend, OR (44°N, 121°W) 100
Bengal, Bay of (ben GAWL), Indian O. (17°N, 90°E) 180
Bengaluru, alternative name for Bangalore (13°N, 78°E) 180
Benghazi (ben GAH zee), Libya (32°N, 20°E) 137
Benguela, Angola (13°S, 13°E) 141
Beni R., Bolivia (14°S, 68°W) 127
Benin, country in Africa (8°N, 2°E) 138
Benin, Bight of, gulf in Africa (6°N, 3°E) 138
Benin City, Nigeria (6°N, 6°E) 138
Bennington, VT (43°N, 73°W) 89
Bentley Subglacial Trench, Antarctica (78°S, 110°W) 200
Benton Harbor, MI (42°N, 87°W) 99
Benue R. (BAYN way), Africa (8°N, 9°E) 138
Berbera, Somalia (10°N, 45°E) 140
Berberati, Central African Republic (4°N, 16°E) 139
Berea (buh REE uh), KY (38°N, 84°W) 90
Berens R., Canada (52°N, 97°W) 69
Berezniki (behr AWZ nyu ke), Russia (59°N, 57°E) 160
Bergen, Norway (60°N, 5°E) 157
Bering Sea (BAYR ing), Pacific O. (57°N, 175°W) 201
Bering Strait, U.S. and Russia (65°N, 168°W) 104

Name (Pronunciation), Description (Lat., Long.) Page

Berkeley, CA (38°N, 122°W) 102
Berkner I., Antarctica (80°S, 45°W) 200
Berkshire Hills, MA (42°N, 73°W) 89
Berlin, Germany (52°N, 13°E) 159
Berlin, NH (44°N, 71°W) 89
Bermejo R., South America (25°S, 61°W) 126
Bermuda Is. (buhr MYOO duh), Atlantic O. (32°N, 65°W) 53
Bern, Switzerland (47°N, 7°E) 159
Besancon (buh ZAN suhn), France (47°N, 6°E) 158
Bessemer, AL (33°N, 87°W) 92
Bethany, MO (40°N, 94°W) 97
Bethel, AK (61°N, 162°W) 104
Bethel Park, PA (40°N, 80°W) 88
Bethlehem, PA (41°N, 75°W) 88
Bettendorf, IA (42°N, 91°W) 97
Bhagalpur (BAHG uhl poor), India (25°N, 87°E) 180
Bhopal (boh PAHL), India (23°N, 77°E) 180
Bhutan (boo TAHN), country in Asia (28°N, 91°E) 180
Biak (bee YAK), island in Pacific O. (1°S, 136°E) 181
Bialystok (bee AHL uh stawk), Poland (53°N, 23°E) 159
Biddeford, ME (43°N, 69°W) 89
Bie Plateau, Angola (13°S, 17°E) 141
Bielefeld (BEE luh felt), Germany (52°N, 9°E) 159
Bien Hoa (bee EHN WAH), Vietnam (11°N, 107°E) 181
Bienville, L. (bee ehn vihl), QC (55°N, 73°W) 71
Big Belt Mts., MT (46°N, 111°W) 101
Big Bend Dam, SD, (44°N, 100°W) 98
Big Bend N.P., TX (29°N, 103°W) 94
Big Black R., MS (33°N, 90°W) 92
Big Blue R., U.S. (41°N, 97°W) 96
Big Cypress Swamp, FL (26°N, 81°W) 93
Big L., ME (45°N, 68°W) 89
Big Lost R., ID (44°N, 114°W) 101
Big Muddy R., IL (38°N, 89°W) 97
Big Sandy R., U.S. (38°N, 83°W) 90
Big Sioux R. (soo), SD (44°N, 97°W) 98
Big Spring, TX (32°N, 102°W) 94
Big Stone L., MN (45°N, 97°W) 98
Big Trout L., ON (54°N, 90°W) 70
Bighorn L., U.S. (45°N, 108°W) 101
Bighorn Mts., U.S. (45°N, 108°W) 101
Bighorn R., U.S. (44°N, 108°W) 101
Bijagos Is., Atlantic Ocean (11°N, 17°W) 138
Bikini Atoll, Pacific O. (12°N, 166°E) 188
Bilbao (bil BAH oh), Spain (43°N, 3°W) 158
Billings, MT (46°N, 109°W) 101
Biloxi, MS (30°N, 89°W) 92
Bimini Is. (BIHM uh nee), Straits of Florida, (26°N, 79°W) 93
Binghamton, NY (42°N, 76°W) 88
Bioko (bee OH koh), island in Gulf of Guinea (4°N, 9°E) 139
Birau, Central African Rep. (10°N, 23°E) 139
Birch Mts., AB (58°N, 113°W) 68
Birmingham, AL (34°N, 87°W) 92
Birmingham, England (53°N, 2°W) 156
Birnie I., Pacific O. (4°S, 172°W) 189
Biscay, Bay of (BIS kay), Europe (45°N, 5°W) 158
Biscay Plain, Atlantic O. (45°N, 5°W) 22
Biscayne N.P. (bis KAYN), FL (25°N, 80°W) 93
Biscotasi L., ON (47°N, 82°W) 70
Bishkek, Kyrgyzstan (43°N, 75°E) 179
Bishop, CA (37°N, 118°W) 102
Biskra, Algeria (35°N, 6°E) 136
Bismarck, ND (47°N, 101°W) 98
Bismarck Archipelago, Pacific O. (3°S, 151°E) 188
Bismarck Sea, Pacific O. (4°S, 147°E) 188
Bissau (bih SAW), Guinea-Bissau (12°N, 16°W) 138
Bitola (BEET uhl yah), North Macedonia (41°N, 21°E) 159
Bitterroot Range, U.S. (47°N, 115°W) 100–101
Bitterroot R., MT (46°N, 114°W) 101
Biwa L., Japan (35°N, 136°E) 183
Biysk (beesk), Russia (53°N, 85°E) 179
Bizerte, Tunisia (37°N, 10°E) 136
Black Canyon of the Gunnison N.P., CO (38°N, 108°W) 103
Black Forest, region of Germany (48°N, 8°E) 159
Black Hills, SD (44°N, 104°W) 98
Black L., SK (59°N, 105°W) 69
Black Mesa (may suh), AZ (37°N, 110°W) 103
Black R., AR (36°N, 91°W) 95
Black R., NY (44°N, 77°W) 88
Black R., Vietnam (22°N, 104°E) 181
Black Sea, Europe and Asia (43°N, 35°E) 160
Black Sea Lowland, Ukraine (46°N, 30°E) 149
Black Volta R., Africa (12°N, 3°W) 138
Black Warrior R., AL (34°N, 87°W) 92
Blackfoot R., MT (47°N, 113°W) 101
Blacksburg, VA (37°N, 81°W) 91
Blagoveshchensk (blah gah VYE she hinsk), Russia (50°N, 128°E) 182
Blair, NE (42°N, 96°W) 96
Blanc, Cape (blangk), Africa (21°N, 18°W) 136
Blanc, Mont (blahn, mawn), France and Italy (45°N, 7°E) 158
Blanca Bay (BLAHNG kuh), Argentina (39°S, 62°W) 126
Blanchard R., OH (41°N, 84°W) 90
Blanco, Cape (BLANG koh), OR (43°N, 125°W) 100
Blanquilla I., Caribbean Sea (12°N, 65°W) 116
Blantyre, Malawi (16°S, 35°E) 141
Blenheim, New Zealand (42°S, 173°E) 195
Blind River, ON (46°N, 83°W) 70
Bloemfontein (BLOOM fahn tayn), South Africa (29°S, 26°E) 141
Bloodvein R., Canada (52°N, 96°W) 69
Bloomington, IL (41°N, 89°W) 97
Bloomington, IN (39°N, 87°W) 90
Bloomington, MN (44°N, 96°W) 99
Blue Mt., PA (41°N, 76°W) 88
Blue Mts, U.S. (45°N, 119°W) 100
Blue Nile, r. in Africa (14°N, 34°E) 140
Blue Ridge, U.S. (36°N, 82°W) 91
Bluefield, WV (37°N, 81°W) 91
Bluefields, Nicaragua (12°N, 84°W) 115
Blumenau (BLU mehn ohu), Brazil (27°S, 49°W) 127
Blytheville, AR (36°N, 90°W) 95
Bo, Sierra Leone (8°N, 11°W) 138
Bo Gulf, Yellow Sea (38°N, 120°E) 182
Boa Vista (boh uh VEESH tuh), Brazil (3°N, 61°W) 127
Bobo Dioulasso (BOH boh doo LAS oh), Burkina Faso (11°N, 4°W) 138
Boca Raton (boh kuh ruh tohn), FL (26°N, 80°W) 93
Bodo, Norway (67°N, 13°E) 157
Bogalusa (boh guh LOO suh), LA (31°N, 90°W) 95
Bogota (boh guh TAH), Colombia (4°N, 74°W) 126
Bogue, Mauritania (17°N, 15°W) 136
Bohemia (boh HEE mee uh), region of Czech Rep. (50°N, 14°E) 159
Bohol (boh HOHL), island in Philippine Sea (9°N, 125°E) 188
Boise (BOY zee), ID (44°N, 116°W) 100
Boise R., ID (44°N, 116°W) 100
Boke, Guinea (11°N, 14°W) 138
Bokna Fiord, Norway (59°N, 6°E) 157
Bolivia (boh LIHV ee uh), country in South America (17°S, 65°W) 127
Bologna (buh LOHN yuh), Italy (44°N, 11°E) 173
Bolzano (bohlt SAHN oh), Italy (47°N, 11°E) 173
Boma, Dem. Rep. Congo (6°S, 13°E) 139
Bombay, alternative name for Mumbai (19°N, 73°E) 180
Bonaire, overseas part of Neth. (12°N, 68°W) 116
Bonavista Bay, NL (49°N, 53°W) 72
Bonifacio, Strait of (bahn uh FAHCH oh), Mediterranean Sea (41°N, 9°E) 159
Bonin Is., Philippine Sea (27°N, 141°E) 188
Bonn, Germany (51°N, 7°E) 159
Bonneville Dam, WA (46°N, 122°W) 100
Boosaaso, Somalia (11°N, 49°E) 140
Boothia, Gulf of (BOO thee uh), NU (72°N, 91°W) 60–61
Boothia Pen., NU (71°N, 94°W) 60–61
Bora-Bora, island in Pacific O. (17°S, 152°W) 189
Borah Pk., ID (44°N, 114°W) 101
Boras, Sweden (58°N, 13°E) 157
Bordeaux (bawr DOH), France (45°N, 1°W) 158
Borgne L. (BAWRN), LA (30°N, 90°W) 95
Borneo, island in South China Sea (0°, 113°E) 181
Bornholm, island in Baltic Sea (55°N, 15°E) 157
Bosnia-Herzegovina (hert suh goh VEE nuh), country in Europe (44°N, 18°E) 159
Bosporus (BAHS puhr uhs), strait in Turkey (41°N, 29°E) 178
Bossier City (BOH zhur), LA (33°N, 94°W) 95
Boston, MA (42°N, 71°W) 89
Boston Mts., AR (36°N, 93°W) 95
Bothnia, Gulf of, Baltic Sea (62°N, 20°E) 157
Botswana, country in Africa (22°S, 24°E) 141
Bouake (BWAH kay), Côte d'Ivoire (7°N, 5°W) 138
Bouar (BOO ahr), Central African Republic (6°N, 16°E) 139
Bouarfa, Morocco (32°N, 2°W) 136
Bougainville (BOO guhn vihl), island in Solomon Sea (6°S, 155°E) 188
Boulder (BOHL duhr), CO (40°N, 105°W) 103
Boulder City, NV (36°N, 115°W) 102
Bountiful, UT (41°N, 112°W) 103
Bounty Is., Pacific Ocean (48°S, 179°E) 195
Bow R. (BOH), AB (51°N, 113°W) 68–69
Bowen, Australia (20°S, 148°E) 195
Bowling Green, KY (37°N, 86°W) 90
Bowling Green, OH (41°N, 84°W) 90
Bowron Lake P.P., BC (53°N, 123°W) 68
Boysen Res., WY (43°N, 108°W) 101
Bozeman (BOHZ muhn), MT (46°N, 110°W) 101
Bradenton, FL (27°N, 83°W) 93
Bradford, England (54°N, 2°W) 156
Braga, Portugal (41°N, 8°W) 158
Brahmaputra R., (brah muh POO truh), Asia (27°N, 92°E) 180
Braila (bruh EE luh), Romania (45°N, 28°E) 159
Brainerd, MN (46°N, 94°W) 98
Brampton, ON (44°N, 80°W) 70
Branco R. (brang koh), South America (0°, 62°W) 127
Brandon, MB (50°N, 100°W) 69
Branford, FL (30°N, 83°W) 93
Branson, MO (37°N, 93°W) 97
Bras d'Or L. (brad AWR), NS (46°N, 61°W) 72
Brasilia (brah SEEL yuh), Brazil (16°S, 48°W) 127
Brasov (brah SHAWV), Romania (46°N, 26°E) 159
Bratislava (brah tuh SLAH vuh), Slovakia (48°N, 17°E) 159
Bratsk Res., Russia (55°N, 102°E) 167
Brattleboro, VT (43°N, 73°W) 89
Braunschweig (BROWN shvyg), Germany (52°N, 10°E) 159
Brazil, country in South America (10°S, 55°W) 127
Brazilian Highlands, Brazil (17°S, 48°W) 127
Brazos R. (BRAZ uhs), TX (32°N, 97°W) 94–95
Brazzaville, Congo Rep. (4°S, 15°E) 139
Bremen (BREHM uhn), Germany (53°N, 9°E) 159
Bremerhaven (brem uhr HAHV uhn), Germany (54°N, 9°E) 159
Bremerton, WA (48°N, 123°W) 100
Brescia (BRESH uh), Italy (46°N, 10°E) 159
Brest, Belarus (52°N, 24°E) 160
Brest, France (48°N, 5°W) 158
Breton Sound (BREHT uhn), Gulf of Mexico (29°N, 89°W) 95
Brewton, AL (31°N, 87°W) 92
Bridgeport, CT (41°N, 73°W) 89
Bridgetown, Barbados (13°N, 60°W) 116
Brindisi (BRIN duh zee), Italy (41°N, 18°E) 159
Brisbane (BRIHS bayn), Australia (27°S, 153°E) 195
Bristol, England (51°N, 3°W) 156
Bristol, VA and TN (37°N, 80°W) 91
Bristol Bay, AK (58°N, 159°W) 104
Bristol Channel, United Kingdom (51°N, 3°W) 156
British Columbia, prov. in Canada (55°N, 125°W) 68
British Isles, Europe (52°N, 7°W) 156
Brittany, region of France (48°N, 4°W) 158
Brno (BUHR noh), Czech Republic (49°N, 17°E) 159
Broadback R., QC (51°N, 79°W) 71
Brockton, MA (42°N, 71°W) 89
Brockville, ON (45°N, 76°W) 70
Broken Arrow, OK (36°N, 96°W) 95
Broken Bow Res., OK (34°N, 95°W) 95
Broken Hill, Australia (32°S, 142°E) 195
Brookings, SD (44°N, 97°W) 98
Brooks Range, AK (67°N, 155°W) 78
Broome, Australia (18°S, 122°E) 195
Brownsville, TX (26°N, 97°W) 95

Name (Pronunciation), Description (Lat., Long.) Page

Brownwood, TX (32°N, 99°W) 94
Browse I., Indian O. (12°S, 123°E) 195
Bruce Peninsula N.P., ON (45°N, 81°W) 70
Brule, L., NL (52°N, 64°W) 72
Brunei (broon EYE), country in Asia (4°N, 114°E) 181
Brunswick, GA (31°N, 81°W) 93
Brunswick, ME (44°N, 70°W) 89
Brussels, Belgium (51°N, 4°E) 158
Bryan, TX (31°N, 96°W) 95
Bryansk (bree ANSK), Russia (53°N, 34°E) 160
Bryce Canyon N.P. (brys), UT (38°N, 112°W) 103
Bucaramanga (boo kuh ruh MAHNG guh), Colombia (7°N, 73°W) 126
Buchanan, Liberia (6°N, 10°W) 138
Buchanan, L., TX (31°N, 98°W) 94
Bucharest (byoo kuh REST), Romania (44°N, 26°E) 159
Budapest (BOO duh pest), Hungary (47°N, 19°E) 159
Buenaventura (bway nuh vehn TOOR uh), Colombia (4°N, 77°W) 126
Buenos Aires (bway nohs EYE rays), Argentina (35°S, 58°W) 126
Buffalo, NY (43°N, 79°W) 88
Buffalo, SD (46°N, 104°W) 98
Buffalo, WY (44°N, 107°W) 101
Buffalo Narrows, SK (57°N, 109°W) 69
Bug R. (boog), Europe (53°N, 22°E) 159
Bujumbura (boo juhm BOOR uh), Burundi (3°S, 29°E) 140
Buka I., Pacific O. (5°S, 155°E) 188
Bukavu, Dem. Rep. Congo (3°S, 29°E) 139
Bulawayo (boo luh WAH yo), Zimbabwe (20°S, 29°E) 141
Bulgaria, country in Europe (43°N, 25°E) 159
Bull Shoals L., U.S. (36°N, 93°W) 95
Bumba, Dem. Rep. Congo (2°N, 22°E) 139
Bunbury, Australia (33°S, 116°E) 195
Bundaberg, Australia (25°S, 152°E) 195
Burao, Somalia (10°N, 46°E) 140
Buraydah, Saudi Arabia (26°N, 44°E) 178
Burgas (boor gahs), Bulgaria (42°N, 27°E) 159
Burkina Faso (bur KEE nuh FAH soh), country in Africa (12°N, 4°W) 138
Burlington, IA (41°N, 91°W) 97
Burlington, NC (36°N, 80°W) 91
Burlington, VT (45°N, 73°W) 89
Burma, alternative name for Myanmar (22°N, 95°E) 181
Burnaby, BC (49°N, 123°W) 68
Burns L., BC (54°N, 126°W) 68
Burntwood R., MB (56°N, 98°W) 69
Bursa, Turkey (40°N, 29°E) 178
Buru (BOO roo), I. in Molucca Sea (3°S, 127°E) 181
Burundi (buh RUHN dee), country in Africa (3°S, 30°E) 140
Butte (byoot), MT (46°N, 113°W) 101
Button Bay, MB (58°N, 93°W) 69
Butuan (boo too AHN), Philippines (8°N, 126°E) 181
Buxoro, Uzbekistan (40°N, 64°E) 178
Buzmeyin, Turkmenistan (38°N, 58°E) 179
Bydgoszcz (BID gawsh), Poland (53°N, 18°E) 159

C

Caballo Res. (kuh BAH yoh), NM (33°N, 107°W) 103
Cabinda (kuh BEEN duh), terr. of Angola (5°S, 12°E) 141
Cabonga Res., QC (47°N, 77°W) 71
Cabora Bassa Dam, Africa (16°S, 32°E) 141
Cabot Strait, between NS and NL (48°N, 60°W) 72
Cacak (CHAH chawk), Serbia (44°N, 20°E) 159
Cacares (KAH tha rays), Spain (39°N, 6°W) 158
Caddo L. (KAD oh), U.S. (33°N, 94°W) 95
Cadillac, MI (44°N, 85°W) 99
Cadiz, Spain (37°N, 6°W) 158
Caen (kahn), France (49°N, 0°) 158
Cagliari (KAHL yuh ree), Italy (39°N, 9°E) 159
Cairns (kayrns), Australia (17°S, 146°E) 195
Cairo (KY roh), Egypt (30°N, 31°E) 137
Cairo (KAY roh), IL (37°N, 89°W) 97
Calais (KAL ay), France (51°N, 2°E) 158
Calcanhar, Point, Brazil (5°S, 35°W) 127
Calcasieu L. (KAL kuh shoo), LA (30°N, 94°W) 95
Calcasieu R., LA (31°N, 93°W) 95
Calcutta (kal KUT uh), alternative name for Kolkata (23°N, 88°E) 180
Caldwell, ID (44°N, 117°W) 100
Calexico, CA (33°N, 116°W) 102
Calgary (KAL guh ree), AB (51°N, 114°W) 68
Cali (KAH lee), Colombia (3°N, 77°W) 126
Calicut, alternative name for Kozhikode (11°N, 76°E) 180
California, state in U.S. (38°N, 121°W) 102
California Aqueduct, CA (36°N, 120°W) 102
California, Gulf of, Pacific O. (28°N, 112°W) 114
Callao (kah YAH oh), Peru (12°S, 77°W) 126
Caloosahatchee R. (kuh loo suh HACH ee), FL (27°N, 82°W) 93
Calumet City (kal yuh MEHT), IL (42°N, 88°W) 97
Cambodia, country in Asia, (13°N, 105°E) 181
Cambridge (KAYM brihj), England (52°N, 0°) 156
Cambridge, MA (42°N, 71°W) 89
Cambridge, OH (40°N, 82°W) 91
Cambridge Bay, NU (69°N, 105°W) 60
Camden, NJ (40°N, 75°W) 88
Cameroon (kam uh ROON), country in Africa (6°N, 12°E) 139
Cameroon Mt., Cameroon (5°N, 9°E) 139
Campbell Plateau, Pacific O. (50°S, 165°E) 22
Campbell River, BC (50°N, 125°W) 68
Campbellton, NB (48°N, 67°W) 72
Campeche (kam PAY chay), Mexico (20°N, 91°W) 114
Campeche, state in Mexico (19°N, 90°W) 114
Campeche, Bay of, Gulf of Mexico (18°N, 94°W) 114
Campina Grande, Brazil (7°S, 36°W) 127
Campinas (kam PEE nuhs), Brazil (23°S, 47°W) 127
Campo Grande (kahm poo GRAN dee), Brazil (20°S, 55°W) 127
Campos (KAM puhs), Brazil (22°S, 41°W) 127
Campos, plain in South America (22°S, 50°W) 127
Camrose, AB (53°N, 113°W) 68-69
Can Tho (kuhn TOH), Vietnam (10°N, 105°E) 181
Canada, country in North America (60°N, 100°W) 60-61
Canadian R., U.S. (36°N, 102°W) 76-77
Canadian Shield, region of Canada (60°N, 101°W) 60-61
Canandaigua L. (kan uhn DAY gwuh), NY (43°N, 77°W) 88
Canary Is., Atlantic O. (28°N, 16°W) 136
Canaveral, Cape, FL (29°N, 80°W) 93
Canberra (KAN behr uh), Australia (35°S, 149°E) 195
Cancun, Mexico (21°N, 87°W) 114
Candlewood, L., CT (41°N, 74°W) 88-89
Caniapiscau Res. (kan ee uh PIHS koh), QC (54°N, 70°W) 71
Caniapiscau R., QC (55°N, 70°W) 71
Cannonball R., ND (46°N, 102°W) 98
Canoas, Brazil (30°S, 51°W) 127
Canso, NS (45°N, 61°W) 72
Cantabrian Mts. (kan TAH bree uhn), Spain (43°N, 6°W) 158
Canterbury, England (51°N, 1°E) 156
Canton (KAN tuhn), OH (41°N, 81°W) 91
Canyon Ferry L., MT (46°N, 112°W) 101
Canyonlands N.P., UT (38°N, 110°W) 103
Cap d'Ambre, cape in Madagascar (11°S, 50°E) 141
Cap Sainte Marie, cape in Madagascar (25°S, 46°E) 141
Cape Breton Highlands N.P., NS (47°N, 63°W) 72
Cape Breton I., NS (47°N, 61°W) 72
Cape Coral, city in FL (27°N, 82°W) 93
Cape Fear R., NC (35°N, 79°W) 91
Cape Girardeau (juh RAHR doh), MO (37°N, 90°W) 97
Cape Plain, Atlantic O. (40°S, 15°E) 22
Cape Town, South Africa (34°S, 18°E) 141
Cape Verde, country in Atlantic O. (16°N, 25°W) 12
Cape Verde Plain, Atlantic O. (15°N, 25°W) 22
Cape York Pen., Australia (13°S, 143°E) 195
Capitol Reef N.P., UT (38°N, 111°W) 103
Caprivi Strip, region of Africa (18°S, 22°E) 141
Caracas (kuh RAH kuhs), Venezuela (11°N, 67°W) 126
Carrara, Italy (44°N, 10°E) 159
Caratasca Lagoon (kahr uh TAHS kuh), Honduras (15°N, 83°W) 115
Carbondale, IL (38°N, 89°W) 97
Carcassonne (kar ka SOHN), France (43°N, 2°E) 158
Carcross, YT (60°N, 135°W) 68
Cardiff (KAHR dif), Wales (52°N, 3°W) 156
Cardston, AB (49°N, 113°W) 68
Caribbean Plate, Caribbean Sea 16
Caribbean Sea (kar uh BEE uhn), Atlantic O. (15°N, 80°W) 106-107
Caribou (KAR uh boo), ME (47°N, 68°W) 89
Caribou Mts., AB (59°N, 115°W) 68
Caribou River P.W.P., MB (59°N, 96°W) 69
Carlsbad, NM (32°N, 104°W) 103
Carlsbad Caverns N.P., NM (32°N, 105°W) 103
Carlyle L. (kahr LYL), IL (39°N, 89°W) 97
Carnarvon, Australia (25°S, 114°E) 195
Caroline Atoll, Pacific O. (10°S, 150°W) 189
Caroline Is., Pacific O. (8°N, 140°E) 188
Carpathian Mts. (kahr PAY thee un), Europe (49°N, 19°E) 159
Carpentaria, Gulf of, Australia (14°S, 140°E) 190
Carson City, NV (39°N, 120°W) 102
Carson R., U.S. (39°N, 120°W) 102
Carson Sink, seasonal lake in NV (40°N, 118°W) 102
Cartagena (kahr tah HAY nah), Colombia (10°N, 75°W) 126
Cartagena, Spain (38°N, 1°W) 158
Cartier I., Indian O. (13°S, 124°E) 195
Cartwright, NL (54°N, 57°W) 72
Cary, NC (36°N, 79°W) 91
Casa Grande (kas uh GRAN dee), AZ (33°N, 112°W) 103
Casablanca (kas uh BLANG kuh), Morocco (34°N, 8°W) 136
Cascade Range (kas KAYD), U.S. (42°N, 122°W) 78
Cascade Res., ID (45°N, 116°W) 100
Casco Bay (KAS koh), ME (44°N, 70°W) 89
Casey Station, Antarctica (66°S, 111°E) 200
Casper, WY (43°N, 106°W) 101
Caspian Depression, Russia (47°N, 47°E) 160
Caspian Sea, Europe and Asia (42°N, 50°E) 149
Cassiar Mts, Canada (59°N, 130°W) 68
Castries, Saint Lucia (14°N, 61°W) 116
Cat I., Bahamas (24°N, 75°W) 93
Catalonia, region in Spain (42°N, 3°E) 158
Catania, Italy (38°N, 15°E) 159
Catanzaro, Italy (39°N, 17°E) 159
Catskill Mts., NY (42°N, 75°W) 88
Cauca R., Colombia (7°N, 76°W) 115
Caucasus Mts. (KAW kuh suhs), Europe and Asia (44°N, 41°E) 151
Cauvery Falls (KOH vuh ree), India (12°N, 77°E) 180
Cauvery R., India (11°N, 79°E) 180
Caxias (KAY sheh ayzh), Brazil (5°S, 43°W) 127
Caxias de Sul (KAY sheh ayzh do SOHL), Brazil (29°S, 51°W) 127
Cayenne (ky EHN), Fr. Guiana (5°N, 52°W) 127
Cayman Is. (KAY muhn), Caribbean Sea (19°N, 81°W) 107
Cayuga L. (kuh OO guh), NY (42°N, 77°W) 88
Cebu (seh BOO), Philippines (10°N, 124°E) 181
Cedar City (SEED uhr), UT (38°N, 113°W) 102
Cedar Creek L., TX (32°N, 96°W) 95
Cedar Falls, IA (42°N, 92°W) 97
Cedar L., MB (53°N, 100°W) 69
Cedar R., IA (42°N, 92°W) 97
Cedar Rapids, IA (42°N, 92°W) 97
Cedros I. (SAY druhs), Mexico (28°N, 115°W) 114
Celebes Sea, Asia (3°N, 122°E) 181
Celtic Sea (KEL tik), Europe (50°N, 8°W) 156
Center Hill L., TN (36°N, 86°W) 90
Central African Republic, country in Africa (7°N, 20°E) 139
Central America, region in North America (15°N, 90°W) 115
Central Lowland, U.S. (41°N, 90°W) 77
Central Lowlands, Australia (22°S, 142°E) 191
Central Makran Range, Asia (26°N, 62°E) 180
Central Patricia, ON (51°N, 90°W) 70
Central Russian Upland, Russia (55°N, 34°E) 149
Central Siberian Plateau, Russia (68°N, 98°E) 170
Central Valley, Chile (36°S, 72°W) 126
Ceram (SAY rahm), I. in Banda Sea (3°S, 129°E) 181
Ceram Sea, Indian O. (2°S, 130°E) 181

Name (Pronunciation), Description (Lat., Long.) Page

Cerf I., Indian O. (9°S, 51°E)....133
Ceuta (SAY oo tuh), terr. of Spain (36°N, 5°W)....158
Ceva-i-Ra, island in Pacific O. (22°S, 174°E)....189
Cevennes, mt. range in France (44°N, 4°E)....158
Chaco Canyon (CHAHK oh), NM (36°N, 108°W)....103
Chad, country in Africa (15°N, 18°E)....132
Chad, L., Africa (13°N, 14°E)....139
Chadron (SHAD ruhn), NE (43°N, 103°W)....96
Chagos Archipelago, island group in Indian O. (6°S, 73°E)....15
Chagos Laccadive Plateau, Indian O. (15°N, 70°E)....22
Chalan Kanoa, Saipan (15°N, 146°E)....188
Chaleur Bay (shuh LOOR), Canada (48°N, 65°W)....72
Chambal R., India (25°N, 76°E)....180
Chamberlain L., ME (46°N, 71°W)....89
Champaign (sham PAYN), IL (40°N, 88°W)....97
Champlain, L. (sham PLAYN), North America (45°N, 73°W)....89
Chandeleur Is. (shan duh LOOR), Gulf of Mexico (30°N, 89°W)....95
Chandeleur Sound, Gulf of Mexico (30°N, 89°W)....95
Chandigarh, India (31°N, 77°E)....180
Chandler, AZ (33°N, 112°W)....103
Chandler, QC (48°N, 65°W)....71
Changchun, China (44°N, 125°E)....182
Changji (chang jee), China (44°N, 87°E)....182
Changsha (chang shah), China (28°N, 113°E)....182
Changuinola, Panama (9°N, 82°W)....115
Channel Is., English Channel (49°N, 3°W)....158
Channel Is., Pacific O. (34°N, 120°W)....102
Channel Is. N.P., CA (34°N, 120°W)....102
Channel-Port aux Basques, NL (48°N, 59°W)....72
Chao Phraya (chow PRY uh), r. in Thailand (15°N, 100°E)....181
Chapala, L., Mexico (20°N, 103°W)....106
Chapel Hill, NC (36°N, 79°W)....91
Chapleau (chap LOH), ON (48°N, 83°W)....70
Chari River (SHAHR ee), Africa (11°N, 16°E)....139
Chariton R. (SHAR uht uhn), U.S.(40°N, 93°W)....97
Charles, Cape, VA (37°N, 76°W)....91
Charleston, IL (40°N, 88°W)....97
Charleston, SC (33°N, 80°W)....93
Charleston, WV (38°N, 82°W)....91
Charlestown, IN (38°N, 86°W)....90
Charlevoix (SHAHR luh voy), MI (45°N, 85°W)....99
Charlotte, NC (35°N, 81°W)....91
Charlotte Amalie (ah MAH lih a), U.S. Virgin Islands (18°N, 65°W)....116
Charlottesville, VA (38°N, 78°W)....91
Charlottetown, PE (47°N, 62°W)....72
Charlton I., James Bay (52°N, 79°W)....71
Chartres (SHAHR truh), France (48°N, 2°E)....158
Charzhou, Turkmenistan (39°N, 64°E)....179
Chatham (CHAT uhm), ON (42°N, 82°W)....70
Chatham Is., poss. of N.Z. (44°S, 178°W)....189
Chattahoochee R., U.S. (32°N, 85°W)....92–93
Chattanooga, TN (35°N, 85°W)....90
Chaudiere R. (shoh DYER), QC (46°N, 71°W)....71
Chautauqua L. (shuh TAW kwuh), NY (42°N, 79°W)....88
Cheat R., WV (40°N, 80°W)....91
Cheboksary (chyeh bawk SAH ri), Russia (56°N, 47°E)....160
Chechnya, Russian province (44°N, 46°E)....161
Cheektowaga, NY (cheek tuh WAH guh), (43°N, 79°W)....88
Chehalis R. (chih HAY luhs), WA (47°N, 123°W)....100
Cheju (CHAY joo), island in East China Sea (34°N, 126°E)....183
Chelan, L. (sheh LAN), WA (48°N, 120°W)....100
Chelyabinsk, Russia (55°N, 61°E)....179
Chemnitz, Germany (51°N, 13°E)....159
Chemung R. (shi MUHNG), NY (42°N, 77°W)....88
Cheney Res. (CHEE nee), KS (38°N, 98°W)....96
Chengdu, China (31°N, 104°E)....182
Chennai, India (13°N, 80°E)....180
Cherbourg (SHEHR boorg), France (50°N, 2°W)....158
Cherepovets (chehr yeh PAW vyehtz), Russia (59°N, 38°E)....160
Cherkasy, Ukraine (49°N, 32°E)....160
Cherkessk, Russia (44°N, 42°E)....161
Chernihiv, Ukraine (51°N, 31°E)....160
Chernivtsi, Ukraine (48°N, 26°E)....160
Chernobyl (chuhr NOH buhl), Ukraine (51°N, 30°E)....160
Chernyakhovsk (chir nyi KHOFSK), Russia (55°N, 22°E)....157
Cherokee L., TN (36°N, 84°W)....90
Cherokees, Lake O' the, OK (37°N, 95°W)....95
Chesapeake (ches uh peek), VA (37°N, 76°W)....91
Chesapeake Bay, U.S. (37°N, 76°W)....91
Chesha Bay, Barents Sea (67°N, 47°E)....160
Chester, PA (40°N, 75°W)....88
Chesterfield Inlet, Hudson Bay (63°N, 91°W)....61
Chesterfield I., Pacific O. (19°S, 160°E)....188
Chesuncook L. (chuh SUHN kook), ME (46°N, 71°W)....89
Chetumal, Mexico (19°N, 88°W)....114
Chetumal Bay (chay tyoo MAHL), Caribbean Sea (18°N, 88°W)....115
Cheyenne (shy AN), WY (41°N, 105°W)....101
Cheyenne R., U.S. (43°N, 105°W)....101
Chi R. (chee), Thailand (16°N, 104°E)....181
Chiang Mai (chee AHNG MY), Thailand (19°N, 99°E)....181
Chiang Rai (chee AHNG RY), Thailand (20°N, 100°E)....181
Chiapas, state in Mexico (17°N, 93°W)....114
Chiba (CHEE buh), Japan (36°N, 140°E)....183
Chibougamau (shuh BOO guh moh), QC (50°N, 74°W)....71
Chic-Chocs Mts., QC (49°N, 67°W)....71
Chicago, IL (42°N, 88°W)....97
Chickamauga L. (chik uh MAW guh), TN (35°N, 85°W)....90
Chickasawhay R. (chik uh SAW way), MS (31°N, 89°W)....92
Chiclayo (chuh KLY oh), Peru (7°S, 80°W)....126
Chico (CHEE koh), CA (40°N, 122°W)....102
Chidley, Cape (CHID lee), Canada (61°N, 64°W)....72
Chihuahua (chih WAH wah), Mexico (29°N, 106°W)....114
Chihuahua (chih WAH wah), state in Mexico (29°N, 108°W)....114
Chihuahuan Desert, Mexico (30°N, 105°W)....114
Chile, country in South America (35°S, 71°W)....126
Chile Basin, Pacific O. (23°S, 80°W)....22
Chilipancingo, Mexico (17°N, 99°W)....114
Chillicothe (chihl uh KAHTH ee), MO (40°N, 94°W)....97
Chillicothe, OH (39°N, 83°W)....90
Chilliwhack (CHIL uh wak), BC (49°N, 122°W)....68
Chiloe I. (chee luh WAY), Chile (43°S, 74°W)....126
Chimborazo, Mt., Ecuador (2°S, 79°W)....126
Chimbote (chim BOH tee), Peru (9°S, 79°W)....126
China, country in Asia (35°N, 105°E)....182
Chinandega (CHEE nan day gah), Nicaragua (13°N, 87°W)....115
Chinchaga R., Canada (58°N, 119°W)....68
Chincoteague Bay (SHING kuh teeg), Atlantic O. (38°N, 75°W)....91
Chindwin R., Myanmar (24°N, 95°E)....181
Chinle Wash (CHIN lee), U.S. (37°N, 110°W)....103
Chios (KEE aws), island in Aegean Sea (38°N, 26°E)....159
Chippewa R., MN (45°N, 96°W)....98
Chippewa R., WI (45°N, 91°W)....99
Chiputneticook Lakes (ship uht NET ih kook), North America (46°N, 68°W)....89
Chisasibi, QC, (54°N, 79°W)....71
Chisinau, Moldova (47°N, 29°E)....160
Chita, Russia (52°N, 114°E)....182
Chitre, Panama (8°N, 81°W)....115
Chittagong, Bangladesh (22°N, 91°E)....180
Chitungwiza, Zimbabwe (18°S, 31°E)....141
Choctawhatchee R. (chahk tuh HACH ee), U.S. (31°N, 86°W)....92
Choiseul I. (shwah ZUHL), Pacific O. (8°S, 158°E)....188
Choloma, Honduras (16°N, 88°W)....115
Choluteca, Honduras (13°N, 87°W)....115
Chon Buri (CHON boo REE), Thailand (13°N, 101°E)....181
Chongjin (chung jeen), North Korea (42°N, 130°E)....183
Chongqing (chuhng chihng), China (29°N, 106°E)....182
Chonos Archipelago, island group in Chile (45°S, 74°W)....126
Chowan R. (chuh WAHN), U.S. (36°N, 77°W)....91
Choybalsan, Mongolia (48°N, 114°E)....182
Christchurch, New Zealand (43°S, 173°E)....195
Christiansted, St. Croix (18°N, 65°W)....116
Christmas I., Indian O. (11°S, 106°E)....181
Christmas I., alternative name for Kiritimati Atoll (2°N, 157°W)....189
Chubut R., Argentina (43°S, 69°W)....126
Chukchi Sea, Arctic O. (70°N, 170°W)....104
Chula Vista (choo luh VIS tuh), CA (33°N, 117°W)....102
Churchill, MB (59°N, 93°W)....69
Churchill, Cape, MB (59°N, 94°W)....69
Churchill Falls, city in NL (53°N, 64°W)....72
Churchill Falls, waterfall in NL (54°N, 64°W)....72
Churchill L., SK (56°N, 108°W)....69
Churchill R., Canada (59°N, 94°W)....69
Chuuk Is., Pacific O. (7°N, 152°E)....188
Cimarron R. (SIM uh rohn), U.S. (37°N, 99°W)....94–95
Cincinnati, OH (39°N, 85°W)....90
Circle, AK (66°N, 144°W)....104
Ciudad Acuna, Mexico (29°N, 101°W)....114
Ciudad Bolivar (syoo DAHD boh LEE vahr), Venezuela (8°N, 64°W)....126
Ciudad del Carmen, Mexico (19°N, 92°W)....114
Ciudad del Este, Brazil (25°S, 58°W)....127
Ciudad Guayana, Venezuela (9°N, 63°W)....126
Ciudad Madero, Mexico (22°N, 98°W)....114
Ciudad Obregon (oh bruh GOHN), Mexico (28°N, 110°W)....114
Ciudad Victoria, Mexico (24°N, 99°W)....114
Claire, L., AB (59°N, 112°W)....69
Clarenville, NL (48°N, 55°W)....72
Clarion, PA (41°N, 79°W)....88
Clark Fork, r. in U.S. (48°N, 116°W)....100–101
Clark Hill L., alternative name for J. Strom Thurman Res. (34°N, 82°W)....93
Clarks Fork, r. in U.S. (45°N, 109°W)....101
Clarksburg, WV (39°N, 80°W)....91
Clarksdale, MS (34°N, 91°W)....92
Clarksville, TN (37°N, 87°W)....90
Clarksville, VA (37°N, 79°W)....91
Clear L., CA (39°N, 123°W)....102
Clearwater, FL (28°N, 83°W)....93
Clearwater Mts., ID (46°N, 116°W)....100
Clearwater R., Canada (57°N, 111°W)....69
Clearwater R., ID (46°N, 116°W)....100
Clearwater River P.P., SK (55°N, 109°W)....69
Clermont-Ferrand (klehr MOHN fuh RAN), France (46°N, 3°E)....158
Cleveland, OH (42°N, 82°W)....91
Cleveland, TN (35°N, 85°W)....90
Cleveland Heights, OH (41°N, 82°W)....91
Clinch R., U.S. (37°N, 83°W)....90–91
Clinton, IA (42°N, 90°W)....97
Clovis, NM (34°N, 105°W)....103
Cluj-Napoca, Romania (47°N, 24°E)....159
Clyde River, NU (71°N, 69°W)....61
Coachella Canal (koh CHEHL uh), CA (33°N, 115°W)....102
Coahuila (koh ah WEE la), Mexico (28°N, 103°W)....114
Coahuila, state in Mexico (28°N, 103°W)....114
Coast Mts., BC (55°N, 120°W)....68
Coast Ranges, U.S. (37°N, 122°W)....78
Coats I., Hudson Bay (62°N, 82°W)....61
Coats Land, region of Antarctica (78°S, 25°W)....200
Coatzacoalcos, Mexico (18°N, 94°W)....114
Cobalt, ON (47°N, 80°W)....70
Coban, Guatemala (15°N, 90°W)....115
Cobh (kohv), Ireland (52°N, 8°W)....156
Cobourg Pen., Australia (12°S, 135°E)....190
Cochabamba, Bolivia (17°S, 66°W)....127
Cochin (koh CHIHN), alternative name for Kochi (10°N, 76°E)....180
Cochrane (KAWK ruhn), ON (49°N, 81°W)....70
Cockburn I. (KOH buhrn), L. Huron (46°N, 83°W)....70
Coco R., North America (14°N, 84°W)....115
Cocos I., Pacific O. (5°N, 87°W)....106
Cocos Plate eastern Pacific O....20
Cod, Cape, MA (42°N, 70°W)....89

Name (Pronunciation), Description (Lat., Long.) Page

Cody, WY (44°N, 109°W) 101
Coeur d'Alene (kawr duh layn), ID (48°N, 117°W) 100
Coeur d'Alene L., ID (47°N, 117°W) 100
Coffeyville, KS (37°N, 96°W) 97
Coffs Harbour, Australia (30°S, 153°E) 195
Coiba I., Panama (7°N, 82°W) 115
Coimbatore (koym buh TOHR), India (11°N, 77°E) 180
Coimbra, Portugal (40°N, 8°W) 158
Cold L., Canada (55°N, 110°W) 69
Colima, Mexico (19°N, 104°W) 114
Colima, state in Mexico (19°N, 104°W) 114
College, AK (65°N, 148°W) 104
College Station, TX (31°N, 96°W) 95
Cologne (koh LOHN), Germany (51°N, 7°E) 159
Colombia, country in South America (3°N, 73°W) 126
Colombo, Sri Lanka (7°N, 80°E) 180
Colon (koh LOHN), Panama (9°N, 80°W) 115
Colorado, state in U.S. (39°N, 107°W) 103
Colorado Plateau, U.S. (37°N, 112°W) 78
Colorado R., Argentina (38°S, 68°W) 126
Colorado R., TX (30°N, 97°W) 94-95
Colorado R., U.S. (34°N, 114°W) 78
Colorado River Aqueduct, CA (34°N, 115°W) 102
Colorado Springs, CO (39°N, 105°W) 103
Columbia, MD (39°N, 77°W) 91
Columbia, MO (39°N, 92°W) 97
Columbia, SC (34°N, 81°W) 93
Columbia, TN (36°N, 87°W) 90
Columbia, Mt., AB and BC (52°N, 118°W) 68
Columbia Mts., BC (52°N, 119°W) 68
Columbia Plateau, U.S. (44°N, 118°W) 78
Columbia R., North America (50°N, 115°W) 54
Columbus, GA (32°N, 85°W) 92
Columbus, IN (39°N, 86°W) 90
Columbus, MS (33°N, 88°W) 92
Columbus, NE (41°N, 97°W) 96
Columbus, OH (40°N, 83°W) 90
Colville R., AK (69°N, 156°W) 104
Colwyn Bay (KAWL wuhn), Wales (53°N, 4°W) 156
Comayagua (koh mah YAH gwah), Honduras (14°N, 88°W) 115
Commander Is., Bering Sea (55°N, 167°E) 169
Como, L. (KOH moh), Italy (46°N, 9°E) 159
Comodoro Rivadavia, Arg. (46°S, 68°W) 126
Comorin, Cape, India (8°N, 78°E) 180
Comoros, country in Indian O. (13°S, 43°E) 141
Comoros Islands, Indian O. (13°S, 43°E) 133
Con Son Is. (kohn sohn), South China Sea (9°N, 106°E) 181
Conakry, Guinea (10°N, 14°W) 138
Concepcion (kuhn sep see OHN), Chile (37°S, 73°W) 126
Conception Bay, NL (47°N, 56°W) 72
Conception, Point, CA (35°N, 121°W) 102
Conchas Res. (KAHN chus), NM (35°N, 104°W) 103
Conchos R., Mexico (29°N, 105°W) 114
Concord, NC (35°N, 81°W) 91
Concord, NH (43°N, 71°W) 89
Concordia, Argentina (31°S, 58°W) 126
Concordia, KS (40°N, 98°W) 96
Concordia Station, Antarctica (75°S, 125°E) 200
Conecuh R. (kuh NAY kuh), AL (31°N, 87°W) 92
Conemaugh R. (KAHN uh moh), PA (41°N, 79°W) 88
Congaree N.P., South Carolina (33°N, 81°W) 93
Congo Basin, Africa (0°, 20°E) 139
Congo Rep., country in Africa (3°S, 15°E) 139
Congo R., Africa (2°N, 20°E) 139
Connecticut, state in U.S. (42°N, 73°W) 88-89
Connecticut R., U.S. (43°N, 73°W) 89
Conroe (KAHN roh), TX (30°N, 95°W) 95
Constance L. (KAHN stuhns), Europe (48°N, 9°E) 159
Constanta, Romania (44°N, 29°E) 159
Constantine, Algeria (36°N, 7°E) 136
Contagem, Brazil (20°S, 44°W) 127
Conway, AR (35°N, 92°W) 95
Cook Inlet, Gulf of Alaska (60°N, 153°W) 104
Cook Is., poss. of N.Z. (20°S, 158°W) 189
Cook, Mt., alternative name for Aoraki 195
Cook Strait, New Zealand (40°S, 173°E) 195
Cooktown, Australia, (16°S, 145°E) 195
Cooper R., SC (33°N, 80°W) 93
Cooperstown, NY (43°N, 75°W) 88
Coos Bay, OR (43°N, 124°W) 100
Coosa R. (koo suh), AL (34°N, 86°W) 92
Copenhagen, Denmark (56°N, 13°E) 157
Copiapo (koh pyah POH), Chile (27°S, 70°W) 126
Coquimbo (ko KIM boh), Chile (30°S, 72°W) 126
Coral Gables, FL (26°N, 80°W) 93
Coral Sea, Pacific O. (15°S, 150°E) 190
Coral Sea Islands Territory, poss. of Australia (16°S, 150°E) 195
Coral Springs, FL (26°N, 80°W) 93
Coralville Res., IA (42°N, 92°W) 97
Corcovado Gulf, Chile (44°S, 75°W) 126
Cordillera Oriental, range of Andes (3°N, 77°W) 126
Cordoba (KAWRD uh buh), Argentina (31°S, 64°W) 126
Cordoba, Spain (38°N, 5°W) 158
Cordova (kawr DOH vuh), AK (61°N, 146°W) 104
Corfu (kawr FOO), Island in Ionian Sea (40°N, 20°E) 159
Corinth, MS (35°N, 88°W) 92
Cork, Ireland (52°N, 9°W) 156
Corn Is., Caribbean Sea (12°N, 83°W) 115
Corner Brook, NL (49°N, 58°W) 72
Cornwall, ON (45°N, 75°W) 70
Coromandel Coast, India (15°N, 81°E) 180
Coronado Bay, Costa Rica (9°N, 85°W) 115
Coronation Gulf, NU (68°N, 112°W) 60
Corpus Christi (kawr puhs KRIHS tee), TX (28°N, 97°W) 95
Corpus Christi Bay, Gulf of Mexico (28°N, 97°W) 95
Corrientes (koh RYEHN tays), Argentina (29°N, 58°W) 126
Corrientes, Cape, Mexico (20°N, 105°W) 106
Corsica, island in Mediterranean Sea (42°N, 9°E) 159
Corsicana (kawr sih KAHN uh), TX (32°N, 96°W) 95
Corteau du Missouri, plateau in North America (49°N, 105°W) 69
Cortes, Sea of, alternative name for Gulf of California (28°N, 112°W) 114
Cortland, NY (43°N, 76°W) 88
Corum, Turkey (41°N, 35°E) 160
Corvallis, OR (45°N, 123°W) 100
Cosenza (koh ZEN suh), Italy (39°N, 16°E) 159
Costa Rica, country in Central America (10°N, 84°W) 115
Côte d'Ivoire (koht deev WAHR), country in Africa (8°N, 5°W) 138
Cotonou (koht uh NOO), Benin (6°N, 2°E) 138
Cottonwood R., KS (38°N, 97°W) 96
Council Bluffs, IA (41°N, 96°W) 96-97
Courtenay, BC (50°N, 125°W) 68
Coventry, England (52°N, 1°W) 156
Covington, KY (39°N, 85°W) 90
Cowlitz R., WA (46°N, 123°W) 100
Cozumel I., Mexico (20°N, 87°W) 114
Craig, AK (55°N, 133°E) 104
Craiova (kruh YOH vuh), Romania (44°N, 24°E) 159
Cranbrook, BC (50°N, 116°W) 68
Crater L., OR (43°N, 122°W) 100
Crater Lake N.P., OR (43°N, 122°W) 100
Crawford, NE (43°N, 103°W) 96
Crawfordsville, IN (40°N, 87°W) 90
Cree L., SK (57°N, 106°W) 69
Crete (kreet), island in Mediterranean Sea (34°N, 25°E) 159
Crete, Sea of, Europe and Asia (36°N, 25°E) 159
Crimean Peninsula, Ukraine (45°N, 34°E) 160
Cristobal Colon, Mt., Colombia (11°N, 74°W) 126
Croatia (kro AY shuh), country in Europe (46°N, 16°E) 159
Cross City, FL (30°N, 83°W) 93
Cross L., MB (55°N, 97°W) 69
Crossville, TN (36°N, 85°W) 90
Crow Agency, MT (46°N, 107°W) 101
Crozet Is. (kro ZAY), Indian O. (46°S, 51°E) 132
Cuando R., Africa (15°S, 20°E) 141
Cuanza R. (KWAN zuh), Angola (9°S, 13°E) 141
Cuauhtemoc (kwou TE mok), Mexico (28°N, 107°W) 94
Cuba (KYOO buh), country in Caribbean Sea (23°N, 80°W) 107
Cubango R., Africa (17°S, 18°E) 141
Cucuta (KOO kuht uh), Colombia (8°N, 73°W) 126
Cuenca (KWENG kuh), Ecuador (3°S, 79°W) 126
Cuernavaca (kwehr nah VAH kah), Mexico (19°N, 99°W) 114
Cuiaba (kyoo yuh BAH), Brazil (16°S, 56°W) 127
Culiacan (koo lyah KAN), Mexico (25°N, 108°W) 114
Cumana, Venezuela (10°N, 64°W) 126
Cumberland, MD (40°N, 79°W) 91
Cumberland Gap, mt. pass in KY and VA (37°N, 84°W) 90
Cumberland, L., KY (37°N, 85°W) 90
Cumberland Plateau, U.S. (36°N, 84°W) 79
Cumberland R., U.S. (36°N, 86°W) 90
Cumberland Sound, Labrador Sea (66°N, 67°W) 61
Cunene R., Africa (17°S, 13°E) 141
Curacao, overseas part of Neth. (12°N, 69°W) 116
Curitiba (koor ih TEE buh), Brazil (25°S, 49°W) 127
Current R., U.S. (37°N, 91°W) 97
Cusco (KOOS koh), Peru (14°S, 72°W) 126
Cut Bank Creek, MT (49°N, 113°W) 101
Cuttack (KUHT uhk), India (21°N, 86°E) 180
Cuyahoga R., OH (42°N, 82°W) 91
Cuyahoga Valley N.P., OH (41°N, 82°W) 91
Cyclades (SIK luh deez), islands in Aegean Sea (37°N, 24°E) 159
Cypress Hills, Canada (50°N, 110°W) 69
Cyprus (SY pruhs), country in Mediterranean Sea (35°N, 33°E) 178
Czech Republic, country in Europe (49°N, 15°E) 159
Czestochowa (chen stuh KOH vuh), Poland (51°N, 19°E) 159

D

Da Nang, Vietnam (16°N, 108°E) 181
Dabola, Guinea (11°N, 11°W) 138
Dahlak Archipelago, island group in Red Sea (16°N, 41°E) 140
Daito Is., poss. of Japan (25°N, 128°E) 188
Dakar, Senegal (15°N, 17°W) 138
Dakhilah Oasis (DAHK luh), Egypt (25°N, 29°E) 137
Dakhla, Western Sahara (24°N, 16°W) 136
Dalbandin (DAL buhn din), Pakistan (29°N, 64°E) 180
Dale Hollow L., TN (37°N, 85°W) 90
Dalhart, TX (36°N, 102°W) 94
Dalian (dah lehn), China (39°N, 122°E) 182
Dallas, TX (33°N, 97°W) 95
Dalles, The (dalz), OR (46°N, 121°W) 100
Daloa, Côte d'Ivoire (7°N, 7°W) 138
Dalton, GA (35°N, 85°W) 92
Daly City, CA (38°N, 122°W) 102
Daly R., Australia (12°S, 130°E) 191
Damascus, Syria (34°N, 36°E) 178
Damavand, Mt., Iran (36°N, 52°E) 178
Dan R., U.S. (37°N, 79°W) 91
Danbury, CT (41°N, 73°W) 89
Danli, Honduras (14°N, 87°W) 115
Dansville, NY (43°N, 78°W) 88
Danube R., Europe (44°N, 27°E) 159
Danube River Delta, Romania (45°N, 30°E) 160
Danville, IL (40°N, 88°W) 97
Danville, VA (37°N, 79°W) 91
Dar es Salaam, Tanzania (7°S, 39°E) 140
Dara, Syria (32°N, 36°E) 178
Dardanelle L., AR (35°N, 93°W) 95
Dardanelles, strait of Europe and Asia (40°N, 25°E) 159
Darfur, region of Africa (13°N, 24°E) 140
Darhan (DAHR khan), Mongolia (49°N, 106°E) 182
Darien, Gulf of, Caribbean Sea (9°N, 77°W) 115
Darling Range, Australia (33°S, 117°E) 191
Darling R., Australia (32°S, 143°E) 191
Darnah, Libya (33°N, 23°E) 137
Darwin, Australia (12°S, 131°E) 195
Dasht-e Kavir, desert in Iran (34°N, 54°E) 178
Dasht-e Lut, desert in Iran (32°N, 58°E) 178
Dasoguz, Turkmenistan (42°N, 60°E) 179
Datong (dah tung), China (40°N, 114°E) 182
Daugavpils, Latvia (56°N, 27°E) 157

Name (Pronunciation), Description (Lat., Long.) Page

Dauphin (DAW fuhn), MB (51°N, 100°W) 69
Davao, Philippines (7°N, 126°E) 181
Davenport, IA (42°N, 91°W) 97
David, Panama (8°N, 82°W) 115
Davie, FL (26°N, 80°W) 93
Davis, CA (39°N, 122°W) 102
Davis Mts., TX (31°N, 104°W) 94
Davis Sea, Antarctica (65°S, 90°E) 200
Davis Station, Antarctica (69°S, 78°E) 200
Davis Strait, Canada and Greenland (67°N, 59°W) 61
Dawson, YT (64°N, 140°W) 60
Dawson Creek, BC (56°N, 120°W) 68
Daxue Mts., China (30°N, 102°E) 182
Dayton, OH (40°N, 84°W) 90
Daytona Beach, FL (29°N, 81°W) 93
Dead Sea, Asia (31°N, 35°E) 178
Dearborn, MI (42°N, 83°W) 99
Dease Lake (dees), BC (58°N, 130°W) 68
Death Valley, CA (36°N, 117°W) 102
Death Valley N.P., CA (36°N, 117°W) 102
Debrecen (DEB ruht sehn), Hungary (47°N, 22°E) 159
Decatur (deh KAY tuhr), AL (35°N, 87°W) 92
Decatur, GA (34°N, 84°W) 93
Decatur, IL (40°N, 89°W) 97
Deccan Plateau, India (18°N, 77°E) 180
Decorah (deh KOHR uh), IA (43°N, 92°W) 97
Defiance, OH (41°N, 84°W) 90
DeKalb, IL (42°N, 89°W) 97
Del Norte (del NOHRT), CO (38°N, 106°W) 103
Del Rio, TX (29°N, 101°W) 94
Delaware, state in U.S. (39°N, 76°W) 91
Delaware Bay, U.S. (39°N, 75°W) 91
Delaware R., U.S. (40°N, 75°W) 88
Delhi (DEL ee), India (29°N, 77°E) 180
Delmarva Pen., U.S. (38°N, 76°W) 91
Dem. Rep. of the Congo, country in Africa (3°S, 24°E) 139
Dempo, mt. in Indonesia (4°S, 103°E) 181
Denakil Depression, lowland in Ethiopia (14°N, 40°E) 140
Denali, AK (63°N, 151°W) 104
Denali N.P., AK (63°N, 150°W) 104
Denison, IA (42°N, 95°W) 97
Denmark, country in Europe (56°N, 9°E) 157
Denmark Strait, Greenland and Iceland (67°N, 27°W) 12
Dennison, OH (40°N, 81°W) 91
Denton, TX (33°N, 97°W) 95
Denver, CO (40°N, 105°W) 103
Derbent, Russia (42°N, 48°E) 161
Derby, Australia (17°S, 124°E) 195
Derry, NH (43°N, 71°W) 89
Des Moines (di MOYN), IA (42°N, 94°W) 97
Des Moines R., IA (43°N, 94°W) 97
Deschutes R. (dih SHOOTS), OR (45°N, 121°W) 100
Dese, Ethiopia (11°N, 40°E) 140
Desna R., Europe (52°N, 32°E) 160
Detroit, MI (42°N, 83°W) 99
Devils L., ND (48°N, 99°W) 98
Devils R., TX (30°N, 101°W) 94
Devils Tower, mt. in WY (45°N, 105°W) 101
Devon I., Baffin Bay (75°N, 85°W) 60-61
Devonport, Australia (41°S, 147°E) 195
Dhaka, Bangladesh (24°N, 90°E) 180
Dhamar, Yemen (14°N, 44°E) 178
Dhaulagiri, mt. in Nepal (29°N, 84°E) 171
D'Iberville, Mt., NL (59°N, 63°W) 72
Dickinson, ND (47°N, 103°W) 98
Diefenbaker L. (DEE fuhn bay kuhr) SK (51°N, 107°W) 69
Diego Garcia, Indian O. (7°S, 72°E) 168
Dien Bien Phu (dyen byen FOO), Vietnam (21°N, 103°E) 181
Diffa, Niger (13°N, 13°E) 138
Digby, NS (45°N, 66°W) 72
Dijon (dee ZHOHN), France (47°N, 5°E) 158
Dili, East Timor (9°S, 126°E) 181
Dillingham, AK (59°N, 159°W) 104
Dillon L., OH (40°N, 82°W) 91
Dinaric Alps, mt. range in Europe (44°N, 17°E) 159
Dire Dawa, Ethiopia (10°N, 42°E) 140
Disappointment Is., Pacific O. (14°S, 141°W) 189
Disappointment, L., Australia (24°S, 123°E) 191
District of Columbia, U.S. (39°N, 77°W) 91
Dixon Entrance, strait between AK and BC (54°N, 133°W) 104
Diyala R., Asia (34°N, 46°E) 178
Diyarbakir, Turkey (38°N, 40°E) 178
Dja R. (JAH), Africa (3°N, 13°E) 139
Djibouti (jih BOO tee), country in Africa (12°N, 43°E) 140
Djibouti, Djibouti (12°N, 43°E) 140
Djougou, Benin (9°N, 2°E) 138
Dnieper Lowland (NEE puhr), Ukraine (53°N, 29°E) 160
Dnieper R., Ukraine (49°N, 34°E) 160
Dniester R., (NEE stuhr), Ukraine (48°N, 28°E) 160
Dniprohes Dam, Ukraine (47°N, 35°E) 160
Dnipropetrovsk (nehp roh pih TRAWFSK), Ukraine (48°N, 35°E) 160
Dobrich, Bulgaria (44°N, 28°E) 159
Dodecanese (doh DEK uh neez), islands in Aegean Sea (37°N, 26°E) 159
Dodge City, KS (38°N, 100°W) 96
Dodoma, Tanzania (6°S, 36°E) 140
Doha, Qatar (25°N, 52°E) 178
Dolak, island in Arafura Sea (8°S, 139°E) 188
Dolores R. (duh LOHR uhs), CO (39°N, 109°W) 103
Dominica, (doh mihn ih CAH), country in Caribbean Sea (16°N, 61°W) 116
Dominican Republic, country in Caribbean Sea (19°N, 71°W) 107
Don R., Russia (47°N, 40°E) 160
Donegal Bay (dahn ih GAWL), Ireland (55°N, 8°W) 156
Donets R., Ukraine (49°N, 38°E) 160
Donetsk, Ukraine (48°N, 38°E) 160
Dongola, Sudan (19°N, 30°E) 140
Dongting L., China (29°N, 112°E) 182
Door Pen., WI (45°N, 87°W) 99
Dordogne R. (dawr DOHN), France (45°N, 1°E) 158
Dore L., SK (55°N, 108°W) 69
Dortmund (DAWRT moont), Germany (52°N, 7°E) 159
Dothan, AL (31°N, 85°W) 92
Douala, Cameroon (4°N, 10°E) 139
Double Mountain Fork, r. in TX (34°N, 102°W) 94
Doubs R. (DOO), France (47°N, 5°E) 158
Douglas, AZ (31°N, 110°W) 103
Douglas, WY (43°N, 105°W) 101
Dourados, Brazil (55°W, 22°S) 127
Douro R., Europe, (42°N, 8°W) 158
Dover (DOH vuhr), DE (39°N, 75°W) 91
Dover, England (51°N, 1°E) 156
Dover, NH (43°N, 71°W) 89
Dover, Strait of, England and France (51°N, 1°E) 158
Drake Passage, Atlantic and Pacific Oceans (60°N, 65°W) 200
Drakensberg, mt. range in South Africa (31°S, 27°E) 141
Drammen, Norway (60°N, 10°E) 157
Drava R., Europe (46°N, 17°E) 159
Dresden (DREZ dehn), Germany (51°N, 14°E) 159
Driftless Area, U.S. (43°N, 91°W) 99
Drobeta-Turnu Severin, Romania (44°N, 25°E) 159
Drumheller, AB (51°N, 113°W) 68-69
Drummond I., L. Huron (48°N, 84°W) 99
Drummondville, QC (46°N, 73°W) 71
Dry Tortugas, islands in Gulf of Mexico (25°N, 83°W) 77
Dry Tortugas N.P., Gulf of Mexico (25°N, 83°W) 93
Dryden, ON (50°N, 93°W) 70
Dubai, United Arab Emirates (25°N, 55°E) 178
Dubawnt L., NT and NU(63°N, 101°W) 69
Dublin, GA (33°N, 83°W) 93
Dublin, Ireland (53°N, 6°W) 156
Dubrovnik (DOO brawv nik), Croatia (43°N, 18°E) 159
Dubuque (duh BYOOK), IA (43°N, 91°W) 97
Ducie Atoll (doo SEE) Pacific O. (26°S, 126°W) 189
Duck Mt. P.P., MB (52°N, 101°W) 69
Duero R. (DWER oh), Europe (42°N, 3°W) 158
Duff Is., Pacific O. (10°S, 167°E) 188
Duke of Gloucester Group, islands in Pacific O. (21°S, 143°W) 189
Duluth (duh LOOTH), MN (47°N, 92°W) 99
Dumont d-Urville Station (do MONT DUHR vil) Antarctica (67°S, 140°E) 200
Dundalk (DUHN dawk), Ireland (54°N, 6°W) 156
Dundee (duhn DEE), Scotland (56°N, 3°W) 156
Dunedin, New Zealand (46°S, 171°E) 195
Durango, Mexico (24°N, 105°W) 114
Durango, state in Mexico (25°N, 106°W) 114
Durant (doo RANT), OK (34°N, 96°W) 95
Durban, South Africa (30°S, 31°E) 141
Durham, NC (36°N, 79°W) 91
Durres, Albania (41°N, 19°E) 159
Dushanbe (du SHAM buh), Tajikistan (38°N, 69°E) 179
Dusseldorf (DOO suhl dawrf), Germany (51°N, 7°E) 159
Dyersburg, TN (36°N, 89°W) 90
Dzerhinsk, Russia (48°N, 38°E) 160
Dzhugdzhur Range, Russia (58°N, 140°E) 170
Dzungarian Basin (zung GAR ee uhn), Asia (45°N, 86°E) 182

E

Eagle L., ME (46°N, 71°W) 89
Eagle Mountain L., TX (33°N, 98°W) 95
Eagle Pass, TX (29°N, 100°W) 94
Eagle R., NL (54°N, 57°W) 72
East Chicago, IN (42°N, 87°W) 90
East China Sea, Asia (30°N, 125°E) 182
East Fork White R., IN (39°N, 86°W) 90
East Lansing, MI (43°N, 84°W) 99
East Liverpool, OH (41°N, 81°W) 91
East London, South Africa (33°S, 27°E) 141
East Nishnabotna R. (nish nuh BAHT nuh), IA (41°N, 96°W) 97
East Pacific Rise, Pacific O. (15°S, 110°W) 22
East Point, GA (34°N, 84°W) 93
East Saint Louis, IL (39°N, 90°W) 97
East Sea, alternative name for Sea of Japan (40°N, 135°E) 183
East Siberian Sea, Arctic O. (73°N, 165°E) 169
East Siberian Uplands, Siberia (66°N, 135°E) 170
East Timor, country in Asia (9°S, 126°E) 181
Easter I., poss. of Chile (27°S, 110°W) 12
Eastern Ghats, mt. range in India (13°N, 78°E) 180
Eastmain R., QC (52°N, 76°W) 71
Eastmain, QC (52°N, 79°W) 71
Eastmain Un, Res. de., QC (52°N, 75°W) 71
Easton, PA (41°N, 75°W) 88
Eastport, ME (45°N, 69°W) 89
Eau Claire (oh KLAYR), WI (45°N, 92°W) 99
Eau Claire, L. á l', QC (56°N, 74°W) 71
Ebro R., Spain (42°N, 2°W) 158
Ecuador (EHK wuh dohr), country in South America (1°S, 78°W) 126
Edea, Cameroon (4°N, 10°E) 139
Edinburg, TX (26°N, 98°W) 94
Edinburgh (ED ihn buh ruh), Scotland (56°N, 3°W) 156
Edirne (ay DIHR nuh), Turkey (42°N, 27°E) 178
Edmond, OK (36°N, 97°W) 95
Edmonds, WA (48°N, 122°W) 100
Edmonton, AB (54°N, 113°W) 68
Edmundston, NB (47°N, 68°W) 72
Edson, AB (54°N, 116°W) 68
Edward, L., Africa (0°, 30°E) 140
Edwards Plateau, TX (31°N, 101°W) 94
Eel R., CA (41°N, 124°W) 102
Efate (ay FAHT ee), I. in Pacific O. (18°S, 169°E) 188
Effingham, IL (39°N, 88°W) 97
Egypt, country in Africa (25°N, 30°E) 137
Eiao, island in Pacific O. (8°S, 141°W) 189
Eighty Mile Beach, Australia (21°S, 119°E) 195
Eildon, L. (EEL duhn), Australia (37°S, 146°E) 195
Ejmiatsin, Armenia (40°N, 44°E) 161
Ekwan R., ON (53°N, 82°W) 70
El Aaiun (eh ly OON), Western Sahara (27°N, 13°W) 136
El Alto, Bolivia (17°S, 69°W) 127
El Centro, CA (33°N, 116°W) 102
El Chichon (chee KOHN), mt. in Mexico (17°N, 93°W) 107

Name (Pronunciation), Description (Lat., Long.) Page

El Djouf, desert in Africa (22°N, 7°W) 136
El Dorado (ehl duh RAH doh), AR (33°N, 93°W) 95
El Hierro, Canary Is. (28°N, 18°W) 136
El Paso, TX (32°N, 106°W) 94
El Progreso, Honduras (15°N, 88°W) 115
El Salvador, country in Central America (13°N, 89°W) 115
Elat, Israel (30°N, 35°E) 178
Elba, island in Tyrrhenian Sea (43°N, 10°E) 159
Elbe R., Europe (54°N, 10°E) 159
Elbert, Mt., CO (39°N, 106°W) 103
Elblag (EL blawng), Poland (54°N, 19°E) 159
Elbrus, Mt., Russia (43°N, 42°E) 161
Elburz Mts., Iran (36°N, 52°E) 178
Elche, Spain (38°N, 1°W) 158
Eldoret, Kenya (1°N, 35°E) 140
Elephant Butte Res., NM (33°N, 107°W) 103
Eleuthera I., Bahamas (25°N, 76°W) 93
Elgin (EL jihn), IL (42°N, 88°W) 97
Elgon, Mt., Africa (1°N, 34°E) 140
Elizabeth, NJ (41°N, 74°W) 88
Elizabeth City, NC (36°N, 76°W) 91
Elizabethton, TN (36°N, 82°E) 91
Elizabethtown, NC (35°N, 79°W) 91
Elk City, OK (35°N, 99°W) 94
Elk City Res, KS (37°N, 96°W) 96
Elk Is. N.P., AB (54°N, 113°W) 68-69
Elkhart, IN (42°N, 86°W) 90
Elkhorn R., NE (42°N, 98°W) 96
Elkins, WV (39°N, 80°W) 91
Elko, NV (41°N, 116°W) 102
Ellef Ringnes I. (el uhf RING nays), Arctic O. (79°N, 102°W) 60
Ellensburg, WA (47°N, 121°W) 100
Ellesmere I., Arctic O. (80°N, 77°W) 61
Ellsworth, ME (45°N, 68°W) 89
Ellsworth Land, region of Antarctica (85°S, 90°W) 200
Elmhurst, IL (42°N, 88°W) 97
Elmira (el MY ruh), NY (42°N, 77°W) 88
Elwell, L., MT (48°N, 111°W) 101
Ely (EE lee), MN (48°N, 92°W) 99
Ely, NV (39°N, 115°W) 102
Elyria (ih LIHR ee uh), OH (41°N, 82°W) 91
Embarrass R. (AHM braw), IL (39°N, 88°W) 97
Emerald, Australia (24°S, 147°E) 195
Emerson, MB (49°N, 97°W) 69
Emi Koussi (ay mee KYOO suh), mt. in Chad (20°N, 19°E) 137
Emperor Seamount, Pacific O. (40°N, 170°E) 22
Emporia (em POHR ee uh), KS (38°N, 96°W) 96
Empty Quarter, alternative name for Rub al Khali (22°N, 53°E) 178
Ems R, Germany (52°N, 9°E) 151
Enderbury I., Pacific O. (2°S, 171°W) 189
Enewetak Atoll (eh NEE wuh tak) Pacific O. (11°N, 162°E) 188
Enfield, CT (42°N, 73°W) 89
Enggano I., Indonesia (5°S, 102°E) 181
England, part of United Kingdom (53°N, 1°W) 156
English Channel, England and France (50°N, 2°W) 156
Enid (EE nid), OK (36°N, 98°W) 95
Ennadai L., NU (61°N, 101°W) 69
Ennedi Plateau (en uh DEE), Africa (18°N, 23°E) 137
Enschede, Netherlands (52°N, 7°E) 151
Ensenada (en suh NAHD uh), Mexico (32°N, 117°W) 114
Entebbe (ehn TEHB ih), Uganda (0°, 32°E) 140
Enugu (ah NOO goo), Nigeria (6°N, 7°E) 138
Epi I. (AY pay) Pacific O. (17°S, 168°E) 188
Equatorial Guinea, country in Africa (2°N, 9°E) 139
Erdenet, Mongolia (49°N, 104°E) 182
Erdine, Turkey (42°N, 26°E) 159
Erebus, Mt. (EHR uh buhs), Antarctica (78°S, 167°E) 200
Erfurt, Germany (51°N, 11°E) 159
Erg Chech, desert in Africa (25°N, 2°W) 136
Erg Iguidi, desert in Africa (26°N, 7°W) 136
Erie, PA (42°N, 80°W) 88
Erie Canal (EER ee), NY (43°N, 77°W) 88
Erie, L., North America (42°N, 82°W) 70
Erimo, Cape, Japan (42°N, 143°E) 183

Name (Pronunciation), Description (Lat., Long.) Page

Eritrea (eh rih TREE yuh), country in Africa (15°N, 39°E) 140
Erromango I. (e ro MAHNG o) Pacific O. (19°N, 169°E) 188
Erzincan, Turkey (40°N, 40°E) 178
Esbjerg (EHS byerhg), Denmark (55°N, 30°E) 157
Escambia R., FL (31°N, 87°W) 92
Escanaba (es kuh NAHB uh), MI (46°N, 87°W) 99
Escarpada Point, Philippines (19°N, 123°E) 181
Escondido (ehs kun DEED oh), CA (33°N, 117°W) 102
Escuintla (ehs KWEEN tlah), Guatemala (14°N, 91°W) 115
Esfahan, Iran (33°N, 52°E) 178
Eskilstuna, Sweden (59°N, 16°E) 157
Eskisehir, Turkey (40°N, 41°E) 178
Esperance (EHS pee ruhns), Australia (34°S, 122°E) 195
Esperanza Station (es puh RAN zah) Antarctica (63°S, 57°W) 200
Espiritu Santo, island in Pacific O. (15°S, 167°E) 188
Espoo, Finland (60°N, 25°E) 157
Essen, Germany (51°N, 7°E) 159
Essex, VT (45°N, 73°W) 89
Esteli, Nicaragua (13°N, 86°W) 115
Estevan (EHS tuh van), SK (49°N, 103°W) 69
Estonia, country in Europe (59°N, 26°E) 157
Eswatini, country in Africa (27°S, 32°E) 141
Ethiopia, country in Africa (10°N, 40°E) 140
Ethiopian Highlands, Africa (10°N, 37°E) 140
Etna, Mt., Italy (38°N, 15°E) 159
Etorofu (eht uh ROH foo), island in Sea of Okhotsk (45°N, 147°E) 183
Etosha Pan, dry lake in Namibia (19°S, 16°E) 141
Euboea (EV yuh), island in the Aegean Sea (39°N, 24°E) 159
Euclid (YOO klid), OH (41°N, 82°W) 91
Eufaula L. (yoo FAW luh), OK (35°N, 96°W) 95
Eugene, OR (44°N, 123°W) 100
Eugenia, Pt., Mexico (28°N, 115°W) 106
Euphrates R., Asia (35°N, 41°E) 178
Eurasian Plate (yoo RAY zhuhn) Europe and Asia 20
Eureka (yoo REE kuh), CA (41°N, 124°W) 102
Europe, continent 148-149
Eutsuk L. (OOT suhk), BC (53°N, 126°W) 68
Evans L., QC (51°N, 77°W) 71
Evanston, IL (42°N, 88°W) 97
Evanston, WY (41°N, 111°W) 101
Evansville, IN (38°N, 88°W) 90
Everest, Mt., China and Nepal (28°N, 87°E) 180
Everett, WA (48°N, 122°W) 100
Everglades City, FL (26°N, 81°W) 93
Everglades N.P., FL (25°N, 81°W) 93
Exeter (EHK suht uhr), England (51°N, 4°W) 156
Eyre, L. (ayr), Australia (29°S, 138°E) 190

F

Fairbanks, AK (65°N, 148°W) 104
Fairmont, MN (44°N, 94°W) 98
Fairmont, WV (39°N, 80°W) 91
Fairweather Mt., BC (59°N, 138°W) 68
Faisalabad (fy sahl uh BAHD), Pakistan (31°N, 73°E) 180
Fakaofo Atoll, Pacific O. (9°S, 171°W) 189
Fakarava Atoll (fah kah RAH vah) Pacific O. (16°S, 146°W) 189
Fakfak, Indonesia (3°S, 132°E) 181
Falcon Res., TX (27°N, 99°W) 94
Faleme R. (fal uh MAY), Africa (13°N, 11°W) 138
Falfurrias (fal FYOOR ee uhs), TX (27°N, 98°W) 94
Falkland Is., (FAWK luhnd) Atlantic O. (52°S, 60°W) 126
Fall River, MA (42°N, 71°W) 89
Fallujah, Iraq (33°N, 44°E) 178
Farafirah Oasis (fuh rahf uh ruh), Egypt (27°N, 28°E) 137
Farah, Afghanistan (32°N, 62°E) 180
Farah, R., Asia (34°N, 63°E) 178
Farallon de Medinilla, island in Pacific O. (16°N, 148°E) 188
Farallon de Pajaros, island in Pacific O. (21°N, 145°E) 188

Name (Pronunciation), Description (Lat., Long.) Page

Farasan Is., Red Sea (17°N, 42°E) 140
Farewell, Cape, Greenland (59°N, 43°W) 61
Fargo, ND (47°N, 97°W) 98
Farmington, ME (45°N, 70°W) 89
Farmington, NM (37°N, 108°W) 103
Faroe Islands, Europe (62°N, 6°W) 146
Farquhar Group, islands in Indian O. (10°S, 51°E) 141
Fawn R., ON (55°N, 88°W) 70
Faya-Largeau, Chad (18°N, 20°E) 137
Fayette (fay EHT), IA (43°N, 92°W) 97
Fayetteville, AR (36°N, 94°W) 95
Fayetteville, NC (35°N, 79°W) 91
Fear, Cape, NC (34°N, 78°W) 91
Federal District, state in Mexico (19°N, 99°W) 114
Federated States of Micronesia, country in Pacific O. (10°N, 150°E) 188
Feira de Santana (fay uhr uh duh san TAN uh), Brazil (12°S, 39°W) 127
Fergus Falls, MN (46°N, 96°W) 98
Fergusson I., Pacific O. (10°S, 151°E) 188
Fernando de Noronha, island in Atlantic O. (4°S, 32°W) 127
Fernie, BC (50°N, 115°W) 68
Ferrara, Italy (45°N, 12°E) 159
Ferraz Station, Antarctica (63°S, 57°W) 200
Feuilles R. (FOO uh yuh), QC (59°N, 71°W) 71
Fez, Morocco (34°N, 5°W) 136
Fianarantsoa, Madagascar (21°S, 47°E) 141
Fiera de Santana, Brazil (12°S, 39°W) 127
Fifth Cataract, waterfall in Sudan (18°N, 34°E) 140
Fiji, country in Pacific O. (20°S, 178°E) 189
Filchner Ice Shelf, Antarctica (82°S, 30°W) 200
Findlay, OH (41°N, 84°W) 90
Finisterre, Cape (fin uh STEHR), Spain (43°N, 9°W) 158
Finland, country in Europe (62°N, 24°E) 157
Finland, Gulf of, Baltic Sea (60°N, 25°E) 157
Finlay R., BC (58°N, 126°W) 68
Firebag Hills, Canada (57°N, 110°W) 69
First Cataract, waterfall in Egypt (24°N, 33°E) 137
Firth of Forth, bay in Scotland (56°N, 3°W) 156
Fitchburg, MA (43°N, 72°W) 89
Fitzroy R., Australia (18°S, 125°E) 195
Flagstaff, AZ (35°N, 112°W) 103
Flagstaff L., ME (45°N, 70°W) 89
Flambeau R. (FLAM boh), WI (45°N, 91°W) 99
Flaming Gorge Res., WY (41°N, 110°W) 101
Flathead L., MT (48°N, 114°W) 101
Flathead R., North America (49°N, 114°W) 101
Flattery, Cape, Washington (48°N, 125°W) 100
Flin Flon, MB (55°N, 102°W) 69
Flinders Ranges, Australia (33°S, 138°E) 191
Flinders R., Australia (18°S, 141°E) 195
Flint, MI (43°N, 84°W) 99
Flint Hills, KS (38°N, 97°W) 96
Flint I., Pacific O. (11°S, 152°W) 189
Flint R., GA (32°N, 84°W) 93
Florence, AL (35°N, 88°W) 92
Florence, Italy (44°N, 11°E) 159
Florence, SC (34°N, 80°W) 93
Flores, Guatemala (17°N, 90°W) 115
Flores, island in Flores Sea (9°S, 121°E) 181
Flores Sea, Indian O. (7°S, 120°E) 181
Florianopolis, Brazil (28°S, 49°W) 127
Florida, state in U.S. (30°N, 83°W) 92-93
Florida Bay, FL (25°N, 81°W) 93
Florida Keys, islands in Caribbean Sea (25°N, 81°W) 93
Florida Pen., FL (28°N, 81°W) 93
Florida, Straits of, U.S. and Cuba (24°N, 81°W) 93
Florina (FLAWR uh nuh), Greece (41°N, 21°E) 159
Florissant, MO (39°N, 90°W) 97
Floyd R., IA (43°N, 96°W) 96
Foggia (FAW juh), Italy (42°N, 16°E) 159
Folsom L., CA (39°N, 121°W) 102
Fond du Lac, WI (44°N, 89°W) 99
Fond-du-Lac (FAHN duh lak), SK (59°N, 107°W) 69
Fond-du-Lac R., SK (59°N, 104°W) 69
Fonseca, Gulf of, Pacific O. (13°N, 88°W) 115
Forest City, IA (43°N, 94°W) 97

Name (Pronunciation), Description (Lat., Long.) Page

Forillon N.P. (foh ree YOHN), QC (49°N, 64°W) 71
Formosa, Argentina (27°S, 58°W) 126
Formosa Reefs, Taiwan Strait (23°N, 118°E) 188
Fort Albany, ON (52°N, 82°W) 70
Fort Chipewyan, AB (59°N, 111°W) 69
Fort Collins, CO (41°N, 105°W) 103
Fort-de-France, Martinique (15°N, 61°W) 116
Fort Dodge, IA (43°N, 94°W) 97
Fort Frances, ON (49°N, 93°W) 70
Fort Lauderdale, FL (26°N, 80°W) 93
Fort Liard (LEE ahrd), NT (60°N, 123°W) 68
Fort McMurray, AB (57°N, 111°W) 69
Fort Myers, FL (27°N, 82°W) 93
Fort Nelson, BC (59°N, 123°W) 68
Fort Nelson R., BC (59°N, 123°W) 68
Fort Peck Dam, MT (48°N, 106°W) 101
Fort Peck L., MT (48°N, 107°W) 101
Fort Pierce, FL (27°N, 80°W) 93
Fort Randall Dam, SD (43°N, 99°W) 98
Fort Resolution, NT (61°N, 114°W) 68
Fort Saint John, BC (56°N, 121°W) 68
Fort Scott, KS (38°N, 95°W) 97
Fort Severn, ON (57°N, 88°W) 70
Fort Simpson, NT (62°N, 121°W) 68
Fort Smith, AR (35°N, 94°W) 95
Fort Smith, NT (60°N, 112°W) 69
Fort Stockton, TX (31°N, 103°W) 94
Fort Vermillion, AB (58°N, 116°W) 68
Fort Walton Beach, FL (30°N, 87°W) 92
Fort Wayne, IN (41°N, 85°W) 90
Fort Worth, TX (33°N, 97°W) 95
Fort Yukon (YOO kahn), AK (67°N, 145°W) 104
Fortaleza, Brazil (4°S, 39°W) 127
Fortescue R. (FAWR tehs kyoo), Australia (21°S, 117°E) 195
Fortune Bay, NL (47°N, 55°W) 72
Fourth Cataract, waterfall in Sudan (19°N, 32°E) 140
Foveaux Strait (foh VOH), New Zealand (47°S, 168°E) 195
Fox R., U.S. (42°N, 88°W) 97
Fox R., WI (44°N, 89°W) 99
Foxe Basin, NU (67°N, 80°W) 61
Foxe Channel, NU (65°N, 80°W) 61
Foxe Pen., Baffin I. (65°N, 76°W) 61
Foz do Iguazu, Brazil (17°S, 12°E) 127
Framingham (FRAY ming ham), MA (42°N, 72°W) 89
France, country in Europe (47°N, 0°) 158
Franceville (frahns VEEL), Gabon (2°S, 14°E) 139
Francis Case, L., SD (43°N, 99°W) 98
Francistown, Botswana (21°S, 27°E) 141
Francois L. (frang SWUH), BC (54°N, 126°W) 68
Frankfort, KY (38°N, 85°W) 90
Frankfurt, Germany (50°N, 9°E) 159
Franklin D. Roosevelt L., WA (48°N, 118°W) 100
Franklin, NC (35°N, 83°W) 90
Franz Josef Land, island group in Arctic O. (82°N, 55°E) 168
Fraser I., Australia (25°S, 153°E) 190
Fraser Plateau, BC (53°N, 125°W) 68
Fraser R., Canada (51°N, 122°W) 68
Frederick, MD (39°N, 77°W) 91
Fredericksburg, VA (38°N, 77°W) 91
Fredericton, NB (46°N, 67°W) 72
Fredonia, NY (42°N, 79°W) 88
Fredrikstad, Norway (59°N, 11°E) 157
Freemantle, Australia (32°S, 116°E) 195
Freeport, IL (42°N, 90°W) 97
Freetown, Sierra Leone (8°N, 13°W) 138
Fremont (FREE mahnt), CA (38°N, 122°W) 102
Fremont, NE (41°N, 96°W) 96
Fremont, OH (41°N, 83°W) 90
French Frigate Shoals, island in Pacific O. (24°N, 167°W) 189
French Guiana (gee AH nuh), overseas state of France (4°N, 53°W) 127
French Lick, IN (39°N, 87°W) 90
French Polynesia, poss. of France (20°S, 140°W) 189
Frenchman R., North America (49°N, 108°W) 69
Fresno, CA (37°N, 120°W) 102
Fria, Cape, Africa (18°S, 12°E) 141
Frio, Cape, Brazil (23°S, 42°W) 121

Name (Pronunciation), Description (Lat., Long.) Page

Frisian Is., Europe (53°N, 5°E) 158
Frobisher Bay, Canada (63°N, 67°W) 71
Frobisher L., SK (56°N, 108°W) 69
Front Range, CO (40°N, 106°W) 78
Frontera (fron TER ah), Mexico (19°N, 93°W) 94
Fuerte R., Mexico (27°N, 109°W) 114
Fuerteventura, Canary Is. (28°N, 13°W) 136
Fuji, Mt. (FOO jee), Japan (35°N, 139°E) 183
Fukui (foo KOO ee), Japan (36°N, 136°E) 183
Fukuoka, Japan (34°N, 130°E) 183
Fukushima (foo kuh SHEE muh), Japan (37°N, 140°E) 183
Fulton, KY (37°N, 89°W) 90
Funafuti (FOO nah FOO tee), Tuvalu (8°S, 179°E) 189
Funchal, Madeira Is. (33°N, 16°W) 136
Fundy, Bay of, North America (45°N, 65°W) 72
Fundy N.P., NB (46°N, 65°W) 72
Furnas Res., Brazil (21°S, 47°W) 120
Furneaux Group (FUHR noh), islands in Bass Strait (40°S, 148°E) 190
Fushun (fyu shoon), China (42°N, 124°E) 182
Futuna (foo TOO nah), island in Pacific O. (15°S, 178°W) 189
Fuzhou (FYU zhoo), China (26°N, 119°E) 182
Fyn (FIN), island in Kattegat (55°N, 10°E) 159

G

Gabes, Gulf of (GAHB uhs), Tunisia (34°N, 10°E) 136
Gabon, country in Africa (1°S, 12°E) 139
Gaborone (gahb uh ROHN ee), Botswana (24°S, 26°E) 141
Gadsden, AL (34°N, 86°W) 92
Gaguan I., Pacific O. (17°N, 146°E) 188
Gainesville, FL (30°N, 82°W) 93
Gairdner, L., Australia (32°S, 136°E) 190
Galapagos Is. (guh LAH puh gohs), Pacific O. (0°, 91°W) 121
Galapagos Rift, Pacific O. (0°, 90°W) 22
Galati (guh LATS ee), Romania (45°N, 28°E) 159
Galdhopiggen, Norway (62°N, 8°E) 157
Galena (guh LEEN uh), IL (42°N, 90°W) 97
Galesburg (GAYLZ buhrg), IL (41°N, 90°W) 97
Galilee, Sea of, Asia (33°N, 36°E) 178
Gallatin R., MT (45°N, 111°W) 101
Gallinas, Point, Colombia (12°N, 72°W) 126
Gallup, NM (36°N, 109°W) 103
Galveston, TX (29°N, 95°W) 95
Galveston Bay, TX (30°N, 94°W) 95
Galway Bay, Ireland (53°N, 9°W) 156
Gambia (GAM bee uh), country in Africa (13°N, 15°W) 138
Gambia R., Africa (13°N, 14°W) 138
Gambier Is. (gamb YAY) Pacific O. (23°S, 135°W) 189
Ganca, Azerbaijan (41°N, 46°E) 161
Gander, NL (49°N, 55°W) 72
Ganges, Mouths of the (GAN jeez), delta in Asia (22°N, 89°E) 180
Ganges Plain, India (26°N, 84°E) 180
Ganges R., India (25°N, 86°E) 180
Gao, Mali (17°N, 0°) 138
Garabogazkol Aylagy, gulf in Caspian Sea (41°N, 53°E) 179
Garda, L., Italy (46°N, 10°E) 159
Garden City, KS (38°N, 101°W) 96
Gardner Pinnacles, island in Pacific O. (25°N, 167°W) 189
Garibaldi, Mt. (gair ih BAL dee), BC (50°N, 123°W) 68
Garibaldi P.P., BC (50°N, 122°W) 68
Garissa, Kenya (1°S, 40°E) 140
Garland, TX (33°N, 97°W) 95
Garonne R. (guh RAHN), France (44°N, 1°E) 158
Garoowe, Somalia (9°N, 48°E) 140
Garoua (guh ROO uh), Cameroon (9°N, 13°E) 139
Garrison Dam, ND (48°N, 101°W) 98
Gary, IN (42°N, 87°W) 90
Gasconade R. (gas kuh NAYD), MO (38°N, 92°W) 97
Gaspe (gah SPAY), QC (49°N, 65°W) 71
Gaspe Pen., QC (48°N, 67°W) 71
Gaspesie P.P., QC (48°N, 64°W) 71
Gaston, L., U.S. (37°N, 78°W) 91
Gastonia, NC (35°N, 81°W) 91

Name (Pronunciation), Description (Lat., Long.) Page

Gates of the Arctic N.P., AK (68°N, 154°W) 104
Gatineau (gat uhn OH), QC (45°N, 76°W) 71
Gatineau R., QC (45°N, 76°W) 71
Gatun L., Panama (9°N, 79°W) 115
Gavin's Point Dam, SD (43°N, 97°W) 98
Gavle, Sweden (61°N, 18°E) 157
Gaza, terr. in Asia (32°N, 34°E) 178
Gaza, Gaza (32°N, 34°E) 178
Gaziantep, Turkey (37°N, 37°E) 178
Gazojak, Turkmenistan (42°N, 61°E) 179
Gbarnga, Liberia (7°N, 9°W) 138
Gdansk (guh DAHNSK), Poland (54°N, 19°E) 159
Gdansk, Gulf of, Poland (55°N, 19°E) 159
Gdynia (guh DIN ee uh), Poland (54°N, 18°E) 159
Geelong (juh LAWNG), Australia (38°S, 144°E) 195
Geita, Tanzania (3°S, 32°E) 140
Gemena, Dem. Rep. Congo (3°N, 20°E) 139
General Santos, Philippines (6°N, 125°E) 181
Genesee R. (jen uh SEE), NY (42°N, 78°W) 88
Geneseo (jen uh SEE oh), NY (43°N, 78°W) 88
Geneva, Switzerland (46°N, 6°E) 159
Geneva, L., Switzerland (46°N, 7°E) 159
Genoa (JEHN oh uh), Italy (44°N, 9°E) 159
George, South Africa (34°S, 23°E) 141
George, L., FL (29°N, 82°W) 93
George, L., NY (44°N, 73°W) 88
George R., QC (58°N, 66°W) 71
George Town, Malaysia (5°N, 100°E) 181
George West, TX (28°N, 98°W) 94
Georgetown, Guyana (7°N, 58°W) 127
Georgetown, KY (38°N, 85°W) 90
Georgetown, MD (39°N, 76°W) 91
Georgia, country in Asia (42°N, 43°E) 161
Georgia, state in U.S. (33°N, 83°W) 92–93
Georgia, Strait of, BC (49°N, 125°W) 68
Georgian Bay, Canada (45°N, 81°W) 70
Georgian Bay Is. N.P., L. Huron (45°N, 80°W) 70
Geraldton, Australia (29°S, 115°E) 195
Germantown, TN (37°N, 90°W) 90
Germany, country in Europe (52°N, 12°E) 159
Gettysburg, PA (40°N, 77°W) 88
Ghadamis, Libya (30°N, 10°E) 136
Ghaghara R. (GAHG uh ruh), Asia (27°N, 83°E) 180
Ghana, Africa (8°N, 2°W) 138
Ghat, Libya (25°N, 10°E) 136
Ghent (gehnt), Belgium (51°N, 4°E) 158
Ghurian (goo REE ahn), Afghanistan (34°N, 62°E) 180
Gibraltar (jih BRAWL tuhr), terr. of United Kingdom (36°N, 5°W) 158
Gibraltar, Strait of, Europe and Africa (36°N, 6°W) 136
Gibson Desert, Australia (24°S, 120°E) 190
Gijon, Spain (44°N, 6°W) 158
Gila R. (HEE luh), U.S. (33°N, 114°W) 102–103
Gilbert Is., Pacific O. (1°S, 174°E) 188–189
Gillam, MB (56°N, 95°W) 69
Gillette (juh LEHT), WY (44°N, 106°W) 101
Gimli, MB (51°N, 97°W) 69
Gisborne, New Zealand (39°S, 178°E) 195
Giza (GEE zuh), Egypt (30°N, 31°E) 137
Gjovik (GYU vehk), Norway (61°N, 11°E) 157
Glace Bay, NS (46°N, 60°W) 72
Glacier N.P., BC (51°N, 118°W) 68
Glacier N.P., MT (49°N, 114°W) 101
Glacier Bay N.P. (glay shuhr), AK (59°N, 137°W) 104
Gladstone, Australia (24°S, 152°E) 195
Glasgow (GLAHZ goh), Scotland (56°N, 4°W) 156
Glasgow (GLAS goh), KY (37°N, 86°W) 90
Glen Canyon Dam, AZ (37°N, 111°W) 103
Glendale, AZ (34°N, 112°W) 103
Glendale, CA (34°N, 118°W) 102
Glendive (GLEHN dyv), MT (47°N, 105°W) 101
Gobi (GOH bee), desert in Asia (44°N, 109°E) 182
Godavari R. (guh DAHV uh ree), India (19°N, 77°E) 180
Goderich (GAHD rich), ON (44°N, 82°W) 70
Gods L., MB (55°N, 94°W) 69
Gods R., MB (55°N, 93°W) 69
Godthab (GAWT hob), alternative name for Nuuk (64°N, 51°W) 52
Godwin Austen, Mt., China and Pakistan (36°N, 77°E) 180

Name (Pronunciation), Description (Lat., Long.) Page

Gogebic Range (goh GEH bik), MI (47°N, 90°W) 99
Goiania (goy AN ee uh), Brazil (17°S, 49°W) 127
Gokceada, i. in Aegean Sea (40°N, 25°E) 159
Golan Heights, terr. in Asia (33°N, 36°E) 178
Gold Coast, Australia (28°S, 153°E) 195
Goldsboro, NC (35°N, 78°W) 91
Gomez Palacio (pah LAH syoh), Mexico
  (26°N, 104°W) 114
Gonder, Ethiopia (13°N, 38°E) 140
Good Hope, Cape of, South Africa (34°S, 18°E) 141
Goodland, KS (39°N, 102°W) 96
Goose L., U.S. (42°N, 121°W) 100
Gore, New Zealand (46°S, 169°E) 195
Gorgan (gohr GAHN), Iran (37°N, 54°E) 178
Gori, Georgia (42°N, 44°E) 161
Gorki Res., Russia (57°N, 43°E) 160
Gosford, Australia (32°S, 154°E) 195
Gota Canal, Sweden (59°N, 15°E) 157
Gotaland, region of Sweden (57°N, 13°E) 157
Goteborg (yuh tuh BAWR yuh), Sweden
  (58°N, 12°E) 157
Gotel Mts., Africa (7°N, 11°E) 138
Gotland, island in Baltic Sea (57°N, 19°E) 157
Goto Is. (GOHT oh), East China Sea (33°N, 129°E) .. 183
Gott Peak, BC (50°N, 122°W) 68
Gouin, Res. (gwan), QC (48°N, 74°W) 71
Governador Valadares, Brazil (19°S, 42°W) 127
Goycay (geh AWK chy), Azerbaijan (41°N, 48°E) 161
Gracias a Dios, Cape, Caribbean Sea (15°N, 83°W) .. 115
Grafton, ND (48°N, 97°W) 98
Graham, TX (33°N, 99°W) 94
Grampian Mts., Scotland (57°N, 4°W) 156
Gran Canaria, Canary Is. (28°N, 16°W) 136
Gran Chaco, plains in central South America
  (24°S, 63°W) 126
Granada, Nicaragua (12°N, 86°W) 115
Granada, Spain (37°N, 4°W) 158
Grand Bahama I., Atlantic O. (27°N, 78°W) 93
Grand Canal, China (36°N, 116°E) 182
Grand Canyon, AZ (36°N, 113°W) 102-103
Grand Canyon N.P., AZ (36°N, 112°W) 103
Grand Coulee Dam, WA (48°N, 119°W) 100
Grand Erg de Bilma, desert in Africa (19°N, 14°E) .. 138
Grand Erg Occidental, desert in Algeria (30°N, 1°E) .. 136
Grand Erg Oriental, desert in Algeria (31°N, 7°E) ... 136
Grand Falls, NB (47°N, 68°W) 72
Grand Forks, ND (48°N, 97°W) 98
Grand Haven, MI (43°N, 86°W) 99
Grand Island, city in NE (41°N, 98°W) 96
Grand I., L. Superior (47°N, 87°W) 99
Grand Junction, CO (39°N, 108°W) 103
Grand L., LA (30°N, 93°W) 95
Grand L., NB (46°N, 67°W) 72
Grand L., OH (41°N, 84°W) 90
Grand Manan I., Bay of Fundy (45°N, 67°W) 72
Grand Rapids, MB (53°N, 99°W) 69
Grand Rapids, MI (43°N, 86°W) 99
Grand R., MI (43°N, 86°W) 99
Grand R., SD (46°N, 102°W) 98
Grand R., U.S. (40°N, 94°W) 97
Grand Teton N.P., WY (44°N, 110°W) 101
Grand Traverse Bay, MI (45°N, 86°W) 99
Grande 2, Res. de la, QC (54°N, 77°W) 71
Grande 3, Res. de la, QC (54°N, 75°W) 71
Grande 4, Res. de la, QC (54°N, 73°W) 71
Grande Bay, Argentina (51°S, 68°W) 126
Grande Prairie, AB (55°N, 119°W) 68
Grande R., Nicaragua (14°N, 84°W) 115
Granville L., MB (56°N, 100°W) 69
Grass River P.P., MB (54°N, 101°W) 69
Grasslands N.P., SK (48°N, 107°W) 69
Grays Harbor, WA (47°N, 124°W) 100
Graz, Austria (47°N, 15°E) 159
Great Abaco I., Atlantic O. (27°N, 77°W) 93
Great Artesian Basin, Australia (24°S, 145°E) 190
Great Australian Bight, gulf in Indian O.
  (34°S, 130°E) 190
Great Barrier Reef, Australia (15°S, 146°E) 190
Great Basin, U.S. (39°N, 117°W) 102
Great Basin N.P., NV (39°N, 114°W) 102
Great Bear L., NT (66°N, 121°W) 60

Great Bend, KS (38°N, 99°W) 96
Great Britain, island in North Sea (52°N, 2°W) 156
Great Dismal Swamp, U.S. (37°N, 76°W) 91
Great Divide Basin, WY (42°N, 108°W) 101
Great Dividing Range, Australia (34°S, 149°E) 191
Great Escarpment, natural feature of Brazil
  (27°S, 49°W) 122
Great Falls, MT (47°N, 111°W) 101
Great Hungarian Plain, Europe (46°N, 18°E) 159
Great Inagua I., Atlantic O. (21°N, 74°W) 107
Great Indian Desert, India (25°N, 71°E) 180
Great Karoo, plateau in South Africa (33°S, 23°E) .. 141
Great Lakes, North America (45°N, 85°W) 53
Great Miami R., OH (39°N, 85°W) 90
Great Plains, North America (50°N, 115°W) 53
Great Rift Valley, Africa (2°S, 35°E) 140
Great Salt L., UT (41°N, 112°W) 103
Great Salt L. Desert, U.S. (41°N, 113°W) 102
Great Sand Dunes N.P., CO (38°N, 104°W) 103
Great Sandy Desert, Australia (19°S, 124°E) 190
Great Sandy Desert, OR (44°N, 121°W) 100
Great Slave L., NT (62°N, 114°W) 68-69
Great Smoky Mts. N.P., U.S. (36°N, 84°W) 90
Great Valley, Appalachian Mts. (38°N, 79°W) 90-91
Great Victoria Desert, Australia (28°S, 126°E) 190
Great Wall, China (38°N, 105°E) 182
Greater Antilles, island group in Caribbean Sea
  (20°N, 77°W) 108
Greater Khingan Range, China (44°N, 119°E) 182
Greater Sunda Is., Indian O. (4°S, 108°E) 181
Greece, country in Europe (38°N, 22°E) 159
Greeley, CO (40°N, 105°W) 103
Green Bay, city in WI (44°N, 88°W) 99
Green Bay, L. Michigan (45°N, 88°W) 99
Green Mts., VT (44°N, 73°W) 89
Green R., KY (37°N, 87°W) 90
Green R., U.S. (42°N, 110°W) 101
Green River, city in WY (42°N, 109°W) 100
Greenland, poss. of Denmark (75°N, 40°W) 52
Greenland Sea, Arctic Ocean (77°N, 1°W) 53
Greensboro, NC (36°N, 80°W) 91
Greensburg, IN (39°N, 86°W) 90
Greenstone, ON (50°N, 87°W) 70
Greenville, Liberia (5°N, 9°W) 138
Greenville, MS (33°N, 91°W) 93
Greenville, NC (36°N, 77°W) 91
Greenville, SC (35°N, 82°W) 93
Greenwood, MS (33°N, 90°W) 92
Greenwood, SC (32°N, 84°W) 93
Grenada, country in Caribbean Sea (12°N, 62°W) ... 116
Grenoble (gruh NOH buhl), France (45°N, 6°E) 158
Gresham, OR (45°N, 122°W) 100
Greymouth, New Zealand (42°S, 171°E) 195
Grinnell (gruh NEHL), IA (42°N, 93°W) 97
Groningen (GROH ning guhn), Netherlands
  (53°N, 7°E) 158
Groote Eylandt (gryoot EYE lund), island in Gulf
  of Carpentaria (14°S, 137°E) 190
Grootfontein, Namibia (20°S, 18°E) 141
Gros Morne N.P., NL (49°N, 58°W) 72
Groton (graht uhn), CT (41°N, 72°W) 89
Grozny (GRAWZ nee), Russia (43°N, 46°E) 161
Guadalajara (gwah duh luh HAHR uh), Mexico
  (21°N, 103°W) 114
Guadalcanal, island in Solomon Sea (9°S, 160°E) .. 188
Guadalquivir R., Europe (38°N, 6°W) 158
Guadalupe (gwah duh LOO peh), Mexico
  (31°N, 106°W) 114
Guadalupe I. (gwah duh LOOP), Mexico
  (29°N, 118°W) 114
Guadalupe Mts., U.S. (32°N, 105°W) 94
Guadalupe Mts. N.P., U.S. (32°N, 105°W) 94
Guadalupe Pk., TX (32°N, 105°W) 94
Guadalupe R., TX (29°N, 97°W) 95
Guadeloupe (gwah duh LOOP), overseas state
  of France (17°N, 62°W) 116
Guadiana R., Spain (39°N, 7°W) 158
Guam, poss. of U.S. (14°N, 143°E) 188
Guanajuato, Mexico (21°N, 101°W) 114
Guanajuato (gwah nah HWAH toh), state in Mexico
  (21°N, 101°W) 114

Guangzhou (gwahng joh), China (23°N, 113°E) 182
Guantanamo (gwahn TAH nuh moh), Cuba
  (20°N, 75°W) 107
Guapore R. (gwahp uh RAY), South America
  (12°S, 65°W) 127
Guardafui, Cape (GWAK duh foo ee), Somalia
  (12°N, 51°E) 140
Guatemala, country in Central America
  (15°N, 90°W) 115
Guatemala City, Guatemala (15°N, 91°W) 115
Guaviare R. (gwav YAHR ee), South America
  (3°N, 73°W) 126
Guayaquil (gwah yah KEEL), Ecuador (2°S, 80°W) .. 126
Guayaquil, Gulf of, Pacific O. (3°S, 80°W) 126
Guelph (gwehlf), ON (44°N, 80°W) 88
Guelmim, Morocco (29°N, 10°W) 136
Guerrero, state in Mexico (18°N, 100°W) 114
Guinea (GIHN ee), country in Africa (10°N, 10°W) .. 138
Guinea, Gulf of, Atlantic O. (0°, 0°) 138
Guinea-Bissau (GIHN ee bih sow), country in Africa
  (12°N, 15°W) 138
Guiana Highlands (gee AH nuh), South America
  (4°N, 65°W) 127
Guiyang (gway yang), China (27°N, 107°E) 182
Gujranwala (gooj ruhn WAHL uh), Pakistan
  (32°N, 74°E) 180
Gulf Coastal Plain, Mexico (20°N, 98°W) 114
Gulf Coastal Plain, U.S. (31°N, 94°W) 76-77
Gulf Islands N.P., BC (48°N, 123°W) 68
Gulfport, MS (30°N, 89°W) 92
Gulu, Uganda (3°N, 32°E) 140
Gumdag, Turkmenistan (39°N, 54°E) 179
Gunisao R. (guhn ih SAY oh), MB (54°N, 97°W) 69
Gunnison R., CO (39°N, 108°W) 103
Guntersville L., AL (34°N, 86°W) 92
Guri Res., Venezuela (8°N, 63°W) 127
Guwahati, India (26°N, 92°E) 180
Guyana, country in South America (5°N, 59°W) 127
Guymon (GY muhn), OK (37°N, 101°W) 94
Gwadar (gah WAH dahr), Pakistan (25°N, 62°E) 180
Gwaii Haanas N.P., BC (52°N, 132°W) 68
Gwalior, India (26°N, 78°E) 180
Gweru, Zimbabwe (19°S, 30°E) 141
Gydan Pen., Russia (84°N, 80°E) 168
Gyor, Hungary (48°N, 18°E) 159
Gyumri, Armenia (41°N, 44°E) 161
Gyzylarbat, Turkmenistan (39°N, 56°E) 179

H

Haapai Group, Pacific O. (20°S, 175°W) 189
Hachinohe (HAHCH ih noh hay), Japan
  (40°N, 142°E) 183
Hadur Shuayb, Mt., Yemen (16°N, 44°E) 178
Haeju (HY joo), North Korea (38°N, 126°E) 183
Hafar al Batin, Saudi Arabia (28°N, 46°E) 178
Hafun, Cape (ha FOON), Somalia (10°N, 51°E) 140
Hagatna, Guam (14°N, 143°E) 188
Hagerstown, MD (40°N, 78°W) 91
Hague, The, Netherlands (52°N, 4°E) 158
Haida Gwaii, islands in Pacific O. (53°N, 132°W) 68
Haifa, Israel (33°N, 35°E) 178
Haikou (hy koh), China (20°N, 110°E) 181
Hail, Saudi Arabia (28°N, 42°E) 178
Hainan, island in South China Sea (20°N, 110°E) ... 182
Haines, AK (59°N, 136°W) 104
Haiphong (hy fong), Vietnam (21°N, 107°E) 181
Haiti (HAY tee), country in Caribbean Sea
  (19°N, 72°W) 107
Hakodate (hahk uh DAHT ee), Japan
  (42°N, 141°E) 183
Haleakala N.P. (HAHL ee ahk uh LAH), HI
  (21°N, 156°W) 104
Halifax, NS (44°N, 63°W) 72
Halil R., Asia (28°N, 57°E) 178
Hall Is., Pacific O. (9°N, 152°E) 188
Hall Pen., Frobisher Bay (63°N, 66°W) 71
Halle (HAHL uh), Germany (52°N, 12°E) 159
Halley Station, Antarctica (76°S, 26°W) 200
Halmahera, island in Philippine Sea (1°N, 128°E) ... 181
Halmahera Sea, Indian O. (0°, 129°E) 190
Halmstad, Sweden (57°N, 13°E) 157

Name (Pronunciation), Description (Lat., Long.) Page   **Name** (Pronunciation), Description (Lat., Long.) Page   **Name** (Pronunciation), Description (Lat., Long.) Page

Hamadan, Iran (35°N, 48°E) 179
Hamamatsu (hahm uh MAHT soo), Japan (35°N, 138°E) 183
Hamar, Norway (61°N, 11°E) 157
Hamburg, Germany (54°N, 10°E) 159
Hamden, CT (41°N, 73°W) 89
Hameenlinna (HEH mayn lihn nay), Finland (61°N, 24°E) 157
Hamersley Range (HAM erz lee), Australia (22°S, 118°E) 191
Hamhung (HAHM hoong), North Korea (40°N, 128°E) 183
Hamilton, AL (34°N, 88°W) 92
Hamilton, New Zealand (37°S, 175°E) 195
Hamilton, OH (39°N, 85°W) 90
Hamilton, ON (43°N, 80°W) 70
Hamilton Inlet, NL (54°N, 58°W) 72
Hammerfest, Norway (71°N, 24°E) 157
Hammond, IN (42°N, 87°W) 90
Hampton, VA (37°N, 76°W) 91
Han R. (hahn), China (33°N, 111°E) 182
Handan, China (37°N, 114°E) 182
Hangzhou, China (31°N, 120°E) 182
Hannibal, MO (40°N, 91°W) 97
Hannover, Germany (52°N, 10°E) 159
Hanoi, Vietnam (21°N, 106°E) 181
Hao Atoll, Pacific O. (18°S, 141°W) 189
Haora (huh O rah), India (23°N, 88°E) 180
Happy Valley–Goose Bay, NL (53°N, 60°W) 72
Harare, Zimbabwe (18°S, 31°E) 141
Harbin, China (46°N, 127°E) 182
Hardanger Fiord (hahr DANG guhr), Norway (60°N, 6°E) 157
Harer, Ethiopia (9°N, 42°E) 140
Hargeysa, Somalia (9°N, 44°E) 140
Harirud, R., Asia (34°N, 61°E) 178
Harlan, KY (37°N, 83°W) 90
Harlingen (hahr ling uhn), TX (26°N, 98°W) 95
Harney Basin, OR (43°N, 120°W) 100
Harney Pk., SD (44°N, 104°W) 98
Harpers Ferry, WV (39°N, 78°W) 91
Harricana R. (har ih KAN aw), QC (51°N, 79°W) 71
Harrisburg, PA (40°N, 77°W) 88
Harrisonburg, VA (39°N, 79°W) 91
Harstad (HAHR stahd), Norway (69°N, 16°E) 157
Hartford, CT (42°N, 73°W) 89
Hartwell L., U.S. (34°N, 83°W) 93
Hasa, region of Saudi Arabia (27°N, 48°E) 178
Hastings, NE (41°N, 98°W) 96
Hastings, New Zealand (40°S, 177°E) 195
Hatchie R., U.S. (36°N, 90°W) 90
Hatteras, Cape, NC (35°N, 76°W) 91
Hatteras I., Pamlico Sound (36°N, 76°W) 91
Hattiesburg, MS (31°N, 89°W) 92
Havana, Cuba (23°N, 82°W) 107
Havasu, L. (hav uh soo), AZ (34°N, 114°W) 102
Haverhill, MA (43°N, 71°W) 89
Havre (HAV uhr), MT (48°N, 110°W) 101
Havre-Saint-Pierre (HAV ruh SAN PYAIR), QC (50°N, 64°W) 71
Hawaii (huh WY ee), state in U.S.(21°N, 157°W) 104
Hawaii, island in Pacific O. (20°N, 156°W) 104
Hawaii Volcanoes N.P., HI (20°N, 156°W) 104
Hawaiian Ridge, Pacific O. (23°N, 165°W) 22
Hay R., Canada (59°N, 119°W) 68
Hay River, city in NT (61°N, 116°W) 68
Hayes R., MB (56°N, 93°W) 69
Hays, KS (39°N, 99°W) 96
Hayward, WI (46°N, 92°W) 99
Hazelton, BC (55°N, 128°W) 68
Hearst, ON (50°N, 84°W) 70
Heart R., ND (47°N, 102°W) 98
Hebgen L., MT (45°N, 111°W) 101
Hebrides (HEHB rih deez), island group in Atlantic O. (57°N, 7°W) 156
Hebron, Israel (32°N, 35°E) 178
Hecate Strait (HEK uht), BC (53°N, 131°W) 68
Hecla P.P., MB (51°N, 99°W) 69
Hejaz, region of Saudi Arabia (24°N, 38°E) 178
Hekla, mt. in Iceland (64°N, 20°W) 148
Helena, MT (47°N, 112°W) 101
Hell's Canyon, Snake R. (45°N, 117°W) 100

Helmand R., Asia (31°N, 64°E) 180
Helsingborg (HEHL sing bawr), Sweden (56°N, 13°E) 157
Helsinki, Finland (60°N, 25°E) 157
Hempstead, NY (41°N, 74°W) 88-89
Henderson, KY (38°N, 88°W) 90
Henderson, NC (36°N, 78°W) 91
Henderson, NV (36°N, 115°W) 102
Henderson I., Pacific O. (24°S, 129°W) 189
Hendersonville, TN (36°N, 87°W) 90
Henrietta Maria, Cape, ON (55°N, 82°W) 70
Henry Mts., UT (38°N, 111°W) 103
Herat (heh RAHT), Afghanistan (34°N, 62°E) 180
Hereford (HUHR furd), TX (35°N, 102°W) 94
Hermosillo (ehr muh SEE yoh), Mexico (29°N, 111°W) 114
Hetch Hetchy Aqueduct, CA (38°N, 121°W) 102
Hialeah (hy uh LEE uh), FL (26°N, 80°W) 93
Hibbing, MN (47°N, 93°W) 99
Hickory, NC (36°N, 81°W) 91
Hickory, L., NC (36°N, 81°W) 91
Hidalgo, state in Mexico (21°N, 100°W) 114
High Level, AB (57°N, 118°W) 68
High Point, NC (36°N, 80°W) 91
Highlands, region of Scotland (57°N, 4°W) 156
Hillsboro, OH (39°N, 84°W) 90
Hilo, HI (20°N, 155°W) 104
Himalayas, mt. range in Asia (28°N, 85°E) 180
Hindu Kush, mt. range in Asia (37°N, 72°E) 180
Hinton, AB (53°N, 118°W) 68
Hirakud Res., India (22°N, 84°E) 180
Hirosaki, Japan (41°N, 140°E) 183
Hiroshima (heer oh SHEE muh), Japan (34°N, 132°E) 183
Hispaniola, island in Caribbean Sea (19°N, 72°W) 108
Hitachi, Japan (37°N, 141°E) 183
Hiva Oa (HEE vah O ah), island in Pacific O. (10°S, 139°W) 189
Hjalmar L. (YEHL muhr), NT (62°N, 115°W) 69
Ho Chi Minh City (ho chee mihn), Vietnam (11°N, 107°E) 181
Hobart, Australia (43°S, 147°E) 195
Hobbs, NM (33°N, 103°W) 103
Hobyo, Somalia (5°N, 48°E) 140
Hoh R., WA (48°N, 124°W) 100
Hohhot (huh ho tuh), China (41°N, 112°E) 182
Hokkaido, island in Sea of Japan (43°N, 143°E) 183
Holguin (awl GEEN), Cuba (21°N, 76°W) 107
Holland, MI (43°N, 86°W) 99
Hollywood, FL (26°N, 80°W) 93
Holston R., TN (36°N, 84°W) 90
Holt, MO (39°N, 94°W) 97
Holyoke (HOHL yohk), MA (42°N, 73°W) 89
Homer, AK (60°N, 152°W) 104
Homestead, FL (25°N, 80°W) 93
Homs, Syria (35°N, 37°E) 178
Homyel, Belarus (52°N, 29°E) 160
Hondo R., North America (18°N, 89°W) 106
Honduras, country in Central America (15°N, 87°W) 115
Honduras, Gulf of, Caribbean Sea (16°N, 88°W) 115
Hong Kong, China (22°N, 114°E) 182
Hongshui R. (hung shay), China (25°N, 105°E) 181
Honiara (hohn ee AHR ah), Solomon Islands (9°S, 160°E) 188
Honolulu, HI (21°N, 158°W) 104
Honshu, island in Sea of Japan (38°N, 140°E) 183
Hood, Mt., OR (45°N, 122°W) 100
Hooghly R. (HOO glee), India (23°N, 88°E) 180
Hoover, AL (33°N, 87°W) 92
Hoover Dam, U.S. (36°N, 115°W) 102
Hope, AR (34°N, 94°W) 95
Hopkinsville, KY (37°N, 87°W) 90
Hormuz, Strait of, Persian Gulf and Gulf of Oman (27°N, 57°E) 178
Horn, Cape, South America (56°S, 68°W) 126
Horn Plateau, NT (62°N, 120°W) 68
Hot Springs, AR (34°N, 93°W) 95
Hot Springs, SD (43°N, 103°W) 98
Hot Springs N.P., AR (34°N, 93°W) 95
Houghton (HOH tuhn), MI (47°N, 89°W) 99

Houma (HOH muh), LA (30°N, 91°W) 95
Houston, MS (34°N, 89°W) 92
Houston, TX (30°N, 95°W) 95
Howland I., poss. of U.S. (1°N, 176°W) 189
Hrodna, Belarus (54°N, 24°E) 160
Huambo, Angola (13°S, 16°E) 141
Huancayo, Peru (12°S, 75°W) 126
Huang He (WANG huh), r. in China (41°N, 110°E) 182
Huanuco, Peru (10°S, 76°W) 126
Huascaran, Mt. (wahs kuh RAHN), Peru (9°S, 78°W) 126
Huber Heights, OH (40°N, 84°W) 90
Hubli-Dharwad (hoob lee dahr WAHRD), India (15°N, 75°E) 180
Hudson Bay, Canada (60°N, 85°W) 69
Hudson Bay Lowlands, Canada (57°N, 93°W) 69
Hudson R., NY (42°N, 74°W) 88
Hudson Strait, Hudson Bay and Labrador Sea (62°N, 70°W) 71
Hue (hoo AY), Vietnam (16°N, 107°E) 181
Huelva (WEHL vah), Spain (37°N, 7°W) 158
Huila, Plateau of, Angola (15°S, 15°E) 141
Hull, England (54°N, 0°) 156
Huludao, China (41°N, 121°E) 182
Humboldt, SK (52°N, 105°W) 69
Humboldt R., NV (41°N, 117°W) 102
Humphreys Peak (huhm freez), AZ (35°N, 112°W) 103
Hungary, country in Europe (47°N, 18°E) 159
Huntington, WV (38°N, 82°W) 91
Huntington Beach, CA (34°N, 118°W) 102
Huntsville, AL (35°N, 87°W) 92
Huntsville, ON (45°N, 79°W) 70
Huntsville, TX (31°N, 96°W) 95
Huron (HYOO ruhn), SD (44°N, 98°W) 98
Huron, L., North America (45°N, 82°W) 70
Hutchinson, KS (38°N, 98°W) 96
Huttonsville, WV (39°N, 80°W) 91
Huumaa, island in Baltic Sea, (59°N, 23°E) 157
Hyco R., NC (36°N, 79°W) 91
Hyderabad, India (17°N, 78°E) 180
Hyderabad, Pakistan (25°N, 68°E) 180

I

I-n-Gall, Niger (17°N, 6°E) 108
I-n-Salah, Algeria (28°N, 4°E) 136
Iasi (YASH ee), Romania (47°N, 28°E) 159
Ibadan, Nigeria (8°N, 4°E) 138
Ibague (ee buh GAY), Colombia (4°N, 75°W) 126
Ibb, Yemen (14°N, 44°E) 178
Iberian Pen., Europe (39°N, 5°W) 158
Ibiza, Balearic Is. (39°N, 1°E) 158
Ica, Peru (14°S, 76°W) 126
Iceland, country in Atlantic O. (65°N, 20°W) 158
Idaho, state in U.S. (44°N, 115°W) 100-101
Idaho Falls, ID (44°N, 112°W) 101
Ifalik Atoll (EE fah leek), Pacific O. (7°N, 144°E) 188
Iguazu Falls (ih GWAH syu), waterfall in South America (26°S, 54°W) 127
Iguidi Desert, Africa (28°N, 7°W) 133
IJsselmeer (EYE suhl mer), l. in Netherlands (53°N, 5°E) 158
Ilesha, Nigeria (8°N, 5°E) 138
Ilha Solteira Res., Brazil (20°S, 52°W) 127
Ili R., Asia (45°N, 77°E) 179
Iliamna L. (ihl ee AM nuh), AK (59°N, 155°W) 104
Illampu, Mt., Bolivia (16°S, 68°W) 127
Illinois, state in U.S. (40°N, 90°W) 97
Illinois R., IL (39°N, 91°W) 97
Ilmen, L., Russia (58°N, 32°E) 160
Iloilo (EE lo EE lo), Philippines (11°N, 123°E) 181
Ilorin (ee luh REEN), Nigeria (9°N, 5°E) 138
Imatra, Finland (61°N, 29°E) 157
Imperatriz, Brazil (6°S, 47°W) 127
Imperial, NE (41°N, 102°W) 96
Imperial Valley, CA (33°N, 116°W) 102
Imphal (IMP huhl), India (25°N, 94°E) 180
Inari, L., Finland (69°N, 28°E) 157
Inchon (IHN chahn), South Korea (37°N, 127°E) 183
Indals R., Sweden (63°N, 15°E) 157
Independence, MO (39°N, 94°W) 97
India, country in Asia (25°N, 80°E) 180

Name (Pronunciation), Description (Lat., Long.) Page

Indian L., ON (47°N, 82°W) ... 70
Indian Ocean ... 15
Indian Plate, India and Indian O. ... 20
Indiana, state in U.S. (40°N, 86°W) ... 90
Indiana, PA (41°N, 79°W) ... 88
Indianapolis, IN (40°N, 86°W) ... 90
Indigirka R., Russia (68°N, 148°E) ... 169
Indio (IN dee oh), CA (34°N, 116°W) ... 102
Indispensable Reefs, Pacific O. (12°S, 161°E) ... 188
Indochina Pen., Asia (15°N, 105°E) ... 181
Indonesia, country in Asia (3°S, 115°E) ... 181
Indore (ihn DOHR), India (23°N, 76°E) ... 180
Indus R., Asia (25°N, 68°E) ... 180
Infiernillo Res., Mexico (19°N, 102°W) ... 114
Inhambane (een ahm BAH neh), Mozambique (24°S, 35°E) ... 141
Innsbruck (ihnz bruk), Austria (47°N, 11°E) ... 159
Inta, Russia (65°N, 60°E) ... 160
Interior Plains, Canada (50°N, 105°W) ... 69
International Falls, MN (49°N, 93°W) ... 98-99
Intracoastal Waterway, canal in LA (30°N, 93°W) ... 95
Inukjuak, QC (58°N, 79°W) ... 71
Inuvik (ih NOO vihk), NT (68°N, 134°W) ... 60
Invercargill (ihn vur KAHR gihl), New Zealand (46°S, 168°E) ... 195
Inverness (ihn vuhr NEHS), Scotland (57°N, 4°W) ... 156
Ioannina, Greece (39°N, 21°E) ... 159
Ionian Is., Greece (38°N, 20°E) ... 159
Ionian Sea, Europe (38°N, 18°E) ... 159
Iowa, state in U.S. (42°N, 94°W) ... 96-97
Iowa City, IA (42°N, 92°W) ... 97
Iowa R., IA (42°N, 92°W) ... 97
Ipoh (EE poh), Malaysia (5°N, 101°E) ... 181
Ipswich, England (52°N, 1°E) ... 156
Iqaluit, NU (64°N, 68°W) ... 71
Iquique (ih KEE keh), Chile (20°S, 70°W) ... 126
Iquitos (ih KEET ohs), Peru (4°S, 73°W) ... 126
Iraklion, Crete (35°N, 25°E) ... 159
Iran, country in Asia (31°N, 54°E) ... 178
Iran, Plateau of, Iran (33°N, 59°E) ... 178
Irapuato (ee rah PWAH toh), Mexico (21°N, 101°W) ... 114
Iraq, country in Asia (32°N, 44°E) ... 178
Irazu, mt. in Costa Rica (10°N, 84°W) ... 115
Irbid, Jordan (33°N, 36°E) ... 178
Ireland, country in Europe (54°N, 8°W) ... 156
Irish Sea, Europe (54°N, 5°W) ... 156
Irkutsk, Russia (52°N, 104°E) ... 182
Iron River, MI (46°N, 89°W) ... 99
Ironton, OH (39°N, 83°W) ... 90
Ironwood, MI (46°N, 90°W) ... 98
Irrawaddy, Mouths of the, delta in Burma (16°N, 95°E) ... 181
Irrawaddy R., Asia (20°N, 94°E) ... 181
Irtysh R. (ir TISH), Russia (58°N, 70°E) ... 170
Irving, TX (33°N, 97°W) ... 95
Isfahan, alternative name for Esfahan (33°N, 52°E) ... 178
Ishim R., Asia (53°N, 68°E) ... 179
Ishpatina Ridge, ON (47°N, 80°W) ... 70
Isiro, Dem. Rep. Congo (3°N, 28°E) ... 139
Iskut R., North America (57°N, 132°W) ... 68
Islamabad, Pakistan (34°N, 73°E) ... 180
Island L., MB (54°N, 94°W) ... 69
Islands, Bay of, NL (49°N, 58°W) ... 72
Isle of Pines, Pacific O. (23°S, 168°E) ... 188
Isle of Youth, Cuba (22°N, 83°W) ... 107
Isle Royale, L. Superior (48°N, 89°W) ... 99
Isle Royale N.P., MI (48°N, 89°W) ... 99
Ismailia (ees may EEL eea), Egypt (31°N, 32°E) ... 178
Isparta (is pahr TAH), Turkey (38°N, 31°E) ... 178
Israel, country in Asia (31°N, 35°E) ... 178
Istanbul, Turkey (41°N, 29°E) ... 178
Istokpoga, L. (ihs tahk POH guh), FL (27°N, 81°W) ... 93
Itabuna (i tah BU nah), Brazil (15°S, 39°W) ... 127
Itacoatiara (ee ta kwa TYAH ra), Brazil (3°S, 58°W) ... 127
Itajai (i tah ZHY), Brazil (27°S, 49°W) ... 127
Italy, country in Europe (42°N, 13°E) ... 159
Itasca, L. (eye TAS kuh), MN (47°N, 95°W) ... 98
Ithaca, NY (42°N, 76°W) ... 88
Ivanovo, Russia (57°N, 42°E) ... 160
Ivory Coast, alternative name for Côte d'Ivoire (8°N, 5°W) ... 138
Ivujivik, QC (62°N, 78°W) ... 71
Iwo (ee woh), Nigeria (8°N, 4°E) ... 138
Iwo To, Pacific O. (25°N, 142°E) ... 188
Izabal, L., Guatemala (15°N, 89°W) ... 115
Izhevsk, Russia (57°N, 53°E) ... 160
Izmir, Turkey (38°N, 27°E) ... 178
Izmit, Turkey (41°N, 30°E) ... 160
Izu Is. (EE zoo), Philippine Sea (34°N, 140°E) ... 183
Izu Trench, Pacific O. (35°N, 140°E) ... 22

J

J. Percy Priest L., TN (36°N, 87°W) ... 90
J. Strom Thurmond Res., U.S. (34°N, 82°W) ... 93
Jabalpur (JUHB uhl poor), India (23°N, 80°E) ... 180
Jaboatao (zhah baw ah toun), Brazil (8°S, 35°W) ... 127
Jackson, AL (32°N, 88°W) ... 92
Jackson, MI (42°N, 84°W) ... 99
Jackson, MS (32°N, 90°W) ... 92
Jackson, OH (39°N, 83°W) ... 90
Jackson, TN (36°N, 89°W) ... 90
Jackson, WY (44°N, 110°W) ... 101
Jacksonville, FL (30°N, 82°W) ... 93
Jacksonville, IL (40°N, 90°W) ... 97
Jacksonville, NC (35°N, 77°W) ... 91
Jaffna, Sri Lanka (10°N, 80°E) ... 180
Jaipur (JY poor), India (27°N, 76°E) ... 180
Jakarta, Indonesia (6°S, 107°E) ... 181
Jalalabad (jah lah LAH bahd), Afghanistan (34°N, 70°E) ... 180
Jalandhar, India (31°N, 76°E) ... 180
Jalapa, Mexico (20°N, 96°W) ... 114
Jalisco, state in Mexico (21°N, 105°W) ... 114
Jaluit Atoll (JAH loo it),Pacific O. (6°N, 170°E) ... 188
Jamaica, country in Caribbean Sea (18°N, 78°W) ... 107
Jamaica Channel, Caribbean Sea (19°N, 76°W) ... 107
Jambi, Indonesia (2°S, 103°E) ... 181
James Bay, Canada (54°N, 81°W) ... 70-71
James R., MO (37°N, 93°W) ... 97
James R., U.S. (46°N, 98°W) ... 98
James R., VA (38°N, 78°W) ... 91
Jamestown, ND (47°N, 99°W) ... 98
Jamestown, NY (42°N, 79°W) ... 88
Jamnagar, India (22°N, 70°E) ... 180
Jamshedpur (JAHM shed poor), India (23°N, 86°E) ... 180
Jan Mayen (yahn MY uhn), island in Greenland Sea (71°N, 8°W) ... 12
Janesville, WI (43°N, 89°W) ... 99
Japan, country in Asia (36°N, 138°E) ... 183
Japan, Sea of, Asia (40°N, 135°E) ... 183
Japura R., South America (3°S, 65°W) ... 127
Jarvis I., poss. of U.S. (0°, 160°W) ... 189
Jasper, AB (53°N, 118°W) ... 68
Jasper N.P., AB (52°N, 117°W) ... 68
Java, island in Java Sea (8°S, 110°E) ... 181
Java Sea, Indian O. (6°S, 113°E) ... 181
Javari R., South America (4°S, 72°W) ... 126
Jawhar, Somalia (3°N, 45°E) ... 140
Jaya Peak, Indonesia (4°S, 137°E) ... 181
Jayapura, Indonesia (2°S, 141°E) ... 181
Jebel Marra, mt. in Sudan (13°N, 24°E) ... 140
Jebel Musa, alternative name for Mt. Sinai (28°N, 34°E) ... 178
Jefferson City, MO (39°N, 92°W) ... 97
Jefferson, Mt., OR (45°N, 122°W) ... 100
Jefferson R., MT (46°N, 112°W) ... 101
Jeffersonville, IN (38°N, 86°W) ... 90
Jelgava, Latvia (57°N, 24°E) ... 157
Jericho (JEHR uh koh), West Bank (32°N, 35°E) ... 178
Jerusalem, Israel (32°N, 35°E) ... 178
Jhansi, India (25°N, 79°E) ... 180
Jiddah, Saudi Arabia (21°N, 39°E) ... 178
Jilin, China (44°N, 127°E) ... 182
Jima, Ethiopia (8°N, 37°E) ... 140
Jinan (jyee nahn), China (37°N, 117°E) ... 182
Jinja, Uganda (0°, 33°E) ... 140
Jizzakh, Uzbekistan (40°N, 68°E) ... 179
Joao Pessoa (zhwow puh SOH uh), Brazil (7°S, 35°W) ... 127
Jodhpur (JAHD puhr), India (26°N, 73°E) ... 180
Joensuu (yoh EHN su), Finland (63°N, 30°E) ... 157
Johannesburg, South Africa (26°S, 28°E) ... 141
John Day, OR (44°N, 119°W) ... 100
John Day Dam, Columbia R. (46°N, 121°W) ... 100
John Day R., OR (45°N, 120°W) ... 100
John H. Kerr Res., U.S. (37°N, 78°W) ... 91
John Redmond Res., KS (38°N, 96°W) ... 96
Johnson City, TN (36°N, 82°W) ... 91
Johnston Atoll, poss. of U.S. (17°N, 168°W) ... 189
Johnstown, PA (40°N, 79°W) ... 88
Johor Baharu (juh HOHR BAHR oo), Malaysia (2°N, 104°E) ... 181
Joinville, Brazil (26°S, 49°W) ... 127
Joliet, IL (42°N, 88°W) ... 97
Joliette, QC (46°N, 73°W) ... 71
Jonesboro, AR (36°N, 91°W) ... 95
Jonkoping (YUHN chuh pihng), Sweden (58°N, 14°E) ... 157
Joplin, MO (37°N, 95°W) ... 97
Jordan, country in Asia (31°N, 37°E) ... 178
Jordan R., Asia (32°N, 35°E) ... 178
Jos Plateau, Nigeria (10°N, 9°E) ... 138
Joseph Bonaparte Gulf, Indian O. (14°S, 128°E) ... 190
Joshua Tree N.P., CA (33°N, 116°W) ... 102
Juan de Fuca Plate, northeastern Pacific O. ... 20
Juan de Fuca Strait, (hwahn duh FYOO kuh), U.S. and Canada (48°N, 125°W) ... 68
Juan Fernandez Is., Pacific O. (33°S, 80°W) ... 121
Juarez (HWAHR ehz), Mexico (32°N, 106°W) ... 114
Juazeiro (zhwu ZEE roo), Brazil (9°S, 41°W) ... 127
Juba, South Sudan (5°N, 31°E) ... 140
Jubba R., Africa (2°N, 42°E) ... 140
Jucar R. (HU kahr), Spain (39°N, 1°W) ... 158
Judith R., MT (48°N, 110°W) ... 101
Juigalpa (hwee GAHL pah), Nicaragua (12°N, 85°W) ... 115
Juiz de Fora, Brazil (22°S, 43°W) ... 127
Juliaca, Peru (15°S, 70°W) ... 126
Juneau (JOO noh), AK (58°N, 134°W) ... 104
Juniata R., PA (40°N, 78°W) ... 88
Jura Mts., France and Switzerland (47°N, 7°E) ... 158
Jurua R. (zhoor WAH), Brazil (7°S, 70°W) ... 127
Jutland, pen. of Denmark (56°N, 9°E) ... 157
Jyvaskyla, Finland (62°N, 25°E) ... 157

K

K2, alternative name for Mt. Godwin Austen (36°N, 77°E) ... 180
Kabale, Uganda (1°S, 30°E) ... 140
Kabalo, Dem. Rep. Congo (6°S, 27°E) ... 139
Kabinakagami R., ON (49°N, 84°W) ... 70
Kabul (KAH bool), Afghanistan (34°N, 69°E) ... 180
Kabwe, Zambia (14°S, 28°E) ... 141
Kadavu I. (kahn DAH voo), Pacific O. (19°S, 178°W) ... 189
Kaduna (kuh DOO nuh), Nigeria (11°N, 7°E) ... 138
Kaedi, Mauritania (16°N, 14°W) ... 136
Kagoshima, Japan (32°N, 131°E) ... 183
Kahoolawe (kah hoh uh LAH wee), island in Pacific O. (21°N, 157°W) ... 104
Kaieteur Falls (ky eh TOOR), Guyana (5°N, 59°W) ... 127
Kailua (ky LOO uh), HI (21°N, 158°W) ... 104
Kailua Kona (ky LOO uh KOH nuh), HI (20°N, 156°W) ... 104
Kainji Dam, Africa (10°N, 5°E) ... 138
Kaiwi Channel (KY wee), HI (21°N, 158°W) ... 104
Kajaani (KAH yay ne), Finland (64°N, 27°E) ... 157
Kakhovka Res., Ukraine (47°N, 34°E) ... 160
Kalaallit Nunaat (KAH lahl leet NOO naht), alternative name for Greenland (75°N, 40°W) ... 52
Kalahari Desert, Africa (23°S, 22°E) ... 141
Kalamai, Greece (37°N, 22°E) ... 159
Kalamazoo, MI (42°N, 86°W) ... 99
Kalemie, Dem. Rep. Congo (6°S, 29°E) ... 139
Kalgoorlie, Australia (31°S, 121°E) ... 195
Kaliningrad (kuh LEE nihn grad), Russia (55°N, 21°E) ... 157
Kalispell, MT (48°N, 114°W) ... 101
Kalisz (KAHL eesh), Poland (52°N, 18°E) ... 159
Kalmar, Sweden (57°N, 16°E) ... 157
Kaluga, Russia (54°N, 36°E) ... 160
Kalyan (kuhl YAHN), India (19°N, 73°E) ... 180
Kama R., Russia (56°N, 53°E) ... 151
Kama Upland, Russia (58°N, 53°E) ... 160

Name (Pronunciation), Description (Lat., Long.)   Page

Kamchatka Pen., Russia (55°N, 160°E)...................169
Kamina, Dem. Rep. Congo (9°S, 25°E)..................139
Kaminak L., NU (61°N, 95°W) 69
Kamloops, BC (51°N, 120°W) 68
Kampala, Uganda (0°, 33°E) 140
Kamskoye Res., Russia (59°N, 57°E)....................160
Kamuela, HI (20°N, 156°W) 104
Kanaaupscow R., QC (55°N, 73°W) 71
Kanairiktok R., NL (54°N, 62°W) 72
Kananga, Dem. Rep. Congo (6°S, 22°E) 139
Kanawha R., WV (38°N, 82°W) 91
Kanazawa (kuh NAHZ uh wuh), Japan (37°N, 137°E) 183
Kanchenjunga (kuhn CHUHN juhng GAH),
  mt. in Nepal (28°N, 88°E)....................................171
Kandahar, Afghanistan (32°N, 66°E) 180
Kandy, Sri Lanka (7°N, 81°E) 180
Kane Basin, North America (79°N, 70°W) 61
Kaneohe (kahn ee oh ee), HI (21°N, 158°W) 104
Kangaroo I., Australia (36°S, 137°E) 190
Kanin Pen., Russia (68°N, 45°E) 160
Kankakee (kang kuh kee), IL (41°N, 88°W) 97
Kankakee R., U.S. (41°N, 88°W) 97
Kankan, Guinea (10°N, 9°W) 138
Kannapolis, NC (35°N, 81°W) 91
Kano, Nigeria (12°N, 8°E) 138
Kanpur, India (26°N, 80°E) 180
Kansas, state in U.S. (38°N, 100°W)...................96–97
Kansas City, KS (39°N, 95°W) 97
Kansas City, MO (39°N, 95°W) 97
Kansas R., U.S. (39°N, 97°W) 96–97
Kanton Atoll, Pacific O. (4°S, 174°W)..................189
Kaohsiung (kah oh syoong), Taiwan (23°N, 120°E) 182
Kaolack (kow lak), Senegal (14°N, 16°W) 138
Kapan, Armenia (38°N, 42°E)................................161
Kapingamarangi Atoll (kah PING ah mahr ang ee),
  Pacific O. (1°N, 155°E)..188
Kapiskau R., ON (53°N, 82°W) 70
Kapuas R., Indonesia (0°, 118°E) 181
Kapuskasing (kap uh skay sing), ON (49°N, 82°W)....70
Kapuskasing R., ON (49°N, 82°W) 70
Kara Kum, desert in Turkmenistan (40°N, 57°E).......179
Kara Kum Canal, Turkmenistan (38°N, 62°E)...........178
Kara Sea, Arctic O. (72°N, 62°E)...........................168
Karachi, Pakistan (25°N, 67°E) 180
Karaj, Iran (36°N, 51°E) 178
Karakol, Kyrgyzstan (42°N, 78°E) 179
Karakoram Pass, Asia (36°N, 78°E) 180
Karakoram Range (kar uh KOHR uhm), Asia
  (36°N, 76°E) 180
Karamay, China (46°N, 85°E) 179
Karbala, Iraq (32°N, 44°E) 178
Kariba Dam, Africa (17°S, 28°E)............................141
Kariba L., Africa (17°S, 28°E)................................141
Karimata Strait, Sumatra and Borneo (1°S, 108°E)......181
Karlstad, Sweden (59°N, 13°E) 157
Karnaphuli Res., India (23°N, 92°E) 180
Karratha, Australia (21°S, 118°E) 195
Kars, Turkey (41°N, 43°E) 161
Karun R., Asia (31°N, 48°E) 178
Kasai R. (kuh SY), Africa (3°S, 17°E).....................139
Kasama, Zambia (10°S, 31°E)................................141
Kasanga (kuh SAHNG guh), Tanzania (8°S, 31°E)........140
Kasba L., NT (60°N, 102°W)................................... 69
Kashi (kah shee), China (40°N, 76°E) 182
Kashmir, region of Asia (34°N, 75°E) 180
Kaskaskia R. (kas kas kee uh), IL (39°N, 89°W) 97
Kasongo, Dem. Rep. Congo (5°S, 27°E) 139
Kaspiysk, Russia (43°N, 48°E) 161
Kassala, Sudan (16°N, 37°E) 140
Kassel, Germany (51°N, 9°E) 159
Katahdin, Mt. (kuh tahd uhn), ME (46°N, 71°W) 89
Katanga Plateau, Dem. Rep. Congo (10°S, 26°E)........139
Katerini, Greece (40°N, 23°E) 159
Katherine, Australia (14°S, 132°E) 195
Kathmandu (kaht mahn DOO), Nepal (28°N, 85°E)....180
Katmai N.P. (KAT my), AK (59°N, 155°W) 104
Katowice (kaht uh VEET suh), Poland
  (50°N, 19°E) 159
Katsina, Nigeria (13°N, 8°E) 138
Kattegat, strait between Sweden and Denmark
  (57°N, 11°E) 157

Name (Pronunciation), Description (Lat., Long.)   Page

Kauai (KOW eye), island in Pacific O.
  (22°N, 159°W) 104
Kauai Channel, HI (22°N, 159°W)......................... 104
Kaula, island in Pacific Ocean (26°N, 160°W)........189
Kaulakahi Channel (kow luh KAH hee), HI
  (22°N, 160°W) 104
Kaunakakai (kow nuh KAH kee), HI (21°N, 157°W) 104
Kaunas, Lithuania (55°N, 24°E)............................157
Kavala (kah VAH lah), Greece (41°N, 24°E)............159
Kaw L., OK (37°N, 97°W) 96
Kawartha Lakes (kuh WAWR thuh), ON
  (45°N, 78°W) 70
Kawasaki, Japan (36°N, 140°E) 183
Kayan R., Indonesia (2°N, 116°E).........................181
Kayes, Mali (14°N, 11°W) 138
Kayseri (ky zuh ree), Turkey (39°N, 35°E)............178
Kazakh Uplands, Kazakhstan (48°N, 75°E) 170
Kazakhstan, country in Asia and Europe
  (48°N, 65°E) 179
Kazan, Russia (56°N, 49°E) 160
Kearney (kahr nee), NE (41°N, 99°W) 96
Kechika R., BC (59°N, 127°W)................................ 68
Keene (keen), NH (43°N, 72°W) 89
Kejimkujik N.P. (kehj uh muh KOO jee), NS
  (44°N, 65°W) 72
Kekaha (kay KAH hah), HI (22°N, 160°W)............. 104
Kelkit R., Asia (41°N, 37°E) 178
Kelowna (kih LOHN uh), BC (50°N, 120°W) 68
Kem, Russia (65°N, 35°E) 157
Kemp, L., TX (34°N, 99°W) 94
Kempt, L., QC (47°N, 74°W) 89
Kenai (KEE ny), AK (61°N, 151°W) 104
Kenai Fjords N.P., AK (60°N, 150°W) 104
Kenai Pen., AK (60°N, 150°W) 104
Kenema, Sierra Leone (8°N, 11°W) 138
Kennebec R., ME (45°N, 70°W) 89
Kennedy, Mt., YT (60°N, 139°W) 68
Kenner, LA (30°N, 90°W) 95
Kennewick, WA (46°N, 119°W) 100
Kenitra (kuh NEE truh), Morocco (34°N, 7°W) 136
Kenogami R. (kuh NAHG uh mee), ON
  (50°N, 85°W) 70
Kenora, ON (50°N, 94°W) 70
Kenosha (kuh NOH shuh), WI (43°N, 88°W) 99
Kent, OH (41°N, 81°W) 91
Kent, WA (47°N, 122°W) 100
Kentucky, state in U.S. (37°N, 87°W)..................90–91
Kentucky L., U.S. (37°N, 88°W) 91
Kentucky R., KY (38°N, 85°W) 90
Kenya, country in Africa (1°N, 37°E) 140
Kenya, Mt., Kenya (0°, 37°E) 140
Keokuk (KEE uh kuhk), IA (40°N, 91°W) 97
Kerch, Ukraine (45°N, 36°E) 160
Kerch, Strait of, Black Sea (44°N, 36°E) 160
Keren, Eritrea (16°N, 38°E) 140
Kerguelen I., Indian O. (56°S, 69°E)...................... 15
Kerguelen Plateau, Pacific O. (50°S, 75°E) 22
Kerki, Turkmenistan (38°N, 65°E) 179
Kermadec Is., poss. of N.Z. (31°S, 177°E)............189
Kermadec Trench, Pacific O. (25°S, 175°E) 22
Kerman, Iran (30°N, 57°E) 178
Kermanshah, Iran (34°N, 47°E) 178
Kesagami L. (kuh SAHG uh mee), ON (50°N, 80°W) 70
Ketchikan, AK (55°N, 132°W) 104
Kettering, OH (40°N, 84°W) 90
Keuka L. (KYOO kuh), NY (42°N, 77°W) 88
Keweenaw Bay (KEE wih naw), L. Superior
  (47°N, 88°W) 99
Keweenaw Pen., MI (47°N, 88°W) 99
Key West, FL (25°N, 82°W) 93
Khabarovsk, Russia (49°N, 135°E)........................182
Khalkis, Greece (38°N, 23°E) 159
Khambhat, Gulf of, Arabian Sea (21°N, 72°E) 180
Khamis Mushayt, Saudi Arabia (17°N, 44°E)..........178
Khania, Crete (35°N, 24°E) 159
Khanka L. (KAHN ka), Asia (45°N, 133°E) 182
Kharijah Oasis, Egypt (25°N, 30°E) 137
Kharkiv, Ukraine (50°N, 36°E) 160
Khartoum (kahr TOOM), Sudan (16°N, 33°E) 140
Khasavyurt, Russia (43°N, 47°E) 161
Kherson (kehr SAWN), Ukraine (47°N, 33°E)..........160

Name (Pronunciation), Description (Lat., Long.)   Page

Khon Kaen (kawn kan), Thailand (17°N, 103°E) 181
Khone Falls, Mekong R. (14°N, 106°E)...................181
Khouribga, Morocco (33°N, 7°W)..........................136
Khujand, Tajikistan (40°N, 70°E) 179
Khulna (KOOL nuh), Bangladesh (23°N, 90°E) 180
Khvoy, Iran (39°N, 45°E).......................................178
Khyber Pass (KY buhr), Asia (34°N, 71°E) 180
Kiang, Malaysia (3°N, 102°E).................................181
Kick-'em-Jenny, volcano in Caribbean Sea
  (12°N, 62°W)...109
Kiel (keel), Germany (54°N, 10°E).........................159
Kiel Canal, Germany (54°N, 9°E) 159
Kielce, Poland (51°N, 21°E)...................................159
Kiev, Ukraine (50°N, 31°E)....................................160
Kiev Res., Ukraine (52°N, 32°E) 160
Kigali, Rwanda (2°S, 30°E) 140
Kigoma (kih GOH muh), Tanzania (5°S, 30°E)........ 140
Kilauea (kee low AY ah), volcano in HI
  (19°N, 155°W) 104
Kilbuck Mts., AK (60°N, 160°W) 104
Kilchu (KIL choh), N. Korea (41°N, 129°E)............183
Kilimanjaro, Mt., Africa (3°S, 37°E) 140
Killarney P.P., ON (46°N, 81°W) 70
Killeen (kil LEEN), TX (31°N, 98°W) 95
Killiniq I., Ungava Bay (61°N, 64°W) 71
Kimberley, BC (50°N, 116°W) 68
Kimberley, South Africa (28°S, 25°E)....................141
Kimberley Plateau, Australia (16°S, 127°E)...........190
Kinabalu, mt. in Malaysia (6°N, 115°E) 181
Kinbasket, L., BC (52°N, 118°W) 68
Kindersley, SK (51°N, 109°W) 69
Kindia (KIHN dee uh), Guinea (10°N, 13°W) 138
Kindu, Dem. Rep. Congo (3°S, 26°E) 139
King George Is., Hudson Bay (57°N, 78°W) 71
King I., Bass Strait (40°S, 144°E) 190
King William I., Arctic O. (69°N, 98°W) 60
Kingman, AZ (35°N, 114°W) 102
Kingman Reef, poss. of U.S. (7°N, 162°W) 189
Kings Canyon N.P., CA (37°N, 119°W) 102
Kingsport, TN (37°N, 83°W) 91
Kingston, Jamaica (18°N, 77°W) 107
Kingston, ON (44°N, 76°W) 70
Kingstown, St. Vincent and the Grenadines
  (13°N, 61°W)...116
Kinshasa, Dem. Rep. Congo (4°S, 15°E).................139
Kinston, NC (35°N, 78°W) 91
Kipawa, L., QC (47°N, 79°W)................................. 88
Kiribati, country in Pacific O. (1°S, 173°W)...........189
Kirikkale, Turkey (39°N, 34°E) 178
Kiritimati Atoll, Pacific O. (2°N, 157°W)...............189
Kirkland Lake, city in ON (48°N, 80°W) 70
Kirksville, MO (40°N, 93°W) 97
Kirkuk (kihr KOOK), Iraq (35°N, 45°E) 178
Kirkwood, MO (39°N, 90°W) 97
Kirov, Russia (59°N, 50°E) 160
Kirovohrad, Ukraine (49°N, 32°E) 160
Kirovsk, Russia (68°N, 34°E) 160
Kirthar Range (kir TAHR), Pakistan (27°N, 67°E) 180
Kiruna, Sweden (68°N, 20°E) 157
Kirwin Res., KS (40°N, 99°W) 96
Kisangani (kee shun GAYN ee), Dem. Rep. Congo
  (1°N, 25°E)..139
Kislovodsk, Russia (44°N, 43°E)............................161
Kismaayo (kis MY yoo), Somalia (0°, 42°E) 140
Kissidougou (KEE see DOO goo), Guinea
  (9°N, 10°W)...138
Kissimmee (kihs IHM ee), FL (28°N, 82°W) 93
Kissimmee, L., FL (28°N, 81°W) 93
Kissimmee R., FL (27°N, 81°W) 93
Kisumu (kih SOO moo), Kenya (0°, 35°E) 140
Kitakyushu (kee TAH KYOO shu), Japan
  (34°N, 131°E)..183
Kitchener, ON (43°N, 81°W) 70
Kitimat, BC (54°N, 129°W) 68
Kittatinny Mts., NJ (41°N, 75°W) 88
Kitty Hawk, NC (36°N, 76°W) 91
Kitwe (KEE tway), Zambia (13°S, 28°E)..................141
Kivu, L. (KEE voo), Africa (2°S, 29°E) 140
Kizil Irmak R., Asia (40°N, 34°E)...........................137
Kjolen Mts., Sweden (65°N, 15°E)..........................157
Klagenfurt (KLAHG uhn foort), Austria
  (47°N, 14°E)..159

Name (Pronunciation), Description (Lat., Long.) Page

Klaipeda (KLY pee da), Lithuania (56°N, 21°E)............157
Klamath Falls (KLAM uth), city in OR (42°N, 122°W)............100
Klamath Mts., U.S. (42°N, 123°W)............102
Klamath, R., U.S. (42°N, 123°W)............100
Klar R., Sweden (61°N, 13°E)............157
Kluane N.P. (kloo AWN ee), YT (60°N, 138°W)............68
Knife R., ND (47°N, 102°W)............98
Knoxville, TN (36°N, 84°W)............90
Kobe (KOH bee), Japan (35°N, 135°E)............183
Kobuk Valley N.P. (koh BOOK), AK (67°N, 160°W)............104
Kochi, India (10°N, 76°E)............180
Kochi (KOH chee), Japan (34°N, 134°E)............183
Kodiak, AK (58°N, 153°W)............104
Kodiak I., Gulf of Alaska (57°N, 154°W)............104
Kohtla-Jarve (KOHT lah YAHR vay), Estonia (59°N, 27°E)............157
Kokkola (KAW koo lee), Finland (64°N, 23°E)............157
Kokomo (koh kuh moh), IN (41°N, 86°W)............90
Kokshetau, Kazakhstan (53°N, 69°E)............179
Kola Pen., Russia (67°N, 38°E)............160
Kolding, Denmark (55°N, 9°E)............157
Kolguyev I., Russia (69°N, 49°E)............160
Kolkata (kahl KAH tuh), India (23°N, 88°E)............180
Kolpino, Russia (60°N, 31°E)............157
Kolwezi (kohl WAY zee), Dem. Rep. Congo (11°S, 25°E)............139
Kolyma Range (kuh LEE muh), Russia (63°N, 160°E)............170–171
Kolyma R., Russia (67°N, 155°E)............170
Komoe R., Africa (10°N, 4°W)............138
Komsomolsk, Russia (51°N, 137°E)............182
Kontum, Plateau of, Vietnam (13°N, 108°E)............181
Konya, Turkey (38°N, 33°E)............178
Konzakovski Kamen, mt. in Russia (60°N, 59°E)............160
Kootenay L., BC (50°N, 117°W)............100
Kootenay N.P. (koot uh nay), BC (51°N, 116°W)............68
Kootenay R., North America (50°N, 115°W)............68
Kopet Dag Mts., Iran (37°N, 58°E)............178
Korce (KAWR chuh), Albania (41°N, 21°E)............159
Korea Bay, Asia (39°N, 168°E)............183
Korea Strait, South Korea and Japan (34°N, 128°E)............183
Korean Archipelago, Korea Strait (34°N, 127°E)............183
Korean Pen., Asia (38°N, 125°E)............169
Korhogo, Côte d'Ivoire (9°N, 6°W)............138
Koroglu Mts., Turkey (41°N, 33°E)............178
Koror, island in Pacific O. (7°N, 134°E)............188
Kosciusko, Mt. (kahz ee UHS koh), Australia (37°S, 148°E)............190
Kosice (KAW shuht say), Slovakia (49°N, 21°E)............159
Kosovo, country in Europe (43°N, 21°E)............159
Kosrae I., Pacific O. (5°N, 163°E)............188
Kostroma, Russia (58°N, 41°E)............160
Kota, India (25°N, 76°E)............180
Kota Kinabalu (KOHT uh kihn uh buh LOO), Malaysia (6°N, 116°E)............181
Kotka, Finland (60°N, 27°E)............157
Kotlas, Russia (61°N, 47°E)............160
Kotzebue (KAHT suh byoo), AK (67°N, 163°W)............104
Kotzebue Sound, AK (67°N, 164°W)............104
Kouchibouguac N.P. (koo shee boo GWAK), NB (47°N, 65°W)............72
Koudougou (koo DOO goo), Burkina Faso (12°N, 2°W)............138
Kouroussa (koo ROO suh), Guinea (11°N, 10°W)............138
Kozhikode, India (11°N, 76°E)............180
Kra, Isthmus of, Asia (10°N, 99°E)............181
Kracheh, Cambodia (12°N, 106°E)............181
Kragujevac, Serbia (44°N, 21°E)............159
Krakow (KRAK ow), Poland (50°N, 20°E)............159
Krasnodar, Russia (45°N, 39°E)............160
Krasnoyarsk, Russia (56°N, 93°E)............167
Kremenchuk, Ukraine (49°N, 33°E)............160
Kremenchuk Res., Ukraine (49°N, 33°E)............160
Krishna R., India (16°N, 75°E)............180
Kristiansand, Norway (58°N, 8°E)............157
Kryvyy Rih, Ukraine (48°N, 33°E)............160
Kuala Lumpur, Malaysia (3°N, 102°E)............181
Kuala Terengganu, Malaysia (5°N, 103°E)............181
Kuantan (KWAHN than), Malaysia (4°N, 103°E)............181
Kuban R., Russia (45°N, 40°E)............160
Kuching, Malaysia (2°N, 110°E)............181
Kufrah Oasis, Libya (23°N, 22°E)............137
Kugaaruk, NU (69°N, 90°W)............61
Kuh-e-Fuladi, mt. in Afghanistan (34°N, 69°E)............180
Kuito, Angola (12°S, 17°E)............141
Kul R., Asia (27°N, 56°E)............178
Kulob, Tajikistan (38°N, 69°E)............179
Kulsary, Kazakhstan (47°N, 54°E)............179
Kumamoto (koom uh MOH toh), Japan (33°N, 131°E)............183
Kumasi (koo MAHS ee), Ghana (7°N, 2°W)............138
Kunashiri, island in Sea of Okhotsk (45°N, 146°E)............183
Kungsbacka (KOONGS BAH kah), Sweden (58°N, 12°E)............157
Kunlun Mts., China (37°N, 80°E)............182
Kunming, China (25°N, 103°E)............182
Kuopio, Finland (63°N, 29°E)............157
Kupang (KOO pang), Indonesia (10°S, 124°E)............181
Kur R., Asia (41°N, 46°E)............161
Kurdistan (koord uh STAN), region of Asia (37°N, 44°E)............178
Kure Atoll, Pacific O. (28°N, 179°W)............189
Kurgan, Russia (55°N, 65°E)............179
Kuri Bay, Australia (15°S, 125°E)............195
Kuria Muria I. (KOOR ee uh MOOR ee uh), Arabian Sea (17°N, 56°E)............178
Kuril Is. (KOO rihl), Sea of Okhotsk (46°N, 152°E)............169
Kuril Trench, Pacific O. (50°N, 155°E)............22
Kursk (koorsk), Russia (52°N, 36°E)............160
Kushiro (KOOSH ee roh), Japan (43°N, 144°E)............183
Kuskokwim Mts., AK (63°N, 156°W)............104
Kuskokwim R., AK (63°N, 155°W)............104
Kusti, Sudan (13°N, 33°E)............140
Kutaisi (koo tuh EE see), Georgia (42°N, 43°E)............161
Kutch, Gulf of (kuch), India (23°N, 70°E)............180
Kuujjuaq, QC (58°N, 69°W)............71
Kuujjuarapik, QC (56°N, 78°W)............71
Kuwait (koo WAYT), country in Asia (29°N, 48°E)............178
Kuwait, Kuwait (30°N, 48°E)............178
Kuybyshev Res. (KWEE buh shehf), Russia (55°N, 50°W)............160
Kwadacha W.P.P., BC (56°N, 127°W)............68
Kwajalein Atoll (KWAH jah lain), Pacific O. (9°N, 168°E)............188
Kwangju (gwawng joo), South Korea (35°N, 126°E)............183
Kwango R., Africa (7°S, 17°E)............139
Kyoga, L. (kee OH guh), Uganda (2°N, 33°E)............140
Kyoto, Japan (35°N, 136°E)............183
Kyrgyzstan, country in Asia (42°N, 75°E)............179
Kyushu (kee YOO shoo), island in East China Sea (33°N, 131°E)............183
Kyzyl (kih ZIL), Russia (52°N, 94°E)............182
Kyzyl Kum Desert (kuh ZIHL KOOM), Kazakhstan (47°N, 62°E)............179

L

La Ceiba, Honduras (16°N, 87°W)............115
La Crosse, WI (44°N, 91°W)............99
La Grande R., QC (54°N, 78°W)............71
La Grange, GA (33°N, 85°W)............92
La Mauricie N.P. (luh mawr ee see), QC (47°N, 73°W)............71
La Palma, Canary Is. (29°N, 19°W)............136
La Paz, Bolivia (16°S, 68°W)............127
La Paz, Mexico (24°N, 110°W)............114
La Plata, Argentina (35°S, 58°W)............126
La Rochelle (lah roh SHEHL), France (46°N, 1°W)............158
La Ronge (luh ROHNZH), SK (55°N, 105°W)............69
La Salle, IL (41°N, 89°W)............97
La Serena, Chile (30°S, 71°W)............126
La Spezia, Italy (44°N, 10°E)............159
La Tuque (luh TYOOK), QC (47°N, 73°W)............71
Laayoune, (lay YOON), alternative name for El Aaiun (27°N, 13°W)............136
Laberge, L. (lah BURZH), YT (61°N, 137°W)............68
Labrador City, NL (53°N, 67°W)............72
Labrador Pen., QC (56°N, 70°W)............71
Labrador Sea, Atlantic O. (57°N, 50°W)............72
Lac La Ronge (LAK la RONZH), SK (55°N, 105°W)............69
Lac La Ronge P.P., SK (55°N, 105°W)............69
Lac Seul (lak SOHL), ON (50°N, 93°W)............70
Laccadive Is., Laccadive Sea (11°N, 73°E)............180
Laccadive Sea, Indian O. (10°N, 75°E)............180
Lachlan R. (LAHK luhn), Australia (33°S, 146°E)............191
Laconia (luh KOH nee uh), NH (43°N, 72°W)............89
Ladoga, L., Russia (61°N, 31°E)............160
Lae (LAH eh), Papua New Guinea (6°S, 147°E)............188
Lafayette (lahf ee ET), IN (40°N, 87°W)............90
Lafayette, LA (30°N, 92°W)............95
Lafourche Bayou (luh FOOSH), r. in LA (30°N, 91°W)............95
Lagos (LAH gohs), Nigeria (6°N, 3°E)............138
Laguna del Carbon, lake in Argentina (49°S, 69°W)............126
Lahore, Pakistan (32°N, 74°E)............180
Lahti (LAH teh), Finland (61°N, 28°E)............157
Lake Charles, city in LA (30°N, 93°W)............95
Lake City, MN (42°N, 92°W)............99
Lake Clark N.P., AK (61°N, 153°W)............104
Lake Havasu City (hav uh soo), AZ (34°N, 114°W)............102
Lake Region, Finland (63°N, 27°E)............157
Lake Superior P.P., ON (47°N, 85°W)............70
Lakeland, FL (28°N, 82°W)............93
Lakewood, CO (40°N, 105°W)............103
Lakewood, OH (41°N, 82°W)............91
Lamar (luh MAHR), CO (38°N, 103°W)............103
Lambarene (lahm buh ray nee), Gabon (1°S, 10°E)............139
Lampedusa (lam puh DOO suh), island in Mediterranean Sea, (36°N, 13°E)............159
Lanai, island in Pacific O. (21°N, 157°W)............104
Lanai City (luh NY), HI (21°N, 157°W)............104
Lancaster, CA (35°N, 118°W)............102
Lancaster, OH (40°N, 83°W)............90
Lancaster, PA (40°N, 76°W)............88
Lancaster Sound, NU (74°N, 85°W)............61
Land's End, cape in England (50°N, 6°W)............156
Lander, WY (43°N, 109°W)............101
Lankaran, Azerbaijan (39°N, 49°E)............161
Lansing, MI (43°N, 85°W)............99
Lanzarote, Canary Is. (29°N, 13°W)............136
Lanzhou (lahn joh), China (36°N, 103°E)............182
Laos (LAH ohs), country in Asia (20°N, 102°E)............181
Lapland, region of Europe (68°N, 20°E)............157
Lappeenranta, Finland (61°N, 28°E)............157
Laptev Sea, Arctic O. (75°N, 125°E)............169
Laramie, WY (41°N, 105°W)............101
Laramie Mts., WY (42°N, 105°W)............101
Laredo, TX (28°N, 99°W)............94
Larisa, Greece (40°N, 22°E)............159
Larkana, Pakistan (28°N, 68°E)............180
Larsen Ice Shelf, Antarctica (68°S, 60°W)............200
Larvik, Norway (59°N, 10°E)............157
Las Cruces (lahs KROO sihs), NM (32°N, 107°W)............103
Las Palmas, Canary Islands (28°N, 15°W)............136
Las Vegas, NV (36°N, 115°W)............102
Lashkargah (lash kah RAHG ah), Afghanistan (32°N, 64°E)............180
Lassen Pk., CA (41°N, 122°W)............102
Lassen Volcanic N.P., CA (41°N, 121°W)............102
Latvia, country in Europe (57°N, 23°E)............157
Lau Group, Pacific O. (17°S, 179°W)............189
Launceston, Australia (41°S, 147°E)............195
Laurel, MS (32°N, 89°W)............92
Laurentian Mts. (law REHN shuhn), QC (47°N, 74°W)............71
Laval (luh VAL), QC (46°N, 74°W)............71
Lawrence, KS (39°N, 95°W)............97
Lawrence, MA (43°N, 71°W)............89
Lawrenceburg, TN (35°N, 87°W)............90
Lawton, OK (35°N, 98°W)............94
Laysan I., Pacific O. (26°N, 172°W)............189
Layton, UT (41°N, 112°W)............103
Le Havre (luh HAHV ruh), France (49°N, 0°)............158
Le Mans (luh MAHN), France (48°N, 0°)............158
Leaf R., MS (31°N, 89°W)............92
Leavenworth (lehv uhn wuhrth), KS (39°N, 95°W)............97
Lebanon, country in Asia (34°N, 37°E)............178
Lebanon, NH (44°N, 72°W)............89
Leduc (leh DOOK), AB (53°N, 114°W)............68–69
Lee's Summit, MO (39°N, 94°W)............97
Leech L., MN (47°N, 94°W)............98
Leeds, England (54°N, 2°W)............156
Leeuwin, Cape (LYOO ihn), Australia (33°S, 115°E)............190
Leeward Is., Caribbean Sea (17°N, 62°W)............116

Name (Pronunciation), Description (Lat., Long.) Page

Leicester (LEHS tuhr), England (53°N, 1°W) 156
Leipzig, Germany (51°N, 12°E) 159
Lek R., Netherlands (52°N, 5°E) 151
Lemhi Range (LEHM hy), ID (45°N, 114°W) 101
Lena R., Russia (69°N, 124°E) 170
Leon, Mexico (21°N, 102°W) 114
Leon, Nicaragua (12°N, 87°W) 115
Leon, Spain (43°N, 5°W) 158
Lerdo, Mexico (25°N, 104°W) 114
Lesbos, island in Aegean Sea (39°N, 26°E) 159
Lesotho, country in Africa (30°S, 28°E) 141
Lesser Antilles, island group in Caribbean Sea (15°N, 62°W) 116
Lesser Slave L., AB (55°N, 115°W) 68
Lesser Sunda Is., Indian O. (9°S, 120°E) 181
Lethbridge, AB (50°N, 112°W) 69
Levis, QC (47°N, 71°W) 71
Levisa Fork (luh vy suh), r. in KY (38°N, 83°W) 90
Lewis and Clark L., U.S. (43°N, 98°W) 98
Lewis Range, MT (48°N, 113°W) 101
Lewis Smith L., AL (34°N, 87°W) 92
Lewiston, ID (46°N, 117°W) 100
Lewiston, ME (44°N, 70°W) 89
Lewistown, MT (47°N, 109°W) 101
Lewisville, TX (33°N, 97°W) 95
Lewisville, L., TX (33°N, 97°W) 95
Lexington, KY (38°N, 85°W) 90
Lexington, VA (38°N, 79°W) 91
Lhasa (LAH suh), China (30°N, 91°E) 182
Lhotse (LUHT say), mt. in Nepal and China (28°N, 87°E) 171
Liard R., Canada (59°N, 126°W) 68
Liberal, KS (37°N, 101°W) 96
Liberia, country in Africa (7°N, 10°W) 138
Liberia, Costa Rica (11°N, 85°W) 115
Libreville, Gabon (0°, 9°E) 139
Libya, country in Africa (26°N, 16°E) 136-137
Libyan Desert, Africa (25°N, 26°E) 137
Licking R., KY (39°N, 84°W) 90
Lida (LEE da), Belarus (54°N, 25°E) 157
Liechtenstein (LIHK tuhn styn), country in Europe (47°N, 10°E) 159
Liege (lee AYZH), Belgium (51°N, 6°E) 158
Liepaja (LEH pah YAH), Latvia (57°N, 21°E) 157
Lifou I., Pacific O. (21°S, 168°E) 188
Ligurian Sea (lih GYOO rih uhn), Europe (44°N, 9°E) 159
Lihue (lih HYOO ee), HI (22°N, 159°W) 104
Likasi, Dem. Rep. Congo (11°S, 27°E) 139
Lille (leel), France (51°N, 3°E) 158
Lillehammer (LEYL eh hahm mehr), Norway (61°N, 10°E) 157
Lilongwe (lih LAWNG way), Malawi(14°S, 34°E) 141
Lima (LEE muh), Peru (12°S, 77°W) 126
Lima (LY muh), OH (41°N, 84°W) 90
Limassol, Cyprus (35°N, 33°E) 178
Limerick, Ireland (53°N, 9°W) 156
Limnos, island in Aegean Sea (40°N, 25°E) 159
Limoges (lee MOHZH), France (46°N, 1°E) 158
Limon (LIH MAWN), Costa Rica (10°N, 83°W) 115
Limon (ly MUHN), CO (40°N, 105°W) 103
Limpopo R. (lihm poh poh), Africa (23°S, 32°E) 141
Lincoln, ME (45°N, 68°W) 89
Lincoln, NE (41°N, 97°W) 96
Lindenhurst, NY (41°N, 73°W) 89
Lindesnes, Cape, Norway (58°N, 7°E) 157
Line Is., Pacific O. (0°, 157°W) 189
Linkoping, Sweden (58°N, 16°E) 157
Linz, Austria (48°N, 14°E) 159
Lion, Gulf of, Mediterranean Sea (43°N, 4°E) 158
Lipari Is., Tyrrhenian Sea (39°N, 15°E) 159
Lipetsk (LYI pehtsk), Russia (52°N, 40°E) 160
Lisbon, Portugal (39°N, 9°W) 158
Lisianski I., Pacific O. (26°N, 174°W) 189
Lismore, Australia (29°S, 153°E) 195
Lithuania, country in Europe (55°N, 23°E) 157
Little Bighorn R., MT (45°N, 108°W) 101
Little Colorado R., U.S. (36°N, 111°W) 103
Little Kanawha R. (kuh NAW wuh), WV (39°N, 81°W) 91
Little Mecatina R., Canada (52°N, 61°W) 72

Name (Pronunciation), Description (Lat., Long.) Page

Little Missouri Badlands, ND (47°N, 103°W) 98
Little Missouri R., U.S. (46°N, 104°W) 98
Little Rock, AR (35°N, 92°W) 95
Little Sioux R. (soo), IA (43°N, 95°W) 96-97
Little Tennessee R., U.S. (36°N, 84°W) 90
Little Wabash R., IL (38°N, 88°W) 97
Liverpool, England (53°N, 3°W) 156
Livingston, L., TX (31°N, 95°W) 95
Livingstone, Zambia (18°S, 26°E) 141
Livorno, Italy (44°N, 10°E) 159
Ljubljana (LYOO blyah nah), Slovenia (46°N, 14°E) 159
Llano Estacado (lahn oh es tuh KAHD oh), plain in U.S. (33°N, 103°W) 94
Llano R., TX (30°N, 99°W) 94
Llanos (LAH nohz), plain in South America (7°N, 71°W) 126
Lloyd George, Mt., BC (58°N, 125°W) 68
Lloydminster, AB (53°N, 110°W) 69
Lloyds R., NL (48°N, 56°W) 72
Lobamba, Eswatini (26°S, 31°E) 141
Lobito, Angola (12°S, 14°E) 141
Lodi (lawd ee), CA (38°N, 121°W) 102
Lodz (looj), Poland (52°N, 19°E) 159
Lofoten Is., Norway (69°N, 15°E) 157
Logan, UT (42°N, 112°W) 103
Logan, WV (38°N, 82°W) 91
Logan, Mt., YT (61°N, 140°W) 60
Logan Mts., YT (62°N, 128°W) 68
Logansport, IN (41°N, 86°W) 90
Loire R. (lwahr), France (48°N, 1°W) 158
Loma Mts., Guinea (8°N, 9°W) 138
Lomami R., Africa (1°S, 25°E) 139
Lombok, island in Flores Sea (9°S, 116°E) 181
Lome (loh MAY), Togo (6°N, 1°E) 138
Lompoc (LAHM pahk), CA (35°N, 120°W) 102
London, England (52°N, 0°) 156
London, ON (43°N, 81°W) 70
Londonderry, Northern Ireland (55°N, 7°W) 156
Londrina, Brazil (22°S, 51°W) 127
Long Bay, SC (34°N, 79°W) 93
Long Beach, CA (34°N, 118°W) 102
Long Branch, NJ (40°N, 74°W) 88
Long I., Hudson Bay (55°N, 80°W) 71
Long I., NY (41°N, 73°W) 88-89
Long I. Sound, U.S. (41°N, 73°W) 89
Long Range Mts., NL (48°N, 59°W) 72
Long Xuyen (lowng SWEE uhn), Vietnam (10°N, 105°E) 181
Longfellow Mts., ME (45°N, 70°W) 89
Longmont, CO (40°N, 105°W) 103
Longs Pk., CO (40°N, 106°W) 103
Longueuil (lawng GAYL), QC (46°N, 74°W) 71
Longview, TX (32°N, 95°W) 95
Longview, WA (46°N, 123°W) 100
Lookout, Cape, NC (35°N, 76°W) 91
Lop Nur (lawp nawr), l. in China (40°N, 90°E) 182
Lorain, OH (41°N, 82°W) 91
Lord Howe I., Tasman Sea (31°S, 159°E) 190
Lord Howe Rise, Pacific O. (30°S, 165°E) 22
Los Alamos (law sal uh mohs), NM (36°N, 106°W) 103
Los Angeles, CA (34°N, 118°W) 102
Los Angeles Aqueduct, CA (35°N, 118°W) 102
Los Mochis, Mexico (26°N, 109°W) 114
Los Roques, island group in Caribbean Sea (12°N, 67°W) 116
Louangphrabang (LWAHNG prah BAHNG), Laos (20°N, 102°E) 181
Loubomo, Congo Republic (4°S, 13°E) 139
Louisbourg, NS (46°N, 60°W) 72
Louisiade Archipelago, Coral Sea (11°S, 153°E) 188
Louisiana, state in U.S. (32°N, 93°W) 95
Louisville, KY (38°N, 86°W) 90
Lowell (LOH uhl), MA (43°N, 71°W) 89
Lower Arrow L., BC (50°N, 118°W) 68
Lower Cook Islands, Pacific O. (18°S, 161°W) 189
Lower Pen., MI (44°N, 85°W) 99
Lower Red Lake, MN (48°N, 95°W) 98
Lower Tunguska R., Russia (65°N, 92°E) 170
Loyalty Is., Pacific O. (21°S, 168°E) 188
Lualaba R., Africa (0°, 26°E) 139

Name (Pronunciation), Description (Lat., Long.) Page

Luanda, Angola (9°S, 13°E) 141
Lubango, Angola (15°S, 13°E) 141
Lubbock, TX (34°N, 102°W) 94
Lubeck, Germany (54°N, 11°E) 159
Lublin, Poland (51°N, 23°E) 159
Lubumbashi, Dem. Rep. Congo (12°S, 27°E) 139
Lucknow (LUHK now), India (27°N, 81°E) 180
Luderitz, Namibia (27°S, 15°E) 141
Ludhiana (lood ee AHN ah), India (31°N, 76°E) 180
Ludington, MI (44°N, 86°W) 99
Lufkin, TX (31°N, 95°W) 95
Luhansk, Ukraine (49°N, 39°E) 160
Lule R. (LOO luh), Sweden (66°N, 21°E) 150
Lulea, Sweden (65°N, 23°E) 157
Lund, Sweden (56°N, 13°E) 157
Lunenburg (LOO nuhn burg), NS (44°N, 64°W) 72
Luoyang, China (35°N, 113°E) 182
Lusaka, Zambia (15°S, 28°E) 141
Luxembourg (LUHK sum burg), country in Europe (50°N, 6°E) 158
Luxembourg, Luxembourg (49°N, 6°E) 158
Luxor, Egypt (26°N, 33°E) 137
Luzon Strait, Philippines and Taiwan (21°N, 121°E) 167
Luzon, island in Philippine Sea (17°N, 121°E) 181
Lviv (luh VAWF), Ukraine (50°N, 24°E) 160
Lyell, Mt., Canada (50°N, 115°W) 68
Lynchburg, VA (37°N, 79°W) 91
Lyndon B. Johnson, L., TX (31°N, 98°W) 94
Lynn (lin), MA (42°N, 71°W) 89
Lynn Lake, city in MB (57°N, 101°W) 69
Lyon (lyawn), France (46°N, 5°E) 158
Lyra Reef, Pacific O. (2°S, 153°E) 188

M

Maan, Jordan (30°N, 36°E) 178
Maas R., Europe (52°N, 5°E) 151
Macapa (mahk uh PAH), Brazil (0°, 52°W) 127
Macau (muh KOW), China (22°N, 113°E) 182
Macdonnell Ranges, Australia (24°S, 130°E) 191
Maceio (mas ay OH), Brazil (10°S, 36°W) 127
MacFarlane R., SK (59°N, 108°W) 69
Machakos, Kenya (2°S, 37°E) 140
Machala, Ecuador (3°S, 80°W) 126
Mackay, Australia (21°S, 149°E) 195
Mackay, L., Australia (22°S, 129°E) 190
Mackenzie, BC (56°N, 123°W) 68
Mackenzie Bay, Canada (70°N, 138°W) 60
Mackenzie Mts., Canada (64°N, 130°W) 60
Mackenzie R., NT (65°N, 125°W) 68
Mackinac, Straits of, MI (46°N, 85°W) 99
Macomb (muh KOHM), IL (40°N, 91°W) 97
Macon (MAY kuhn), GA (33°N, 84°W) 93
MacRobertson Land, region of Antarctica (70°S, 60°E) 200
Madaba, Jordan (31°N, 36°E) 178
Madagascar, country in Africa (20°S, 45°E) 141
Madang (mah DAHNG), Papua New Guinea (5°S, 146°E) 188
Madeira Falls (muh DEER uh), waterfall in Brazil (10°S, 65°W) 127
Madeira Is., Atlantic O. (33°N, 17°W) 136
Madeira R., Brazil (8°S, 64°W) 127
Madison, IN (39°N, 86°W) 90
Madison, WI (43°N, 89°W) 99
Madison R., MT (45°N, 112°W) 101
Madisonville, KY (37°N, 88°W) 90
Madras, alternative name for Chennai (13°N, 80°E) 180
Madre Lagoon, Mexico (25°N, 98°W) 106
Madrid, Spain (40°N, 4°W) 158
Madurai (mahd uh RY), India (10°N, 78°E) 180
Maewo I., Pacific O. (15°S, 168°E) 188
Mafia (MAHF ee uh), island in Indian O. (8°S, 40°E) . 140
Magadan, Russia (60°N, 151°E) 167
Magdalen Is. (MAD uh layn), Gulf of Saint Lawrence (47°N, 62°W) 72
Magdalena R., Colombia (7°N, 75°W) 126
Magdeburg, Germany (52°N, 12°E) 159
Magellan, Strait of, South America (53°S, 70°W) 126
Magnitogorsk (mahg NYI toh gohrsk), Russia (53°N, 59°E) 160
Magpie R., QC (50°N, 65°W) 71

Name (Pronunciation), Description (Lat., Long.) Page

Mahajanga, Madagascar (15°S, 46°E) 141
Mahalapye, Botswana (23°S, 28°E) 141
Mahilyow, Belarus (54°N, 30°E) 160
Mai-Ndombe, L., Dem. Rep. Congo (2°S, 19°E) 139
Maiduguri (my doo guh ree), Nigeria (12°N, 13°E) 138
Main R. (MYN), Germany (50°N, 5°E) 159
Maine, state in U.S. (45°N, 70°W) 89
Maine, Gulf of, Atlantic O. (43°N, 68°W) 72
Maitri Station, Antarctica (71°S, 12°E) 200
Maji, Ethiopia (6°N, 36°E) 140
Majorca, Balearic Is. (39°N, 3°E) 158
Majuro (mah JOO ro), Marshall Islands (7°N, 171°E) 188
Majuro Atoll, Pacific O. (7°N, 171°E) 188
Makassar, Indonesia (5°S, 119°E) 181
Makassar, Strait of, Borneo and Sulawesi (3°S, 117°E) 181
Makgadikgadi Pans, dry lakes in Botswana (21°S, 25°E) 141
Makhachkala, Russia (43°N, 48°E) 161
Makin I. Pacific O. (3°, 173°E) 189
Makkah, alternative name for Mecca (21°N, 40°E) 178
Makkovik, NL (55°N, 59°W) 72
Makurdi (mah KOOR dee), Nigeria (8°N, 9°E) 138
Malabar Coast, India (14°N, 74°E) 180
Malabo, Eq. Guinea (4°N, 9°E) 139
Malacca, Strait of, Sumatra and Malay Pen. (4°N, 100°E) 181
Malaga, Spain (37°N, 4°W) 158
Malaita I. (mah LAY tah), Pacific O. (9°N, 161°E) 188
Malakal, South Sudan (10°N, 32°E) 140
Malakula I. (MAH lah KOO lah), Pacific O. (16°S, 168°E) 188
Malang (muh LAHNG), Indonesia (8°S, 113°E) 181
Malanje, Angola (10°S, 16°E) 141
Malaren, L., Sweden (59°N, 17°W) 157
Malatya (ma LAH tuh), Turkey (39°N, 38°E) 178
Malawi, country in Africa (13°S, 34°E) 141
Malawi, L., alternative name for Lake Nyasa (11°S, 35°E) 141
Malay Pen., Asia (5°N, 101°E) 181
Malaysia, country of Asia (3°N, 102°E) 181
Malden I., Pacific O. (4°S, 155°W) 189
Maldives, country in Indian O. (3°N, 74°E) 180
Male (MAH lay), Maldives (4°N, 74°E) 166
Malheur L. (mal HOOR), OR (43°N, 119°W) 100
Mali (MAH lee), country in Africa (16°N, 2°W) 132
Malindi (muh LIHN dee), Kenya (3°S, 40°E) 140
Malmo, Sweden (56°N, 13°E) 157
Malpelo I., Pacific O. (4°N, 81°W) 126
Malta, country in Europe (36°N, 15°E) 159
Malta, MT (48°N, 108°W) 101
Maltese Is., Mediterranean Sea (36°N, 15°E) 148
Mammoth Cave N.P., KY (37°N, 86°W) 90
Mamore R. (mahm uh RAY), South America (14°S, 65°W) 127
Man, Côte d'Ivoire (7°N, 8°W) 138
Man, Isle of, poss. of United Kingdom (54°N, 5°W) 156
Manado, Indonesia (1°N, 125°E) 181
Managua, Nicaragua (12°N, 86°W) 115
Managua, L., Nicaragua (12°N, 86°W) 115
Manakara, Madagascar (22°S, 48°E) 141
Manama, Bahrain (26°N, 51°E) 178
Manassas (muh NAS uhs), VA (39°N, 77°W) 91
Manaus, Brazil (3°S, 60°W) 127
Manchester, CT (42°N, 72°W) 89
Manchester, England (53°N, 2°W) 156
Manchester, KY (37°N, 84°W) 90
Manchester, NH (43°N, 71°W) 89
Manchurian Plain, China (45°N, 125°E) 182
Mand R., Asia (29°N, 52°E) 178
Mandalay, Myanmar (22°N, 96°E) 181
Mandan, ND (47°N, 101°W) 98
Mandara Mts. (mahn DAH ruh), Africa (10°N, 14°E) 138
Mandurah, Australia (32°S, 117°E) 195
Mangaia I., Pacific O. (22°S, 158°W) 189
Mangalore (MANG guh lawr), India (13°N, 75°E) 180
Manhattan, KS (39°N, 97°W) 96
Manicouagan Res. (man uh KWAHG uhn), QC (52°N, 68°W) 71
Manicouagan R., QC (51°N, 68°W) 71

Name (Pronunciation), Description (Lat., Long.) Page

Manihiki Atoll (mah nee HEE kee), Pacific O. (10°S, 158°W) 189
Manila, Philippines (14°N, 121°E) 181
Manisa (MAH ny sah), Turkey (39°N, 28°E) 159
Manistee R. (man uh STEE), MI (44°N, 86°W) 99
Manitoba, prov. in Canada (57°N, 95°W) 69
Manitoba, L., Canada (51°N, 98°W) 69
Manitou Is. (MAN uh too), L. Michigan (45°N, 86°W) 99
Manitoulin I. (man uh TOO luhn), L. Huron (46°N, 83°W) 70
Manitowoc (man uht uh wahk), WI (44°N, 88°W) 99
Maniwaki (man uh WAW kee), QC (46°N, 76°W) 71
Mankato (man KAY toh), MN (44°N, 94°W) 98
Mannar, Gulf of (muh NAHR), Asia (8°N, 79°E) 180
Mannheim, Germany (49°N, 9°E) 159
Manokwari, Indonesia (1°S, 134°E) 181
Manouane, L. (mah NOO uhn), QC (51°N, 71°W) 71
Manra I. (MAHN rah), Pacific O. (4°S, 171°W) 189
Mansel I., Hudson Bay (62°N, 80°W) 71
Mansfield, OH (41°N, 83°W) 91
Mansfield, PA (42°N, 77°W) 88
Mansfield, Mt., VT (45°N, 73°W) 89
Manta, Ecuador (1°S, 80°W) 126
Manukau, New Zealand (37°S, 175°E) 195
Manus I., Pacific O. (2°S, 146°E) 188
Maoke Mts. (mow kay), New Guinea (4°S, 139°E) 191
Maple Creek, city in SK (50°N, 109°W) 69
Maputo, Mozambique (26°S, 33°E) 141
Mar del Plata, Argentina (38°S, 58°W) 126
Maraba, Brazil (5°S, 49°W) 127
Maraca I., Brazil (2°N, 51°W) 127
Maracaibo (mar uh KY boh), Venezuela (11°N, 72°W) 126
Maracaibo, L., Venezuela (10°N, 72°W) 126
Maracay, Venezuela (10°N, 68°W) 126
Maradi, Niger (13°N, 7°E) 138
Marajo I., Brazil (1°S, 49°W) 127
Marakei Atoll (mah RAH kay), Pacific O. (2°N, 173°E) 189
Marambio Station, Antarctica (64°S, 57°W) 200
Marand, Iran (38°N, 46°E) 161
Maranon R., Peru (5°S, 75°W) 126
Maras, Turkey (37°N, 37°E) 178
Marathon, ON (49°N, 86°W) 70
Marawi, Sudan (118°N, 32°E) 140
Marcy, Mt., NY (44°N, 74°W) 88
Mare I. (ma RAY), Pacific O. (22°S, 167°E) 188
Margarita I., island in Caribbean Sea (11°N, 64°W) 126
Margherita Peak, mt. in Dem. Rep. Congo (0°, 30°E) 139
Maribor, Slovenia (47°N, 16°E) 159
Mariana Is., Pacific O. (17°N, 145°E) 169
Mariana Trench, Pacific O. (15°N, 145°E) 22
Marias R. (muh RY uhs), MT (48°N, 111°W) 101
Marie Byrd Land, region of Antarctica (78°S, 120°W) 200
Marie Galante, Guadeloupe (16°N, 61°W) 116
Marietta, GA (34°N, 85°W) 92
Marietta, OH (39°N, 82°W) 91
Marion, IN (41°N, 86°W) 90
Marion, OH (41°N, 83°W) 90
Marion, VA (37°N, 82°W) 91
Marion, L., SC (33°N, 80°W) 93
Maritsa R., Europe (42°N, 26°E) 159
Mariupol, Ukraine (47°N, 37°E) 160
Mark Twain L., MO (40°N, 92°W) 97
Markermeer (MAHR kuhr mer), l. in Netherlands (53°N, 5°E) 151
Markham, ON (44°N, 79°W) 70
Marmara, Sea of (MAHR muhr uh), Black and Mediterranean Seas (41°N, 28°E) 178
Marne R. (mahrn), France (48°N, 4°E) 158
Maro Reef, Pacific O. (25°N, 171°W) 189
Maroa (mah ROH ah), Venezuela (3°N, 68°W) 126
Marotiri Is., Pacific O. (28°S, 143°W) 189
Maroua (muh ROO uh), Cameroon (11°N, 14°E) 139
Marquesas Is. (mahr KEH sahs), Pacific O. (9°S, 141°W) 189
Marquette, MI (47°N, 87°W) 99
Marrakech, Morocco (32°N, 8°W) 136
Marseille (mahr SAY), France (43°N, 5°E) 158

Name (Pronunciation), Description (Lat., Long.) Page

Marshall, MN (44°N, 96°W) 98
Marshall, TX (33°N, 94°W) 95
Marshall Is., country in Pacific O. (10°N, 165°E) 188
Marshalltown, IA (42°N, 93°W) 97
Marshfield, WI (45°N, 90°W) 99
Martaban, Gulf of (MAHR tah BAHN), Andaman Sea (17°N, 97°W) 181
Martensville, SK (52°N, 107°W) 69
Martha's Vineyard, MA (41°N, 71°W) 89
Martin, L., AL (34°N, 86°W) 92
Martinique (mahr tuh NEEK), overseas state of France (15°N, 61°W) 116
Martinsburg, WV (39°N, 78°W) 91
Martinsville, VA (37°N, 80°W) 91
Martre, L. la, NT (63°N, 120°W) 68
Mary, Turkmenistan (38°N, 62°E) 179
Maryborough, Australia (26°S, 153°E) 195
Maryland, state in U.S. (39°N, 77°W) 91
Marysville, KS (40°N, 97°W) 96
Maryville, TN (36°N, 84°W) 90
Masan, South Korea (35°N, 129°E) 183
Masaya, Nicaragua (12°N, 86°W) 115
Mascarene Is. (mas kuh REEN), Indian O. (21°S, 57°E) 133
Mascarene Plateau, Indian O. (10°S, 60°E) 22
Maseru (MAZ uh roo), Lesotho (29°S, 27°E) 141
Mashhad, Iran (36°N, 60°E) 178
Masira (muh SIHR uh), island in Arabian Sea (21°N, 59°E) 178
Masira, Gulf of, Arabian Sea (19°N, 58°E) 178
Mason City, IA (43°N, 93°W) 97
Massachusetts, state in U.S. (42°N, 72°W) 89
Massachusetts Bay, MA (42°N, 71°W) 89
Massawa, Eritrea (16°N, 39°E) 140
Masset, BC (54°N, 132°W) 68
Massif Central, mt. region in France (45°N, 3°E) 158
Massillon, OH (41°N, 82°W) 91
Mata Utu, Wallis and Futuna (13°S, 176°W) 189
Matadi, Dem. Rep. Congo (6°S, 13°E) 139
Matagalpa, Nicaragua (13°N, 86°W) 115
Matagami, QC (50°N, 78°W) 71
Matagorda Bay (mat uh GAWRD uh), Gulf of Mexico (29°N, 96°W) 95
Matamoros, Mexico (26°N, 97°W) 114
Matane (muh TAN), QC (49°N, 68°W) 71
Mato Grosso Plateau, Brazil (13°S, 58°W) 127
Mattagami R. (muh TAG uh mee), ON (48°N, 81°W) 70
Mattoon, IL (39°N, 88°W) 97
Maturin (maht uh REEN), Venezuela (10°N, 63°W) 126
Maug Is. (moug), Pacific O. (20°N, 143°E) 188
Maui (MOW ee), I. in Pacific O. (21°N, 156°W) 104
Mauke I. (mou kay), Pacific O. (20°S, 158°W) 189
Maumee R. (maw MEE), U.S. (41°N, 84°W) 90
Maun, Botswana (20°S, 24°E) 141
Mauna Kea (mow nuh KEE uh), mt. in HI (20°N, 156°W) 104
Mauna Loa, mt. in HI (19°N, 155°W) 104
Mauritania, country in Africa (20°N, 10°W) 136
Mauritius, country in Indian O. (20°S, 57°W) 132
Mawlamyine, Myanmar (16°N, 98°E) 181
Mawson Station, Antarctica (68°S, 63°E) 200
May, Cape, NJ (39°N, 75°W) 88
Mayaguez, Puerto Rico (18°N, 67°W) 116
Mayfield, KY (37°N, 89°W) 90
Maykop, Russia (45°N, 40°E) 160
Mayotte, island in Indian O. (13°S, 45°E) 141
Maysville, KY (39°N, 84°W) 90
Mazar-e Sharif (muh ZAHR ee shuh reef), Afghanistan (37°N, 67°E) 180
Mazatlan, Mexico (23°N, 106°W) 114
Mbabane (em buh BAHN), Eswatini (26°S, 31°E) 141
Mbala (em BAH luh), Zambia (9°S, 31°E) 141
Mbandaka (em bahn DAHK uh), Dem. Rep. Congo (0°, 18°E) 139
Mbarara, Uganda (1°S, 31°E) 140
Mbeya (em BAY uh), Tanzania (9°S, 33°E) 140
Mbomou R. (em BOH moo), Africa (5°N, 24°E) 139
Mbuji-Mayi (em BOO jee MY ee), Dem. Rep. Congo (6°S, 24°E) 139
McAllen, TX (26°N, 98°W) 94
McComb, MS (31°N, 90°W) 92

Name (Pronunciation), Description (Lat., Long.) Page

McConaughy, L., NE (41°N, 102°W) ... 96
McCook, NE (40°N, 101°W) ... 96
McGrath, AK (63°N, 155°W) ... 104
McKean I., Pacific O. (4°S, 178°W) ... 189
McKenzie, TN (36°N, 89°W) ... 90
McKenzie R., OR (44°N, 122°W) ... 100
M'Clintock Channel, NU (72°N, 103°W) ... 60
M'Clure Strait, Arctic O. (75°N, 120°W) ... 60
McMillan, L., NM (33°N, 104°W) ... 103
McMinnville, TN (36°N, 86°W) ... 90
McMurdo Station, Antarctica (78°S, 167°E) ... 200
Mead, L., U.S. (36°N, 114°W) ... 102
Meadow Lake, city in SK (54°N, 108°W) ... 69
Meadow Lake P.P., SK (54°N, 108°W) ... 69
Mealy Mts., NL (53°N, 59°W) ... 72
Mecca, Saudi Arabia (21°N, 40°E) ... 178
Medan, Indonesia (4°N, 98°E) ... 181
Medellin, Colombia (6°N, 76°W) ... 126
Medford, OR (42°N, 123°W) ... 100
Medicine Bow Mts., WY (41°N, 106°W) ... 101
Medicine Hat, AB (50°N, 111°W) ... 69
Medina, Saudi Arabia (24°N, 40°E) ... 178
Mediterranean Sea, Europe, Africa, and Asia (35°N, 5°E) ... 133
Medora (mih DOHR uh), ND (47°N, 104°W) ... 98
Meerut (MAY ruht), India (29°N, 78°E) ... 180
Mega, Ethiopia (4°N, 38°E) ... 140
Mekele, Ethiopia (14°N, 39°E) ... 140
Meknes, Morocco (34°N, 6°W) ... 136
Mekong, Mouths of the (may kawng), delta in Vietnam (10°N, 106°E) ... 181
Mekong R., Asia (17°N, 105°E) ... 170
Melbourne (MEHL buhrn), Australia (38°S, 145°E) ... 195
Melbourne, FL (28°N, 81°W) ... 93
Melekeok, Palau (7°N, 135°E) ... 188
Melezes, R., QC (57°N, 72°W) ... 71
Melfort, SK (53°N, 105°W) ... 69
Melilla (muh LEE uh), terr. of Spain (35°N, 3°W) ... 158
Melville, SK (51°N, 103°W) ... 69
Melville I., Arctic O. (75°N, 110°W) ... 60
Melville I., Australia (11°S, 131°E) ... 190
Melville, L., NL (54°N, 59°W) ... 72
Melville Pen., NU (68°N, 84°W) ... 61
Memphis, TN (35°N, 90°W) ... 90
Memphremagog L. (mehm fruh MAY gahg), QC (45°N, 73°W) ... 89
Menasha, WI (44°N, 88°W) ... 99
Mendocino, Cape, CA (40°N, 124°W) ... 102
Mendoza, Argentina (33°S, 69°W) ... 126
Menihek Lakes, NL (54°N, 67°W) ... 72
Menominee Range (muh NAHM uh nee), U.S. (46°N, 89°W) ... 99
Mentawai Is., Indonesia (2°S, 100°E) ... 181
Mentor, OH (42°N, 81°W) ... 91
Meramec R. (MEHR uh mak), MO (38°N, 91°W) ... 97
Merauke, Indonesia (9°S, 140°E) ... 181
Merca, Somalia (2°N, 32°E) ... 140
Merced (muhr SED), CA (37°N, 121°W) ... 102
Meredith, L., TX (36°N, 102°W) ... 94
Mergui Archipelago (muhr GWEE), Myanmar (12°N, 97°E) ... 181
Merida (MER uh duh), Mexico (21°N, 90°W) ... 114
Merida, Venezuela (9°N, 71°W) ... 127
Meridian, MS (32°N, 89°W) ... 92
Merredin, Australia (32°S, 119°E) ... 195
Merrillville, IN (42°N, 87°W) ... 90
Merrimack R., NH (43°N, 72°W) ... 89
Mersin, Turkey (36°N, 34°E) ... 178
Meru, Kenya (0°N, 38°E) ... 140
Mesa (MAY suh), AZ (33°N, 112°W) ... 103
Mesa Verde N.P. (may suh VUR dee), CO (37°N, 108°W) ... 103
Mesabi Range (muh SAHB ee), MN (47°N, 93°W) ... 99
Mesopotamia (mehs uh puh TAY mee uh), region of Iraq (32°N, 45°E) ... 178
Messina (muh SEE nuh), Italy (38°N, 15°E) ... 159
Messina, Strait of, Mediterranean Sea (38°N, 16°E) ... 159
Meta Incognita Pen., NU (63°N, 69°W) ... 71
Meta R., South America (4°N, 72°W) ... 126
Metairie, LA (30°N, 90°W) ... 95
Methow R. (MET how), WA (48°N, 120°W) ... 100

Name (Pronunciation), Description (Lat., Long.) Page

Metz, France (49°N, 5°E) ... 158
Meuse R. (myooz), France (49°N, 5°E) ... 158
Mexicali, Mexico (33°N, 115°W) ... 114
Mexico, country in North America (24°N, 103°W) ... 114
Mexico, state in Mexico (19°N, 100°W) ... 114
Mexico City, Mexico (19°N, 99°W) ... 114
Mexico, Gulf of, Atlantic O. (25°N, 90°W) ... 106-107
Mexico, Plateau of, Mexico (24°N, 103°W) ... 109
Meymaneh, Afghanistan (36°N, 65°E) ... 180
Mezen R., Russia (65°N, 45°E) ... 160
Miami, FL (26°N, 80°W) ... 93
Miami Beach, FL (26°N, 80°W) ... 93
Michigan, state in U.S. (45°N, 85°W) ... 99
Michigan City, IN (42°N, 87°W) ... 90
Michigan, L., U.S. (42°N, 87°W) ... 99
Michipicoten I. (MIHSH uh puh KOHT uhn), L. Superior (48°N, 86°W) ... 70
Michoacan, state in Mexico (18°N, 104°W) ... 114
Mid-Atlantic Ridge, Atlantic O. (0°, 20°W) ... 22
Mid-Pacific Mountains, Pacific O. (20°N, 180°) ... 22
Middle Loup R. (loop), NE (42°N, 100°W) ... 96
Middlesboro, KY (37°N, 84°W) ... 90
Middletown, OH (40°N, 84°W) ... 90
Midland, MI (44°N, 84°W) ... 99
Midland, TX (32°N, 102°W) ... 94
Midway, islands in Pacific O.(28°N, 179°W) ... 189
Milan, Italy (45°N, 9°E) ... 159
Mildura (mihl DOOR uh), Australia (34°S, 142°E) ... 195
Miles City, MT (46°N, 106°W) ... 101
Milford, DE (39°N, 75°W) ... 91
Milford Res., KS (39°N, 97°W) ... 96
Milford Sound, New Zealand (45°S, 168°E) ... 195
Milk R., North America (48°N, 109°W) ... 101
Mille Lacs L. (mil LAKS), MN (46°N, 94°W) ... 98
Millville, NJ (39°N, 75°W) ... 88
Millwood Res., AR (34°N, 94°W) ... 95
Milwaukee, WI (43°N, 88°W) ... 99
Minami Tori Shima, poss. of Japan (26°N, 155°E) ... 188
Minatitlan (mee nah tee TLAHN), Mexico (18°N, 95°W) ... 114
Minch, The, strait in Hebrides Is. (58°N, 6°W) ... 156
Mindanao (mihn duh NAH oh), island in Philippine Sea (8°N, 126°E) ... 181
Mindoro (mihn DOHR oh), island in South China Sea (13°N, 121°E) ... 181
Mingacevir, Azerbaijan (41°N, 47°E) ... 161
Mingacevir Res., Azerbaijan (41°N, 47°E) ... 161
Mingan Archipelago N.P. Reserve, QC (50°N, 64°W) ... 71
Minneapolis, MN (45°N, 93°W) ... 98-99
Minnesota, state in U.S. (46°N, 95°W) ... 98-99
Minnesota R., MN (45°N, 95°W) ... 98
Mino R., Europe (43°N, 8°W) ... 158
Minorca, Balearic Is. (40°N, 4°E) ... 158
Minot (MY naht), ND (48°N, 101°W) ... 98
Minsk, Belarus (54°N, 28°E) ... 160
Minto, L., QC (57°N, 76°W) ... 71
Miquelon (MIK uh lahn), island in Atlantic O. (47°N, 56°W) ... 72
Miramichi, NB (47°N, 65°W) ... 72
Miramichi R. (mihr uh muh SHEE), NB (47°N, 65°W) ... 72
Mirim L., South America (33°S, 53°W) ... 127
Mirnyy Station, Antarctica (67°S, 93°E) ... 200
Mishawaka, IN (42°N, 86°W) ... 90
Miskigum R., OH (40°N, 82°W) ... 91
Miskito Cays, islands in Caribbean Sea (15°N, 83°W) ... 115
Miskolc (MISH kohlts), Hungary (48°N, 21°E) ... 159
Misratah (mis uh RAHT uh), Libya (32°N, 15°E) ... 137
Missinaibi R. (mis uh NY bee), ON (50°N, 83°W) ... 70
Mississagi R. (mihs uh SAHG ee), ON (46°N, 83°W) .. 70
Mississauga, ON (44°N, 80°W) ... 70
Mississinewa L., IN (41°N, 86°W) ... 90
Mississippi, state in U.S. (32°N, 90°W) ... 92
Mississippi R., U.S. (32°N, 92°W) ... 77
Mississippi R., Delta of the, LA (29°N, 89°W) ... 95
Missoula, MT (47°N, 114°W) ... 101
Missouri, state in U.S. (38°N, 94°W) ... 97
Missouri City, TX (29°N, 96°W) ... 95
Missouri R., U.S. (42°N, 96°W) ... 78-79
Mistassibi R., QC (51°N, 72°W) ... 71

Name (Pronunciation), Description (Lat., Long.) Page

Mistassini, L., QC (51°N, 73°W) ... 71
Mitchell, SD (44°N, 98°W) ... 98
Mitchell R., Australia (16°S, 143°E) ... 195
Mitchell, Mt., NC (36°N, 82°W) ... 91
Mitumba Mts., Africa (11°S, 27°E) ... 139
Mo i Rana, Norway (66°N, 13°E) ... 157
Moa, island in Banda Sea (9°S, 129°E) ... 181
Moab, UT (39°N, 110°W) ... 103
Moala Group, Pacific O. (19°S, 180°) ... 189
Moanda, Gabon (2°S, 13°E) ... 139
Mobile, AL (31°N, 88°W) ... 92
Mobile Bay, AL (31°N, 87°W) ... 92
Mobridge, SD (46°N, 100°W) ... 98
Modena (MAWD ee nuh), Italy (45°N, 11°E) ... 159
Modesto, CA (38°N, 121°W) ... 102
Mogadishu, Somalia (2°N, 45°E) ... 140
Mogollon Rim (muhg ee OHN), AZ (34°N, 111°W) ... 103
Mohave, L. (muh HAHV ee), U.S. (33°N, 115°W) ... 102
Mohawk R., NY (43°N, 74°W) ... 88
Moisie R. (mwa ZEE), QC (52°N, 67°W) ... 71
Mojave Desert (muh HAH vee), CA (35°N, 117°W) ... 102
Mokpo (MAHK poh), S. Korea (35°N, 126°E) ... 183
Molde, Norway (63°N, 7°E) ... 157
Moldova, country in Europe (47°N, 28°E) ... 160
Moline, IL (42°N, 90°W) ... 97
Molokai, island in Pacific O. (21°N, 157°W) ... 104
Molopo R. (muh LOH poh), Africa (27°S, 21°E) ... 141
Molson L., MB (54°N, 97°W) ... 69
Molucca Islands, Molucca Sea (2°S, 128°E) ... 181
Molucca Sea, Indian O. (1°S, 125°E) ... 181
Mombasa, Kenya (4°S, 40°E) ... 140
Mona I., Caribbean Sea (18°N, 68°W) ... 116
Mona Passage, Caribbean Sea (18°N, 68°W) ... 116
Monaco, country in Europe (44°N, 7°E) ... 158
Monchegorsk (MOHN cheh gawrsk), Russia (69°N, 34°E) ... 157
Monclova, Mexico (27°N, 101°W) ... 114
Moncton (MUHNG tun), NB (46°N, 65°W) ... 72
Mongolia, country in Asia (46°N, 101°E) ... 182
Mongolian Plateau, Mongolia (47°N, 110°E) ... 182
Mongu, Zambia (15°S, 23°E) ... 141
Mono L. (MOH noh), CA (38°N, 119°W) ... 102
Monongahela R. (muh nahn guh HEE luh), U.S. (40°N, 80°W) ... 88
Monroe, LA (32°N, 92°W) ... 95
Monroe, NC (35°N, 81°W) ... 91
Monroe L., IN (30°N, 86°W) ... 90
Monroeville, PA (40°N, 80°W) ... 88
Monrovia, Liberia (6°N, 11°W) ... 138
Mont Tremblant P.P., QC (46°N, 75°W) ... 71
Montana, state in U.S. (47°N, 113°W) ... 100-101
Montauk Point (mahn tawk), NY (41°N, 72°W) ... 89
Montego Bay, city in Jamaica (18°N, 78°W) ... 107
Montenegro, country in Europe (43°N, 19°E) ... 159
Monterey, CA (37°N, 122°W) ... 102
Monterey Bay, CA (37°N, 122°W) ... 102
Monterrey, Mexico (26°N, 100°W) ... 114
Montes Claros, Brazil (17°S, 44°W) ... 127
Montevideo (mahn tuh vih DAY oh), Uruguay (35°S, 56°W) ... 127
Montgomery, AL (32°N, 86°W) ... 92
Mont-Laurier, QC (47°N, 76°W) ... 71
Montmagny (mo mah NYEE), QC (47°N, 71°W) ... 71
Montpelier (mahnt PEEL yuhr), VT (44°N, 73°W) ... 89
Montpellier (mohn pehl YUH), France (46°N, 4°E) ... 158
Montréal, QC (46°N, 73°W) ... 71
Montserrat, island in Caribbean Sea (17°N, 62°W) ... 116
Moorhead (MOHR hed), MN (47°N, 97°W) ... 98
Moose Jaw, SK (51°N, 106°W) ... 69
Moose L., MB (54°N, 100°W) ... 69
Moose R., ON (51°N, 82°W) ... 70
Moosehead L., ME (46°N, 70°W) ... 89
Moosonee, ON (51°N, 81°W) ... 70
Mopti, Mali (15°N, 4°W) ... 138
Morava R., Europe (49°N, 18°E) ... 159
Moravia (muh RAY vee uh), region of Czech Rep. (49°N, 17°E) ... 159
Moray Firth, bay in Scotland (58°N, 4°W) ... 156
Moreau R. (MOHR oh), SD (45°N, 102°W) ... 98
Morehead, KY (38°N, 83°W) ... 90
Morehead City, NC (35°N, 77°W) ... 91

Name (Pronunciation), Description (Lat., Long.)	Page
Morelia, Mexico (20°N, 101°W)	114
Morelos, state in Mexico (18°N, 99°W)	114
Morgantown, WV (40°N, 80°W)	91
Morioka (mohr ee OH kuh), Japan (40°N, 141°E)	183
Morocco, country in Africa (32°N, 7°W)	136
Morogoro (moh roh GOH roh), Tanzania (7°S, 38°E)	140
Moroni, Comoros (11°S, 43°W)	141
Morotai I. (muh RO tay), Indonesia (2°N, 129°E)	181
Mortlock Is., Pacific O. (6°N, 154°E)	188
Moscow (MAHS koh), ID (47°N, 117°W)	100
Moscow (MAHS kow), Russia (56°N, 38°E)	160
Moses L., WA (47°N, 119°W)	100
Moshi, Tanzania (3°S, 37°E)	140
Mosquito Coast, Nicaragua (13°N, 84°W)	115
Mosquito Gulf, Caribbean Sea (9°N, 81°W)	115
Moss, Norway (59°N, 11°E)	157
Mossendjo, Congo Republic (3°S, 13°E)	139
Mossoro, Brazil (5°S, 37°W)	127
Mostar (MOH stahr), Bos. (43°N, 18°E)	159
Mosul (moh SYOOL), Iraq (36°N, 43°E)	178
Mouila, Gabon (2°S, 11°E)	139
Moultrie, L. (MOHL tree), SC (33°N, 80°W)	93
Moundou (MOON doo), Chad (7°N, 16°E)	139
Mount Carleton P.P., NB (48°N, 67°W)	72
Mount Desert I., Atlantic O. (44°N, 68°W)	89
Mount Edziza P.P., BC (57°N, 130°W)	68
Mount Gambier, city in Australia (38°S, 141°E)	195
Mount Isa, city in Australia (20°S, 139°E)	195
Mount Pleasant, city in SC (33°N, 80°W)	93
Mount Rainier N.P. (ruh NEER), WA (47°N, 122°W)	100
Mount Revelstoke N.P., BC (51°N, 118°W)	68
Mount Vernon, city in IL (38°N, 89°W)	97
Moyale (moh YAHL ee), Kenya (3°N, 39°E)	140
Mozambique (moh zuhm BEEK), country in Africa (18°S, 34°E)	141
Mozambique, Mozambique (15°S, 41°E)	141
Mozambique Channel, Indian O. (20°S, 40°E)	141
Mtwara (ehm TWAHR uh), Tanzania (10°S, 40°E)	140
Mu Us Desert, China (39°N, 109°E)	182
Muchinga Mts., Africa (13°S, 31°E)	141
Mulhouse (muh LOOZ), France (48°N, 7°E)	158
Multan (mool TAHN), Pakistan (30°N, 71°E)	180
Mumbai (muhm BY), India (19°N, 73°E)	180
Mun R. (MOON), Thailand (15°N, 102°E)	181
Muncho Lake, city in BC (59°N, 126°W)	68
Muncie, IN (40°N, 86°W)	90
Munich, Germany (48°N, 12°E)	159
Munising (MYOO nuh sing), MI (46°N, 87°W)	99
Munster (MOON stuhr), Germany (52°N, 8°E)	159
Muonio R., Sweden and Finland (67°N, 23°E)	157
Murcia (MUHR shuh), Spain (38°N, 1°W)	158
Murdo (MUHR doh), SD (44°N, 101°W)	98
Mures R. (MYOOR esh), Europe (46°N, 24°E)	159
Murfreesboro, TN (36°N, 86°W)	90
Murgab R. (moor GAHB), Asia (37°N, 63°E)	178
Murian, L., Iran (27°N, 59°E)	178
Murmansk, Russia (69°N, 33°E)	160
Murray, L., SC (34°N, 81°W)	93
Murray R., Australia (34°S, 142°E)	190
Murzuq, Libya (26°N, 14°E)	137
Muscat (muhs KAT), Oman (24°N, 59°E)	178
Musgrave Ranges, Australia (25°S, 130°E)	191
Muskegon (muhs KEE guhn), MI (43°N, 86°W)	99
Muskegon R., MI (43°N, 86°W)	99
Muskogee (muh SKOH gee), OK (36°N, 95°W)	95
Muskwa R., BC (59°N, 123°W)	68
Musselshell R., MT (46°N, 108°W)	101
Mut, Egypt (25°N, 29°E)	137
Muynak, Uzbekistan (44°N, 59°E)	179
Mwanza, Tanzania (3°S, 33°E)	140
Mweru, L., Africa (9°S, 29°E)	139
Myanaung (MYAN awng), Myanmar (18°N, 95°E)	181
Myanmar (myahn MAHR), country in Asia (22°N, 95°E)	181
Myitkyina (mee chee NOH), Myanmar (25°N, 97°E)	181
Mykolayiv, Ukraine (48°N, 32°E)	160
Myrtle Beach, SC (34°N, 79°W)	93
Mysore, India (12°N, 77°E)	180
Mzuzu, Malawi (12°S, 34°E)	141

N

Name (Pronunciation), Description (Lat., Long.)	Page
Naberezhnyye Chelny, Russia (56°N, 52°E)	160
Nablus, West Bank (32°N, 35°E)	178
Nacala, Mozambique (15°S, 41°E)	141
Nacogdoches (nak uh DOH chuz), TX (32°N, 95°W)	95
Nagano (nah GAHN oh), Japan (37°N, 138°E)	183
Nagasaki (nahg uh SAHK ee), Japan (33°N, 130°E)	183
Nagoya (nuh GOY uh), Japan (35°N, 137°E)	183
Nagpur, India (21°N, 79°E)	180
Nahanni N.P. (nah HAHN ee), NT (62°N, 126°W)	68
Naikoon P.P., BC (54°N, 132°W)	68
Nain, NL (56°N, 62°W)	72
Nairobi, Kenya (1°S, 37°E)	140
Najd, region of Saudi Arabia (25°N, 43°E)	178
Najran, Saudi Arabia (17°N, 44°E)	178
Nakhodka (nah KOT kuh), Russia (43°N, 133°E)	183
Nakhon Ratchasima (nah KAWN rah chah sih MAH), Thailand (15°N, 102°E)	181
Nakuru (nah KOOR oo), Kenya (0°, 36°E)	140
Nalchik (nah CHIK), Russia (44°N, 44°E)	161
Nam Dinh (nahm deen), Vietnam (20°N, 106°E)	181
Namangan, Uzbekistan (41°N, 72°E)	179
Namib Desert, Africa (22°S, 14°E)	141
Namibe, Angola (15°S, 12°E)	141
Namibia, country in Africa (20°S, 17°E)	141
Namonuito Atoll (NAH mon wee to), Pacific O. (9°N, 150°E)	188
Nampa, ID (44°N, 117°W)	100
Nampo, North Korea (39°N, 125°E)	183
Nampo Is., Pacific O. (29°N, 140°E)	188
Nampula, Mozambique (15°S, 39°E)	141
Namtu (NAHM too), Myanmar (23°N, 97°E)	181
Nan Range, China (24°N, 112°E)	182
Nanaimo (nuh NY moh), BC (49°N, 124°W)	68
Nanchang (nahn chang), China (29°N, 116°E)	182
Nanchong (nahn chung), China (31°N, 106°E)	182
Nancy, France (49°N, 6°E)	158
Nanga Parbat (nun GAH PUHR bet), mt. in Pakistan (35°N, 75°E)	171
Nanjing, China (32°N, 119°E)	182
Nanning (nahn ning), China (23°N, 108°E)	182
Nantes (nants), France (47°N, 2°W)	158
Nantucket I., Atlantic O. (41°N, 70°W)	89
Nantucket Sound, MA (42°N, 70°W)	89
Nanumanga I. (NAH noo MAHNG ah), Pacific O. (6°S, 176°E)	189
Nanumea Atoll (NAH noo MAY ah), Pacific O. (5°S, 176°E)	189
Naococane, L., QC (53°N, 71°W)	71
Napa, CA (38°N, 122°W)	102
Naperville, IL (42°N, 88°W)	97
Napier, New Zealand (39°S, 177°E)	195
Naples, FL (26°N, 82°W)	93
Naples, Italy (41°N, 14°E)	159
Narbonne, France (43°N, 3°E)	158
Narmada R., India (23°N, 74°E)	180
Narodnaya, Mt., Russia (65°N, 60°E)	160
Narragansett Bay, RI (41°N, 71°W)	89
Narva (NAHR vah), Estonia (59°N, 28°E)	157
Narvik, Norway (68°N, 17°E)	157
Nashua (NASH uh wuh), NH (43°N, 71°W)	89
Nashville, TN (36°N, 87°W)	90
Nasik, India (20°N, 74°E)	180
Nasiriyah, Iraq (31°N, 46°E)	178
Naskaupi R., NL (54°N, 62°W)	72
Nass R., BC (55°N, 129°W)	68
Nassau, Bahamas (25°N, 77°W)	93
Nassau I., Pacific O. (12°S, 165°W)	189
Nasser, L., Africa (23°N, 33°E)	137
Natal (nuh tahl), Brazil (6°S, 35°W)	127
Natashquan R., Canada (52°N, 62°W)	72
Natchez (NACH ez), MS (32°N, 91°W)	92
Natchitoches (NAK uh tahsh), LA (32°N, 93°W)	95
Natuna Besar Is., South China Sea (4°N, 108°E)	181
Nauru, country in Pacific O. (1°S, 167°E)	188
Nawoiy, Uzbekistan (40°N, 65°E)	179
Naxcivan, Azerbaijan (39°N, 46°E)	161
Nay Pyi Taw, Myanmar (20°N, 96°E)	181
Nayarit (nah yah REET), state in Mexico (23°N, 105°W)	114
Nazareth, Israel (33°N, 35°E)	178
Nazca Plate, southeastern Pacific O.	20
Nazca Ridge, Pacific O. (20°S, 80°W)	22
Nazret, Ethiopia (9°N, 39°E)	140
N'Djamena (ehn JAHM uh nuh), Chad (12°N, 15°E)	139
Ndola (en DOH lah), Zambia (13°S, 29°E)	141
Nebraska, state in U.S. (42°N, 100°W)	96-97
Nechako R., BC (54°N, 125°W)	68
Neches R. (NEH chez), TX (31°N, 95°W)	95
Necker I., Pacific O. (24°N, 164°W)	189
Neenah, WI (44°N, 89°W)	99
Negev, desert in Asia (31°N, 35°E)	178
Negro R. (NAY groh), Argentina (39°S, 66°W)	126
Negro R., South America (1°S, 65°W)	127
Negros, island in Philippine Sea (10°N, 122°E)	181
Neiva, Colombia (3°N, 75°W)	126
Nejanilini L., MB (60°N, 98°W)	69
Nelson, BC (50°N, 117°W)	68
Nelson, New Zealand (42°S, 173°E)	195
Nelson R., MB (56°N, 97°W)	69
Neman R., Belarus and Lithuania (55°N, 23°E)	160
Nemuro (NEHM uh ROH), Japan (43°N, 145°E)	183
Nemuro Strait, Japan (44°N, 145°E)	183
Nen R., China (47°N, 124°E)	182
Nendo I., Pacific O. (11°S, 166°E)	188
Nengonengo Atoll, Pacific O. (19°S, 142°W)	189
Neosho R. (nee OH shuh), U.S. (38°N, 95°W)	96-97
Nepal, country in Asia (28°N, 84°E)	180
Nesselrode, Mt., North America (59°N, 134°W)	68
Netherlands, country in Europe (52°N, 5°E)	158
Neumayer Station, Antarctica (71°S, 8°W)	200
Neuquen, Argentina (39°S, 68°W)	126
Neuse R. (NOOS), NC (35°N, 77°W)	91
Nevada, state in U.S. (39°N, 118°W)	102
Nevinnomyssk, Russia (45°N, 42°E)	161
New Albany, IN (38°N, 86°W)	90
New Bedford, MA (42°N, 71°W)	89
New Bern, NC (35°N, 77°W)	91
New Braunfels (BROWN fulz), TX (30°N, 98°W)	94
New Britain, CT (42°N, 73°W)	89
New Britain, Papua New Guinea (5°S, 152°E)	188
New Brunswick, NJ (41°N, 74°W)	88
New Brunswick, prov. in Canada (46°N, 66°W)	72
New Caledonia, island in Pacific O. (22°S, 166°E)	188
New Caledonia, poss. of France (22°S, 166°E)	188
New Castle, PA (41°N, 80°W)	88
New Delhi (DEHL ee), India (28°N, 77°E)	180
New Georgia Group, I. in Pacific O. (9°S, 157°E)	188
New Glasgow (GLAS goh), NS (46°N, 63°W)	72
New Guinea, island in Pacific O. (5°S, 141°E)	188
New Hampshire, state in U.S. (44°N, 72°W)	89
New Hanover, island in Pacific O. (3°S, 150°E)	188
New Haven, CT (41°N, 73°W)	89
New Hebrides, islands in Pacific O. (16°S, 167°E)	188
New Hebrides Trench, Pacific O. (23°S, 172°E)	22
New Iberia, LA (30°N, 92°W)	95
New Ireland, island in Bismark Sea (3°S, 152°E)	188
New Jersey, state in U.S. (40°N, 74°W)	88
New London, CT (41°N, 72°W)	89
New Madrid, MO (37°N, 90°W)	97
New Mexico, state in U.S. (35°N, 107°W)	103
New Orleans, LA (30°N, 90°W)	95
New Plymouth, New Zealand (39°S, 174°E)	195
New Providence I., Bahamas (25°N, 77°W)	93
New R., VA (37°N, 81°W)	91
New Siberian Is., Russia (75°N, 140°E)	169
New South Wales, state in Australia (31°S, 145°E)	195
New York, state in U.S. (43°N, 78°W)	88-89
New York City, NY (41°N, 74°W)	88
New Zealand, country in Pacific O. (40°S, 175°E)	195
Newark, DE (40°N, 76°W)	91
Newark, NJ (41°N, 74°W)	88
Newark, OH (40°N, 82°W)	91
Newburgh, NY (42°N, 74°W)	88
Newcastle, Australia (33°S, 152°E)	195
Newcastle, South Africa (28°S, 30°E)	141
Newcastle upon Tyne, England (55°N, 2°W)	156

Name (Pronunciation), Description (Lat., Long.) Page

Newfoundland, island in Gulf of Saint Lawrence (48°N, 56°W) ... 72
Newfoundland and Labrador, prov. in Canada (53°N, 60°W) ... 72
Newport, OR (45°N, 124°W) ... 100
Newport, RI (41°N, 71°W) ... 89
Newport News, VA (37°N, 76°W) ... 91
Newton, KS (38°N, 97°W) ... 96
Nezhualcoyotl, (NAY tsah wahl koh YOHT uhl), Mexico (20°N, 98°W) ... 92
Nezpique R. (NEHZ peek), LA (30°N, 93°W) ... 95
Ngaoundere, Cameroon (8°N, 14°E) ... 139
Ngatik Atoll, Pacific O. (6°N, 158°E) ... 188
Ngulu Atoll (NGOO loo), Pacific O. (8°N, 137°E) ... 188
Nha Trang (nya trahng), Vietnam (12°N, 109°E) ... 181
Niagara Falls, city in NY (43°N, 79°W) ... 88
Niagara Falls, city in ON (43°N, 79°W) ... 88
Niagara Falls, waterfall in North America (43°N, 79°W) ... 70
Niamey (nyah MAY), Niger (14°N, 2°E) ... 138
Niangua R. (ny ANG gwuh), MO (38°N, 93°W) ... 97
Nias, island in Indian O. (1°S, 99°E) ... 181
Nicaragua, country in Central America (13°N, 86°W) ... 115
Nicaragua, L., Nicaragua (11°N, 86°W) ... 115
Nice (NEES), France (44°N, 7°E) ... 158
Nicobar Is. (NIHK uh bahr), Bay of Bengal (9°N, 93°E) ... 180
Nicosia (nihk uh SEE uh), Cyprus (35°N, 33°E) ... 178
Niger (ny juhr), country in Africa (17°N, 10°E) ... 132
Niger Delta, Nigeria (5°N, 6°E) ... 138
Niger R., Africa (12°N, 4°E) ... 138
Nigeria, country in Africa (10°N, 7°E) ... 138
Nihoa, island in Pacific O. (23°N, 162°W) ... 189
Niigata (nee GAHT uh), Japan (37°N, 139°E) ... 183
Niihau (NEE how), I. in Pacific O. (22°N, 160°W) ... 104
Nikunau I. (nee koo NOU), Pacific O. (1°S, 176°E) ... 189
Nile R., Africa (28°N, 31°E) ... 134
Nile River Delta, Egypt (31°N, 31°E) ... 137
Nimes (NEEM), France (44°N, 4°E) ... 158
Ninety East Ridge, Indian O. (20°S, 170°E) ... 22
Ningbo, China (30°N, 122°E) ... 182
Ninigo Group, Pacific O. (1°S, 144°E) ... 188
Ninnescah R. (NIN ehs kah), KS (37°N, 97°W) ... 96
Niobrara R., U.S. (42°N, 103°W) ... 96
Nipawin, SK (53°N, 104°W) ... 69
Nipigon, ON (49°N, 88°W) ... 70
Nipigon, L., ON (50°N, 89°W) ... 70
Nipissing, L., ON (47°N, 80°W) ... 70
Nis (nish), Serbia (43°N, 22°E) ... 159
Niteroi, Brazil (23°S, 43°W) ... 127
Niuatoputapu Group (NYOO aah TAW poo TAH poo), islands in Pacific O. (16°S, 174°W) ... 189
Niue, poss. of New Zealand (20°S, 167°W) ... 189
Niulakita I. (NYOO lah KEE tah), Pacific O. (11°S, 180°) ... 189
Niutao I. (NEE oo TAH o), Pacific O. (6°S, 177°E) ... 189
Nizhniy Novgorod (nizh nee NAHV guh rahd), Russia (56°N, 43°E) ... 160
Nizhniy Tagil, Russia (58°N, 60°E) ... 160
Nodaway R., U.S. (41°N, 95°W) ... 97
Nogales (noh GAL uhs), AZ (32°N, 111°W) ... 103
Nogales, Mexico (31°N, 111°W) ... 114
Nome, AK (65°N, 165°W) ... 104
Nonacho L., NT (62°N, 111°W) ... 69
Nopiming P.P., MB (51°N, 95°W) ... 69
Norfolk, NE (42°N, 97°W) ... 96
Norfolk, VA (37°N, 76°W) ... 91
Norfolk I., Tasman Sea (29°S, 168°E) ... 190
Norfolk L., U.S. (36°N, 92°W) ... 95
Norilsk, Russia (69°N, 88°E) ... 166
Normal, IL (41°N, 89°W) ... 97
Norman, OK (35°N, 97°W) ... 95
Norman, L., NC (36°N, 81°W) ... 91
Norman Wells, NT (65°N, 128°W) ... 60
Normandy, region of France (49°N, 0°) ... 158
Norris L., TN (36°N, 84°W) ... 90
Norrkoping (NAWR chuhp ing), Sweden (59°N, 16°E) ... 157
North America, continent ... 53
North American Basin, Atlantic O. (35°N, 60°W) ... 22

Name (Pronunciation), Description (Lat., Long.) Page

North American Plate, North America and Atlantic O. .. 20
North Battleford, SK (53°N, 108°W) ... 69
North Bay, ON (46°N, 79°W) ... 70
North Canadian R., U.S. (36°N, 99°W) ... 94
North Cape, New Zealand (34°S, 174°E) ... 195
North Cape, Norway (71°N, 25°E) ... 157
North Carolina, state in U.S. (36°N, 82°W) ... 90-91
North Cascades N.P., WA (48°N, 121°W) ... 100
North Channel, L. Huron (46°N, 83°W) ... 70
North Channel, Scotland and Northern Ireland (55°N, 6°W) ... 156
North Charleston, SC (33°N, 80°W) ... 93
North China Plain, China (34°N, 115°E) ... 182
North Dakota, state in U.S. (47°N, 100°W) ... 98
North Fork., r. in Texas (34°N, 102°W) ... 94
North I., New Zealand (37°S, 175°E) ... 195
North Korea, country in Asia (40°N, 127°E) ... 183
North Little Rock, AR (35°N, 92°W) ... 95
North Loup R. (loop), NE (42°N, 100°W) ... 96
North Macedonia, country in Europe (42°N, 22°E) ... 159
North Platte, NE (41°N, 101°W) ... 96
North Platte R., U.S. (42°N, 104°W) ... 96
North Sasketchewan R., Canada (53°N, 110°W) ... 68-69
North Sea, Europe (57°N, 3°E) ... 148
North Sea Canal, Netherlands (53°N, 5°E) ... 151
North West Cape, Australia (22°S, 113°E) ... 190
Northampton, MA (42°N, 73°W) ... 89
Northeast Pacific Basin, Pacific O. (30°N, 145°W) ... 22
Northern Cook Islands, Pacific O. (11°S, 160°W) ... 189
Northern Dvina R. (duh vee NAH), Russia (64°N, 43°E) ... 160
Northern European Plain, Europe (52°N, 10°E) ... 148-149
Northern Indian L., MB (57°N, 97°W) ... 69
Northern Ireland, part of U.K. (55°N, 7°W) ... 156
Northern Mariana Is., commonwealth of U.S. (17°N, 145°E) ... 188
Northern Rocky Mts. P.P., BC (58°N, 125°W) ... 68
Northern Sporades, islands in Aegean Sea (38°N, 23°E) ... 159
Northern Terr., Australia (18°S, 133°E) ... 195
Northern Uvals, Russia (61°N, 50°E) ... 160
Northfield, MN (44°N, 93°W) ... 99
Northumberland Strait, Gulf of Saint Lawrence (46°N, 63°W) ... 72
Northwest Pacific Basin, Pacific O. (40°N, 155°E) ... 22
Northwest Territories, Canada (65°N, 120°W) ... 68-69
Norton, KS (40°N, 100°W) ... 96
Norton Sound, AK (64°N, 165°W) ... 104
Norwalk, CT (41°N, 73°W) ... 89
Norway, country in Europe (60°N, 8°E) ... 157
Norwegian Sea, Arctic and Atlantic Oceans (64°N, 0°) ... 148
Norwich (NAWR ich), CT (41°N, 72°W) ... 89
Norwich, England (53°N, 1°E) ... 156
Noto Pen., Japan (37°N, 137°E) ... 183
Notre Dame Bay, NL (50°N, 55°W) ... 72
Notre Dame Mts. (noh truh DAHM), QC (47°N, 70°W) ... 71
Nottaway R., QC (51°N, 78°W) ... 71
Nottingham, England (53°N, 1°W) ... 156
Nottingham I., NU (63°N, 79°W) ... 71
Nouadhibou, Mauritania (21°N, 17°W) ... 136
Nouakchott (nwahk SHAHT), Mauritania (18°N, 16°W) ... 136
Noumea (noo may AH), New Caledonia (22°S, 166°E) ... 188
Nova Iguazu (ee gwuh SOO), Brazil (23°S, 43°W) ... 127
Nova Scotia, prov. in Canada (44°N, 63°W) ... 72
Novaya Zemlya (noh vuh yuh ZEM lee uh), islands in Kara Sea (72°N, 55°E) ... 168
Novi Sad (noh vee SAHD), Serbia (45°N, 20°E) ... 159
Novokuznetsk, Russia (54°N, 87°E) ... 179
Novolazarevskaya Station (no vo LAH zuh REV skah yuh), Antarctica (71°S, 12°E) ... 200
Novorossiysk (nohv uh ruh seesk), Russia (45°N, 38°W) ... 160
Novosibirsk, Russia (55°N, 83°E) ... 179
Nubian Desert, Africa (21°N, 33°E) ... 137
Nueces R. (noo aY suhs), TX (28°N, 99°W) ... 94
Nueltin L., NU (60°N, 100°W) ... 69
Nueva Guinea, Nicaragua (12°N, 84°W) ... 115
Nuevo Casas Grandes, Mexico (30°N, 108°W) ... 94

Name (Pronunciation), Description (Lat., Long.) Page

Nuevo Laredo, Mexico (28°N, 100°W) ... 114
Nuevo Leon, state in Mexico (26°N, 100°W) ... 114
Nugaal Valley, Africa (9°N, 48°E) ... 140
Nuku Hiva (NOO koo HEE vah), island in Pacific O. (9°S, 140°W) ... 189
Nuku'alofa (NOO koo ah LO fah), Tonga (22°S, 176°W) ... 189
Nukulaelae Atoll (NOO koo LYE lye), Pacific O. (9°S, 180°) ... 189
Nukunonu Atoll (NOO koo NAH noo), Pacific O. (9°S, 172°W) ... 189
Nukus, Uzbekistan (43°N, 60°E) ... 179
Nullarbor Plain, Australia (32°S, 125°E) ... 190
Numaykoos Lake P.W.P., MB (58°N, 96°W) ... 69
Nunavut (NOON uh voot), terr. in Canada (65°N, 95°W) ... 69
Nunivak I., AK (60°N, 166°W) ... 104
Nuremberg (NYUR em behrg), Germany (49°N, 11°E) ... 159
Nuuk (nuk), Greenland (64°N, 51°W) ... 52
Nyala, Sudan (12°N, 25°E) ... 140
Nyasa, L., Africa (13°S, 35°E) ... 141
Nyiragongo, mt. in Dem. Rep. Congo (1°S, 29°E) ... 139
Nzerekore, Guinea (7°N, 9°W) ... 138

O

Oahe Dam, SD (44°N, 100°W) ... 98
Oahe, L. (oh WAH hee), U.S. (45°N, 101°W) ... 98
Oahu, island in Pacific O. (22°N, 158°W) ... 104
Oak Ridge, TN (36°N, 84°W) ... 90
Oakland, CA (38°N, 122°W) ... 102
Oamaru, New Zealand (45°S, 171°E) ... 195
Oaxaca (wah HAH kah), Mexico (17°N, 97°W) ... 114
Oaxaca, state in Mexico (17°N, 97°W) ... 114
Ob Bay, Russia (67°N, 72°E) ... 168
Ob R., Russia (64°N, 67°E) ... 170
Oba, ON (49°N, 84°W) ... 70
Obuasi, Ghana (6°N, 2°W) ... 138
Ocala (oh KAL uh), FL (29°N, 82°W) ... 93
Ocean City, MD (38°N, 75°W) ... 91
Oceania, island region of Pacific O. ... 188-189
Oceanside, CA (33°N, 118°W) ... 102
Ocmulgee R. (ohk MUHL gee), GA (32°N, 84°W) ... 93
Oconee L. (oh KOH nee), GA (33°N, 83°W) ... 93
Oconee R., GA (33°N, 83°W) ... 93
Odense (OH thehn seh), Denmark (55°N, 10°E) ... 157
Oder R., Europe (53°N, 14°E) ... 159
Odessa (oh DES uh), TX (32°N, 102°W) ... 94
Odessa, Ukraine (46°N, 31°E) ... 160
Oeno Atoll, Pacific O. (24°S, 131°W) ... 189
Ogaden, plateau in Ethiopia (7°N, 45°E) ... 140
Ogbomosho (ahg buh MOH shoh), Nigeria (8°N, 4°E) ... 138
Ogden, UT (41°N, 112°W) ... 103
Ogdensburg, NY (45°N, 76°W) ... 88
Ogeechee R. (oh GEE chee), GA (32°N, 81°W) ... 93
Ogooue R. (oh guh WAY), Gabon (1°S, 10°E) ... 139
O'Higgins Station, Antarctica (64°S, 57°W) ... 200
Ohio, state in U.S. (40°N, 83°W) ... 90-91
Ohio R., U.S. (40°N, 81°W) ... 90-91
Oil City, PA (41°N, 80°W) ... 88
Ojos del Salado (oh hohz dehl suh LAHD oh), mt. in South America (27°S, 69°W) ... 126
Oka R., Russia (55°N, 41°E) ... 151
Oka-Don Plain, Russia (54°N, 43°E) ... 160
Okanagan L. (oh kuh NAHG uhn), BC (50°N, 120°W) ... 68
Okanogan, WA (48°N, 120°W) ... 100
Okanogan, R., North America (49°N, 120°W) ... 100
Okavango Swamp, Africa (20°S, 23°E) ... 141
Okeechobee, L., FL (27°N, 81°W) ... 93
Okefenokee Swamp (oh kuh fuh NOH kee), GA (31°N, 82°W) ... 93
Okhotsk, Sea of, Asia (55°N, 150°E) ... 167
Oki Is., Sea of Japan (36°N, 133°E) ... 183
Okinawa, island in East China Sea (26°N, 128°E) ... 182
Okino Tori Shima, poss. of Japan (21°N, 136°E) ... 188
Oklahoma, state in U.S. (35°N, 99°W) ... 94-95
Oklahoma City, OK (35°N, 98°W) ... 95
Okotoks, AB (51°N, 114°W) ... 68
Olanchito, Honduras (15°N, 87°W) ... 115
Oland (UHR land), I. in Baltic Sea (57°N, 17°E) ... 157

Name (Pronunciation), Description (Lat., Long.) Page

Olathe (oh LAY thuh), KS (39°N, 95°W) ... 97
Old Crow, YT (67°N, 140°W) ... 60
Old Hickory L., TN (36°N, 87°W) ... 90
Olean (OH lee an), NY (42°N, 78°W) ... 88
Olenek R., Russia (68°N, 110°E) ... 170
Olsztyin (AWL shtehn), Poland (54°N, 20°E) ... 159
Olt R. (awlt), Romania (45°N, 24°E) ... 159
Olympia, WA (47°N, 123°W) ... 100
Olympic Mts., WA (48°N, 124°W) ... 100
Olympic N.P., WA (48°N, 124°W) ... 100
Olympus, Mt., Greece (40°N, 22°E) ... 159
Omaha, NE (41°N, 96°W) ... 96
Oman, country in Asia (20°N, 56°E) ... 178
Oman, Gulf of, Arabian Sea (25°N, 59°E) ... 178
Omdurman, Sudan (16°N, 32°E) ... 140
Omineca Mts. (oh mih NEHK uh), BC (57°N, 126°W) ... 68
Omsk, Russia (55°N, 73°E) ... 179
Onega Bay, Russia (64°N, 36°E) ... 160
Onega, L., Russia (62°N, 35°E) ... 160
Onega R., Russia (64°N, 39°E) ... 160
Oneida L., NY (43°N, 76°W) ... 88
O'Neill, NE (42°N, 99°W) ... 96
Oneonta, NY (42°N, 75°W) ... 88
Onitsha (oh NIHCH uh), Nigeria (6°N, 7°E) ... 138
Onotoa Atoll (o no TO ah), Pacific O. (2°S, 176°E) ... 189
Ontario, CA (34°N, 118°W) ... 102
Ontario, OR (44°N, 117°W) ... 100
Ontario, prov. in Canada (50°N, 90°W) ... 70
Ontario, L., North America (44°N, 77°W) ... 88
Ontong Java Atoll (AWN tawng JAH vah), Pacific O. (5°S, 160°E) ... 188
Ootsa L., BC (54°N, 126°W) ... 68
Opasquia P.P. (oh PAS kwee uh), ON (53°N, 94°W) ... 70
Opinaca R. (oh PIHN uh kaw), QC (52°N, 78°W) ... 71
Opiscoteo L. (oh pisk oh TEE oh), QC (53°N, 68°W) ... 71
Oradea (aw RAHD yah), Romania (47°N, 22°E) ... 159
Oraibi (oh RY bee), AZ (36°N, 110°W) ... 103
Oral, Kazakhstan (51°N, 51°E) ... 179
Oran, Algeria (36°N, 1°W) ... 136
Orange, Australia (34°S, 149°E) ... 195
Orange R., Africa (28°S, 18°E) ... 141
Orange Walk, Belize (18°N, 89°W) ... 115
Orangeburg, SC (33°N, 81°W) ... 93
Oranjestad, Aruba (13°N, 70°W) ... 116
Orcadas Station, Antarctica (61°S, 45°W) ... 200
Orchila I., Caribbean Sea (12°N, 66°W) ... 116
Ordu, Turkey (41°N, 38°E) ... 178
Ore Mts., Europe (51°N, 13°E) ... 159
Orebro (OO ree broh), Sweden (59°N, 15°E) ... 157
Oregon, state in U.S. (44°N, 123°W) ... 100
Orel, Russia (53°N, 36°E) ... 160
Orem, UT (40°N, 112°W) ... 103
Orenburg, Russia (52°N, 55°E) ... 160
Orinoco R., South America (8°N, 66°W) ... 126
Orkney Is., Atlantic O. (59°N, 3°W) ... 156
Orlando, FL (29°N, 81°W) ... 93
Orleans, France (48°N, 2°E) ... 158
Ormond Beach, FL (29°N, 81°W) ... 93
Ornskoldsvik, Sweden (63°N, 19°E) ... 157
Oroluk Atoll (OR ah look), Pacific O. (8°N, 155°E) ... 188
Orsha, Belarus (54°N, 30°E) ... 157
Orsk, Russia (51°N, 59°E) ... 160
Oruro, Bolivia (18°S, 70°W) ... 127
Osage R. (oh SAYJ), U.S. (38°N, 94°W) ... 97
Osaka, Japan (35°N, 136°E) ... 183
Osceola (ah see OH luh), IA (41°N, 94°W) ... 97
Osh, Kyrgyzstan (41°N, 73°E) ... 179
Oshkosh, WI (44°N, 88°W) ... 99
Osijek (OH see yek), Croatia (46°N, 19°E) ... 159
Oskemen, Kazakhstan (50°N, 83°E) ... 179
Oslo, Norway (60°N, 11°E) ... 157
Ossa, Mt., Tasmania (42°S, 146°E) ... 190
Osterdal R., Sweden (62°N, 13°E) ... 157
Ostersand, Sweden (63°N, 14°E) ... 157
Ostrava (AW struh vuh), Czech Republic (50°N, 18°E) ... 159
Ostrowiec (aw STRAW vyets), Poland (51°N, 21°E) ... 159
Osumi Is. (OH suh mee), East China Sea (30°N, 131°E) ... 183
Osumi Strait, Philippine Sea (31°N, 131°E) ... 183

Name (Pronunciation), Description (Lat., Long.) Page

Oswego (ah SWEE goh), NY (43°N, 76°W) ... 88
Otish Mts., QC (52°N, 70°W) ... 71
Otoskwin R., ON (52°N, 89°W) ... 70
Otranto, Strait of, Mediterranean Sea (40°N, 19°E) ... 159
Ottawa, Canada (45°N, 76°W) ... 70
Ottawa Is., Hudson Bay (60°N, 80°W) ... 71
Ottawa R., Canada (46°N, 78°W) ... 70
Ottumwa (uh TUHM wuh), IA (41°N, 92°W) ... 97
Ouachita, L. (WAHSH uh taw), AR (35°N, 93°W) ... 95
Ouachita Mts., U.S. (35°N, 95°W) ... 79
Ouachita R., AR (33°N, 93°W) ... 95
Ouagadougou (wah guh DOO goo), Burkina Faso (12°N, 2°W) ... 138
Ouargla (WAHR gluh), Algeria (33°N, 5°E) ... 136
Ouesso, Congo Republic (2°N, 16°E) ... 139
Oujda (ooj DAH), Morocco (35°N, 2°W) ... 136
Oulu (OW loo), Finland (65°N, 26°E) ... 157
Ourense, Spain (42°N, 8°W) ... 158
Outardes R. (oo TAHRD), QC (51°N, 69°W) ... 71
Ouvea Atoll, Pacific O. (21°S, 167°E) ... 188
Overland Park, KS (39°N, 95°W) ... 97
Oviedo, Spain (43°N, 6°W) ... 158
Owasco L. (oh WAHS koh), NY (43°N, 77°W) ... 88
Owen Sound, ON (44°N, 81°W) ... 70
Owens L., CA (36°N, 118°W) ... 102
Owensboro, KY (38°N, 87°W) ... 90
Owyhee, L., OR (44°N, 117°W) ... 100
Owyhee Mts. (oh WY ee), ID (43°N, 117°W) ... 100
Owyhee R., OR (44°N, 117°W) ... 100
Oxford, England (52°N, 1°W) ... 156
Oxford, MS (34°N, 90°W) ... 92
Oxford, OH (39°N, 85°W) ... 90
Oxnard, CA (34°N, 119°W) ... 102
Oyem, Gabon (2°N, 12°E) ... 139
Ozark Plateau, U.S. (37°N, 94°W) ... 79
Ozarks, L. of the, MO (38°N, 93°W) ... 97

P

Paarl (pahrl), South Africa (34°S, 19°E) ... 141
Pachuca, Mexico (20°N, 99°W) ... 114
Pacific-Antarctic Ridge, Pacific and Southern O. (60°S, 180°) ... 22
Pacific Ocean ... 14–15
Pacific Plate, Pacific O. ... 20
Pacific Range, mts. in BC (51°N, 126°W) ... 68
Pacific Rim N.P., BC (49°N, 126°W) ... 68
Padang (PAHD ahng), Indonesia (1°S, 100°E) ... 181
Padre I., TX (27°N, 97°W) ... 95
Padua (PAD yoo uh), Italy (45°N, 12°E) ... 159
Paducah (puh DOO kuh), KY (37°N, 89°W) ... 90
Pagadian (pah gah DEE ahn), Philippines (8°N, 123°E) ... 181
Pagan Is. (pah GAHN), Pacific O. (18°N, 146°E) ... 188
Pago Pago, American Samoa (14°S, 171°W) ... 189
Pagoda Point, Myanmar (15°N, 98°E) ... 181
Pahala (puh HAH luh), HI (19°N, 155°W) ... 104
Pailolo Channel (py LOH loh), HI (21°N, 157°W) ... 104
Painted Desert, AZ (36°N, 111°W) ... 103
Pakistan, country in Asia (30°N, 70°E) ... 180
Palatka, FL (30°N, 82°W) ... 93
Palau (pah LOW), country in Pacific O. (8°N, 135°E) ... 188
Palawan, island in Sulu Sea (10°N, 119°E) ... 169
Palembang, Indonesia (3°S, 105°E) ... 181
Palermo, Italy (38°N, 13°E) ... 159
Palikir, Federated States of Micronesia (7°N, 158°E) ... 188
Palk Strait (pawk), Asia (10°N, 80°E) ... 180
Palm Springs, CA (34°N, 117°W) ... 102
Palma, Balearic Is. (40°N, 3°E) ... 158
Palmas, Cape, Africa (4°N, 8°W) ... 138
Palmer Land, Antarctica (72°S, 63°W) ... 200
Palmerston Atoll, Pacific O. (18°S, 163°W) ... 189
Palmerston North, New Zealand (40°S, 176°E) ... 195
Palmyra Atoll, poss. of U.S. (6°N, 162°W) ... 189
Palu, Indonesia (1°S, 120°E) ... 181
Pamirs, (puh MIHRZ), mt. range in Asia (38°N, 73°E) ... 179
Pamlico Sound, NC (35°N, 76°W) ... 91
Pampa, TX (36°N, 101°W) ... 94
Pampas, plain in Argentina (34°S, 62°W) ... 126

Name (Pronunciation), Description (Lat., Long.) Page

Pamunkey R. (puh MUHNG kee), VA (38°N, 77°W) ... 91
Panama, country in Central America (8°N, 82°W) ... 115
Panama Canal, North America (10°N, 80°W) ... 115
Panama City, FL (30°N, 86°W) ... 92
Panama City, Panama (9°N, 80°W) ... 115
Panama, Gulf of, Pacific O. (10°N, 80°W) ... 115
Panama, Isthmus of, North America (10°N, 80°W) ... 115
Panay (pan EYE), island in Philippine Sea (11°N, 122°E) ... 181
Panevezys (PAHN yeh VAY zhees), Lithuania (56°N, 24°E) ... 157
Panuco R. (PAHN uh koh), Mexico (22°N, 99°W) ... 106
Panzhihua (pan ji huah), China (26°N, 102°E) ... 182
Papeete (puh PEE tee), French Polynesia (20°S, 150°W) ... 189
Papua, Gulf of, Coral Sea (9°S, 145°E) ... 188
Papua New Guinea, country in Pacific O. (5°S, 143°E) ... 188
Para R., Brazil (54°N, 41°E) ... 127
Paracel Is. (par uh SEHL), South China Sea (17°N, 112°E) ... 181
Paradise, NV (36°N, 115°W) ... 102
Paraguana Pen., South America (12°N, 70°W) ... 116
Paraguay, country in South America (23°S, 58°W) ... 127
Paraguay R., South America (19°S, 57°W) ... 127
Parakou (pa ra KOO), Benin (9°N, 3°E) ... 138
Paramaribo, Suriname (6°N, 55°W) ... 127
Parana, Argentina (32°S, 61°W) ... 126
Parana R., South America (23°S, 54°W) ... 127
Parent, QC (48°N, 75°W) ... 71
Paricutin Volcano (puh REE kuh teen), mt. in Mexico (19°N, 102°W) ... 106
Parinas, Point (puh REEN yuhs), Peru (5°S, 81°W) ... 126
Paris, France (49°N, 2°E) ... 158
Paris Basin, region of France (49°N, 2°E) ... 158
Park Falls, WI (46°N, 90°W) ... 99
Park Range, CO (40°N, 107°W) ... 103
Parker Dam, U.S. (34°N, 114°W) ... 102
Parkersburg, WV (39°N, 82°W) ... 91
Parma, Italy (45°N, 10°E) ... 159
Parma, OH (41°N, 82°W) ... 91
Parnaiba R., Brazil (7°S, 45°W) ... 127
Parnu, Estonia (58°N, 24°E) ... 157
Parry Sound, ON (45°N, 80°W) ... 70
Parsnip R., BC (55°N, 122°W) ... 68
Pas, The (pah), MB (54°N, 101°W) ... 69
Pasadena, CA (34°N, 118°W) ... 102
Pasadena, TX (30°N, 95°W) ... 95
Pascagoula, MS (31°N, 89°W) ... 92
Pascagoula R. (pas kuh GOO luh), MS (31°N, 89°W) ... 92
Pasco, WA (46°N, 119°W) ... 100
Passo Fundo, Brazil (28°S, 52°W) ... 127
Pasto, Colombia (1°N, 77°W) ... 126
Patagonia, plateau in Argentina (48°S, 71°W) ... 126
Paterson, NJ (41°N, 74°W) ... 88
Pathein, Myanmar (17°N, 95°E) ... 181
Pathfinder Res., WY (42°N, 107°W) ... 101
Patna, India (26°N, 85°E) ... 180
Patos Lagoon, Brazil (31°S, 51°W) ... 127
Patrai, Greece (38°N, 22°E) ... 159
Patuxent R., MD (39°N, 77°W) ... 91
Pau (poh), France (43°N, 0°) ... 158
Paulo Afonso Falls, waterfall in Brazil (9°S, 38°W) ... 127
Pavlodar, Kazakhstan (52°N, 77°E) ... 179
Pawtucket, RI (42°N, 71°W) ... 89
Payette R., ID (44°N, 116°W) ... 100
Payne, L., QC (59°N, 73°W) ... 71
Pea R., AL (31°N, 86°W) ... 92
Peace R., Canada (57°N, 117°W) ... 68–69
Peace R., FL (27°N, 82°W) ... 93
Peace River, city in AB (56°N, 117°W) ... 68
Pearl and Hermes Atoll, Pacific O. (28°N, 176°W) ... 189
Pearl Harbor, Oahu, HI (21°N, 158°W) ... 104
Pearl Is., Gulf of Panama (55°N, 130°W) ... 115
Pearl R., MS (32°N, 90°W) ... 92
Pechora, Russia (65°N, 58°E) ... 160
Pechora Basin, Russia (67°N, 56°E) ... 160
Pechora R., Russia (67°N, 53°E) ... 160
Pecos (PAY kuhs), TX (31°N, 104°W) ... 94
Pecos R., U.S. (31°N, 103°W) ... 74
Pecs (paych), Hungary (46°N, 18°E) ... 159

Name (Pronunciation), Description (Lat., Long.) Page

Pee Dee R., U.S. (34°N, 79°W) 93
Peipus, L., Europe (58°N, 28°E) 160
Pekanbaru, Indonesia (1°N, 101°E) 181
Pelee, Mt. (puh LAY, mawn), Martinique (15°N, 61°W) 116
Pelly Crossing, YT (63°N, 137°W) 60
Pelly Mts. (PEHL ee), YT (62°N, 134°W) 68
Pelly R., YT (62°N, 132°W) 68
Peloponnesus (PEHL uh puh NEE suhs), peninsula in Greece (37°N, 22°E) 159
Pelotas, Brazil (32°S, 52°W) 127
Pemadumcook L., ME (46°N, 69°W) 89
Pematangsiantar, Indonesia, (3°N, 99°W) 181
Pemba, island in Indian O. (5°S, 40°E) 140
Pemba, Mozambique (13°S, 40°E) 141
Pembina (PEHM buh nuh), ND (49°N, 97°W) 98
Pembina R., North America (49°N, 97°W) 98
Pembroke, ON (46°N, 77°W) 70
Penas, Gulf of, Chile (47°S, 78°W) 126
Pend Oreille, L. (pahn duh RAY), ID (48°N, 116°W) 100
Pend Oreille R., U.S. (48°N, 117°W) 100
Pendleton, OR (46°N, 119°W) 100
Pennsylvania, state in U.S. (41°N, 79°W) 88
Penobscot Bay, ME (44°N, 69°W) 89
Penobscot R., ME (45°N, 69°W) 89
Penrhyn Atoll (PEN rin), Pacific O. (9°S, 158°W) 189
Pensacola, FL (31°N, 87°W) 92
Pentecost I., Pacific O. (16°S, 168°E) 188
Penticton, BC (50°N, 120°W) 68
Penza, Russia (53°N, 45°E) 160
Peoria, IL (41°N, 90°W) 97
Pereira, Colombia (5°N, 76°W) 126
Peribonka R. (pehr uh BAWNG kuh), QC (51°N, 71°W) 71
Perm, Russia (58°N, 57°E) 160
Perpignan (pehr pee NYAHN), France (43°N, 3°E) 158
Perry L., KS (39°N, 96°W) 97
Persian Gulf, Arabian Sea (28°N, 51°E) 178
Perth, Australia (31°S, 116°E) 195
Perth Amboy, NJ (41°N, 74°W) 88
Peru, country in South America (8°S, 75°W) 126
Peru-Chile Trench, Pacific O. (20°S, 70°W) 22
Perugia (puh ROO juh), Italy (43°N, 12°E) 159
Pescara (pays KAH rah), Italy (42°N, 13°E) 159
Peshawar (puh SHAH wuhr), Pak. (34°N, 27°E) 180
Peter Pond L., SK (56°N, 109°W) 69
Peterborough, ON (44°N, 78°W) 70
Petersburg, AK (57°N, 133°W) 104
Petersburg, VA (37°N, 78°W) 91
Petit Mecatina, R. du, QC (52°N, 61°W) 72
Petrified Forest N.P., AZ (35°N, 110°W) 103
Petrolina, Brazil (9°S, 40°W) 127
Petropavl, Kazakhstan (55°N, 69°E) 179
Petropavlovsk-Kamchatskiy, Russia (53°N, 159°E) 167
Petrozavodsk, Russia (62°N, 34°E) 160
Phenix City (FEE niks), AL (32°N, 85°W) 92
Philadelphia, MS (33°N, 89°W) 92
Philadelphia, PA (40°N, 75°W) 88
Philippine Islands, Philippine Sea (14°N, 125°E) 169
Philippine Plate, western Pacific O. 20
Philippine Sea, Pacific O. (15°N, 135°E) 167
Philippine Trench, Pacific O. (10°S, 125°E) 22
Philippines, country in Asia (13°N, 123°E) 181
Phnom Penh (nawm pehn), Cambodia (12°N, 105°E) 181
Phoenix (FEE niks), AZ (33°N, 112°W) 103
Phoenix Is., Pacific O. (4°S, 174°W) 189
Pickwick L., U.S. (35°N, 88°W) 90
Pico de Orizaba, mt. in Mexico (19°N, 97°W) 106
Pico Duarte, mt. in Dominican Republic (19°N, 71°W) 107
Piedmont (peed mahnt), U.S. (35°N, 83°W) 77
Piedras Negras, Mexico (29°N, 101°W) 114
Pierre, SD (45°N, 100°W) 98
Pietermaritzburg (peet uhr MAHR uhts buhrg), South Africa (30°S, 30°E) 141
Pigeon R., North America (48°N, 90°W) 70
Pikes Peak, CO (39°N, 105°W) 103
Pikeville, KY (37°N, 83°W) 90
Pilcomayo R., South America (25°S, 59°W) 127
Pinatubo, Mt. (pihn uh TOO boh), Philippines (15°N, 120°E) 181
Pindus Mts., Greece (40°N, 21°E) 159

Name (Pronunciation), Description (Lat., Long.) Page

Pine Barrens, NJ (40°N, 75°W) 88
Pine Bluff, AR (34°N, 92°W) 95
Pine Creek Res., OK (34°N, 95°W) 95
Pine Ridge, SD (43°N, 102°W) 98
Pines, L. O' the, TX (33°N, 95°W) 95
Ping R., Thailand (17°N, 99°E) 181
Pinsk, Belarus (52°N, 26°E) 160
Pipmuacan Res., QC (50°N, 70°W) 71
Piraeus (py ree uhs), Greece (38°N, 24°E) 159
Pisa (PEE zuh), Italy (44°N, 10°E) 159
Pit R., CA (42°N, 122°W) 102
Pitcairn Is., Pacific O. (25°S, 130°W) 189
Pitesti, Romania (45°N, 25°E) 159
Pitt I., Hecate Strait (54°N, 130°W) 68
Pittsburg, KS (37°N, 95°W) 97
Pittsburgh, PA (40°N, 80°W) 88
Pittsfield, MA (42°N, 73°W) 89
Piura, Peru (5°S, 81°W) 126
Pivhennyy Buh R., Ukraine (48°N, 30°E) 160
Placentia (pla SEHN shih uh), NL (47°N, 54°W) 72
Placentia Bay, NL (47°N, 55°W) 72
Plamas, Brazil (10°S, 48°W) 127
Plano (PLAY noh), TX (33°N, 97°W) 95
Platte R., U.S. (41°N, 99°W) 96
Plattsburgh (PLATS buhrg), NY(45°N, 74°W) 88–89
Playgreen L., MB (54°N, 98°W) 69
Plenty, Bay of, New Zealand (36°S, 177°E) 195
Ploiesti (plaw YESHT), Romania (45°N, 26°E) 159
Plovdiv, Bulgaria (42°N, 25°E) 159
Plum, PA (40°N, 80°W) 88
Plymouth (PLIHM uhth), England (50°N, 4°W) 156
Plymouth, IN (41°N, 86°W) 90
Plymouth, MA (42°N, 71°W) 89
Plzen (puhl zehn), Czech Republic (50°N, 13°E) 159
Po R., Italy (45°N, 12°E) 159
Pocatello (poh kuh TEHL oh), ID (43°N, 113°W) 101
Pocono Mts. (POH kuh noh), PA (41°N, 75°W) 88
Podgorica, Montenegro (42°N, 19°E) 159
Pohnpei Is. (PAHN pay), Pacific O. (7°N, 158°E) 188
Point Pelee N.P. (pee lay), ON (42°N, 83°W) 70
Pointe des Monts, cape in QC (49°N, 67°W) 71
Pointe Louis-XIV, QC (55°N, 80°W) 71
Pointe-Noire (pwant nuh WAHR), Congo Republic (5°S, 12°E) 139
Poland, country in Europe (52°N, 20°E) 159
Polar Bear P.P., ON (55°N, 83°W) 70
Polar Plateau, Antarctica (85°S, 90°E) 200
Polokwane, South Africa (24°S, 29°E) 141
Pomeroy (PAHM roy), OH (39°N, 82°W) 91
Pomme de Terre Res. (pohm dee TEHR), MO (38°N, 93°W) 97
Pomona Res. (puh MOHN uh), KS (39°N, 96°W) 97
Pompano Beach (PAHM puh noh), FL (26°N, 80°W) 93
Ponca City (pahng kuh), OK (37°N, 97°W) 95
Ponce (PAWN say), Puerto Rico (18°N, 67°W) 116
Ponta Grossa, Brazil (25°S, 50°W) 127
Pontchartrain, L., LA (30°N, 90°W) 95
Pontiac, IL (41°N, 89°W) 97
Pontiac, MI (43°N, 83°W) 99
Pontianak, Indonesia (0°, 109°E) 181
Pontic Mts., Turkey (41°N, 37°E) 178
Poopo, L., Bolivia (19°S, 67°W) 127
Poplar Bluff, MO (37°N, 90°W) 97
Popocatepetl Volcano (poh poh kuh TAY peh tuhl), mt. in Mexico (19°N, 99°W) 106
Porcupine Hills, Canada (53°N, 102°W) 69
Porcupine R., North America (67°N, 145°W) 104
Pori, Finland (61°N, 22°E) 157
Porlamar (por la MAR), Venezuela (11°N, 64°W) 116
Port Alberni, BC (49°N, 125°W) 68
Port Angeles, WA (48°N, 124°W) 100
Port Arthur, TX (30°N, 94°W) 95
Port-au-Prince, Haiti (19°N, 72°W) 107
Port Augusta, Australia (33°S, 138°E) 195
Port Blair, Andaman Is. (12°N, 93°E) 180
Port Elizabeth, South Africa (34°S, 26°E) 141
Port Gentil (pawr zhawng TEE), Gabon (1°S, 9°E) 139
Port Harcourt, Nigeria (5°N, 7°E) 138
Port Hardy, BC (51°N, 127°W) 68
Port Hawkesbury (HAWKS buhr ee), NS (46°N, 61°W) 72

Name (Pronunciation), Description (Lat., Long.) Page

Port Hedland, Australia (20°S, 119°E) 195
Port Hope Simpson, NL (53°N, 56°W) 72
Port Huron (HYOOR uhn), MI (43°N, 83°W) 99
Port Lincoln, Australia (35°S, 136°E) 195
Port-Louis, Mauritius (20°S, 58°E) 132
Port Macquarie, Australia (31°S, 153°E) 195
Port McNeil, BC (51°N, 127°W) 68
Port Moresby, Papua New Guinea (9°S, 147°E) 188
Port Nelson, MB (57°N, 69°W) 70
Port Nolloth, South Africa (29°S, 17°E) 141
Port-of-Spain, Trinidad and Tobago(11°N, 62°W) 116
Port Orange, FL (29°N, 81°W) 93
Port Said (sah EED), Egypt (31°N, 32°E) 137
Port Saint Lucie, FL (27°N, 80°W) 93
Port Sudan, Sudan (20°N, 37°E) 140
Port-Vila, Vanuatu (18°S, 169°E) 188
Portage, MI (42°N, 86°W) 99
Portage la Prairie (PORT ihj luh PREH ree), MB (50°N, 98°W) 69
Portland, ME (44°N, 70°W) 89
Portland, OR (46°N, 123°W) 100
Porto Alegre, Brazil (30°S, 51°W) 127
Porto Velho, Brazil (9°S, 64°W) 127
Porto, Portugal (41°N, 9°W) 158
Porto-Novo, Benin (6°N, 2°E) 138
Portsmouth (POHRT smuhth), England (51°N, 1°W) 156
Portsmouth, NH (43°N, 71°W) 89
Portsmouth, OH (39°N, 83°W) 90
Portsmouth, VA (37°N, 76°W) 91
Portugal, country in Europe (37°N, 8°W) 158
Posadas, Argentina (28°S, 56°W) 126
Possum Kingdom L., TX (33°N, 99°W) 94
Potholes Res., WA (47°N, 119°W) 100
Poti (PAW tee), Georgia (42°N, 42°E) 161
Potomac R., U.S. (38°N, 77°W) 91
Potosi, Bolivia (20°S, 66°W) 127
Potsdam, Germany (52°N, 13°E) 159
Potsdam, NY (45°N, 75°W) 88
Poughkeepsie (puh KIHP see), NY (42°N, 74°W) 88
Povungnituk, R. de, QC (61°N, 75°W) 71
Powder R., OR (45°N, 118°W) 100
Powder R., U.S. (45°N, 106°W) 101
Powder River Basin, U.S. (45°N, 106°W) 101
Powell, L., U.S. (37°N, 111°W) 103
Powell River, city in BC (50°N, 125°W) 68
Poyang L., China (29°N, 116°E) 182
Poznan, Poland (52°N, 17°E) 159
Prague, Czech Republic (50°N, 14°E) 159
Prairie Dog Town Fork, r. in U.S. (35°N, 101°W) 94
Prairie du Chien (PRER ee duh SHEEN), WI (43°N, 91°W) 99
Pratt, KS (38°N, 99°W) 96
Prescott, AZ (35°N, 113°W) 103
Presque Isle (preh SKYL), ME (47°N, 68°W) 89
Pretoria, South Africa (25°S, 28°E) 141
Pribilof Is. (prib uh lawf), Bering Sea (57°N, 170°W) 104
Price, UT (40°N, 111°W) 103
Primrose L., Canada (55°N, 110°W) 69
Prince Albert, SK (53°N, 106°W) 69
Prince Albert N.P., SK (54°N, 106°W) 69
Prince Charles I., Canada (68°N, 74°W) 61
Prince Edward Island, prov. in Canada (47°N, 63°W) 72
Prince Edward I. N.P., PE (46°N, 63°W) 72
Prince Edward Is., Indian O. (47°S, 38°E) 132
Prince George, BC (54°N, 123°W) 68
Prince of Wales I., Arctic O. (73°N, 99°W) 60
Prince of Wales I., Gulf of Alaska (56°N, 133°W) 104
Prince Patrick I., Arctic O. (77°N, 120°W) 60
Prince Rupert, BC (54°N, 130°W) 68
Prince William Sound, Gulf of Alaska (61°N, 147°W) 104
Princess Royal I., Hecate Strait (53°N, 129°W) 68
Princeton, IN (38°N, 88°W) 90
Principe, island in Gulf of Guinea (2°N, 8°E) 139
Pripyat Marshes, Europe (53°N, 26°E) 160
Pripyat R., Europe (52°N, 28°E) 160
Pristina (PRISH tih nah), Kosovo (43°N, 21°E) 159
Progress Station, Antarctica (69°S, 76°E) 200
Prokopyevsk, Russia (54°N, 87°E) 179

Name (Pronunciation), Description (Lat., Long.) Page

Providence, RI (42°N, 71°W) 89
Providencia I., I. in Caribbean Sea (14°N, 82°W) 115
Provo, UT (40°N, 112°W) 103
Prudhoe Bay, AK (70°N, 148°W) 104
Prut R., Europe (47°N, 28°E) 159
Pskov, Russia (58°N, 28°E) 160
Pucallpa, Peru (8°S, 75°W) 126
Puebla, Mexico (19°N, 98°W) 114
Puebla, state in Mexico (19°N, 98°W) 114
Pueblo, CO (38°N, 105°W) 103
Puerto Armuelles (PWEHR toh ahr moo AY lays),
  Panama (8°N, 83°W) 115
Puerto Barrios, Guatemala (16°N, 89°W) 115
Puerto Cabezas, Nicaragua (14°N, 83°W) 115
Puerto Montt, Chile (42°S, 73°W) 126
Puerto Princesa (PWER to prin SE sah), Philippines
  (10°N, 119°E) 181
Puerto Rico, commonwealth of U.S. (18°N, 67°W) 116
Puerto Rico Trench, Atlantic O. (20°N, 65°W) 22
Puerto Vallarta (PWAIR tuh vuh YAHR tuh),
  Mexico (19°N, 105°W) 107
Puget Sound (PYOO jeht), WA (48°N, 123°W) 100
Pukapuka Atoll (POO kah POO kah), Pacific O.
  (15°S, 139°W) 189
Pukapuka Atoll, Pacific O. (11°S, 166°W) 189
Pukaskwa N.P., ON (48°N, 86°W) 70
Pullman, WA (47°N, 117°W) 100
Pulusuk Atoll (PUL ah sook), Pacific O.
  (7°N, 149°E) 188
Pune (POO nuh), India (19°N, 74°E) 180
Punta Arenas, Chile (53°S, 71°W) 126
Punta Gorda (puhn tuh GAWR duh), FL
  (27°N, 82°W) 93
Punta Parinas, Peru (6°S, 81°W) 126
Puntarenas (punt ah RAY nahs), Costa Rica
  (10°N, 85°W) 115
Purgatoire R. (PUHR guh twahr), CO
  (37°N, 104°W) 103
Purus R. (puh ROOS), Brazil (6°S, 65°W) 127
Pusan, South Korea (35°N, 129°E) 183
Putrajaya, Malaysia (2°N, 102°E) 181
Putumayo R., South America (2°S, 74°W) 126
Puvirnituq, QC (60°N, 77°W) 71
Pyatigorsk, Russia (44°N, 43°E) 161
Pymatuning Res., OH and PA (42°N, 81°W) 91
Pyongyang, North Korea (39°N, 126°E) 183
Pyramid L., NV (40°N, 119°W) 102
Pyrenees, mt. range in Europe (43°N, 0°) 158

Q

Qaanaaq (kah NAHK), Greenland (78°N, 70°W) 52
Qabis, Tunisia (34°N, 10°E) 136
Qaidam Basin, China (37°N, 95°E) 182
Qaraghandy, Kazakhstan (50°N, 72°E) 179
Qarshi, Uzbekistan (39°N, 66°E) 179
Qasr al Farafirah, Egypt (27°N, 28°E) 137
Qatar (KAH tahr), country in Asia (25°N, 51°E) 178
Qattara Depression, lowland of Egypt
  (29°N, 27°E) 137
Qazvin, Iran (36°N, 50°E) 178
Qeshm I., island in Arabian Sea (27°N, 56°E) 178
Qilian Mts, China (39°N, 98°E) 182
Qingdao, China (36°N, 120°E) 182
Qinghai L. (zhing hy), China (37°N, 100°E) 182
Qiqihar, China (47°N, 168°E) 182
Qom (kohm), Iran (34°N, 51°E) 178
Qostanay, Kazakhstan (53°N, 64°E) 179
Qu'Appelle R. (kwa PEHL), Canada (50°N, 102°W) 69
Quba, Azerbaijan (41°N, 49°E) 161
Québec, prov. in Canada (50°N, 70°W) 71
Québec, QC (47°N, 71°W) 71
Queen Adelaide Archipelago, Chile (52°S, 75°W) 126
Queen Bess, Mt., BC (51°N, 123°W) 68
Queen Charlotte Is., alternative name for
  Haida Gwaii (53°N, 132°W) 68
Queen Charlotte Sound, BC (51°N, 130°W) 68
Queen Charlotte Strait, BC (51°N, 128°W) 68
Queen Elizabeth Is., Arctic O. (76°N, 100°W) 60-61
Queen Maud Gulf, NU (68°N, 100°W) 60
Queen Maud Land, region of Antarctica
  (73°S, 30°E) 200

Name (Pronunciation), Description (Lat., Long.) Page

Queensland, state in Australia (22°S, 145°E) 195
Queenstown, South Africa (32°S, 27°E) 141
Quelimane (kehl uh MAHN uh), Mozambique
  (18°S, 37°E) 141
Queretaro (keh RAY tah roh), Mexico
  (21°N, 100°W) 114
Queretaro, state in Mexico (21°N, 100°W) 114
Quesnel (kuh NEHL), BC (53°N, 122°W) 68
Quesnel L., BC (53°N, 121°W) 68
Quetico P.P., ON (48°N, 92°W) 70
Quetta, Pakistan (30°N, 67°E) 180
Quezaltenango (keh zahl teh NAHN goh),
  Guatemala (15°N, 92°W) 115
Quezon City (KAY sohn), Philippines (15°N, 121°E) 181
Qui Nhon (kwee NYAWN), Vietnam (13°N, 109°E) 181
Quinault R., WA (47°N, 124°W) 100
Quincy, IL (40°N, 91°W) 97
Quincy, MA (42°N, 71°W) 89
Quintana Roo, state in Mexico (20°N, 89°W) 114
Quito (KEE toh), Ecuador (0°, 78°W) 126
Qunghirot, Uzbekistan (43°N, 59°E) 179
Quqon, Uzbekistan (41°N, 71°E) 179
Qurghonteppa, Tajikistan (38°N, 69°E) 179
Qyzylorda, Kazakhstan (45°N, 66°E) 179

R

Raas Caseyr, alternative name for Cape Guardafui
  (12°N, 51°E) 140
Rabat, Morocco (34°N, 7°W) 136
Rabaul (rah BOUL), Papua New Guinea
  (4°S, 152°E) 188
Race, Cape, NL (47°N, 52°W) 72
Racine, WI (43°N, 88°W) 99
Radom, Poland (51°N, 21°E) 159
Raft R., ID (42°N, 113°W) 101
Raiatea, island in Pacific O. (17°S, 152°W) 189
Rainier, Mt. (ruh NEER), WA (47°N, 122°W) 100
Rainy L., North America (49°N, 93°W) 70
Rainy R., North America (49°N, 94°W) 99
Raipur (RY poor), India (21°N, 82°E) 180
Raivavae I. (RY vah VAH ay), Pacific O.
  (24°S, 148°W) 189
Rajang R. (RAHJ ahng), Malaysia (3°N, 113°E) 181
Rajasthan Canal, India (28°N, 72°E) 180
Rajkot (RAHJ koht), India (22°N, 71°E) 180
Raleigh, NC (36°N, 79°W) 91
Ralik Chain, Pacific O. (7°N, 167°E) 188
Ramallah, West Bank (32°N, 35°E) 178
Ramsey L., ON (47°N, 82°W) 70
Rancagua, Chile (34°S, 71°W) 126
Ranchi, India (23°N, 85°E) 180
Randers, Denmark (56°N, 10°E) 157
Rangeley L. (RAYNJ lee), ME (45°N, 71°W) 89
Rangiroa Atoll (rahng ee RO ah), Pacific O.
  (15°S, 148°W) 189
Rangoon, alternative name for Yangon
  (17°N, 96°E) 181
Rankin Inlet, Canada (63°N, 94°W) 61
Rapa I., Pacific O. (28°S, 144°W) 189
Rapid City, SD (44°N, 103°W) 98
Rappahannock R., VA (38°N, 77°W) 91
Raquette R. (RAK uht), NY (44°N, 75°W) 88
Rarotonga I. (rah raw TAWNG ah), Pacific O.
  (21°S, 163°W) 189
Ras al Hadd, cape in Oman (22°N, 60°E) 178
Ras Dashen, mt. in Ethiopia (13°N, 38°E) 140
Rasht, Iran (37°N, 50°E) 178
Ratak Chain, Pacific O. (11°N, 171°E) 188
Rathbun Res., IA (41°N, 93°W) 97
Raton, NM (37°N, 104°W) 103
Ratz, Mt., BC (57°N, 132°W) 68
Rawaki I., Pacific O. (4°S, 171°W) 189
Rawalpindi (rah wuhl PIHN dee), Pakistan
  (34°N, 72°E) 180
Rawlins, WY (42°N, 107°W) 101
Reading (REHD ing), PA (40°N, 76°W) 88
Recife (reh SEE fuh), Brazil (8°S, 35°W) 127
Red Deer, AB (52°N, 114°W) 68
Red Deer R., Canada (51°N, 112°W) 68-69
Red L., MN (48°N, 95°W) 75
Red L., ON (51°N, 94°W) 70

Name (Pronunciation), Description (Lat., Long.) Page

Red Lake R., MN (48°N, 96°W) 98
Red R., Asia (23°N, 105°E) 181
Red R., North America (50°N, 97°W) 60
Red R., U.S. (34°N, 99°W) 94-95
Red River Valley, U.S. (47°N, 97°W) 98
Red Sea, Africa and Asia (19°N, 40°E) 133
Redding, CA (42°N, 122°W) 102
Redwood N.P., CA (41°N, 124°W) 102
Reef Is., Pacific O. (11°S, 166°E) 188
Reggio di Calabria (REH joh dee kuh LAH bree uh),
  Italy (38°N, 16°E) 159
Regina (ruh JY nuh), SK (51°N, 105°W) 69
Reidsville, NC (36°N, 80°W) 91
Reims (reemz), France (49°N, 4°E) 158
Reindeer L., SK (57°N, 102°W) 69
Rend L., IL (38°N, 89°W) 97
Rennell I. (ren NEL), Pacific O. (12°S, 161°E) 188
Rennes (rehn), France (48°N, 1°W) 158
Reno, NV (40°N, 120°W) 102
Republican R., U.S. (40°N, 101°W) 96
Resistencia, Argentina (27°S, 59°W) 126
Resolute, NU (75°N, 95°W) 60
Resolution I., Hudson Str. (62°N, 64°W) 71
Reunion, overseas state of France (21°S, 56°E) 132
Revelstoke, BC (51°N, 118°W) 68
Revillagigedo Is. (rih VIHL uh guh GEED oh),
  Pacific O. (18°N, 111°W) 106
Rexburg, ID (44°N, 112°W) 101
Reyes, Point, CA (38°N, 123°W) 102
Reykjavik (RAY kyuh veek), Iceland (64°N, 22°W) 158
Reynosa, Mexico (26°N, 98°W) 114
Rezekne, Latvia (57°N, 27°E) 157
Rhine R., Europe (52°N, 7°E) 159
Rhinelander, WI (46°N, 89°W) 99
Rhode Island, state in U.S. (42°N, 71°W) 89
Rhodes, island in Mediterranean Sea (36°N, 28°E) 159
Rhodope Mts. (RAHD uh pee), Europe
  (42°N, 25°E) 159
Rhone R., Europe (44°N, 4°E) 158
Ribeirao Preto, Brazil (21°S, 48°W) 127
Rice Lake, WI (46°N, 92°W) 99
Richland, WA (46°N, 119°W) 100
Richlands, VA (37°N, 82°W) 91
Richmond, IN (40°N, 85°W) 90
Richmond, VA (38°N, 77°W) 91
Ridgecrest, CA (35°N, 118°W) 102
Riding Mt. N.P., MB (51°N, 100°W) 69
Riga (REE guh), Latvia (57°N, 24°E) 160
Riga, Gulf of, Baltic Sea (58°N, 23°E) 160
Rigolet (rihg uh LEHT), NL (54°N, 58°W) 72
Rijeka (ree YEHK uh), Croatia (45°N, 14°E) 159
Rimini, Italy (44°N, 13°E) 159
Rimouski (rim OO skee), QC (48°N, 69°W) 71
Rio Branco, city in Brazil (10°S, 68°W) 127
Rio Bravo del Norte (ree oh BRAHV oh dehl NORT ee),
  r. in North America, (29°N, 108°W) 114
Rio Colorado, r. in Mexico and U.S. (32°N, 115°W) 114
Rio Cuarto, city in Argentina (33°S, 64°W) 126
Rio de Janeiro (REE oh day zhuh NAIR oh),
  city in Brazil (23°S, 43°W) 127
Rio de la Plata, r. in South America (35°S, 57°W) 126
Rio Gallegos (RIH oh gah LAY gohs),
  city in Argentina (52°S, 69°W) 120
Rio Grande, city in Brazil (31°S, 52°W) 127
Rio Grande (REE oh GRAN day),
  r. in U.S. and Mexico (28°N, 100°W) 78-79
Rio Grande Rise, Atlantic O. (30°S, 35°W) 22
Rio Hondo, r. in NM (34°N, 104°W) 103
Rio Muni (ree oh MOO nee),
  region of Eq. Guinea (2°N, 10°E) 139
Rio Rancho, city in NM (35°N, 107°W) 103
Riverina, Australia (35°S, 146°E) 195
Riverside, CA (34°N, 117°W) 102
Riverton, WY (43°N, 108°W) 101
Riviera (rihv ee EHR uh), coastal region of Europe
  (44°N, 7°E) 159
Riviere-du-Loup (ree vee EHR duh LOO), QC
  (48°N, 70°W) 71
Rivne, Ukraine (51°N, 26°E) 160
Riyadh (ree AHD), Saudi Arabia (25°N, 47°E) 178
Roanoke (ROH uh nohk), VA (37°N, 80°W) 91

Name (Pronunciation), Description (Lat., Long.)   Page

Roanoke R., U.S. (36°N, 77°W) 91
Robson, Mt., Canada (53°N, 119°W) 68
Rochester, MN (44°N, 92°W) 99
Rochester, NH (43°N, 71°W) 89
Rochester, NY (43°N, 78°W) 88
Rock Hill, SC (35°N, 81°W) 93
Rock Island, IL (41°N, 90°W) 97
Rock R., U.S. (42°N, 90°W) 97
Rock Springs, WY (42°N, 109°W) 101
Rockall, island in Atlantic O. (58°N, 14°W) 158
Rockford, IL (42°N, 89°W) 97
Rockhampton, Australia (23°S, 151°E) 195
Rockville, MD (39°N, 77°W) 91
Rocky Mount, NC (36°N, 78°W) 91
Rocky Mountain N.P., CO (40°N, 106°W) 103
Rocky Mts., North America (45°N, 110°W) ... 54
Roebuck Bay, Australia (19°S, 120°E) 190
Rogue R. (rohg), OR (42°N, 123°W) 100
Rojo, Cape, Mexico (21°N, 97°W) 106
Rolla (RAHL uh), MO (38°N, 92°W) 97
Rolling Fork, r. in KY (38°N, 86°W) 90
Roma, Australia (27°S, 149°E) 195
Romaine R., QC (50°N, 64°W) 72
Romania, country in Europe (46°N, 25°E) 159
Rome, GA (34°N, 85°W) 92
Rome, Italy (42°N, 13°E) 159
Rome, NY (43°N, 75°W) 88
Rondonopolis, Brazil (16°S, 55°W) 127
Ronne Ice Shelf, Antarctica (78°S, 65°W)....200
Roraima, Mt., South America (5°N, 61°W) 126
Rosario, Argentina (33°S, 61°W) 126
Rose Atoll, Pacific O. (14°S, 168°W) 189
Roseau (roh ZOH), Dominica (15°N, 61°W) 116
Roseburg, OR (43°N, 123°W) 100
Ross Barnett Res., MS (32°N, 90°W) 92
Ross Bay Junction, NL (53°N, 66°W) 72
Ross Ice Shelf, Antarctica (82°S, 180°) 200
Ross L., WA (49°N, 121°W) 100
Ross Sea, Antarctica (75°S, 180°) 200
Rossignol L., NS (44°N, 65°W) 72
Rosso, Mauritania (17°N, 16°W) 136
Rostock, Germany (54°N, 12°E) 159
Rostov-na-Donu (ruh STAHV nah DAH noo),
    Russia (47°N, 40°E) 160
Roswell, GA (34°N, 84°W) 93
Roswell, NM (33°N, 105°W) 103
Rota I., Pacific O. (14°N, 145°E) 188
Rotorua, New Zealand (38°S, 176°E) 195
Rotterdam, Netherlands (52°N, 4°E) 158
Rotuma I. (ro TOO mah), Pacific O. (13°S, 178°E)....189
Rouen (roo AHN), France (49°N, 1°E) 158
Rough River Res., KY (38°N, 86°W) 90
Round Rock, TX (31°N, 98°W) 95
Rouyn-Noranda (ROO uhn nuh RAN duh), QC
    (48°N, 79°W) 71
Rovaniemi (ROH vah NYEH mih), Finland
    (66°N, 26°E) 157
Rub al Khali (ROOB al KAH lee), region of
    Saudi Arabia (22°N, 53°E) 178
Rubtsovsk, Russia (52°N, 81°E) 179
Ruby Mts., NV (40°N, 116°W) 102
Rufiji R. (roo fee jee), Tanzania (8°S, 37°E) 140
Rugby, ND (48°N, 100°W) 98
Rugen (ROO guhn), Island in Baltic Sea
    (54°N, 14°E) 157
Rukwa, L. (RUHK wuh), Tanzania (8°S, 32°E) 140
Rupert R., QC (51°N, 79°W) 71
Rururtu I. (roo ROO too), Pacific O.
    (23°S, 151°W) 189
Ruse (ROO say), Bulgaria (44°N, 26°E) 159
Rushmore, Mt., SD (44°N, 103°W) 98
Russell, MB (51°N, 101°W) 69
Russia, country in Europe and Asia (60°N, 60°E).....12-13
Rustavi, Georgia (42°N, 45°E) 161
Rutland, VT (44°N, 73°W) 89
Ruvuma R. (ruh VUH mah), Africa (11°S, 40°E) 141
Rwanda, country in Africa (2°S, 30°E) 140
Ryazan, Russia (55°N, 40°E) 160
Rybinsk Res., Russia (59°N, 38°E) 160
Ryukyu Is. (ree OO kyoo), Pacific O. (26°N, 128°E) 188
Rzeszow (zhah shahf), Poland (50°N, 22°E)....159

Name (Pronunciation), Description (Lat., Long.)   Page

S

Saanich, BC (48°N, 124°W)............................. 68
Saaremaa, island in Baltic Sea (58°N, 23°E) 157
Saberi L., Asia (32°N, 61°E) 178
Sabha, Libya (26°N, 15°E) 137
Sabine L. (suh BEEN), U.S. (30°N, 94°W) 95
Sabine R., U.S. (32°N, 95°W) 95
Sable, Cape, FL (25°N, 81°W) 93
Sable, Cape, NS (44°N, 65°W) 72
Sable I., Atlantic O. (43°N, 59°W) 72
Sacandaga Res. (sak uhn DAY guh), NY (43°N, 74°W) 88
Sachigo L., ON (54°N, 92°W) 70
Sachigo R., ON (55°N, 89°W) 70
Sachs Harbour, NT (72°N, 125°W) 60
Sacramento, CA (39°N, 122°W) 102
Sacramento Mts., U.S. (33°N, 106°W) 103
Sacramento R., CA (40°N, 122°W) 102
Sacramento Valley, CA (40°N, 122°W) 102
Sado (SAHD oh), island in Sea of Japan
    (38°N, 138°E) 183
Safi, Morocco (32°N, 9°W) 136
Sagar (SAHG uhr), India (24°N, 79°E) 180
Saginaw (SAG uh naw), MI (44°N, 84°W) 99
Saginaw Bay, MI (44°N, 84°W) 99
Saguaro N.P., AZ (32°N, 111°W) 103
Saguenay (sag uh NAY), QC (48°N, 71°W) 71
Saguenay R., QC (48°N, 71°W) 71
Sahara, desert in Africa (24°N, 10°E) 136-137
Sahel, region of Africa (14°N, 10°E) 139
Saimaa, L. (SY mah), Finland (61°N, 28°E) 157
Saint Ann's Bay, NS (42°N, 61°W) 72
Saint Anthony, NL (51°N, 56°W) 72
Saint-Augustin R. (sant oh goos TEEN), Canada
    (51°N, 59°W) 72
Saint Augustine, FL (30°N, 81°W) 93
Saint Barthelemy, Guadeloupe (18°N, 63°W) 116
Saint Catharines, ON (43°N, 79°W) 70
Saint Charles, MO (39°N, 90°W) 97
Saint Clair, L., ON (43°N, 83°W) 70
Saint Clair R., ON (48°N, 82°W) 99
Saint Cloud, MN (46°N, 94°W) 98
Saint Croix (kroy), island in Caribbean Sea
    (18°N, 65°W) 116
Saint Croix R., North America (45°N, 69°W) ... 89
Saint Croix R., U.S. (45°N, 93°W) 99
Saint Elias, Mt. (ee LY uhs), North America
    (60°N, 141°W) 104
Saint Elias Mts., YT (61°N, 138°W) 68
Saint Etienne (san tay TYEHN), France (45°N, 5°E)....158
Saint Francis R., AR (36°N, 90°W) 95
Saint Francis R., North America (47°N, 69°W) 89
Saint George, UT (37°N, 114°W) 102
Saint George's, Grenada (12°N, 62°W) 116
Saint George's Bay, NL (48°N, 59°W) 72
Saint George's Channel, Ireland and Wales
    (52°N, 6°W) 156
Saint Helena, island in Atlantic O. (15°S, 5°W) 132
Saint Helens, Mt., WA (46°N, 122°W) 100
Saint Ignace I. (IHG nuhs), L. Superior
    (49°N, 88°W) 70
Saint Jean, L. (san ZHAHN), QC (49°N, 72°W) 71
Saint Joe R., ID (47°N, 116°W) 100
Saint John, NB (45°N, 66°W) 72
Saint John R., Canada and U.S. (47°N, 69°W) 89
Saint John's, Antigua and Barbuda (17°N, 62°W)........116
Saint John's, NL (48°N, 53°W) 72
Saint Johns R., FL (30°N, 82°W) 93
Saint Johnsbury (jahnz ber ee), VT (44°N, 72°W) 89
Saint Joseph, MI (42°N, 87°W) 99
Saint Joseph, MO (40°N, 95°W) 97
Saint Joseph, L., ON (52°N, 91°W) 70
Saint Joseph R., U.S. (41°N, 85°W) 99
Saint Kitts and Nevis (NEE vihs),
    country in Caribbean Sea (17°N, 63°W)......116
Saint Lawrence, Gulf of, Atlantic O. (48°N, 62°W) 72
Saint Lawrence I., Bering Sea (63°N, 170°W) 104
Saint Lawrence Is. N.P., ON (44°N, 76°W) 70
Saint Lawrence R., Canada and U.S. (48°N, 70°W) 71
Saint Louis, MO (39°N, 90°W) 97

Name (Pronunciation), Description (Lat., Long.)   Page

Saint-Louis (sang loo ee), Senegal (16°N, 16°W) 138
Saint Louis R., MN (47°N, 93°W) 99
Saint Lucia, country in Caribbean Sea
    (14°N, 61°W)...116
Saint Malo (san muh LOH), France (49°N, 2°W) 158
Saint Malo, Gulf of, France (49°N, 3°W) 158
Saint Martin, island in Caribbean Sea (18°N, 63°W) ...116
Saint Mary's Bay, NL (47°N, 54°W) 72
Saint Matthew I., Bering Sea (60°N, 172°W) 104
Saint Matthias Group, islands in Pacific O.
    (1°S, 149°E) 188
Saint Maurice R. (san moh REES), QC
    (48°N, 74°W) 71
Saint Paul, MN (45°N, 93°W) 99
Saint Paul I., Indian O. (39°S, 78°E) 15
Saint Peters, MO (39°N, 91°W) 97
Saint Petersburg, FL (28°N, 83°W) 93
Saint Petersburg, Russia (60°N, 30°E)..........160
Saint Pierre, island in Atlantic O. (47°N, 56°W)....72
Saint Pierre and Miquelon (MIK uh lahng),
    terr. of France (47°N, 56°W) 72
Saint Quentin, France (50°N, 4°E) 158
Saint Vincent, Cape, Portugal (37°N, 9°W) 158
Saint Vincent and the Grenadines,
    country in Caribbean Sea (13°N, 62°W) 116
Sainte Foy, QC (47°N, 71°W) 71
Sainte Genevieve (sant JEHN uh veev), MO
    (38°N, 90°W) 97
Sainte-Marguerite R. (mahr GREET), QC
    (50°N, 67°W) 72
Saipan I., Pacific O. (15°N, 146°E) 188
Saitama, Japan (36°N, 140°E) 183
Sajama, Mt., Bolivia (18°S, 69°W) 127
Sakai, Japan (35°N, 135°E) 183
Sakakah, Saudi Arabia (30°N, 40°E) 178
Sakakawea, L., ND (48°N, 102°W) 98
Sakami, L., QC (53°N, 77°W) 71
Sakhalin I., Russia (50°N, 143°E) 167
Saki, Azerbaijan (41°N, 47°E) 161
Salada Lagoon, Mexico (33°N, 116°W) 114
Salado R., Argentina (26°S, 64°W) 126
Salalah, Oman (17°N, 54°E) 178
Salamanca, Spain (41°N, 6°W) 158
Salavat, Russia (53°N, 57°E) 160
Salekhard, Russia (66°N, 67°E) 160
Salem (SAYL uhm), MA (43°N, 71°W) 89
Salem, OR (45°N, 123°W) 100
Salerno, Italy (41°N, 15°E) 159
Salina (suh LY nuh), KS (39°N, 98°W) 96
Salinas (suh LEE nuhs), CA (37°N, 122°W) 102
Salisbury (SAWLZ behr ee), Australia (35°S, 138°E) 195
Salisbury, MD (38°N, 76°W) 91
Salisbury, NC (36°N, 81°W) 91
Salisbury I., NU (64°N, 76°W) 71
Salluit, QC (62°N, 75°W) 71
Salmon (SAM uhn), ID (45°N, 114°W) 101
Salmon Falls Creek Res., ID (42°N, 115°W)...................101
Salmon R., ID (46°N, 116°W) 100-101
Salmon R. Mts., ID (44°N, 115°W) 101
Salt Basin, TX (32°N, 105°W) 94
Salt Lake City, UT (41°N, 112°W) 103
Salt R., AZ (34°N, 112°W) 103
Salt R., KY (38°N, 86°W) 90
Salt R., MO (40°N, 92°W) 97
Salta, Argentina (25°S, 65°W) 126
Saltillo (sahl TEE yoh), Mexico (25°N, 101°W)............114
Salto, Uruguay (31°S, 58°W) 120
Salton Sea, CA (33°N, 116°W) 102
Saluda R. (suh LOOD uh), SC (34°N, 82°W)....93
Salvador, Brazil (13°S, 38°W) 127
Salween R., Asia (18°N, 97°E) 170
Salyan, Azerbaijan (40°N, 49°E) 161
Salzburg, Austria (48°N, 13°E) 159
Sam Rayburn Res., TX (31°N, 94°W) 95
Samar (SAH mahr), island in Philippines
    (12°N, 126°E) 181
Samara, Russia (53°N, 50°E) 160
Samarinda, Indonesia (1°S, 117°E) 181
Samarqand, Uzbekistan (40°N, 67°E) 179
Samarra, Iraq (34°N, 44°E) 178
Samoa, country in Pacific O. (10°S, 172°W) 189

Name (Pronunciation), Description (Lat., Long.) Page

Samos (SAH mahs), island in Aegean Sea (38°N, 27°E) 159
Samothrace (sahm uh THRAHK ee), i. in Aegean Sea (40°N, 26°E) 159
Samsun (sahm SOON), Turkey (41°N, 36°E) 178
San Ambrosio Island, Pacific O. (26°S, 80°W) 121
San Andres I., Caribbean Sea (13°N, 82°W) 115
San Angelo (san AN juh loh), TX (31°N, 100°W) 94
San Antonio, TX (29°N, 98°W) 94
San Antonio, Cape, Argentina (37°S, 57°W) 126
San Antonio R., TX (29°N, 97°W) 95
San Bernardino, CA (34°N, 117°W) 102
San Blas, Cape, FL (30°N, 86°W) 92
San Carlos Res. (KAHR luhs), AZ (33°N, 110°W) 103
San Clemente (kluh MENT ee), island in Pacific O. (33°N, 119°W) 102
San Cristobal, island in Pacific O. (11°S, 162°E) 188
San Cristobal, Venezuela (8°N, 72°W) 126
San Cristobal, volcano in Nicaragua (12°N, 87°W) 109
San Cristobal de las Casas, Mexico (17°N, 93°W) 114
San Diego, CA (33°N, 117°W) 102
San Felix I., Pacific O. (26°S, 80°W) 121
San Fernando, Trinidad and Tobago (10°N, 61°W) 115
San Francisco, CA (38°N, 123°W) 102
San Ignacio, Belize (17°N, 89°W) 115
San Isidro, Costa Rica (9°N, 84°W) 115
San Joaquin R., CA (38°N, 121°W) 102
San Joaquin Valley, CA (37°N, 121°W) 102
San Jorge, Gulf of, Atlantic O. (46°S, 67°W) 126
San Jose (san hoh ZAY), CA (37°N, 122°W) 102
San Jose, Costa Rica (10°N, 84°W) 115
San Jose I., Mexico (25°N, 111°W) 106
San Juan (san HWAHN), Argentina (32°S, 68°W) 126
San Juan, Puerto Rico (19°N, 66°W) 116
San Juan Is., Puget Sound and Strait of Georgia (48°N, 123°W) 100
San Juan Mts., U.S. (38°N, 107°W) 103
San Juan R., Nicaragua and Costa Rica (11°N, 85°W) 115
San Juan R., U.S. (39°N, 108°W) 103
San Justo (HUS toh), Argentina (35°S, 59°W) 126
San Lorenzo, Paraguay (25°S, 57°W) 127
San Lucas, Cape, Mexico (23°N, 110°W) 114
San Luis, Argentina (33°S, 66°W) 126
San Luis, Mexico (33°N, 115°W) 114
San Luis Obispo (san LOO uh suh BIS poh), CA (35°N, 121°W) 102
San Luis Potosi, Mexico (22°N, 101°W) 114
San Luis Potosi, state in Mexico (23°N, 102°W) 114
San Marcos (san MAHR kuhs), TX (30°N, 98°W) 94
San Marino, country in Europe (44°N, 12°E) 159
San Mateo, (san muh tay oh), CA (38°N, 122°W) 102
San Matias, Gulf of, Atlantic O. (42°S, 64°W) 126
San Miguel, El Salvador (14°N, 88°W) 115
San Miguel de Tucuman (too koo MAHN), Argentina (27°S, 65°W) 126
San Miguel R. (san muh GEHL), CO (38°N, 108°W) 103
San Pedro, Côte d'Ivoire (4°N, 6°W) 138
San Pedro R. (san PAY droh), AZ (33°N, 111°W) 103
San Pedro Sula, Honduras (15°N, 88°W) 115
San Rafael (san ruh FEHL), CA (38°N, 123°W) 102
San Salvador, El Salvador (14°N, 89°W) 115
San Salvador de Jujuy, Argentina (23°S, 66°W) 126
San Salvador I., Atlantic O. (24°N, 75°W) 107
San Sebastian, Spain (43°N, 2°W) 158
Sanaa (sah NAH), Yemen (15°N, 44°E) 178
SANAE IV Station, Antarctica (71°S, 3°W) 200
Sanaga R., Cameroon (5°N, 12°E) 139
Sand Hills, NE (42°N, 102°W) 96
Sand Lakes P.W.P., MB (58°N, 100°W) 69
Sand Sea of Calanscio, desert in Africa (28°N, 21°E) 137
Sandakan (san DAHK uhn), Malaysia (6°N, 118°E) 181
Sandnes, Norway (59°N, 6°E) 157
Sandspit, BC (53°N, 132°W) 68
Sandusky, OH (41°N, 83°W) 90
Sandusky R., OH (41°N, 83°W) 90
Sandy City, UT (40°N, 112°W) 103
Sandy L., ON (53°N, 93°W) 70
Sanford, FL (29°N, 81°W) 93
Sanford, ME (43°N, 69°W) 89
Sanford, NC (35°N, 79°W) 91
Sangamon R. (SANG guh muhn), IL (40°N, 90°W) 97
Sangha R., Congo Rep. (3°N, 16°E) 139
Sangre de Cristo Mts., U.S. (38°N, 106°W) 103
Sankuru R., Africa (4°S, 23°E) 139
Santa Ana, CA (34°N, 118°W) 102
Santa Ana, El Salvador (14°N, 90°W) 115
Santa Barbara, CA (35°N, 120°W) 102
Santa Barbara Channel, CA (34°N, 120°W) 102
Santa Catalina, island in Pacific O. (33°N, 118°W) 102
Santa Clarita, CA (34°N, 118°W) 102
Santa Cruz (sant uh krooz), Bolivia (18°S, 63°W) 127
Santa Cruz, CA (37°N, 122°W) 102
Santa Cruz, Canary Is. (28°N, 15°W) 136
Santa Cruz Is., Pacific O. (11°S, 167°E) 188
Sante Fe (san tuh FAY), Argentina (32°S, 61°W) 126
Santa Fe, NM (36°N, 106°W) 103
Santa Isabel, island in Pacific O. (8°S, 159°E) 188
Santa Margarita I., Mexico (24°N, 112°W) 107
Santa Maria, Brazil (30°S, 54°W) 127
Santa Maria, CA (35°N, 120°W) 102
Santa Marta, Colombia (11°N, 74°W) 126
Santa Rosa, CA (38°N, 123°W) 102
Santander, Spain (43°N, 4°W) 158
Santarem, Brazil (3°S, 55°W) 127
Santee R., SC (33°N, 80°W) 93
Santiago, Chile (34°S, 71°W) 126
Santiago, Panama (8°N, 81°W) 115
Santiago de Cuba, Cuba (20°N, 76°W) 107
Santiago del Estero, Argentina (27°S, 64°W) 126
Santo Domingo, Dominican Republic (19°N, 70°W) 107
Santo Domingo, Ecuador (0°, 79°W) 126
Santos, Brazil (24°S, 47°W) 127
Sao Bernardo do Campos, Brazil (24°S, 47°W) 127
Sao Francisco R. (sown frahn SEE skoo), Brazil (14°S, 44°W) 127
Sao Luis (sown loo EES), Brazil (3°S, 44°W) 127
Sao Paulo (sown POW loo), Brazil (24°S, 47°W) 127
Sao Tome (sown taw MEH), island in Gulf of Guinea (0°, 7°E) 139
Sao Tome, Sao Tome & Principe (0°, 7°E) 139
Sao Tome and Principe (PREEN see puh), country in Gulf of Guinea (1°N, 7°E) 139
Saone R. (SOHN), France (46°N, 5°E) 158
Sapporo, Japan (43°N, 141°E) 183
Sarajevo (sahr uh YAY voh), Bos (44°N, 18°E) 159
Saransk, Russia (54°N, 45°E) 160
Sarasota, FL (27°N, 82°W) 93
Saratoga Springs, NY (43°N, 74°W) 88
Saratov, Russia (52°N, 46°E) 160
Sarawak (suh RAH wahk), region of Malaysia (2°N, 112°E) 181
Sardinia, island in Mediterranean Sea (40°N, 9°E) 159
Sargodha (suhr GOHD uh), Pakistan (32°N, 73°E) 180
Sarh, Chad (9°N, 18°E) 139
Sarnia, ON (43°N, 82°W) 70
Saskatchewan, prov. in Canada (54°N, 106°W) 69
Saskatchewan R. (sas kach uh wahn), Canada (53°N, 104°W) 69
Saskatoon, SK (52°N, 107°W) 69
Sassandra R. (suh SAN druh), Côte d'Ivoire (7°N, 7°W) 138
Sassari (SAHS uh ree), Italy (41°N, 9°E) 159
Sata, Cape, Japan (31°N, 131°E) 183
Satilla R., GA (31°N, 82°W) 93
Satu Mare (SAHT oo MAHR uh), Romania (48°N, 23°E) 159
Saudi Arabia, country in Asia (24°N, 44°E) 178
Sault Sainte Marie (SOO saynt muh REE), MI (46°N, 84°W) 99
Sault Sainte Marie, ON (47°N, 84°W) 70
Sava R., Europe (46°N, 15°E) 159
Savaii, island in Pacific O. (14°S, 172°W) 189
Savannah, GA (32°N, 81°W) 93
Savannah R., U.S. (33°N, 82°W) 93
Savannakhet (suh vahn uh KEHT), Laos (17°N, 105°E) 181
Savu Sea, Indian O. (9°S, 122°E) 190
Sawatch Range, CO (39°N, 106°W) 103
Sayan Mts., Russia (53°N, 95°E) 170
Saylorville Res., IA (42°N, 94°W) 97
Scandinavian Pen., Europe (61°N, 12°E) 157
Schefferville (SHEF uhr vil), QC (55°N, 67°W) 71
Schenectady (skuh nek tuh dee), NY (43°N, 74°W) 88
Schreiber, ON (49°N, 87°W) 70
Scioto R. (sy oht uh), OH (40°N, 83°W) 90
Scotia Plate, southern Atlantic O. 20
Scotia Sea, Atlantic O. (55°S, 50°W) 121
Scotland, part of United Kingdom (57°N, 5°W) 156
Scott Station, Antarctica (80°S, 167°E) 200
Scottsbluff, NE (42°N, 104°W) 96
Scottsdale, AZ (34°N, 112°W) 103
Scranton, PA (42°N, 76°W) 88
Sea Is., Atlantic O. (32°N, 81°W) 93
Seaford, DE (39°N, 76°W) 91
Seal R., MB (59°N, 95°W) 69
Seattle, WA (48°N, 122°W) 100
Sebago L. (suh bay goh), ME (44°N, 71°W) 89
Sebastian Vizcaino Bay, Baja California (28°N, 115°W) 114
Sechelt, BC (49°N, 123°W) 68
Second Cataract, waterfall in Sudan (22°N, 31°E) 137
Sedalia (sih DAYL yuh), MO (39°N, 93°W) 97
Segou, Mali (13°N, 6°W) 138
Seine R. (sayn), France (49°N, 1°E) 158
Sekondi (she KUHN dee), Ghana (5°N, 2°W) 138
Seldovia, AK (59°N, 152°W) 104
Selenge R. (sehl ung GAH), Mongolia (49°N, 102°E) 182
Selkirk, MB (50°N, 97°W) 69
Selma, AL (32°N, 87°W) 92
Selvas (sel vuhz), forest region in Brazil (5°S, 65°W) 127
Semarang (suh MAHR ang), Indonesia (7°S, 110°E) 181
Semeru, mt. in Indonesia (8°S, 113°E) 181
Semey, Kazakhstan (50°N, 80°E) 179
Seminoe Res., WY (42°N, 107°W) 101
Seminole, L. (sehm uh nohl), U.S. (31°N, 85°W) 92
Semnan, Iran (35°N, 54°E) 179
Sendai (sen DY), Japan (38°N, 141°E) 183
Seneca L. (sen ih kuh), NY (42°N, 77°W) 88
Senecaville Res., OH (40°N, 81°W) 91
Senegal, country in Africa (15°N, 15°W) 138
Senegal R., Africa (16°N, 14°W) 138
Sennar, Sudan (13°N, 34°E) 140
Sennar Dam, Africa (14°N, 34°E) 140
Senneterre (sehn TEHR), QC (48°N, 77°W) 71
Seoul (sohl), South Korea (38°N, 127°E) 183
Sept-Iles (set EEL), QC (50°N, 66°W) 71
Sequoia N.P., (sih kwoy uh), CA (36°N, 119°W) 102
Serasun Strait, Malaysia (2°N, 109°E) 181
Serbia, country in Europe (45°N, 20°E) 159
Serengeti Plain (sehr uhn geht ee), Tanzania (3°S, 35°E) 140
Serov, Russia (60°N, 61°E) 160
Serowe, Botswana (22°S, 27°E) 141
Serrai (SEHR ray), Greece (41°N, 24°E) 159
Setubal (suh TOO bahl), Portugal (31°N, 9°W) 158
Seul, L. (sool), ON (50°N, 93°W) 70
Sevan, L., Armenia (40°N, 45°E) 161
Sevastopol, Ukraine (44°N, 33°E) 160
Severn R., ON (55°N, 89°W) 70
Severnaya Zemlya, Is. in Arctic O. (80°N, 95°E) 168
Severodvinsk, Russia (64°N, 40°E) 160
Severomorsk, Russia (69°N, 33°E) 157
Sevier Bridge Res. (suh vir), UT (38°N, 112°W) 103
Sevier L., UT (39°N, 113°W) 102–103
Sevier R., UT (38°N, 112°W) 103
Seville, Spain (37°N, 6°W) 158
Seward, AK (60°N, 150°W) 104
Seward Pen. (soo uhrd), AK (65°N, 165°W) 104
Seychelles (say SHEHL), country in Indian O. (5°S, 55°E) 132
Sfax, Tunisia (35°N, 11°E) 136
Shache, China (38°N, 77°E) 182
Shackleton Ice Shelf, Antarctica (65°S, 105°E) 200
Shanghai, China (31°N, 121°E) 182
Shantou (SHAHN to), China (23°N, 117°E) 182
Shark Bay, Australia (25°S, 113°E) 190
Sharpe, L., SD (44°N, 100°W) 98
Shasta L., CA (41°N, 122°W) 102

Name (Pronunciation), Description (Lat., Long.) Page

Shasta, Mt., CA (42°N, 122°W) 102
Shatt al Jarid, seasonal lake in Africa (33°N, 9°E) 136
Shawnee, OK (35°N, 97°W) 95
Shebele R., Africa (6°N, 43°E) 140
Sheboygan, WI (44°N, 88°W) 99
Sheffield, England (53°N, 1°W) 156
Shelburne, NS (44°N, 65°W) 72
Shelby, NC (35°N, 82°W) 91
Shelbyville, TN (35°N, 86°W) 90
Shelbyville, L., IL (39°N, 89°W) 97
Shenandoah N.P., VA (39°N, 78°W) 91
Shenandoah R., VA (39°N, 78°W) 91
Shenyang, China (42°N, 123°E) 182
Sherbrooke, NS (45°N, 62°W) 72
Sherbrooke, QC (45°N, 72°W) 71
Sheridan, WY (45°N, 107°W) 101
Sherman, TX (34°N, 97°W) 95
Shetak, L., MN (44°N, 96°W) 98
Shetland Is., North Sea (61°N, 2°W) 156
Sheyenne R. (shy EN), ND (48°N, 99°W) 98
Shiawassee R. (shy uh waws ee), MI (43°N, 84°W) 99
Shihezi, China (45°N, 87°E) 179
Shijiazhuang (shihr jah wahng), China (38°N, 115°E) 182
Shikoku, island in Sea of Japan (34°N, 134°E) 183
Shinyanga (sheen YAHNG guh), Tanzania (4°S, 33°E) 140
Shiraz, Iran (30°N, 52°E) 178
Sholapur (SHOH luh poor), India (18°N, 76°E) 180
Shreveport, LA (33°N, 94°W) 95
Shymkent, Kazakhstan (42°N, 70°E) 179
Sialkot (see AHL koht), Pakistan (33°N, 74°E) 180
Siauliai (SHOU lye), Lithuania (56°N, 23°E) 157
Siberia, Asian Russia (65°N, 120°E) 166-167
Sibu (SEE boo), Malaysia (2°N, 112°E) 181
Sichuan Basin (sich oo ahn), region of China (30°N, 105°E) 182
Sicily, island in Mediterranean Sea (37°N, 14°E) 159
Sidi Bel Abbes (SEE dee BEHL uh BEHS), Algeria (35°N, 1°W) 136
Sidney, NE (41°N, 103°W) 96
Sidney Lanier, L., GA (34°N, 84°W) 93
Sidon, Lebanon (34°N, 35°E) 178
Sidra, Gulf of, Mediterranean Sea (32°N, 19°E) 137
Sierra de Gredos, mt. range in Spain (41°N, 5°W) 158
Sierra de Guadarrama, mt. range in Spain (42°N, 4°W) 158
Sierra Leone, country in Africa (8°N, 12°W) 138
Sierra Madre, mt. range in southeastern Mexico, (16°N, 94°W) 106
Sierra Madre del Sur, mt. range in southern Mexico (27°N, 100°W) 106
Sierra Madre Occidental, mt. range in western Mexico (28°N, 107°W) 114
Sierra Madre Oriental, mt. range in Mexico (28°N, 102°W) 114
Sierra Morena, mt. range in Spain (36°N, 5°W) 158
Sierra Nevada, mt. range in Spain (37°N, 3°W) 158
Sierra Nevada, mt. range in U.S., (38°N, 120°W) 78
Sierra Vista, AZ (32°N, 111°W) 103
Sikasso, Mali (11°N, 6°W) 138
Sikeston (SYK stuhn), MO (37°N, 90°W) 97
Sikote-Alin Mts. (SEE kuh TAY uh LEEN), Russia (44°N, 135°E) 171
Silver City, NM (33°N, 108°W) 103
Silver Spring, MD (39°N, 77°W) 91
Silvies R. (SIHL veez), OR (44°N, 119°W) 100
Simcoe, L., ON (44°N, 79°W) 70
Simeropol, Ukraine (45°N, 34°E) 160
Simeulue (see muh LOO uh), island in Indian O. (3°N, 96°E) 181
Simpson Desert, Australia (26°S, 137°E) 190
Sinai, Mt., Asia (28°N, 34°E) 137
Sinai Pen. (SY ny), Asia (29°N, 33°E) 178
Sinaloa (see nah loh ah), state in Mexico (25°N, 108°W) 114
Singapore, country in Asia (1°N, 104°E) 181
Sinuiju (SHIHN ee joo), North Korea (40°N, 125°E) 183
Sioux City (soo), IA (43°N, 96°W) 96
Sioux Falls, SD (44°N, 97°W) 98
Sioux Lookout, ON (50°N, 92°W) 70
Sipiwesk L., MB (55°N, 98°W) 69
Sir James MacBrien, Mt., NT (63°N, 128°W) 68

Name (Pronunciation), Description (Lat., Long.) Page

Sisseton, SD (46°N, 97°W) 98
Sistan Marsh, Iran (32°N, 61°E) 178
Sitka, AK (57°N, 135°W) 104
Siwah, Egypt (29°N, 26°E) 137
Siwah Oasis (SEE wuh), Egypt (30°N, 25°E) 137
Sixth Cataract, waterfall in Sudan (16°N, 33°E) 140
Sjaelland (SHEHL luhn), island in Kattegat (56°N, 12°E) 157
Skagerrak, strait between Norway and Denmark (57°N, 9°E) 157
Skagit R. (SKAJ uht), WA (48°N, 122°W) 100
Skagway, AK (60°N, 135°W) 104
Skaneateles L. (skan ee AT luhs), NY (43°N, 76°W) 88
Skeena Mts., BC (57°N, 130°W) 68
Skeena R., BC (55°N, 128°W) 68
Skelleftea, Sweden (65°N, 21°E) 157
Skien (SKI ehn), Norway (59°N, 10°E) 157
Skopje (SKOP yeh), North Macedonia (42°N, 22°E) 159
Skunk R., IA (41°N, 91°W) 97
Slamet, mt. in Indonesia (7°S, 109°E) 181
Slave Lake, AB (55°N, 115°W) 68
Slave R., Canada (60°N, 111°W) 68-69
Sleeper Is., Hudson Bay (58°N, 80°W) 71
Sliven, Bulgaria (43°N, 26°E) 159
Slovakia, country in Europe (49°N, 19°E) 159
Slovenia, country in Europe (46°N, 15°E) 159
Smallwood Res., NL (54°N, 64°W) 72
Smith, AB (55°N, 114°W) 68
Smith Mountain L., VA (37°N, 80°W) 91
Smithers, BC (55°N, 127°W) 68
Smoky Hill R., U.S. (39°N, 100°W) 78-79
Smoky R., AB (54°N, 119°W) 68
Smolensk, Russia (55°N, 32°E) 160
Smyrna (SMUHR nuh), GA (34°N, 85°W) 92
Snake R., U.S. (47°N, 118°W) 100-101
Snake River Plain, ID (43°N, 114°W) 101
Snares, The, islands in New Zealand (48°S, 167°E) 195
Snowbird L., NT (62°N, 103°W) 69
Sobat R., Africa (9°N, 32°E) 140
Sobradinho Res., Brazil (10°S, 42°W) 127
Sobral, Brazil (4°S, 40°W) 127
Sochi (SAWCH ih), Russia (44°N, 40°E) 161
Society Is., Pacific O. (17°S, 152°W) 189
Socorro (suh KAW roh), NM (34°N, 107°W) 103
Socorro I., Mexico (19°N, 110°W) 114
Socotra, island in Arabian Sea (12°N, 54°E) 178
Sofia, Bulgaria (43°N, 23°E) 159
Sogne Fiord (SAWNG nuh FYAWRD), Norway (61°N, 6°E) 157
Sokhumi, Georgia (43°N, 41°E) 161
Sokode (soh KOH day), Togo (9°N, 1°E) 138
Sokoto (SOH kuh toh), Nigeria (13°N, 5°E) 138
Soldotna (sol DAWT nuh), AK (60°N, 151°W) 104
Soledad, Colombia (11°N, 75°W) 126
Solomon Islands, country in Pacific O. (9°S, 160°E) 188
Solomon R., KS (39°N, 98°W) 96
Solomon Sea, Pacific O. (8°S, 154°E) 190
Somali Pen., Somalia (10°N, 50°E) 140
Somalia, country in Africa (5°N, 47°E) 140
Somaliland, Somalia (10°N, 47°E) 140
Somerset, KY (37°N, 85°W) 90
Somerset I., Arctic O. (73°N, 93°W) 60-61
Songhua R., China (46°N, 125°E) 182
Songkhla, Thailand (7°N, 101°E) 181
Sonora, state in Mexico (30°N, 110°W) 114
Sonoran Desert, U.S. and Mexico (33°N, 113°W) 114
Sonsorol Is., Pacific O. (5°N, 133°E) 188
Sorocaba, Brazil (23°S, 47°W) 127
Sorol Atoll, Pacific O. (8°N, 141°E) 188
Sorong, Indonesia (1°S, 131°E) 181
Soufriere Hills, volcano in Montserrat (13°N, 61°W) 109
Souris R. (soor uhs), U.S. and Canada (49°N, 102°W) 98
Sousse, Tunisia (36°N, 11°E) 136
South Africa, country in Africa (30°S, 25°E) 141
South America, continent 121
South American Plate, South America and Atlantic O. 20
South Australia, state in Australia (28°S, 133°E) 195

Name (Pronunciation), Description (Lat., Long.) Page

South Bend, IN (42°N, 86°W) 90
South Carolina, state in U.S. (34°N, 80°W) 93
South China Sea, Asia (15°N, 115°E) 167
South Dakota, state in U.S. (45°N, 100°W) 98
South Fiji Basin, Pacific O. (25°S, 170°E) 22
South Georgia, island in Atlantic O. (54°S, 37°W) 122
South Georgia Ridge, Atlantic O. (55°S, 45°W) 22
South Henik L., NU (62°N, 97°W) 69
South Hill, VA (37°N, 78°W) 91
South I., New Zealand (45°S, 170°E) 195
South Korea, country in Asia (36°N, 128°E) 183
South Loup R. (loop), NE (41°N, 100°W) 96
South Orkney Is., Southern O. (60°S, 45°W) 200
South Ossetia, region in Georgia (42°N, 44°E) 161
South Pass, WY (43°N, 109°W) 101
South Platte R., U.S. (41°N, 104°W) 103
South Saskatchewan R., Canada (51°N, 110°W) 68-69
South Shetland Is., Southern O. (62°S, 60°W) 200
South Sioux City (soo), NE (43°N, 96°W) 96
South Sudan, country in Africa (8°N, 30°E) 140
Southampton, England (51°N, 1°W) 156
Southampton I., Hudson Bay (64°N, 84°W) 61
Southeast Indian Ridge, Indian O. (50°S, 135°E) 22
Southeast Pacific Basin, Pacific O. (50°S, 135°E) 22
Southern Alps, New Zealand (45°S, 169°E) 195
Southern Indian L., MB (57°N, 99°W) 69
Southern Ocean 200
Southwest Indian Ridge, Indian O. (35°S, 55°E) 22
Southwest Pacific Basin, Pacific O. (30°S, 150°W) 22
Soweto, South Africa (26°S, 28°E) 141
Soya Pt., Japan (46°N, 142°E) 183
Spain, country in Europe (40°N, 5°W) 158
Spartanburg, SC (35°N, 82°W) 93
Spatsizi Plateau W.P.P., BC (57°N, 128°W) 68
Spear, Cape, NL (48°N, 53°W) 72
Spencer, IA (43°N, 95°W) 97
Spencer Gulf, Indian O. (35°S, 137°E) 190
Split, Croatia (43°N, 16°E) 159
Spokane (spoh kan), WA (48°N, 117°W) 100
Spokane R., WA (48°N, 118°W) 100
Spoon R., IL (41°N, 90°W) 97
Sprague R. (sprahg), OR (42°N, 122°W) 100
Spratly Is., South China Sea (9°N, 112°E) 181
Spring Hill, FL (29°N, 83°W) 93
Springbok, South Africa (30°S, 18°E) 141
Springdale, AR (36°N, 94°W) 95
Springfield, IL (40°N, 90°W) 97
Springfield, MA (42°N, 73°W) 89
Springfield, MO (37°N, 93°W) 97
Springfield, OH (40°N, 84°W) 90
Springfield, OR (44°N, 123°W) 100
Spruce Grove, AB (54°N, 114°W) 68
Sri Jayewardenepura Kotta, Sri Lanka (7°N, 80°E) 180
Sri Lanka, country in Asia (8°N, 81°E) 180
Srinagar, India (34°N, 75°E) 180
Stamford, CT (41°N, 74°W) 88-89
Stanley, ND (48°N, 102°W) 98
Stanley Falls, waterfall in Dem. Rep. Congo (1°N, 26°E) 139
Stanley Pool, lake in Africa (4°S, 16°E) 139
Stanovoy Mts. (STAN uh voy), Russia (55°N, 125°E) 169
Stara Zagora (ZAH goh rah), Bulgaria (42°N, 26°E) 159
Starbuck I., Pacific O. (6°S, 156°W) 189
State College, PA (41°N, 78°W) 88
Staten I., Argentina (53°S, 64°W) 126
Statesville, NC (36°N, 81°W) 91
Staunton, VA (38°N, 79°W) 91
Stavanger, Norway (59°N, 6°E) 157
Stavropol, Russia (45°N, 42°E) 160
Steamboat Springs, CO (40°N, 107°W) 103
Steens Mt., OR (42°N, 119°W) 100
Steinbach (styn bak), MB (50°N, 97°W) 69
Stephens L., MB (56°N, 95°W) 70
Stephenville, NL (49°N, 59°W) 72
Steppes, plains in Europe and Asia (50°N, 40°E) 149
Sterling, IL (42°N, 90°W) 97
Steubenville, OH (40°N, 81°W) 91
Stevens Point, WI (44°N, 90°W) 99
Stewart, BC (56°N, 130°W) 68

Name (Pronunciation), Description (Lat., Long.) Page

Stewart I., Pacific O. (47°S, 168°E) 195
Stikine R. (stik EEN), BC (58°N, 131°W) 68
Stillwater, OK (36°N, 97°W) 95
Stockholm, Sweden (59°N, 18°E) 157
Stockton, CA (38°N, 121°W) 102
Stockton L., MO (38°N, 94°W) 97
Stockton Plateau, TX (30°N, 102°W) 94
Stone Mt., GA (34°N, 84°W) 93
Storm Lake, IA (43°N, 95°W) 97
Stornoway, Scotland (58°N, 6°W) 156
Strasbourg (STRAHS boorg), France (49°N, 8°E) 158
Stratford-upon-Avon, England (52°N, 2°W) 156
Strathcona P.P., BC (49°N, 125°W) 68
Stuart L., BC (55°N, 125°W) 68
Stuttgart, Germany (49°N, 9°E) 159
Subotica (SOO buh TEET suh), Serbia (46°N, 20°E) 159
Sucre (SOO kray), Bolivia (19°S, 65°W) 127
Sudan, country in Africa (13°N, 30°E) 132
Sudbury, ON (47°N, 81°W) 70
Sudd, region of Sudan (8°N, 30°E) 140
Suez (soo EHZ), Egypt (30°N, 33°E) 137
Suez Canal, Egypt (31°N, 33°E) 137
Suez, Gulf of, Egypt (30°N, 33°E) 137
Suffolk, VA (37°N, 77°W) 91
Suhaj, Egypt (27°N, 32°E) 178
Suhar, Oman (24°N, 57°E) 178
Sukhona R., Russia (60°N, 43°E) 160
Sukkur (SOOK uhr), Pakistan (28°N, 69°E) 180
Sula Is., Molucca Sea (2°S, 125°E) 181
Sulaiman Range (SOOL eye MAHN), Pakistan (69°N, 30°E) 180
Sulawesi (soo LAH wuh see), island in Molucca Sea (2°S, 120°E) 181
Sulaymaniyah, Iraq (36°N, 45°E) 178
Sulphur R., TX (33°N, 95°W) 95
Sulu Archipelago, Celebes Sea (6°N, 121°E) 188
Sulu Sea, Asia (8°N, 120°E) 181
Sumatra, island in Indian O. (0°, 102°E) 181
Sumba, island in Savu Sea (9°S, 120°E) 181
Sumbawa (soom BAH wuh), island in Flores Sea (8°S, 117°E) 181
Summerside, PE (46°N, 64°W) 72
Sumqayit, Azerbaijan (41°N, 50°E) 161
Sumter, SC (34°N, 80°W) 93
Sunda Strait, Java and Sumatra (6°S, 106°E) 181
Sundsvall (SOHNDS vahl), Sweden (62°N, 19°E) 157
Sunnyside, WA (46°N, 120°E) 100
Sunnyvale, CA (37°N, 122°W) 102
Sunrise Manor, NV (36°N, 115°W) 102
Superior, WI (47°N, 92°W) 99
Superior, L., North America (48°N, 88°W) 99
Superior Upland, ON (49°N, 88°W) 70
Surabaya, Indonesia (8°S, 113°E) 181
Surat (SOOR uht), India (21°N, 73°E) 180
Surat Thani (soor aht AN ee), Thailand (9°N, 99°E) 181
Suriname, country in South America (4°N, 56°W) 127
Surrey, BC (49°N, 123°W) 68
Surt, Libya (31°N, 17°E) 137
Surtsey I. (SURT see), Atlantic O. (63°N, 21°W) 148
Susquehanna R., U.S. (40°N, 76°W) 88
Sutton L., ON (54°N, 85°W) 70
Suva, Fiji (18°S, 178°W) 189
Suwanee R., FL (30°N, 83°W) 93
Suwarrow Atoll, Pacific O. (13°S, 163°W) 189
Suwon, South Korea (37°N, 127°E) 183
Svalbard, poss. of Norway (77°N, 20°E) 201
Svir R., Russia (61°N, 34°E) 160
Swains I., Pacific O. (11°S, 171°W) 189
Swan Is., Caribbean Sea (18°N, 84°W) 115
Swan River, MB (52°N, 101°W) 69
Swanson Res., NE (40°N, 101°W) 96
Sweden, country in Europe (60°N, 15°E) 157
Sweetwater R., WY (42°N, 108°W) 101
Swift Current, SK (50°N, 108°W) 69
Switzerland, country in Europe (47°N, 8°E) 159
Sydney, Australia (34°S, 151°E) 195
Sydney, NS (46°N, 60°W) 72
Syktyvkar (sik tif KAHR), Russia (62°N, 51°E) 160
Syowa Station, Antarctica (69°S, 40°E) 200
Syr Darya, r. in Kazakhstan (46°N, 65°E) 170
Syracuse, NY (43°N, 76°W) 88
Syria, country in Asia (35°N, 38°E) 178
Syrian Desert, Asia (32°N, 39°E) 178
Szczecin (SHCHET seen), Poland (53°N, 15°E) 159
Szeged (SEG ed), Hungary (46°N, 20°E) 159

T

Tabasco, state in Mexico (18°N, 93°W) 114
Table Rock L., U.S. (36°N, 93°W) 97
Tabora, Tanzania (5°S, 33°E) 140
Tabriz, Iran (38°N, 46°E) 178
Tabuaeran Atoll, Pacific O. (4°N, 159°W) 189
Tabuk (tuh BOOK), Saudi Arabia (28°N, 37°E) 178
Tacna, Peru (19°S, 70°W) 126
Tacoma, WA (47°N, 123°W) 100
Taconic Mts. (tuh KAHN ihk), NY (42°N, 74°W) 88-89
Tadoule L., MB (59°N, 98°W) 69
Tadoussac (TAD uh sak), QC (48°N, 70°W) 71
Taegu (TAG oo), South Korea (36°N, 129°E) 183
Taejon (tah JAWN), South Korea (36°N, 127°E) 183
Taganrog (tah gahn RAWK), Russia (47°N, 39°E) 160
Tagus R., Europe (40°N, 4°W) 158
Tahat, Mt., Algeria (24°N, 6°E) 136
Tahiti, island in Pacific O. (20°S, 150°W) 189
Tahoe, L., U.S. (39°N, 120°W) 102
Tahoua, Niger (16°N, 5°E) 138
Taichung (TY choong), Taiwan (24°N, 121°E) 182
Taipei (ty pay), Taiwan (25°N, 122°E) 182
Taiwan, country in Asia (24°N, 121°E) 182
Taiwan Strait, Taiwan and China (24°N, 120°E) 182
Taiyuan (TY yoo ahn), China (38°N, 112°E) 182
Taizz, Yemen (14°N, 44°E) 178
Tajikistan, country in Asia (38°N, 69°E) 179
Tajumulco (tah hoo MOOL koh), mt. in Guatemala (15°N, 92°W) 115
Takamatsu, Japan (34°N, 134°E) 183
Taklimakan Desert, China (38°N, 80°E) 182
Taku R., North America (59°N, 134°W) 68
Talaud Is., Indonesia (4°N, 128°E) 181
Talca, Chile (33°S, 72°W) 126
Talcahuano, Chile (37°S, 73°W) 126
Taldyqorghan, Kazakhstan (45°N, 77°E) 179
Tallahassee, FL (31°N, 84°W) 93
Tallinn, Estonia (59°N, 25°E) 157
Tallulah (tuh LOO luh), LA (32°N, 91°W) 95
Tamale, Ghana (9°N, 1°W) 138
Tamanrasset, Algeria (23°N, 7°E) 136
Tamaulipas (tah mah oo LEE PAHS), state in Mexico (24°N, 99°W) 114
Tambora, Mt (TAHM buh ruh), Indonesia (8°S, 118°E) 181
Tambov, Russia (53°N, 41°E) 160
Tampa, FL (28°N, 82°W) 93
Tampa Bay, Gulf of Mexico (28°N, 82°W) 93
Tampere (TAHM puh ray), Finland (61°N, 24°E) 157
Tampico, Mexico (22°N, 98°W) 114
Tamworth, Australia (31°S, 151°E) 195
Tan-Tan, Morocco (28°N, 12°W) 136
Tana, L., Ethiopia (12°N, 37°E) 140
Tanami Desert, Australia (20°S, 130°E) 190
Tanana R. (TAN uh naw), AK (65°N, 148°W) 104
Tanezrouft (TAH nehz ruhft), region of Algeria (24°N, 1°E) 136
Tanga, Tanzania (5°S, 39°E) 140
Tanganyika, L., Africa (7°S, 30°E) 140
Tangier (tan JEER), Morocco (36°N, 6°W) 136
Tanimbar Is., Arafura Sea (8°S, 131°E) 181
Tanna I., Pacific O. (19°S, 169°E) 188
Tanzania, country in Africa (5°S, 35°E) 140
Taongi Atoll, Pacific O. (15°N, 169°E) 188
Taos (TAH ohs), NM (36°N, 106°W) 103
Tapachula, Mexico (15°N, 92°W) 114
Tapajos R., Brazil (6°S, 57°W) 127
Tar R., NC (36°N, 78°W) 91
Tarakan (tahr uh KAHN), Indonesia (3°N, 118°E) 181
Taranto, Italy (40°N, 17°E) 159
Taranto, Gulf of, Ionian Sea (40°N, 17°E) 159
Tarawa, Gilbert Islands (2°N, 173°E) 189
Taraz, Kazakhstan (43°N, 71°E) 179
Tarbagatay Mts., Asia (48°N, 84°E) 179
Targu Mures, Romania (47°N, 25°E) 159
Tarija, Bolivia (22°S, 65°W) 127
Tarim Basin, China (40°N, 85°E) 182
Tarim R., China (41°N, 81°E) 182
Tarragona, Spain (41°N, 1°E) 158
Tartu (TAR too), Estonia (58°N, 27°E) 157
Tartus, Syria (35°N, 36°E) 178
Tashkent, Uzbekistan (41°N, 69°E) 179
Tasman Sea, Pacific O. (30°S, 165°E) 190
Tasmania, island in Australia (41°S, 143°E) 190
Tasmania, state in Australia (42°S, 147°E) 195
Tatlatui P.P., BC (57°N, 127°W) 68
Tatnam, Cape, MB (57°N, 91°W) 69
Tatshenshini-Alsek W.P.P., BC (59°N, 138°W) 68
Tau I. (TAH oo), Pacific O. (14°S, 169°W) 189
Taunton (tawnt uhn), MA (42°N, 71°W) 89
Taupo, L., New Zealand (39°S, 176°E) 195
Taurus Mts. (taw ruhs), Turkey (37°N, 33°E) 178
Tawakoni, L., TX (33°N, 96°W) 95
Taylor, Mt., NM (35°N, 108°W) 103
Taylorville, IL (40°N, 89°W) 97
Taymyr Pen., Russia (75°N, 105°E) 168
Tbilisi (tuh BIHL uh see), Georgia (42°N, 45°E) 161
Tegucigalpa (tuh goo see GAHL puh), Honduras (14°N, 87°W) 115
Tehachapi Mts. (tuh hach uh pee), CA (35°N, 119°W) 102
Tehran, Iran (36°N, 51°E) 178
Tehuacan (tay wah KAHN), Mexico (18°N, 97°W) 114
Tehuantepec, Gulf of (tuh WAHN tuh pehk), Pacific O. (16°N, 95°W) 114
Tehuantepec, Isthmus of, Mexico (17°N, 95°W) 108
Tejen, Turkmenistan (37°N, 61°E) 179
Tel Aviv, Israel (32°N, 35°E) 178
Tema (tay muh), Ghana (6°N, 0°) 138
Temagami, L., ON (47°N, 80°W) 70
Temiscaming (tuh mihs kuh ming), QC (47°N, 79°W) 71
Tempe (tem pee), AZ (33°N, 112°W) 103
Temple, TX (31°N, 97°W) 95
Temuco, Chile (39°S, 73°W) 126
Tenerife, Canary Is. (29°N, 17°W) 136
Tennant Creek, Australia (20°S, 134°E) 195
Tennessee, state in U.S. (36°N, 88°W) 90-91
Tennessee R., U.S. (35°N, 87°W) 90
Tennessee Tombigbee Waterway, MS (35°N, 88°W) 92
Tepic (tay PEEK), Mexico (22°N, 105°W) 114
Teraina I. (te RAY nuh), Pacific O. (5°N, 160°W) 189
Terek R., Russia (44°N, 45°E) 161
Teresina, Brazil (5°S, 43°W) 127
Termiz, Uzbekistan (37°N, 67°E) 179
Ternopil, Ukraine (50°N, 26°E) 160
Terra Nova N.P., NL (49°N, 54°W) 72
Terrace, BC (55°N, 129°W) 68
Terre Haute (ter uh HOHT), IN (39°N, 87°W) 90
Terrebonne Bay (TEHR uh bahn), Gulf of Mexico (29°N, 91°W) 95
Teslin, YT (60°N, 133°W) 68
Teslin R., Canada (61°N, 133°W) 68
Tete, Mozambique (16°S, 34°E) 141
Tethys Ocean, ancient ocean 171
Teton Range (TEE tahn), WY (44°N, 111°W) 101
Tetouan (tay twahn), Morocco (36°N, 6°W) 136
Tetovo, North Macedonia (42°N, 21°E) 159
Texarkana, AR and TX (33°N, 94°W) 95
Texas, state in U.S. (32°N, 100°W) 94-95
Texas City, TX (29°N, 95°W) 95
Texoma, L., U.S. (34°N, 97°W) 95
Thailand (TY land), country in Asia (17°N, 100°E) 181
Thailand, Gulf of, South China Sea (10°N, 102°E) 181
Thames (tehmz), r. in England (51°N, 1°E) 156
Thames R., ON (43°N, 82°W) 70
Thane (TAHN uh), India (19°N, 73°E) 180
Tharthar, L., Iraq (33°N, 43°E) 178
Thasos (THAH sahs), island in Aegean Sea (41°N, 25°E) 159
Thayetmyo, Myanmar (19°N, 95°E) 181
Thelon R., Canada (64°N, 100°W) 63

Name (Pronunciation), Description (Lat., Long.) Page

Theodore Roosevelt L., AZ (34°N, 111°W) 103
Theodore Roosevelt N.P., ND (47°N, 104°W) 98
Thermopolis (thuhr MAHP uh lus), WY (44°N, 108°W) 101
Thessaloniki (theh suh loh NEE kee), Greece (41°N, 23°E) 159
Thief River Falls, MN (48°N, 96°W) 98
Thies (TY ehs), Senegal (15°N, 17°W) 138
Thimphu (thim PYOO), Bhutan (28°N, 90°E) 180
Third Cataract, waterfall in Sudan (20°N, 30°E)......... 140
Thiruvnanthapuram, India (8°N, 77°E) 180
Thomasville, GA (31°N, 84°W) 93
Thompson, MB (56°N, 98°W) 69
Thompson R., BC (51°N, 121°W) 68
Thousand Is., St. Lawrence R. (44°N, 76°W) 88
Thrace, region in Greece and Turkey (41°N, 26°E)......159
Three Gorges Dam, China (31°N, 111°E)..........182
Three Kings Is., New Zealand (34°S, 171°E)..........195
Three Points, Cape, Ghana (5°N, 2°W) 138
Three Sisters, mts. in OR (44°N, 122°W)..........100
Thule (TOO lee), alternative name for Qaanaaq (78°N, 70°W)..........52
Thunder Bay, city in ON (48°N, 89°W) 70
Tianjin, China (39°N, 117°E) 182
Tiaret, Algeria (36°N, 1°W)..........136
Tiber R., Italy (42°N, 12°E) 159
Tibesti Mts., Africa (22°N, 18°E)..........137
Tibet, region of China (32°N, 84°E)..........182
Tibet, Plateau of, China (30°N, 90°E) 182
Tiburon I., Gulf of California (29°N, 112°W)..........114
Tien Shan, mt. range in Asia (42°N, 78°E) 170
Tierra del Fuego (tih EH ruh dehl foo AY go), archipelago of South America (54°S, 70°W)..........126
Tifton, GA (31°N, 84°W) 93
Tigris R., Asia (35°N, 43°E) 178
Tihamah, region of Saudi Arabia (18°N, 43°E)..........178
Tijuana (tee WHAN uh), Mexico (33°N, 117°W)..........114
Tiksi, Russia (72°N, 129°E)..........167
Tillamook, OR (45°N, 124°W) 100
Tillery, L., NC (35°N, 80°W)..........91
Timaru, New Zealand (44°S, 171°E)..........195
Timbuktu, Mali (17°N, 2°W) 136
Timisoara (tee mish WAHR uh), Romania (46°N, 21°E) 159
Timmins, ON (48°N, 81°W) 70
Timon, Brazil (4°S, 43°W)..........127
Timor, island in Timor Sea (9°S, 125°E)..........181
Timor Sea, Indian O. (11°S, 125°E)..........181
Tims Ford L., TN (35°N, 86°W).......... 90
Tindouf, Algeria (28°N, 8°W)..........136
Tinian I., Pacific O. (15°N, 146°E)..........188
Tippecanoe R., IN (41°N, 87°W) 90
Tirana (tih RAH nuh), Albania (41°N, 20°E) 159
Tiraspol, Moldova (47°N, 30°E)..........160
Tisdale, SK (53°N, 104°W).......... 69
Tississat Falls, waterfall in Ethiopia (12°N, 38°E)....... 140
Tisza R. (TIHS aw), Hungary (47°N, 20°E) 159
Titicaca, L., South America (16°S, 70°W)..........126
Titusville (TY tuhs vil), FL (29°N, 81°W) 93
Tlaquepaque (tlah keh PAH keh), Mexico (21°N, 103°W)..........114
Tlaxcala (tlahs KAH lah), Mexico (20°N, 98°W)..........114
Tlaxcala, state in Mexico (20°N, 98°W)..........114
Tobago, island in Trinidad and Tobago (11°N, 61°W)..........116
Tobruk (toh BROOK), Libya (32°N, 24°E) 137
Tocantins R. (toh kuhn TEHNS), Brazil (10°S, 48°W)..........127
Tocoa (toh KOH ah), Honduras (16°N, 86°W)..........115
Tofino (toh FEE noh), BC (49°N, 126°W) 68
Togo, country in Africa (8°N, 1°E) 138
Tok, AK (63°N, 143°W) 104
Tokelau, poss. of New Zealand (8°S, 176°W)..........189
Tokyo, Japan (36°N, 140°E) 183
Toledo, OH (42°N, 84°W)..........90
Toledo Bend Res., U.S. (32°N, 94°W) 95
Toliara, Madagascar (23°S, 44°E)..........141
Toluca (tuh LOO kuh), Mexico (19°N, 100°W)..........114
Tolyatti, Russia (54°N, 49°E)..........160
Tomah (TOH muh), WI (44°N, 90°W) 99
Tombigbee R., U.S. (32°N, 87°W) 92
Tonga, country in Pacific O. (20°S, 175°W)..........189

Name (Pronunciation), Description (Lat., Long.) Page

Tongatapu Group (TAWNG ah TAH poo), islands in Pacific O. (21°S, 175°W)..........189
Tongjoson Bay, Japan (40°N, 128°E)..........183
Tonkin, Gulf of, South China Sea (20°N, 108°E) 181
Tonle Sap (tahn lay SAHP), lake in Cambodia (13°N, 104°E) 181
Tonopah (tohn uh pah), NV (38°N, 117°W) 102
Toowoomba (tu WOOM buh), Australia (28°S, 152°E)..........195
Topeka, KS (39°N, 96°W) 96-97
Torbat-e Heydariyah, Iran (35°N, 59°E).......... 180
Torne R., Sweden (68°N, 21°E).......... 157
Torngat Mountains N.P. Reserve, NL (59°N, 65°W)....72
Toronto, ON (44°N, 79°W) 70
Toronto Res., KS (38°N, 96°W) 96
Torrance, CA (34°N, 118°W) 102
Torrens, L., Australia (31°S, 138°E)..........190
Torreon, Mexico (25°N, 103°W)..........114
Torres Is., Pacific O. (13°S, 167°E) 188
Torres Strait, New Guinea and Australia (10°S, 141°E)..........195
Tortuga I., Venezuela (11°N, 65°W)..........116
Torun, Poland (53°N, 19°E)..........159
Toubkal, mt. in Morocco (31°N, 8°W)..........136
Touggourt (too goort), Algeria (33°N, 6°E) 136
Toulon (too LOHN), France (43°N, 6°E) 158
Toulouse (too LOOZ), France (44°N, 1°E) 158
Tours (toor), France (47°N, 1°E) 158
Townsville, Australia (19°S, 147°E) 195
Towson, MD (39°N, 77°W) 91
Toyama (toh YAHM uh), Japan (37°N, 137°E) 183
Trabzon, Turkey (41°N, 40°E) 178
Trail, BC (49°N, 118°W) 68
Tralee (truh LEE), Ireland (52°N, 10°W) 156
Trans-Alaskan Pipeline, AK (67°N, 150°W) 104
Transylvanian Alps, mt. range in Europe (45°N, 23°E) 159
Traverse City, MI (45°N, 86°W) 99
Traverse, L., MN (46°N, 97°W) 98
Travis, L., TX (30°N, 98°W) 94-95
Trento, Italy (46°N, 11°E) 159
Trenton, NJ (40°N, 75°W) 88
Tres Marias Is., Pacific O. (21°N, 107°W)..........106
Tres Marias Res., Brazil (18°S, 46°W)..........121
Tres Puntas, Cape, Argentina (47°S, 66°W) 126
Trieste (tree est), Italy (46°N, 14°E) 159
Trindade, island in Atlantic O. (21°S, 29°W)..........124
Trinidad, CO (37°N, 104°W) 103
Trinidad, island in Trinidad and Tobago (10°N, 61°W)..........116
Trinidad and Tobago, country in Caribbean Sea (11°N, 62°W)..........116
Trinity Bay, NL (48°N, 54°W)..........72
Trinity R., CA (41°N, 123°W) 102
Trinity R., TX (32°N, 96°W) 95
Tripoli, Lebanon (34°N, 36°E) 178
Tripoli, Libya (33°N, 13°E) 136
Trivandrum (truh VAN druhm), alternative name for Thiruvnanthapuram (8°N, 77°E).......... 180
Trois-Rivieres (trwah ree vyer), QC (46°N, 73°W) 71
Tromso, Norway (69°N, 19°E) 157
Trondheim, Norway (64°N, 10°E)..........157
Trondheims Fiord, Norway (64°N, 9°E)..........157
Trout L., ON (51°N, 93°W) 70
Troy, AL (32°N, 86°W) 92
Troy, NY (43°N, 74°W) 88
Truckee R., U.S. (39°N, 120°W)..........102
Trujillo (troo hee yoh), Peru (8°S, 79°W) 126
Truk Is., alternative name for Chuuk Is. (7°N, 152°E)..........188
Truro, NS (45°N, 63°W) 72
Tshwane, alternative name for Pretoria (25°S, 28°E) ...141
Tsimlyansk Res., Russia (47°N, 43°E)..........160
Tsugaru Strait (soo GAH roo), Japan (42°N, 140°E) ...183
Tsumeb, Namibia (19°S, 18°E) 141
Tsushima (soo shee muh), island in Korea Strait (34°N, 129°E) 183
Tuamoto Archipelago, island group in Pacific O. (20°S, 140°W)..........189
Tuaranga, New Zealand (38°S, 176°E)..........195
Tubuai I., Pacific O. (23°S, 149°W)..........189
Tucson (TOO sahn), AZ (32°N, 111°W) 103

Name (Pronunciation), Description (Lat., Long.) Page

Tucumcari (too kum kahr ee), NM (35°N, 104°W) 103
Tucurui Res., Brazil (4°S, 49°W) 127
Tufts Plain, Pacific O. (50°N, 145°W)..........22
Tug Fork, r. in U.S. (38°N, 82°W) 91
Tula, Russia (54°N, 38°E) 160
Tulcan (tool KAHN), Ecuador (1°N, 78°W) 126
Tulsa, OK (36°N, 96°W) 95
Tunduru (tuhn doo roo), Tanzania (11°S, 37°E) 140
Tunis (TOO nihs), Tunisia (37°N, 10°E) 136
Tunisia, country in Africa (34°N, 10°E) 136
Tupelo (toop uh loh), MS (34°N, 89°W) 92
Turan Lowland, Kazakstan (43°N, 60°E)..........179
Turbat (TUHR but), Pakistan (26°N, 63°E) 180
Turin (too rihn), Italy (45°N, 8°E) 159
Turkana, L., Africa (4°N, 36°E) 140
Turkey, country in Asia and Europe (39°N, 35°E) 178
Turkey R., IA (43°N, 92°W).......... 97
Turkmenbashy, Turkmenistan (40°N, 53°E)..........179
Turkmenbat, Turkmenistan (38°N, 63°E) 178
Turkmenistan, country in Asia (40°N, 57°E)..........179
Turks and Caicos Is., Atlantic O. (22°N, 72°W)..........107
Turku, Finland (61°N, 22°E)..........157
Turlock, CA (37°N, 121°W) 102
Turneffe Is., Belize (17°N, 88°W) 115
Turpan Depression (toor pahn), China (42°N, 90°E) 182
Turtle Mts., ND (49°N, 100°W) 98
Tuscaloosa, AL (33°N, 87°W) 92
Tuttle Creek L., KS (39°N, 97°W).......... 96
Tutuila I., Pacific O. (14°S, 171°W)..........189
Tuvalu, country in Pacific O. (5°S, 174°E)..........189
Tuxtla Gutierrez, Mexico (17°N, 93°W)..........114
Tuz, L. (tooz), Turkey (39°N, 33°E)..........178
Tver, Russia (57°N, 36°E) 160
Tweedsmuir P.P., BC (53°N, 127°W) 68
Twin Falls, ID (43°N, 115°W) 101
Twin Falls, NL (54°N, 65°W)..........72
Tyler, TX (32°N, 95°W) 95
Tyre, Lebanon (33°N, 35°E)..........178
Tyrrhenian Sea (tih ree nee uhn), Mediterranean Sea (39°N, 12°E) 159

U

Ua Pou, island in Pacific O. (9°S, 140°W) 189
Ubangi R., Africa (3°N, 19°E)..........139
Uberlandia, Brazil (19°S, 48°W)..........127
Ucayali R. (ook uh yah lee), Peru (7°S, 75°W) 126
Udaipur (oo DY poor), India (25°N, 74°E).......... 180
Udon Thani, Thailand (18°N, 103°E)..........181
Uele R., Africa (4°N, 24°E) 139
Ufa, Russia (55°N, 56°E) 160
Uganda, country in Africa (2°N, 32°E) 140
Uige, Angola (8°S, 15°E) 141
Uinta Mts. (yoo IHN tuh), UT (41°N, 110°W) 103
Ujelang Atoll (oo je LAHNG), Pacific O. (10°N, 161°E) 188
Ujiji (oo JEE jee), Tanzania (5°S, 30°E).......... 140
Ukhta, Russia (63°N, 54°E) 160
Ukiah (yoo ky uh), CA (39°N, 123°W) 102
Ukraine, country in Europe (49°N, 30°E)..........160
Ulaanbaatar (oo lahn bah tahr), Mongolia (48°N, 107°E) 182
Ulan Ude (oo lahn oo DAY), Russia (52°N, 108°E)......182
Uliastay (OOL yoh sty), Mongolia (48°N, 97°E)..........182
Ulithi Atoll (oo LEETH ee), Pacific O. (10°N, 139°E) 188
Ulm (OOLM), Germany (48°N, 10°E) 159
Ulsan (OOL sahn), South Korea (36°N, 129°E) 183
Ulungur R. (oo loon gyoor), Asia (47°N, 85°E) 182
Uluru, Australia (25°S, 131°E)..........190
Ulyanousk (oo LYAH nawfsk), Russia (54°N, 48°E)...160
Ume R., Sweden (64°N, 18°E) 157
Umea, Sweden (63°N, 21°E) 157
Umm as Samim, Oman (21°N, 56°E)..........178
Umnak I. (oom nak), Bering Sea (53°N, 169°W) 104
Umtata (oom tah tuh), South Africa (32°S, 29°E) 141
Unalakleet (uhn uh LAK leet), AK (64°N, 161°W) 104
Unalaska (uhn uh las kuh), AK (54°N, 167°W) 104
Unalaska I., Bering Sea (54°N, 166°W) 104
Ungava Bay, Hudson Strait (60°N, 68°W) 71
Ungava Pen., QC (61°N, 75°W).......... 71

Name (Pronunciation), Description (Lat., Long.) Page

Unimak I. (YOO nuh mak), Bering Sea (55°N, 164°W) ... 104
United Arab Emirates, country in Asia (24°N, 53°E) .. 178
United Kingdom, country in Europe (55°N, 3°W) ... 156
United States, country in North America (40°N, 100°W) ... 74–75
University City, MO (39°N, 90°W) ... 97
Unzen, Mt. (OON zen), Japan (33°N, 130°E) ... 183
Upington, South Africa (28°S, 21°E) ... 141
Upolu, island in Pacific O. (14°S, 172°W) ... 189
Upper Arlington, OH (40°N, 83°W) ... 90
Upper Arrow L., BC (51°N, 118°W) ... 68
Upper Iowa R., IA (43°N, 92°W) ... 97
Upper Klamath L. (KLAM uth), OR (42°N, 122°W) ... 100
Upper Pen., MI (46°N, 86°W) ... 99
Upper Red Lake, MN (48°N, 95°W) ... 98
Uppsala (UHP suh lah), Sweden (60°N, 18°E) ... 157
Uraba, Gulf of, Caribbean Sea (8°N, 76°W) ... 115
Ural Mts., Russia (64°N, 59°E) ... 160
Ural R., Europe and Asia (48°N, 52°E) ... 160
Uranium City, SK (60°N, 109°W) ... 69
Urbana (uhr BAN uh), IL (40°N, 88°W) ... 97
Urganch, Uzbekistan (42°N, 61°E) ... 179
Urmia, L., Iran (38°N, 46°E) ... 178
Uruguay, country in South America (33°S, 56°W) ... 126
Uruguay R., South America (29°S, 57°W) ... 127
Urumqi, China (43°N, 88°E) ... 182
Uspallata Pass, Argentina (33°S, 70°W) ... 126
Ust-Urt Plateau, Kazakhstan (44°N, 55°E) ... 179
Utah, state in U.S. (39°N, 113°W) ... 102–103
Utah L., UT (40°N, 112°W) ... 103
Ute Res. (yoot), NM (35°N, 103°W) ... 103
Utica (YOO tih kuh), NY (43°N, 75°W) ... 88
Utikuma L., AB (56°N, 116°W) ... 68
Utrecht (YOO trekt), Netherlands (52°N, 5°E) ... 158
Uvea I., Pacific O. (13°S, 176°W) ... 189
Uvs L., Mongolia (50°N, 94°E) ... 182
Uwajima (oo wuh JEE muh), Japan (33°N, 133°E) ... 183
Uzbekistan, country in Asia (42°N, 63°E) ... 179
Uzhhorod, Ukraine (49°N, 22°E) ... 160

V

Vaal R. (vahl), South Africa (27°S, 27°E) ... 141
Vaasa (VAHS uh), Finland (63°N, 22°E) ... 157
Vacaville (VAK uh vil), CA (38°N, 122°W) ... 102
Vachon, R., QC (61°N, 73°W) ... 71
Vadodara, India (22°N, 73°E) ... 180
Vadso, Norway (70°N, 29°E) ... 157
Vaigach I., Russia (70°N, 60°E) ... 160
Vail, CO (40°N, 106°W) ... 103
Vaitupu I. (vy TOO poo), Pacific O. (8°S, 179°E) ... 189
Val-d'Or, QC (48°N, 78°W) ... 71
Valdai Hills, Russia (58°N, 33°E) ... 160
Valdes Pen., Argentina (43°S, 64°W) ... 126
Valdez, AK, (61°N, 146°W) ... 104
Valdosta, GA (31°N, 83°W) ... 93
Valencia, Spain (39°N, 0°) ... 158
Valencia, Venezuela (10°N, 68°W) ... 126
Valentine, NE (43°N, 101°W) ... 96
Valladolid (vahl yah dhoh LEEDH), Spain (42°N, 5°W) ... 158
Vallejo (vuh LAY oh), CA (38°N, 122°W) ... 102
Valletta (vuh LEHT uh), Malta (36°N, 15°E) ... 159
Valley City, ND (47°N, 98°W) ... 98
Valparaiso, Chile (33°S, 72°W) ... 126
Valparaiso, IN (41°N, 87°W) ... 90
Van, Turkey (38°N, 43°E) ... 178
Van, L., Turkey (39°N, 43°E) ... 178
Vanadzor, Armenia (41°N, 44°E) ... 161
Vancouver, BC (49°N, 123°W) ... 68
Vancouver, WA (46°N, 123°W) ... 100
Vancouver I., BC (50°N, 127°W) ... 68
Vanderhoof, BC (54°N, 124°W) ... 68
Vanern, L., Sweden (59°N, 13°E) ... 157
Vanikolo Is. (vah nee KAW lo), Pacific O. (11°S, 167°E) ... 188
Vanua Levu (vah NOO AH LAY voo), island in Pacific O. (17°S, 179°E) ... 189
Vanuatu (vah noo AH too), country in Pacific O. (19°S, 169°E) ... 188

Name (Pronunciation), Description (Lat., Long.) Page

Varanasi (vuh RAHN uh see), India (26°N, 83°E) ... 180
Varanger Fiord, Norway (70°N, 30°E) ... 157
Vardo (VAHR duhr), Norway (70°N, 31°E) ... 147
Varna, Bulgaria (43°N, 28°E) ... 159
Varzea Grande, Brazil (16°S, 57°W) ... 127
Vasteras (VEHS tehr ohs), Sweden (60°N, 17°E) ... 157
Vatican City, country in Europe (42°N, 12°E) ... 159
Vattern, L., Sweden (58°N, 14°E) ... 157
Vavau Group (vah VAH oo), Pacific O. (19°S, 174°W) ... 189
Vaxjo, Sweden (57°N, 15°E) ... 157
Velikiy Novgorod, Russia (59°N, 32°E) ... 160
Velikiye Luki, Russia (56°N, 31°E) ... 160
Venezuela, country in South America (7°N, 65°W) ... 126
Venezuela, Gulf of, Caribbean Sea (12°N, 71°W) ... 107
Venice, Italy (45°N, 12°E) ... 159
Ventspils (VENT peels), Latvia (57°N, 22°E) ... 157
Ventura (ven toor uh), CA (34°N, 119°W) ... 102
Veracruz (vehr uh KROOZ), Mexico (19°N, 96°W) ... 114
Veracruz, state in Mexico (21°N, 97°W) ... 114
Verde, Cape, Senegal (14°N, 18°W) ... 138
Verde R., AZ (34°N, 112°W) ... 103
Verdigris R. (VUHR duh gruhs), U.S. (37°N, 96°W) ... 96–97
Vereeniging (fuh REEN ih king), South Africa (27°S, 28°E) ... 141
Verkhoyansk (vehr kuh YANSK), Russia (68°N, 133°E) ... 167
Verkhoyansk Range, Russia (70°N, 130°E) ... 15
Vermilion R., IL (41°N, 89°W) ... 97
Vermillion, SD (43°N, 97°W) ... 98
Vermillion L., MN (48°N, 93°W) ... 98
Vermillion R., SD (43°N, 97°W) ... 98
Vermont, state in U.S. (44°N, 73°W) ... 89
Vernon, BC (50°N, 119°W) ... 68
Verona, Italy (45°N, 11°E) ... 159
Versailles (vehr SY uh), France (49°N, 2°E) ... 158
Vesuvius, Mt., Italy (41°N, 14°E) ... 159
Viangchan, alternative name for Vientiane (18°N, 103°E) ... 181
Vichy (VISH ee), France (46°N, 3°E) ... 158
Vicksburg, MS (32°N, 91°W) ... 92
Victoria, BC (48°N, 123°W) ... 68
Victoria, Seychelles (5°S, 56°E) ... 132
Victoria, state in Australia (37°S, 143°E) ... 195
Victoria, TX (29°N, 97°W) ... 95
Victoria Falls, waterfall in Africa (18°S, 26°E) ... 141
Victoria I., Arctic O. (74°N, 110°W) ... 60
Victoria, L., Africa (1°S, 33°E) ... 140
Victoria Land, region of Antarctica (73°S, 160°W) ... 200
Victoria R., Australia (16°S, 130°E) ... 191
Viedma, Argentina (41°S, 63°W) ... 120
Vienna, Austria (48°N, 16°E) ... 159
Vientiane (vyehn TYAHN), Laos (18°N, 103°E) ... 181
Vietnam, country in Asia (17°N, 107°E) ... 181
Vigo, Spain (42°N, 9°W) ... 158
Vijayawada (vihj uh yuh WAHD uh), India (17°N, 81°E) ... 180
Vila Velha, Brazil (20°S, 40°W) ... 127
Vilanculos, Mozambique (22°S, 35°E) ... 141
Viljandi (VIL yahn dee), Estonia (58°N, 26°E) ... 157
Villa Nueva, Guatemala (14°N, 91°W) ... 115
Villahermosa (vee yuh ehr MOH zuh), Mexico (18°N, 93°W) ... 114
Villavicencio (VEEL yah vee SEN syoh), Colombia (4°N, 74°W) ... 126
Vilnius, Lithuania (55°N, 25°E) ... 157
Vina del Mar, Chile (33°S, 72°W) ... 126
Vincennes (vin senz), IN (39°N, 87°W) ... 90
Vineland, NJ (39°N, 75°W) ... 88
Vinh, Vietnam (18°N, 106°E) ... 181
Vinnytsya, Ukraine (49°N, 28°E) ... 160
Vinson Massif, mt. in Antarctica (79°S, 86°W) ... 200
Virden, MB (50°N, 102°W) ... 69
Virgin Is., Caribbean Sea (18°N, 65°W) ... 116
Virgin R., U.S. (37°N, 114°W) ... 102
Virginia, state in U.S. (37°N, 80°W) ... 90–91
Virginia Beach, VA (37°N, 76°W) ... 91
Virginia City, NV (39°N, 120°W) ... 102
Visalia (vih sayl yuh), CA (36°N, 119°W) ... 102
Visby (VIHS bee), Sweden (58°N, 18°E) ... 157

Name (Pronunciation), Description (Lat., Long.) Page

Viscount Melville Sound, NU (74°N, 110°W) ... 60
Vishakhapatnam (vih shahk uh PUHT nuhm), India (18°N, 83°E) ... 180
Vistula R., Europe (53°N, 20°E) ... 159
Viti Levu, island in Pacific O. (18°S, 178°W) ... 189
Vitoria, Brazil (20°S, 40°W) ... 127
Vitoria da Conquista, Brazil (15°S, 41°W) ... 127
Vitoria-Gasteiz, Spain (43°N, 3°W) ... 158
Vitsyebsk, Belarus (55°N, 30°E) ... 160
Vladikavkaz, Russia (43°N, 45°E) ... 161
Vladimir, Russia (56°N, 40°E) ... 160
Vladivostok, Russia (43°N, 132°E) ... 183
Vlore, Albania (40°N, 20°E) ... 159
Volcano Is., Pacific O. (24°N, 141°E) ... 188
Volga R., Russia (48°N, 46°E) ... 160
Volga Upland, Russia (52°N, 45°E) ... 160
Volgograd, Russia (49°N, 44°E) ... 160
Volgograd Res., Russia (50°N, 46°E) ... 160
Vologda, Russia (59°N, 40°E) ... 160
Volos (VOH lahs), Greece (39°N, 23°E) ... 159
Volta, L., Ghana (7°N, 0°) ... 138
Voronezh (vuh RAWN ish), Russia (52°N, 39°E) ... 160
Vosges Mts. (vohzh), France (48°N, 7°E) ... 158
Vostok I. (VAHS tahk), Pacific O. (10°S, 153°W) ... 189
Vostok Station, Antarctica (78°S, 107°E) ... 200
Voyageurs N.P., MN (49°N, 93°W) ... 99
Vryheid (VRY hyt), South Africa (28°S, 31°E) ... 141
Vyatka R. (VYAHT kah), Russia (59°N, 51°E) ... 151
Vyborg, Russia (61°N, 29°E) ... 160
Vychegda R. (VI cheg dah), Russia (62°N, 48°E) ... 160

W

Wa, Ghana (10°N, 30°W) ... 138
Wabakimi P.P., ON (51°N, 90°W) ... 70
Wabasca R., AB (57°N, 114°W) ... 68
Wabash R., U.S. (38°N, 88°W) ... 90
Wabuk Point, ON (56°N, 85°W) ... 70
Waco (WAY koh), TX (32°N, 97°W) ... 95
Waconda L., KS (40°N, 98°W) ... 96
Wad Medani, Sudan (14°N, 34°E) ... 140
Waddenzee (VAH duhn zay), bay in Netherlands (53°N, 5°E) ... 151
Waddington, Mt., BC (51°N, 123°W) ... 68
Wadi al Batin, r. in Asia (28°N, 46°E) ... 178
Wadi al Masilah, r. in Asia (16°N, 50°E) ... 178
Wagga Wagga, Australia (35°S, 147°E) ... 195
Wahpeton (WAW puh tuhn), ND (46°N, 97°W) ... 98
Waigeo I., Indonesia (0°N, 131°E) ... 181
Wailuku, HI (21°N, 156°W) ... 104
Wainwright (WAYN ryt), AB (53°N, 111°W) ... 69
Waipahu (wy PAH hoo), HI (21°N, 158°W) ... 104
Wakayama (wahk uh YAHM uh), Japan (34°N, 135°E) ... 183
Wake, poss. of U.S. (19°N, 167°E) ... 188
Wakkanai (wahk uh NY), Japan (45°N, 142°E) ... 183
Wales, part of United Kingdom (53°N, 4°W) ... 156
Walla Walla, WA (46°N, 118°W) ... 100
Wallis and Futuna, poss. of France (13°S, 176°W) ... 189
Wallis Is., Pacific O. (13°S, 176°W) ... 189
Wallkill R., NY (41°N, 74°W) ... 88
Wallowa Mts. (wuh LOW uh), OR (45°N, 117°W) ... 100
Walpole I., Pacific O. (23°S, 172°E) ... 188
Walter F. George Res., AL and GA (32°N, 85°W) ... 92
Walvis Bay, Namibia (23°S, 15°E) ... 141
Walvis Ridge, Atlantic O. (30°S, 5°E) ... 22
Wappapello L., MO (37°N, 90°W) ... 97
Wapsipinicon R. (wahp suh PIN uh kuhn), IA (92°N, 43°W) ... 97
Wapusk N.P., MB (58°N, 93°W) ... 69
Warner Robins, GA (33°N, 84°W) ... 93
Warren, AR (34°N, 92°W) ... 95
Warren, MI (43°N, 83°W) ... 99
Warren, OH (41°N, 81°W) ... 91
Warren, PA (42°N, 79°W) ... 88
Warsaw, Poland (52°N, 21°E) ... 159
Warta R. (VAHRT uh), Poland (52°N, 17°E) ... 159
Warwick, RI (42°N, 71°W) ... 89
Wasatch Range, U.S. (41°N, 111°W) ... 103
Wash, The, bay in England (53°N, 0°) ... 156
Washington, D.C. (39°N, 77°W) ... 91
Washington, PA (40°N, 80°W) ... 88

Name (Pronunciation), Description (Lat., Long.) Page

Washington, state in U.S. (47°N, 123°W) 100-101
Washington, Mt., NH (44°N, 71°W) 89
Waskaganish, QC (52°N, 79°W) 71
Waterbury, CT (42°N, 73°W) 89
Wateree L. (WAWT uh ree), SC (34°N, 81°W) 93
Waterford, Ireland (52°N, 7°W) 156
Waterloo, IA (43°N, 92°W) 97
Waterloo, ON (43°N, 81°W) 70
Waterton Lakes N.P., AB (49°N, 114°W) 68
Watertown, NY (44°N, 76°W) 88
Watertown, SD (45°N, 97°W) 98
Waterville, ME (45°N, 70°W) 89
Watseka (waht SEE kuh), IL (41°N, 88°W) 97
Watson Lake, YT (60°N, 129°W) 68
Watts Bar L., TN (36°N, 85°W) 90
Waukegan (waw KEE guhn), IL (42°N, 88°W) 97
Wausau (WAW saw), WI (45°N, 90°W) 99
Wauwatosa (waw wuh toh suh), WI (43°N, 88°W) 99
Waw, South Sudan (8°N, 28°E) 140
Wawa, ON (48°N, 85°W) 70
Waycross, GA (31°N, 82°W) 93
Weddell Sea, Antarctica (70°S, 45°W) 200
Wei R. (way), China (35°N, 106°E) 182
Weirton (WIRT uhn), WV (41°N, 81°W) 91
Weiss L., AL (34°N, 86°W) 92
Welch, WV (37°N, 82°W) 91
Welkom (VEL kum), South Africa (28°S, 27°E) 141
Welland Canal, ON (43°N, 79°W) 70
Wellesley Is., Australia (16°S, 139°E) 190
Wellington, New Zealand (41°S, 175°E) 195
Wellington I., Pacific O. (49°S, 75°W) 121
Wells Gray P.P., BC (52°N, 121°W) 68
Wenatchee, WA (47°N, 120°W) 100
Wenzhou (wuhn joh), China (28°N, 121°E) 182
West Allis, WI (43°N, 88°W) 99
West Bank, terr. in Asia (32°N, 35°E) 178
West Grand L., Maine (45°N, 68°W) 89
West Indies, island group in Caribbean Sea (22°N, 78°W) 108
West Jordan, UT (41°N, 112°W) 103
West Lafayette (lahf ee ET), IN (40°N, 87°W) 90
West Memphis, AR (35°N, 90°W) 95
West Palm Beach, FL (27°N, 80°W) 93
West Plains, MO (37°N, 92°W) 97
West Siberian Plain, Russia (60°N, 75°E) 168
West Virginia, state in U.S. (39°N, 81°W) 90-91
Westbrook, ME (44°N, 69°W) 89
Western Australia, state in Australia (25°S, 120°E) 195
Western Dvina R. (dvee NAH), Europe (56°N, 26°E) 160
Western Ghats, mt. range in India (14°N, 75°E) 180
Western Plateau, Australia (25°S, 125°E) 191
Western Sahara, adm. by Morocco (25°N, 13°W) 136
Westport, New Zealand (42°S, 172°E) 195
Wetar (WEH tahr), island in Banda Sea (7°S, 126°E) 181
Wetaskiwin (wih TAS kuh wihn), AB (53°N, 113°W) ... 68
Wewak (WEE wak), Papua New Guinea (3°S, 144°E) 188
Weyburn (WAY buhrn), SK (50°N, 104°W) 69
Whangarei, New Zealand (36°S, 174°E) 195
Wheaton, MD (39°N, 77°W) 91
Wheeler L., AL (35°N, 87°W) 90
Wheeler Pk., NM (37°N, 105°W) 103
Wheeler Pk., NV (39°N, 114°W) 102
Wheeling, WV (40°N, 81°W) 91
White Bay, NL (50°N, 57°W) 72
White L., LA (30°N, 93°W) 95
White Mts., NH (44°N, 71°W) 89
White R., AR (36°N, 92°W) 95
White R., IN (39°N, 87°W) 90
White R., SD (43°N, 102°W) 98
White R., TX (36°N, 102°W) 95
White R., U.S. (40°N, 109°W) 103
White Nile, r. in Africa (14°N, 33°E) 140
White Nile Dam, Africa (15°N, 33°E) 140
White Plains, NY (41°N, 74°W) 88
White River, ON (49°N, 85°W) 70
White Sea, Russia (66°N, 40°E) 160
White Sulphur Springs, MT (47°N, 111°W) 101
White Sulphur Springs, WV (38°N, 80°W) 91
White Volta R., Africa (13°N, 1°W) 138
Whitecourt, AB (54°N, 116°W) 68

Name (Pronunciation), Description (Lat., Long.) Page

Whitefish Bay, L. Superior (47°N, 85°W) 99
Whitehorse, YT (61°N, 135°W) 68
Whiteshell P.P., MB (50°N, 95°W) 69
Whitewater R., U.S. (39°N, 85°W) 90
Whitney, L., TX (32°N, 97°W) 95
Whitney, Mt., CA (37°N, 118°W) 102
Wholdaia L., NT (61°N, 104°W) 69
Whyalla, Australia (33°S, 138°E) 195
Wichita (WIHCH uh taw), KS (38°N, 97°W) 96
Wichita Falls, TX (34°N, 98°W) 94
Wichita Mts., OK (35°N, 99°W) 94
Wick, Scotland (58°N, 3°W) 156
Wicklow Mts., Ireland (53°N, 6°W) 156
Wiesbaden (VEES bahd uhn), Germany (50°N, 8°E) 159
Wight, Isle of (wyt), English Channel (51°N, 1°W) 156
Wilkes-Barre (WIHLKS bair ee), PA(41°N, 76°W) 88
Wilkes Land, region of Antarctica (70°S, 120°E) 200
Willamette R., OR (45°N, 123°W) 100
Willapa Bay (WIHL uh paw), Pacific O. (47°N, 124°W) 100
Willemstad, Curacao (12°N, 69°W) 116
William "Bill" Dannelly Res., AL (32°N, 87°W) 92
Williams Lake, city in BC (52°N, 122°W) 68
Williamsburg, VA (37°N, 75°W) 91
Williamsport, PA (41°N, 77°W) 88
Williston, ND (48°N, 104°W) 98
Williston L., BC (56°N, 123°W) 68
Willmar, MN (45°N, 95°W) 98
Willmore W.P.P., AB (54°N, 119°W) 68
Willow, AK (62°N, 150°W) 104
Willowlake R., NT (63°N, 123°W) 68
Wilmington, DE (40°N, 76°W) 91
Wilmington, NC (34°N, 78°W) 91
Wilson, NC (36°N, 78°W) 91
Wilson L., AL (35°N, 88°W) 92
Winchester, KY (38°N, 84°W) 90
Winchester, VA (39°N, 78°W) 91
Wind Cave N.P., SD (44°N, 103°W) 98
Wind R., WY (43°N, 109°W) 101
Wind River Range, WY (43°N, 110°W) 101
Windhoek (VINT hook), Namibia (23°S, 17°E) 141
Window Rock, city in AZ (35°N, 109°W) 103
Windsor, NL (49°N, 56°W) 72
Windsor, ON (42°N, 83°W) 70
Windward Is., Caribbean Sea (13°N, 62°W) 116
Windward Passage, Caribbean Sea (20°N, 74°W) 107
Winisk L., ON (53°N, 87°W) 70
Winisk R., ON (54°N, 86°W) 70
Winkler, MB (49°N, 98°W) 69
Winnebago, L., WI (44°N, 89°W) 99
Winnemucca, NV (41°N, 118°W) 102
Winnipeg, MB (50°N, 97°W) 69
Winnipeg, L., MB (53°N, 98°W) 69
Winnipeg R., Canada (50°N, 96°W) 69
Winnipegosis, L. (wihn uh puh GOH suhs), MB (52°N, 100°W) 69
Winnipesaukee, L., NH (44°N, 71°W) 89
Winona, MN (44°N, 92°W) 99
Winston-Salem, NC (36°N, 80°W) 91
Winter Haven, FL (28°N, 82°W) 93
Wisconsin, state in U.S. (45°N, 90°W) 99
Wisconsin Dells, WI (44°N, 90°W) 99
Wisconsin R., WI (44°N, 90°W) 99
Wloclawek (vlawt SLAH vehk), Poland (53°N, 19°E) 159
Wolf Point, MT (48°N, 106°W) 101
Wollaston L. (WOOL uh stuhn), city in SK (58°N, 103°W) 69
Wollongong, Australia (34°S, 151°E) 195
Wonsan (WUHN sahn), North Korea (39°N, 127°E) 183
Wood Buffalo N.P., Canada (59°N, 114°W) 68-69
Woodland Caribou P.P., ON (51°N, 95°W) 70
Woodlark I., Pacific O. (9°S, 152°E) 188
Woods, L. of the, Minnesota and ON (49°N, 95°W) 98
Woodward, OK (36°N, 99°W) 94
Woomera, Australia (31°S, 137°E) 195
Wooster, OH (41°N, 82°W) 91
Worcester (WOOS tuhr), MA (42°N, 72°W) 89
Worthington, MN (44°N, 96°W) 98

Name (Pronunciation), Description (Lat., Long.) Page

Wounded Knee, SD (43°N, 103°W) 98
Wrangel I., Chukchi Sea (71°N, 180°) 169
Wrangell, AK (56°N, 132°W) 104
Wrangell Mts. (RANG guhl), North America (62°N, 142°W) 104
Wrangell-Saint Elias N.P. (ee LY uhs), AK (60°N, 141°W) 104
Wright Patman., L., TX (33°N, 95°W) 95
Wroclaw (VRAWTS lahf), Poland (51°N, 17°E) 159
Wuhan, China (31°N, 114°E) 182
Wuxi (woo shee), China (32°N, 120°E) 182
Wuyi Shan (woo yih shahn), mts. in China (26°N, 116°E) 182
Wuzhou, China (24°N, 111°E) 182
Wyndham (WYND uhm), Australia (16°S, 128°E) 195
Wyoming, state in U.S. (43°N, 109°W) 101
Wyoming, MI (43°N, 86°W) 99
Wyoming Range, WY (43°N, 110°W) 101
Wytheville (WITH vil), VA (37°N, 81°W) 91

X

Xai-Xai, Mozambique (25°S, 34°E) 141
Xankandi, Azerbaijan (40°N, 47°E) 161
Xi Jiang R. (shee jee ahng), China (24°N, 107°E) 182
Xiamen (shee ah muhn), China (25°N, 118°E) 182
Xian (shyee an), China (34°N, 109°E) 182
Xiang R. (shee ang), China (29°N, 111°E) 182
Xingu R. (sheeng GYOO), Brazil (5°S, 53°W) 127
Xining (shee ning), China (37°N, 102°E) 182
Xuzhou (shyoo joh), China (34°N, 117°E) 182

Y

Yablanovyy Mts. (YAHB luh nuh VEE), Russia (53°N, 115°E) 170
Yakima (YAK ih maw), WA (47°N, 121°W) 100
Yakima R., WA (46°N, 120°W) 100
Yakutat (YA koo tat), AK (60°N, 140°E) 104
Yakutsk, Russia (62°N, 130°E) 167
Yalta (YAWL tuh), Ukraine (45°N, 34°E) 160
Yalu R. (YAH loo), Asia (41°N, 125°E) 183
Yamal Pen., Russia (84°N, 70°E) 168
Yamoussoukro (yahm uh SOO kroh), Côte d'Ivoire (7°N, 5°W) 138
Yampa R., CO (40°N, 109°W) 103
Yamuna R. (YAH muh nuh), India (27°N, 78°E) 180
Yanbu, Saudi Arabia (24°N, 38°E) 178
Yangon (yahng GOHN), Myanmar (17°N, 96°E) 181
Yangtze R., China (31°N, 110°E) 182
Yankton (YANG tuhn), SD (43°N, 97°W) 98
Yaounde (yah oon DAY), Cameroon (4°N, 12°E) 139
Yap Is., Pacific O. (11°N, 138°E) 188
Yaqui R. (YAH kee), Mexico (28°N, 110°W) 114
Yaren District, Nauru (1°S, 167°E) 188
Yarmouth, NS (44°N, 66°W) 72
Yaroslavl, Russia (58°N, 40°E) 160
Yasawa Group, Pacific O. (17°S, 177°W) 189
Yathkyed L. (yath ky EHD), NU (63°N, 98°W) 69
Yazd, Iran (32°N, 54°E) 178
Yazoo City, MS (33°N, 90°W) 92
Yazoo R., MS (33°N, 89°W) 92
Yekaterinburg, Russia (57°N, 61°E) 160
Yellow R., alternative name for Huang He (41°N, 110°E) 182
Yellow Sea, Asia (36°N, 123°E) 183
Yellowknife, NT (62°N, 114°W) 68
Yellowstone L., WY (44°N, 110°W) 101
Yellowstone N.P., WY (45°N, 110°W) 101
Yellowstone R., U.S. (46°N, 109°W) 101
Yemen, country in Asia (16°N, 44°E) 178
Yenisey R., Russia (68°N, 86°E) 170
Yerevan, Armenia (40°N, 45°E) 161
Yevlax, Azerbaijan (41°N, 47°E) 161
Yichang (yee chang), China (31°N, 112°E) 182
Yingkou (ying ko), China (41°N, 122°E) 183
Yining, China (44°N, 81°E) 179
Yoho N.P., BC (51°N, 117°W) 68
Yokohama, Japan (36°N, 140°E) 183
Yolotan, Turkmenistan (37°N, 62°E) 179
Yonkers, NY (41°N, 74°W) 88
York, England (54°N, 1°W) 156

Name (Pronunciation), Description (Lat., Long.)   Page

York, PA (40°N, 77°W) 88
York, Cape, Australia (11°S, 143°E) 190
Yorkton, SK (51°N, 102°W) 69
Yorktown, VA (37°N, 76°W) 91
Yosemite Falls (yoh sehm ih tee), CA
  (38°N, 120°W) 102
Yosemite N.P., CA (38°N, 120°W) 102
Youngstown, OH (41°N, 81°W) 91
Ysyk-Kol, lake in Kyrgyzstan (42°N, 77°E) ... 179
Yuan R., China (25°N, 110°E) 182
Yuba City (YOO buh), CA (39°N, 122°W) 102
Yucatan (yoo kuh TAHN), state in Mexico
  (21°N, 89°W) 114
Yucatan Channel, Mexico and Cuba (22°N, 84°W) 107
Yucatan Pen., Mexico (20°N, 90°W) 114
Yukon R., North America (64°N, 160°W) 104
Yukon, terr. in Canada (63°N, 135°W) 68
Yuma, AZ (33°N, 115°W) 102
Yumen, China (40°N, 97°E) 182
Yunnan Plateau (yoo NAHN), China
  (26°N, 103°E) 182

Name (Pronunciation), Description (Lat., Long.)   Page

Z

Zabol, Iran (32°N, 61°E) 178
Zacatecas (sah kah TAY kahs), Mexico
  (23°N, 103°W) 114
Zacatecas, state in Mexico (24°N, 103°W) .. 114
Zadar (ZAHD ahr), Croatia (44°N, 15°E) 159
Zagora, Morocco (30°N, 6°W) 136
Zagreb, Croatia (46°N, 16°E) 159
Zagros Mts., Asia (35°N, 47°E) 178
Zahedan (zah ay DAHN), Iran (30°N, 61°E) .. 178
Zahlah, Lebanon (34°N, 36°E) 178
Zambezi R., Africa (16°S, 33°E) 141
Zambia, country in Africa (15°S, 25°E) 141
Zanesville, OH (40°N, 82°W) 91
Zanzibar, city in Tanzania (6°S, 39°E) 140
Zanzibar, island in Indian O. (6°S, 40°E) 140
Zapopan, Mexico (21°N, 103°W) 114
Zaporizhzhya (zah po REEZH zhyah), Ukraine
  (48°N, 35°E) 160
Zaragoza, Spain (42°N, 1°W) 158
Zaranj, Afghanistan (31°N, 62°E) 180

Name (Pronunciation), Description (Lat., Long.)   Page

Zaria (ZAHR ee uh), Nigeria (11°N, 8°E) 138
Zaysan, L., Kazakhstan (48°N, 84°E) 179
Zhangjiakou (JAHNG zhee ah koh), China
  (41°N, 115°W) 182
Zheleznodorozhny (zhil yihzh nuh dah ROHZH nih yee),
  Russia (63°N, 51°E) 160
Zhengzhou (jung joh), China (35°N, 114°E) .. 182
Zhezqazghan (zhez kahz GAHN), Kazakhstan
  (48°N, 69°E) 179
Zhongshan Station (SHONG shang), Antarctica
  (69°S, 76°E) 200
Zhytomyr (ZHEE TOH meer), Ukraine (50°N, 29°E) 160
Zibo (dzee bwo), China (37°N, 118°E) 182
Ziguinchor (zee gan SHOHR), Senegal
  (13°N, 16°W) 138
Zimbabwe, country in Africa (20°S, 30°E) 141
Zinder, Niger (14°N, 9°E) 138
Zion N.P. (ZY uhn), UT (37°N, 113°W) 102–103
Zouirat, Mauritania (23°N, 12°W) 136
Zugdidi, Georgia (43°N, 42°E) 161
Zuni R. (ZOO nee), U.S. (35°N, 110°W) 103
Zurich (ZOO rik), Switzerland (47°N, 9°E) 159

Abbreviations

&	and
AB	Alberta
A.D.	Anno Domini (year of the Lord)
adm.	administered by
AIDS	Acquired Immunodeficiency Syndrome
AK	Alaska
AL	Alabama
Alb.	Albania
a.m.	ante meridiem (before noon)
Am. Samoa	American Samoa
Ang.	Angola
AR	Arkansas
Arch.	archipelago
Arg.	Argentina
Arm.	Armenia
Aus.	Austria
Austr.	Australia
AZ	Arizona
Azer.	Azerbaijan
B.C.	Before Christ
BC	British Columbia
Bos., Bosnia	Bosnia-Herzegovina
Bulg.	Bulgaria
C	Celsius
C. Afr. Rep.	Central African Republic
CA	California
cm	centimeter
CO	Colorado
Congo Rep.	Congo Republic
Cro.	Croatia
CT	Connecticut
Cz., Cz. Rep.	Czech Republic
D.C.	District of Columbia
DE	Delaware
Dem. Rep. Congo	Democratic Republic of the Congo
Den.	Denmark
Dom. Rep.	Dominican Republic
E	East
elev.	elevation
Eq. Guinea	Equatorial Guinea
Est.	Estonia

F	Fahrenheit
Fk.	Fork
FL	Florida
Fr.	France or French
ft.	foot or feet
GA	Georgia (U.S. state)
GDP	Gross Domestic Product
GMT	Greenwich Mean Time
HI	Hawaii
HIV	Human immunodeficiency virus
I., Is.	island, islands
IA	Iowa
ID	Idaho
IL	Illinois
IN	Indiana
in.	inch or inches
Intl.	International
km	kilometer or kilometers
KS	Kansas
Kos.	Kosovo
KY	Kentucky
L.	lake
LA	Louisiana
Lat.	Latvia
Liech.	Liechtenstein
Lith.	Lithuania
Lux.	Luxembourg
m	meter or meters
MA	Massachusetts
MB	Manitoba
MD	Maryland
ME	Maine
Mex.	Mexico
MI	Michigan
mi.	mile or miles
mm	millimeter or millimeters
MN	Minnesota
MO	Missouri
Mol.	Moldova
Mon.	Montenegro

MS	Mississippi
MT	Montana
Mt., Mts.	mount, mont, mountain, or mountains
N	North
N. Mac.	North Macedonia
Nat.	National
NB	New Brunswick
NC	North Carolina
ND	North Dakota
NE	Nebraska
Neth.	Netherlands
NH	New Hampshire
NJ	New Jersey
NL	Newfoundland and Labrador
NM	New Mexico
Nor.	Norway
N.P.	National Park
NS	Nova Scotia
NT	Northwest Territories
NU	Nunavut
NV	Nevada
NY	New York
N.Z.	New Zealand
O.	ocean
OH	Ohio
OK	Oklahoma
ON	Ontario
OR	Oregon
PA	Pennsylvania
Pak.	Pakistan
PE	Prince Edward Island
Pen.	peninsula
Pk.	peak
p.m.	post meridiem (after noon)
Pop.	Population
Port.	Portugal
poss.	possession
P.P.	Provincial Park
Prov.	Province, Provincial
Pt.	point
P.W.P.	Provincal Wilderness Park

QC	Québec
R.	river
Ra.	range
Rep.	republic
Res.	reservoir
RI	Rhode Island
S	South
S. Afr.	South Africa
SC	South Carolina
SD	South Dakota
Sd.	sound
Serb.	Serbia
SK	Saskatchewan
Sl., Slovak.	Slovakia
Slov.	Slovenia
Sp.	Spain
sq.	square
St., Ste.	Saint, Sainte
Str.	strait
Switz.	Switzerland
Terr.	territory
TN	Tennessee
TX	Texas
U.A.E.	United Arab Emirates
U.K.	United Kingdom
U.S.	United States
US$	United States dollars
UT	Utah
VA	Virginia
Ven.	Venezuela
VT	Vermont
W	West
WA	Washington
WI	Wisconsin
W.P.P.	Wilderness Provincial Park
WV	West Virginia
WY	Wyoming
YT	Yukon